Virginia Historical Society
Documents

Volume 4

THE DIARY OF
Colonel Landon Carter
OF SABINE HALL

1752–1778

Colonel Landon Carter (1710–1778) of Sabine Hall
Attributed to Charles Bridges. T. Dabney Wellford, R. Carter Wellford, and Hill B. Wellford, owners.

The Diary of

COLONEL
LANDON CARTER

of Sabine Hall, 1752-1778

Edited with an Introduction by
JACK P. GREENE

VOLUME I

Published for
THE VIRGINIA HISTORICAL SOCIETY
THE UNIVERSITY PRESS OF VIRGINIA
Charlottesville 1965

Published with the assistance of the
Old Dominion Foundation

First Published 1965
The University Press of Virginia
Library of Congress Catalog Card Number: 64-19201
Printed in the United States of America

For My Father and Mother

Merui, sed intus tantum fruor.

In spite of my merit, I have only inward satisfaction.

PREFACE

I FIRST encountered the enormous manuscript diary of Colonel Landon Carter of Sabine Hall nine years ago while I was combing the manuscript collections at Alderman Library at the University of Virginia in search of material for another book. I had already read the brief excerpts from the diary published by Lyon G. Tyler in the *William and Mary College Historical Magazine,* 1st. Ser., XIII–XXI (1904/5–1912/13). I had assumed that Tyler had published the most important parts of the diary, but even a hurried examination of the manuscript indicated that he had included considerably less than 5 per cent of the total document. A subsequent and more thorough analysis revealed, in fact, that he had published, in many cases inaccurately, only random snatches drawn mostly from Carter's comments on the main events of the revolutionary controversy from 1774 to 1776. He had ignored the valuable and unique private minutes of the sessions of the House of Burgesses for 1752–55, the farm record book for 1756–58, the daybook for 1763–64, and the diary and daybook for 1766–67, the last of which had somehow found its way to the William L. Clements Library at the University of Michigan. So impressive was the unpublished material, in particular those portions of the diary that cover in great detail the last eight years of Carter's life from 1770 to 1778, that I sought and obtained permission to edit and publish it from the William L. Clements Library and from the Reverend T. Dabney Wellford, a direct descendant of Landon Carter and owner of those portions of the diary deposited at Alderman Library, who had himself planned to edit the diary and had already begun the work of transcribing and preliminary editing.

Through many years of association with the diary I have gained an increasing respect for it as a source for the study of colonial and revolutionary Virginia. Covering about half of the period from 1752 to 1778, it is neither so complete as that of George Washington nor so light and entertaining as that of William Byrd II of Westover. But it is more intimate and more revealing than either. It is full of information on agriculture, slavery, medical practice, scientific activity, social life, and politics, and it is probably the richest account of the day-to-day life of any single member of the colonial Virginia gentry. From its pages and from other surviving papers it is possible to delineate the primary character traits and personal values of Carter; to determine to a large extent what motivated him, what major problems he faced, how he sought to solve them, and how well he succeeded; and even to look at his world in much the way he must have seen it. Perhaps for no other Virginia planter of the colonial period is such an undertaking possible, and the introductory sketch attempts to present what is hoped will appear to the reader of the diary as a plausible psychological and intellectual portrait.

In editing the diary and in quoting from other sources in the introduction I have in general followed the expanded method as described in *The Harvard Guide to American History* (Cambridge, 1955), 98–99, except that I have modernized punctuation wherever it seemed necessary to render the text understandable. In identifying persons and items mentioned in the text I have given references only in those cases in which I have had to use sources not listed in Earl G. Swem's *Virginia Historical Index* (2 vols.; Roanoke, 1934–36) or Lester J. Cappon and Stella F. Duff's *Virginia Gazette Index* (2 vols.; Williamsburg, 1950) or sources not readily available in the county records on microfilm in the Virginia State Library at Richmond. In identifying medicines I have relied upon contemporary pharmacopoeias, especially John Quincy, *Pharmacopoeia Officinalis & Extemporanea* (London, 1749).

A great many individuals and institutions have assisted me in this enterprise. For permission to publish the diary I am indebted to the Reverend T. Dabney Wellford of Sabine Hall near Warsaw, Virginia, and to Howard Peckham, director of the William L. Clements Library. Mr. Wellford, my wife Sue, and Irby B. Brown each transcribed portions of the diary. Grants-in-aid from the Henry E. Huntington Library and Colonial Williamsburg, Inc., enabled me to collect materials for the introduction and annotations. Michigan State University provided funds to pay for the transcription of the diary, and the Virginia Historical Society for typing the final copy. The staff of Alderman Library, in particular Francis L. Berkeley, Jr., Anne Freudenberg, Russell M. Smith, Robert E. Stocking, and William H. Runge, were especially helpful during my several sojourns in Charlottesville, as was D. Alan Williams. Genevieve Miller helped me with the identification of medical references. Leon Golden, Francis R. Bliss, and particularly Donald R. Laing, Jr., translated the Latin and Greek passages in the diary. John M. Hemphill II, Jane

Carson, and Thad W. Tate, Jr., steered me to useful sources of information on the Carters. W. W. Abbot, Keith B. Berwick, Robert M. Calhoon, Charles R. Crowe, Emory G. Evans, Norman S. Grabo, Winthrop D. Jordan, Donald R. Laing, Jr., Frank Rosengarten, Jean Paul Smith, and Thad W. Tate, Jr., read and criticized the introduction. Mrs. Frank M. Yatsu typed the text of the diary, and Meredyth Bacon the introduction. Judith Hope Reynolds made the index. William M. E. Rachal, editor of publications for the Virginia Historical Society, assisted me throughout the preparation of these volumes. Finally, I am grateful to the Wellford family for their hospitality and for making the surviving portions of Landon Carter's personal library available to me during my visits to Sabine Hall.

J. P. G.

Cleveland, Ohio
March 10, 1964

CONTENTS

Volume I

Volume II

ILLUSTRATIONS

Volume II

INTRODUCTION

INTRODUCTION

VITA

FEW children in colonial America were born with greater advantages than Landon Carter. His father, Robert "King" Carter, was one of the wealthiest Americans of his generation and perhaps the most prominent and most successful of that remarkable group that rose to dominance in Virginia during the last decades of the seventeenth century and provided the foundations for the famous Virginia gentry of the eighteenth century. By the time Landon—his fourth son, the third by his second wife, Elizabeth Landon Willis—was born on August 18, 1710, King Carter was already one of the most commanding figures in the colony, distinguished both by his enormous wealth and by a political career that stretched back over three decades and included service as justice of the peace for Lancaster County, vestryman in Christ Church Parish, speaker of the House of Burgesses, treasurer, and councilor. As agent for the Northern Neck proprietary after 1703, King Carter added those quantities of land to his already extensive holdings that would total some 333,000 acres at his death in 1732.[1]

That Landon, like his four brothers, would have an excellent education and a generous inheritance was never open to doubt. In late 1719 or early 1720 when he was nine he went with two older brothers, Robert and Charles, to London, where he received at the private school of Solomon Low the usual classical education given to young gentlemen in England. At school he dem-

---

[1] The best published treatment of Robert "King" Carter is Louis B. Wright, *The First Gentlemen of Virginia: Intellectual Qualities of the Early Colonial Ruling Class* (San Marino, Calif., 1940; reissued Charlottesville, 1964), 248–85, but see also the short sketch in Louis Morton's excellent study of King Carter's grandson, *Robert Carter of Nomini Hall: A Virginia Tobacco Planter of the Eighteenth Century* (Williamsburg, 1941), 3–31. A contemporary estimation of King Carter's wealth is in the *Gentleman's Magazine,* II (1732), 1082.

onstrated so good a memory and such a strong inclination for learning that his father, already disposed to "make learning" an important "part of his portion," allowed him to stay on at school for four more years after his brothers had returned home in 1723. When he returned to Virginia in May 1727 at age sixteen, his father discovered him to be "a lad of good morals and of an agreeable, obligeing behaviour," "well advanced" in his education, and "very well qualified to enter upon any business." His father thought for a time of apprenticing him to a London business house "to breed him up a Virginia merchant" but eventually decided to teach him the business of plantation management so that he could follow in the footsteps of himself and his three older sons.[2] After at least a brief stay at the College of William and Mary,[3] Landon lived with his father at the family seat at Corotoman and apparently managed some of his father's Northumberland lands until 1732, when his father died. In the same year Landon, age twenty-two, married Elizabeth, daughter of the late John Wormeley, scion of another leading Virginia family, of Rosegill in Middlesex County across the Rappahannock from Corotoman.[4]

King Carter left Landon a bounteous legacy. Through both his wife and his brothers and sisters, Landon was as well connected as any man in the colony. His sisters had married into the Burwell, Harrison, Page, Braxton, and Fitzhugh families, and his oldest two brothers into the Hills and Churchills.[5] Moreover, his father had provided him with a sizable estate. He already owned over 15,000 acres in the western part of the Northern Neck, his share of two large grants of 41,550 and 50,212 acres made by his father in 1724 and 1730 to Landon, his younger brother George, and seven of Landon's nephews.[6] In addition, his father bequeathed to him at least eight fully equipped and operating plantations: Round Hill in King George County; Bloughpoint, Jones Place, and Old Place in Northumberland County; and Hickory Thicket,

---

[2] Robert "King" Carter to William Dawkins, July 14, 1720, in Louis B. Wright, ed., *Letters of Robert Carter, 1720–1727* (San Marino, Calif., 1940), 25; same, Jan. 28, 1724, as quoted in *Virginia Magazine of History and Biography,* XXXI (1923), 39–40; to Landon Carter (hereafter L. C.), July 5, 1723, in Robert Carter Letter Book, 1723–1724, Virginia Historical Society, Richmond; to John Falconar, May 16, 1727, and Dec. 16, 1727, and to James Bradley, May 17, 1727, in Robert Carter Letter Book, 1727–1728, Alderman Library, University of Virginia, Charlottesville; Robert Carter Diary, May 25, 1727, Alderman Lib.

[3] *A Provisional List of Alumni, Grammar School Students, Members of the Faculty, Members of the Board of Visitors of the College of William and Mary in Virginia, from 1693–1888* (Richmond, 1941), 11.

[4] L. C. Diary, May 12, 1776, p. 1039; Walter Ray Wineman, *The Landon Carter Papers in the University of Virginia Library: A Calendar and Biographical Sketch* (Charlottesville, 1962), 47.

[5] Morton, *Robert Carter,* 21–29.

[6] William Waller Hening, ed., *The Statutes at Large: Being a Collection of All the Laws of Virginia* (13 vols.; Richmond, 1823–35), V, 300–2.

the Fork, Mangorike, and Lansdowne in Richmond County.[7] Landon chose
Lansdowne for his temporary seat. Taking "an old brick building tore down
in many places and at an expence of some hundreds" repairing it, he appears to
have moved there sometime in late 1733 or early 1734.[8]

For the next two decades Carter devoted himself primarily to raising a
family, improving his estate, and establishing himself as one of the leading
men in Richmond County. All together, he had seven children that survived
into adulthood. Elizabeth bore him four, Robert Wormeley, Landon, John,
and Elizabeth, before her early death at age twenty-seven in January 1740. His
second wife, the fifteen-year-old Maria, daughter of Councilor William Byrd
II of Westover, lived only a little over two years after their marriage in 1742
but bore Carter another daughter, Maria. His third wife, whom he married in
1746, was a neighborhood spinster, Elizabeth, daughter of the deceased
Thomas Beale. She bore two daughters, Judith and Lucy, before she died in
the mid-1750s.[9] Through his marriages Carter added to his landholdings. His
first wife brought him a thousand-acre plantation, Rings Neck, on the York
River in King and Queen County,[10] and his second, a tract in Charles City
County. By purchase he added several pieces in Richmond County and one in
Westmoreland County,[11] and with the death of his brother George in 1741 he
fell heir to two lots in Williamsburg, additional land in the western part of the
Northern Neck, and two plantations: Ripon Hall in York County and the
Park in Stafford County.[12] At the same time he was increasing the number of
his slaves and livestock, building a mill and other outbuildings on his property,
and seating his unoccupied lands in Prince William and Frederick counties.[13]
By 1750 he possessed an immense, and still growing, estate, totaling over 35,000
acres in the Northern Neck alone.[14] As soon as he had the "wherewithall"—

[7] Will of Robert Carter, Aug. 22, Oct. 11, 1726, Sept. 12, 1728, June 9, July 23, 1730, and
inventory of Robert Carter [1732], "Carter Papers," *Va. Mag. of Hist. and Biog.,* V (1897–98),
409–28, VI (1898–99), 1–22, VII (1899–1900), 66–68.

[8] L. C. Diary, Aug. 9, 1777, p. 1123. L. C. was still living in Lancaster Co. in May 1733 but had
moved to Richmond Co. by September 1734. See Indenture of lease between Edward Barradall and
L. C. "of Lancaster County," May 28, 1733, Sabine Hall Collection, Alderman Lib., and H. R.
McIlwaine, ed., *Executive Journals of the Council of Colonial Virginia* (5 vols.; Richmond, 1925–45),
IV, 331 (Sept. 5, 1734).

[9] Wineman, *Landon Carter Papers,* 46–48; Epitaph for Elizabeth Carter, 1740, Carter Family Papers,
Folder 1, College of William and Mary Library, Williamsburg, Va.; *Tyler's Magazine,* IX (1928), 284.

[10] Surveyor's plat of "Ring's Quarter," King and Queen Co., 1729, Carter Family Papers, Folder 3.

[11] See Wineman, *Landon Carter Papers,* 9–24.

[12] Copy of will of George Carter, Jan. 2, 1741, Sabine Hall Col.; will of Robert Carter, Sept. 12, 1728,
June 9, 1730, "Carter Papers," *Va. Mag. of Hist. and Biog.,* VI (1898–99), 11–17. See also
L. C. Diary, Aug. 9, 1777, p. 1123.

[13] See Wineman, *Landon Carter Papers,* 9–14, and petition of L. C., Feb. 2, 1736, Richmond Co.
court Order Book 1732–39, X, 360 (Feb. 2, 1736), Richmond Co. Courthouse, Warsaw, Va.

[14] See L. C.'s Account of Lands to Lord Fairfax, Sept. 29, 1767, Carter Family Papers, Folder 3.

almost certainly sometime after his first wife's death in 1740—he built, perhaps with the help of architect Richard Taliaferro, a dwelling house "of taste," an airy and elegant Georgian structure high on a hill that looked southward over six gardened terraces to the Rappahannock River three miles below. This new family seat and the plantation surrounding it he called Sabine Hall.[15]

But Carter in the tradition of his fellow gentry did not spend all of his energies on private affairs. Like his father and his older brothers, he early assumed an important role in the public life first of his county and then of the colony. In September 1734, within a year after he had settled at Lansdowne, Lieutenant Governor William Gooch and the Virginia Council appointed him justice of the peace and member of the quorum on the Richmond County court.[16] In this position he helped to dispense justice and administer the county until his death over forty-four years later. Sometime during the following decade the vestry of Lunenburgh Parish elected him to the vestry, and Gooch appointed him county lieutenant in command of militia. The former post he held until his death and the latter until new militia regulations that decreased his control over the troops prompted him to resign in early 1776.[17] He also held a variety of less important positions in the county as his colleagues on the bench designated him to supervise the building and repair of roads, the construction of a new courthouse, or the collection of a list of tithables.[18] Less immediately successful in securing elective office, he was rejected by the voters of Richmond County three times, in 1735, 1742, and 1748, before they finally returned him in 1752 to represent them in the House of Burgesses in Williamsburg.[19]

[15] An excellent description of Sabine Hall is in Thomas Tileston Waterman, *The Mansions of Virginia, 1706–1776* (Chapel Hill, 1946), 127–36, 422. Waterman suggests that the house was built by Taliaferro (*ibid.*, 103, 107). His further suggestion—and here he follows earlier historians—that Sabine Hall was built for L. C. by his father in 1730 is clearly wrong. The entry in the L. C. Diary, Aug. 9, 1777, p. 1123, shows that King Carter did not provide a dwelling house for L. C., and the letter of John Carter to L. C., Mar. 3, 1740, Sabine Hall Col., indicates that L. C. had not yet moved from Lansdowne to Sabine Hall.

[16] *Exec. Journals of Council of Col. Va.*, IV, 331 (Sept. 5, 1734); Richmond Co. court Order Book, 1732–39, X, 226 (Jan. 6, 1735), 1748–52, XII, 128 (July 4, 1748), XVIII, 23 (Aug. 4, 1777).

[17] See Richmond Co. court Order Books, 1752–55, XIII, 22 (Mar. 5, 1753); L. C. to Lord Botetourt, Nov. 1, 1768, and to John Dixon and William Hunter, Jr., May 1776 (?), Sabine Hall Col.; and Norborne Berkeley, Baron de Botetourt, to L. C., July 31, 1769, Emmet Collection, 6197, New York Public Library, New York.

[18] See Richmond Co. court Order Books, 1732–39, X, 636 (July 4, 1738), 1748–52, XII, 194 (Aug. 7, 1749), 1756–62, 336 (May 5, 1760).

[19] Richmond Co. poll, July 21, 1735, Fairfax Papers, Brock Collection, Box 227, Henry E. Huntington Library, San Marino, Calif.; Henry R. McIlwaine and John P. Kennedy, eds., *Journals of the House of Burgesses of Virginia* (13 vols.; Richmond, 1905–15), *1742–49*, 34–35 (May 24, 1742); Richmond Co. court Order Book, 1748–52, XII, 353; Lucille Griffith, *Virginia House of Burgesses, 1750–1774* (Northport, Ala., 1963), 83–90, 222–23.

With his election to the Burgesses Carter's public career took a new turn. Thenceforth he operated at two levels, never neglecting his duties in Richmond County but increasingly concentrating his attention upon concerns of the colony as a whole. Immediately upon his entry into the Burgesses he became one of its most active members, and during a legislative career that stretched over sixteen years until 1768, when he finally failed of reelection because, as he put it, he did not "familiarize" himself "among the People,"[20] only Speaker John Robinson, Peyton Randolph, Richard Bland, his brother Charles Carter of Cleve, and Edmund Pendleton consistently played more important parts in the counsels of the House.[21] At his first session he secured appointment to the powerful standing committees for privileges and elections and for propositions and grievances, and after 1756 he was usually chairman of the standing committee on courts of justice.[22] As a writer of some reputation he helped prepare formal addresses, and along with Richard Bland he became the public defender of the House, publishing pamphlets and newspaper essays upholding its stand on the pistole fee, paper currency, and the Two-Penny Act.[23] A strong advocate of vigorous measures against the French during the French and Indian War,[24] he also consistently and adamantly opposed British encroachments upon American rights after 1763. He claimed the distinction of first raising the alarm against the Stamp Act in the Burgesses and of inspiring that body in the fall of 1764, six months before Patrick Henry's famous resolutions of the following May, to protest that measure in petitions to the King, Lords, and Commons.[25] Over the following decade he poured forth a

[20] L. C. Diary, Apr. 1, 1776, pp. 1008–9.

[21] See Jack P. Greene, "Foundations of Political Power in the Virginia House of Burgesses, 1720–1776," *William and Mary Quarterly*, 3d Ser., XVI (1959), 486–506.

[22] See *Burgesses Journals, 1752–58, 1758–61, 1761–65, 1766–1769, passim;* Hening, ed., *Statutes,* VI, 454, 524, VII, 13, 76, 276, 289, 568.

[23] See Jack P. Greene, "Landon Carter and the Pistole Fee Dispute," *Wm. and Mary Qtly.*, 3d Ser., XIV (1957), 66–69, for the establishment of L. C.'s authorship of both *A Letter from a Gentleman in Virginia, to the Merchants of Great Britain, Trading to that Colony* (London, 1754) and an essay in the *Maryland Gazette* (Annapolis), Oct. 24, 1754. His authorship of *A Letter to a Gentleman in London, from Virginia* (Williamsburg, 1759), a defense of the paper currency act passed by the Virginia Assembly in 1758, is indicated by obvious similarities of style and organization to his other writings. Other evidence for his authorship of this tract is presented by John M. Hemphill, II, in *Wm. and Mary Qtly.*, 3d Ser., XV (1958), 410. L. C.'s two pamphlets on the Two-Penny Act are *A Letter to the Right Reverend Father in God, the Lord B——p of L——n* (Williamsburg, 1760) and *The Rector Detected* (Williamsburg, 1764).

[24] See L. C. to George Washington, Apr. 27–29 (?), 1756, in Stanislaus Murray Hamilton, ed., *Letters to Washington and Accompanying Papers* (5 vols.; Boston and New York, 1898–1902), I, 236, and L. C. Diary, Aug. 22, 1754, May 14, 1755, pp. 111–12, 123–24.

[25] On this point see L. C. Diary, July 14, 25, 1776, February 23, 1777, pp. 1057, 1063, 1082–83; L. C. to George Washington, Oct. 31, 1776, in Peter Force, ed., *American Archives* (Washington, 1837–53), 5th Ser., II, 1304–07.

steady stream of essays in support of the American cause.[26] From September 1774 through the middle of 1775 he was chairman, usually by "unanimous" election, of the series of committees that administered the county in the months after the breakdown of royal authority and enforced the Continental Association.[27] Though he sharply disagreed with Thomas Paine's *Common Sense,* preferring to be compelled to independence rather than to seek it actively, he continued to give wholehearted support to the American cause after the Declaration of Independence, his spirits rising and falling with the tide of American fortunes in the war.[28]

When Carter died on December 22, 1778, at the age of 69,[29] a eulogist could have pointed to the accomplishments of a full and active life. He had obviously been more than an ordinary man. A devoted and tireless public servant, he had played a significant part in every important political event in Virginia during his career in the Burgesses between 1752 and 1768 and through his writings had perhaps helped sustain the determined resistance to Britain over the succeeding decade. He was almost certainly the most prolific and most published author of his generation in Virginia and perhaps in any of the colonies south of Pennsylvania, producing at least four major pamphlets and nearly fifty essays for the *Virginia Gazettes, Maryland Gazette,* and other newspapers in both England and America. His scientific writings had won for him election to the American Philosophical Society in 1769 and to the Virginia

---

[26] L. C. published mainly in the *Virginia Gazettes* both under his own name and under a variety of pseudonyms, including C—R—, L—C—, B—E—, Honest Buckskin, An American, An Associating Planter, Experience, and probably others. Political pieces in the *Gazettes* that can be definitely identified as his either from manuscript drafts in the Sabine Hall Col. and Carter Family Papers or through pseudonyms known to have been used by Carter are in Alexander Purdie and John Dixon's *Va. Gaz.,* Apr. 4, Aug. 1, Oct. 17, Nov. 6, 1766, Apr. 20, July 13, 1769, Mar. 22, 1770, Oct. 3, 1771, and July 28, 1774; William Rind's *Va. Gaz.,* Sept. 1, 1768, June 1, Sept. 14, 1769, Apr. 26, June 14, Dec. 13, 1770; Nov. 11, 1773, and Apr. 7, May 12, 1774, and Purdie's *Va. Gazette,* Feb. 12, 1775, Mar. 28, 1777. Pieces in the *Md. Gaz.* are in the issues for Oct. 24, 1754, and May 8, 1766. In addition there is evidence that L. C. may have published essays in the *Maryland Journal* (Baltimore) and the *Pennsylvania Evening Post* (Philadelphia) in 1777. (See Francis Lightfoot Lee to L. C., Feb. 28, Apr. 15, 1777, Lee-Ludwell Papers, Va. Hist. Soc.) He also published at least one piece and probably more in London (Diary, undated 1774, p. 917, and Francis Lightfoot Lee to William Lee, April 6, 1770, Brock Col., Box 4). That he wrote and undoubtedly published many other essays on the debate with Britain is clear from the numerous manuscript drafts scattered in the various collections of his papers. In the Sabine Hall Col. alone there is the draft of a long pamphlet on the Stamp Act, dated Nov. 30, 1765, plus at least twelve shorter essays ranging over virtually every important issue between 1765 and 1776. There are three other pieces in the Carter Family Papers (Folders 3 and 104) and one each in the Wellford Collection in the library at Sabine Hall, Warsaw, Va., and in the Brock Col. (L. C. to Joseph Royle, June 3, 1765).

[27] *Va. Gaz.* (Purdie), Feb. 17, May 19, June 2, 1775, (Dixon), Jan. 14, 1775; Robert Wormeley Carter Diary, Sept. 22, 1774, American Antiquarian Society, Worcester, Mass.

[28] See L. C. Diary, June 14, 1776, pp. 1049–50; L. C. to George Washington, July 30, 1777, Washington Papers, LII, 101, Library of Congress, Washington, D.C.

[29] Family Bible, Sabine Hall.

Society for the Promotion of Useful Knowledge when it was founded in 1773.[30] All of his children had made acceptable marriages, and he had provided for them amply, giving large dowries to his four daughters and large estates to his three sons. Including property already transferred to his sons before his death, he left an estate consisting of nearly 50,000 acres of land, perhaps as many as 500 slaves, and a large amount of additional wealth in livestock, buildings, and personal possessions—a fortune second to few in the state.[31]

But these accomplishments could not gloss over a sense of bitter disappointment that nagged Carter throughout his final years. For some reason he had failed—and he knew he had failed—to make any lasting impression upon his generation, to achieve that recognition among his contemporaries that would assure him of a place in history. That his disappointment was well founded is attested by his subsequent obscurity, an obscurity that may on the surface seem to be deserved. Even a full biography with the traditional plea for recognition of a long-neglected figure would not raise him to that position to which he aspired and to which he liked to think he might be entitled. Neither would it add much to what is already known about the configuration of Virginia society during his lifetime. There is little in the general pattern of his life to distinguish him from any number of his contemporaries among the Virginia gentry. With some slight changes, a few minor substitutions of names, dates, places, details, his biography might be any of theirs. Yet for history to say no more about Landon Carter would do him a grave injustice. What distinguishes him from his fellows, what may yet attain for him the recognition of which he thought he had been deprived is his diary, a diary that served first as a simple record of day-to-day activities, then increasingly as a companion to which in the loneliness of old age he could confide his thoughts and lay bare his frustrations. For unlike similar documents of his contemporaries his diary has a reflective quality and an openness that provide, perhaps better than any other single source, a suitable vehicle for a journey into the mind of one member of Virginia's eighteenth-century plantation gentry. An analysis of the individual psychology of one or even several members of a group can probably never be an adequate substitute for the study of the social

---

[30] *Proceedings of the American Philosophical Society, Held at Philadelphia, for Promoting Useful Knowledge* (Philadelphia, 1884), XXII (July 1835), Part III, No. 119, 19–20 (Nov. 15, 1768), 35 (Apr. 21, 1769); and *Va. Gaz.* (Rind), Apr. 14, 1774.

[31] L. C.'s will is in *Va. Mag. of Hist. and Biog.*, XXIX (1921), 361–62. His inventory is in the Sabine Hall Col. For the property of his sons a few years after his death, see Jackson T. Main, "The One Hundred," *Wm. and Mary Qtly.* 3d Ser., XI (1954), 372. His children's marriages are described in Wineman, *Landon Carter Papers*, 47–48.

psychology of the whole group, but a probing of the basic motivations, preoccupations, aspirations, fears, and impressions of Landon Carter, an identification and explanation of his central assumptions, attitudes, beliefs, values, tastes, ideals of behavior, and ethical imperatives, may at least serve as a beginning toward a clearer understanding of the psychology of one of the most important groups in the American past.

THE IMPERFECTION OF EVERY CREATED BEING

One of the most distinctive features of the personality of Landon Carter was an intense and abiding distrust of men. Whence it derived, how deep it lay within his past, are now impossible to determine, but it was an integral part of his character by the time he began keeping a diary at age forty-one. It may have been no more than the expression of an extreme shyness that he sought to mask by bold disdain for others, but whatever its origins it manifested itself in a pronounced reserve and caution in his personal relationships, an almost total cynicism about the motives and actions of his fellow men, a profound skepticism that made it impossible for him to accept anything not confirmed by his own experience, and a constant and thorough scrutiny of his own behavior. This cluster of traits and the deeper distrust with which they were associated were intimately connected with his conception of human nature.

Until the latter part of the eighteenth century it was, of course, traditional in the western world for man to have a low opinion of himself. The imperfection of man in contrast to the perfection of the gods or God had been in turn a cornerstone of Greek, Hebrew, and Christian theology, and the innate and total depravity of man was central to most Protestant theologies as they developed in the sixteenth and seventeenth centuries. Though there were some indications of the emergence of a more genial view of man as early as the last decades of the seventeenth century, few seventeenth- or eighteenth-century men in either Europe or America seriously entertained the proposition that man was naturally good or held out the hope for human progress that was so characteristic of the nineteenth century—an era appropriately styled by A. O. Lovejoy as "the Age of Man's Good Conceit of Himself." Rather, they persisted in the conception that man was both corrupt and irrational; dominated by his passions, prejudices, vanity, and interest; and perpetually deluded in thinking himself rational.[32]

That Carter shared this view of human nature was to be expected; few

[32] An excellent discussion of seventeenth- and eighteenth-century conceptions of human nature is in Arthur O. Lovejoy, *Reflections on Human Nature* (Baltimore, 1961), especially 1–34.

men depart radically from the general intellectual milieu in which they live. But his conception of man was not merely a reflection of the views of theologians or philosophers; he found it in every corner of life, in the indifference and ingratitude of his overseers, the indolence and drunkenness of his slaves, the avarice and dishonesty of British merchants, the thirst for power of the clergy.[33] Everywhere he looked he constantly saw men "intoxicated with either ambition, malice, avarice, or some of the other modes of corruption," falling into error "either through temper or interest," sacrificing truth to their own vanity, sinking ultimately into depravity.[34] It was not that men were innately evil; they were merely weak and imperfect, fallible in their understanding, confined in their vision, unhappy even in their structures. Thus constituted, they could scarcely avoid falling into corruption, and "Corruption once tasted" led directly to the grossest "species of barbarity, injustice and Plunder." Vice was simply a concomitant of human nature.[35]

Carter's analysis of himself only confirmed his judgment of man. His own greatest weakness, a constant reminder of his and man's imperfection, was an almost ungovernable temper that had already acquired for him a reputation as "a passionate man" before he was twenty-five years old.[36] The repeated and occasionally violent quarrels with his neighbors, overseers, and family—each in turn "a scandalous affair,"[37] a blatant display of his own vicious tendencies—troubled him deeply and brought him continual anguish. The recurrent outbursts between him and his eldest son, Robert Wormeley, who was, as Carter remarked, "perhaps . . . equally unhappy in temper" with himself, turned Sabine Hall during the last fifteen years of Carter's life into a scene of "eternal fretting at nothing and indeed quarrelling about as little" and drove him alternately to denounce his son as his "dayly curse" and to resolve either to "remove out of his Company or forever hold my tongue."[38] "Sorry indeed and very sorry I am," he wrote in his diary in September 1775, "ever to let anything

[33] See L. C. Diary, Apr. 27, 1766, Sept. 28, 1770, Apr. 7, Sept. 11, 1771, Mar. 9, 1776, July 7, 1777, Aug. 31, 1778, pp. 291–92, 505, 556, 625–26, 997–98, 1107, 1148–49; *Letter to B——p of L——n*, 55.

[34] L. C. on parliamentary taxation, n.d., Wellford Col., Sabine Hall; L. C. to Joseph Royle, June 3, 1765, Brock Col.; *Md. Gaz.*, Oct. 24, 1754.

[35] L. C. Diary, Apr. 13, May 28, July 26, 1776, Feb. 11, Apr. 27, 1777, pp. 1016, 1045, 1065–66, 1075, 1102–3; *Letter to a Gentleman in London*, 20–21; *Letter to B——p of L——n*, 6, 17; *Rector Detected*, 16; L. C. on councilors' refusal to join association, [1774–75], Sabine Hall Collection.

[36] John Randolph to L. C., Mar. 3, 1735, *Va. Mag. of Hist. and Biog.*, III (1885–96), 357. See also similar hints in William Byrd II to L. C., July 26, 1742, in Moncure D. Conway, *Barons of the Potomac and Rappahannock* (New York, 1892), 193–94.

[37] L. C. Diary, Sept. 5, 1775, p. 937–38.

[38] See, for instance, L. C. Diary, July 6, 1766, June 23, 1773, Feb. 15–16, 1776, pp. 314–15, 763, 983–84; Robert Wormeley Carter Diary, Aug. 25, 1766, Col. of Wm. and Mary Lib.

whatever alarm me into indecencies. But the man who is of a hasty temper must be ever thinking of it if he intends to conquer it or it will forever keep him under."[39] Though he could occasionally comfort himself with the knowledge that he had gained a temporary victory over his temper, no amount of resolution and effort, of remorse or contrition, seemed to enable him to make the victory complete, and he could find consolation only in the knowledge that his weakness could be "imputed to those frailties which are incident to human nature."[40] But it was not merely his temper or his passions that he had to contend with. "I think," he wrote to George Washington in May 1776, "that in general we are too much tinctured with either the interest or the vanity which most of us acquire from our cradles. I speak as from myself; it has cost me more labour to conquer such habits than ever *Hercules* had. Such an *Augean* stable is the whole world almost!"[41] If he judged men harshly, he also saw in them reflections of his own imperfections and tried to judge himself by the same standards. There could, after all, be no greater folly than for a man to fancy "that he does not bray."[42]

The overwhelming evidence of "the imperfection of every created being" meant simply that no man, no matter what his position or responsibilities, could be expected to overcome all his evil tendencies. If a governor turned out to be "avaricious and designing," if a clergyman displayed an insatiable thirst for power, if a king "should incline to be a despot," it was primarily because they were men. By the same token, all human institutions—the British Parliament, the Virginia Assembly, the Richmond County court—could be expected to be fallible precisely because they were composed of men. "Injustice and Oppression will always be the product of an earthly Supremacy," Carter wrote in 1776, "and I am confident however Romantic writers may be as to the morality of their heroes among men, there never was that created being either single or collected . . . who ever did or even could discharge so divine a duty with impartiality and disinterestedness. I do not say there are not, nor ever were good men," he added, "but if we consider the human machine, we are not without Perpetual opportunities, though we should discover the Spirit of men to be willing to do good . . . of Observing and indeed feeling the weakness of flesh." Clearly, man could never be any more than man.[43]

This profound conviction of man's inherent weakness colored Carter's

[39] L. C. Diary, Sept. 20, 1775, p. 946.
[40] L. C. Diary, June 16, 1771, June 23, 1773, Feb. 11, 1777, pp. 577–78, 763, 1075.
[41] L. C. to Washington, May 9, 1776, in Force, ed., *Am. Archives*, 4th Ser., VI, 389–92.
[42] L. C. to Alexander Purdie, Feb. 14, 1774, Sabine Hall Col.
[43] L. C. Diary, Apr. 27, 1777, pp. 1102–3; *Md. Gaz.*, Oct. 24, 1754; *Letter to B——p of L——n*, 55; *Rector Detected*, 16; L. C. to Dixon and Hunter, May 1776 (?), Sabine Hall Col.

entire personality. Knowing that no man was "incapable of Error," he preferred to rely on his own experience rather than "upon the possitive though not always very certain accounts" of others. Seeing "every day . . . stronger reasons for" his "great caution in this world" and convinced from "more than 50 years real Observation" that there was no genuine friendship, he chose to remain aloof even at the risk of alienating his closest associates rather than to put himself in the power of imperfect men. In choosing to be aloof, he may also have hoped to hide his own imperfections and a deep sense of guilt he felt at not being able to overcome them.[44]

VIRTUE IS THE BEST POLICY

Man's imperfections, his inability ever to be *completely* good, did not mean that he was incapable of improvement. The very knowledge of his weakness was itself the greatest spur to overcome it, and the quest for virtue and honor—the determination to bridle one's passions, to resist all temptations to corruption, to act with reason and deliberation, to avoid self-delusion, to rise above a narrow concern for one's self-interests, perhaps even to become in the eyes of one's fellowmen a praiseworthy man by whose very acts and example society might be bettered—the striving to harness man and make him serviceable to himself and to society was the most important, and the most difficult, challenge confronting mankind. But it was the determination to surmount these difficulties—to meet and to overcome the challenge—that gave nobility to man, and with Landon Carter this determination was compulsive.

Carter's relentless pursuit of improvement was probably the dominant feature of his personality; certainly it was the central concern of what he referred to less than two years before his death as "the whole plan of my life."[45] Reflecting back over his first sixty-five years in June 1775, he characterized himself in Alexander Purdie's *Virginia Gazette* as a "sensible Gentleman, who has lived to an extreme age, preserving an unexceptionable character, as well in his publick capacity as in his private life."[46] This strong commitment to the ideal of a virtuous and honorable life, a consuming desire both to overcome his own weaknesses and to distinguish himself among men by contributing to the happiness and safety of his family and the public, was at the root of most of his behavior. "Be convinced from a life of long experience," he warned the

---

[44] L. C. Diary, Jan. 9, Feb. 9, 1776, Aug. 1, 1777, pp. 967, 977, 1120; *Md. Gaz.*, Oct. 24, 1754; L. C. to 2 in the Corner, [1769–70], Sabine Hall Col.

[45] L. C. Diary, July 28, 1777, p. 1117.

[46] *Va. Gaz.* (Purdie), June 30, 1775.

Virginia councilors in a public letter in late 1774, "that in all endeavours whatever, Virtue like honesty is the best Policy." Dishonesty and vice might well produce some "temporary advantage," but they also brought grave penalties: "the fatal *but,* in a good Character that could hardly be forgotten among men," a persistent gnawing "in some leizure hour of reflection" of that "living worm in man Called Consciousness."[47] But more dreadful than the loss of reputation or the pangs of a guilty conscience was the prospect that virtue once lost might never be recovered, that temptation once succumbed to might never be overcome, that, as Carter suggested in warning against submission to the Tea Act in February 1774, corruption unless it was resisted might even "in time get the better of all Virtue." That this prospect was no idle fear was repeatedly illustrated during Carter's last years—years when his entire structure of values seemed to be under assault by the combined forces of political corruption in Great Britain and social decay in Virginia—by the abandonment of his sons, Robert Wormeley and John, to gambling; the passion of his personal body servant, Nassau, for drink; the failure of his overseers to tell him the truth; the decline all around him among friends and associates of the traditional sense of public duty; the continual machinations of "departments of ill designing men" in British politics. It was only too apparent that vice, as he lamented in his diary in October 1774, was "a thing most easily learned and but seldom . . . got over."[48]

The attainment of virtue by creatures so strongly attracted to vice required enormous strength of character and unusual self-discipline, qualities Landon demanded from both himself and others. He liked to think of himself as "a *Steady* friend to Society" and admired those men who, like his son-in-law William Colston, seemed to be of a *"steady* turn of mind."[49] For weakness, whether the weakness of his "upland friend" for sacrificing a "Vast estate" to satisfy the demands of an extravagant wife or that of his grandson Landon for his "constant and extravagant" indulgence of an "outrageous" temper, he had only contempt.[50] And inconstancy and vacillation—playing "wanton with the *Wind,*" as Carter felicitously phrased it in *The Rector Detected*—were perhaps the grossest forms of weakness. He was disturbed to discover in 1752 during his first session in the House of Burgesses that his fellow politicians "should

[47] L. C. Diary, Mar. 1, 1774, pp. 798–99; L. C. on councilors' refusal to sign the Continental Association, [1774–75], Sabine Hall Col.

[48] See L. C. Diary, Mar. 7, 1772, Sept. 23, 1773, May 2, Oct. 8, 1774, Apr. 8, 1776, Apr. 16, 1777, pp. 657, 778, 800, 868–69, 1013, 1091–92; *Va. Gaz.* (Rind), Sept. 1, 1768; L. C. to Purdie and Dixon, Feb. 14, 1774, Sabine Hall Col.

[49] L. C. Diary, July 19, 1776, pp. 1059–60; L. C. to Dixon and Hunter, May 1776 (?), Sabine Hall Col.

[50] L. C. Diary, June 16, 1771, Feb. 8, 1776, pp. 577–78, 977.

run like Bowls," and he denounced the "famous Mr. Richd. Bland" as "a Shuttle Cock and without faith" for not remaining "steady in one instance to the Opinion he set out upon this Session unless it was immediately determined."[51] Although he had no illusions about his own infallibility and repeatedly asserted his eagerness to recede from error, he was strongly convinced, as he declared in condemning the Stamp Act in the *Maryland Gazette* in 1766, that *"Right* and *Wrong"* were "so immutable in their Ideas, and so much at variance in their Natures" that it was inexcusable either to confuse one with the other or not to adhere tenaciously to an opinion one had once decided was right.[52] Refusing to sanction even the slightest sacrifice of truth, he disputed with neighbors over trifles, insisting that "truth and justice have no virtue" if they did "not shine in a farthing as well as in a million."[53] The man in quest of virtue could ill afford to give an inch, to relax for a moment, to permit even the slightest indulgence of any weakness. Although all faults could be attributed to man's natural imperfections, not attempting to overcome them reduced "Things to a *primitive State of Barbarity*" and opened the door to all vice. Any "Sharper" could say "when he is detected in cheating at a Gaming-Table, that others would do the same, had they the same Opportunity or Advantage," Carter declared in *The Rector Detected,* and "every Bunter" could "justify her Course of Life, by saying that no Woman could be chaste if she did not dread the Loss of her Reputation."[54] But every man was obliged to attempt to overcome his natural imperfections, and without a continual and steady effort he had little chance of success.

But strength and discipline alone were not sufficient to overcome those imperfections. Given the almost certain probability of self-deception, of incorrectly perceiving the *real* reasons for his behavior, it was necessary for man to subject his motives and deportment to a rigorous examination to make sure that "Malice" had not taken "possession of his heart" or that he had not unwittingly yielded to his passions. "Always in your Leisure hours," Carter advised the twenty-three-year-old George Washington in 1755, "regard the inward Man." Only through the kind of careful self-study recommended by this injunction could one hope to know himself well enough to subdue his baser tendencies. Even a comprehensive and persistent probing of the inner self might not produce the necessary self-knowledge. There was no more difficult task than to know one's self, and Carter was persuaded, as he wrote to

[51] L. C. Diary, Apr. 11, 14, 1752, pp. 99, 101; *Rector Detected*, 12.
[52] See L. C. Diary, Dec. 26, 1774, p. 905; *Rector Detected*, 5; *Md. Gaz.*, May 8, 1766.
[53] L. C. Diary, Jan. 25, 1770, Oct. 5, 1774, pp. 350, 865.
[54] *Rector Detected*, 23.

a more mature Washington in May 1776, that no more "truly sublime compliment" could be paid to any man than "That he was a master of himself!"[55] This drive for self-mastery, though less pronounced in Carter than in some of his contemporaries such as John Adams, contributed to a strong tendency toward introversion, to a painful concern to discover how he was doing in his struggle with his passions in his pursuit of distinction.[56]

Perhaps the best weapon man had in the struggle for self-mastery was reason. For Landon reason was that "improvement . . . which in every body is impressed by nature," that faculty which permitted man, alone among all creatures, "to govern" his instincts, to employ, as Carter suggested in some informal comments on René Le Bossu's *Traité du poème épique,* "the knowledge and experience and hopes and fears of Effects and consequences . . . to promote or avoid . . . Causes according as they are known or Suspected to be advantageous or detrimental to us." That reason was continually hindered in its operations by passions, prejudices, vanities, and interests within man or by the constraint of tradition or "some Superior or Ascendant Power"[57] upon him did not have to mean, as Alexander Pope had suggested in his *Essay on Man,* that man need *always* be animated by his passions rather than his reason.[58] Indeed, Carter insisted that every man was obliged to use his reason, however unreliable it might be, to check his passions and to guard against habits and tendencies, arguments and practices, that were "Vastly against all or any spark of reason."[59] However difficult the task might be, and he never suggested that it might be easy, it was essential for the attainment of virtue and distinction; and he insisted that wisdom and "real sensibility" came only to the man "who knowing his human machine" endeavored "by his reason to counteract it" so that he might never sacrifice "his good sence" to his passions or permit those passions to exceed the bounds of his reason.[60]

The ideal of moderation had traditionally been regarded as one of man's most useful devices for curbing his passions, and Carter made it his constant concern to live up to that ideal. He was thoroughly persuaded, as he wrote in his diary in August 1770, that "Extremes in any thing are bad."[61] Without

[55] L. C. Diary, Feb. 6, 1776, p. 976; L. C. to Washington, Oct. 7, 1755, in Hamilton, ed., *Letters to Washington,* I, 108; May 9, 1776, in Force, ed., *Am. Archives,* 4th Ser., VI, 389–92.

[56] See L. C. Diary, June 16, 1771, June 23, 1773, Aug. 12–13, 1777, pp. 577–78, 762–63, 1125.

[57] L. C. Diary, Mar. 6, 13, 1752, Feb. 15, 1770, pp. 75, 84–85, 357; L. C., "Jotting on Epick defined from Bossue," n.d., Wellford Col.; L. C. to George Washington, May 9, 1776, in Force, ed., *Am. Archives,* 4th Ser., VI, 389–92.

[58] For an analysis of this aspect of Pope's thought, see Lovejoy, *Reflections on Human Nature,* 42–45.

[59] L. C. Diary, Mar. 9, 1752, p. 78; *Letter from a Gentleman in Virginia,* 13; L. C. to Old Friend, May 14, 1769, Sabine Hall Col.

[60] L. C. Diary, June 16, 1771, May 10, 1774, pp. 577–78, 809; *Letter to B——p of L——n,* 3.

[61] L. C. Diary, Aug. 14, 1770, Oct. 13, 1774, pp. 465, 875–76.

restraint, without a strong determination to maintain the utmost prudence in one's appetites, habits, and behavior, one could, despite his reason, indulge himself in the rankest of his passions until he had either suffered himself to fall prey to the "most abandonned of all Vices" or perhaps even destroyed himself completely. The penalty for the "imprudent habits of that kind of intemperance generally called good living" was no less than the corruption of "the whole machine with one kind of Morbidity or another," and the failure to moderate one's desire for wealth and power could result only in "a dropsical thirst" which increased the more it was indulged.[62] Nor were the "horrid" consequences of self-indulgence limited to one's self; a man's intemperate actions might ruin his family or plunge his entire country, as Carter inferred in his *Letter to the B——p of L——n* in 1760, "into Confusion and Despair."[63] A strict adherence to the goals of moderation and prudence was essential for the man in pursuit of distinction, and Carter sought not only to maintain "every degree of temperance" in his own behavior but also to appear "to the whole World as a constant Enemy to . . . *all Kinds of extravagant Life.*"[64]

One of the most pernicious forms of extravagance in the world of Landon Carter was the pursuit of pleasure, and his firm belief that "good living" could never be combined successfully with the quest for distinction manifested itself in a deep antagonism to most diversions. To be sure, he had his own pleasures: smoking his pipe, riding out to view his plantations, studying and writing, maintaining a table of quality, conversing with friends and visitors about matters of moment, providing a week-long entertainment for all of his neighborhood friends each January, even having an occasional dram with other leading men of the county at the ordinary after court or militia muster.[65] But these and most other amusements he permitted himself were either useful or infrequent, and those he preferred most were useful. His reading and writing, certainly his own greatest diversions, were always purposeful. They had to provide some "Agreeable instruction," and his dictum that poetry should have "some moral truth . . . as the foundation of the Work" accurately expressed his attitude toward all forms of literature and all varieties of knowledge.[66] He had no taste for frivolity. A play to which Peyton Randolph and his older brother Charles Carter of Cleve dragged him in Williamsburg in 1752 was a surfeit of "Stupidity and nonsense delivered from the mouths of Walking Statues"; a dinner with several Essex County friends at Whitlock's Ordinary

[62] L. C. Diary, Sept. 28, 1770, Apr. 19, 1771, Apr. 8, 1776, pp. 505, 558–59, 1012–13.
[63] L. C. Diary, Sept. 14, 1774, p. 857–58; *Letter to B——p of L——n,* 37.
[64] L. C. Diary, Sept. 11, 1770, Dec. 31, 1771, Oct. 13, 1774, pp. 487, 642, 876; *Rector Detected,* 13.
[65] See, for instance, L. C. Diary, Jan. 14, Nov. 25, 1770, June 25, 1774, pp. 346, 527, 835.
[66] L. C., "Epick defined from Bossue," n.d., Wellford Col.

in Hobbs Hole was "time . . . very disagreeably spent among some laughing Gentlemen."[67] For Carter life was too serious for levity and the quest for distinction too difficult to waste many moments in nonpurposeful endeavors. But what he found even more disagreeable than the useless and the trivial, what he even more stoutly disdained, was the intemperate devotion that he constantly observed in his sons Robert Wormeley and John, in his grandson Landon, and in many of the younger generation of Virginians to those "bewitching" diversions—cards, dancing, liquor, horse racing, "running about"— that not only served no useful purpose and "at best" produced no more than "some serious and Mortifying reflexion how idly, injuriously, and simply" one had spent his time, but also became ends in themselves and thereby led men away from "the more solid improvements of the mind, the Body and the estate" which could be expected to "effect something Permanent that will be injoyed hereafter."[68]

Just as Carter was opposed to all diversions that became ends in themselves and served no useful purpose, so also was he hostile to "v[ai]n shew," empty ceremony, and concern for form rather than substance. In November 1770 he offered no apologies to especially important guests, the John Randolph and Philip Ludwell Lee families, for not serving wine with dinner when he had "neither estate nor constitution to Justifie the use of it," and in September 1772 he was disturbed to see the wife of one of his plantation managers "act the part of a fine Lady in all her towering aparell with at least two maids besides her own girl to get the dinner and wait upon her," preferring instead to "have seen the diligent industrious woman." English education, he came to believe by the 1770s, epitomized all the evils and emptiness of ostentation. "The general importers of it nowadays," he recorded in his diary, "bring back only a stiff priggishness with as little good manners as possible," a concern for nothing more important than "the particular cut of a waistcoat, the multi oval trim of a hat, or the cast of a buckle," and knowledge of nothing but "the foppishness of fancy." An excessive interest in appearances, like a devotion to frivolous pleasures, could never be expected to produce anything more than "bodily and momentary injoyments" that died "away with the hour generally, if they" did "not introduce some horrid conclusion."[69]

Even more alarming than the possibility that one might, by devoting himself exclusively to the pursuit of pleasure, waste his entire life away in

[67] L. C. Diary, Apr. 15, 1752, Feb. 20, 1771, pp. 103, 539.

[68] L. C. Diary, June 27, 1772, Feb. 12, Sept. 14, 1774, Mar. 8–9, 1776, pp. 703, 795, 857–58, 996–98.

[69] L. C. Diary, Mar. 23, Nov. 21, 25, 1770, Sept. 14, 1772, Sept. 14, 1774, pp. 372–73, 525, 527, 728, 857–58.

"folly, idleness, and dissipation" was the danger that he could in time lose his freedom by becoming a slave to his passions. The man "that loveth drink," Carter declared in July 1766, "must love every thing, to get at it" and, like the man with a passion for gaming, could "so continue as to sell the part of the Community he lives in and at last sell himself" just to satisfy his lust. Carter complained in February 1774 that Robert Wormeley had become through his devotion to gaming "every man's man but his own." "No affrican is so great a slave," Carter declared the following October, as the man with a "Passion for gaming." Gaming, along with the avarice that Carter was convinced produced it, could also destroy a man's freedom by reducing him to beggary, for the man who gamed risked losing "his own Liberty" quite as much "as his fortune," and if a man lost his estate, nothing could "keep him free and independent."[70] Carter's lifelong exposure to Negro slavery provided him with a constant and vivid reminder of just how "miserable" and abject the slave was,[71] and he was persuaded that the only certain way to avoid being reduced to such a wretched condition was to take "constant care" never to be left "without the Cork Jacket of Independence." He was invulnerable, he declared in 1759, as long as he had his "excellent little Fortress . . . built on a Rock . . . of *Independency*" for protection, and the preservation of his independence was with Carter an obsession, in many ways his most prized and most jealously guarded possession. "Independency," he wrote in 1769, was the "base or footstool on which Liberty can alone be protected," and for Carter there was absolutely no doubt that the man without liberty could never be a man of virtue.[72]

The pursuit of distinction required not only that a man maintain his independence but also that he always act with disinterestedness and impartiality. Nothing was any more destructive to virtue nor more pervasive in man than the desire for wealth and power—what in the eighteenth century was generally subsumed under the term *ambition*—and the narrow concern for selfish interests that usually attended it. Carter never ceased to be impressed by the "Predominancy of Gain among mankind," and for him no one group illustrated the evils it produced better than merchants. Mostly "Men of low and selfish Notions," they were "well vined in the sinister modes of gain," driven "by an uncommon Kind of Partiality," masters of "the arts of Speculation and deception," and "no otherwise *interested in the Country,* than in the

[70] L. C. Diary, July 5, 1766, June 6, 1773, Feb. 12, Oct. 9, 1774, Mar. 9, 1776, Sept. 2, 1777, pp. 314, 755–56, 795, 870, 997–98, 1129.
[71] Instances of this kind of reaction to Negro slavery may be found in L. C. Diary, July 10, Sept. 19, 1771, pp. 589, 636; L. C. to Mr.——, Nov. 30, 1765, Sabine Hall Col.
[72] *Letter to a Gentleman in London,* 27; L. C. to Purdie and Dixon, Fall, 1769, Folder 3, Carter Family Papers; L. C. to Wm. Rind, Oct. 1773, Sabine Hall Col.

dirty demands" they had against it. "It is . . . well known," he warned the public in September 1776 in arguing against the encouragement of mercan-tile enterprise in Virginia, "that the *Lex Mercatoria* indulged to any extent, must soon introduce a manifest interruption of the *Jus Commune* in any State." Trade, he declared in May 1774 in exasperation against his British creditors, "is a Profession that kicks Conscience out of doors like a fawning Puppy," and the man who abandoned conscience, who permitted himself to be governed by "self and gain alone," could be expected to "Sacrifice . . . every duty, whether Moral or religious" to his self-interest. Any man who "makes an *Idol of his Interest,*" Carter cautioned in *The Rector Detected,* "must make a *Martyr* of his *Integrity.*"[73]

Of "all the Failings incident to human Nature," however, the most pernicious—"the worst disposition to be possessed of in the world"—was man's insatiable "thirsting after . . . Power," his "innate disposition to rule," to be the "sole determiner in all things." This "partial Fondness for Power incon-troulable" appeared everywhere: in Speaker John Robinson's attempt to domi-nate the proceedings of the House of Burgesses; in the clergy's attempts to secure the disallowance of the Two-Penny Act, a law the Virginia legislature had considered necessary for "the Welfare of the Community"; in British merchants' acting as "lording Tyrants over their unfortunate Debtors"; in Parliament's extravagant claims to supremacy over the colonies in the Declara-tory Act; in "the secret inclination of some" members of the new republican government in 1776 "to an arbitrary sway"; in the desire of Robert Wormeley to dominate life at Sabine Hall. Wherever this "Grasp" for "Power" appeared, it was certain that both public good and private virtue would be sacrificed to self-interest and partial ends.[74] The failure to check one's ambition—to subdue one's desire for wealth and power—was an open invitation to corruption. One might by dint of purely selfish ambition become wealthy and powerful and in the process acquire fame and *apparent* distinction among men. But in the very process he would necessarily have forfeited the impartiality and disinterest that were the central characteristics of *real* distinction. Carter reserved his admiration for those men who sought to "ennoble their Lives by *real* Good-ness." "I only wish that every one was, as you have shown yourself to be," he wrote George Washington in May 1776, "not so much in quest of praise and

[73] L. C. Diary, Sept. 28, 1770, May 20, 1774, Jan. 31, 1776, Aug. 8, 1777, pp. 505, 813, 970, 1122; *Letter to a Gentleman in London,* 6–7, 9, 27; *Rector Detected,* 24; L. C. to Wm. Rind, Oct. 1773, and to Purdie, Feb. 14, 1774, and Sept. 1776, Sabine Hall Col.

[74] L. C. Diary, Mar. 13, 1752, Sept. 18, 1775, May 29, 1776, pp. 84–85, 944–45, 1046; *Md. Gaz.,* Oct. 24, 1754; *Letter to a Gentleman in London,* 11; *Letter to B——p of L——n,* 55; *Va. Gas.* (Rind), Sept. 1, 1768, (Purdie and Dixon), July 28, 1774.

emolument to yourself as of *real* good to your fellow-creatures." For himself he disdained "all Praise or Commendation" that did not arise from the true glory of genuine *"public Virtue,"* preferring that *"contented Condition"* that arose only from the knowledge that one actually was, and not only appeared to be, virtuous.[75]

This desire to *be* and not merely just to *seem* could not be fulfilled by the simple checking of one's passions, by a constant devotion to the ideals of reasonableness, moderation, independence, and disinterestedness; it required positive accomplishments for the benefit of one's family and country, accomplishments that came only through hard work. Throughout his life Carter seems to have adhered closely to his father's injunction to him as a lad of thirteen studying at Low's School in London to be "a good Boy and mind your Book" and to "Improve your time Suitable to the charge I am at upon you."[76] Believing that "a constant diligence" not only would "effect great matters" but also would check the natural human tendency toward "degenerating into indolence" and prevent man from falling "into a disponding way" and making "even the common cares of life a very heavy weight upon himself," he demanded hard work and a careful use of time both from himself and from everyone around him.[77] At court it was he who always acted as the "Spur" to the other justices, resorting to cajolery, threats, and a continual "calling out" to secure some "order and dispatch of Publick business," to rouse his fellows out of "their lazyness" and "spirit" them "up to a diligent discharge of their duty to the public."[78] On his plantations he held his overseers and slaves to a rigorous schedule. He prided himself on never getting a day behind in his plantation work, and he always planted the fullest crop possible, persuaded that those who planted short crops expecting to produce larger yields by more thorough working only accelerated the natural human tendency to degenerate "into indolence when there is not a visible necessity to be otherwise." On the same theory he always sought to keep his slaves busy, believing that there was "nothing so certain as spoiling your slaves by allowing them but little to do; so sure are they from thence to learn to do nothing at All." He reluctantly permitted the use of mechanical implements, for he was convinced that "Carts and plows only serve to make Overseers and people extremely lazy." "It is a certain truth," he wrote in his diary in April 1770, "that wherever they are in great abundance there is the least plantation work done . . . for both Over-

[75] *Letter to a Gentleman in London,* 12; *Letter to B——p of L——n,* 40; *Rector Detected,* 33; L. C. to Washington, May 9, 1776, in Force, ed., *Am. Archives,* 4th Ser., VI, 389–92.

[76] King Carter to L. C., July 5, 1723, Robert Carter Letter Book, 1723–24, Va. Hist. Soc.

[77] L. C. Diary, Feb. 28, Apr. 30, Sept. 11, 1771, pp. 544, 566, 625–26.

[78] L. C. Diary, May 9, 1770, Apr. 14, 1772, Mar. 1, 1774, pp. 405, 668–69, 799.

seers and Negroes imagine this or that work will be quickly done with the plows and Carts and of course are very little solicitous to do their proper parts of the business."[79] Nor did he demand any more work from others than he did from himself. His careful and in many cases direct supervision of his plantation work and his painstaking diligence in recording his agricultural successes and failures in his diary so that he "might correct . . . his . . . errors" leave no doubt that he held himself to the same high standards of industry.[80]

For the man of distinction learning was as important as hard work; it served both as a means to acquaint oneself with the past mistakes and successes—the accumulated knowledge—of man and as a base for adding to that knowledge. "It is the business of man," Carter wrote in his diary in February 1771, "to find out causes where he can in order to prevent any evil that may attend," and much of his adult life seems to have been devoted to that end. His early success at Low's School, the considerable amount of erudition sprinkled through his enormous literary output, the copious annotations in the margins of his large collection of books at Sabine Hall, his "particular Respect" for "Men of Learning," his attempt to establish a free school in Richmond County, his extreme sensitivity about his intellectual achievements, his presumption in the midst of the War for Independence in asking Washington for a map of the fighting area to gratify his "geographical genius," his attribution of the chronic "Vertiginous disorder" of his later years to his "too great a desire for knowledge, an intense reading and observing upon all things," the diary itself—all testify both to his learning and to a passionate devotion to the pursuit of knowledge which probably exceeded that of most of his contemporaries among the Virginia gentry. This devotion derived not only from his desire to excel but also from his usual reserve and introversion and from the sheer pleasure he received from reading and writing. In his diary for April 1777 he remarked that before the deterioration of his eyes he had never been less alone than when by himself—"*Nunquam minus Solus, quam cum solus*"—and he probably always felt more comfortable at home among his books than he did in company. Nor did this tendency decrease as he grew older, for the "desire to read" became, especially during the last decade of his life, the chief antidote to the loneliness of old age.[81]

A man who was convinced of the imperfection of every man could also be

[79] L. C. Diary, Apr. 12, Aug. 14, 1770, Sept. 11, 1771, May 27, 1772, June 25, 1774, May 12, 1776, pp. 386–87, 465–66, 625–26, 694–95, 834, 1038–39.

[80] L. C. Diary, May 29, 1772, p. 697.

[81] L. C. Diary, Feb. 24, 1771, Aug. 18, Sept. 2, 22, 1772, Feb. 24, 1776, Apr. 13, 1777, pp. 540, 713, 720, 731, 987, 1090; *Rector Detected*, 24; L. C., "Proposals for establishing a free school in Richmond County," n.d., Sabine Hall Col.; L. C. to Washington, Nov. 2, 1776, in Force, ed., *Am. Archives*, 5th Ser. III, 482.

expected to believe in the imperfection of every author, and Carter was a thoroughly skeptical reader. He was willing to accept "the possitive though not always very certain accounts of the learned," as he wrote during a controversy over the transit of Venus in 1769 and 1770, only when they did not contradict his experience. Although he thought that theory was necessary to explain practice, he was at heart a complete empiricist and always insisted on the primacy of experience over theory. The very "Imperfectness of theory," he told Dr. Walter Jones in May 1772 in defending the great Leiden physician Hermann Boerhaave against Jones's teacher, Dr. William Cullen of Edinburgh, meant that there was always "room for experience to improve it"; and he was persuaded, he wrote in his diary in July 1775, that "reasoning on General Principles . . . is cursed nonsense in every Science whatever, for General Principles are like General rules, subject to multitudes of Exceptions and perhaps no two instances can happen but must differ from those Principles according to Attending Circumstances."[82] To know anything, then, required a thorough and precise knowledge of all its complexities, all its subtleties.

The same obsession with thoroughness that caused him to plow his land deeper and to work his fields oftener and more systematically than anyone else and the same concern for accuracy that made him keep exact records of business transactions and a detailed diary manifested themselves in his own writings in tediousness and verbosity. Anyone who reads his pamphlets and essays will recognize the probable justice of Thomas Jefferson's charge that Carter's "speeches, like his writings were dull, vapid, verbose, egoistical, smooth as the lullaby of the nurse, and commanding, like that, the repose only of the hearer." Though Carter undoubtedly could and did, as he said on one occasion, mouth "as Caesar till I shook the Senate" and awaken even Jefferson, he always preferred, as he wrote in his *Letter to a Gentleman in London* in 1759, to rely upon the "evident Truth" of his argument rather than any "extraordinary Eloquence" to persuade his readers and hearers. He could not write shorter essays, he declared in his piece on the weevil fly published in the American Philosophical Society *Transactions,* because they would be "less clear and intelligible." The lack of specific information was perhaps the most serious failing in a writer. "It is amongst the oddities in Authors, whether travellers, Essayists, or Naturalists," he complained in July 1775, that "they all write as if every reader knew beforehand what they were writing of as well as themselves; for this reason in hardly any one instance do they give any Particulars." Without "Particulars" their writings were not fully useful to the reader. Completeness and exactness were the ways to truth, and Carter in his

[82] L. C. Diary, Mar. 17, 1771, May 26, 1772, July 22, 1775, Feb. 6, 1776, pp. 548, 692–93, 926, 976; L. C. to 2 in the Corner, [1769–1770], Sabine Hall Col.

preoccupation with truth and his suspicion of form always made a point, as he declared in *The Rector Detected,* of penning his arguments "with such Precision and Plainness . . . that every Reader, the least acquainted with the Subject I have written upon, might understand them."[83]

Carter's desire to push back the boundaries of knowledge was symptomatic of the greater obligation he felt to serve the public; devoted public service was the hallmark of the man of virtue, the characteristic that distinguished the man of real quality from the man who was merely in search of fame, wealth, and power. Carter thought both that man "was at first created" for the performance of "social duties" and that the responsibility for those duties fell squarely upon "the polite and more considerate part" of society, that group which had the time, resources, and virtue to care for the concerns of the public expertly and impartially. It was to the upper classes that a country looked "for Prudent advice and assistance," for "Patterns or examples," and there was nothing more "commendable" than "to let men see our good works that they may take example by them in their conduct to each other and to the happiness and safety of their Country."[84] This concept of upper-class leadership carried with it a heavy burden of responsibility, and Carter was one member of the Virginia gentry who shouldered that burden eagerly and with the same high seriousness with which he accepted his obligation to lead a virtuous life. He repeatedly sought to use his learning for the benefit of the public, publishing the results of his scientific and agricultural experiments in the *Gazettes,* using his skill in medicine to minister to his "whole neighbourhood," advising friends and acquaintances about the law, supporting measures to encourage arts and manufactures in the colony.[85]

Carter's most conspicuous public service was in the political realm. As a

[83] L. C. Diary, Apr. 20, 1752, May 25, 29, 1772, Oct. 5, 1774, July 27, 1775, pp. 107, 692, 697, 865, 930; Stan V. Henkels, ed., "Jefferson's Recollections of Patrick Henry," *Pennsylvania Magazine of History and Biography,* XXXIV (1910), 406; *Letter to a Gentleman in London,* 28; *Rector Detected,* 3–4; L. C., "Observations concerning the fly weevil, that destroys wheat," *Transactions of the American Philosophical Society,* Old Ser., I (1771), 217; L. C. to My Friend, [1774?], Sabine Hall Col.

[84] L. C. Diary, Nov. 6, 1771, Oct. 6, 1774, Sept. 11, 1775, Feb. 23, 1777, pp. 638, 866–67, 941, 1084; Hening, ed., *Statutes,* VII, 289, 568; L. C. to Purdie and Dixon, Fall 1769, Carter Family Papers, Folder 3; L. C. to Wm. Rind, Aug. 1772, Sabine Hall Col.

[85] L. C. Diary, Sept. 11, 1771, Sept. 14, 1775, pp. 625–26, 942–43. Known or highly probable writings on agricultural and scientific subjects by Carter are in *Trans. Am. Phil. Soc.,* Old Ser., I (1771), 218–24, on the fly weevil; in the *Va. Gaz.* (Rind), Sept. 14, 1769, on a hurricane, July 26, 1770, on the transit of Venus, Nov. 19, 1772, on the fly weevil, and on Apr. 14, 1774, on the care of lightning victims; *Va. Gaz.* (Purdie and Dixon), Aug. 30, Sept. 13, 20, Oct. 4, Dec. 13, 1770, Jan. 31, 1771, on the transit of Venus, and Dec. 3, 1772, on the prevention of the plague; *Md. Gaz.,* Dec. 21, 1758, Apr. 5, 1759, on the corn moth, Mar. 10, 1763, on lucern. Manuscript pieces by Carter include letters to Purdie and Dixon, Oct. 1, 1770, on the transit of Venus, Carter Family Papers, Folder 3, to 2 in the Corner, 1770, on the transit of Venus, in the Sabine Hall Col., as well as undated essays on the body fluids and the cultivation of hops in the Sabine Hall Col.

justice of the peace he continually endeavored to improve the quality and the efficiency of the administration of the county. In January 1735 at the second meeting after his appointment to the court he sought to remedy certain deficiencies by securing an order empowering him "to send to England for what law books he shall think necessary for Richmond County" and "to acquire a table of weights and measures according to colony law." For the rest of his life he was constantly trying to secure some "order and dispatch of Publick business" and to preserve "order an[d] decency . . . in the Co[unty]." The same devotion to duty that caused him to worry about "the possibility of a wrong Judgement . . . either through temper or interest" also drove him to leave a sick bed to attend court so that he might not contribute to the delay of the administration of justice. Even after independence, when he felt that the ingratitude of many people in the county had given him ample cause to withdraw from the court, he could not, despite strong resolutions to the contrary, "desert" his "Duty to" his "Country," and when a "worthy member begged" him to "come to give weight and order to the Proceedings," he re-sumed his place on the bench, convinced from the observations of a long life that "order and comfort arises from the appearance only of some good man." Nor was he any less devoted to his duties as a burgess. To be a burgess was an "honour" in itself, but just to have the post was not enough for Carter; only by being "a *diligent"* and, he might have added, unusually active "Member of the assembly" could he think himself "truely meritorious." In seventeen years of service, he declared in 1774, he had missed the meeting of the House only when he was sick or when he wished to protect himself "in the small Pox time." The same "true Sense of the Duty he" owed "to his Country" drove him to take up his pen to defend the Burgesses and the colony in each of the long series of controversies that preceded the outbreak of the War for Independ-ence. His greatest satisfaction seems to have been the knowledge that he had done his duty to his community, and the role he delighted in most was, as he signed himself in a letter to Alexander Purdie's *Virginia Gazette* in September 1776, as the public's "most devoted and Assiduous Servant in all my endeav-ours for their real good."[86]

Even with the strictest adherence to this elaborate structure of values, the most intense devotion to self-discipline, self-mastery, reason, moderation, im-provement, independence, disinterestedness, hard work, learning, and public

---

[86] Richmond Co. court Order Books, X, 1732–39, 230 (Jan. 7, 1735); L. C. Diary, Apr. 6, 1772, Mar. 1, 1774, Feb. 15, Aug. 8, 1777, pp. 668, 799, 1076–77, 1121; *Letter from a Gentleman in Virginia,* 3–5; *Rector Detected,* 3–4; L. C. to Joseph Royle, June 3, 1765, Brock Col., Huntington Lib.; L. C. to Wm. Rind, Oct. 1773, to My Friend, (1774?), to Dixon and Hunter, July 1776, and to Purdie, Sept. 1776, Sabine Hall Col.

service, Carter knew from repeated experience that no man could achieve true distinction or measurable success in his earthly enterprises without the help and favor of God. No seventeenth-century New England Puritan was any more deeply impressed with the omnipotence of God and the ultimate dependence of man upon God's will than Landon Carter. He was not, as he admitted to George Washington in October 1776, "enthusiastically religious" in the conventional sense. He was a devout Anglican who took his duties as vestryman in Lunenburgh Parish seriously, but his bitter attacks on the clergy during the controversy over the Two-Penny Act and his repeated embroilments with local ministers William Kay and Isaac Giberne were indicative of his antagonism to and suspicion of the clergy. Although he believed strongly in a close connection between church and state so that the religious power might remedy "the Imperfections of the Civil," he favored toleration and was opposed to burdening non-Anglicans with the support of the established church. Nor does he seem to have had much interest in formal theology, preferring instead the "Practical godliness" so strongly recommended to him by his father.[87] Though he had little use for many of the trappings of religion, he was an intensely religious man. His piety permeates the diary. He was continually thanking God for his blessings, asking forgiveness for his sins, seeking divine favor in his endeavors. He could not help worrying that he might have "imperfectly conceived" God's commands or that he might "have possibly deserved" any "inconveniency" that befell him. His religion was his chief comfort in the face of adversity and failure, his source of inspiration whenever he fell into a "disponding way," and when during his last ten years a "multitude of infirmities" brought him severe pain and the resulting confrontation with the certainty of death even "Produced a long dream of entertaining many dead People" and made each symptom seem like "a harbinger of death," his religion gave him hope and helped him keep up the "Cheerful" appearance that, as he noted in October 1774, he believed was his "only insincerity."[88]

Religion also served Carter as a handmaiden in his quest for distinction. Though he had no doubt that God was supreme and that man was completely at His mercy, he liked to believe that God was also just and favored the man who helped himself, who used his "skill, care, and diligence" as fully as he might and who sought to live by His word as closely as an imperfect

---

[87] L. C. Diary, Mar. 10, 1752, Aug. 19, 1771, June 4, 1774, pp. 81, 616–17, 819–21; Carter to Washington, Oct. 21, 1776, in Force, ed., *Am. Archives*, 5th Ser., II, 1304–7; *Letter to B———p of L———n*, 4, 7, 14–16, 24; King Carter to William Dawkins, July 14, 1720, in Wright, ed., *Letters of Robert Carter*, 25; William Kay to Bishop of London, June 14, 1752, in William S. Perry, ed., *Papers relating to the History of the Church in Virginia, 1650–1776* (Hartford, 1870), 389–91.

[88] L. C. Diary, Aug. 14, 18, 1770, Feb. 27–28, Apr. 29, July 15, Aug. 18, 1771, May 16, July 2, Aug. 18, 1772, June 23, 1773, Oct. 1, 9, 1774, Sept. 11, 16, 1775, Feb. 15, 1776, Aug. 12–13, 1777, Aug. 18, 21, 1778, pp. 465, 468–69, 543–44, 565, 591–93, 615, 684, 704, 713, 763, 860, 870, 940–41, 943, 988, 1125–26, 1145–46.

being might. By doing his best to live a virtuous life and obey God's commands, however, a man could control his destiny only up to a point; in the last analysis it was God's will that would be done, and a man could do no more than use "his best endeavour" and "trust in his God." "In all things," Carter wrote in his diary in February 1772, "I do the best I can and relye on Superiour mercy for the success of my endeavours." When God did not reward his efforts, a man could only accept his misfortune with resignation and humility, knowing that no human was "too great to brook misfortunes" at the hand of God, that, as Carter prayed in July 1771, "if God favors, all will be well. And if he should not what sensible Mortal could think of Existing a moment."[89]

However God might finally choose to reward or punish his efforts, Carter never for a moment ceased trying to do everything in his power to make himself worthy of any favors God might wish to bestow upon him, and the quest for virtue and distinction meant more to him than even love or friendship. Neither his affection for his immediate family nor the fatherly attachment he felt toward some of his overseers ever prevented him from trying to hold them to a strict adherence to the same rigid code by which he lived. Though he had genuine compassion and a deep sense of responsibility for his slaves, he never hesitated to use the whip or any other punishment "not barbarous"—even to frightening Toney the carpenter into work by having him "make his own Coffin to be laid up in and buryed"—to keep them to their duty. Keeping Negroes busy was especially important, not only because they might meditate their freedom or their "master's destruction" if they had too much idle time, but also because they were less honest and more imperfect than white men. Unlike other men, who were "spurred on to diligence by rewards," "kindness to a Negroe" seemed to be "the surest way to spoil him," and only by maintaining strict discipline could the master fulfill his responsibility to the slaves to keep them from lapsing into a life of dishonesty and vice. "Indeed, Slaves are devils," Carter declared in disgust in August 1778, "and to make them otherwise than slaves will be to set devils free." He was one Virginia planter who had no inclination to permit his Negroes, as he sarcastically commented in July 1776, to "glut" their "genius for liberty which" they were "not born to."[90]

Carter held his friends and associates outside his family to the same standards. He insisted both that every "Proper individual" was "obliged to

[89] L. C. Diary, Aug. 2, 22, Sept. 19, 1770, July 15, Aug. 13, 1771, Feb. 11, May 8, Aug. 7, Sept. 24, Oct. 14, 1772, Feb. 28, 1777, pp. 459–60, 472, 493–94, 591–93, 611, 653, 677, 710, 733, 740, 828, 1088.

[90] L. C. Diary, Apr. 27, May 4, 1766, June 28, Aug. 14, 21, Sept. 28, 1770, July 10, Sept. 17, 19, 1771, May 27, 1772, June 14, 1774, July 13, 1776, Apr. 20, 1777, Aug. 31, 1778, pp. 292, 295, 429–30, 465–66, 471, 505, 589, 632–33, 635–36, 694–95, 827, 1056, 1095–96, 1148–49; *Rector Detected*, 25; L. C. to Dixon and Hunter, May 1776 (?), Sabine Hall Col.; epitaph on Elizabeth Carter, 1740, Carter Family Papers, Folder 1.

Judge" for "the benefit of the Community" and that all men should be judged by merit and not by friendship. In his conviction that candidness was the best policy and that for men "to be so much on the guard, as to be always concealed" was "contemptible," he never tried to hide his disapproval. The result was that he was never a popular man. Indeed, some responded to him with intense dislike and perhaps even actual hate. William Jordan, a Richmond County freeholder, vowed in 1742 that he "would give a Hogshead, or a Hundred Gallons of Rum, rather than Mr. Carter . . . should go Burgess; and that he never should go Burgess." To his indentured secretary, Owen Griffith, Carter was a "Boisterous Tyrant"; and someone else bitterly satirized him in two long poems in Purdie and Dixon's *Virginia Gazette* in 1767. Carter's trouble was that he demanded perfection from men knowing that they, like himself, would always be imperfect, and his "stern behavior" and apparent cynicism offended people and made them uncomfortable. "How might he be revered," an anonymous and friendly critic suggested in verse in November 1768 just before Carter's constituents turned him out of the Burgesses, "Would he strive rather to be loved than feared." "Let him relax," he added, "and we are all his own." But relax was the very thing Carter could never do. His vigil over himself was constant, and if he was critical of the weaknesses of others, it was because he was intimately acquainted with his own imperfections. He never demanded anything from others that he did not ask of himself, and he was persuaded that no man was more honest or more "Patriotic" than "the man who owns he had split upon a rock, and . . . points it Out to others, that they may avoid it." If others objected to his judgments, it was because they either failed to consider them impartially and with "good sense" or deliberately sacrificed truth and justice for friendship. For Landon Carter either alternative was impossible. He could never, as he replied to his anonymous critic, permit justice to "pine, or Right give up its whole./To purchase love, so painful to the Soul." For the man in quest of honor and virtue neither love nor friendship nor applause was worth the forfeiture of integrity.[91]

A NOBLE STRUGGLE

Landon Carter seems to have been irresistibly drawn to politics. For forty-four years from 1734 until his death in 1778 he was actively involved in

---

[91] L. C. Diary, Mar. 14, 1770, Mar. 9, 15, 31, 1776, pp. 368, 997, 1001–2, 1007–8; *Letter to B——p of L——n*, 35; *Va. Gaz.* (Purdie and Dixon), June 11, Aug. 13, 1767; *Burgesses Journals, 1742–49*, 34–35 (May 24, 1742); "Verses before Election" and Carter's reply, Nov. 1, 1768, and Owen Griffith to L. C., Dec. 21, 1771, Sabine Hall Col.

the political life of the colony, and his keen sense of public responsibility, his conviction that devoted public service was the most important mark of the man of distinction, his tendency to immerse himself in any question or problem he encountered, his penchant for thorough and systematic analysis, and his compulsion to write all of his observations down that they might be of some service either to himself or to the public—all of these characteristics combined to produce a body of formal and informal political comment that exceeds in quantity that of any other Virginian of his generation and probably reveals more fully than the writings of any other individual the framework of political assumptions and ideas within which his generation of Virginians operated. To what extent those ideas derived from his reading and his early experience in the relatively stable political environment of Richmond County and Virginia in the years before 1754 is now impossible to say, but they were certainly amplified and enlarged, if not in many cases fully articulated for the first time, in response to the dramatic events of subsequent decades: the French and Indian War; the pistole fee, paper money, and Two-Penny Act controversies; the pre-Revolutionary debate with Britain; war and independence. They grew out of and were dependent upon his conception of human nature, and they represented in general an attempt to apply to the public realm those values and standards of behavior around which and on which he thought all men should build their private lives. Just as the greatest challenge to man as an individual was to protect himself from his own evil tendencies, so the principal end of government was to protect men from each other, and the central question behind most of Carter's political inquiries was how a government necessarily composed of imperfect men could ever fulfill that end. That this was the basic dilemma of man in society became increasingly manifest with each new succession of events between 1754 and 1778, and its apparent insolubility only made the search for a solution the more compelling. Indeed, man's persistence in the search even in the face of almost certain failure was perhaps, as Carter suggested in mid-1776, his most "noble Struggle."[92]

Carter's notions about politics rested upon two assumptions about the nature of man: first, that he was a social being drawn naturally and inevitably into associations with other men and, second, that he was an imperfect creature who, if left entirely to his own devices, could not be expected to act for the good of society as a whole. Few men could see beyond their own narrow horizons or could rise above "the general proneness in Mankind, to favour their own Errors." But much more dangerous than this natural weakness was the conscious malevolence of "men of a depraved Turn." They invariably

[92] L. C. to Dixon and Hunter, May 1776 (?), Sabine Hall Col.

sought to "shake off every Restraint," and their passion for fame or money or power was so great that "even halters about" their necks could scarcely prevent "them from broaching the most destructive measures" to society. To promote happiness and order by securing the life, liberty, and property of every individual from the arbitrary rule of such men, to seek to operate upon the principles of freedom and justice rather than oppression and injustice, and to disappoint "every *avaritious, merciless* Man, in his Desires of preying upon the Necessities of the People" were, then, the primary functions of government.[93]

For a government to fulfill these functions it was absolutely necessary, Carter was convinced, that it always attend to the general "Good of the Community" rather than to the particular needs of any individual or group within the community. It was upon this principle that Carter built his defense of the Two-Penny Act against the attacks of the clergy and the Bishop of London in 1760. That law, he argued in his *Letter to the B——p of L——n,* "was a Thing absolutely necessary to be done" for the welfare of the colony and was "therefore just in itself." To oppose it because it injured a small group within the colony, as the clergy had done, was to demonstrate a willingness "to pave the Way to egregious Extortion on a whole Community" to benefit "but a very few Individuals," and it was a "great Absurdity," he argued, to suppose "that a Part is greater than its Whole; or, in other Words, that some Individuals ought to be considered, even to the Destruction of the Community, which they compose." That doctrine, he declared, was "worthy of those alone who are confined within the narrow Circle of private Profit, and have no Relish for *publick Good,* that interferes with their dirty Schemes of Gain." Later in the controversy he used the same argument in *The Rector Detected* against the Crown's right to disallow laws colonial legislatures had thought necessary for the good of the colonies. "For let the Prerogative be carried to what Height it will," he contended, "it cannot, without great Injustice, be construed to the Destruction of the Prince's Virtue; which I shall not stick to define to be that Goodness which inclines him . . . to acquiesce at all Times in the Agreement of his Subjects amongst themselves, in any Part of his Dominions, when that Agreement does not affect his own *royal Right* in any *sensible* Manner, or the Rest of his Subjects of his Kingdom in any Manner *whatever.*" Even the royal prerogative had always to give way before the public good. Almost immediately after the outbreak of the War for Independ-

---

[93] L. C. Diary, Feb. 24, 1776, pp. 986–87; L. C. on taxation, n.d., Wellford Col.; L. C., to Botetourt, Nov. 1, 1768, to Purdie, Feb. 14, 1774, and Sept. 1776, to Dixon and Hunter, May 1776 (?), Sabine Hall Col.; L. C. to Washington, Oct. 21, 1776, in Force, ed., *Am. Archives,* 5th Ser., II, 1304–7; *Letter from a Gentleman in Virginia,* 3–5, 16, 33–35; *Md. Gaz.,* Oct. 24, 1754; *Letter to a Gentleman in London,* 25; *Letter to B——p of L——n,* 5, 17, 43, 59; *Va. Gaz.* (Rind), Apr. 4, 1766.

ence in early 1775 Carter declared in his diary that he thought the welfare of the community justified the suppression and perhaps even the expulsion and punishment of any "Traytors in opinion to their Country." Anyone not choosing to join the Continental Association or refusing to take an oath of allegiance to his country was, as he declared in February 1777, certainly "an enimy to his Country." Rejecting the argument that "Tories . . . only differed in Opinion" and that that difference might somehow be "for the good of the Country," he contended that to permit a part of the community to differ in opinion from the majority when the very being of that community was at stake "might be destructive of the whole." "One or a few" could never "be better Judges of" the public "Good than was the multitude," and if that good required the suspension of "Private Justice" or the suppression of the individual liberty of the minority that opposed it, then it was, as in the case of the Two-Penny Act, "a Thing absolutely necessary to be done" and "therefore just in itself."[94]

The "Good of the Community" demanded not only that its corporate interests always be preferred to those of any part of it but also that no group within it—and especially no group with political power—ever be granted any special privileges. Such a grant might appear initially to be for the welfare of the public and might even opeate in a salutary way so long as those to whom it was made were "undebauched by corruption." But given the "frail nature" of man and especially his "innate disposition" to seek power over his fellow creatures, no individual or group of men, however virtuous or deserving they might seem, could be trusted not to turn such privileges to their own private advantage and to use them to establish a despotism or "a mere Aristocratic power." In Carter's eyes aristocracy, which he defined as the rule of a small group for their own private ends, was "an Arbitrary and an Oppressive" form of government.[95] This belief that no men could be trusted with too much power led Carter to advocate rotation in office after independence and to oppose attempts by any group to secure special privileges. Thus, in August 1772 he attacked the ruling of the Virginia Council that a councilor could be tried only in the General Court in Williamsburg or in the court of the county in which he lived. To make such an "extraordinary distinction . . . between a councellor and a Commoner," he charged, carried "an Aristocratical Complexion"; and he warned that "such a vast extension of power . . . united in one set of men" might introduce great "inconveniency to the Community."

[94] *Letter to a Gentleman in London,* 20–21; *Letter to B——p of L——n,* 5, 19, 29, 50–51, 55; *Rector Detected,* 23, 30.

[95] L. C. Diary, July 29–30, 1775, Feb. 20, 1777, pp. 931–33, 1078–79; *Letter to B——p of L——n,* 19.

Even if the councilors who made the ruling managed to resist the temptation to seek still greater privileges and more power, they might be replaced by "men of great extravagance, always dextrous in the slavery which they generally introduce to support themselves," and then, Carter cautioned, "poor Denmark let thy unhappy history apply the fatal conclusion." "No Judicious Constitution" could ever "give the least countenance" to such a "partial privilege." One of the "most essential" tasks of government, Carter had declared in *The Rector Detected* back in 1764, was "the Preservation of the greater Number of Individuals against an almost certain Oppression from the lesser Number," and the only certain way to prevent the lesser number from gaining the ascendancy was to preserve the absolute legal equality of all subjects. In attacking the Council's ruling, Carter emphasized the obligation assumed by the justice of the peace in his oath "to *do equal right to the poor and to the rich, after their cunning, wit, and power according to law.*" That obligation underlined the greater responsibility of a government to make sure that no group was ever accorded any special status, privilege, exemption, or benefit. "Subjects have no Pretence, one more than another," he declared in 1759 in his *Letter to a Gentleman in London;* "they must all equally enjoy an Advantage, or suffer a Calamity whenever it attends a Community." Such an equality was the best guarantee against the emergence of an authority within the state that could not be controlled by the public.[96]

But if a good government avoided giving any advantages to or placing too much power in the hands of the rulers or any other special group, it also had to be careful not to place too much influence in the hands of the people in general, and Carter was as opposed to "popularity"—by which he seems to have meant both the tendency for men with political ambitions to seek office by catering to the whims of the people and the demand of the voters that their representatives act in direct accordance with their sentiments—as he was to aristocracy. As early as October 1754 he argued in a debate with the "favourers of Popularity" over the nature of representation in the House of Burgesses that in all cases except those that "related particularly to the interest of the Constituents alone" a representative should "be Governed" not by the collective "sentiments of his Constituents" but by "his own Reason and Conscience." Obviously, a man who permitted himself to be closely bound by his constituents could not act with that spirit of disinterestedness and impartiality that Carter thought necessary for every public servant, and he was deeply suspi-

---

[96] L. C. Diary, May 9, 1774, May 29, 1776, pp. 808, 1046; *Letter to a Gentleman in London*, 10; *Rector Detected*, 22; L. C. to William Rind, Aug. 1772, and to Dixon and Hunter, May 1776 (?), Sabine Hall Col.; Francis Lightfoot Lee to L. C., Nov. 9, 1776, Emmet Col.

cious of the motives of any man who permitted himself to be so bound. It was clear to Carter that such a man would promise anything to the freeholders and even practice the most "rascally deceit" to "suit" his "ambitious schemes" to be "chosen a representative only to carve a good plan for himself." Such a hypocrite, once in office, could be expected to serve not the public but himself either by conspiring with men of similar hue to establish "an Aristocratic Power" or by selling himself to his country's enemies, forgetting "poor Liberty" in the process and delivering the country "into slavery." Carter had no doubt, as he wrote to George Washington in October 1776, that "popularity" was as real an "enemy to freedom" as the most corrupt ministers in Great Britain. Nor was it worth while for a man of virtue to play the game in the hope of eventually bringing the people back to their senses. Though his son Robert Wormeley "kissed the arses of the people and very servilely accommodated himself to" them, they "shamefully" and ungratefully threw him out of office at "a kind of April fool" election on April 1, 1776, after seven years of faithful service. "But it is the nature of Popularity," Carter cynically wrote in his diary after the election; "She I long ago discovered to be an adulteress of the first order; for at any time let her be most sacredly wedded to one man she will even be grogged by her gallant over his shoulder."[97]

Perhaps the least desirable feature of popularity was its direct effect upon the people. By early 1776, as a result of the forces set in motion by the breakdown of royal authority and the American opposition to Britain, they had become so "Poisoned" by popularity and had fallen into such disorder that they preferred to rely for their defense upon "the incontroulable will of every individual humble" rather than submit to the direction even of "the greatest and most devoted constitutional Patriot that has for ages appeared." This rejection of qualified and disinterested leaders, coupled with the tendency, also produced by popularity, for each individual to pursue his own private interest "Neck or nothing" in the attempt to get ahead, led to the total neglect of public concerns. In short, as Carter lamented in March 1776, "the Public is . . . neglected . . . as the People may be concerned."[98]

Because the people in general could not be trusted to care for the interests of the public or the community, government had to depend for leadership upon the patriot, and the patriot had to have those qualities Carter invariably claimed for himself in his public writings: virtue, honor, a sense of justice,

[97] L. C. Diary, Oct. 17, 1754, Mar. 28–29, Apr. 1, 4, 1776, Feb. 4, Apr. 27, 1777, pp. 116–17, 1006–10, 1073, 1102–3; *Rector Detected,* 8; L. C. to Washington, Oct. 21, 1776, in Force, ed., *Am. Archives,* 5th Ser., II, 1304–7.

[98] L. C. Diary, Mar. 29, Apr. 9, 1776, Aug. 8, 1777, Aug. 5, 1778, pp. 1006, 1015, 1121, 1141; L. C. to Dixon and Hunter, May 1776 (?), Sabine Hall Col.

impartiality, disinterestedness, independence. In every public action he had to be moved, as Carter claimed to be during the pistole fee controversy, by no "Interest less than that of a whole Country"; he had to be, like Carter thought George Washington was, "resolved never to forget" the "citizen in the . . . rulers." He could not be attached to any party, because parties, Carter thought in common with most of his contemporaries, were the instruments of partial and interested men whose commitments to factional and private ends invariably prevented them from considering the public interest objectively and impartially. Every "good man," Carter contended in urging the Virginia councilors to join the Continental Association, "ought to act under all appointments relative to the Public."[99]

Even patriots, however, could not always be trusted to act in the best interests of the public. John Robinson, speaker of the House of Burgesses and treasurer of Virginia from 1738 to 1766, was a case in point. A man of great charity, benevolent intentions, "amiable dignity," and "many brilliant virtues," Robinson, Carter noted upon his entry into the Burgesses in 1752, frequently used the influence of his position to push measures through the House that Carter thought were unwise. Though he complained about Robinson's willingness to use his "weight" to overcome "reason" and disapproved of any man's having such a stranglehold upon the House, he was not especially alarmed, because Robinson seemed to be entirely without any "vitious Principles." The revelation at Robinson's death in 1766 that he had, apparently solely out of charity, loaned large sums of public money to his friends showed just how dangerous the concentration of so much power in the hands of even an honest man could be. That Robinson's actions had "proceeded from nothing fraudulent in the Gentleman, but from the humane disposition [of] charity" did not make them, at least in Carter's eyes, any less "condemnable" nor any less harmful to the public. The lesson in this incident was clear: neither the firmest patriot nor the most virtuous man could be trusted with "uncontroulable Power."[100]

Both because "Man left to his own Will over his Fellow Creatures" could, as Carter observed in his *Letter to a Gentleman in London* in 1759, "sometimes fall into such Depravations of Mind, as to become more cruel than the most Savage Beast of Prey" and because even those men who overcame their vicious

[99] L. C. Diary, Mar. 21, Apr. 11, 1752, pp. 89, 98–99; *Letter from a Gentleman in Virginia,* 3–5, 35; *Letter to B——p of L——n,* 10; *Md. Gaz.,* Oct. 24, 1754; L. C. to Washington, May 9, 1776, in Force, ed., *Am. Archives,* 4th Ser. VI, 389–92; L. C. on councilors' refusal to join association, [1774–75], Sabine Hall Col.

[100] L. C. Diary, Mar. 13, 1752, May 23, 1776, pp. 84–85, 1042–43; *Va. Gaz.* (Purdie and Dixon), Aug. 1, 1766.

nature could by falling victim to their many imperfections inadvertently injure their fellows, all men—both rulers and ruled—had to be restrained. If it were closely connected with the "civil Power" and "Civil Society," a "Religion that deters from Evil, and encourages good Actions" could, Carter thought, help remedy their imperfections, but in the last analysis reliance had to be placed primarily upon law, statutory law to minister to the general welfare of the community by establishing and maintaining an "Equitable and Just" relationship among men and fundamental law—the constitution—to guarantee to the governed those basic rights that would insure that they would never be subjected to "the voluntary Mercy" of any individual or exposed to the unlimited power of an "uncontroulable" government. The fallibility "of human Understanding, as to Causes, Effects, and Consequences," Carter repeatedly argued against all attempts to limit the lawmaking power of the Virginia Burgesses, inevitably meant that statutory law had to be continually revised and altered as necessity, reason, and justice required; but the constitution, though it might sometimes have to "be aided, extended or qualified . . . to support and preserve the Community," had to be kept "as sacred as possible." As the guarantor of man's basic rights and as the instrument by which he hoped to balance harmful elements against each other—e.g., in the manner of the "Pure British Constitution" to check the tendencies toward aristocracy and popularity by mixing them together in such a way as to keep them in a constant state of equilibrium so that man might be preserved from man, that men could live under a government of impartial laws rather than of partial men—the constitution was, at least for Carter, man's most precious possession.[101]

This strong attachment to the constitution and to constitutionalism was at the heart of Carter's intense opposition to British policy after 1764. In each successive crisis from the first announcement of the Stamp Act until independence he cast himself in the role, as he wrote in September 1768, of an American "greatly struggling in the cause of liberty, to save" the "constitution from being overturned." The issue, as Carter saw it, was clear: by attempting to tax the colonies "out of the constitutional road" Parliament had threatened to destroy *"the fundamental laws of the Constitution,"* and Americans by insisting upon their "Privilege of being solely governed and taxed by Laws made with the Consent of the Majority of their own Representatives, accord-

---

[101] L. C. Diary, Mar. 6, 1752, p. 75; *Letter from a Gentleman in Virginia,* 11–12, 19, 22–23, 29; *Md. Gaz.,* Oct. 24, 1754; *Letter to a Gentleman in London,* 14–15, 19–21; *Letter to B———p of L———n,* 5–7, 15–16, 19, 46, 50–51, 53, 55; L. C. on taxation, n.d., Wellford Col.; L. C. to William Rind, Aug. 1772, and to Dixon and Hunter, May 1776 (?), Sabine Hall Col.; L. C. to George Washington, May 9, Oct. 21, 1776, in Force, ed., *Am. Archives,* 4th Ser., VI, 389–92, 5th Ser., II, 1304–7.

ing to the *Englishman's* inherent Birthright" were simply striving to preserve those laws and protect the "purity of the . . . constitution." To Carter the most "essential" element in that constitution was the people's right of representation, their right "freely" to "enjoy and occupy their own Properties, by being Governed and Taxed only by such laws as" their representatives agreed to. Because that right was "inherent by Birth in every *Englishman,*" those Englishmen who had migrated to the colonies had brought it with them, and the Crown, finding it "impossible for the Subject when he emigrated, to enjoy such a Right . . . in a *British* Parliament," had established "either by *Charters* or *Instructions*" the "several Legislative constitutions in the Colonies," not "as a grant of new Rights," but as "a confirmation of the people's original Right of Government." Americans, then, exercised their right of representation, not through Parliament to which they neither did nor could send representatives, but through their own representative assemblies. Thus, Carter insisted, well in advance of most other American writers who were content at the time of the Stamp Act to deny Parliament's right to tax the colonies, that Parliament could neither tax nor legislate for the internal affairs of the colonies. From the Stamp Act on, he wrote to Richard Henry Lee in 1775, he had never made any distinction between "the right of giving money and the right of making laws." Through either taxation or legislation "without representation" a man might be deprived of his liberty and property without his consent, and for that reason, as he declared in arguing against the Stamp Act, men had to be exempt "from the force of *any* Law, made without the consideration of their Representatives."[102]

That no group of Englishmen should be *"governed and taxed"* by any body or any group over which they had no control derived, of course, out of Carter's general belief that there could be no uncontrollable power in any justly constituted state. "Wherever there is a superiority in Power (considered either literally or figuratively)," he declared in 1765 while attacking the notion that Parliament had unlimited authority over the empire, "Justice seldom prevails" and "Might" usually "overcomes Right," but he warned against confusing the *"Right of exercising"* with *"the power of effecting . . . such measures."* Parliament undoubtedly could command the strength to force the colonies to submit to its authority, but such an "extravagant" exercise of power could never be justified by the constitution. Carter already conceived of the empire as a series of distinct political entities united with Britain only through the Crown, and in such a political organization it was clear that no one part of

---

[102] L. C. Diary; May 29, 1776, p. 1046; L. C. to Mr.——, Nov. 30, 1765, and to R. H. Lee, Feb. 25, 1775, Sabine Hall Col.; *Md. Gaz.,* May 8, 1766, *Va. Gaz.* (Rind), Sept. 1, 1768.

the realm could have any greater privileges or any more power than any other part, just as no well-ordered government could permit any group or individual within it to have any greater advantages or immunities than the rest of the public. There had to be an "equality of constitutional rights . . . in the whole realm"; colonists had to be equal to Britons, and colonial legislatures, Carter strongly inferred, had to be equal to Parliament. "From my earliest acquaintance with the legislative body of my Country," Carter wrote, "I have looked upon them as an assembly, inheriting every liberty that could appertain to Britons, or the Sons of Britons." He rejected out of hand any suggestion that the Virginia House of Burgesses was "a poor epitomé of British greatness" with *"only a Corporation Right to make Bye-Laws, subject to every whimsical Alteration of some pretended supreme Legislature."* So long as the "KING OF THE WHOLE REALM" exercised that "actual Supremacy . . . in every Legislation" which "the Constitution" had provided for in giving him authority to call and dissolve parliaments in and veto laws from "any Part of the Realm," there was no "Necessity . . . for a further supremacy" in Parliament. In any case, however, such a supremacy would invariably be unjust and unconstitutional, not only because it would introduce a basic inequality of rights between Britons and Americans by setting up a power over the Americans that they would be unable to control, but also because it violated *"that Fundamental"* of the *"Constitution"*—the liberty of "every Englishman" not to be governed and taxed "by any law that has not had the actual consideration of his Representatives."[103]

The Stamp Act crisis produced in Carter, as in many other Americans, a deep suspicion that corruption had taken hold in Britain and that out of that corruption had emerged a sinister conspiracy "to reduce the subjects of Great Britain" to "slavery . . . though beginning only by degrees with those in America," and each subsequent stroke at American freedom over the next decade only convinced Carter of the justice of that suspicion. The Declaratory Act of 1766 was "the bill of might"—a wanton and unjustified assertion of authority conceived only to pave the way for the "base purposes" of ministerial conspirators. Unable to believe that George III himself had any "design to oppress us," Carter could only conclude during the long dispute over the Townshend Acts that "departments of ill designing men" had blocked the channel to the throne and were deliberately and vilely misrepresenting "American intentions" to further their "enslaving schemes of tyranny and

[103] *Letter to a Gentleman in London*, 10; *Letter to B——p of L——n*, 44; L. C. to Joseph Royle, June 3, 1765, Fairfax Papers, III, Brock Col.; L. C. to Mr. ——, Nov. 30, 1765, Sabine Hall Col.; *Md. Gaz.*, May 8, 1766; *Va. Gaz.* (Rind), Apr. 4, 1766.

oppression." The circular letter of Secretary of State Lord Hillsborough order-ing the "rescinding, erasing, &c." of "resolutions in favour of liberty, made by the several Assemblies in the colonies" against the Townshend Acts seemed to be calculated to blot "out all traces to posterity, should they unhappily be born under slavery, that their ancestors did every thing that their weak situation could admit of, to support and maintain their rights to freedom." Britain, Carter was persuaded by May 1769, had sunk into a "universal state of dissipa-tion," and he warned against any compromise that would leave the constitu-tional issue in any doubt, not only because he believed strongly that there could never "be any half way between Slavery and freedom," but also because it would permit "the perpetrators of such an unhappy circumstance" to "draw the curtain of Respect over the destructiveness of their intentions" so that they might bring them forth again "under the banners of a planned Corruption" when the public had relaxed its guard.[104]

The mounting evidence of the internal corruption of Great Britain and of a ministerial plot against American and British liberty was perhaps the most important factor in Carter's estrangement from the mother country. In 1760 he could declare with complete sincerity that "Loyalty is the very Genius of the Country," and even as late as 1765 he could report with probable accuracy in one of his essays against the Stamp Act that the "Colonies . . . glory in their connection with" Britain. But Carter also pointed out in 1765 that the most valuable and unique feature of that connection was Britain's historic preservation of "the Religion and Liberties of the people" of the colonies "in their full enjoyment," and, though he adamantly denied that Americans had any intention of seeking independence, as various British politicians had charged, he did warn in September 1768 that "the desire of independency" might be the eventual result, as it had frequently been throughout history, "of impatience in suffering" over an extended period of time.[105]

The repeal of the bulk of the Townshend duties in 1770 and the period of quiet that followed, at least in Virginia, did not allay Carter's suspicions, especially because he had begun to be convinced that the same corruption that had gripped Great Britain was gaining ground in Virginia. "Pride and Lux-ury," he observed as early as 1754, "always find an Entrance in with Riches," and he thought that the steady rise in wealth in Virginia over the previous

---

[104] L. C. Diary, May 29, 1770, p. 418; *Va. Gaz.* (Rind), Sept. 1, 1768; L. C. to Old Friend, May 14, 1769, Sabine Hall Col.

[105] *Letter to a Gentleman in London*, 25; *Letter to B——p of L——n*, 38; *Va. Gaz.* (Rind), Sept. 1, 1768; L. C. to Mr. ——, Nov. 30, 1765, Sabine Hall Col.

century was by the 1760s undermining the old "Principles of order and society," the old standards of virtue and industry, and substituting in their place dissipation, "extravagance and folly." The whole society seemed to be in decline: parents neglected to discipline their children, and children in turn neglected their "duty to Parents"; "Ladies" had "grown too delicate to look into family affairs," and Carter himself had grown too "delicate in taste"; the younger generation, even those like Robert Wormeley who had been "well educated," had forsaken reading and learning for pleasure and "loungings," and the resulting loss of intellectual vitality had produced "a sameness in action, speech, reasoning, and expression that you would think every body only learnt from one another." Worst of all, Carter noted a sharp decline among the gentry in their devotion to public service so that "the Public duty" hardly seemed "to be anybody's concern" and few thought that there was "any kind of duty or trust in the offices they undertake." Members of the Richmond County court showed not "the least inclination even to incomode the least private concern for the sake of the public," and the burgesses, as Carter observed in April 1772, sat up "regaling or gaming till 12 every night, and rise very late, mostly unprepared and in the morning very unfit for business, by which means designing men carry on scandelous and injurious laws that take up much time, which unless they had been thrown out would ruin the Country." "Thus does Social Virtue gradually die away," he lamented, "and al[ways] some imperious obstinacy succee[d]."[106]

For a time after he became governor of Virginia in 1768 Norborne Berkeley, Baron de Botetourt, seemed as if he might be able both to frustrate the sinister schemes of the ministry and to rescue Virginians from their own corruption. "Pitcht upon to be the Agent of a dirty tyrranic Ministry," Botetourt "resisted such an employment and . . . became the instrument of a dawning happiness." "Through his active and exemplary virtue," Carter thought, "order everywhere revived out of that confusion that our own dissipative indolence had thrown us into." But Botetourt's death in the fall of 1770, Carter feared, would both enable "those devils" in the ministry again to inaugurate their attempts "to distress this Colony" and permit "corruption" once more to "begin the great work of enslaving this Country and in it all America." "And when we get into the way of corruption," Carter despaired, "he will [be] the cleverest man that gets the most by it. Clients will turn bribers; and the transition from the sale of private justice to that of Public

---

[106] L. C. Diary, Mar. 23, May 9, 1770, Mar. 28, 1771, Apr. 14, Oct. 3, 25, 1772, June 29, 1773, May 12, 1776, pp. 372–73, 405, 553, 668–69, 736, 744, 765, 1038–39; *Letter from a Gentleman in Virginia*, 28–29; Carter to Purdie and Dixon, Fall 1769, Carter Family Papers, Folder 3.

liberty will [be] but easy and short." Carter liked to think that Americans might "be better situated as to avoiding of such a corruption," but he knew from experience and observation that "human nature, in America," differed "not in its frailties from the same unhappiness in other lands." Experience had also taught him that only a strict adherence to tested values could avoid such a corruption in any man and in any society.[107]

That the men in power in Britain had deserted those values became increasingly clear in the crucial years after 1773. The Tea Act of that year left Carter with no doubt that his earlier suspicions had been correct. "Nothing seems more rational," he wrote in February 1774, "than to conclude that those noble Parliament leaders, presuming on the Peaceable disposition of the Americans during those years [following the partial repeal of the Townshend duties in 1770] have ventured by a combination with the East India Company to attempt to fix this duty upon America, as a Precedent for some other Purpose as yet concealed." That purpose was revealed as the crisis deepened. By the summer of 1774 Carter could no longer escape the conclusion that George III was "one grand Corupter of mankind, who has from his first exertion of his disposition only shewn that he wants to establish this Slavery nearer home, by supplying himself with a new fund for Corruption" so that he might buy the people by giving them pensions and places supported, ironically, "with their own money." "Pensions and Places in Government," he angrily charged after learning of Parliament's passage of the Coercive Acts to punish Boston for the Tea Party, "are like Opiates and other various forms, not administered to remove, but to stupify some painful sensation of a disorder, till a spotted despotism like the [inevitable] Mortification concludes the dreadful scene." A "designing favourite"—a Lord North, a Lord Mansfield, or any one of the other "monsters of Corruption" who assisted the King in his base enterprises—was, Carter wrote, "an occult Cancer in a State that secretly pervades about till every spring is enervated out of its Constitutional tone."[108]

To combat such corruption obviously required strong and determined action, and Carter, never much given to compromise, was now ready to go to any extreme to root it out and destroy it. Just as he had argued during the Stamp Act crisis for a more limited definition of Parliamentary authority than any other American leader, with the possible exception of his fellow Virginian Richard Bland, and had stubbornly resisted during the agitation over the Townshend duties a movement by Virginia politicians Edmund Pendleton and Robert Carter Nicholas "for meeting the Parliament half" after it had

[107] L. C. Diary, Oct. 15, 20, 1770, pp. 512, 516; *Va. Gaz.* (Rind), Apr. 26, 1770.
[108] L. C. to Purdie, Feb. 14, July 18, 1774, and to ——, [1774 or 1775], Sabine Hall Col.

only partially repealed the duties, so in 1774 and 1775 he recommended the most drastic measures possible, convinced from the history of Britain itself that it was far better to "run into mere civil war, regardless of every thing" than "suffer . . . a precedent" against liberty "to gain the least [ground]." The Boston Tea Party, for instance, was precisely the kind of remedy the situation called for. For the Bostonians to have used tea "with the Parliamentary duty laid upon it" would by establishing "a Precedent for the fleecing . . . of" their "Properties" have cost them no less than their "whole Liberty." "There can be no Liberty without some Property not subject to be taken away from us every moment," Carter contended. Such a precedent had to "be for ever lookt upon" to be "as deadly as the most infected bale of goods"; and like all infected commodities, the tea by virtue of the *"Lex Prima Natura"—"The Law of Self Preservation"*—had to be destroyed. When some of the Virginia burgesses formed an association in May 1774 not to import any East India Company goods Carter resolved to "be hearty in it," and he insisted both in conversation with people in the county and in letters to newspapers that Americans should "have as little Commerce with" the people of Great Britain "as Possible; and farther to refuse to do them the service to determine their suits for debts since they had consented to a Manifest Violation of our whole Constitution." Only by some dramatic action of this type, he argued, could they be brought to protest "this Arbitrary Proceeding of their Parliament." By the summer of 1774 he was advocating resistance to the death if it became necessary. "I am resolved to be free or cease to exist," he wrote to Alexander Purdie in July, "I meane not by my own hand but by the hand of those who are to take my liberty from me; for one thing I certainly feel that if I am not to be free life must be a burden to me, and that he who is to take my liberty from me must be an equal enimy to my life."[109]

As it gradually became clear during the summer and fall of 1774, first by the appointment of General Thomas Gage as governor of Massachusetts and then by his military preparations, that the British government was willing to resort to armed force to secure American compliance with the Coercive Acts, Carter seems to have become more and more alienated from both the British government and the British people. However distressing to a loyal and devoted Englishman might be the conclusion that "our mother country" suddenly had to be called "our enemies," it could no longer easily be avoided. That "natural Affection"—the most "noble base to build upon in every human System of Politicks"—which had preserved among the colonists "for near 200

---

[109] L. C. Diary, May 29, 1770, June 3, 8, Aug. 8, 1774, pp. 418, 817–19, 821–22, 847; L. C. to Purdie, Feb. 14, July 18, 1774, Sabine Hall Col.; L. C. on taxation, n.d., Wellford Col.

years a joyous content, wrapt up in a cordial and filial respect," now seemed to have given way to complete indifference; and "indifference carried too far," Carter wrote in his diary in December 1774, "often becomes a cornerstone to hatred." Though Carter's own hatred was not yet strong enough to alienate him completely from Britain, he was arguing by October 1774 that "the duty to a Prince was cancelled by the duty to one's country," and the country he referred to was quite obviously not Great Britain but Virginia and not just Virginia as Virginia but as a part of "British America (as the Colonies are called)." Moreover, the obvious willingness of the British to use force caused him to advocate meeting force with force. "Drawn swords in the hands of freedom," he observed during the winter of 1774–75, could have truly "wonderful effects," and after Lord Dunmore, then royal governor of Virginia, had stealthily removed the powder from the public magazine in Williamsburg on April 20, 1775, Carter urged that force be used to recover it. Resisting force with force, he declared, "is the first law of nature, and such an one, that even despotism should never even fancy it can dismay." With Gage's attack upon Lexington and Concord on April 19 and Dunmore's subsequent burning of warehouses on Virginia rivers and his attempts to create a general slave uprising by promising freedom to those slaves who would flee to his banner, Carter became convinced that the British would stop at no *"inhumanity"* or *"barbarity"* even to "Murder . . . of the aged and tender infants" and the spilling of "the blood of innocents" to "subdue America" and he thought anything was justifiable to "put to flight those British Butchers." That the British might in the end be too strong for the Americans did not matter. It was far better, he wrote in his diary in July 1775, "not to deserve this Slavery by resisting it than tamely to submit to it." Besides, he had complete faith, as he reiterated until his death in 1778, that God would favor the Americans "not from any Peculiar goodness in us, but in the cause we are engaged in." The British government had both "violated" the "rights of Nature" and sought by an "Ungrateful stretch of Power" to introduce "the most hateful of iniquities, a Tyrannic despotism in the King who rules In Great Britain with mony, and would Govern America with an iron Sceptre." "Unless the devil" were "more Powerful than the God of Justice," British corruption, if not American virtue or strength of arms, would insure American success.[110]

Carter's ardor for the American cause seems never to have weakened, but

[110] L. C. Diary, Aug. 8, Oct. 29, Dec. 24, 1774, July 30, Sept. 20, 1775, Apr. 4, 23, July 16, 1776, pp. 847, 890–91, 901, 932–33, 945–46, 1011, 1023–24, 1058; L. C. to Purdie, July 18, 1774, Sept. 1776; to the Independent Company of Volunteers of Richmond County, Apr. 28, 1775; to Dear Sir, Apr. and May, 1775; and to———, [1774–1775], and L. C.'s note on strife, 1775, Sabine Hall Col.; L. C. to Washington, Oct. 21, 1776, in Force, ed., *Am. Archives*, 5th Ser., II, 1304–7.

he did not think independence the best way to prosecute that cause, and from the moment he first read Thomas Paine's open advocacy of independence in *Common Sense* in February 1776 until independence was actually declared by Virginia the following May he argued vigorously against it. His opposition was not simple. From the beginning of the dispute he had denied that there was any foundation to the British charge that Americans were aiming at independence, writing as late as May 1775 that "we are averse to all foreign connections and only wish . . . (the navigation act submitted to)" to "be restored to an harmonious reconciliation." Always contemptuous of inconstancy and always reluctant to change his mind or go back on his word, Carter wanted to keep the dispute on the original issue, "constitutional freedom," and he did not want to put the "original justice" of "the American cause" in question, to have it in "the least sullied," by switching goals in the middle of the conflict. "What an Opprobrium must this be to the Gentlemen of the Congress, who not only denied their tendency to independency when they were charged with it by writers," he scolded in March 1776, "but have over and over again told the whole British World that they only desired to be reinstated as they were in 1763." Such insincerity placed Americans only slightly above the British. Also apprehensive lest any aid received from foreign powers as a result of independence come with strings attached that would be "equally injurious" to American liberty, he was especially concerned because everyone who favored independence seemed also to favor a republican form of government and to "declare against the English constitution, as a form of Government which freedom cannot exist under from its arbitrary tendency." "A great Stickler for that Authority," Carter could not stand to see "the Pure British Constitution . . . so reprobated" and insisted that there was as much of an arbitrary tendency in a "Republican form" as in a limited monarchy. Even after independence had become a reality and he could no longer profitably oppose it, he chose to think that he had been compelled to it by British tyranny "rather than to ever have it out of choice, because," he insisted, "as a constitution of government none was so good as the British, and though we need not be under the control of its now depraved arbitrariness, yet it would be best for us to embrace the same mixed form."[111]

Carter's fear of independence and republicanism and his commitment to a "mixed form" of government derived, of course, from his longstanding con-

[111] L. C. Diary, Feb. 14, 24, Mar. 28, May 23, June 14, 1776, pp. 980–81, 986–87, 1006, 1042–43, 1049–50; L. C. to Purdie and Dixon, Fall 1769, Carter Family Papers, Folder 3; L. C. to Purdie, July 18, 1774, and to Dear Sir, Apr. and May 1775, Sabine Hall Col.; L. C. to George Washington, May 9, 1776, in Force, ed., *Am. Archives,* 4th Ser., VI, 389–92; L. C.'s endorsement on R. H. Lee to L. C., June 2, 1776, in James C. Ballagh, ed., *The Letters of Richard Henry Lee* (2 vols.; New York, 1912), I, 200.

viction that a "mixed form" was the best instrument for balancing the several interests in society against one another and for neutralizing the passions of individual men; both his fear and his commitment were intensified, however, by his observation that the tendencies in Virginia toward moral decay and corruption that he had noted over the previous decades seemed to have been increased rather than lessened by the pressures of the revolutionary agitation. "The Representatives of the people," he noted during the agitation over the Tea Act in May 1774, seemed to "go out of their way of their duty instead of into it." "Such is the nature of Public Virtue in this Colony where there is such a Cry for Liberty," he complained, "there is hardly a man to be met with who pays the least regard to it." Even in early 1776 with Dunmore's forces threatening the riversides the Richmond County Committee of Safety and the officers of the regiment stationed at Richmond County courthouse seemed to be more interested in gaming than in protecting the county. "It is a melancholly thing to think of," Carter declared, "but [at] a time when [t]here is the greatest occasion for sensibility and thoughtfulness, we see nothing but folly, idleness and dissipation." He was appalled in April 1776 when even his own family objected to his grandson and "courageous NameSake['s]" responding to the call to duty and going off with a band of "memorable Young heroes" to repel Bartlett Goodrich, Dunmore's Tory lieutenant. "For God's sake," he protested, "what is Patriotism, if it is only to lie in a chamber, and provide against no danger, and run no Risks?" He was sure that George III "would be Glad of such Subjects in America." To Carter, the disinterested patriot and public servant who always sought to put the interests of the whole community first, this lack of spirited patriotism, the apparent discord in the face of such a "Prodigeous cause for Unanimity," and a perpetual display of selfishness that seemed to indicate that each individual was more interested in having "his own estate secured" than in saving his country meant that Virginia must indeed have gotten "into the way of corruption," and such a development boded only ill for the future of Virginia.[112]

To Carter there appeared to be a close connection between this decline of public spirit with its attendant "internal Contentions" and the "republican form we all seem to be hurrying into." That segment of society usually referred to by Carter as "commoners" had, he reported in May 1776, come to expect that "Independency" would "be a form of Government that, by being independent of the rich men, every man would then be able to do as he pleased," and the various manifestations of such sentiments in Richmond

---

[112] L. C. Diary, May 2, 1774, Feb. 9, Mar. 9, 13, 15–16, Apr. 23–24, 1776, pp. 800, 977, 997–98, 1000–1004, 1023–26.

County left him convinced that they would result in nothing but "Confusion." On April 1, 1776, at the election of delegates to the convention that declared independence and adopted a new constitution for Virginia, the voters of the county turned out their old representatives, Robert Wormeley Carter and Francis Lightfoot Lee, for Hudson Muse and Charles McCarty—the one, in Landon Carter's estimation, "a worthless, though impudent, fellow" and the other "a most silly though goodnatured fool"—purely, Carter suspected, with the expectation that the new representatives would vote for "an intire independence in which no Gentleman should have the least share." As if to confirm those suspicions a "certain G. R. when asked" a month later "to lend his fire lock to go against" a British tender in the Rappahannock River "asked the People if they were such fools to go to protect the Gentlemen's houses on the river side" and announced that "he thought it would be better if they were burnt down." Carter could only interpret such behavior as manifesting a desire to exclude the gentlemen—the men not only of wealth but also of virtue, learning, experience, and distinction—from their traditional exercise of political leadership. He was fearful that without some independent and disinterested gentlemen in the government demagogues would manipulate the commoners for their own selfish interests and perhaps even establish "an Aristocratic Power" that would result in a tyranny as objectionable as the British. "My only dread has been on account of this separation which" Great Britain, "her King, her ministry and her Parliament have barbarously driven us into," he wrote in his diary in late May 1776, lest "from the secret inclination of some to an arbitrary sway themselves we might fall into a worse situation from internal oppression and commotions than might have been obtained by a serious as well as cautious reconciliation." "Certainly," he continued, "it behooves him who admires Peace, order, and moderation in Government to be cautious of such People, for it is morally certain that there are such, and without the utmost timely care they will work themselves into the Hydra of Power."[113]

To prevent such a development Carter thought that "some good form of Government" had to be devised as soon as independence was declared. He did not agree with John Adams' suggestion in his *Thoughts on Government* that remedies to the "many evils that" might "possibly attend his proposal" to establish new constitutions might be left "to times of more tranquility." Adams had drawn a parallel between "corporeal and political bodies," suggest-

[113] L. C. Diary, Mar. 28–29, Apr. 1, 9, May 1, 29, 1776, pp. 1006–9, 1015, 1030–31, 1046; L. C. to George Washington, May 9, 1776, in Force, ed., *Am. Archives,* 4th Ser., VI, 389–92, and July 30, 1777, Washington Papers, LII, 101.

ing that time and nature would "be as active in the operations of the latter as she generally is in the former." But Carter did not think the analogy a valid one. He agreed that in the corporeal body "a tranquil waiting" for "the effects of nature" would "most probably" remove the cause of a disease. But the "body politick," he argued, had to contend, not with a beneficent nature that could be counted on for assistance, but with "a second" human "nature, vicious in all its distinctions." To insure that men would not yield to that nature, would not succumb to "the common temptations of the natural passions," it was absolutely necessary, as he wrote George Washington in May 1776, to "prevent such evils in the very beginning, or never expect to do it at all," and the best way to do so was to adopt a constitution which would establish the same "mixed form" of government as the British. No other form, Carter believed, could sufficiently check the various elements in society against each other in such a way as to insure that the government would always operate for the benefit of the entire society.[114]

In the situation of mid-1776 Carter was especially concerned that the tendencies toward popularity be counterbalanced by the forces of disinterest and impartiality. He did not want to have "to trust an ignorant representative to do what he pleases under a notion of leaving his constituents independent." "Do we not see that as social beings, we must necessarily be dependent on one another," he wrote in a public letter to the convention probably in May 1776, and that unless "every individual in this state of freedom has an equal Capacity in the several essential parts of it by which we are to preserve this (not unfitly Stiled) bark of freedom" there is a "necessity of reposing every here and there in the State, a limited as well as an accountable, though not a confined power, that the sails, rigging, tar, and halon of the Vessel may be all skilfully as well as properly Conducted." A well-run ship of state had to have a strong power— limited, of course, by the constitution—placed in the hands of those men of more than common capacity, those men with sufficient learning and public spirit to navigate it properly; and such a power, Carter argued, would in no way be "a restriction on freedom," for "without some such thing," he believed, "freedom must destroy by its own confusion." "No Authority need be"—and he might have added ever ought to be—"uncontroulable. But certainly the controul ought not to lodge with those only who are to be governed by it."[115]

Making a constitution, then, was a momentous enterprise that could at best be only partly successful. No matter how well the job was done, "Injustice

[114] L. C. to George Washington, May 9, 1776, in Force, ed., *Am. Archives,* 4th Ser., VI, 389–92.
[115] L. C. to Dixon and Hunter, May 1776 (?), Sabine Hall Col.; L. C. to George Washington, May 9, 1776, in Force, ed., *Am. Archives,* 4th Ser., VI, 389–92.

and Oppression" would "always be the product of an earthly supremacy" because it would always be in the hands of imperfect men. Yet Carter was persuaded that with the proper mixing of various interests it was possible for imperfect men to construct a workable, if not in all respects completely satisfactory, political instrument. But they could only do so, he felt, by eschewing popularity, recognizing that all members of society were dependent upon one another, and making sure that political leadership was entrusted to men of real distinction within a framework that sufficiently limited their power so that they could never arbitrarily oppress their constituents or pursue measures that were disastrous to the community. That the Virginia Convention did not do so well as Carter had hoped was apparent in the years after independence. He was distressed, he wrote in October 1776, that the constitution had not provided for a proper separation between legislative, executive, and judicial powers. "All three powers" seemed to be "crowding to form one tribunal," and the legislature seemed to be usurping all power "according to some democratick, assumed retrospection." Worst of all, as he objected in July 1777, it had failed to stop "the growth of licencious freedom" or to provide against "some sordid self providing creatures, who have been creeping into Legislation by every deception Possible."[116]

Whatever the weaknesses of the Virginia constitution, however, Carter vastly preferred it "to *slavery* and *oppression*" under Great Britain. Indeed, as the war progressed, his antagonism to George III and his followers in both Britain and America increased. "If ever a war began on the Principles of robbery this did," he declared in February 1777, expressing the hope that "every American" would "dispise every Attempt" at a reconciliation "and forever hug that independency which they have been compelled to, that has thus providentially brought about a Seperation from such a Tyrant, and his adherents." "I every day see more and more of the unhappy base tendency of that G[eorge] 3d," he noted in his diary in April 1777, and for that reason he had no qualms about having disavowed his "allegiance to him." "For my part I think every contract especially about Government is reciprocal with conditions on both sides," he wrote in July 1777; "Allegiance was mine and the condition for it was Justice and freedom together with a Paternal affection. If that is broken or denied me, I am absolved."[117]

That Carter was glad after independence to have been "providentially"

---

[116] L. C. to Dixon and Hunter, May 1776 (?), Sabine Hall Col.; L. C. to George Washington, Oct. 21, 1776, in Force, ed., *Am. Archives,* 5th Ser., II, 1304-7, and July 30, 1777, Washington Papers, LII, 101.

[117] L. C. Diary, Feb. 13, 20, 23, 25, Apr. 20, July 15, 1777, pp. 1075, 1078-79, 1082-87, 1096, 1112; L. C. to Purdie, Sept. 1776, Sabine Hall Col.

separated from Britain did not mean that he had no regrets. It could not have been easy for a man in his mid-sixties who had long prided himself on being an Englishman suddenly to disavow his allegiance and break his emotional ties, and he continued to wonder how Great Britain "in a mere Zenith of trade" with an "empire over almost the whole world" could have so quickly lost its traditional "contempt for Slavery." The answer, he finally decided, was moral decline, the causes of which were "exactly the same" as those that brought about the fall of the Roman Empire, "the only Power to be found in History equal with themselves in extent of dominion." In the case of Rome, the "want of a rival in power (to wit) the destruction of Cathage; brought on all the luxuries and extravagances of trade; so that as by effeminacy and bribery Rome dwindled in freedom, Dictators and Emperors grew mighty; and death, barbarity, Servitude and debauchery, the concomitants of Despotism, Prevailed, to their entire exterpation." Similarly, "Britain, being able by the assistance of her vast Empire, to check, if not Subdue her only rival Powers, France and Spain; and by that means encreasing in trade, instead of Paying off those debts which this successful grasp of empire had occasioned, has run mad with the luxuries of this vast trade; and by sinking into effeminacy and bribery to support that extravagance, have now raised a mere Nero in his despotic inclinations over them." Without some external force to check the natural human tendencies to indolence and evil, nations, like men, seemed to fall into depravity, and more than any other single factor it was the conviction that Britain had degenerated into such a state that seems to have accounted for Carter's joy at having broken the connection. For Landon Carter the American Revolution was a moral drama. With his fellow Americans he was waging a war on corruption, a battle against nothing less than the imperfect nature of man. Such a war was a "noble struggle" indeed, and the ultimate goal was a political utopia on earth: a political society that would embody those values and those ethical imperatives on which he had sought to build a life of virtue.[118]

ONLY INWARD SATISFACTION

Driven into public life by societal demands and his compulsion for distinction, Landon Carter was never completely comfortable there. His uncompromising and stern nature, his insistence upon keeping a proper distance from men lest too intimate a relationship somehow contaminate him or deprive him of his independence and impartiality, and the extraordinary standards of

[118] L. C. Diary, Feb. 25, 1777, p. 1085–86.

behavior he demanded from others tended to alienate even his closest associates and thereby precluded the development of strong and enduring friendships and prevented him from ever attaining the warm admiration of the public. Without either, Carter not surprisingly came to feel, especially in his later years, lonely, neglected, and unappreciated. Although he continued as always to pride himself on never having "courted Public applause,"[119] his ego was so great that it required constant feeding. He thought he had done well in life and was proud of his accomplishments as a provider for his family, a planter and man of learning, a public servant, and a virtuous and honorable man. But he was never so sure of the worth of his accomplishments as to be able to scorn completely the opinions of other men—with the result that he constantly demanded reassurance in the form of recognition and respect from his associates. Although he received considerable recognition and no little respect, it was never enough. Puzzled and hurt by the failure of his contemporaries to pay him that regard which he thought his achievements merited, he became so sensitive that the merest slight or the smallest insult sent him scurrying to his plantation and his study for refuge from a hostile and malevolent world. He seems always to have been plagued by a tension deep within him between a sense of responsibility to the public and a desire to retreat to the familiar and friendly privacy of his plantation, by a consuming need for recognition from the outer world and a desire to remain uncorrupted by that world; and his feelings of neglect and his disappointment at having failed to obtain more recognition from his fellowmen during his last decade only accentuated his tendencies toward withdrawal, turning him inward and driving him to seek comfort in his diary and his memories. Lonely, self-pitying, and even a trifle bitter and resentful, he eventually became somewhat paranoiac, willing to suspect everyone—his family, overseers, neighbors, colleagues on the bench—of conspiring to ignore and persecute him. They seemed to have rejected, not only him, but his whole system of values, and his only comfort was the inward satisfaction of knowing that, at least by his standards, he deserved better treatment.

By any standards Carter's accomplishments were impressive, and he was well aware that few of his contemporaries either in Virginia or elsewhere in the English colonies exceeded him in material success. "I cannot help taking notice," he proudly observed in July 1770, of "the care I have taken of my family, the paying off Children's fortunes, and putting out 3 sons with an Estate very well to pass in the world, still maintaining a large family at home,"

---

[119] L. C. Diary, July 14, 1776, p. 1057.

at a cost of about £400 per year, "and all this without being in debt but a very
trifle." That debt, which had amounted to around £1,000 in 1766, apparently
had been paid off by June 1776, and he could boast in September 1776 that even
though Dunmore—"Lord Pilferer"—had robbed him of "a full thousand
Pounds in Valuable slaves," he had "many more, besides stocks of all kinds,
land Productions not a few, and other reputables (for even a treasury chest) to
furnish out a distress." For his extraordinary success he was thankful to God,
but he did not underestimate the importance of his own efforts. He could not
help but agree with Captain Burgess Ball's estimate in July 1777 that he "was
by far the best Planter about," and he had no doubt that "such a success could
only be produced by great and sensible experience." Nor was he any less
pleased with his public achievements. He was proud, he remarked in March
1774, of his record on the Richmond County court, particularly of the "order
and dispatch" he had promoted in the "Publick business" and of the "success
in the order an[d] decency I have Preserved in the Co[unty]." During
his seventeen years in the House of Burgesses, he could boast to a critic in 1774,
he had served his constituents faithfully and diligently without engaging "in
any teinted affair," and that service, he declared two years later, had brought
him far more "contentment" than was generally "allowed to mankind."[120]

Carter's accomplishments were, moreover, recognized by others. Richard
Bland wrote a poem to him in 1758 in which he complimented him on his
tracts defending the Burgesses in the pistole fee controversy and pronounced
him both his "Country's surest Friend" and "A Friend to Virtue and a Foe to
Vice." Lieutenant Governor Francis Fauquier was equally pleased with his
various political writings in the early 1760s, and in 1765 Richard Henry Lee
addressed him as "one of the best friends, as well as one of the most able of the
community." The American Philosophical Society thought his essay on the
weevil fly "ingenious and accurate," and on the basis of the same essay Dr.
Thomas Bond, the Philadelphia physician, reportedly entertained "the highest
opinion of" his "Genius and Abilities" and remarked that the world was
"greatly obliged to" him. Even after he had been turned out of the Burgesses,
fellow politicians continued to seek his advice, deferring to him as a man of
"great Abilities and Experience," of "abilities with good intentions," of "Wisdom and experience." Carter reveled in such tributes, and there is no question,
as Francis Lightfoot Lee observed, that he loved "to be tickled." During his
first session in the House of Burgesses he took great delight in any compli-

[120] L. C. Diary, July 6, 1766, July 19, Aug. 18, 1770, Mar. 12, 1771, Sept. 24, 1772, Mar. 1, May 20,
1774, Apr. 9, 1776, July 14, 1777, pp. 314–15, 468–69, 548, 733, 799, 812–13, 1014–15, 1110–11;
L. C. to "My Friend," [Feb. 1774], to Dixon and Hunter, May 1776 (?), and to Purdie, Sept. 1776,
Sabine Hall Col.

ments on his speeches or written addresses. When "Some Gentlemen told" him, "and not a few, so handsome a Speach and so Close an answer they had never met with," he eagerly recorded it in his diary, and on another occasion he thought "the Praise of Everybody and a Vote of the whole house but three" certainly "intitles me to value myself." He received with great relish Dr. Bond's reported praise of his weevil fly essay, and when his nephew Carter Braxton wrote in October 1776 that he would always value Carter's advice because he was a man "whose Experience in Life and Knowledge of Mankind justly entitle him to the Esteem of all admirers of Literature," Carter found it a most "agreeable letter." Carter's love of praise meant, of course, that he was susceptible to flattery. In 1770 Francis Lightfoot Lee wrote to his brother William, who as a tobacco merchant in London was trying to get Carter's business away from his rival, William Molleson, that Molleson kept Carter's loyalty "chiefly by flattery." According to Lee, Molleson "praises" Carter's "writings, publishes them in some London paper, then asks ten thousand pardons, for taking so great a liberty, but his love for mankind obliges him to make them as public as possible." Lee doubted that Carter's consignments were "worth so great a sacrifice."[121]

But praise did more than simply tickle Carter; it seems to have been essential to his happiness and peace of mind. Respect and attention sustained him; disapproval and neglect threw him into fits of anger and despair. Criticism was almost unbearable. He could not understand, for instance, how "men not remarkt for ever having read more than an adjudged case or two or perhaps than have no other real boast than the making of a Plant of tobacco or two should think themselves at Liberty to criticize" an address he had written for the House of Burgesses when his skill in writing had been so frequently complimented, and his extreme sensitivity to criticism was at the root of most of the violent disputes in which he became involved at one time or another with almost everyone he was ever closely associated with. This inability to accept criticism gracefully was not simply the result of an insufferable arrogance, as some of his contemporaries seem to have thought. He never regarded

[121] L. C. Diary, Mar. 10, Apr. 15, 1752, Oct. 18, 1774, pp. 80, 102, 880; Fauquier to L. C., June 3, 1760, Miscellaneous Papers, Colonial Williamsburg, Inc.; John Tayloe to L. C., Apr. 26, 1764, Sabine Hall Col.; Richard Lee of Lee Hall to L. C., Mar. 7, 1772, Sept. 20, 1774, Apr. 20, June 9, 1776, Lee-Ludwell Papers, Va. Hist. Soc.; Francis Lightfoot Lee to L. C., Oct. 21, 1775, Jan. 14, 1777, and Carter Braxton to L. C., Oct. 17, 1776, Lee Transcripts, II, 70, 104, IV, 308, Va. Hist. Soc.; Braxton to L. C., Apr. 14, 1776, Fogg Autograph Collection, Maine Historical Society, Portland, Me.; F. L. Lee to William Lee, Apr. 6, 1770, Brock Col., Box 4; R. H. Lee to L. C., June 22, 1765, in Ballagh, ed., *R. H. Lee Letters*, I, 7–8; Richard Bland's poem on L. C., June 20, 1758, in Conway, *Barons of the Potomac and Rappahannock*, 138–41; *Proc. of Am. Phil. Soc.*, XXII (July 1835), Part III, No. 119, 19–20 (Nov. 15, 1768).

his own imperfections lightly or considered himself above reproach, but he could see that he had accomplished more than most men and he brooded about the failure or refusal of men of lesser accomplishments to pay him greater deference. The apparent gap between his conception of himself and the way he appeared to others seems to have produced considerable uncertainty within him about the actual importance of his accomplishments, to have raised doubts about his own evaluations of himself; and the only way he could bridge that gap or allay his doubts was to obtain constant reassurance and approval from others. Carter's sensitivity to criticism and dependence upon praise had still other ingredients. There is good evidence to suggest that they were closely related to his failure to match the accomplishments of his father. He had enormous respect for King Carter, who was over fifty when he was born and who was probably the most commanding figure in Virginia when he died, and his realization that his own achievements, however substantial they might have been, fell far short of those of his father, that he would never make the mark upon his generation that his father had made upon the previous one, and that he would consequently never be accorded that respect and recognition that were given to his father probably caused stirrings of guilt and frustration that were intensified by disapproval and relieved only by praise. In addition, he was so wary of other men, so prone to suspect them of acting with malicious or evil intent, that he could never trust anyone sufficiently to develop a relationship that was close enough to permit easy criticism. Whatever the reasons, Carter seems to have become more and more sensitive with each passing year until by the 1770s the smallest disagreement, the most inconsequential slight, deeply wounded his ego, and he came to regard each of them in turn as a personal affront, a questioning of his abilities, a belittling of his accomplishments, or a direct attack upon his whole structure of values. Much of his world came to seem hostile and ungrateful, and *"Ingratitude"* appeared to him to be no less than *"the Devil,"* "the basis of every species of evil."[122]

The wounds that sank deepest, the instances of ingratitude that hurt the most, were those that came from his family, and particularly from his eldest son Robert Wormeley. What he found most disappointing and most frustrating was his inability to impress his own values and drives upon his children and the apparent rejection by his family of the entire code around which he had built his life. It was becoming clear to him during his last decade that Robert Wormeley had degenerated into a mere "man of Pleasure." "He has

[122] L. C. Diary, Apr. 15, 1752, Sept. 11, 1770, June 25, 1774, Mar. 10, May 12, 1776, pp. 102, **487,** 835–36, 998, 1038–39; *Letter from a Gentleman in Virginia*, 4.

truely got the name of Wild Bob," he complained in his diary in February 1774, "for there is not one kind of business he cares for but that of gaming and running about." When he did not "moor" himself "to an idle gaming table or figit about from house to house," he either concerned himself with "some trifling imployment" or slept "all day," never seeking to improve his time "now and then in some useful reading or conversation." For Carter, Robert Wormeley's "abandoned devotion" to gaming and pleasure spelled only misfortune and ruin for his family. The "married gamester," Carter lamented in March 1776, "keeps his family in the Perpetual fear of starving," and neither of his sons—John nor Robert Wormeley—seemed to have any sense of family responsibility. Both, he wrote in June 1774, had "wives very big with large gangs of children and yet they play away and play it all away."[123]

Even more serious than the prospect of economic ruin was the possibility of the eventual moral corruption, perhaps even the total decay, of the family. In Carter's opinion the "bad example" set by Robert Wormeley had "murdered" a "fine Genius" in his son Landon. Carter had already begun to suspect by the early 1770s that unless Robert Wormeley drastically altered his behavior young Landon would "in a very little time become the most outrageous of all children that ever lived" and would eventually revenge "the ill usage I have ever received from his Parent," and by the middle 1770s these suspicions were well on the way to being confirmed. Young Landon's stay at the College of William and Mary in 1772 and 1773 only further "improved his talk for triflings and loungings," and by September 1774 no amount of persuasion could induce him to give up "one moment" of his pleasure. "Like father like Son," Carter despaired in March 1776; "I wonder everybody can't go to hell by themselves without endeavouring to carry his Children there." Soon, he predicted in February 1774, neither son nor grandson would be any better than "the rest of mankind, some of whom are but Idiots." For the principal heir in two successive generations thus to forsake distinction for dissipation could only result "in an intire mortification" of the family and it would not, he feared, take "many generations to compleat the Catastrophe."[124]

Carter did not sit idly by and watch the degeneration of his family. His concern for its welfare, his conception of himself as its conscience—the one shield against its almost certain corruption—and his refusal ever to be content with failure drove him to try every means at his disposal, reason, cajolery,

---

[123] L. C. Diary, Sept. 28, 1770, Feb. 12, June 16, 1774, Mar. 13, 16, May 9, July 26, 1776, pp. 505, 795, 830, 1000–1001, 1004, 1036, 1064.

[124] L. C. Diary, June 16, 1771, June 25, 1772, June 29, 1773, Feb. 12, Sept. 14, 1774, Mar. 10, 13, 1776, pp. 577–78, 702, 765, 795, 857–58, 998, 1000–1001.

threats, demands, special favors, to dissuade Robert Wormeley from pursuing his destructive habits, to persuade him to recognize the necessity of closely adhering to his own rigid structure of values. "God send that those who wait for my estate may wait long enough," he prayed in December 1774, "for I would willingly save a Soul or two alive before I die," and he vowed to his grandson at that time that he "never would give over striving to save him whilst under my roof." But his repeated and more or less perpetual campaigns for the salvation of his son and grandson seemed only to increase their defiance and produced in Carter acute frustration and a suspicion that Robert Wormeley did things deliberately because "he knows it fluxes me" and was "fond of torturing his father." When company came, Robert Wormeley endeavored "to get them to Cards" so that Carter could not have "a word's conversation of any one of them," and at dinner he picked "out all titbits, then asks everybody to have them and at last asks his father." Robert Wormeley refused even to admit that Carter was "a tollerable manager" of his plantations. "Every thing that I do must be excessively wrong," Carter complained in July 1770, "although vastly superior in the produce to any proportion of his profit and much greater than better lands have produced for any number of years in my Neighbourhood." He finally came to regard Robert Wormeley as his "most vexatious tyrant," and what disturbed him the more was that "everybody" seemed "to take a Pleasure that he is so." Such "species of filial disrespect," such evident ingratitude, were to Carter "past all bearing," and by March 1776 he was ready to believe that Robert Wormeley would put him "out of the way" if the law did not "Prevent Parricide." "Good God," he declared in his diary, "that such a monster should have descended from my loins."[125]

How justified Carter's reactions were, how accurately they caught the spirit and intent of his son's behavior, is now impossible to tell. Certainly, Robert Wormeley had ample provocation; Carter's insistence upon constantly "advising" a mature man could have driven anyone to take reprisals. He seemed unable to understand, as Robert Wormeley reminded him in March 1776, that a "40 year old man . . . was not a child to be controuled," arrogantly insisting that even "40 ought to hear reasons" and having complete confidence that his reason and experience were superior to those of his son. Carter undoubtedly believed that he was "a kind, an indulgent and an humane Parent," but he demanded a standard of conduct that few men could meet. It is also probable that Carter's extreme sensitivity to criticism and disagreement

[125] L. C. Diary, July 19, 1770, Oct. 3, 1772, Aug. 12, Dec. 24-25, 1774, Feb. 15-16, Mar. 16, 1776, pp. 447-48, 736, 848-49, 902-04, 983-84, 1004.

caused him to misinterpret many innocent acts and remarks as insult and disrespect and that he tended to magnify such things on the part of his son, to find them all the harder to bear, because they stood in such stark contrast to the great regard he had always held for his own father. But whatever the causes and nature of the storms at Sabine Hall, there is no question that to Carter they were much more than minor domestic spats. He was convinced both that his son was deliberately disrespectful and that he had rejected almost everything he had stood for, and this belief wounded him deeply and caused him repeated anguish and bewilderment. He seemed unable to push it out of his consciousness. It became the dominant theme in his diary, and he even came to conceive of the diary as a record of the "evident misconduct" and "extraordinary manouvres" of his son. He continued to hope for a change in his son's behavior. But his hopes were in vain. There was no apology, no reconciliation, no amendment by Robert Wormeley. "I have tried every way to be better treated," he lamented in August 1774, "but cannot even Purchase it of him; many are the Pounds that I have paid out of my Pocket for him; but nothing will do."[126]

Frustrated at his inability to effect a reformation in his son and puzzled how to account for such ingratitude and disrespect, Carter searched everywhere for explanations. One obvious cause was Robert Wormeley's constant attachment to gaming, his fondness for keeping company with "Pernicious . . . Gamesters and Spendthrifts; who by taking no care, are reducing themselves, whilst I am keeping as well as I can, my buckle and thong together." But the primary cause Carter finally fixed upon was the "Princesslike art" of Robert Wormeley's wife, Winifred Travers Beale. To Carter, at least in his declining years, most women were Eve figures who had, as he remarked in August 1772, "nothing in the general in view, but the breeding contests at home." "I don't think there can be a more treacherous, interprising, Perverse, and hellish Genius than is to be met with in A Woman," he declared in April 1777 in response to a report that some Philadelphia ladies had tried to help the British by spiking American guns; "Madam Eve we see at the very hazard of Paradise suffered the devil to tempt her; and of such a tendency has her sex been." Nor did any woman have any more "of the devil" in her than his daughter-in-law. She was the epitome of the temptress, and she was largely responsible for the "prodigeous vein of contradiction" in Robert Wormeley. "I have had 3 women to wife," he declared in July 1777, "but never one of them,

---

[126] L. C. Diary, June 23, 1773, Aug. 12, 1774, Sept. 18, 1775, Feb. 15–16, Mar. 9, 15, Apr. 3, 1776, pp. 762–63, 848–49, 944–45, 983–84, 997–98, 1001–2, 1009–10.

like Lady Fat, [a] Lady for lying and scolding, and thus it is I do suppose, by the husband's warping to her temper has he turned a mere bulldog." Furthermore, Carter suspected that she might even have been part of the conspiracy with her father William Beale and her brother Reuben that resulted in Reuben's marriage to Carter's daughter Judith against Carter's express wishes. The whole Beale family, in fact, seemed to be endeavoring by some "concealed . . . scheme" to persecute Carter by ruining his children. Never taking "any care to educate their own" and seeing "others exceeding them," they tried, Carter charged in December 1774, purely "out of revenge . . . every treachery to decoy young people off from Duty." "I never knew many of them possessed with any justice or Principle," he wrote in his diary in June 1773, and their "hellish machinations" only confirmed him in his judgment that it was "as necessary to consult the Pedigree of men and women, as it is that of Mules and horses. A good breed of either must be great riches."[127]

It was not only the machinations of his daughter-in-law and her family and the disrespect of Robert Wormeley that Carter had to endure. His overseers became so impudent and disrespectful that they deliberately disobeyed his "express orders" and tried to tell him how to run his own plantations. Even in his own house no one followed his directions or tried to take "the least care of any one thing." By September 1775 he could only conclude that there was a general "Combination against" him that extended over his entire plantation. Even more difficult to bear was the neglect of his children and grandchildren in his declining years. "Everybody," he ruefully concluded in April 1777, "is for themselves." His daughters visited him only infrequently and never stayed very long, and his grandchildren were not even grateful enough to keep him company when he was "alone" in his "extreme age and great infirmity." "In virginia," he complained in November 1763, "a man dyes a month sooner in a fit of any disorders because he can't have one soul to talk to. If he has children some are one way and some another. And without a wife, who has a sick man to converse with?" "It is a pity," he lamented in September 1772, "that old age . . . should be so contemptible in the eyes of the world" that even the children of "the aged" seemed "to despise them." "Some few," he thought, "fancy they ought to behave otherwise, and do so in the main, but not amongst my really ungrateful children," and he was thankful that his "limbs as yet" served him "to ride out" and his "eyes by the help of glasses" enabled him "to read and dispise them in my turn." Indeed, things had

[127] L. C. Diary, Aug. 18, Oct. 3, 1772, June 23, 1773, Aug. 12, Oct. 5, Dec. 21, 1774, Apr. 27, July 7, 1777, pp. 713, 736, 762–63, 848–49, 865, 900, 1103, 1106–7.

gotten to such a pitch that he even came to think, as he declared in April 1772, that "families desired their old Parents to die."[128]

Had Carter had more esteem and approval from the public, the neglect and disrespect of his family might not have weighed so heavily on his mind, but ingratitude seemed to have taken hold of his whole world. In September 1772 his friend, lawyer Richard Parker, insulted him openly in court, and, though he later made a public apology, Carter could only infer from the event that "with some people no Person nor behaviour can be intitled to a decent respect." "I have been a slave to everybody in the County," he reflected after the incident, "and yet without either Severity or arbitrariness in my behaviour nor anything but a resolution to do my duty, I am the most insulted of any man in it." In response to the report that Dr. Bond had said that Carter's pamphlet on the weevil fly had "immortalized" him and that "all Europe" had "actually addressed" him "upon it" and so venerated him "as to Pronounce" him "the greatest Natural Philosopher of this age" with "almost Universal knowledge," Carter wrote in his diary that "if the Gent has preserved the truth I may say that in me is verified the saying that A Prophet is not without honour save in his own Country; for here I publish my discoveries on the Weavil fly, and it was hardly so much noticed, as to encourage but here and there a sensible gentleman to experience its good effects." Though he later decided when the reported address failed to appear that Dr. Bond must be "either a talker or a deceiver," he had hoped the report was true because, as he remarked when he first heard it, it would have given him great happiness in his old age to see his "endeavour to serve mankind so generally acknowledged." But Carter was never to receive the kind of acknowledgment he craved so much, and the ingratitude of his country preyed heavily upon his mind. The best he could hope for was that, as he wrote in March 1774, "however disrespected by many about," he would be wanted after his death "by many people who may now wish me gone" to help check "a prodigeous stride to a Lawless behaviour" that he saw arising in the county. "I often think of the old Roman who received every disgrace untill he was drove from his Country," he wrote in February 1776, "and yet when ignorance brought those who insulted him into a state of dispair, he alone was capable Of and did reprove them and again reinstated that happiness which they had lost."[129]

[128] L. C. Diary, Apr. 25, 1758, Nov. 23, 1763, Apr. 6, Sept. 2, 1772, Sept. 9, 1773, Oct. 6, Dec. 30, 1774, Sept. 21, 1775, Apr. 17, July 14, 1777, pp. 221–22, 242, 668, 720, 767–68, 866–67, 907, 947, 1092, 1010–11.

[129] L. C. Diary, Sept. 9, 11, 1772, Mar. 1, Oct. 18, 1774, Feb. 6, 1776, pp. 726–27, 799, 880, 976; Richard Lee to L. C., Sept. 20, 1776, Apr. 20, 1776, Lee-Ludwell Papers.

But such hopes were small comfort, especially when after independence Carter was deprived even of the credit for his greatest moment in history, his attack in the fall of 1764 upon Parliament's proposed stamp duties and his role in persuading the House of Burgesses to send petitions of protest to the King, Lords, and Commons at that time. He was disturbed to learn in July 1776 that Governor Patrick Henry, who had, of course, been instrumental in pushing the famed Virginia resolutions against the Stamp Act through the House of Burgesses in May 1765, had been credited at the Virginia Convention with being "the first who opened the breath of liberty to America." Carter was pleased that it had been "with truth replied, and Proved that that breath was first breathed and supported by a person not then taken notice of," but, although he claimed the merit accorded to Henry for himself, he was proud, he wrote in his diary, that he had never, like Henry, "courted Public applause; and if any endeavour assists my country, I care not who enjoys the merit of it." Rather than participate in any schemes of popularity, he preferred to do "without honour" from "his own country," convinced that "virtue will ever carry its own reward." Despite his professions, however, Carter was especially bothered by this incident, and it came to serve as a symbol of his failure to receive that respect, gratitude, and recognition he was convinced were rightfully his.[130]

For six months after the incident he was seeking reassurances, first from Francis Lightfoot Lee, then from George Washington and probably from others that he really had been "first, in *America*," to attack the Parliamentary vote "to tax the Colonies with certain stamp duties" and that Henry had not even been at that assembly but had "only assisted in the resolves after the stamp act came in." To see another receive the distinction for so signal an honor as being the first to protest "such an unconstitutional stretch of Power in . . . Parliament" was scarcely bearable. He was proud to have played a role like Cato's in spiriting his countrymen up to a defense of their freedom, but it was unjust and painful to be deprived of Cato's just reward, the reward of "never" being "forgotten." Finally, in September 1776 Carter was driven to assert in a public essay his claim of being "uncontrovertably the first admonisher of this impending combined despotism, in a memorable as well as Public Assembly." Though his many "instances of duty" to society had been "so remarkably requited with a disregard," he had faith, he told the public, that "the God who assists the 13 united States of America, in maintaining their Just claims" would "not desert a faithful servant to mankind though now something enfeebled with Years," and in the meantime he would "injoy a comfort, in even a Conscious (though Unattended) *Merui.*" *"Haec, ego Primus ten-*

---

[130] L. C. Dairy, July 14, 1776, p. 1057.

tavi" (I was the first to try this), he concluded his essay, *"tulis alter honorem"* (but another received the honors). Though it included the characteristic scorn of public applause, this essay was in essence a plea for public recognition, but it obviously failed in its intent and Carter continued to brood about the refusal of the public to appreciate his important contribution to the Revolutionary movement. In February 1777 when William Dennis, a British ship captain temporarily interned in the neighborhood, displayed some talent at making portraits in "Chalk and Charcoal," Carter persuaded him to "take" his "figure" and he "produced a serious, thoughtful old gentleman holding in his right hand a paper thus inscribed: America, Freedom suported Against the British Stamp Act. *Merui, sed intus tantum fruor."* The Latin "motto" meant, "in spite of my merit, I have only inward satisfaction," and Carter, as he explained in his diary, intended it to allude "to the evident ingratitude of others as to him who first opened this door to freedom, to leave him [on]ly the inner satisfaction as a rewa[rd]."[131]

Carter's growing conviction that the only reward one might expect on earth was inward satisfaction only intensified what appears to have been a life-long tendency toward withdrawal. Uncomfortable with other men and afraid that too close a contact with a corrupt world would somehow stain his virtue, he seems to have been devoted to the ideal of his plantation as a rural retreat where he might enjoy a life of quiet meditation and uncorrupted virtue on the Horatian model. He named his house Sabine Hall after Horace's sheltered "Sabine vale" in the hills behind Rome where, as Horace wrote in his poem "Contentment," he could expect to live undisturbed by the rush for "fame," and "worth," and "Praise," away from the "doubled wealth and doubled care" of Rome.[132] Carter seems to have found unusually congenial the central character's advice in Joseph Addison's play *Cato* always to retreat from "a corrupted state"

> To thy paternal seat, the Sabine field
> Where the great Censor toiled with his own hands,
> And all our frugal ancestors were blessed
> In humble virtues, and a rural life.
> There live retired, pray for the peace of Rome:
> Content thyself to be obscurely good.
> When vice prevails, and impious men bear sway,
> The post of honor is a private station.[133]

---

[131] L. C. Diary, July 25, 1776, Feb. 23–24, 1777, pp. 1063, 1082–84; L. C. to Purdie, Sept. 1776, Sabine Hall Col.; L. C. to Washington, Oct. 21, 1776, in Force, ed., *Am. Archives,* 5th Ser., II, 1304–7.

[132] "Of Contentment," conveniently in Francis R. B. Godolphin, ed., *The Latin Poets* (New York, 1949), 256.

[133] Act IV, scene 4, ll. 140–51.

Whenever politics took a turn he could not sanction, he always declared his intention to retire, as he declared in 1776, to his "Private station" at Sabine Hall: "This only Post of honour." Thus, according to Richard Bland, he decided for reasons not now entirely clear, to withdraw from public life in 1758 after two terms in the House of Burgesses, professing that he would "envy not . . . the great,"

> Their Pomp, their Luxury, their pageant state,
> But bless'd with all that Heav'n below can give
> A mind contented and a taste to live,
> [He'd] . . . smile superior on their empty show,
> Their seeming pleasure and their real woe
> At Sabine Hall, retir'd from public praise,
> [He'd] . . . spend in learned ease [his] . . . future days.

Similarly, in 1765 he thought it better "to retire and lament in private" rather than to be "publickly . . . concerned" as a burgess in consenting to reduce his country to slavery by submitting to the Stamp Act, and in the months after Lexington and Concord he not only threatened but actually did withdraw "from public business," giving up his lieutenancy for the county because of his objections to the provisions for court martials in a new militia law and quitting the county court because the people were "Poisoned by . . . Popularity." Despite a sincere desire to withdraw entirely from the public arena, it was hard for Carter to bring himself to do it. His devotion to public service was too intense and his ambition to win distinction by meritoriously serving the community was too great. Both in 1758 and 1765 he ran for reelection and won, justifying his decision to stay in public life on the grounds that his resignation might bring an inferior man to office or, as Francis Lightfoot Lee wrote in urging him not to retire in 1775, that if he could not "do all the good" he "could wish" he could "at least endeavour to prevent all the mischief in" his power. Even after he had left the court in 1775 and vowed never to return he did resume his commission in 1777, unable to resist a plea by a "worthy member" for him to "come to give weight and order to the Proceedings." When he did leave the Burgesses in 1768 it was because he was turned out by the voters, and even his semiretirement after 1775 could be attributed, as Carter himself inferred in 1776, not to his own decision but to his inability to get along with the younger men in the county, an inability he preferred to attribute to "something factious and imperious in the sway of mankind."[134]

[134] L. C. Diary, May 9, 1774, Sept. 4, 1775, Feb. 6, 1776, Apr. 7, Aug. 8, 1777, pp. 808, 937, 976, 1089, 1121; Richard Bland's poem on L. C., June 20, 1758, in Conway, *Barons of the Potomac and Rappahannock*, 138–41; R. H. Lee to L. C., June 22, 1765, in Ballagh, ed., *R. H. Lee Letters*, I, 7–8; L. C. to

But Carter's gradual retirement to a "Private station" after he was turned out of the House of Burgesses in 1768 did not—because of his passion for distinction, could not—bring him the contentment he had wished for. Rather, it only afforded him more time to fret over the ingratitude and disrespect that seemed to be his portion in life and that had been at least in part responsible for driving him out of public life. With time "heavy on his hands" and constantly at odds with most of the members of his family, he turned more and more to his diary for comfort and asylum and there repeatedly speculated about the causes of his distress. Simple envy of his "good Estate" and his general success in life, he thought, was in part responsible, as was his age, which, given the universal "practice of moderns . . . of worshiping the rising sun and disregarding the setting," made it impossible to merit "anything from the rising generation." He even entertained the possibility that there might be no such thing as real gratitude, that esteem might be no more than "a Species of love not really merited," a "passion that enslaves the mind without . . . conviction." What did not occur to him, however, was that the primary reason why he failed to win the admiration and respect of his contemporaries might have been his strict devotion—to the exclusion of any other considerations—to those values on which he sought to build a life of virtue, values that served not only as a shield to protect him from the public's hostility but also as a barrier that deprived him of its love. Whenever it came to a choice, he preferred to rely upon his "good conscience" for "shelter" rather than upon the esteem of the public, to be respected because of his integrity rather than to be loved, because, like Speaker John Robinson, he "was a jewil of a man." To adhere to his code, to avoid offending his own conscience, to know he had done what was right and good, were more important to Carter than the feelings or respect of any man. At least in part, then, he failed to win the praise of the public because he had succeeded too well in keeping to his personal values. He attained a large measure of that praiseworthiness he coveted so much only at the sacrifice of the praise that he seemed to need so badly. To be sure, he derived some comfort in "being but now and then obscurely good" in his "Private station"—in the inward satisfaction he derived from knowing that he merited more than he received. But few men take comfort in knowing they deserve more than they receive, and Landon Carter appears to have done so least of all.[135]

Joseph Royle, June 3, 1765, Brock Col.; Francis Lightfoot Lee to L. C., Oct. 21, 1775, Lee Transcripts, II, 70, Va. Hist. Soc.; L. C. to Dixon and Hunter, May 1776 (?), Sabine Hall Col.

[135] L. C. Diary, Sept. 11, Oct. 9, 1772, Mar. 1, Dec. 13, 21, 1774, June 17, 1775, Feb. 6, Mar. 8, July 25, 1776, Feb. 23, July 8, 1777, pp. 727, 738, 799, 895–96, 900, 923, 976, 996, 1063, 1082–83, 1109; L. C.'s reply to poem, Nov. 1, 1768, and L. C. to Dixon and Hunter, May 1776 (?), Sabine Hall Col.

JOURNAL PRIVATELY KEPT OF THE HOUSE OF BURGESSES

February 1752—June 1755

JOURNAL

February 1752 to June 1755

FEBRUARY 1752

27. Thursday.

Assembly held under Mr. Dinwiddie
February 27, 1752[1]

Members' Names According to the Counties Alphabetically

ACCOMACK	Edmund Allen	George Duglass
ALBERMARLE	Joshua Frye	Allen Howard
AMELIA	Thos. Tabb	Wood Jones
AUGUSTA	Jno. Maddison	Jno. Wilson
BRUNSWICK	Drury Stith	Jno. Willis
CAROLINE	Edmund Pendleton	Lunsford Lomax
CH[ARLE]S CITY	Ben Harrison	Richard Kennon
CHESTERFIELD	Richd. Eppes	Jno. Bolling
CULPEPER	Jno. Spotswood	Wm. Green
CUMBERLAND	George Carrington	Samuel Scot
ELIZABETH CITY	Wm. Westwood	Jno. Tabb
ESSEX	Francis Smith	Ths. Waring
FAIRFAX	Hugh West	Gerard Alexr.
FREDERICK	G[eorge William] Fairfax	Gabriel Jones
GLOSTER	B[everley] Whiting	Jno. Page
GOOCHLAND	Jno. Payne	Jno. Smith

[1] These minutes are printed from the original journal in the Sabine Hall Col., Alderman Library, University of Virginia, Charlottesville. They fill approximately one-fourth of a quarto-sized volume that also includes the diary for 1756–58. The official journals of the House of Burgesses for the period covered by these minutes are in *Burgesses' Journals, 1752–1758,* 1–276.

Members' Names According to the Counties Alphabetically (cont.)

HANOVER	Jno. Chisswell	John Symme
HENRICOE	Wm. Randolph	Bowler Cocke
JA[MES] CITY	Carter Burwell	Benjamin Waller
ISLE WIGHT	Robt. Burwell	Ths. Gale
K[ING] GEORGE	Charles Carter	Ths. Turner
K[ING] AND QUEEN	Jno. Robinson *Speaker*	Philip Johnson
[KING WILLIAM	John Martin	Bernard Moore]
LANCASTER	Edwin Conway	Joseph Chinn
LOUISA	Abram Venable	Thos. Walker
LUNENBURGH	William Byrd	Clemen. Reade
MIDDLESEX	Ralph Wormeley	Christopher Robinson
NANSEMOND	Leml. Reddick	Anth. Holloday
NEW KENT	Richd. Adams	James Power
NORFOLK	Robt. Tucker	Saml. Boush junr.
NORTHAMPTON	Littleton Eyre	Jno. Kendal
NORTHUMBERL[AN]D	Presley Thornton	Spencer Ball
ORANGE	George Taylor	Benj. Cave
P[RINCE] GEORGE	Richd. Bland	Stephen Dewey
P[RIN]CESS ANN	An. Walke junr.	Ed. Hacke Moseley
P[RINCE] WILLIAM	Thos. Harrison	Jo. Blackwell
RICHMOND	Jno. Woodbridge	Landon Carter
SO[UT]HAMPTON	Ethelred Taylor	Thos. Jarrell
SPOTSILVANIA	William Waller	Rice Curtis
STAFFORD	William Fitzhugh	Peter Hedgeman
SURRY	Robt. Jones	Auge. Clayborne
WARWICK	William Harwood	W[illiam] Digges
WESTMORELAND	Jno. Bushrod	Robert Vaulx
YORK	Jno. Norton	Dudley Digges
JAMES TOWN	Edward Travis	
NORFOLKBOROUGH	Jno. Hutchings	
WILLIAMS BOURGH	Armistead Burwell	
COLLEDGE	Peyton Randolph	

The Members returned from the Several Countys etc. with the Returns made by the Sherrifs went up to the Council Chamber, where by a Particular Committee to the Council from the Governor, they took the oaths to the Government Appointed by Law, and having obtained a Certificate thereof they all returned to the house and waited untill the Governour[2] by a Message Comanded their Attendance in the Council Chamber, where having paid a Compliment he directed them to Return to the House and Choose a Speaker. Note: the Clerk[3] appointed by the Governor also took the oaths.

The Mace lay under the table.

Carter Burwell[4] then put the House in mind of the Command to choose a Speaker and Recommended Mr. J[ohn] Robinson[5] to which the house agreed. The Speaker led to the Chair by two Members Where he Expressed his Thanks for the Honor done him.

C[harles] Carter[6] then moved that Some of their Members be appointed to wait on the Governor and let him know that in Obedience to His Honor's Command They had made Choice of a Speaker and to know when they might be permitted to Present him. Two Members sent up with this Message.[7] The Governor's Answer sent by his own Messenger[8] to attend immediately. The Speaker in behalf of the house begged his Protection etc.

The Governor's Speach with a promise of Protection.

The Speaker brought down a Copy of the Governor's Speach and read it Standing. The Clerk the Same.

Mr. Bland[9] moved for an Address of Thanks. Mr. Bland, Mr. C[arter] Burwell, Mr. Conway,[10] Mr. Wormeley[11] and L[andon] Carter appointed to draw it.[12]

[2] Robert Dinwiddie (1693–1770) was lieutenant governor of Virginia from November 1751 to January 1758. For a biography see Louis Knott Koontz, *Robert Dinwiddie* (Glendale, Calif., 1941).

[3] John Randolph, Jr. (1728–84), lawyer and son of Sir John Randolph (1693–1737) and Susanna Beverley, was clerk of the House of Burgesses, 1752–66; burgess for Lunenburgh Co., 1769, and the College of William and Mary, 1775–76; and attorney general of Virginia, 1766–76.

[4] Carter Burwell (1716–56), planter and son of Nathaniel Burwell (1680–1721) and Elizabeth Carter, was burgess for James City Co., 1742–55. He was Landon Carter's nephew.

[5] John Robinson (1704–66), planter and son of John Robinson (1683–1749) and Katherine Beverley, was speaker of the House of Burgesses, 1736–65, and burgess for King and Queen Co., 1727–65. For a brief biography see William M. Dabney, "John Robinson, Speaker of the House of Burgesses and Treasurer of Virginia" (M.A. thesis, University of Virginia, 1941).

[6] Charles Carter of Cleve (1707–64), planter and son of Robert "King" Carter (1663–1732) and Judith Armistead, was burgess from King George Co., 1734–64. He was Landon Carter's brother. For a sketch see Robert Leroy Hillrup, "A Campaign to Promote the Prosperity of Colonial Virginia," *Va. Mag. of Hist. and Biog.*, LXVII (October 1959), 410–28.

[7] Charles Carter and Carter Burwell, *Burgesses' Journals, 1752–1758,* 4 (Feb. 27, 1752).

[8] Nathaniel Walthoe (d. 1770) was clerk of the Council, 1744–70.

[9] Richard Bland (1710–1776), lawyer-planter and son of Richard Bland (1665–1729) and Elizabeth Randolph, was burgess for Prince George Co., 1742–76, and delegate to the First Continental Congress. The best published treatment is Clinton Rossiter, *Seedtime of the Republic* (New York, 1953), 147–80.

[10] Edwin Conway (1681/82–1763), planter and son of Edwin Conway and Sarah Walker, was burgess for Lancaster Co., 1710–18, 1723–55.

[11] Ralph Wormeley of Rosegill (1715–90), planter and son of John Wormeley (1689–1726), was burgess for Middlesex Co., 1742–64.

[12] For a copy of the Governor's speech and the Burgesses' reply see *Burgesses' Journals, 1752–1758,* 5–9

The Chaplain Appointed; Then door Keepers by their Petitions as it was a New Assembly.[13] Upon a division, the Ays on the left of the Chair, the No on the Right. The House adjourned till 11 next day. No motion Put till Seconded. Rise before the Speakers addressed for leave to speak. Spoke for the first time in the debate about the Door Keeper.

28. *Friday.*

Persons Appointed to draw up the Address having obtained Leave reported the Same. Received Amended only in the word Merit and the word Obtained inserted. Committees Appointed: Conway first of Priviledges; C[harles] Carter of Propositions; Lomax[14] of trade; B[everley] Whiting[15] of Courts of Justice; Frye[16] of Claims. Note: the Chairman is Generally him who is first Appointed. Nevertheless in the Choice of the Committee. Palmer Contends against Anderson Styth for the Clerkship for Committee Courts of Justice.[17] Vote for Palmer. Spoke in this debate. Claims Certyfyd delivered to the Clerk. Those not Certyfyed According to Law but Sworn to before a Justice Referred to the Committee Claims by Motion. Some Undue Elections Complained of by Motion on a Petition. Note: I drew the chief part of the address.

Persons that drew the address by the motion of Waller[18] Order[ed] to wait on the Governor and know when he would have the Same Presented. A Claim refused because, although Sworn to by the taker up of the Negroe, yet as it was assigned to another and the Asignees not Sworn rejected. I find those who can't attend the Court of Claims ought to have the reasons Certyfyd of their not attending that so their Claims may be received. House adjourned.

(Feb. 27–28, 1752). Also appointed to the committee to draw the reply was Peyton Randolph (1721–75), lawyer and son of Sir John Randolph and Susanna Beverley. He was burgess for Williamsburg, 1748–49, 1761–75, and for the College of William and Mary, 1752–61; speaker of the House of Burgesses, 1766–75; president of the First Continental Congress; and attorney general of Virginia, 1748–66.

[13] Rev. Thomas Dawson (d. 1761) was chaplain. He was rector of Bruton Parish, 1743–59; commissary and member of the Council, 1752–61; and president of the College of William and Mary, 1752–61. The doorkeepers were Thomas Broadrib (d. 1762) of Sussex Co., William Francis, Andrew Lindsay, and Robert Wager (*Burgesses' Journals, 1752–1758*, 5–6 [Feb. 27, 1752]).

[14] Lunsford Lomax (1705–72), planter and son of John Lomax and Elizabeth Wormeley, was burgess for Caroline Co., 1742–55.

[15] Beverley Whiting (1707–55), lawyer-planter and son of Henry Whiting and Anne Beverley, was burgess for Gloucester Co., 1738–55.

[16] Joshua Fry (1700–54), planter-teacher and son of Joseph Fry of Somerset, England, was professor of natural philosophy and mathematics at the College of William and Mary, 1732–37, and burgess for Albemarle Co., 1746–54.

[17] The committee selected John Palmer (d. 1759), lawyer and bursar of the College of William and Mary. His competitor, Anderson Stith (d. 1768), lawyer, was a son of John Stith (d. ante 1759) and Elizabeth Anderson.

[18] Probably Benjamin Waller (1710–86), lawyer and son of Col. John Waller (1670–1754) and Dorothy King. He was burgess for James City Co., 1744–61; clerk of the general court of Virginia, ca. 1745–76; and judge of state admiralty and general courts, 1776–85.

29. Saturday.

The House met. The Chairman of Propositions having returned Some Reports of the resolutions of that Committee. Some were agreed to, in Particular the Rejecting of the Caroline and Essex Petitions for a Stint law. Great Arguments thereon Carried for the Report. Spoke in this against the Petition. The Chairman for Privileges etc. also gave in his report of the Resolutions of the Committee. The Form: The Committee of Blank having had under their Consideration Sundry [blank], Also having come to Sundry resolutions he was ready to report them when the House thought Proper to receive them. Many Writs Wrong as to Simple mistakes, one for K[ing and] Q[ueen County] for not mentioning the Place of Election. Motion for Sending for the Sherif carried in the Negative. Amended at the table. Spoke against Sending. The Sheriff of Nancemond[19] sent for, because he had not annexed his return by a Schedule but had wrote it on the Writ. Note: here the prevailing reason seemed to be that the Clerk could not amend it because he could not write the Sheriff's Name. Therefore he was sent for in Custody. The other not sent for. The case was the Sheriff, instead of writing the endorsement on the writ, wrote a return also on the writ as well as schedule. Spoke in all these debates against Sending. Colo. Carter against. Mr. Conway and Waller the same.

Mr. Bland reported the Waiting on the Governor to know when he'd receive the address. His answer also. Several Certificates not Certyfyd in Court produced by motion. I introduced one of Jno. Jennings[20] Sworn to before Colo. Tayloe.[21] I observe thus far every motion must be seconded before there can be any question put upon it or any debate upon and so of Persons speaking against such motion. Mr. Speaker Putteth not all Questions Standing. That for adjourning in these words: Gentlemen is it your Pleasure to adjourn? Then, all you etc. The Address was read by the Person presenting the Same, which was the first in the Committee for drawing the Same. Thence twice by the Clerk. Then by the Speaker. And so the Governor's Speech. When a Division happens, if 'tis relating to things intirely in the house, vizt, about Clerks etc., Ays on one Side No's on the other. But, if 'tis about any matter in the House that Some are against and some for, those against the resolution in the house,

---

[19] Probably Josiah Riddick was sheriff of Nansemond Co. See *Exec. Journals of Council of Col. Va.,* 318 (June 13, 1750).

[20] John Jennings was a resident of Richmond Co. (Richmond Co. Court Order Books, 1752–62, pp. 56, 153, 215, Virginia State Library, Richmond). His claim was for taking up a runaway servant (*Burgesses' Journals, 1752–1758,* 9, [Feb. 29, 1752]).

[21] John Tayloe of Mount Airy (1721–79), planter and son of John Tayloe (1687–1747) and Elizabeth Fauntleroy, was a member of the Council, 1757–76, and a neighbor of Landon Carter.

such as the Reports of any Committee, Go out of the house on the division. Tellers are appointed of each Party. One going out is Stopped and Counteth those within. Another from within counteth those who went out as they come in. Resolution to take into Consideration on Monday the Governor's Speech.

MARCH 1752

2. *Monday.*

Bland reported to the Committee that they had waited on the Governor to know when he'd receive the House's address who was pleased to say on This day 12 o'Clock. Pursuant to a Message for that Purpose, the Speaker and House went up and Presented the address, who trembled exceedingly then returned and reported what was done and so read the Governor's Answer.

Chairman Committee Propositions reported the resolution of the Committee on the Essex Petition and Propositions for a Town at Leyton's. I disagree to the report of the Committee who had rejected it. Waring[22] Seconded and a large debate thereon. Yet Carryed against me because the Person owning the Land was a Minor. No division.

Agreeable to the order of the day to take into Consideration the Governor's Speech, Mr. Conway motioned for the House to resolve itself into a Committee of the House. Mr. [Charles] Carter made Chairman. The Speaker on a bench next the Chair. Then the Governor's Speech read twice by the Clerk and then Paragraph by Paragraph. Speaker motioned with respect to Exchange. Pendlet[on][23] with respect to Courts of Justice. The method in these Committees: to move to the Consideration for a Resolution etc. and not for an amendment to any Particular thing but to whole Acts in General. And here they must be Seconded. The Committee by motion adjourned and the Speaker taking the Chair, the Chairman reported that the Committee had directed him to move for leave to sit again tomorrow. Agreed. This Evening, being of the Committee of Privileges and Elections, we Examined the Alegations of Sundry Petitioners for Controverted Elections, Mr. Randolph our Clerk being by the House permitted to appear as Council. We fixed the days for hearing and limitted the petitioners to particulars in their Charges though against my opinion, for as either Accusation, if here, would do so he was at Liberty to make use

---

[22] Thomas Waring (d. 1754), planter, was a burgess for Essex Co., 1736–40, 1752–54.

[23] Edmund Pendleton (1721–1803), lawyer and son of Henry Pendleton (1683–1721) and Mary Taylor, was burgess for Caroline Co., 1752–76; delegate to the First Continental Congress, and president of the Virginia Conventions, 1774–76. An excellent biography is David John Mays, *Edmund Pendleton, 1721–1803: A Biography* (2 vols.; Cambridge, Mass., 1952).

of All. Many thought with me but we were over ruled. Note: there is a Standing rule of the House that the Person Complaining shall give ten days notice of the things and Persons he intends to object to with respect to a Scrutany. Also a great debate whether the Evidences should come down. It was resolved both because it was not objected to by the Parties. But in the Complaint about the Rioters they were ordered to Town. That is the Evidences before the Committee; and I observe it is a rule that when the Parties do not agree to it All the Evidences come down. Hedgeman[24] made a Strange Speech relating to the Town aforesaid, being against it. C[harles] Carter against it [as were] Bland [and] Lomax. For it: myself, Reddick,[25] Martin,[26] Waring.

All the best Judges say the Address of the House is by [far] preferable to the Council's. And So Say I by much.

3. *Tuesday.*

House sat at 11. Committee of Priviledges by their Chairman make their Report Relating to the Petition of Richd. Bowker[27] of an Undue Election as also of A Riotous Election In which Report the Committee set for the time appointed. Mr. Bland moved to have the Petitioner Confined to one thing, vizt, the Riot. If so, Many Charges will be saved. Mr. Martin Supported the motion. I supported the Resolution of the Committee. Mr. Waller said that the House had agreed to the Committee's Report. It Could not now be altered.

House go into a Committee of the Whole House and then agree to Ask leave to Sit again. The Speaker resumed the Chair. The Chairman reported. The House agreed to the Report. A Select Committee to draw and prepare a bill pursuant to one of the Resolutions, vizt, that for an Assize Law. Mr. Whiting and All the Lawyers on that Committee with myself.[28] Note: here

[24] Peter Hedgeman (d. 1765), planter, was burgess for Prince William Co., 1732–40, and Stafford Co., 1742–58.

[25] Lemuel Riddick (1711–75), planter-lawyer, was burgess for Nansemond Co., 1736–68, 1769–75.

[26] John Martin (d. 1756), lawyer, merchant, and planter, was burgess for Caroline Co., 1730–34, 1738–40, and for King William Co., 1752–56.

[27] Richard Booker (d. 1760), planter and son of Edward Booker, failed in his effort to contest the election of Wood Jones (*Burgesses Journals, 1752–1758*, pp. 13, 58 [Mar. 3, Apr. 1, 1752]). He was later burgess for Amelia Co., 1756–60.

[28] This committee consisted of Peyton Randolph, Benjamin Waller, James Power, Beverley Whiting, Edmund Pendleton, Robert Jones, Landon Carter, Richard Bland, Stephen Dewey, George Douglass, William Waller, Lemuel Riddick, Augustine Claiborne, and John Martin (*Burgesses' Journals, 1752–1758*, 14 [Mar. 3, 1752]). James Power (d. 1757), lawyer and emigrant from Ireland, was burgess for King William Co., 1742–47, and for New Kent Co., 1752–58. Robert Jones, lawyer, was burgess for Surry Co., 1748–55. Stephen Dewey, lawyer, was burgess for Prince George Co., 1752–55; he later moved to North Carolina. George Douglass (d. 1758), lawyer and emigrant from Scotland around 1715, was burgess for Accomack Co., 1742–55. William Waller (1714–60), lawyer-planter and brother of Benjamin Waller, was burgess for Spotsylvania Co., 1742–53, 1756–60. Augustine Claiborne (1721–87), lawyer-planter and son of Thomas Claiborne (1680–1732), was burgess for Surry Co., 1748–53.

was a division whether it should be a Select Committee or that of the Courts Justice. Carryed for a Select Committee. Ays Went out because the Courts of Justice Committee are of the house and as a Rule the opposers to any thing in the house go out.

The other Resolution of the Committee of the Whole House referred to the Committee of Propositions to draw up the bill, vizt, for Regulating Exchange etc.

Note: I observe Every Chairman first informs the house of their Comittee's having had under their Consideration Several (things) to them referred and have come to Several Resolutions thereupon Which he is ready to Report when the house is pleased to receive them. The leave being given, he Reports.

Note also: the Consideration of any matter in any Committee's report may be referred to another day or lye on the table as was twice done this day to some Resolutions of the Committee Propositions. This day Spoke against a resolution for Inspecting Shingles etc. from the Committee of trade and only because the Person Supporting the same informed the house that the Colonys abroad Seized such things if they were not Inspected. I sayd this was a law in itself.[29]

Spoke also against the Report from the Committee Priviledges and Elections about ordering Evidences to be executed with respect to some Voter's pretensions who had been sworn before. But this the Speaker told me was a standing order of the House of Commons (*Sed tame[n] Quam*).[30] I never read any such and in my Speach I argued strongly against it because, were that the case, the oath could have no Signification unless it were to deter some men of tender Consciences from Voting. Besides, as the Law gave a remedy to any Person against the Person taking the Oath if he took it falsely, it would in effect be declaring on such enquiry the Person Perjured if before he was properly arraigned at Law; and I did not know but a Vote of the house might be admitted as Evidence. This was not answered by any Member in the House but upon a Private Conference with the Speaker, who did not disallow of my reasoning but said our oath was the same with the Oath prescribed by Act of Parliament in England. And yet the same proceeding was used as in the before mentioned Report of the Committee.

4. *Wednesday.*

Sat with the Committee of Propositions. There resolved to the reasonableness of the 2 propositions of Richmond and Charles City, vizt, for the restrain-

---

[29] The Burgesses passed a bill at this session in compliance with this resolution. See Hening, ed., *Statutes*, VI, 233–35.

[30] "But nevertheless how?"

ing the Number of dogs kept by Negroes and Servants. Also to the Removal of Naylor's Warehouse to Cat Point. Mr. Woodbridge,[31] Waller and others joyned me in Supporting these Propositions in the Committee. The Committee rejected a Proposition for dividing Amelia County but as it was only for want of Explanation as to the Place where the division was to be made.

Mr. William Randolph[32] moved to have the Consideration of that part of the Committee's resolution referred or rather recomitted. Therefore, the Speaker proposed the giving it Back to the Chairman and not taking notice of it in the Journal of the House. I seconded Mr. Randolph.

On the Sitting of the House I moved that the Chair might admonish the members of that house that the rising and going out confusedly upon an adjournment before the Speaker was contrary to the Rules of Parliamentary decency. Mr. Waller then moved for the rules to be hung up. Agreed the Clerk should do it but not to be noticed in the Journal because it should not appear as a reflection. The Chairman of the Committee of Claims moved for the Instruction of the house as to the allowance to be made and the Number of Guards to be allowed in the County Courts for the Guarding of Criminals in the County Gaols. B[enjamin] Waller moved to leave it to the discretion of the Committee. Will Waller and myself and Others against it. We shewed the Law left it to the Sherrifs and as the Courts do always Levy the same on the People they must be the best Judges whether the Charge was extravagant. On a division the Question for directing the Committee to allow according to the Allowance Certyfyed by the Courts was carried by a very Great Majority but not entered in the Journals. The reasons I know not.

Mr. Power, observing many Petitions still Crowding in against Sitting members for Undue Practices at Election, Moved that in case such Petitions should be judged frivolous and Vexatious the Petitioner should make the sitting member satisfaction. This I seconded. And Colo. [Charles] Carter and Conway opposing it with some others, I spoke largely and shewed it to be the standing Rule of the house of Commons and that, although this house had formerly rejected it, it was no rule they should now do it. Here I was answered with some uncommon distinctions on My Arguments on which I moved for leave to Replye. Many Cryed out no leave, But on the Question leave was granted by a large Majority. And then I supported my former observations against the distinctions made upon, and the motion was Carried by a great Majority. However, it was only entered as a Standing order and no notice

---

[31] John Woodbridge (1706–69), planter and son of William Woodbridge, was burgess for Richmond Co., 1736–69.

[32] William Randolph of Wilton (1719–61), planter and son of William Randolph of Turkey Island (1681–1742) and Elizabeth Beverley, was burgess for Henrico Co., 1752–61.

taken of any Motion. Sat this evening in the Committee of Privileges and Elections to set a day for Hearing the Petition of Eppes[33] against Stephen Dewey. The Petition of the Barbar's Prentices for a Law to prevent Shaving on Sundays rejected by a great Majority. Only one Nay, (to wit) Mr. C[hristopher] Robinson.[34] Mr. Martin introduced this Petition very sacredly. B[enjamin] Waller and I opposed it strongly because I could not look upon it as any Profanation of the Sabbath to go Clean into the house of my God. Colo. Carter spoke also against it. The Speaker whispered me I might be shaved on Saturdays. Came home very Sick.

5. *Thursday.*

Blooded and took a Purge. Sat up bolstered all night. Could not attend the house. Therefore this day's work borrowed from the Journals. I learned from Conversation That the Committee of the Courts of Justice this day made a report that it was reasonable that the law for killing Crows and Squirrels should be revived and that this resolution was agreed to by a great Majority notwithstanding Sundry Members spoke largely and well against. But some voted to Please their Constituents and others, particularly the Townsmen of Northfolk, voted for it by a Perswasion that grain would grow cheaper by it. Accordingly, was ordered to be brought in for that Purpose.

This day also two Motions introduced, two resolves to ballance that of yesterday, vizt, that as every frivolous and vexatious Petitioner against a Sitting Member should make Satisfaction to the Sittings so that, if the Sitting Member had procured his Election by any kind of Bribery or should prevent any Evidence from giving Testimony to the house in such case, that then the house would proceed against him with the Outmost Severity. Colo. Carter introduced these motions, and as they are also with the other standing orders of the House of Commons I, had I been there, should have been for them. I am told the Gentleman was some time without a Second but the motions met with no Opposition. The rest I refer to the Journals. Only by accident a Member rising a little out of time upon being checkt by the Speaker was taken so Speachless as not to recover it.

6. *Friday.*

As soon as the House Sat I moved for an order to Settle the bounds of Richmond County between that County and the Countys of King George,

[33] Francis Eppes, planter and son of Francis Eppes, Sr. (d. 1734), was burgess for Prince George Co., 1736–49. He failed in his attempt to contest the election of Stephen Dewey (*Burgesses' Journals, 1752–1758,* 17, 63 [Mar. 5, 30, 1752]).

[34] Christopher Robinson of Hewick (1705–68), planter and son of Christopher Robinson (1681–1727), was burgess for Middlesex Co., 1752–58.

Westmoreland, and Northumberland, that Persons Proper be appointed by the said County Courts in Conjunction with Richmond County Court and to Report their Proceedings therein to their Respective Courts. This was done upon the Plan of an order in 1738 but never executed. Woodbridge Seconded. The Same order passed for King George, Stafford, and Westmoreland respectively.[35]

The Chairman of the Committee Claims moved for the directions of the House with regard to the allowances to be made to Countys for the imprizonment of Persons committed for Breaches of the house for that the Committee had been informed that former Committees never allowed them. Mr. Waller spoke for the Allowance. I seconded him. Then B[enjamin] Waller mentioned an order formerly made against it and said it might be thought a Reflection on the dignity of the house to alter that order but he leaned to an alteration. Colo. Carter Strongly against it. Conway doubted whether it could be done. Colo. Carter said it would in effect be charging the house with injustice to former Claimers of this Nature. I answered All and declared against law obligatory on Parliaments, that Precedents and orders made were only demonstrations of what was done heretofore and no farther directory of what was to be done than as they came within the bounds of Good reason and Justice; that we could not be thought reflecting on the dignity of the house by Contradicting former orders for every order was Governed by its own Circumstances, and unless the Journals had minuted every Circumstance no man could properly call it a Contradiction; and as to the Injustice Chargeable on former Assemblys, if we ever could suppose this house could do injustice, the continuing of it would never extenuate it; that it was Clear, breakers of the Peace were in the Eye of the law Criminals, and, if they were insufficient to bear the Charges of a Prosecution, the Law had directed the Public should; if this was thought unreasonable, a new law might alter it, but, as the debate was upon what was already, the law was the directory. The Question Potion [?]. A great Majority for the Committee's allowing them and accordingly an order made for that they should always be allowed except where the Person imprisoned had sufficient, which is according to the Law.

Chairman of Propositions reported the Richmond and James City Propositions for destroying Negroes' dogs reasonable. A great debate hereon in which Colo. Carter, myself, Martin and others Spoke fully but to no Purpose. It was rejected by two voices. The reason, many members were absent. Mr. Chairman also reported the Proposition from Northumberland for Masters of Convicts to pay their Servants charges in cases of felonies rejected. Here Colo.

---

[35] For this order see *ibid.*, 19 (Mar. 6, 1752). The 1738 order may be found in *ibid., 1727–1740*, 383, (Dec. 20, 1738).

Carter, myself, and Hedgeman argued strongly for the Proposition. Martin, Reddick, and others against us. But we Carryed it by a great Majority reasonable and We Were appointed to prepare and draw up a bill.[36] No further business. The House adjourned.

7. Saturday.

Mr. Chairman of Propositions Sat in Committee where we examined Propositions and Petitions both Certyfyed by the County Court Clerks and also others Referred to the Consideration of the Committee by house. Many Resolutions thereupon. Some Reject[ed] and some Reasonable. One for a Ferry at Donaphan's Rejected. Lomax and Pendleton Spoke against it. This it Seems had been before in former Sessions. Therefore, there was a Crye for rejecting as soon as it was read, but I thought otherwise, vizt, that Public Conveniences ought always to be considered. Another for a New district on Notoway rejected not under the cognisance of the house. Other Petitions for a Ferry from and to Port Royal to be free referred to another day because Mr. Waller had something to say against and he was upon the Committee of Claims. The reason was one Roy[37] who owned and kept a Ferry Just by had Petitioned against the Town Petition.

In the House, the Chairman of Propositions reported Sundry Resolutions of the Committee, vizt, one Proposition from the County of Richmond for removing the Warehouse from Naylor's Hole to Cat Point to which the house Agreed. I rose and explained to the House the reasonableness of the Proposition: that it had been moved in former Assemblys and had passed the house but for some reasons not known it had been Stopped in its Passage upstairs, that now the Proprietor had throw[n] the Present Warehouses on the County, that the Landing was so bleak that it was always dangerous for boats to come on Shoar and the making of Wharfs was a Perpetual Charge to the Country.

Also the Propositions for a New Warehouse at Boleling's Point, or at Bland ford or at Mon ford or at Fisher's on Appomatox were read and the three last disagreed by the house, that is, Reject[ed]. Here I argued to refer them to the Committee of the Whole house, who had this day been appointed to amend and continue the tobacco Law,[38] but not Seconded. A Petition was

[36] Appointed to this committee were Charles Carter, Landon Carter, and Peter Hedgeman (*ibid.*, *1752–1758*, 21 [Mar. 6, 1752]).

[37] Thomas Roy (d. 1772) was a tobacco inspector and operator of a warehouse, ferry, and tavern in Port Royal, Caroline Co. See T. E. Campbell, *Colonial Caroline* (Richmond, 1954), pp. 83, 106–7, 140, 484.

[38] The final version of the tobacco law, the subject of much debate at this session, is printed in Hening, ed., *Statutes*, VI, 222–27.

introduced by W[illiam] Waller from the Fredericksburg Merchants to oblige the Planters to tye up all their tobacco in bundles not exceeding 6 leaves and not to put Stem and leaf tobacco in one hogshead. I opposed it and so did Conway and Will Randolph because it seemed to be a Whim, and I sayd it lookt as if it was intended to introduce the making of Several Sorts of tobacco so that by such steps of Indulgence we should come to that and at last leave our whole Substance in the Power of the Inspector. It was ordered to lye on the Table and to Cut all Short. A Vote passed that every Proposition relating to the amendment of the tobacco Law should lye and be referred to the Consideration of the Whole house who were to sit in Committee for that Purpose on Wednesday next. A large Vote for a Bridge from Bolling's Point which I agreed to in order to take away the necessity of a new Warehouse Petitioned for. Some Acts had their first reading, vizt, one for fairs in the town of Alexandria.[39] The Act for dividing P[rince] George Passed the House. The new County called Dinwiddie.[40]

When the first Person in a Committee appointed to prepare any bill is prepared, he acquaints The house with it and lays it on the Table. And then at Leisure The Clerk reads first the title, which is only Endorsed on the back and wrote in no Other part of the bill, Then the bill, On which The Speaker takes the bill, opens the nature of it to the House first by Title, Then Preamble, and next the Enacting Clause, and telling the House how oft it hath been read and what the next question will be (vizt, whether it shall be read a 2d time) or whether it shall be engrossed or read a third time. If any one, before the person puts the question, desires to debate further on the bill, he moves to have it Committed.

9. *Monday.*

The bill for laying a duty on Negroes[41] Committed upon a third reading to a Committee of the Whole house. No Arguments this day. Nothing done but read over the Report of the Committee of Propositions which lay on the Table on Saturday. I moved for leave to bring in a bill for restraining and Lessening the number of Doggs in Northumberland, Westmoreland, Richmond, Lancaster, and King George. Not Seconded by my Colleague who had told me he would. But it seems he had thought himself affronted, for in the arguments I used in the proposition for removing Naylor's Hole Warehouse to Cat Point I informed the House of its having passed the house and being Stopt

---

[39] For the final version of this act see *ibid.*, IV, 286–87.
[40] For the final version of this act see *ibid.*, VI, 254–56.
[41] For the final version of this bill see *ibid.*, 217–21.

upstairs. The Petitioners moved it to a Subsequent Assembly and the next time that it was sent down it was lost I supposed for want of Proper information of the facts. He says I said for want of being properly Supported. I said no more than what I said in the Committee before, and then he did not make any objection. He talkt to me of this, and I told him I intended nothing but the truth and I believe it was the whole truth for he owned he did not know how the place stood.

Sat This Evening in Committee Priviledges and Elections to hear the point debated about the James Town Election of Travis,[42] Where one Harris was Judged a Legal Voter notwithstanding he lived so far from the Town as that the bounds must take near 700 Acres to take in his Land. There was no Evidence of this being the Town, but the man who Swore he heard it always reckoned so and, because he said his Father and he had used to Vote, it was adjudged a Good Vote. Vastly against all or any spark of reason that I could Frame to myself. Again the 2d Point was whether Persons having lots in the Towns without Houses should vote. It was determined that in James Town they might because the Acts of Assembly only related to qualifications necessary for a County and all Particular Acts take in no other but those Towns that are mentioned. Here I could by no means agree with them. That as to James Town, although nothing was said in the Law, yet in the Act in 1736[43] the Proviso there explained what the Law was, and no proviso Enacts anything new. And in that Proviso the right of Voting was by a house and Lots. The other Point as to the Returning officer to be moved to the house. Note: the Candidates were five to 4, and the officer swore the Majority Governed him or else he would have returned the Petitioners. This Point left to the house.

10. *Tuesday.*

This day the Committee of Propositions sitting in the house very late. The house did not sit till after 12 o'clock, When the Chairman for Priviledges and Elections gave in his Report of Yesterday's debate about James Town Election. At a Proper time I moved that the matter might be recommitted for a further debate, having been instructed to say that the Petitioners had now Evidence Nearly to Ascertain the bounds of the Town and, as to the Evidence given by Harriss to the antiquity of his Voting, he had mistaken a part of his Age for that he had asserted he had voted 42 years for a member he could not be of Age

---

[42] Lewis Burwell of Kingsmill (d. 1784), planter, son of Lewis Burwell (d. 1743), and burgess for James City Co., 1758–74, was the petitioner against Travis. Edward Champion Travis (1721–70), planter, was burgess for Jamestown, 1752–59, 1761–65. For the disposition of this case see *Burgesses' Journals, 1752–1758*, 12, 25–41 (Mar. 2, 14, 18, 1752). The exact identity of Harris is unknown.

[43] This act is in Hening, ed., *Statutes*, IV, 475–78.

at that time; That as the difference between the Sitting Member and the Petitioner Burwell was but one Vote, if it could be Shewn that one vote was illegal, the number of Votes must be equal and in such case the returning officer had declared he would return Burwell; that I lookt upon it as a thing sacred in itself and a matter of such Moment to a Country whose interest it was to Support the Freedom of Elections I was in hopes the house would indulge the Petitioner. Mr. Martin Seconded the motion. Hedgeman, as he always is, was violent against it. He was sure he had heard all that could be said and he wanted to hear no more. Colo. Carter spoke for a recommitment. Conway against it. Mr. Attorney Spoke handsomely for it, saying he must own the Opinion he gave in the Committee was but upon slight Circumstances although the best that appeared and that, if the Petitioner made to appear what he had instructed the Gentleman who made the motion to say, he should be of opinion the Sitting Member had no right to a Seat in the house. A division And above ⅔ of the house followed me.

A Petition Complaining of Undue Practices in Colo. Chiswell[44] and Jno. Symmes[45] for Hanover from Henry Robinson[46] was presented by Mr. Power. Received and Referred to the Committee of Elections.

Several Petitions for allowances for Negroes who dyed after outlawry rejected.

Colo. Carter first of the Committee for Preparing a bill to make masters or owners of Convicts lyable for the costs attending any prosecution for felony against them gave in the bill which was read the first time by the Clerk. And, as soon as the Speaker read the title of the bill and told us that the question would be whether it should [be] read the Second time, Mr. Martin rose and, indecent to all bills unless Such as are very offensive, Opposed it in a very long Speach, first doubting the Power of the Governor to Pass Such a bill, then charging it as an affront to offer such a bill to him, then shewing were this bill to pass People would not b[u]y them and the Captains or Persons transporting them here would loose by them, then charging the Preamble with a Seeming Falshood in setting forth that most of the felonies committed here were perpetrated by Convicts, Then representing it as a thing that would Compell

---

[44] John Chiswell (d. 1766), planter, iron manufacturer, and son of Charles Chiswell, was burgess for Hanover Co., 1742–55, and for Williamsburg, 1756–58.

[45] John Syme (1728–1805), planter and son of John Syme (d. 1731), was burgess for Hanover Co., 1756–68, 1773–76; member of the Virginia Conventions, 1774–76; and later member of the state legislature. He was the half-brother of Patrick Henry.

[46] Henry Robinson (1718–56), planter and son of Councilor John Robinson (1683–1749), was burgess for Hanover Co., 1752–56. His petition was successful. The House declared Chiswell and Syme not duly elected, and in a new election the voters returned Robinson and Chiswell (*Burgesses' Journals, 1752–1758*, 61–62 [Mar. 26, 1752]).

the Government, whom he called our Mother Country, to send them nowhere but to Virginia, Then Alledging that they made the best of Servants, Concluded with being fixed Against the bill. Mr. Woodbridge, to the Surprize of everybody, Seconded him. Many said they could see he was set against me. Upon which I rose and, if the Praise of Everybody and a Vote of the whole house but three intitles me to value myself, I answered Mr. Martin as Close as the method he took Could bear. As to his doubts about the Governor's Power, unless he could assert his own Knowledge, it was raising a doubt without foundation; that the Governor must know his own Power and if his instructions were such as forbid him to pass such laws to be sure he would let us know it; And, as the affront Charged on the bill must depend on the Governor's instructions, if they did not forbid the Passing of such bills, all notion of an affront must fall; that it was on the Contrary an affront to suppose that a Gentleman that had so handsomely promised us every assistance that by his instruction he could be unwilling to pass a bill that the Country had so modestly framed when by the Gentleman's own arguments it might be a means to prevent peoples' buying them here; That the not buying them would be of Service because of the great propensity to Villany that the most of them discovered; That the Statutes for Transportation were not Calculated to make a trade for Captains to bring them in here but for Prevention of the former practice of hanging them; and further that the Acts Set forth they were for the better Cultivating of the Colonys; That even as to the transporter what with the Government's Allowance and a mere moderate Charge in buying them he would be a gainer; That the bill would not absolute[ly] prevent the buying them but that it would Operate as a Caution to those who bought them to give less for them that so in case they proved bad they might not be so great loosers; That as to the Preamble it could not be suspected of Falshood since it was a Preamble taken from [an] Act that had received the sanction of this house, which a Lawyer might have been presumed to have known; That the Observation as to the Mother [Country] was Charging her with being a very U[n]-natural Parent when her Children for whom she had once Calculated a benefit from Mature age and great Experience had found now Exceedingly Prejudicial. I say that she should think them disobedient for this your attempt to perswade me of the injuries you received. She Could say I will send them to you and you only. I then observed that Our Sovereign Whilst he Considered the interest of his Eldest daughter would not disregard the Prayers of her descendants, and I did not doubt but if this house would agree to Complain the redress would be obtained. Some Gentlemen told me and not a few so handsome a Speach and so Close an answer they had never met with.

Robert "King" Carter (1663–1732), Father of Colonel Landon Carter
Attributed to Sir Godfrey Kneller. T. Dabney Wellford, R. Carter Wellford, and
Hill B. Wellford owners.

Elizabeth Wormeley Carter (1714–1740), First Wife of Colonel Landon Carter
Attributed to Charles Bridges. T. Dabney Wellford, R. Carter Wellford, and Hill B. Wellford, owners.

Maria Byrd Carter (1727–1744), Second Wife of Colonel Landon Carter
Copy by William Dering after Charles Bridges. T. Dabney Wellford, R. Carter Wellford, and Hill B. Wellford, owners.

Probably Elizabeth Beale Carter, Third Wife of Colonel Landon Carter
By unknown artist. T. Dabney Wellford, R. Carter Wellford, and Hill B. Wellford, owners.

A Proposition from Augusta desiring the Minister's Sallery to be encreased, although agreed to by the Committee, was rejected Unanimously. Here Mr. Maddison[47] who had told me the whole affair came to me. I insisted upon his Opening the facts. He did. Then the Plain, homespun Mr. Wilson[48] from Augusta greatly Surprized us when, in a modest and Even stirring way, [he] set forth the Poverty of the People and shewed himself to be a singed Cat, for from the sight of the man no one could imagine such a thing and really he spoke exceeding Pertinent, Plain and fluent. I then opened and kept myself from the Censure of the house because it was a Parson's Sallery and having paid all defference to the Cloth argued upon the infancy of that Part of the Country, shewed them that the law had been fond and favourable to encourage them, that as they laboured under disadvantages their Pastor ought to bear a Part. Further, I took notice that the Majority of the People [were] favoured by the tolleration act[49] and, though it was necessary to preserve the Established Church, yet it would be Cruel to load tender Consciences with a greater burthen than they could bear for besides this Minister's Sallery they had their own Pastors to Pay and that at Present the Proposition was too soon by many years and had better be rejected at this time till a greater Number of the Church of England should settle there and make the burthen more Equal. Power changed and Came Over. And so did Waller and Conway. In short, the whole house, but not a voice was heard in favor of the resolution.

11. *Wednesday.*

The Chairman of Priviledges reporting that the Committee had set a day for hearing the Complaint of Robinson against Chisswell and Symms for an undue Election. Pendleton moved for a recommitment and that the Committee might be instructed to proceed on Certain Bonds inserted in the Complaints, that is to determine whether the Passing of them was illegal or not, setting forth that it would save time, for, if they were illegal, then the Election might be void, if not, then the Petitioner might proceed to his other Allegations. Power Seconds. I opposed a recommitment, alledging it was no matter of Equity, that it was a mere Simple Rule in the Power of the Committee. I was not for having the Committee in those things Circumscribed for that would be making it to Appear ridiculous. That the Frugality mentioned was well enough in the mouths of Gentlemen who Accustomed themselves to

[47] John Madison (d. 1783), planter and son of John Madison and Isabella Todd, was burgess for Augusta Co., 1748–54.

[48] John Wilson (1702–73), planter, was burgess for Augusta Co., 1748–72.

[49] Carter almost certainly refers here to the English Toleration Act of 1689. That act is conveniently published in Andrew Browning, ed., *English Historical Documents, 1660–1714* (New York, 1953), 400–3.

read only one side of the Question. Then I put the Supposition the Other way and All would be to do over again. Mr. Attorney and the other Lawyers chewed the Expression over and endeavoured to return it, but they could not. It was too true. Carryed the motion by a large Majority. Several Private bills presented and read the first time and appointed to be read a Second. Then the House resolved itself into a Committee for the Amendments of the tobacco [law] and settled many Warehouses and enlarged many Inspectors' Sallerys. Here opposed the building a Warehouse at a Place called Westham 7 miles from Navigation. Paid the Person supporting the same a great Compliment. This day when I was out Dixon[50] got his friends to fix his Warehouse at Falmouth.

12. *Thursday.*

This day the Committee Priviledges sat and appointed a day for hearing the Complaint of Francis West[51] against the Election of Bernard Moore[52] and Jno. Martin.

Very Little business in the house any more than the reading over sundry bills a 2d time. All Private bills Committed for docking Intails. There arose a dispute on one of them to prevent the lands settled in Lien being sold hereafter by *ad quod Damnum.*[53] Mr. Attorney Spoke handsomely against the necessity of the Clause which was in my opinion Just, but as it was only an Argument by the by no question was put but the usual one for an amendment.

The House went into a Committee and debated sundry amendments in the tobacco Law. Every one proposed by a Certain Gentleman[54] agreed to *Natu Signisque Loquuntur.*[55] If any dared to Oppose, some Severe Expression unbecoming his dignity was immediately thundered out. For Example, Carter Burwell spoke for amendment to that part of the law that directed the Captains to make out 2 Manifests, vizt, now it would be necessary for three because the Naval officers were obliged to send home three. I seconded him. Here that Gentleman rose, ridiculed the thing that our assembly should be imployed to make laws because an Act of Parliament required a thing to be done. Let the

---

[50] John Dixon (d. 1757), merchant from Bristol, England, came to Virginia before 1727, acquired large landholdings, owned a warehouse at Falmouth, and returned to England sometime before his death.

[51] Francis West, planter and son of Thomas West (*ca.* 1670–1743), was burgess for King William Co., 1748–49, 1756–58. For the Burgesses' action on his complaint see *Burgesses' Journals, 1752–1758*, 30 (Mar. 11, 1752).

[52] Bernard Moore of Chelsea (b. 1720), planter and son of Augustine Moore (1685–1743), was burgess for King William Co., 1744–58, 1761–65, 1769–71.

[53] A chancery writ used to assess damages to land for some public use.

[54] A reference to Speaker John Robinson.

[55] "They speak in accord with signs of rank."

officers do it. I modestly answered that it was not inconsistent with this Assembly to do it since the Very Law which they were amending was Actually Calculated for Preventing Frauds in his Majestie's Customs and I presumed the sending 3 Manifests was only for the better Securing the Customs. Upon which he told the Chairman I had no other method of Arguing but by making wrong Observations that I might hold forth upon for what he said did not relate to his Majestie's Customs. After this I opposed an Amendment for Certyfying the Sort of tobacco, vizt, whether tyed or untyed by the Inspectors, Shewing the great Partiality in Inspectors and I would not leave any more in their Power. Vaulx[56] Seconded me and argued Against me, but this Gentleman According to his Usual Way told the Committee I only argued against inspectors in General. To this I answered in return of his Compliment that my words were plain enough but the affectation of blindness I observed was Sometimes a proper method to furnish out a Speach with. Here he sayd I was witty and so the question was put and Carryed Against me. He also overruled an Amendment of William Randolph's, I believe because I seconded it, to oblige the Inspectors [so that] they would not receive any other fee or reward. This was unanimously agreed to till that Gentleman spoke, and all that he said against it [was] that it would make a great alteration in the Law, and then it ran against the Amendment. Afterwards I proposed an Amendment that Inspectors should not be Concerned in the Picking of tobacco Condemned by them for fee or reward. Here he did not know what to say and told us plainly an amendment of that sort was already made, on which the Chairman Sayd it passed in the Negative. However, it was enough he shewed himself Against it and so by a Great Majority the Amendment was lost although many other Gentlemen said in the house they knew many to have gotten above 15 or 16,000 [pounds of] tobacco per annum that way. Of this Sort went it all day. Whatever he agreed to was Carryed and whatever he Opposed dropt. Which I suppose to be one reason why so many things are Committed to the Whole House for he beckons before such Motions a Member whom he knows, and up he comes and having his lesson, moves for a Committment to the Whole House. Two Amendments to Oblige Inspectors to Sell all the tobacco found in their houses above three years old [and] to give a Certificate of the Persons' Names to whom they gave notes to the Court and of the marks and Numbers which is to be advertized and then to be payd into the treasury to be repayd the Owner whenever he Appeared. The other to forbid the taking out transfer notes after the notes for Crop were once taken out for the same tobacco.

[56] Robert Vaulx (d. 1754), planter and son of Robert Vaulx, was burgess for Westmoreland Co., 1752–54.

13. *Friday.*

This day went into the Committee of Propositions and there heard the most Surprizing debate that ever was about the Division of the County of Surry. Many Evidences Concerning the nature of the affair to and for The division and so Confused that I could not form any Opinion. I therefore referred myself for the debates in the house. Accordingly, as soon as the house Sat, The Chairman made the Report of the Committee resolutions, which were that the Proposition for dividing were reasonable. After the Ceremony for Reading were over, Mr. Robert Jones, a bold Asserter, spoke long, and Mr. Bland answered him. The former against the Resolution of the Committee. The other Against and Mr. Auge. Clayborne also against the Division. In which debate I observed the most uncommon Assertions and Contradictions of each Other imaginable, which being of a Piece with what Passed in the Committee I gave my Opinion for the Division which was Carryed by a great Majority. Mr. Wormeley Petitioned for payment of a Negroe Shot on an Insurrection, which was allowed. After this the Committee of the Whole House about the tobacco Law in which I waited till the 52d Section which lays the Clogg on Cutting tobacco. Here I moved for an Amendment That Inspectors might Inspect the tobacco at the Warehouses or Cutting Cellars of the Person manufacturing the Same. To enforce this amendment I shewed it must be inconsistant with Any Country to restrain their own Manufactures and Clogg them and that, as this Clause was framed to prevent the Exportation of trash, the same would still be done and the Sanctity of the Oath would still be preserved for it was not desired that anything should be altered. And as I told Colo. Thornton[57] so it happened. The Byg man[58] arose in Opposition after Mr. Woodbridge had Seconded me and by throwing the most absurd arguments endeavoured to Overset me, such as Everyman might Expect to have the Inspectors at his own door and much such Stuff that I will be hanged if one impartial Creature could say was in the least applicable to the debate. I told the Chairman that I expected Opposition and was so Unhappy as to know the very Spot from Whence it should Issue but surely the Gentleman must be a better Judge of reasoning than to say there was any Parallel between the Amendment proposed in this debate and that of every Planter for Every Planter was not obliged to Carry his Comodity twice to a Market; but I was in hopes the

---

[57] Presley Thornton (1721–69), planter and son of Col. Anthony Thornton and Winifred Presley, was burgess for Northumberland Co., 1748–61, and member of the Council, 1761–69.

[58] A reference to Speaker John Robinson.

Committee would not always be bore down with weight without reason. Mr. Ben. Waller, who had promised me to be silent in the debate and who had before declared he knew nothing of tobacco, Observing that the Speaker would now loose his Point and taking a Nodd and with the most ridiculous supposition that a man might Set up a Cutting Engine in Goochland, expressed his dislike to the Amendment. And so with this Union of Interest only 25 on a division were for the Amendment. I must Observe Colo. Carter Burwell pusht me with his cain to make the motion and then Opposed it saying inspectors might be influenced at a man's own house Although they Could not be so in Inspecting Flower etc. which is the method prescribed by Law. So fair well to Committees of the whole house. For there he sits and what he can't do himself he prompts others to do by his nodds, nay to hollow out aloud, as the division must run to whichsoever side he sits, is enough to throw the side he is off, and I'll suffer death if in these days he looses a motion. It is not only my observation. Even his friends told me it would be so. And I did hear that Some Sessions agoe he lost a motion in the Committee of the Whole house and he gave such proofs of his Resentment that no Stone was unturned to Please the Worthy Gentleman. I observed a Silent Joaker[59] on his right hand never to leave him. Now I'll be hanged if in such a Multitude of Motions etc. it could be possible that two people without any other influence than that of bare reason could always be so exactly of one Opinion. How unhappy must a Country be should such a man be byasd with vitious Principles. I do absolutely declare that the use of any but one Member is Needless for 'tis but only get all things into this Grand Committee and then he's all in All.

14. *Saturday.*

Nothing this [day] but reading some bills Engrossed and passing them to be sent up to the Council, Who it seems have nothing to do. Several of these were Private bills and as most of them came from Lawyers I am of Opinion they were paid for drawing them. In [one] of these bills is a Clause to prevent the Sale of the Lands settled in Lieu of the others by *Ad quod damnum.*[60] I opposed this because I would not have it be made a presumptive reason that An *Ad quod damnum* could interfere with an intail settled by Act of Assembly. Should any Argument of its being prevented by a Special Clause shew in other cases it would Operate, it might be a means of Injuring all those cut off without such a Clause. The Law against the Convicts read a Second time

[59] Probably Benjamin Waller.
[60] A chancery writ used to assess damages to land for some public use.

and committed because it seemed to Carry a Retrospection, but Mr. Vaulx had other reasons for committing of it, vizt, I believe for destroying it, which no doubt we shall hear. The bill for Lessening the Number of Doggs in some particular Counties read the first time. Our Wise heads are full of Observations upon the distinction in the bill between Doggs and bitches, but nothing Yet said. No doubt they will get them ready to bring them forth. Colo. Carter, intending to Cross York, moved for the putting off the order of the day untill Tuesday as [he] was Chairman of the Committee and perhaps could not attend as such soon enough on Monday. But Mr. Speaker nodded to B[enjamin] Waller and by their Joint interest it was put off only till Monday, and, if the Chairman could not Attend, another might be appointed. This would be ill manners to any but a Carter, but to these it seems it is not. A Gentleman told me that the Members all Agree that the Bashaw used me ill in the Committee of the whole house.

16. *Monday.*

This day the Dogg bill had the 2d reading And the Convict Bill Committed for Amendments. This as much as might be to oblige Mr. Vaulx, who I think, has an inclination of oversetting the bill, although he seemed to lean in his Arguments in his first speach which he [made] this day for an Amendment. Myself, Westmoreland Members,[61] Mr. Woodbridge, Hedgeman, Fitzhugh,[62] Thornton and Ball[63] the Committee for amending. The rest of the day spent in reading the resolutions of the Committee of the Whole house on the Amendments of the tobacco law. R[obert] Jones moved for the Consideration of them to be put off till next day as it was a thing of Consequence and the house thin. B[enjamin] Waller Opposed it, but Carryed against him. After the house broke up, I told Waller it was illnatured to Oppose so reasonable a motion upon which with great Warmth he vowed he'd throw out my Dogg bill as he called it. Upon this I defyed him.

17. *Tuesday.*

Very ill all day. Blooded and Purged. My cold Worse and Worse. Blood quite Corrupted. Nothing from the house could I hear. Colo. Thorn[ton] came to see me and told me people were much disturbed to see me so Opposed without Cause.

[61] Robert Vaulx and John Bushrod (d. 1760) were the members from Westmoreland Co. Bushrod, planter and son of John Bushrod (d. 1720), was burgess for Westmoreland, 1748–55.

[62] William Fitzhugh (1721–98), planter and son of George Fitzhugh (d. 1722), was burgess for Stafford Co., 1748–58, and in 1759 moved to Maryland where he became a member of the Council.

[63] Spencer Ball (ca. 1700–67), planter, was burgess for Northumberland Co., 1748–67.

18. *Wednesday.*

Went to the house. Chairman from Committee Priviledges report the Examination in Burwell's Complaint against Travis, the James Town Member. An old Act of Assembly was found which declared the Peninsula to be the bounds of the Town and directed who should Vote.[64] These Qualifications being repealed by the Act in 1705,[65] I gave up the matter. This day Mr. Power in behalf of Frank West moved for leave to withdraw his Petition of Complaint against Martin and Moore because he said he was sick. Martin Then moved for satisfaction according to the Resolution of the house. I seconded him. Waller, Power, and Colo. Carter spoke for it and Carryed that the Petition was frivolous and Vexatious. I then came home, having had a bad fever. 'Twas this day Colo. Carter Carryed it for a free Ferry to Port Royal [66] but lost the Petition for a Ferry from Donaphan's to Battalie's.

19. *Thursday.*

Dogg Bill, having been read a third time and Engrossed, now came to the last question whether it was to Pass or not. Upon which I got the blanks filled up and then Made an Anticipating Speach in which I raised all the Objections started without doors and answered them. Upon [which] the Buffoon Reddick got up and because he was Ridiculous to make people laugh Pleased many and Concluded with a Verse that now he hoped to send it to the Lethean Shoar where he hoped never to hear of it more. Upon which I replyed that it was a humane failing not to know at what people laught nor at home [whom?] but, if he delighted in being a laughing stock, I gave him joy of it, and for his Verse I would agree to dubb him the Laureat of the house; that I could blush for him but as I saw a strange[r] to Shame I would pay him no such Compliment. The Grype Doctor's Petition was read and agreed to on Conditions of Tryal.[67] My bill Passed and by order I waited on the Council to Present [it], which I did in the [following terms:] Gentlemen of the Council, The House of Burgesses have passed a bill intitled An Act etc., and, reading the title concluded, to which they desiring Concurrence. Many bills Passed and Sent up and others ordered for a 3d Reading and Engrossing. Bland moved

[64] The act here referred to is almost certainly "An Act limmitting the bounds of James Cittie," passed in June 1676 and printed in Hening, ed., *Statutes*, II, 362.

[65] The act of 1705 is in *ibid.*, III, 236–46.

[66] The act to establish this ferry is in *ibid.*, VI, 296.

[67] This petition claimed to have discovered a medicine to cure the dry grypes (*Burgesses' Journals, 1752–1758*, 33–34 [Mar. 14, 1752]). The dry grypes, also called the iliack passion, were a form of lead poisoning caused by rum distilled through lead pipes. See Wyndham B. Blanton, *Medicine in Virginia in the Seventeenth Century* (Richmond, 1930), 66, 217.

for Council to be heard at the barr against the bill for a Bridge over Appomattox,[68] which was denied him. Myself, Attorney and Colo. Carter carryed it against him. This day The Chairman of Priviledges reported the Resolution of the Committee upon The Petition of Wall[69] of Brunswick against John Willis[70] for an Undue Election. The resolution was that the Sitting Member had on the Scrutiny a Majority of the Voters and therefore duly Elected. The House agreed to this and A motion was made to vote the Petitioner Frivolous according to the order of the House a former day but it Passed in the Negative.

20. *Friday.*

Mr. Willis's Costs amounting to £100, a motion was this day made by Bland to Consider of Wall's Petition Again. Upon which Waller moved the Chair to inform the house as to the Rules of Parliament, whether a thing once determined Could be brought on again that Session. Bland quoted a Case, vizt, The last Session for Appointing an Agent to Solicit an Address to Parliament at home, relating to the last penny where upon one day one Agent was Appointed and the Next The order reversed.[71] The Speaker said he remembered the case but at the same time he thought it was Unparliamentary. Therefore, Mr. Bland's motion of this day overruled. Mr. Attorney then varyed it, and as the thing determined Yesterday was whether the Petition of Wall was Frivolous or not yet in another Shape the house might receive a motion for paying the Sitting Member his costs. This was Seconded, and Colo. Carter Supported it by shewing that the resolution of the House in the Case of West against Martin and Moore this Session was double, vizt, one for making it frivolous, the Other for Paying costs, and therefore agreeable to the former order of the house. Had the Petition been frivolous, the Petitioner should make Satisfaction. Some thing other than Costs must be meant or why should there be two resolutions on it, one for Satisfaction, the other for Costs. This was so artfull that even the Cunning of Waller could not obstruct, and so the Sitting Member Willis got Costs. Upon which Waller moved that it might be generally resolved that in All cases where the Petitioner failed He should pay Costs. I saw the favour intended to a Person in the House Petitioned against and therefore I seconded him with him an amendment that if the Sitting Member

---

[68] The final version of this act is in Hening, ed., *Statutes,* VI, 293–94.

[69] John Wall (d. 1761), planter, was burgess for Brunswick Co., 1736–47. For the Burgesses' action on his petition see *Burgesses' Journals, 1752–1758,* 43 (Mar. 19, 1752).

[70] John Willis (d. 1769), planter and son of Francis Willis (b. 1690), was burgess for Brunswick Co., 1752–55.

[71] The proceedings on this address may be traced in *Burgesses' Journals, 1742–1749,* 366, 380, 385–86 (Apr. 17, 27, May 2, 1749), although there is no mention of any attempt to appoint an agent.

was removed he should also pay Costs. I knew this would appear equitable and as it would not serve his Purpose he must withdraw his Motion. Accordingly, it was done and no notice taken of it in the Journals. I heard this day the Council threw the dog bill out 4 to 3. No reasons given for it and indeed I must believe they had none unless it was to save Doggs which some are fond of.

21. *Saturday.*

The Chairman of the Privileges reported the resolution of the Committee of Eppes against Dewy, vizt, Notwithstanding of Dewy's Son-in-Law giving the Liquor that was brought to the Election away All the time of Voting, yet, as it did not Appear that Dewy ordered it, he was duly Elected. We had great arguments on this. First, the Chairman had omitted Some part of the facts in the Report. Therefore, I moved for a recommitment and with reason asserted that Otherwise, as few of the Committee might meet and the house were not to go out of the Report for facts, the Committee would be Sole judges. However, Party prevaled and this was carryed against me. Then I debated that those facts reported were within the law against treating and any Other Construction might render the law useless, for a Son need not want his father's Orders and now the road for Evasion would be so plain every Man must be a fool that could not hit it. As to the Precedents of Former Assemblys brought, should they be binding, it would be to suppose that an Assembly could not Err, and though the cases were in Point, Yet I had heard those Gentlemen who mentioned them call them hard judgments. Besides they proved too much, for they not only shewed that the House never turned out the Sitting Member when the treating was not by his orders but further that the house never punished Anybody. For in the case quoted, Carter against Fanteleroy,[72] the Committee Reported that the Person that treated declared he had always ordered it and that he would do it, and Yet the house did positively resolve that it was not at [all] infringing the freedom of Elections. This debated. Ended against me a very large Majority, but they seemed to be fewer than before. After this, Waller, who sayd he would not Concern himself because Dewy was his father-in-Law, forgot himself and moved for Costs which Colo. Carter, myself, C[arter] Burwell, and Conway Opposed Violently, but we lost it by 2. So now, Who will Petition again? No treating but from a man's own hands and then a load of Costs.

[72] In this case Landon Carter contended that friends of William Fauntleroy (1684–1757) had furnished rum to some of the voters in Richmond Co. to entice them to vote for him for burgess. The Burgesses' action on this case may be followed in *ibid.*, 14, 34–35 (May 12, 24, 1742). Fauntleroy, planter and son of William Fauntleroy, was burgess for Richmond Co., 1736–49.

31. *Tuesday*.

To this day my health hath made it necessary to be abroad at Mr. Pages,[73] where I endeavoured by reading etc. to recover my health. I heard in the time many Controverted Elections were tryed and that Colo. Chisswell and Mr. Syme of Hannover were thrown out for having signed a bond to overturn a report spread about them that they designed to divide the Parish or County.[74] This body hath so little in it That I can't forbear saying with others that the Petitioners, being allyed to the Chair, had great weight, for certainly a Promise not to do such a thing was what the Constitutents had a right to demand and a bond is only a Promise brought within the reach of the Judge. By its penalty it differs not also. This I have heard to be granted on all hands, but they say Mr. Waller argued that the bonds given to Church of England men would be of no consequence but to new Light men they were. We need go no farther to account for this Piece of Art than to say that, having declared beforehand he thought them nothing, it was necessary for him to evade when his attachment to the C[hair] required a Compliment. In this time also they moved for a Present to the Governour in which they were so Cunning as to design it when I was absent for they knew I should oppose it. Mr. Bland told me So. Mr. Attorney moved it, and it was luckly lost. Waller, Hedgeman, C[harles] Carter and Conway opposed it.

This day got to the house. Heard the Surry Bill was overset, the Council's making an amendment and Adhearing to it relating to the naming the Upper and lower County. And upon [this] the bill was thrown out. The bill for the free ferry at Roystown read a Second time. Will. Waller proposed a Clause of obliging the Proprietors of that Ferry to contract with Roy. This I opposed and shewed that it was modestly called doing Mr. Roy Justice but it was intended to destroy the bill. Here I spoke long. Power, Lomax, and C[harles] C[arter] with me. Pendleton and B[enjamin] Waller against. So also against engrossing the bill. But we Carryed both and the bill engrossed. Obtained an order to the Committee of Claims for Levying on Pinkard[75] the money due to the witnesses he summoned against me when he endeavoured to get me indicted. Obtained also an Allowance in full for a Wharf built by the Court of

---

[73] Probably the home of Landon Carter's nephew, John Page (1720–74) of North End in Gloucester Co. A lawyer-planter and son of Mann Page (1691–1730) and Judith Carter, Landon's sister, John Page was burgess for Gloucester Co, 1752–68, and member of the Council, 1768–74.

[74] See *ibid., 1752–1758,* 61–62 (Mar. 26, 1752).

[75] Probably Thomas Pinkard (d. 1787), planter of Lancaster Co. and son of Thomas Pinkard (d. 1727). Pinkard, after Charles Carter had sought to indict him for forcible entry, had tried to indict Landon Carter before the General Court for a "Challenge." Both Charles Carter and Pinkard failed to obtain their indictments, and the Burgesses required them to pay the expenses of the witnesses (*ibid.,* 66 [Mar. 31, 1752]).

Eliza[beth] City, The Committee Claims having pretended to curtail the Accounts. The rest of this day spent in reading bills a Second time and then the house rose. Mr. Fitzhugh in my absence by way of Alarum made a motion to remove the Seat of Government which was Seconded and leave given to bring in a bill by a Vast Majority.

APRIL 1752

1. *Wednesday.*

Many bills read the Second time particularly the Lumber bill which I objected to and compelled the Persons Concerned to have it Committed. Mr. Lemuel [Riddick] Shewed himself again and endeavoured to Ridicule All that Conway, Charles Carter, Hedgeman, and myself could say till I took him to Pieces and made him sensible of the danger his bill was in. Then he struck in with a Merry Speach of the Attorneys and Agreed for a Commitment. The Bill relating to the damage on Protested bills and other Sterling debts when paid in Cash read a Second time but being only *ex parte*[76] it was recommitted.

Several other bills brought in, one for an Addition to this Church and an Organ.[77] I opposed it and so did some Others, but it was Carryed for a 2d reading. The Book of Claims came in this day. Crow and Squirrel bill read a 2d time.

2. *Thursday.*

Colo. Carter by way of Amendment brought in a Clause to sever[?] the Priviledge annexed to James City or James Town in sending a Member. Every[one] cryed out agreed; and, no Argument being put upon it, when the division [took place], it was Carryed against the Amendment. After reading a few bills, adjourned and Went to a Race in York Town Where Colo. Tayloe's Mare, Jenny Cameron,[78] won the Purse.

3. *Friday.*

Engrossed bills read and sent up and Some returned Agreed to, but the Crow and Squirrel bill dyed in its Passage. So no more of that. The Amendments made by the Council to the bills for Continuing and Amending the tobacco Law considered. The House agreed to all but that Clause that prohibited the paying of any hogshead Mixt that is Stemmed and leaf for any debt

[76] "On one side" or "on the interest of one side."

[77] The final version of this act is in Hening, ed., *Statutes*, VI, 230–31.

[78] A sketch of Jenny Cameron is in Fairfax Harrison, *The Equine F. F. Vs.* (Richmond, 1928), 141–43.

whatsoever. This I opposed might and Main and called it an Explanation of Some bold Strokes I had observed in the Committee of the Whole and declared the Law would in effect Starve every poor man in the Country. Conway, C[harles] Carter and Phil. Johnson[79] Opposed it. We carried it by a great Majority, and now we are threatened with the loss of the Whole law by the Council, but let them do it. The Book of Claims took us up above 3 hours reading no farther than the Letter C in the Accounts Alphabetically Stated.

The Method:

Every County Debit	*Ditto Credit*
To the Claims in their County both Public and private.	By every person owing a Claim living in the said County Although the person he owes it to lives in another County.

By this means the Levy is Properly made on every man by his own Sherrif, and to whomsoever the Claim is due by this transferring the ballance from one County to another he gets his Claim where he lives. Note: the discounts off every Claim in any County is taken according to the County Allowance where the Claimer lives.

4. Saturday.

Went on with the book of Claims. In it discovered many Claims for Runaway Servants not regularly certifyed by the Clerk but they were overruled and all Allowed. One made by a person not a Justice disallowed. This day for the first time a Call of the house moved and passed on Monday next. Two of the Persons, vizt, Farrow and Nevil,[80] that were ordered to be taken into Custody on Account of the Prince William Election were brought to the bar and there Specially reprimanded by the Speaker and then discharged paying fees.

Many and long debates about Quarterly Courts in Cumberland and Car-

---

[79] Philip Johnson (d. 1769), planter and son of William Johnson, was burgess for King and Queen Co., 1752–58, and James City Co., 1761–65.

[80] Abraham Farrow (d. 1786), planter and son of Abraham Farrow, and Joseph Nevill, probably the same Joseph Neville who was burgess for Hampshire Co., 1773–75, were residents of Prince William Co. Along with Henry Peyton (d. 1781), planter, son of Valentine Peyton (d. 1751), and burgess for Prince William Co., 1756–61, Farrow and Nevill were charged with acting riotously and unlawfully, assaulting the sheriff, and intimidating the freeholders during the Prince William election. The Burgesses ordered the sergeant at arms, Thomas Hall, to take all three into custody. Farrow and Nevill confessed at the bar of the house, where Speaker Robinson reprimanded them and discharged them after they paid fees. Apparently Peyton never made a similar confession (*Burgesses' Journals, 1752–1758,* 57–58, 73 [Mar. 25, Apr. 4, 1752]).

oline. I stedfastly withstood them. Will. Randolph, C[harles] Carter, Riddick, Conway, and R[obert] Burwell[81] with me. Pendleton, Lomax, and Robt. Jones against me. However, we threw it out. This day The Council Sent down and Insisted on their Amendment to the Act Continuing etc. the Tobacco Law so that I must believe some Coughs will ensue. I talked much with the Speaker, who is for this Amendment, but it was only to prevent his Opinion having any weight with some I saw in his Company. Several Members protested to me that they would dye before they would agree to it. In the debate about the Quarterly Courts, Robert Jones, who I believe has Convinced every body of his impudence, answered me and said I knew nothing of the Method of bringing a Suit to tryal and he did. I replyed that it pleased me to find a Gentleman Pique himself on a little Mechanical knowledge, which to be sure all the forms of Pleadings must be allowed to be on; [that] we could not imagine they were so eazy to be learned in the Spare hours that some people had behind Counters; That Attorneys were always lookt upon as so many Copyers and their knowledge only lay in knowing from whom to Copy Properly. We had also an instance of an engrossed bill's being amended. Moved for by Waller. For Authority he called upon the Chair. This day there was a great omission. In the bill for Erecting a lighthouse sent up to the Council And amended by them,[82] although it was what we call a money bill and only in the power of the House, yet they amended it, and it was not toucht by one Member till it was too late. I spoke to Several, and no one shewed any disposition to second me till Colo. Carter came in. Then he hit it, but it was too late. The house had agreed to the Amendments.

6. *Monday*.

This day Went on with the book of Claims. Passed several bills and sent them up to the Council. Most of them returned Agreed to. Ben. Waller then moved for the Call of the house ordered on Saturday, which I opposed and Richd. Bland because there was no need of it and the house was full. Mr. Bland brought in the bill for removing the seat of Government which was read once and Voted by a large Majority for a Second reading, and it had it. The Attorney, Riddick, and Waller against. Waller was trapped in his own art. He began by saying he should not make many observations on the bill but rung An Alarum about money Which I roasted him about. A motion made for Committing the bill to a Committee of the Whole house. It Passed in the Affirmative.

[81] Robert Carter Burwell (d. 1777), planter and son of Nathaniel Burwell (1680–1721) and Elizabeth Carter, was burgess for Isle of Wight Co., 1752–58, and member of the Council, 1764–76.

[82] This bill called for a lighthouse at Cape Henry. The final version of it is in Hening, ed., *Statutes*, VI, 227–29.

7. Tuesday.

This morning I cut early into the book of Claims and objected to the Committee's rejecting Ben. Rust's[83] Account for putting over Criminals. Over Ruled because it is not mentioned in the law and not ever allowed. I endeavoured much but to no Purpose. Got £100 Allowed to Colo. Tayloe. No opposition, Although Power ready for it. Allowed our Clerk £325. Walthoe £100. Propositions £80. Court of Justice £50. And so on. A great debate for allowing Robinson,[84] Master of the Colledge, £15, then £12.10, for his leaving his room when it Appeared he never left his room on Account of the house. These motions were made and over ruled as fast as Made. Mr. Preston[85] had left his room and was therefore Allowed £20. R[alph] Wormeley then moved a 2d time for £500 to the Governour. Seconded by Bland. I objected to the Regularity of it, And so did Pendleton. The Speaker said the former motion not being entered it was as no motion and therefore it might be moved again. I differed with the Chair and shewed it was only the Practice of the bar. Bland then harrangued in behalf of the Governour [as did] Power [and] Martin. I answered them all. Spoke long and modestly. It was over ruled again. So now it is to be hoped the Gentlemen are Satisfyed. Immediately the House resolved into a Committee and the removing bill was read and blanks filled up. First Vote James River or York. York Carryed it. Then New-Castle and so On to filling up the bill. In the God Sped of this Joys came New[s] from England that ten of the Acts passed last Session ordered to be repealed by Proclamation. 57 passed the Royal Assent, and many lay unobserved.[86] This was a great damp and will be the Cause of a Sum to the Governor to get these things represented [at] home that they are injurious to us and also of a much longer Assembly. Yesterday Reddick turned Rhyming buffoon again and had the happyness to be the Ass of the house.

8. Wednesday.

This day, after reading a few engrossed bills to send up and receiving others Just put in, The Governor sent us a Message by Mr. Walthoe That he commanded the immediate attendance of the house in the Council Chamber.

[83] Benjamin Rust (d. 1754) was a small planter and resident of Richmond Co.

[84] Rev. Thomas Robinson (1718-ante 1765), Anglican minister, took a B.A. at Queen's College, Oxford, and in 1741 joined the faculty of the College of William and Mary, where he was master of the grammar school.

[85] Rev. William Preston (d. 1778), Anglican minister, received an M.A. from Queen's College, Oxford, and came to Virginia in 1744 to become professor of moral philosophy at the College of William and Mary. He also was minister of James City Parish from 1755 until his return to England in 1757.

[86] This proclamation, or, more accurately, order in council, was issued Oct. 31, 1751, and may be found in the Public Record Office, London, Colonial Office Papers 5/1327, pp. 155-160B.

Upon Which we waited upon him, and in a kind manner he communicated us a List of the 57 Acts that had received the Royal Assent and of the ten that had been repealed. By the by I must observe that an Act of Assembly is now a trifling thing both from the possibility of getting them passed the Royal Assent or repealed in a Clandestine manner, for, although the Royal Assent must be obtained and is Necessary to some Acts, yet they are so few in Number that it is a hardship to burthen any Country with it for every Little footy Law that is in the Nature of it temporary or indeed Necessary to be altered, because sometimes it may be necessary to enact Laws that will not remedy the Evil or produce the Good intended. In such case, to be sure, the People ought to have the power incontrollable of Amending or repealing them. But after the Royal Assent [is] obtained, it seems, Although they may be amended or Repealed, yet it must always be with a Salvo to his Majesty until his Royal Pleasure shall be known. By which means the force of the Act must be suspended for a long time and of Course the want of Property remedy in any Case as before must needs be a very great injury. And the repealing of a Law not affecting the Mother Country but purely relating to the trade of or general or Particular good of the Country where it is enacted, I say, passing such a repeal without the application of that People is to do them an injury. And Whoever sees the List of those Assented to or Repealed will agree with me. For most of those assented to are temporary by express Clause. Some indeed expired before assented and others temporary in their Nature, that is, Acts only to License the doing of some immediate thing which, When done, the Act Naturally ceases. Those repealed are of the Same Stamp. Besides the suffering, such a Method of underhand practice must be introductory of All imaginable Bribery etc.

After the Governour presented the Papers before mentioned to the Speaker, the House went down and [the Speaker], resuming the Chair, told us the Governor's kind treatment of us. They were read by the Clerk, and Colo. Carter moved that Conference might be desired with the Council upon the Subject Matter of those papers, setting forth the unhappyness of the Country under the Repeal of Some of the Laws. He was sent up to desire one. Upon Which the Council by their Messenger sent us word they had agreed to A Conference and were ready to attend in the Conference Chamber. Conferrees were Appointed, vizt, Colo. Carter, Mr. Bland, Mr. Attorney, Mr. Whit[ing], Mr. B[enjamin] Waller, and myself, who all went up to the Conference Chamber door. And the Conferees on the side of the Council entering, those on the part of the House followed after, and, being seated, their first Conferree, C[harles] Carter, delivered the Message of the House, that a Committee of the House should meet a Committee of the Council [which] should be appointed to examin into the Acts repealed by his Majestie's instructions and also those Passed and make report of such as by them shall be necessary to be reenacted, and then came down. The Council then sent a Message to desire a Conference on the Subject Matter of the last Conferrence. We met as before, when Mr. [John] Blair,[87] manager in behalf of the Council, told us the Council had appointed himself and Messrs. [William and Thomas] Nelson[88] to be a Committee for the Purpose desired by the house with a Power of sitting from day to day. The Conferrees returned and reported the Conferance. A Committee of the Same Persons were immediately appointed, and, upon Notice Given of it to the Council, they agreed to meet in the Evening and settle the time when the Committee should meet. The House then Re[a]d some more bills and then the order of the day, vizt, the Committment of the New Town bill, was moved for, and the House immediately resolved into a Committee and went upon Amendments to the Bill, Which were, upon the Speaker's resuming the Chair, reported. And great endeavours used by Reddic[k] and The Attorney to get the Amendment for the place to be on James River. But Martin, Will. Randolph, Chs. Carter, and myself opposed it, and the Amendments all passed. After this a Small bill or two and other trifling motion[s], and then the house adjourned. Note: when the House receives a Message from the Governour, he [Speaker Robinson] puts not on his hat as in the Case of a Message from the Council. This day by a resolve of the House Colo. C[harles] Carter, Mr. Bland, Mr. Attorney, Mr. Wormeley, and myself went to return the thanks of this House for his great kindness in communicating the Papers of the Repealed Laws etc. to the house. To which he replyed he was very glad to find the houses of Approbation of what he had done and he should always make it his Study to serve this Country.

9. *Thursday.*

Colo. Carter and the Committee before mentioned met the Council in the Conference Chamber, vizt, Blair and the two Nelsons and there, having debated and considered What was Expedient to be done in the Present case, vizt, for the relief of the Country under the unhappy Scituation of the Re-

---

[87] John Blair (1687–1771), merchant and son of Archibald Blair (1660–1734), was burgess for Jamestown, 1734, and for Williamsburg, 1736–40; member of the Council, 1743–71; and acting governor, 1758, 1768.

[88] William Nelson (1711–72), merchant-planter and son of Thomas Nelson (1667–1745), was burgess for York Co., 1742–45; member of the Council, 1745–72; and acting governor, 1770–71. His brother, Thomas Nelson (1716–87), lawyer, merchant, and planter, was burgess for York Co., 1745–49, secretary of Virginia, 1742–76; member of the Council, 1749–76; and secretary of the Commonwealth. A biographical treatment is Emory G. Evans, "The Nelsons: A Biographical Study of a Virginia Family in the Eighteenth Century" (Ph.D. dissertation, University of Virginia, 1957).

pealed Laws, and came to the following resolutions, vizt, That the proceedings and Process of the General Court to the time of Repealing and every thing Consequent thereon ought to be made Valid; That a Representation should be made to his Majesty of our Unhappyness that so he might be pleased to give instructions to his Governor to recommend such of those laws as shall be represented usefull and necessary to our assembly to be again reenacted, it having before adjudged in the Carolina Case[89] that that was the only method to be used, and also to lay before him the inconveniencys that may attend the giv[ing] the Royal Assent to such laws that are in their Nature temporary and subject to many Alterations and Amendments; That The Governour be addressed thereupon to desire his kind Assistance to get those matters favourably recommended to the King. As soon as the house sat, Colo. Carter reported the Governour's return to the house's thanks; Also the Report of the Above Committee. Then a motion made for a joynt address with the Council to the king agreed to. That to the Governor agreed to, but not Joint because it must be delivered by the Whole house, and in such case the Speaker could not Present it and it would be [an] indignity taken should the Council present it. The same Committee appointed to draw the representation and Address. The removing bill passed the house 44 to 34. Sundry pretended to be against it and went out just before the question. Mr. W[illiam] Randolph went home. Mr. Byrd,[90] Mr. John Willis and others at the door. Mr. Bland at last kept his Vote but was mighty faltering.

The book of Claims returned Passed from the Council. Then sent to be Passed by the Governor by William Waller. The Governor askt him if there was no money Levyed for the Governor.

In Pursuance of the Committee report, leave was given for the bill to make the proceedings and process of the Court Valid from the Commencement to the Repeal of the General Court. This Bill three times read, engrossed, Passed below and above, enrolled, and received the Governour's hand, who,

[89] Carter probably refers to the Privy Council's disallowance on Oct. 31, 1751, of two South Carolina laws: "An Additional Act to an Act . . . for enlarging the Qualifications of the Electors as well as of the Persons to be Elected to Serve as Members of the General Assembly" of March 1747, and "An Additional Act to an . . . Act for preventing as much as may be the Spread of Contagious Distempers and to revive and continue An Act for the establishing of a Market in tht Parish of St. Philip Charles Town and for preventing engrossing, forestalling regrating and unjust Exactions in the said Town and Market" of June 1747. On this same day the Privy Council disallowed the ten Virginia laws because they amended or explained laws previously disallowed. See Board of Trade to Crown, Aug. 6, 1751, and Order in Council, Oct. 31, 1751, Transcripts of Records relating to South Carolina in the British Public Record Office, South Carolina Archives Department, Columbia, XXIV, 372–73, 380–82. The two laws are printed in Thomas Cooper and David J. McCord, eds., *Statutes at Large of South Carolina* (10 vols.; Columbia, 1836–41), III, 692–96.

[90] William Byrd III (1728–77), planter and son of William Byrd of Westover (1674–1744), was burgess for Lunenburgh Co., 1752–54, and member of the Council, 1754–76.

being advertized of it, came to the Council Chamber and sent the house he commanded their Attendance and directed the Speaker to bring with him such Acts as were ready for his signing. The House waited on him, and he signed the Act.[91] Mr. Speaker signed also a Space below. After this the house adjourned.

10. *Friday.*

Met the Council in Committee. Reasoned upon Several of the Repealed Acts and Resolved that the following Acts were reasonable and ought to be reenacted, vizt, Slaves Personal Estate, distribution of Intestate Estates, General Court Law. Act Limitation useless because it differed Little from those in force.[92] I was against the Reasonableness of the first but no one Else openly. As Soon as the Committee broke up, I was taken so ill that I was obliged to come home and Could not Attend the house. I heard the house insisted on their Amendments to the Council's Amendments. Had I been there, I would have adhered and so I desired others to do.

11. *Saturday.*

Our Committee this day did nothing excepting to desire Mr. Waller to give the reasons for the making some of those Acts that are repealed and to shew the General reasons for the others. Also the two Nelsons to draw the Representation to his Majesty. Many methods were proposed of Addressing his Majesty but, as it is seeming to Prescribe to his Prerogative, the most humble is to be used. Some did think as if they would shew the Circumstances the Colony was then in as being under the direction of one who was averse to many of those laws and of Course had suppressed the true reason of their being enacted.[93] But I opposed this as a thing uncertain and improper to impeach the Memory of a person dead without great Proof. The Elder and Younger Nelsons both said it could be proved. Nothing to do in the house this day only to sit and hear engrossed bills and to reject them as being now against the assent given to some at home and the repeal of Others which interfere and will not be passed. The foolish Lumber law Passed. This day our Town bill went

---

[91] This act is in Hening, ed., *Statutes*, VI, 229–30.

[92] The formal titles of these four laws were respectively "An Act Declaring Slaves to be Personal Estate," "An Act for the Distribution of Intestate Estates," "An Act for Establishing the General Court, and for regulating and settling the Proceedings therein," and "An Act for Limitations of Actions, and avoiding of Suits." None of them are printed in Hening but may be found in Colonial Office Papers 5/1394.

[93] Carter here refers to Sir William Gooch (1681–1751) who was lieutenant governor of Virginia, 1727–49. For a brief sketch see Percy S. Flippin, "William Gooch, Successful Royal Governor of Virginia," *Wm. and Mary Qtly.*, 2d Ser., V (1925), 225–58, VI (1926), 1–38.

up, and we did not hear of one advocate for it. Such is the Chance of a Poor Colony where the upper house as they call themselves [are] all in a Neck.[94] It is remarkable that some, who were Once Burgesses and hearty for a Removal, as Councillors are against it. 'Tis a pity men should run like Bowls. The famous Mr. Richd. Bland is a Shuttle Cock and without faith. I met with a thing this day called a Rider to a bill. When the bill is engrossed and can't be amended Substantially, if 'tis necessary to alter it and yet save it, a clause is proposed to be added which is produced, engrossed, and read as the bill, and the question put upon it whether it shall pass as a Rider. If it does, then it passes again in the bill. But it seems two riders are not allowable to one bill. We threw out the bill amending the Exchange Act[95] because it was improper in the Preamble and gave leave for one to amend the Execution Act.[96]

13. *Monday.*

This day the Select Committee met as Usual and run over some of the reasons, drawn up by Mr. Waller to be annexed to the Representation preparing to be made to his Majesty relating to the Repealed Acts of Last Session, and then adjourned. In the house nothing of any consequence, having hardly more to do than the preparing many bills not very public for the passing. However, there was a most extraordinary Engrossed bill sent down from the Council for

[94] By "all in a Neck," Landon Carter meant that the councilors all lived on the peninsula between the James and York rivers. Actually, only six of them, John Blair, William Nelson, Thomas Nelson, William Dawson (1704–52), Philip Ludwell (1716–67), and Peter Randolph (1713–67) lived there. Four others, however, lived not far away on the peninsula between the York and Rappahannock rivers: William Beverley (1698–1766) and Richard Corbin (1708–90) lived in King and Queen Co.; Philip Grymes (d. 1762) lived in Middlesex Co.; and Lewis Burwell (1710–56) and John Lewis II (1694–1753) lived in Gloucester Co. Only William Fairfax (1691–1757) lived in the Northern Neck, the region between the Rappahannock and Potomac rivers. Dawson, an Anglican minister, came to Virginia in 1729 as professor of moral philosophy at the College of William and Mary. He became president of the College in 1743 and was a member of the Council, 1745–52. Ludwell, planter and son of Philip Ludwell (1672–1727), was burgess for Jamestown, 1742–49, and member of the Council, 1752–67. Randolph, planter and son of William Randolph (1681–1742) and Elizabeth Beverley, was burgess for Henrico Co., 1749, and member of the Council, 1749–67. Beverley, planter and son of Robert Beverley (1673–1722) and Ursula Byrd, was burgess for Orange Co., 1734–40, and for Essex Co., 1742–49. Corbin, planter and son of Gawin Corbin (1669–1745), was burgess for Middlesex Co., 1748–49, member of the Council, 1751–76, and receiver general of Virginia, 1754–76. Grymes, planter and son of John Grymes (1691–1748) and Lucy Burwell, was burgess for Middlesex Co., 1748, receiver general of Virginia, 1749–54, and member of the Council, 1749–62. Burwell, planter and son of Nathaniel Burwell (1680–1721), was burgess for Gloucester Co., 1742–43, member of the Council, 1743–56, and acting governor. Lewis, planter and son of John Lewis I (1669–1725) of Warner Hall, was a member of the Council, 1748–53. Fairfax, planter and cousin of Lord Fairfax, proprietor of the Northern Neck, came to Virginia in 1734 as agent and estate manager for his cousin. He was burgess for Prince William Co., 1742–43, and member of the Council, 1743–57.

[95] The law, "An act for ascertaining the damage upon protested bills of exchange; and for the better recovery of debts due on promissory notes; and for the assignment of bonds, obligations, and notes," was passed in October 1748 and is in Hening, ed., *Statutes,* VI, 85–87.

[96] This law, "An Act declaring the law concerning Executions; and for relief of Insolvent debtors," was passed in October 1748 and is in Hening, ed., *Statutes,* V, 526–40.

the concurrence of the House which was calculated to take the Power of Granting ordinary Licenses into the Visitors of the Colledge in order as it was set forth to prevent the entertainment given to the Collegians. But we opposed it so well as being no ways conducive to the end proposed that only 7 were found for it, and of Course it fell to the Ground. There was also an amendment proposed by the Council to our bill (for preventing frivolous and vexatious indictments by obliging the Persons failing to pay the costs of such indictments) that of confining it solely to indictments brought in the General Court.[97] This was disagreed to without one Vote for it. All the Other business of this day was purely form.

14. *Tuesday.*

Our Select Committee met as usual and agreed to the reasons drawn by Waller with some amendments as to the reasons for reenacting the Repealed Act making negroes Personal Estate. They are in my opinion the most Specious and Partial that can be imagined, running all upon the transitory Nature of Slaves and those Clauses in the Old Law that for the sake of trade etc. where they were made Personal, although in the General they were real. I endeavoured to shew that they were in the same Act that intended them to be personal made in some Cases real. Therefore, the arguments would turn against them, for, if it was a real Objection that they were not real in all Cases under the Old Act, it might with equal justice [be said that] they were not in all cases Personal under this Act. But reasons here could not avail so they were adopted and it would be easier to remove the Capitol than to convince the Majority of those Concerned. I did hear Mr. B[everley] Whiting was against this Act for Personal Estate, but I found his constant friend, Mr. Sp[eaker], was too near him, and in my own Observations I could discover the securing an Estate was the only motive with some. But this in Private. Our Representation to the King drawn up by the Messrs. Nelsons was read and Criticized. Colo. C[harles] Carter observed they had in the recital of that part of the King's Commission to Lord Albermarle giving a Power to hold Assembly the title given to the House of Burgesses, vizt, that they should be called the General Assembly,[98] and moved to have it inserted, but the Majority of the Committee was against it. The thing was not Material either way, but I believe his reasons were that in after days no traces should be found where the house had

---

[97] For the final version of this bill see *ibid.,* VI, 246.

[98] This provision in the commission of William Anne Keppel (1702–54), 2nd Earl of Albemarle and governor-in-chief of Virginia, 1737–54, actually reads "the Persons so elected [by the freeholders and planters in Virginia] and qualifyed shall be Called and Deemed the General Assembly of that our Colony and Dominion" (Colonial Office Papers 5/1366, p. 155).

consented to Anything that might be construed against their power and Authority. At least these were my reasons for joyning with him. This Representation[99] is no ways disagreeable to me and the Gentlemen that drew it hit the Sence of the Committee, but whether it will meet the desired Effect is what I doubt of because it all runs against a thing done by the Advice of the board of trade and of the Privy Council at home and it is not easy to imagine the King would consent to undo what they have advized him to do or that those boards to whom this Representation and these reasons are to be referred by express instruction to the Governor which Was produced to our Committee would be easly perswaded to contradict their own advice. However, *Audendum Si vis Esse Aliquid.*[100] In the house nothing but form in Passing bills excepting in the bill for Repairing the W[illia]msburg Church, which went as for engrossing, Orgain and all. And in Particular Mr. Richard Bland, who so strongly opposed it, became an Advocate for it. But this is no news with that Gentleman, and whoever pays any regard to his word in any matter stands nine Chances out of ten of being deceived. I have not found him steady in one instance to the Opinion he set out upon this Session unless it was immediately determined. This may be owing to his having played so much with the bar as to beget in him a Shew of harranguing without any Sincerity. I can't but say I was a little astonished to see the amendments proposed yesterday by the Council to the bills against frivolous and vexatious indictments so universally disagreed to and yet this day, when they came down again, insisted upon without one word in favour of them. A large majority For them. It must be opposition or else some other practice, for 'tis impossible to suppose such a Change in the opinions of so many without something secret transacted, and yet the play in this Case is not worth the Candle. Yesterday a motion was made by Bland for a bill to pay the Burgesses' Sallerys in money[101] and Seconded by Mr. Waller, at which Old Ned Conway began and held forth above a quarter of an hour against any such bill because, as he sayd, his County were able to pay him and had more Titheables now than When they used to pay in tobacco. I answered all the reasons given by him and also one that I said I believed he did not care to speak out, that was, should the Burgesses be paid in tobacco as the Law now stood they would instead of 10/ per day get 20/. Upon which the old Gentleman with much indecent Warmth got up and said he rose to let that Gentleman know he told an Untruth. Upon which, observing some Consternation in the house, I laughed and indeed favoured the Old illmannerly fool.

[99] A copy of this representation is in Colonial Office Papers 5/1327, ff. 231–33.

[100] "If you want to be something, you must be daring."

[101] The final version of this act is in Hening, ed., *Statutes*, VI, 251–52.

We had this day a small tryal of Mr. Waller, a man of a Popular and qualifyed Genius, in filling up the bill for appointing a Speaker [treasurer].[102] It was proposed to give 6 instead of 5 per Cent, but Waller's popularity, although it did not amount to more than £50 per Annum, would not let him agree to it. And so we had a Staggering Speach full of Opposition and excuses, and he went so far as to beg pardon in the house and hoped the Speaker would not take it amiss after it went in favour of the Opposition. However, he was Nicked in the 2d motion, for the next blank to fill up was that for his [Treasurer Robinson's] Allowance per annum for passing the Inspectors' Accounts, which was proposed to be £150 so that this 50 more is full equal to the 1 per Cent.

15. *Wednesday.*

Our Committee this day agreed to their Representation and reasons, and our Address to the Governor was presented to the House, who as every Conjurer thought he had reason strove to amend every word, but I say in Vain. Mr. Pendleton, although it was to the Governor, was never for speaking of the King but with the Majesty at the heals of it, and this the wise Carter Burwell warmly espoused. But I never heard such nonsence, and, lucky for the reputation of the house, these blades were over Ruled or we should have had his Majesty in every case from the Nominative to the Ablative. 'Tis strange that impudence has no boundary, no not even ignorance can't Stop it. The Committee Appointed for this address, I believe, were as well chosen as they could be out of the house, vizt, Mr. Whitinge, C[harles] Carter, Bland, Waller, Mr. Attorney, and myself, and, though I drew it, yet it met with a Strict Scrutiny. For of that Sort, I have much compliment paid, and, after all this, Men not remarkt for ever having read more than an adjudged case or two or perhaps that have no other real boast than the making of a Plant of tobacco or two should think themselves at Liberty to criticize and argue for their Nonsence in spight of the Shame of Others.[103] Our house passes bills now by tale, though indeed they are not of much consequence. After this address was received by the house, Mr. Bland drew up a motion and made it for £600 to the Governour. And, as it pursued the address wherein we had particularly desired a very great favour, vizt, his Countenance and Solicitation [at] home, a thing that could not be done without great expence and expence from a Man although a Governour yet one that hath not as yet been benefited by the Colony, these reasons made me argue for it. And the famous Mr. Waller

---

[102] The final version of this bill is in *ibid.*, VI, 248–50.
[103] For a copy of this address see *Burgesses' Journals, 1752–1758,* 89 (Apr. 15, 1752).

declared himself for it, but as it was moved by another, which he Called ill timing of it, he argued strongly against and got a Previous question put whether the question should be put. I do assert this is the most Popular Gentleman I know. His whole sum that he would pay of this money would amount to about 10½ or Eleven pence were it immediately to be levyed by the Poll, and yet he opposed it. I cannot help suspecting that I saw some other person concerned in it, for Carter Burwell whispered a great deal and then as well as he could, poor man, harrangued for it. Waller does it only to Please the humour of the Plebeians who have a strange notion now of Governours. Indeed, Gooch gave them some reason. The bill for repairing the Church passed with its orgain. Some Mountaineers thought an organ was some strange instrument or Rather Monster and so voted only to have an opportunity of seeing one. The repair is to cost £300 and the Organ £200 Sterling, and, when it is got, who is to play upon it? Not in the bill at present. The Gentlemen intend to find one and all other Charges, but I humbly conceive these are but promises and at a future day the money will be askt of us. Yet our fools could not believe this, although I told them the Whole in a long speach. Besides experience had informed us that these instruments could not stand long in this Country. Dust, Spiders, and dirt daubers would Stop up all the Pipes, and when it should be out of Repair what artificer had we to mend it. Again, no doubt, Mr. Waller's frying pan man Davenport[104] had Ingenuity enough to do it, for he told us truely that he could play upon it. This evening by order of the house we waited upon the Governor to know when he would appoint to receive our address, and he told us he would send Word tomorrow. From thence Charles Carter and the Attorney dragged me to the Play, and there I was surfeited with Stupidity and nonsense delivered from the mouths of Walking Statues.[105]

16. *Thursday*.

This day the Labours of our Committee were produced into the house after this Manner: The Committee on the Part of the Council took the Address and reasons agreed on and agreed to them in full Council. Then a Message came to desire a Conference upon the Subject of the Joint Committee. The Members of the former Conference, being again Appointed Managers, went up and received from those on the Part of the Council the Address and representation to the King And the Reasons agreed on. And so Report was

[104] The exact identity of this man is unknown.

[105] Playing that week at the new Williamsburg Theatre was the comedy, "Constant Couple or a Trip to the Jubilee," by Mrs. Beccely's Players. Also on the boards were a dance, "The Drunken Peasant," and a farce, "The Lying Valet." See *Va. Gaz.*, Apr. 17, 1752.

made of the same to the house, which were read and severally Agreed on, that is, we would not be fond of Criticizm. This day we presented our Address to the Governor and received his Answer and a recommendation from him to appoint an Agent. As soon as his honor's thanks were read by the Speaker in the house, a motion was made to Present him with £500, which was Carryed, it being remarkable that the bellowing Club distinguished themself off. I crackt a Joke upon some of them that Vext them. I told them that I was very Glad to find that they had slept on the arguments offered yesterday and, although there was no difference between the two motions of yesterday and today, yet they could find enough to say in Excuse for some hours. However, as every one tended the same way, I would make one Speach for them all. This vexed many. The next matter that came on was the debate for an Agent which I moved and shewed, I think, the reasons for one to be very convincing. I put them in mind of the Evils we had suffered for want of a Person to have objected to some arguments that no doubt had been used to get the repeal of the Laws we now complain of. And, as we Cannot say this will [be] the only evil, to be sure we ought to be forewarned and forearmed against it. That to say that the Gentleman that had been imployed was unfaithfull was saying nothing because in other instances in life bad servants could not be an argument for no Servants at all, [though] it might be one for a Change. The Attorney spoke also very handsomely upon the Subject, indeed, but we might both have whistled, for there was so small a number of us it was not worth dividing. Many bills were passed for the Council's Concurrence, and many sent up to them came down agreed to. But one for settling the tobacco allowed to Evidences in the back Counties with a large amendment to make the same allowance to all the officers by which the Parson, as we were told, would get more. And this was the whole reason for the Alterations, but the compliment it received was disagreed to unanimously. However, no doubt the Upstairs Gentry will insist, and then our tame creatures must give it up, I suppose. By a Message from the Council we understand that we are supposed to address the King on the death of his Son and Daughter. 'Twould have been indecent not to have joined but I am of opinion 'tis old and stale. However, our Committee was appointed, vizt, the Members of the former to meet and Prepare one in conjunction with the Council.

17. *Friday*.

Our business now is trifling, only passing and sending up bills. Our Committee for drawing up our address to the King met and did nothing. 'Twas then Agreed that Mr. Attorney and I should prepare something against next morning, but he is a Gentleman too Lazy. And therefore I sent to Mr.

Corbin, and he came over and Assisted in the first Paragraph a little. But the two last were intirely my own. So we got it ready for the Council tomorrow.[106] This day an Odd affair happened, vizt, to the bill sent up to the Council relating to making provision for Officers' fees in the back Counties. The Council had an inclination to do something for Parsons and so by amendment thrust in a Clause to raise the payment of the Levies which before was in money at 3/4 to 10/ per Cent. As this would have ruined the People, the house disagreed to it. The Council sent it again and insisted on their Amendment, and this day by Means of Mr. Power and Mr. Waller it came to be debated whether we should not recede with an amendment to that Amendment. I then rose and told the house after an amendment disagreed to by the house was sent back, if we receded, it must be to the whole from [for?] 'tis receding from our disagreement, and, as that was to the whole, this receding must be to the whole, which was in express words agreeing to the amendment in whole, and therefore no amendment could be allowed. Upon which I moved to adhere to our disagreement. Waller and Carter Burwell then was only for insisting the latter, saying the Council by adhering too soon last session had put the house out of temper all the remaining part of the Session. Wm. Randolph and I shewed it was only returning the Compliment of the Council this session, for they had more than once receded before insisting. I told the house the favourers of this Amendment had gone beyond their mark, for, if we insisted, it would be only turning the Argument, for the Council must then Adhere or recede to the whole. In the first case, the bill would fall as we wanted it. In the second case, the bill must pass without the Amendments. And Waller finding this to cut the matter short came out upon Adhering. Note: the Speaker was askt as to the Regularity of Receding in Part. He said he thought it was Parliamentary but never remembered it here. But in this perhaps he favoured the amendment too much.

18. *Saturday.*

Had a debate about allowing John Palmer, Clerk of the Select Committee £97 cash, then £20 cash. Then on £10 carryed. Yesterday a resolution for £500 to the Governor because given as a fee was refused by him and this day we changed the Words, as it would appear to us all that he would do the Services we required, vizt, the Soliciting our Representation to the King. This day we voted one hundred pounds Sterling to James Abercrombuy Esqr.[107] to be our agent in the Particular affair of the Representation, and then I left the

---

[106] For a copy of this address see Colonial Office Papers 5/1338, f. 111.

[107] James Abercromby served as London agent for Virginia, North Carolina, and South Carolina at various times between 1738–74. See Ella Lonn, *The Colonial Agents of the Southern Colonies* (Chapel Hill, 1945).

house and came to Court to put in my order from home for an Appeal to the King in Council in the cause of Kay against the Parish tenants of Lunenburgh Parish.[108] Mr. Nelson moved to have time to Consider of it, and said the Court was not to be hurryed into Judgment by any body. I told him neither should I be Scared out of my right. I claimed it as a Subject of Great Britain. It was an order of the King in Council to an inferior Court and, if they would not Obey it, I would take the Papers and applye again to my Sovereign for redress. As to the other things he said, I answered them fully and as the Governour afterwards told me much to his Satisfaction. Ludwell handsomely moved for an immediate obedience, and so did Corbin, Randolph and Grymes. Then it was granted. I have now heard these Gentlemen intend to make Representation home against it.

20. Monday.

This Morning we met as Usual. The Speaker proposed his bond and Security as treasurer in the Clerk's Office, signed it, and, vizt, himself and three Securitys, and sent it to the Governor. When the house Sat, the first of the Committee[109] to whom the Enrolled bills were comitted for Examination Reported 55 Acts with these words, that the Persons appointed had examined the Enrolled bills and had found them correct except in some matters of grammar or English which they had Corrected. They were then Received per the house and then Sent up by the Reporter (vizt, B[everley] Whitinge, who seems to have been chairman because he was so of the Courts of Justice) to the Council and Presently sent down in the same bundle as agreed to. It may be presumed they took it for granted they were right. Some Short time Walthoe brought a Message from the Governor Commanding the immediate attendance of the house and directing the Speaker to carry up Such bills and Resolves as were prepared for his Consent. We all went up in a body, and after Silence the Speaker addressed himself to the Governor in these words: Sir, in obedience to your Honor's Commands, the House of Burgesses now wait upon [you] and have brought with us such Bills and Resolves that have passed their

---

[108] The altercation that formed the background to this case is described by Carter's opponent, Rev. William Kay (d. 1764), Anglican minister and graduate of Trinity and Emmanuel Colleges, Cambridge, in a letter to the Bishop of London, June 14, 1752, in Perry, ed., *Hist. Col. Relating to Am. Col. Church,* 389–91.

[109] This committee consisted of Beverley Whiting, Richard Bland, William Waller, Peyton Randolph, Robert Jones, Gabriel Jones, Clement Reade, Augustine Claiborne, John Madison, and Edmond Pendleton (*Burgesses' Journals, 1752–1758,* 73 [Apr. 3, 1752]). Gabriel Jones (1724–1806), lawyer, and son of John Jones, was burgess for Frederick Co., 1748–53, Augusta Co., 1756–58, 1769–71; and Hampshire Co., 1758–61. He was later a member to the Virginia Convention to ratify the Federal Constitution. Clement Reade (1707–63), lawyer-planter, was burgess for Lunenburg Co., 1748–54, 1758–63.

house and Received the Consent of the Council, and they humbly desire Your Honor will be pleased to Pass them. Note: The Mace stood on his left and the Clerk behind and all the bills were Chaptered before according to the Speaker's directions. I could not discover What method he followed. He then layd them open bill by bill and the Governor signed each, and the Speaker, as Speaker, some distance below. But three of the bills, after the rest was signed, he also presented with an Apology, vizt, that they had passed the Assembly before the Arrival of the Royal Assent to Sundry Acts with which these seemed to interfere. The house therefore had directed him to present them Separately. To which the Governor was pleased to Say he had been advized by his Council not to pass them. Then the Governor made us a proroguing Speach and Prorogued us to the last thursday in October. And every Man with Joy Returned homewards. With Joy, I say, for only they can tell the fatigue of such long attendance and attachement to one particular business. Thus ends the business of this Assembly and, I think, from the Arguments Noted and the Several observations made, anyone may prepare himself for another.

AUGUST 1754

22. *Thursday.*

There have been two sessions of assembly since, vizt, one beginning November 1753 and ending in the same year, The other beginning [February 1754] and ending very soon after the other. On the first I was prevented sitting above two days, being seized in my Way down with a Violent fever and of a dangerous continuance with as bad a relapse, so that I had no part in the same.

I did not attend the Second by reason of the Small pox's being in Town.

In the first of these sessions arose that grave dispute between the Governour and the Country relating to the Pistole charged on Pattents issuing out of the Secretary's office for Lands as a fee for the use of the Seal. This gave cause to the Sending home Peyton Randolph, Esqr. as Agent for the Country. Some Compliments of this kind were paid to me, but my weak state of health and the Largeness of my Family made me decline having any motion made on my Account. The History of this Assembly is very full in the Journals.[110]

In the Second Session that Act was fraimed which laid a tax of 5/ for ev-

---

[110] Brief summaries of the pistole fee dispute are to be found in Koontz, *Robert Dinwiddie*, 201–35; Glenn C. Smith, "The Affair of the Pistole Fee, Virginia, 1752–55," *Va. Mag. of Hist. and Biog.*, XLVII (1940), 209–21; and Jack P. Greene, ed., "The Case of the Pistole Fee: The Report of a Hearing on the Pistole Fee Dispute before the Privy Council, June 18, 1754," *ibid.*, LXVI (1958), 399–422.

ery Wheel on any Carriage contrived for ease or Luxury and 15d not taxable in the bill of Costs for every suit brought in County Courts and 2/6 in the General Court, this to raise a sum to maintain forces against the French then taking possession of all the Lands West of the Allegany Mountains.[111]

Some time after the first of these Assemblys I wrote a Pamphlet by way of Letter to the Virginia Merchants setting the affair of the Pistole and the Arguments in favour of it in a true light. This Pamphlet was printed in London and sent in here.[112]

This Assembly was called by the Governour to gain a Farther Supplye for the raising a greater Force against the French, who carried on their encroachments with more Violence than ever and had encountered our men twice on the lands on the River Ohio. The first was only a Skirmish of a few, in which Colo. Washington took and killed every man but one.[113] Amongst the prisoners was one La Force,[114] who became famous on account of many Relations handed to us from those Parts by Some of our Friendly Indians of his being the Chief director and mover of all the Schemes of the French in that Part of the Country. He was brought a Prisoner to W[illia]ms burgh with 23 others.

The Second might be called an Engagement, and, as the ill success that attended it on our Side gave foundation to many different relations (either from a Politic view of not disheartening our people from farther attempts to protect those lands to the Crown of Great Britain or from a desire of preserving the Glory of the former action unsullyed), I endeavoured to come at as true a Story as I could by enquiring privately of many of the Officers, vizt, Capt. Pyrony, Capt. Polston, and Afterwards Colo. Washington and Colo. Stevens who were all in the engagements.[115]

---

[111] This act is in Hening, ed., *Statutes*, VI, 417–20.

[112] This pamphlet was entitled *A Letter from a Gentleman in Virginia, to the Merchants of Great Britain, Trading to that Colony* (London, 1754). That this is the pamphlet Carter wrote is demonstrated in Jack P. Greene, "Landon Carter and the Pistole Fee Dispute," *Wm. and Mary Qtly.*, 3d Ser., XIV (1957) 66–69.

[113] George Washington (1732–99) obviously needs no identification. Perhaps the best biographical treatment is Douglas Southall Freeman, John A. Carroll, and Mary W. Ashworth, *George Washington* (7 vols.; New York, 1948–1957).

[114] Commissary La Force was a French officer in the West. For his part in the Ohio skirmishes see *ibid.*, I, 303, 307, 308, 311, 324, 337, 358, 369, 373–76, 435.

[115] Ens. William Chevalier La Peyroney (d. 1755), Lt. William Polson, and Capt. Adam Stephen (1724–91) were officers under Washington who played prominent roles in the West during the French and Indian War. Polson was later promoted to captain, but little is known of his background or subsequent career. La Peyroney was a French Protestant who was promoted to captain in August 1754 and killed July 9, 1755, at Braddock's defeat. Stephen was a Scot and a doctor trained at Edinburgh who was later promoted to colonel. During the War for Independence he served as a brigadier general and later as major general of American forces before his dismissal for being intoxicated during the battle of Germantown. He was a member of the Virginia Convention to ratify the Federal Constitution in 1788. A sketch of Stephen's early life is in Freeman, Carroll, and Ashworth, *George Washington*, I, 345–46.

The Facts appeared to be this: The Indians who pretended Friendship, however willing they might be to continue so, observing the Superiority of the French on those Lands and the Slow motions of Great part of our Army, dreaded their own fate should the French prove victorious. And they, taking part against them, privately informed them of our Weakness, which encouraged [the French] to march out of their Fort they had taken from the Ohio Company.[116] And though at a great distance off, Yet by coming down the Ohio to a place Called Red Stone Creek they had at that place well nigh Surprized our People there, who were not more than 300 in number and had been by Superior orders, though it now seems to be contradicted, Clearing a large road to that Creek in order for the marching of the whole Forces and embarking there in order for an Attack upon the French in that Fort. Our Governour it seems was the Sole director of the Plan to be pursued, and he, too Sanguin on the Success of the first Skirmish, had ordered Washington to prepare these roads that there might [be] no obstruction to the marches of the whole body which with the two New York Independent Company[s] were expected would amount in All to 600 men. Had this number Joyned Washington, in all probability the whole French Scheme would have been happyly render[ed] abortive for one Seven year at least. For the Certain bravery of those few of our men that were engaged would, when aided by double there Number, [have] been vastly an over match for the French, who had evacuated most of their other Forts to make this Vigorous push; and the timorous Indians, instead of being compelled by Policy to take up arms against us, would by such a defeat as we might, as is above related, have expected been at least for some time our Friends and might have been imployed in driving the few remaining French from the Ohio.

But alas, Colo. Washington and his three hundred men instead of being joyned were totally neglected and left quite without Provision whilst the others were encamped, some in one town and some in another place a great way on this side the Appelachian or Allegany mountains, and this under the Conduct of one Innis,[117] a Gentleman Preferred only from a National Attachment by All the Accounts I ever heard.

In this Condition was Washing[ton] with many of his Small Force out on

---

[116] Valuable studies of the Ohio Company and its role in western affairs after its formation in the late 1740s are Kenneth P. Bailey, *The Ohio Company of Virginia* (Glendale, Calif., 1939) and Alfred P. James, *The Ohio Company: Its Inner History* (Pittsburgh, 1959). Other useful information is available in Lois Mulkearn, ed., *George Mercer Papers* (Pittsburgh, 1954).

[117] Col. James Innes, a Scot and a resident of New Hanover Co., N.C., had served in 1740 in the Cartagena expedition. Dinwiddie appointed him commander-in-chief over the forces serving in Virginia in 1754 after Col. Joshua Fry's death. See Koontz, *Robert Dinwiddie*, 118.

the Forage for bread when he was informed by an express from one of the Rangers that the French to the Number of 900 men besides 200 Indians had gone down the Ohio and would be upon him in a few days. Upon this he immediately decamped from Red Stone Creek, sent for his Foragers in, and order[ed] a Rendevous at the Camp at the Meadows near where he had the first Skirmish. But before his decampment the French had near reached him, for they got to the place of the encampment on Red Stone Creek within little more than a day after he left it. And they had certainly returned back (imagining the Colo. had gone to joyn the reinforcements that the Indians had informed them were expected), had not some Irish Papist deserted from our Army and informed them of the distressed Scituation of our Small Army, at the most only 300 men and some of them Seperated upon Forage, as was before related, and the others quite fatigued with a long March to regain the Camp at the Meadows and also by dragging their Swivels after them which their horses were quite Unable to do. So that our Army had scarce gained the Camp, which by some was Called a Fort but was only a small place a little railed in and in noways fortifyed, being, as I before observed, obstructed by the orders for Clearing the roads, when their Sentinel gave the Alarm by firing his Piece. Here the Colo. intended, from the knowlege he had of the Mercyless-ness of the Enemy, intended to Sell the English blood as dear as Possible but was prevented by the Cowardice of his next Officer[118] of whom may be read in the Journals of the H[ouse of] B[urgesses]. For, instead of bringing up the 2d division to make the Attack with the first, he marched them or rather fright-ened them back into the trenches, so that the Colo. at the head of the Carolina Independent Company[119] was greatly exposed to the French Fire and were forced to retire to the same trenches, where they were galled on All sides by 1,100 French and Indians who never came to an Open ground but fired from behind trees. This made a long engagement. About 30 were killed on our side and above 60 wounded on the side of the French. It is not yet know[n] how many, but [by] their Calling a Parley diverse times it must be certain they received some great loss. Upon Calling out for that Rascal Vanbraam[120] (who

[118] Lt. Col. George Muse of Caroline Co. was one of four district adjutants of Virginia and second in command to Washington at this engagement. His name is conspicuously absent from the list of officers commended by the House of Burgesses (*Burgesses' Journals, 1752–1758*, 198 [Aug. 30, 1754]), but the reasons for his omission had not hitherto been known (Freeman, Carroll, and Ashworth, *George Washington*, I, 413).

[119] Capt. James MacKay (d. 1787) was head of the South Carolina Independent Company. For his part in the engagement and in the western skirmishes see *ibid.*, I, 385–97, 408–13, 419–20. See also Robert A. Brock, ed., *The Official Records of Robert Dinwiddie* (2 vols.; Richmond, 1883–84), 146.

[120] Capt. Jacob Van Braam (b. 1725) emigrated to Virginia from Holland in 1752. A teacher of French, it was not hitherto known that he was also a servant. Like Muse, he was omitted from the Bur-gesses' list of officers to be commended because of his suspected treachery (*Burgesses' Journals, 1752–*

was himself the only unpardonable blunder that Washington made by making a Confidant of him, for he was a poor juggling Servant, but by understand[ing] French and having attended the Colo. on his Embassy made in the Spring[121] to the Fort he became a Favourite and was preferred), I say, when the French called for this Rascal, he went and brought terms of Capitulation, which he deceived the Colo. in, for he read them quite different in English from what they were in French. These terms being signed upon the Faith of that Dutch Dog and Pyronée, the only French Linguist being dangerously wounded so that he could not be of any Service untill the whole was over, and our men being Cool from Action together with the hardships they indured from violent rains and the many wounded, our Army marched in with the most disgraceful Capitulation that ever was made and such that any brave man could not knowingly have preferred to death.[122]

Under these Circumstances were we when our Governor called us together in August And upon our meeting told us the necessity there was for a Farther Supply.

'Tis hard to point out the true disposition of the House at this time. They Suffered in General great declarations of their intentions to protect themselves against the Insults of the French and went farther in every design of preparing for the intention of raising money, for they desired and Obtained a view of all Copys relating to the orders that had been given by the Governour and the methods taken pursuant to the design of the Aid of ten Thousand pounds. Yet when they came in a Committee of the Whole house to consider of the thing, The Speaker, to whom it seems it is a Compliment due of moving first, Sat still and so did every one Else, untill, observing something like a Party that were not for Laying anything, I got up and moved that the Committee should resolve that the sum of £20,000 should be levyed for the defence of the Country. As soon as this was Seconded, the Speaker, very strongly Supported, moved that the question should be put upon £10,000, Alledging that he did not imagin any sum we could raise would be sufficient and therefore, as it would be but throwing money away, he was [for] throwing away the least Sum. I soon

---

1758, 198 [Aug. 30, 1754]), but he was later acquitted of the charge after his return to Virginia in 1760 following a four-year internment as a prisoner of war. See Brock, ed., *Dinwiddie Papers,* I, 51. See also Freeman, Carroll, and Ashworth, *George Washington,* I, 277, 406–11.

[121] The embassy to De St. Pierre, the French commander at Fort Le Boeuf, was made in the winter, not in the spring. Washington left Virginia early in November 1753 and returned to Williamsburg about the middle of January 1754. Van Braam accompanied him as interpreter. Washington's journal of this mission was printed in Williamsburg in 1754. A recent facsimile edition is *The Journal of Major George Washington* (Williamsburg, 1959; paperback reprint, Charlottesville, 1963).

[122] An excellent study of the terms of capitulation is Freeman, Carroll, and Ashworth, *George Washington,* I, 546–49.

perceived by the Speaches made by others that they were also for nothing and that every one had forged a most Specious reason. Waller alledged we had told the king when we gave £10,000 that we were very poor and the levying £20,000 or any Sum now would be telling a lye and much more of the like, which is but a low Popular argument and Could only Serve such a Purpose. And so I answered him, for, Although [we] were poor and had said so, Yet that would not convey an Idea that we had nothing to loose, and our Levying now could only shew that, poor as we were, we were so Much Alarumed with the visible danger that we were resolved to give up all in the Cause rather than to be the Subjects of a Foreign Prince. Having got them in this dilemma, that though they wanted no Levy they had proposed a Sum, I moved for a question on the first motion, to which the Speaker with Warmth moved for the Previous question, whether the question on the first motion should be put or no. I knew this would trye his Strength and argued against it, and he carried the Point, so that the question was put on the £10,000 and it went in the negative. And £20,000 voted in Committee And afterwards agreed to by the house. And a bill drawn accordingly.

This Bill passed a Strict Scrutiny and every thing Calculated with a seeming Harmony. 'Tis true I formed a Scheme of Treasury bills to issue for the Sum of £20,000 which should be made payable only at such time as it might be imagined the money could be raised on our tobacco, but this met with few Espousers from the great aversion to Paper money. But no one Argument could Support such an objection, for it could last no longer than one Year, and these notes would only be Current for so long a time. And Persons unable to give long Credit would be able thereby to deal for ready money because they would go immediately into Payment from one to the Other. And the man of Circumstance would be glad to take them because a better security Could not be had. However, Popular prejudice prevailed, and the Proposition dropt, and I joyned heartily for the Bill as it stood.

After this Bill was prepared and Considered by the Committee of the whole House, The Party (against it or not I know not) added a Clause for the Payment of the £2,500 to Peyton Randolp[h], Esqr., sent home in 1753 as an Agent. It seems when the Complaint was made against the Pistole taken by the Governour for Patents for Lands granted out of the King's Grants this Gentleman was sent home as an Agent and the above Sum was voted him. But the Council would not pass the Resolve, so that the House at that time ordered the money to be paid by the Treasurer and resolved to support it.[123] The Re-

---

[123] An account of this dispute may be found in Dinwiddie to Abercromby, Sept. 1, 1754, in Brock, ed., *Dinwiddie Papers*, I, 298–301. On Randolph's agency see Greene, ed., "The Case of the Pistole Fee," *Va. Mag. of Hist. and Biog.*, LXVI (1958), 399–405.

Charles Carter of Cleve (1707–1764),
Brother of Colonel Landon Carter *By
Gustavus Hesselius. C. Hill Carter,
owner.*

Peyton Randolph (1721–1775)
*By John Wollaston. Virginia Historical
Society, owner.*

Archibald Cary (1721–1787)
*Attributed to Charles Bridges. For-
merly owned by Virginia State Library
and destroyed in fire at Governor's
Mansion.*

Benjamin Harrison of Brandon (1726?–
1791)
*By Charles Willson Peale. W. Gordon
Harrison, Richmond, owner.*

Edmund Pendleton (1721–1803)
Miniature by William Mercer. Virginia Historical Society, owner.

George Wythe (1726–1806)
By unknown artist. Colonial Williamsburg, Inc., owner.

John Robinson (1704–1766), Speaker of
the House of Burgesses
Miniature by unknown artist. Virginia Historical Society, owner.

Benjamin Waller (1716–1786)
Miniature by unknown artist. Virginia Historical Society, photo.

fusal of the Council still Continuing and some hard language having passed without door by the Governour, the House pitched upon this expedient to have it confirmed by tacking it to that Bill. Against this Tack I argued Strongly that it was giving up the Point to the Council, Who claimed a Negative or Concurrence in any [and] all money Votes, Against which there was a Precedent in Lord Howard's days.[124] And such a point ought never to be rendered even doubtfull and this Clause would confirm it against the rights of the House, A very dangerous thing perhaps in future. Again it was no proper time in the hour of imminent danger to hazard the passing this bill, because by it it was proposed that the Country should be defended and it was more than Probable the Council would not agree to it because they had at first no just reason to refuse to assent to the Resolve and Persons discovering such pure Obstinacy were likely to Continue in it. But this, I was privately assured, would not be the Case, and Colo. Carter Burwell and others were confident from some private Conversation with the Secretary[125] that it would be the only way to get the money paid. I believed the informer, that he was told so, but could not give Credit to the Intention, because I think I know mankind and very few deceive me—at least that Honorable Gentleman could not. I conjectured it to be all Artifice to draw the house into a Confession of the Council's right and after the Bill should pass our House their point would be gained and yet no bill would pass above for it needed not their Consent. It was enough to their end so as it passed our house.

Accordingly, after the Bill passed with this Clause it went up, and in one hour we heard it was unanimously rejected. Then many were amazed, and in the Mouths of many nothing was heard but there's no believing mankind.

Those who would not give up the Cause fell upon a very prudent stratagem to give the world a full view of the matter and justifye the behaviour of the house in not providing for the defence of the Country. The French and Indians had during the Sessions come in and drove off some of the Inhabitants, and they had sent an Express with a Petition to the house Complaining of the grievance and desired some Speedy relief.[126] The House immediately took this Petition into Consideration And Resolved that the Bill already Passed had provided the relief required by the Petition And also that a Message be sent to inform the Council of the said Petition and Resolve and to desire they would expedite the Passing that bill. To this they sent a written message telling us

---

[124] Francis Howard, Baron of Effingham (d. 1694), was governor of Virginia, 1684–92. The precedent Carter refers to was probably the payment to Philip Ludwell in 1691 for his services as agent for the Burgesses against Effingham in 1688. In this connection see *Burgesses' Journals, 1660–1693,* lxiii–lxiv.

[125] Councilor Thomas Nelson (1716–87) was secretary.

[126] For a summary of this petition, which was from the inhabitants of the upper part of Augusta Co., see *ibid., 1752–1758,* 202 (Sept. 3, 1754).

they had rejected the Bill on Account of that Clause with much Specious reasoning for it (see the Message on the Journals).[127] And in a few days the house were Called up and Prorogued by the Governour, Nothing being done except a few private bills.

This Proroguation Speach carried all the Venom and all the Falsehood of an Angry Passionate man, and to mend the matter it was Spoke only to the House as, if the Council had obeyed orders in what they did, So that many of the Council were in doubt whether they should rise. However, As this could not have been deemed a Prorogation, it being directed only to one part of the Assembly, the Printer was by the Governor's orders made to insert Gentlemen of the Council.[128]

Every Burgess, I am sure, retired full of Revenge, and in the month of September I wrote a Paper Published in Maryland Setting the matter in a true and faithfull light, which has met with much Applause.[129]

OCTOBER 1754

17. Thursday.

The Assembly met this day, And to give an Idea of what is to be expected I will venture to call it the Harmonious Session. The Affair of the Pistole having been determined at home and both Partys having got something, both seemed to hugg themselves with a Victory: The Governor in that he had got leave to Charge a fee on all Pattents (granted after the date of the order of Council that consented to this fee) that are not under a hundred Acres or that lye on this side the Allegany Mountains, And also the King's Attorney turned out for presuming to go home as an Agent; And The Country in that they had Stopped the fee on those pattent[s] granted before that day (which were not a few) and on all lands beyond the Allegany and all Pattents under 100 acres, And farther an Assurance that, if the Attorney asked for his Place, he was to have it again, And also that the Treasurer's Accounts should be passed with the Article of £2,500, the bone of contention, in it.[130] I say these things were

---

[127] For the Burgesses' resolve and the Council's message see *ibid.*, 202–3 (Sept. 3–4, 1754).

[128] This speech is printed in *ibid.*, 205 (Sept. 5, 1754).

[129] This paper was published in the Oct. 24, 1754, issue of the *Md. Gaz.* See Greene, "Landon Carter and the Pistole Fee Dispute," *Wm. and Mary Qtly.*, 3d Ser., XIV, 68.

[130] The imperial decision in the pistole fee case is set forth in Board of Trade to Dinwiddie, July 3, 1754, in Colonial Office Papers 5/1367, ff. 94–100. However, the agreement to pass the treasurer's account with the article to pay Randolph the sum promised him for his agency was not part of the imperial ruling but the product of a *quid pro quo* between Dinwiddie and the Council on one hand and the Burgesses on the other. For an analysis of this decision see Greene, "The Case of the Pistole Fee," *Va. Mag. of Hist. and Biog.*, LXVI (1958), 404–5.

confidently asserted to the House, But his Honor could not forget his Rod at the last Prorogation and, though he did not openly use it, Yet some twiggs of it were imployed in the Speach at the Opening of this Session.[131] When that Speach came to be considered, A motion was made for the Usual Compliment of an Address, but as I was affraid the resolution would be too mild upon too easy a Credulity and, remembering how barefacedly things were retorted last Session, I seconded the motion with an amendment, And so the business of Address drawing was laid on my shoulders which by the Private directions of many members I endeavoured to Sprinkle with a proper resentment but all in implication work. It Passed *Nemine Contradicente,*[132] and the Governor looked upon it as Wormwood and Molasses. However, being tired with heat and perceiving the House disposed to Levy money, he returned only a mild answer.[133]

As to our House, we had no Contest about the money bill. It went for £20,000 to be raised Part in April (that is) 2/6 Per Poll or 30 pounds tobacco and the same in December next. This was sent up, but not till we saw the T[reasurer's] Accounts passed nor without this, as it was the Olive Branch. We would not give the bill the 3d reading untill that came in. At last it appeared and, every member being satisfyed, the Bill passed and went up, where it was also Passed.[134] But note: not Unanimously in Council for the *Par Nobile Fatrum*[135] and Ludwell protested against it *More Magnatum.*[136] How true then was my Prediction last Session that men Purely obstinate will continue to be so. Thus do they endeavour to make Lords of themselves. But, as it [is] *ex Parte* doing, they must be weak hereafter that shall call this a Precedent.

We received the Compliments this Session from Washington and his officers in return for our Thanks transmitted them last August And desired the Governor to Recommend them for Preferment to his Majesty.[137] All but George Muse, a Rank Scoundrel and Coward, and that Dutch Dogg Vanbraam, now in the Service of the French as we hear from all parties whilst poor Stobo is in confinement as an hostage because we refused to return La Force

---

[131] This speech is printed in *Burgesses' Journals, 1752–1758*, 209–10 (Oct. 17, 1754).

[132] "Unanimously."

[133] Also on the committee to draw the address were John Martin and James Power (*ibid.*, 210 [Oct. 17, 1754]). The address and the governor's reply are printed *ibid.*, 211, 213 (Oct. 18, 21, 1754).

[134] The final version of this act is printed in Hening, ed., *Statutes*, VI, 435–38.

[135] "A noble pair of brothers" (Horace, *Satires*, II. 3. 243). Probably a reference to Thomas and William Nelson.

[136] "In the manner of bigwigs."

[137] The compliments of Washington and his officers are printed in *Burgesses' Journals, 1752–1758*, 217–18 (Oct. 24, 1754). The committee to recommend the officers for preferment consisted of Charles Carter, Landon Carter, William Fitzhugh, Richard Bland, and William Randolph (*ibid.*, 219 [Oct. 25, 1754]).

agreeable to Stobo's letter,[138] who wrote not to Consider him but to keep La Force.

The Governour Assured us he had done as we desired and would continue to recommend them. But *Fronti Nulla fides,*[139] for 'tis Certain Colo. Washington after many fair Promises was told he could expect nothing but command under all that bore his Majesty's Commission. Upon which he advised with a Number of us as his friends, and we one and All advised him not to Serve on such dishonourable terms. On this he went to the Governor to acquaint him with it, but, being unluckily interrupted by Colo. Sharpe,[140] Who came out to give him written orders to repair to his Post, he was forced to tell him his Errand and afterwards Governor Dinwiddie, who turned Short and told him it was very well this last Circumstance afforded excuse to the Court friends to say that Colo. Washington had behaved ill in giving up his Commission to Sharp when he received it from the Governor, and this was the reason of his Honor's treatment. But in Fact it is all a lye, for a Commission he never had but one unsigned since the death of Colo. Frye,[141] and they were very humble Servants who could take an Accident without its Circumstances and work it up into such a dress. But the Case was there were Many fair Promises publicly made, broken, and some excuse was better than none. The truth of the Whole is the darling Innis was and is on Purpose imployed to Serve a particular end and this cannot be effected without him. At least Washington was no Proper Person because not a Countryman, and any Opportunity was Catched at to keep in the one and disengage the other. In Short, Such a vast Sum of money is too tempting and it must leave a Small Wash or Stain behind it.

Hitherto the Session was Harmonious but an affair happened to occasion great debates, vizt, the Bill for a Stint Law, which, as I imagin it will be the subject of a future Assembly, I will take but little notice of, only that it made much division amongst us. In the debates on it we had many difinitions on Casuistry and the question was Whether a Representative was obliged to follow the directions of his Constituents against his own Reason and Conscience or to be Governed by his Conscience. The Arguments for implicit

---

[138] Capt. Robert Stobo (1727–70), son of a Glasgow merchant, was one of Washington's subordinate officers who became a favorite fictional hero. A facsimile of the letter mentioned by Carter, the original of which is in the archives of the District of Montreal, is included in Freeman, Carroll, and Ashworth, *George Washington,* I, between pp. 437 and 438. For a sketch of Stobo see George M. Kahrl, "Captain Robert Stobo," *Va. Mag. of Hist. and Biog.,* XLIX (1941), 141–51, 254–68.

[139] "There is no trusting to appearances."

[140] Lt. Col. Horatio Sharpe (1718–90) was governor of Maryland, 1753–69, and commander-in-chief of Crown forces in America from 1754 until the arrival of Gen. Edward Braddock in Virginia in February 1755. A biography is Matilda Edgar, *A Colonial Governor of Maryland* (London and New York, 1912).

[141] Col. Joshua Fry, who died sometime earlier in 1754.

obedience were that the first institution of a Representative was for the avoiding the Confusion of a Multitude in assembly. He, therefore, was to Collect the sentiments of his Constituents and whatever that Majority willed ought to be the rule of his Vote. Thus argued the favourers of Popularity, who were all headed by the Speaker, for these were nearly his own words. The Admirers of Reason and Liberty of Conscience distinguished upon it and said, where the matter related particularly to the interest of the Constituents alone, there implicit obedience ought to Govern, but, where it was to affect the whole Community, Reason and Good Conscience should direct, for it must be absurd to Suppose one part of the Community could be apprized of the good of the whole without Consulting the whole. For that Part, therefore, to order an implicit vote must be absurd and the Representative acting accordingly could only augment the Absurdity because he must suppose his people so perverse as not to be moved by Reasons ever so good that might be advanced by other parts of the Community. Many other Arguments do so naturally arise to support this last and best Opinion that I need not insert them. Be it as it will, nothing but Art could effect anything to prevent the passing of this Bill, confessedly pernicious even by most who espoused it upon the reasoning before mentioned. And by Suffering the abettors of it to Clog [it] with many gross absurdities, such as prodigious deductions from all Public tobacco and officers' fees and by moving to put off the 3d reading of it to a day known to the Proposer too far off for that session to take any farther notice of it because of the Certain Proroguations, it fell; and to palliate the thing it was ordered to be printed for the Perusal and Consideration of the Inhabitants, I hope never to Appear again. The merit of this last artifice is due to Colo. Charles Carter, Supported by Waller and, I think I may say, myself and others.

MAY 1755

1. *Thursday.*

The House met and were called up as Usual to receive the Governor's Speach,[142] which as soon as reported by the House met the Usual Compliment from Bland for an Address. A Committee for the same was Appointed. Bland first, and, though I spoke nothing to it, 'twas my Fate to be ordered to joyn in this disagreeable task at this time.[143]

[142] This speech is printed in *Burgesses' Journals, 1752–1758,* 231–32 (May 1, 1755).

[143] In addition to Bland and Landon Carter, Charles Carter, William Randolph, and Benjamin Harrison were on this committee (*ibid.,* 232–33 [May 1, 1755]). Benjamin Harrison (1726–91), planter and son of Benjamin Harrison (d. 1744) and Anne Carter, was burgess for Charles City Co., 1748–76;

Vote for the House next day to reso[l]ve into a Committee tomorrow to consider the weighty matters in the Governour's Speach.

2. *Friday.*

Bland Reported the Speach and 'tis all his own. To him therefore be the prais. I think it Stale and huskey.[144] Committees revived except that for trade which I attackt on account of its uselessness and had it sunk. Order of the day put off till tomorrow.

3. *Saturday.*

Order of the day Put off till Wednesday.

5. *Monday.*

Present the Address to the Governour. Committee of trade revived to please Old Lomax, who seemed much dejected at loosing his Chairman's Place; And to give him something to do, ordered many Petitions from Claims to his Committee to enquire into the Allegations. Petitions upon Petitions received.

6. *Tuesday.*

A petition of R[obert] Bolling's[145] relating to his Burnt Warehouses occasioned some debate. First the Referring it to a Committee was rejected without argument. Then a Strange contradictory motion by Bland, supported by W[illiam] Randolph and the Attorney and Wyth,[146] was made for letting it lye on the table. I argued the Irregularity and the Confusion that would ensue from such a Precedent. The Gentlemen built much on the Act of Assembly which gave relief to All sufferers by Fire,[147] but I endeavoured to shew those

member of the First and Second Continental Congresses; signer of the Declaration of Independence; speaker of the Virginia House of Delegates, 1778–1781, 1785; governor, 1781–84; and delegate to the Virginia Convention to ratify the Federal Constitution.

[144] For this address see *ibid.*, 235 (May 2, 1755).

[145] Robert Bolling (1730–75), merchant-planter and son of Robert Bolling II (1686–1749) and Anne Meriwether, was the proprietor of a warehouse in Prince George Co. He was burgess for Dinwiddie Co., 1756–58, 1761–69, 1772–74. For an extract of his petition see *ibid.*, 239 (May 6, 1755).

[146] George Wythe (1726–1806), lawyer-scholar, was burgess for Williamsburg, 1754–55; the College of William and Mary, 1758–61; and Elizabeth City Co., 1761–68. During his later career he was clerk of the Burgesses, 1769–75; professor of law at the College of William and Mary, a position beginning in 1779; delegate to the Second Continental Congress; signer of the Declaration of Independence; delegate to the Federal Constitutional Convention; vice-president of the Virginia Convention to ratify the Federal Constitution; and chancellor of Virginia, 1787–1801. An excellent study of his early career is William Edwin Hemphill, "George Wythe, the Colonial Briton" (Ph.D. dissertation, University of Virginia, 1937).

[147] The act referred to is "An Act, for reducing the Laws made, for amending the Staple of Tobacco . . . ," passed in May 1742; and the particular provision in question is paragraph XLIII. See Hening, ed., *Statutes*, V, 150.

words only extended to the Persons suffering in their tobacco Carryed to Warehouses, that the Proprietors were only Landlords and their Rent was their Consideration.

The Question therefore being regularly for rejecting, it was Accordingly rejected. Several Petition[s] from disbanded Soldiers thrown out. The reason is plain. We gave £30,000 and the Officers had pocketed the money and the Poor soldiers thrown on us as an artfull way to get more money. A Petition for the Country to pay for a Negroe because he had hanged himself after he had burnt his Master's tobacco house rejected, although supported by Waller and the Lawyers except Wyth, because not within the letter nor meaning of the Act[148] relating thereto.

Note: the Committee Claims, having a New chairman, vizt, Ruffin,[149] brought in by Mr. Waller a query whether a deduction should be made from the tobacco to be paid to the takers up of Runaways, Although it had ever been so levyed ever since the tobacco law, which was determined by the house that the deduction should be according to the deductions prescribed in the tobacco law in that County where the Runaway should be taken up.[150] Now came on the debate of the Stint Law and the Worthy Members for it so bent upon pleasing their Constituents that it was remarkable to hear them without doors exclaiming against and yet plum for it on every motion within. So that when the Report from the Committee Propositions was read, which had rejected the 9 Petitions for it, The Majoryty disagreed to that resolution and immediately voted the bringing in a Bill. Their Captain Spokesman and draughtsman[151] sat up all night and got it ready next morning for the Assent of his Committee, and in they came with it to the House with every blank for every fine etc. and even for the time of its taking place and continuance filled up. And they had learnt to be so jealous of the Opposers of this Bill that they were sure to object to any thing though for the good of the Bill that could be proposed. So that discovering the many inconsistencys [in] it and being fearfull least they of their own Accord should go into a Committment of it, I proposed a Comittment from a Confidence that they would Oppose it. This accordingly happened, and with much Ostentation Capt. Pendleton told us we should have

---

[148] The act referred to here is "An Act directing the trial of Slaves committing capital crimes . . . ," and the particular provision in question is paragraph X. See *ibid*. VI, 107.

[149] John Ruffin (d. 1775), planter and son of Robert Ruffin (d. 1721), was burgess for Surry Co., 1754–55.

[150] Provisions governing rewards for taking up runaways are to be found in paragraph XVII in "An Act for the better government of servants and slaves," passed in November 1753 and printed in Hening, ed., *Statutes*, VI, 363.

[151] Probably Edmund Pendleton. He was chairman of a committee to bring in the law. See *Burgesses' Journals, 1752–1758*, 245 (May 8, 1755).

nothing to do with our Bill as he called it. When I saw him intent, in order, as I pretended, to save time, I receded, and it had its Second reading, was engrossed etc. for a third Reading, which was put off until the 14th day of May for a full house, When we made heavy battle against it.

14. *Wednesday*.

Colo. C[arter] Burwell beyond [began] the Attack [upon the Stint Law] by a Well digested paper which he read on the unreasonableness of their hopes from such a bill and the Certainty of the great Injury which must attend the Planter. Some rediculed a written Speach without, but for my part I think a good thing had better be read than not heard at all as it was so pertinent. Colo. C[harles] Carter engaged with the 2d division and endeavoured indeed very handsomely to rally those Members that make no tobacco for their endeavouring to force the Planters into such Methods of living as must affect their Merchandize and destroy their Present Market. I brought up the Rear and shewed the Unreasonableness of a Stint Law in General because it laid a prohibition on the Staple, A thing never to be done except where the Advantage was certain and as experience was against it highly Injurious. Then by a Close push on their Center, I mean their Bill, I shewed it to be such a lump of inconsistancys and hardships as to render it as unpalatable as Pudding Cookt in a hurry. The Close attention of the house to these arguments from every quarter alarumed and Confounded their Captain so much that, when he attempted to Rally, it was so faint as to Convince his party of their Weakness and on the Vote for rejecting it 51 went out and only 40 staid in so that instead of 7 Majority against us, which was on the former vote, 11 were for it, which brought forth this Witty saying, that 11 makes 7.

The Act for dissolving the Vestry of Cople Parish came into the house by a Petition last Session, and, although it had all the Malice and venom that ever a Petition was stuffed with, it passed both below and above stairs.[152] Such I find was the General Aversion to Colo. Lee[153] that the most trifling act perhaps of his life should extend without one fresh Circumstance of Complaint to many Years after his death. And so pleasing is Revenge that it seems as if an opportunity was wanted to exercise it on his Memory. The History is this: Colo. Lee was a Vestryman in that Parish and for many months in the year, nay we'll say altogether, removed into the upper parish of that County. This re-

[152] An extract of this petition is printed in *ibid.,* 220 (Oct. 28, 1754). The act is in Hening, ed., *Statutes,* VI, 517.

[153] Thomas Lee (1690–1750), planter and fifth son of Councilor Richard Lee (1647–1714) and Leatitia Corbin, was burgess for Westmoreland Co., 1726–33; member of the Council, 1733–50; president of the Council and acting governor, 1749–50; and leading factor in the Ohio Company, 1749–50.

moval made him a non resident and his seat in Vestry of Course vacated by it. But this he refused to submit to and had interest enough to Secure himself against a new Election. It seems Colo. Lee, though not the casting voice, had also agreed to Choose one Oldham a Vestryman in the time And that many Years had passed since and no one illegal or Arbitrary act said to be done in Vestry. Yet the being a Vestryman against law, as they called it, was motive enough for this New Act. 'Twas in Vain to Oppose it. Every Unwary Ear was engaged. I attempted with some others to shew that the Allegations were trifling, but it seems I differed from a Certain Person[154] who had in his day drank very large drafts of Rancour and Revenge against Colo. Lee, and it was little less than throwing away time to oppose it. But how the Bill got downstairs again is to me a great mistery, for they had once before thrown it out, and, as there was not any fresh Cause of Complaint, 'tis amazing, as their Ears are above the Sleepy insinuations of those who concerned themselves below. But we may suppose that although they could not be influenced yet they might have warped with resentment. This Act if properly considered is a good lesson for those who fancy power, for it is a testimony that there wants nothing but perseverance and sooner or later they or their Adherents feel the effects of it. C[harles] Carter, B[enjamin] Waller, J[ames] Power, myself, and indeed many a Speaker against this bill, but it had weight enough to pass every thing.

The dividing of Prince William was also a matter that to my great astonishment went down prodigiously. It had all the arguments against it: the Poverty of the people; the want of Proper Justices; instead of a proper division across, one up and down; and a division directly contrary to the Prayer of the Petitioners.[155] And Yet, though my Brother, Hedgman, and myself argued these things every motion and shewed it could only answer one purpose, vizt, the encreasing of Burgesses, Yet it could not be stopt. In short, the Job appeared more in this and the last bill than in anything I ever saw in the house. However, I appeared in Council against it and I believe gave some reason why it should not Pass, and it never came down stairs.

A Petition for dividing Hanover[156] came also in but there was such a General dislike to divisions of Countys that, although some had slyly passed,

---

[154] Probably Speaker John Robinson. There had been a long rivalry, mostly over western lands, between the Robinson-Randolph faction on one hand and the Lees on the other. The evidence for such a faction is presented in David Alan Williams, "Political Alignments in Colonial Virginia, 1698–1750" (Ph.D. dissertation, Northwestern University, 1959), 329–37.

[155] For the Burgesses' action on this bill see *Burgesses' Journals, 1752–1758,* 255, 263 (May 15, 21, 1755).

[156] For the Burgesses' action on this petition see *ibid.,* 261 (May 21, 1755).

Yet I could not help attacking this *in Principio*[157] because I now found by experience That referring Petitions by way of Compliment is only giving time to the promoters to aid them by an extra and private solicitation. This we experienced, for the thing fell by this means when I could afterwards perceive it would have gone had there been time for negotiation. I sustained much resentment on this Account, and I once thought after 6 or eight days had passed that we must have had it more public. But anger with some folks is like Sweet small ail. It runs out as soon as it has vent, and I am pleased to find that I may hope to vote again as I think proper without offence to anyone.

A petition from the Clergy was introduced by Mr. Attorney under the Pompous Appellation of the Venerable body's praying an augmentation of their Sallerys and very prudently confessing in the Petition the dissolute behaviour of many of them, imputing it to the poorness of their livings;[158] It was easy to see that it was more duty than inclination that governed in the Specious introduction. Wormeley, not knowing I am persuaded the Consequences of such a Motion, was for its lying on the table. But Waller, who had experienced the arts that might and had been used before in favour of that body, argued for an immediate Consideration and to be rejected. Colo. W[illiam] Randolph, Colo. C[harles] Carter, and myself all on the same side in the debate. Carter Burwell much for a reference and called it a Compliment to that body; I would not wholly disagree that some of them were respectable, and, if anyone would find out a Cullender to separate the bad from the Good, I would then Join with the Petitioners. And in a very small space of time this Petition was rejected by almost the whole house. But it did not sleep here, for when it was found to be unsuccessfull then it was represented as a matter introduced by the impudence of Warrington[159] and Cam[m][160] and great pains were taken to trye to get it Erased out of the Journals that the Confession contained in it might not be a future proof of the badness of Clergymen here. And it was said to be false and Scandalous. And indeed, what I cannot omit, the printing of our Journals seemed to wait upon this last motion for an erasure perhaps untill the house was thinner or till a party could be made in favour of it. For ask the Printer[161] where the Journals were? He'd Answer he

---

[157] "Primarily."

[158] For an extract of this petition and the Burgesses' action on it see *ibid.*, 257 (May 15, 1755).

[159] Rev. Thomas Warrington (d. 1769) was an Anglican minister at Hampton, Elizabeth City Co., and kept a school.

[160] Rev. John Camm (1718–79), Anglican minister and son of Thomas Camm of Hornsea, England, was professor of divinity, 1749–77, and president, 1771–77, of the College of William and Mary; member of the Virginia Council, 1775–76; and defender of the clergy in the dispute over the Two-Penny Act, 1759–65.

[161] William Hunter (d. 1761), son of William Hunter of Hampton, was public printer and editor of the *Va. Gaz.*, 1750–61.

could not get them from the Clerk. Ask the Clerk and he'd tell you the Speaker had not ordered him to deliver them. And I will say, he that recollects the affair need not ask him. It was better than 8 days between the coming in of the Petition, its rejection, and the motion for the Erasure. And, had not the motion been timely checked by one made previous for Adjournment, I doubt not but we should have heard much murmuring about this delay of our Journals. The Erasure was refused and the Petition is attended with a *Valeat Quantum potest*[162] on our Journals.

I will now Comprehend the Votes and Arguments for the Supplye which we brought by Resolution from the Committee of the whole House to £6,000. I cannot but express my concern that men should be inconsistant in their Actions, a specimen of which this affair affords me. And to represent it truely I will go a little back to two former Sessions from whence the inconsistancy I mean will appear. When the £10,000 was granted, it was so disagreeable a Subject that much art was used to get one penny raised for the defence of the Country. And, although we had then certain intelligence our Enemy had taken our lands, no steps were to be taken to endeavour to stop them. Our People were too poor to defend themselves. But by a side Glance the money was raised And, being not enough, two Short Sessions last year were imployed to raise £20,000 more. Then, indeed, the great struggle was whether it should be nothing, £10,000 or 20. It went for the 20 against the Clamours of poverty, I might rather say Popularity, for as the people had not been then tryed no one could say much in the point as to poverty. And, as there was certainly a necessity to shew our enemy that we should not easyly be persuaded to part with what we had, I joyned with and was indeed Active for the 20, that we might shew our mother Country our own Sensibility of danger and excite their Care. All this had its effect, Men, money, and Arms Came over. But now, when it seems to be the only time to own our Poverty and when we have experienced it, we have grown on a Sudden Rich without one visible sign of Riches. And I must say it was no small art that fixed the Sum to £6,000, and there seems a view to a much greater sum. However, it would Obnubilate patriotism to Open the door and let it in at once. It may be said that those who were for giving before are now against it. I own it in some sort and have this reason: before we knew not exactly our Poverty, we had no kind of defence, no steps from home, and our indolence lulled them of which our enemys were taking great advantage. Now we have found ourselves poor. Many steps have been taken, if not effectual, to rout, at least to check, the enemy, and our Mother Country are strongly engaged. But say they: shall we leave off and be enactive because our Friends are willing to help us? I answer that what we

[162] "Let it be effective as much as possible."

have not, we cannot give, which must be a just excuse. Rais[e] the money, that is shew where it is to be had, and I am ready. In short, I own it is a difficult point to determin in and it is possible that there may be error. I have consented to this small sum in hopes that by way of lottery or some such means it may be got. And for this Purpose A bill has been framed agreeable to the Resolution to raise the sum. It has been once read and would have either been passed or Rejected had it not been for the following Accident[163]:

JUNE 1755

2. *Saturday.*

On Wednesday last Mr. Speaker had advice of his Lady's dangerous indisposition and was obliged to crave an early sitting that by means of an adjournment he might go home. The next day the members without a Speaker met and Adjourned themselves to the day following. The day following we met again without a Speaker, and, as we were not clear in our Precedents for adjournment to a long day, I moved to the Clerk, to whom in such case we are to address ourselves, to make a Precedent, for all Precedents must have had a beginning and there could not happen a more necessary occasion. And therefore the motion for Adjournment was Carryed to this day with a *Nemine Contradicente* In hopes the Speaker may be down. And I wish he can, for I really see some evils will arise if he don't. But as they can't be very far off it is needless to express them.

[163] The Burgesses finally passed this measure, "An Act for raising the sum of six thousand pounds, by a Lottery, for the further protection of his majesty's subjects, against the insults and incroachments of the French," on June 30 after a three-week recess because of the illness of Speaker Robinson's wife; the bill was formally approved by Governor Dinwiddie on July 9, 1755 (*Burgesses' Journals, 1752–1758,* pp. 285, 293). The act is printed in Hening, ed., *Statutes,* VI, 453–61.

THE DIARY OF
LANDON CARTER OF
SABINE HALL

September 21, 1756—October 24, 1758

THE DIARY

1756

SEPTEMBER 1756

21. *Tuesday.*[1]

It has continued drye weather so long that 'tis needless to repeat it only that we have the addition of hot and foggy mornings which has introduced amongst us some of the most obstinate irregular fevers that ever I met with. To this day 67 of my family and people have been laid up with them and frequently relapsed. Some few have turned to regular intermittants at last, but my dear Suky[2] lyes now dangerous ill with one. On the 2d day she had severe Convulsions. It has continued a week on her and all yesterday till 12 at night there was more probability of her dying than living. All but the Doctor[3] despaired but her fever rose again and she continues dangerous ill notwithstanding every evacuation has been made and even blisters used. This day two were applyed to her Ears. God only knows her fate.

I suspected my Wheat that was catched in the rain and shewed a little sprouting would not come up, but I sowed 2 acres and ¼ a fortnight agoe of it and the dews and foggs have brought it up as fine as ever I saw.

OCTOBER 1756

3. *Sunday.*

It has continued drye weather then Cold and hot to this day, and I believe the rain is now come. The wind is to the Eastward of the North and raining in plenty and Cold withall. Therefore, to Conclude our Observation about the

---

[1] Printed from the original diary in the Sabine Hall Col. Those portions of the diary from Sept. 21, 1756, to Oct. 24, 1758, fill the final three-fourths of the quarto-sized volume that includes the private minutes of the Burgesses' proceedings.

[2] Susannah Carter (d. April 1758) was the daughter of Landon Carter and his third wife, Elizabeth Beale.

[3] Probably Doctor Nicholas Flood (d. 1776), long "an eminent practicioner and Consultant" in Richmond Co. (Wyndham B. Blanton, *Medicine in Virginia in the Eighteenth Century* [Richmond, 1931], 382).

weather to this day, from the 23d of July to this time we have had only two showers, one in August very slight, the other in September of no Continuance and quickly soaked up. My daughter still in her fever the 19th day but I think she has mended in her strength a little. God send this moisture that we are now to expect may disperse and so remove the present prodigious unhealthy Constitution of air. I have been sick myself ever since the 2d of September and far from being recovered yet, and now above 80 of us young and Old have felt the effects of the Season, which has been attended with violent irregular fevers of a most bilious nature. Nay such quantitys have attended that some have many days (notwithstanding plentifull evacuations of it by Vomits when they were first taken) voided it upwards and downwards till they were near Spent, and I don't find above 2 or 3 cases that the bark[4] has opperated at all favourably, for if the fever has been checked a day or two by it the Patient has been intirely Sallow, and all ages the same. Neither do I know of any certain success attending any Physician. Do what they could the byle would flow again and the disorder return and I have seen patients of Amson's[5] [and] Flood's etc. so that we must conclude that the Epedemic Constitution of the air was the Sole Cause of it, which 'tis to be observed was all along drye, hot and foggy at nights excepting now and then a day when the smallest change though but a Cold drye air would revive the Sick. Note: many Children swelled after the fevers left them but I thank God none of mine as yet.

This drye weather has given a sufficient proof of the Justness of my arguments against those Gentlemen who from mere Vulgar Error have fallen into such a fondness for double geered mills as to build them on every run not considering the quantity of their water but have formed to themselves a Confidence that less water and more searvice done by them than by single geered. I say this has proved my argument that the Multiplication of wheels must encrease the resistance by Friction and of Course make the encrease of the Vis Matrix or first mover necessary and therefore more water expended to turn them than Single geered require, for my mill is single geered and the Course of her Run could not in 12 hours raise more than one inch of water, and Yet she has with that inch workt every day and all day except Sundays, when she became a gainer so much as to allow her more water, and all the mills I have heard of have been quite drye Grinding only 1 day or so in a Week.

Now to Prove this in a Philosophical way:

By experiments in Natural Philosophy on the Axis in Peritrochio it is found that the diameter of the wheel and the diameter of the Axis are the ratio

---

[4] Jesuits', Peruvian, or cinchona bark was a bitter bark containing quinine from Andean trees of the genus *Cinchona* used in treating agues and fevers.

[5] Doctor John Amson practiced in Williamsburg.

on which the whole is founded, that is, by so much as the diameter of the wheel exceeds that of the Axis by so much the easyer will the weight be raised. Of Course the Smaller the diameter of the Axis the sooner will a weight be raised by a wheel of any given diameter, and on the Contrary the larger the axis the more force must be required on the same given wheel. This granted, it follows that as in double geered mills the Communication must be by wheels placed on the Axis and of course the diameter of the axis is encreased to the diameter of that communicating wheel for wherever that power touches there is the axis. And every other wheel added to this communicating wheel is still a full or encrease of the diameter of the Axis. Therefore by this encrease the diameter of the axis becomes at last equall to the diameter of the wheel to which the vis matrix is applyed or exceeds it and of Course the vis Matrix must be encreased.

This Appears plain by laying a Watch flat on the table. The vis matrix is the main Spring; every wheel added is the encrease of the diameter of the Axis till at last a wheel of no greater resistance than the strength of a fine hair stops the vis matrix. Now the Common method of reasoning is to argue from the last wheel or resistance given and make that the moving power, but 'tis a base and inverted reasoning for the moving power is below, and to trye the force of the resistance of each wheel take away the ballance or Cock wheel and then the watch which before moved Slow will run down, take away the next wheel and it will run faster and take away all but the wheel next the barrel where the Spring is and it will flye in a jurk almost imperceptible. If it should be asked of what use are double geered mills and why are they used abroad, I answer 'tis only where they can encrease their moving power and Are not in danger of wanting water. Then there use is evident because every multiplyed wheel adds to the revolution of the Stone, but in Virginia where drye spells and hot suns do almost evaporate the water everywhere they are of no use but a prejudice except in Winter where it frequently rains. But in the summer where there is a head of water they grind a day or two faster than a single mill, but in a week's drye weather they can't grind at all when the Single mill shall grind Constantly. Again as a Single mill, from what has been said, will go with less water the buckets may be made Smaller and the water wheels lighter, which can't be in double geered, for their buckets must be large enough to admit of water enough to move the mill at all.

7. *Thursday.*

The rain that fell the 3d day proved very trifling. It did little more than introduce a Northwest that cooled the air but did not moisten the earth. It has been drye ever since; there has been a drizzling shower or two this day. We have been endeavouring to get some wheat ground plowed but with great difficulty. I am trying to find whether the dressing the ground with Pea vines will produce so well as is talkt of. The land we are plowing is all well covered over with Virginia pea vines and I have persons before the plow chopping them that the plow may turn them under, but they don't seem to make a great Covering and are really hard to turn under the Clods. Our Fotter not yet all in. Such overseers I have never seen. They began the 7th of last month and have had no hindrance but a little stripping in the morning. They pretend it was stacked a good way off but that was not their labour. They brought it no farther than where they would have stackt it and I brought [it] in place after with my Carts.

8. *Friday.*

A fine Rain this day and almost all night.

9. *Saturday.*

Young Colo. Charles Carter[6] and with him a large family came here.

13. *Wednesday.*

These terrible fevers continue and every body relapsing and those not sick before taken ill. My little girls just mending again. Suky very low. My Son Robert[7] taken ill. They now are attacked with vomitings and Purgings.

20. *Wednesday.*

This makes just two months since my family was attackt with this irregular and bilious fever and there is still ill in my family—my sons Robert, John,[8] My daughters Judy[9] and Suky—and without doors several Slaves. Judy and Johnny have relapsed and are in no way of recovery as yet. I have found that after the vomits have workt plentifully rattle snake in powder given to the Slaves has been of great Service the next morning, but it is more operative in

---

[6] Charles Carter, Jr., of Ludlow, planter and son of Charles Carter (1707–64) of Cleve, was Landon Carter's nephew. He lived in King George Co. and was burgess for that county, 1756–68, 1769–71.

[7] Robert Wormeley Carter (1734–97) of Sabine Hall, planter and oldest son of Landon Carter and his first wife Elizabeth Wormeley (1714–40), was burgess for Richmond Co., 1769–76, member of the Richmond Convention, 1775, and delegate from Richmond Co., 1775–87. He married Winifred Travers Beale of Richmond Co. and inherited the Sabine Hall estate. For an account of his career see Louis Morton, "Robert Wormeley Carter of Sabine Hall: Notes on the Life of a Virginia Planter," *Journal of Southern History*, XII (1946), 345–65.

[8] John Carter (d. 1789), later of Sudley, Prince William Co., was a planter and the third son of Landon Carter and Elizabeth Wormeley. He married Janet Hamilton.

[9] Judith Carter, daughter of Landon Carter and Elizabeth Beale, later married her cousin Reuben Beale of Richmond Co.

some than others.[10] 10 grains three times a day even in some large boys has only produced a breathing Sweat and great discharges of urin and insensibly as it were secreted the byle and Carryed it down its proper Channel, but in some grown persons who have been much relaxed the like quantity of 10 grains has produced a profuse sweat all night. With such therefore the quantity should be lessened. I wish my own fears did not prevent my giving it to my Children or that I was Physician enough to correct its acrid pungent taste for I believe it affects the throat glands not a little. No rain since the 8th of the month but now great dews which hang in fogs in the morning.

23. Saturday.

Rain this day but Small. My two Children Judy and Suky and Johnny very ill. Jordan's[11] Cow calved this night a Cow Calf by my Bull but well markt.

26. Tuesday.

The second frost I have had here this Year. We began to sow wheat the 15th and have been sowing as we could get plowed ever since. We shall be a week longer here. The weather is drye, the wheat only coming up where first sown.

NOVEMBER 1756

2. Tuesday.

The drye weather still continues and I am affraid ⅘ths of my wheat sown is destroyed by it for it is only here and there come up and on examining the rest I find a black speck where the sprout should be. In short I never sowed wheat with satisfaction to myself since I have been a farmer. The ground all Cloddy and drye quite to the bottom of the Furrows.

3. Wednesday.

Rain from 5 last night to this morning and raining. God be thanked.

4. Thursday.

The fine Rain yesterday was succeeded by a Violent Northwest and at night a hard black frost so that Wheat is not much benefitted by it. Note:

---

[10] Rattlesnake powder was made from *Polygala senega,* a vegetable plentiful in the southern colonies. John Tennent, who came to Virginia from England in 1725, advocated its use in treating pleurisy and gout. It was also used for cases of snake bite (Blanton, *Medicine in Virginia in the Eighteenth Century,* 122, 244).

[11] Probably William Jordan (d. 1757), a resident of Richmond Co.

though the rains have been few this year yet all of them have been followed by Cold winds and now frosts as the winter Advances.

6. *Saturday*.

Finished sowing wheat here this morning and the plows gone to put in my Son's wheat at Landsdown.[12] The quantity sown here is

	bushels
At the house white wheat———————————————————	5¾
In the piece this side the barn of white wheat———————	27
In the piece facing the barn of Morgan's[13] wheat———————	52
" " " beyond the barn white wheat———————	19¾
" " " " " " Morgan's wheat———————	6
" " " " " " wheat made at Harrison's[14]———	35
	145½
Sown at Morgan's————————————————————————	5½
	151

which at 2 bushels to the acre should be 72 acres and better, but I know the Ground is full 80 acres if not more, so that my Young seedsman is not a Certain hand as Dick Edwards[15] was and I am affraid has sowed much too thin.

8. *Monday*.

Rain a very fine one and the 9th a sharp Northwest so that moisture without warmth adds nothing to the growth in the Farm. Began to so[w] wheat yesterday at Landsdown but stopped by the rain.

12. *Friday*.

Went up to Bull Hall[16] this day. Left Manuel plowing my Fork Land[17] for Wheat, where it seems they sowed better than 18 bushels so that after the rate

---

[12] A plantation belonging to Robert Wormeley Carter in Richmond Co. A survey of this tract dated Jan. 20, 1735, is in the Sabine Hall Col.

[13] Probably David Morgan, one of Landon Carter's overseers.

[14] Probably Benjamin Harrison (1726–91) of Berkeley, Landon Carter's nephew.

[15] Richard Edwards from time to time during the 1750s and 1760s managed Landon Carter's Richmond Co. plantations. He married Ann Hamilton in March 1764.

[16] Bull Hall was the plantation house on a tract of land on Bull Run Creek belonging to Landon Carter, Jr., second son of Landon Carter and Elizabeth Wormeley. Young Landon married Judith Fauntleroy.

[17] A tract of land in Richmond Co. belonging to Landon Carter. A survey of the Fork Quarter dated July 10, 1759, is in the Sabine Hall Col.

of 2 bushels to the Acre the piece held 9 acres. Sowed after this Morgan's Wheat quantity 5 bushels.

15. *Monday.*

Reached Bull Hall. My Son Landon met me on Broad run about 7 miles from home. We got to the Hall by Sunset, found all well there and every thing better than I ever found since Sibley's[18] death. Corn all measured and housed. We reckon they will certainly make at least 30 hogsheads there and if I mind Patrick[19] he will make 20 hogsheads.

19. *Friday.*

Left Bull and settled Simon Churchill[20] at Park Quarter.

23. *Tuesday.*

Got home. No rain ever since I went [from] home. Corn not gathered quite here such has been the Lazyness of our People.

24. *Wednesday.*

Rain all this night very hard. It did snow a little but quickly over. 2 Calves dropt at the barn Yesterday and 4 days agoe.

25. *Thursday.*

Raining this morning.

DECEMBER 1756

13. *Monday.*

Not yet done plowing my next year's Ground. We had the beginning of this month very hard frosts and Cold winds for about 5 days and a Slight Spitting of Snow but ever since very fine weather indeed.

15. *Wednesday.*

We are trying to raise hoggs at the Mill and have got 21 piggs from 3 sows. I am making a tall punchioned place of about [blank] ground. These punchions I intend to Cap at top with a rail let in and pin them to a middle rail

[18] Probably John Sibley (d. 1750), long an overseer in the Carter family.

[19] Patrick was probably one of Landon Carter's overseers.

[20] Simon Churchill was one of Landon Carter's overseers. Park Quarter was a tract of land in Stafford Co.

within that they may not be dugg out and I will have shelters for them to go in and they shall be lockt up every night.

17. *Friday.*

This day began with a warm rain but about 10 o'clock changed with the wind to a Cold snow which lasted till 3 then grew excessive Cold. Wind Northwest and remained so all night.

18. *Saturday.*

A hard Frost. Ground Covered with Snow but moderate warm at 12 though no thaw except in the Sun. The Crop of Wheat made this year, that is, what is threshed out, is as follows:

	bushels		*[bushels]*
At Morgan's	60	To be deducted out Sown	151
At the Fork	192	Sold Dr. Flood	26
At the House	58½	Spencer Watts[22]	3
White Wheat	53½	Longwith[23]	3
Red Wheat	31	Note: we sowed at the Fork of	
Stone house field	699	my son's Wheat from Lands-	
Riverside point[21] threshed	66	down	18½
" " "	500		
	1660		
" " "	051½		
" " "	1711½		

20. *Monday.*

It began to Snow last night about 7 o'Clock and Continued, Snowing, raining and blowing hard all night. This morning Snowing fast and a hard gale at Northwest. Left off at 12 and a fine evening overhead.

21. *Tuesday.*

A fine day Overhead and [so the] 22nd.

[21] Both the Stone House field and Riverside Point were part of the Sabine Hall estate in Richmond Co. A map and survey of the Riverside field dated Nov. 14, 1738, is in the Sabine Hall Col.

[22] Spencer Watts was one of Landon Carter's overseers.

[23] John Longwith was overseer of Landon Carter's Northumberland plantations.

23. *Thursday.*

Began to Snow last night at Dark and snowed till midnight, then rain and Continued so till 8 this day.

27. *Monday.*

The first working day for some time past.

31. *Friday.*

Very fine weather ever since and so continues till the 3d January 1757.

THE DIARY

1757

JANUARY 1757

3. Monday.

Ended in a Cold Northwest and frose hard and excessive Cold all night.

4. Tuesday.

Violent wind Northwest, very hard Frost and severely cold. In short, the plowed ground looks grey as if divested of all Richness. Mr. Armour[1] came here the 1st of this month.

5. Wednesday.

Fine day the former part but cold the latter part. A lamb this day from a black Ewe. The lamb white.

7. Friday.

As fine a morning as I ever saw only the ground damp with the long frosts giving way. Capt. Payne[2] fired against my house last night at 8 o'Clock.

Note: we have made out of the oats stacked without doors 918 bushels, which is a great Crop, and if the within doors now yields in the same proportion according to its dimensions we shall not fail of turning out better than 50 bushels to the acre.

[11. *Tuesday.*]

Fine weather these 4 days and so to the 16.

---

[1] Mr. Armour was probably one of Carter's overseers or tenants.
[2] Perhaps Capt. William Payne who commanded several merchant vessels trading to Virginia in the 1750s.

[16. *Sunday.*]

Another lamb last night. 1 lamb this day.

17. *Monday.*

No plowing these 4 days although the weather fine. The ground too hard. The weather has continued very Cold, drye and the Ground hard Frozen till the

21. *Friday.*

when it rained great part of the night and turned to a very great thaw insomuch that our houses were all dripping within doors. The wind at South and there is a prospect of working in the Ground tomorrow. My threshers of oats made a shift to thresh no more per day than they did when the days were 20 minutes shorter and the oats then all taken out of Stack without doors where they must have been a little toughened by Weather and now these oats are in a mow close by the floor fine and drye. This was such evident lazyness that I ordered them Correction which they took three days running and then by setting them on different floors to discover the lazy fellow they returned me 40 bushels per day. This I minute down to shew that things are often judged impossible when obstinacy alone is the Cause of it.

23. *Sunday.*

Very Cold after the rain yesterday. 4 calves at the barn, 3 at Watts' and 1 at Matheny's.[3]

24. *Monday.*

This day a milch Cow very fat and well drowned in a Small ditch, push[ed] in head foremost by the rest of the Cattle. It should seem as if the keeping Cattle fatt was an injury to them. They are so wanton as to always to be running and poking at one another. This was a fine Cow and the place miry but she was pinned down by her horns.

We have 11 lambs this day. Two more fallen, but one dyed. The rains are now every day and ground prodigious wet.

25. *Tuesday.*

Rained all night. No working at anything and so to the

---

[3] Matheny, whose first name remains a mystery, was either one of Carter's overseers or tenants.

27. *Thursday.*

A prospect for a fine day but cold.

29. *Saturday.*

But an indifferent day and rain at night. Mr. Nelson Barclay[4] came here.

31. *Monday.*

Rain yesterday, rain last night and this morning. Thunder, Lightning and rain. Rain all the evening with more lightning and Thunder to the Southeast. I have been some days plowing in 4 bout ridges [in] my new corn field taken in this year at the Riverside exactly 5½ distance. Therefore the work for the people is only howing up the lacings as they are called. I should have finished this sooner to have began my plowing for oats, but, as the Corn field I am to turn out is stumpy and is what I intend to sow in oats besides my farm lot, I shall make the overseer repay this work by levelling that field down pretty light and then sowing and harrowing in the oats.

FEBRUARY 1757

1. *Tuesday.*

A Cold day, the ground all afloat very bad at 10. Snow, hail, sleet, rain, wind and Ice. The 2d the same. The 3d very Cold. The 4th more so although fair.

5. *Saturday.*

Snow in the night. The ground Covered but a fine clear Sun this day.

6. *Sunday.*

Rain this morning. I observe as usual that Snows in February are too late for wheat, for mine this year carryed a fine verdure untill this week and now it seems quite withered. So it proved in '55 and '56.

[4] Nelson Berkeley of Airwell in Hanover Co., planter and son of Edmund Berkeley (d. 1745) and Mary, daughter of Secretary Thomas Nelson of Barn Elms, married Elizabeth Wormeley Carter, eldest daughter of Landon Carter and his first wife, Elizabeth Wormeley. He was justice of the peace and sheriff in Hanover Co.

7. *Monday.*

Very hard frost. And a very fine day.

9. *Wednesday.*

I went to the Fork quarter, find the overseer there is but a Chattering fellow, promises much but does little, for which I have given him a piece of my mind. He protests he will mend. But 5 lambs there although we have 31.

The dam we are making across that marsh is a heavy work on the side next the Fork. 'Tis miry marsh and sinks much. We shall, it may be, by tomorrow night get across but it must be raised higher because of its shrinking. I find the tide has rose near the top. Had all my tobacco beds hoed up again and laid off, raked and ready for sowing. If the wind lyes, I shall also sow at home. Watts has been 4 days hoing his old Corn field. A fine day this if the Southerly wind did not blow quite so hard. A great prospect for much rain. Therefore gave positive orders to keep the seed ready prepared for the plant patches and sow as soon as the wind lyes if 'tis in night. At home prepared with the tobacco seed the following garden seeds: Onions, Cabbages, Sugar loaf ditto, Savoys, radishes, Lettice Coss, and Cabbage and of these a good quantity for use.

Sowed my tobacco seed at the riverside in the afternoon. Not quite 2 quarts of seed Sowed at home. It rained all night abundance.

10. *Thursday.*

A very Cloudy morning and very hollow wind from the North as if more rain.

11. *Friday.*

A clear day but airish till night and then excessive Cold, Stormy and a Smart Snow for about an hour at night. I went to Dr. Flood's with my daughter Betty and little Suky and stayed there, the weather being prodigious Cold, till Monday, when I came home followed by Dr. Flood and his Lady.

14. *Monday—20. Sunday.*

Monday Just as I got home my son Robert informed me that a fellow of mine from the Park quarter had come to his mill the 11th where he found him in the evening and ordered him to me the next day, that the fellow told him he had got the Small pox the 12th, being Saturday, upon which he looked at him and saw many pimples in his face like pins heads and imagined it to be the same eruptive disorder that had been amongst my negroe children, but, on the fellow's complaining of very sore eyes, great pain in the head and severe pain in the small of his back with a fever, he was ordered to go and lye in the weaver's house, intending to put him in the hospital the next morning. This was not quite cautious enough, for although the weaver had had the small pox yet some negroe boys lay there also. The fellow's pains and fever was very bad all night and a very sore throat. The next day, vizt, sunday, he was confined in the hospital and victuals put at his door and wood. It was as before observed very cold and he had no Covering given him, which I suppose was the cause the eruptions made no great progress. On monday the 14th I ordered the weaver to go in and take care of him, but he had presently got so drunk that I was obliged to order the Smith who had had the Small pox to take the fellow under his care and to go and live there constantly with him and contrived that the fellow should have clean straw and warm blankets and that no one should go anigh the hospital nor come from it. Dr. Flood examined the fellow this night but could not speak positively of the distemper then because all eruptions resemble one another except in the first Period and, as he had been much exposed to Cold weather, this disorder had not seemed to be quite so regular as the small pox from the first symptoms. He found by talking with the fellow that the negroe Children at the Park quarter had had the same disorder but had not lain by it, but this could be only the chicken pox about every where, but talking with the fellow the 15th he found he had been runaway ever since the third of the month, that he had attempted to go to Bull run but was stopt by Cedar run and that the small pox was about in that neighborhood and in many parts of Prince William and Stafford Countys. Landon had wrote to me the 4th of the month and made no mention of the Small pox nor of any distemper at the Park. This day the Doctor pronounced the disorder the small pox and found the man must have had eruptions on him the thursday before, which was the tenth of the month, and if we allow 4 days before when the Symptoms must have seized him and one day, retarding their progress by reason of the fellow's being exposed in the very Cold weather, these Symptoms must have begun on the fifth so that he must have catched the infection before he says he run away from his quarter, for I am persuaded it would not in two days have tinctured the blood so as to occasion high fevers, pains, etc., which the fellow says he had before he run away, and as his overseer whipped him for not waking he came away with them. Now though 'tis needless to enquire how negroes get these things yet from his own mouth his is reconciliable, for he says an old woman dyed of it in the neighbourhood of the quarter and that one James Kentan or Kendal had it close by the quarter when it was brought down by some opekan Waggons.[5] Let the Stage of this order be therefore what I have reckoned it must be from the tenth at least 5 days and inclusive 6 days to this day. The pock came out plentifully on him. His face much swelled and his eyes greatly inflamed, but his fever abated greatly and many Pustles on his back and leggs.

The 16th, which the Doctor looked on as the 7th day, he was all full and the fever in a manner quite gone but a great soreness down the jaws, in his head and throat very sore and his ribbs quite down his right side so sore as to render it difficult to tell whether it was not really a great pain.

17th. The 8th day the pustles on the face began to flatten and the Doctor called it a most favourable sort. Note: he was restless the day and night before last so that last night by the Doctor's orders he only took 3 spoon fulls Syrrop of Diacodiane[6] in a glass of madeira wine.

18th. The 9th day by the Doctor's reckoning. The pustles on the face drying and those on his leggs and back flattening, the swelling in his face much abated and the inflamation in his eyes much lessened also.

19th. The 10th the fellow very wek all this day by his keeper's account. Note: ever since the 17th he has been very fetid. All hands kept at a great distance and very Cloudy rainy weather.

20th. This day also very well, which is by Accounts the 11th and with those in which the disorder proves mortal, as I have read, the fatal period.

Note: as far as this day the fellow only took the above opiad and no sort of medicin. His food was always gruel, thin broths, mush and beer and only once a little small beer with a little wine in it because the Doctor found him sickish. I shall esteem myself very lucky here if it spreads not because of the 1st imprudence in my son's seeking him last saturday's evennight, vizt., the 12, and his lying in the same house with two negroe boys that night, for the eruption were out upon him and as we have no one Symptom of Complaint and it is now 9 days since I hope in God we shall escape. Indeed the Doctor spoke as fully as he could to Comfort us that 'tis seldom catching till about the 7th or 8th day and so on from that time till the whole is over and everything well purged of infection. This man has had only a stool or two now and then.

The 18th, Poor Landon from Bull run wrote me a letter dated the 12th describing the case of a sick woman much like this only there appeared no

---

[5] "Opekan Waggons" were wagons from Opequon in Frederick County.

[6] Syrup of diacodion or diacodium is the syrup from poppies or opium and was formerly used as a narcotic.

eruption but upon a great lump that had swelled on her neck full of little pimples the day before. She was then in a Violent fever and the use of her limbs almost taken away with pain and distracted in her head and Eyes. It seems she had been out of order a week before but drove out to work by her overseer Boyce Edison and made to wade in the run and at night was taken with an ague and these pains the next day. She was blooded and had taken a great deal of rattle snake decoction, 2 spoon fulls every two hours, to procure a sweat, which was improper in the Small pox. I dispatched away the boy immediately to admonish them of the small pox, informing them of the fellow here that had come from those parts with it, and my hopes are that he may get there before the Eruptions are ripe enough to spread the Contagion. I have also given instructions how to conduct themselves if it should be it. And Yesterday I sent off Mr. Austin Brokenbrough's[7] man with letters to Dr. Wallace[8] to go up there and if it is the disorder to bring Landon down if it is not broke out upon him till he can see whether he has catched it. I also wrote to Landon on the Subject and if he has got it I have begged the Doctor to stay with him and I will satisfy him for his trouble besides being greatly obliged to him. I wrote largely on the care and method to be used and related what we have done here and now have composed myself to meet the worst, knowing that God is Mercyfull and that he requires no more of us but our own proper humane Care and that he will protect where it shall seem good to his infinite wisdom.

Mr. Wormeley came here the 18th and stayed till this day. Prodigious bad weather, mere deluges of rain to this day.

20. Sunday.

A very fine day and so the 21st.

21. Monday.

The Small pox man very well. Dr. Flood came here at night.

---

[7] Austin Brockenbrough (b. 1738) was a planter and son of Capt. William Brockenbrough (1715-78), justice of the peace, long-time resident of Richmond Co., and son of Austin Brockenbrough (d. 1717), and Elizabeth, daughter of Moore Fauntleroy. A lieutenant in Washington's 1st Virginia Regiment during the French and Indian War, he married Lucy, daughter of John Champe of "Lamb's Creek," King George Co. He lived in King George Co., where he was a justice of the peace. A loyalist during the Revolution, he removed to England but returned to Virginia after the war.

[8] Dr. Michael Wallace (1719-67) of Ellerslie in King George Co. Born in Scotland and indentured to Dr. Gustavus Brown of Charles City Co., Maryland, he married Elizabeth, daughter of Dr. Brown, and practiced in Falmouth and the adjacent area (Blanton, *Medicine in Virginia in the Eighteenth Century*, 77).

22. Tuesday.

A raw Cold morning. Dr. Flood gave the Man his Purge, being a bolus.[9]
This is the 13th day from the Eruptions.

23. Wednesday.

The fellow in the Small pox continues mending. 'Tis his 14th day. His
purge workt well. Not with standing it has been clear, drying weather ever
since the rain which fell Saturday 19 to this day, yet our land is hardly solid
enough to bear riding with out miring such a rain was it. I can't remember the
like for four year past and this day there is a very great [fog], which all this
winter have foreboded more rain, although I must own I have discovered fogs
to be a sign of drye weather in Summer, and I suppose there is a Substantial
reason, for both in Summer the natural moisture of the earth is so rarifyed that
it ascends and by the Continued heat disperses away into air as the rare faction
continues, but in winter these vapours arise from a warmth but in such
prodigious quantitys that they presently condense in the atmosphere naturally
moist for want of a due proportion of heat in winter, and then by their weight
they fall again either in Snow or rain at the region of air is at to hot or cold.

Betty Oliver very ill. This is a fine wench but now much affected. She had
first a fever in the summer of the raging bilious kind from which she was
releived as others were by evacuants, but her pregnancy preventing a repiti-
tion of them she relapsed with the Season into an inflamatory disorder for
which she was twice blooded and recovered so as to imploy herself about light
works. A week before her lying in she was attacked with a numbness in her
right side from her hips and into her side but she describing it only by a
pain and her being loaded she was again bled and mended till she lay in, at
which time the infant was imprudently or unskillfully taken away from her in
a wrong position and this Numbness returned with a swelling in her groin.
Her Lochial evacuations were very great, and as she was attended with hysterical Symptoms I ordered her some Nervins which releived her, and I always heard she was better and even yesterday 'twas said she was much mended
and walkt about clear of a fever, but at night she was again taken very ill
and this morning I visited her [and] found a prodigious rattling Cold on
her, a very feverish pulse and her Nerves greatly affected. She protested she
never went out to expose herself. Note: as she was purged since her lying in
by Dr. Flood's directions, I never attempted to do anything of that kind but

---

[9] A bolus is a portion of masticated food ready to swallow or a medicine prepared in the form of a
large pill.

just to procure a motion or two per day with rhubarb given in small quantitys with castor[10] etc. which had every good affect, but it is to be fear[ed] there is a Collection of matter internally in the swelling in her groin, for she says it keeps to its state, feels soft and as if it was hollow. I sent for Dr. Flood, who I expected was at Mr. Faunteleroy's.

The boy Samson also very ill. His case was an ague and then a fever two days on the 12th of the month when I was abroad, for which they gave him a vomit which occasioned an intermission for two days, when he went out after his cattle at night but relapsed again into a Cold fit and a fever, and as there were many twitching symptoms in his belly and his pulse very irregular I gave him 24 grains Pulvis Bazilicus,[11] believing there might be worms contributing to the disorder, and if there were not the evacuation could not be hurtfull, but this gave no indication of the disease. His head remained affected and by watching his pulse Narrowly every now and then yesterday I imagined there must be a load of boil, for which I gave him a penny weight of Ipecacuana.[12] This worked once upwards and brought off a quantity of green byle and tending downwards much went off by stool, and I think his pulse much mended, not so strong in the beats and soft and plyable to the touch. Note: I have two days before endeavoured to loosen this bile by medecin and Collect it for the purpose and I hope it will answer.

Began this day to sow oats at least a week later than ever I did since the first and second year of my farming. The reasons are the prodigious wet weather latterly and a prodigious Corn field I broke up with my Farm plows. The quantity I have ordered to be sowed is after the rate of 4 bushels to one acre and ⅛ of an Acre because each land makes just 1,344 square yards and 'twould be a fraction too nice for my negroe Sower to calculate by the hand. Therefore I have ordered a bushel in each land.

24. *Thursday.*

The Small pox patient taked his second purge ordered by Dr. Flood, this day being his 15th day. The boy Samson continued all yesterday in the same fever before described without any alteration and at night his head was much disturbed and the fever high. I [He?] was this day some thing confined in, the

---

[10] Castor is a creamy, orange-brown substance with a strong penetrating odor. It consists of the dried preputial follicles of beaver glands and their secretions and was formerly used as a stimulant and spasmodic.

[11] Pulvis basilicus, the royal powder, was a compound used as a laxative. It was particularly recommended for worms.

[12] Ipecacuana is an emetic and expectorate made from the root of *Cephaëlis ipecacuanha,* a plant found in Brazil.

fever being of the inf[l]amatory kind, and had near 4 ounces blood taken from his arm. It had a deep floridness inclining to a black Colour but with no Symptoms as if attended with a Cold and I could wish my fears had permitted me to have drawn more off. His head grew quite easy and his pulse more soft to the touch but his skin drye and the fever still continuing. I changed his drink to barley water, observing but little serum in his blood, of which I ordered him to drink plentifully and every two hours gave him 60 drops of Spiritus Mindererius[13] to act as a neutralsalt to remove obstructions that such a viscid blood must Occasion and in order to promote a breathing moisture, but as yet that is not effected although the boy acknowleges himself much better. Nature perhaps by these little helps will be more at liberty to act. Note: he had a griping in the night and threw off 3 bilious stools.

Betty Oliver mended much yesterday after taking the Sal Ammoniae[14] but in the night the Hysteric Symptoms returned and with them a fever. She says she was near Choaked by the usual lumps rising. She expectorated a great deal of viscid matter and is this morning quite easy and cheer full. I was in hopes the Ammoniae would have assisted her nerves from their peculiar quality assigned to them in Spasmodick Symptoms, and it is noted likely, but they were prevented, although she is pretty full in Complaining, being of the kind of Moaning weak hearted Constitution. Note: she says the swelling in her groin has not been uneasy to her these 2 days.

No Touring out to day. The wind hard at Southwest and seems to be brewing up much rain. We sowed only 4 bushels yesterday.

28. Monday.

Very Cold frost, hard Northwest. So yesterday and the day before rain all day. Lost 2 lambs last night. I am puzzled to account for the smallness of my Lambs this year. They used before to be large. I penned hardly any sheep last year and they lookt exceeding well. They have been all well fed this year. Had field of wheat to feed on whilst Lambing and young Clover. They all lay warm and drye but not all of them have had Lambs by near 50 Ewes. If this not owing to the prodigious drowth last year from July to October, I can't tell to what to impute it. Note: I had large fields of Clover opened to them in the drowth and it had such an affect on my Cattle as to make them dung plentifully and are very strong and I always expected drye weather the best for

---

[13] Spirit of Mindererus is diluted acetic acid neutralized with ammonia. It was used as a stimulant or applied locally for bites and stings of venomous insects and reptiles.

[14] Sal ammoniac is a salt found in hot countries and was used as an aperient for all kinds of obstructions.

sheep. The Ram indeed may be old but he was well kept all the winter before. I must trye and change him and see what effect young rams have on breeding. I have 2 very fine ones yeaned last april. These I intend to turn on land though Old Ram shall be Cut in the Summer.

We have sown only 31 bushels oats which if my directions of 4 bushels to an acre will amount to better than 7 acres. I am greatly surprized at the behaviour of my threshers. I had a Stack of oats without doors that must needs have been very tough and though it was not near half the dimensions of my mow within nor higher than the Eves of my barn when my mow was up to the wind beams yet out of the stack they got 918 bushels and out of the mow only ♌ [15] (Character Algebraic), which is in no proportion. I examined the straw and there is scarce a head that has not half the grain left in it. They have been severely whipped day by day. They have all encouragement given them but they are such Villains that they will not thresh them cleaner so that I intend to thresh the straw that is left over again. These were the first oats housed. Had no rain upon them from the Cutting before they were housed and therefore could not be so much shattered as the last Cutting and easyer to thresh, but they hear others don't thresh so much and the farmer from Mr. Wormeley's, I am certain, when he comes up is always inculcating this injury to me so that I must send the wench he comes after up to Bull run, for I see I shall do nothing here if he has opportunity of stealing up. I observe negroes tyre with the Continuance of the same work so that I will double their Number next year and make it quickly off hand and then perhaps they will do better, for they certainly threshed Cleaner and as much when they began as they do now.

Small pox man 19 days from his Eruptions. All his Scabs etc. gone these three or four days and he perfectly well only kept up to Purifye him.

MARCH 1757

1. *Tuesday.*

'Tis now my usual time for observing on my Crops of Wheat on the ground. I am of opinion this last month is the most pernicious month in the whole Year to a farmer that Cultivates low stiff lands for if it proves drye the harsh and suddain changes from heat to severe frosts do evidently kill great part of his wheat on the Ground and if it proves wet as this has been to an

---

[15] The exact meaning or origin of this symbol is unknown. From the context of the sentence one might conjecture that it stands for 1,500.

excessive degree then his Land naturally spews by the rapidness of the Frosts and thousands of roots are destroyed by them as soon as the Sun grows warm, which is now my Case although I thought to ballance this inconveniency by sowing thicker than Common, but I am affraid that will barely do. However I perceive I shall make some amends by strength, for the dung land wheat seems to be getting into a pretty tollerable Verdure. As to the Cultivation or manuring by Pea vines which is so much recommended in books of husbandry I much question whether I shall ever trye that method again. I tended full 10 acres that way on Peas last year and then chopped and plowed in their vines wich were very rank and sowed my wheat early, but it looks but poorly in Comparision of the dunged ground. However I won't call it a fair tryal for although the pea dressing was a pritty good one yet I did not think in plowing it came up to what the dressing by tending to tobacco is. Note: I wish I had laid all my land this year down in 4 bout ridges. It would have Suited the wet weather better. Began this evening to turn my dung at my house. Sent 3 hands to help my son and Scour his oat field ditches and watch them for this year's Crop.

2. Wednesday.

Oats sown to this day 66½ bushels which is better than 16 acres at 4 bushels to the acre.

This day my Fork overseer came to give me notice of a Sick Cow which is the 2d of his Cattle taken in the same way. The 1st was a Steer that had been fattening and turned out because I found I should not want him. The ailment at first appeared like a pouch in the hollow of the lower jaw Just above the joyning of the teeth socket. From thence it spread up to each eye and Ear and the Creature attended with a prodigious itching that made him rubbed the hair off. A Salaver dribbled from his mouth very frothy and Slimy and there was a frequent likking with his tongue which fretted of his hair. I did not hear of it till he had one Jordan to bleed it, on which it instantly dyed. In oppening of it there was a great deal of Yellow waky jelly about the head and in the throat. This Cow he says was but just taken as he came here but when I went to see it I am sure it must have been so a day or two. I ordered a knife to be thrust through the pouch and then came out a great deal of thin Yellow matter. I entered a trowel of bacon Rhind but the Creature was so far gone that although it occasioned a great discharge yet it dyed swelled all over. 'Twas very observable that this Creature never was penned but having brought a very fine calf about 3 weeks before was Put into a Shed open below. There certainly came from her an effluvium that alarmed the other Cattle for 'twas with great difficulty that we could keep them from coming to the place she was in. About

4 years agoe when Ben Smith was my overseer I had 22 cattle taken in the same manner to all appearance, but it being immediately discovered and the [t]rowel timely inserted they all recovered. 'Twas then called the Watery Murrain and not improperly, I believe, for there constantly gluted from the Bowels yellow fetid water.

3. *Thursday.*

And that year I observe was remarkable for being Cold and very wet even till the Month of April when this distemper raged amongst many cattle. I have ordered mine to be all tarried on the ropes. I have been this year very unlucky at this Fork quarter. 1 creature dyed Early gored to death; another swelled in the body and dyed in November. 2 oxen Got into a hole in the Creek and was drowned and now these 2 make in all 6. Yet they are in very great heart and have plenty of food.

Sowed this day 23 bushels oats which make the quantity sown 89½ bushels. They appear thick sown.

4. *Friday.*

Mr. Garland[16] surveyed my Stone house field and the field at the Sasafras bottom. The stone house field contains of tendible land some what better than 47 acres so that when wet and that in Tobacco each quarter will have 23½ acres which at 3 foot and ¼ to a tobacco hill makes 96,914 hills which is too short a quantity, so that at such times care must be taken that they get about their quarters at least 18,086 hills as there are 10 hands and the overseer at each place. We have divided this field by stakes stuck in the ground where we are to begin to Cowpen next week for next year tobacco after this. An acre is 4,124 hills at 3¼.

The Sasafras field holds now only 41½ acres so that when this cropped in tobacco there will want 57,954 hills so that some other piece of Land ought to be joyned to it, for it will be at least 28,977 hills short at each planta[tion?] of 10,000 per head allowing for the overseers' share and ½.

Oats sowed to day are 102 bushels which should be more than 25 acres at 46 the acre, but I am afraid he has sowed near 5 as we make but 41 acres in it.

5. *Saturday.*

We are still turning the dung at the house and they will not finish before monday 12 o'clock, which will make 5 days compleat with 5 hands, but three of them are my runaways who I have been obliged to make work in Chains.

---

[16] Probably William Garland (d. 1766), surveyor of Richmond Co., who did several surveys of Landon Carter's land. Some of them are in the Sabine Hall Col.

There is a very great quantity of Dung and better. It smells well, as the farmers call it. I believe next year if I live so long I shall contrive to do this work more expeditiously the way I have always thought on, but in this as well as all other projects I have gone upon I have always been willing to see how things would turn out before I engaged myself in too much expense about them and, having now experienced the great advantage farming has been of to my Lands as well as profitable to my self by making good reasonable Crops of tobacco, wheat, and Oats when I could hardly make corn before, I intend to put my Cowyards into good order after the following manner.

A line of Cowstalls double so as to hold 20 head of Cattle and a Crib between that each may feed by itself and from the Outer posts of these stalls I intend to raise a roof so that the food as well as the Creatures will be sheltered from the rains and snows and from the piercing winds which I imagin will be equall to any food I can give them. These stalls shall be raised with earth a foot above the level of the yard and a causeway much like the hacks of a brick yard shall be carryed all round. These stalls shall be Constantly littered and cleaned out every monday and the litter thrown into the spaces between the stalls of the Raised hacks which shall be also strewed with straw after every rain and every morning after the Cattle are turned out of their stalls. They shall be drove Gently about in these spaces and then turn out to browse about for the Conveniency of making these to all my yards as some of them will be moveable, Pent to suit the grounds I am to manure. I propose to have the lovering only thetched and the whole made so as they can be taken to pieces and carryed to the next year's ground.

Levelled down with my hoes a piece of Old Corn field that I turn out to sow in oats and I think if it does not rain before they are sowed they may be well enough Covered to bring a good Crop and I do assert that oats want no other Cultivation but to be well covered but not too deep. My experience teaches me that a hardy, swardy Land just turned in is better than twice or thrice plowing the same Land but I know who Combat this. However let them make more Oats than I do to an Acre and I use no other method. Two years ago I broke up about 60 acres of old worn out Corn field and made it very fine. It proved a very drye year so as the oats grew and came in with only one shower the Crop was not much indeed, but of the Scattered oats that year, which I only harrowed in July the same year and fed down all the winter, I got above 100 of large Cart loads of good hay the next, very tall and well set, and I should have saved them for a Crop, but I had too many growing in my farm and could not mow them had they stayed to ripen, so I took the spare opportunity and made them into hay.

6. *Sunday*.

Rained great part last night. The Ground again a float. A very hard wind this morning. The weather Cleared up with a hard Northwest at 7 o'clock in the morning that blew down all our fences every where. The rains that we have had now near two months together are not only very frequent, for the most part twice a week and some times all the week, but they fall in prodigious quantitys so that our low grounds have been too wet to move in and our high lands so sobbed and miry that it was impossible to work them. I have been 10 days with hard labour getting in a few oats and have done but little and I am affraid broke the hearts of my horses although they now eat double what they ever had before and have done so these two months. Yesterday I was levelling an old corn field and though it was upon a very visible declivity yet I found the earth could but just crumble and in many places miry, and last week was the best weather we have had this winter. I mention all these things that I may see in the end whether 'tis a fault in husbandry or accidents of weather that disappoint my expectations. Tomorrow was to have been a general day for turning my dung every where but now I must go all hands to putting up my fences.

7. *Monday*.

The destruction made in my fencing by yesterday's Puff of wind is much greater than I imagin. At my Riverside plantation there is near two days' hard work to repair and in my Farm I am certain 'twill take as much time, but Watts's plantation is better off. The reason, I suppose, is the shelter of the woods. This year's and last year's hard gales makes me think I shall at last be obliged to take to Chestnut posts and rails, for no other fencing seems to standing but what is well drove into the Ground. Note: my Wattled ground down more.

Watts is turning his dung. It seems to be very short and good but not thick in the field. I thought they had littered fast enough but now I fear to the Contrary. We are obliged to double our plows. The ground is to wet and tough.

Just now I examined my drained marshes and I find I am under a necessity of some improvement, for the Common trunks doe not discharge the water from these prodigious wet spells fast enough for the time of year and the basons at the lower part of them to contain the water that falls into the meadow get so quickly full that we are under a necessity to provide them a discharge, which I see can't be done through the doors because they have no good foundation to joyn wood Work. I am therefore contriving to empty the basons by the side of the Canals but so as not to admit of any Communication between them, for should that be the case the water will naturally run into one another and of Course the Canals as they take the runs at the head and must be discharging, every low tide will fill the basons. The method to be effect is as follows:

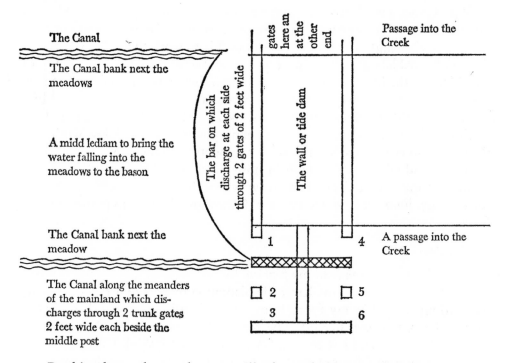

By this scheme the trunk gates will take up fraim and all 11 feet, that is

For the two end posts:	2 feet	Note: the division between
For the three gates:	6	the bason gate and the
For the division between the bason gate		trunk gates are to joyn
and the Canal gates:	2	well to the Canal bank and
For the Post between the trunk gates:	1	be well plank double and
	11.	rammed within.

EXPLANATION:

The numbers 1, 2, 3 are the gates where the water enters the cistern or conduit. Here the trunk gates are to open within the Conduit. Numbers 4, 5,

6 are the gates discharging the water and open outwards. The cross work is made to hold Flood gates to shut down occasionally which I have found necessary on great Spring tides. They who choose to work pieces of a lesser square in scantling will shorten the wedth of the fraims in proportion to the dimensions of their posts.

A side draft of the before mentioned gates Explained:

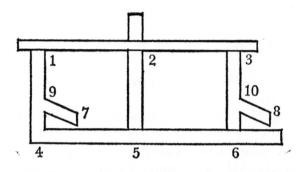

1, 2, 3 are two side Cap sills, their length as wide as the wall or tide dam. 4, 5, 6 are two mudd sills two feet longer than the Cap sills. Into these cap and mudd sills are ten notched three posts—1/4, 2/5, 3/6, long enough to answer from the bottom of their Canal, which ought to be even with the very lowest of low water, to the top of your tide wall. 7, 8 are trunk gates of which there should be 6, three playing or opening into the Conduit and three opening into the Creek, although only two can be here represented, this being only a side view. Besides the posts mentioned above there are to be a proper Number of 4 inch studds tenonted in to the Cap and mudd sills for the Conveniency of nailing the plank to to secure the work from blowing up, for the fraim is to be set in the main land for the sake of a foundation. The end mudd sills described in the first draft are to tenon into these side sills to be 11 foot from out to out into these end sills, their tenons, one post to divide the two Canal gates and two small ones at such a distance as is before described for the dividing the bason gates and the Canal gates, which are to be double planked. And these posts all head in Cross Cap sills 11 foot long from out to out. The trunk gates, 8, do all shut down 6 inches below the Conduit floor for which purpose the mudd sills on the side next the creek are all cut down 6 inches and two feet from the end and on this 2 foot is a sort of a platform to prevent the water's burrowing as it runs out. The floor of the Conduit should be nailed down in 2 inch rabbits cut in all the mudd sills and a Sufficient Number of Sleepers laid level with the side rabbits Cross wise.

THE SCANTLING

2 Mudd sills for the sides the wedth of the tide wall and 2 feet longer 8 square.

2 end sills long enough to fraim 11 foot from out to out or less if the discharge of water is not expected to be very great. This should gove[r]n for then the gates instead of 2 feet may be but 18 inches wide or still less, 8 square.

8 posts the higth of the Canal from the bottom to the top of the tide dam Square 6 inches.

6 ditto ditto for dividing the bason trunks from the Canal trunks. These need be only Studds 4 by 3.

2 Cap sills 12 feet long 8 square. 4 Cross ditto two feet wider than the end sills Square 6 inches.

4 Bridge Pieces to answer the Cross cap sills 6 square and Lower sleepers the wedth of the end mudd sills. 32 studds the higth of the side post these need be only 3 square. Plank not a great deal.

This will be called Costly doings because the work should be well done, and, if we consider that this will be also draining the meadow and what advantages will arise from such rich lands in the power of water always, I don't think it a great deal, and without some such Contrivance I am satisfyed it cannot be done. We may trye one fraim for a year and if at a middling diameter such as 9, 12 or 14 inches for the gates and if we find that answers the other Canal may go on discharging out of a Common trunk.

8. *Tuesday.*

Yesterday we had a fine day and every prospect for good weather but at 8 at night without wind it overcast and rained in the night and this morning.

Betty Oliver, who was thought to be on the Recovery a little, has relapsed this weak and continues to return into all her old Symptoms which are severely Hysterical. She took a week vomit last night by Dr. Flood's orders, it brought off much Yellow bile, and drank wine whey with Cammonile Flowers[17] infused in it to work it and after it was done some wine and water to strengthen her. She said it gave her great ease in her stomach and fell a Sleep.

Samson was left a week agoe and better by Dr. Flood. Took all his

---

[17] Camomile or chamomile flowers are the flower heads of the plant *Anthemis nobilis* with properties due to a volatile oil, a camphor, and a bitter principle. Used in coughs and spasmodic infantile complaints.

medicine. I wrote the Doctor a Complaint he made about his throat and that I thought his fevers had not left him but perhaps this would be the case for some time. He wrote me word that he believed he'd recover with out any more medicin. Therefore I left off going to see him but sent him victuals punctually and I was always told he was clear of a fever and a great deal better till yesterday curiosity led me to see him and I think him much worse. His fever still high although without any Complaint but much weaker and this morning the same. A moisture over him but it does not seem as if it came naturally from his pores for the flesh is drye beneath and had a great soarness all within him. I have ordered him a vomit for no Doctor can I get to him. Flood is gone to Corotoman[18] from Court yesterday. I sent him word of it yesterday but he said he could not come. Therefore I must trye my self.

9. *Wednesday.*

Betty Oliver mended all day yesterday and was distracted for an Opiate last night. I deceived her with wine and brown sugar water. She slept well till midnight and then was Siezed with an ague and fever, a new Symptom not before discoverable in her disorder from beginning to ending. If this should not have been a rigor I shall hope the disorder is terminating into an inter-mittant but then the ague is to me a demonstration of obstructions in the Hepatic duct and I suppose we shall see some discharge upwards or down-wards of green bile. She goes on with Flood's hysteria medicine.

Samson better, I think, today. His vomit yesterday brought off much viscid Phlegm and a powerfull sweat which I hope has opened the pores. I endeavoured to keep this up by weak wine diluters and twice threw in a Spoon full of rattle snake decotion. His sweat continued all night and till 9 this day. His flesh feels cooler and his pulse not so quick.

My turning of dung has been interrupted three day by the blowing down of my fences and now by the rain and I can't finish plowing nor harrowing in what Oats I have sowed for the rain. As to dung making I now can positively pronounce this rule to be observed. The Pens ought to be very large at least 40 yards Square for every 60 Cattle. It is not only evident by the difference of the goodness and quantity of the dung but also rational, for although all the dung and the stall of the Cattle in a small square would seem to make the litter richer yet when we consider they by that means make it miry and the necessity of laying more litter greater we shall find that it will grow so thick and compact as not to rott or shorten the Straw a bitt which has been this year's

[18] Corotoman was the home plantation of Robert "King" Carter in Lancaster Co.

case. In the large pen there was a much greater quantity of litter spread and yet not thick but it was all trod short, but in the small pen the same quantity of cattle, the litter was as green as it was when put in and this is owing to the necessity there is in the small pen of the Cattle standing still and of coarse lyable to be gored by each other and in the large they travel about drop their dung etc. every where and lye all about so that they expend the same quantity or more of litter and have it well trod which is one good step to rotting it. And though we may be fond of the dung and Urin of Creatures yet if we can get rotten vegetables we get the same. We get what makes those salts in their dung, their bodys being only the distillers and affect the putrefaction the sooner; so that I say the salts of the same number of Cattle is in the large pen added to a greater quantity of rotten Vegetables and in the lesser 'tis thrown on a smaller quantity not rotten.

I lookt into my wheat manured with pea vines last year and find it all near killed. The reason is the vines did not rot soon. Kept the ground light and as the Farmers call it Frowy and then the rains and Frosts destroyed the roots of the wheat. This is the reason they choose not in England to sow wheat on Clover sward till it is well rotted and the soil is made Compact again.

This day tallow became the topick of Conversation and out of 7 grass beeves and three fatten ones that were allowed to be as fat as need to be there has only been produced 26 pounds so that my house keeping goes on finely. I sold Dr. Flood 2 beaves out of the same stall that neated me £10.13/2.

10. *Thursday.*

Rain yesterday, All last night and this day till 2. Prodigious wet before but now miry.

Betty Oliver disappoints all our hopes, a Cold Rigor siezed her again, and is thought to be a dying. Samson easy but pulse quick yet and low. He [is] very week but I am in hopes mending. Look Cheerfull in the face and his muscles not so flat as two days agoe. Neither is his flesh hot as before. The weight of a backwoods beef: 414 pounds, tallow 38 pounds.

13. *Sunday.*

Oats sown in the Old Cornfield, 16 bushels. Betty Oliver dyed 3 days agoe.

14. *Monday.*

Go from home in order to attend the Assembly but met an account of its Prorogation till the 28th of April.

27. Sunday.

Returned home this day having taken this Opportunity of Visiting the Gloucester Gent[19] and Mr. Ralph Wormeley.

It has been almost one intire rainy Spell whilst I was down and yet low as those lands are things appear incomparably fine such is the Prodigeous richness of the land all along in that Neck from Mr. Warner Lewis's[20] to Mr. Francis Willis[21] and along that prodigeous level Neck. The sight of these lands makes me quite sick of my own heavy stiff white Clay. However by dint of a little Cleaner husbandry I find I am able to follow them with the Corn fan and manure.

As it was impossible for much work to be done here since I went, I need only say they seem not to have attempted it.

28. Monday.

Mr. Willis and Mr. Carter of Nomony[22] here, the Former excessively surprized at my quantitys of Manure.

29. Tuesday.

Rain at Northeast in very great Plenty. *Nota Bene.* This moon changed on Saturday and I think the old Observation is a good one if it comes in 7 year it is too soon. Went this day with Frank Willis to Mr. Carter's Nomony.

30. Wednesday.

Excessive hard rain all night.

31. Thursday.

Fair but

APRIL 1757

1. Friday.

a prodigeous prospect for rain and from Northeast.

[19] Probably John Page of North End.

[20] Warner Lewis (b. 1720), planter in Gloucester Co. and son of Councilor John Lewis, married Eleanor Bowles, daughter of James Bowles of Maryland and widow of Col. William Gooch, son of Governor William Gooch.

[21] Francis Willis (b. 1690), planter and son of Henry Willis, was burgess for Gloucester Co., 1727–40, 1745–49.

[22] Robert Carter of Nomini Hall (1728–1804), planter and son of Robert Carter II, was a member of the Council, 1764–76. An excellent biography is Morton, *Robert Carter of Nomini Hall.*

2. *Saturday*.

The Skye very heavy and the air very Cold so that we shall in all probability have another small deluge. We can do no kind of work to any advantage. If we hill our Corn ground, they are beat flat and hard the next day. If we level old Corn ground for oats 'tis made a quaggmire before we can sow and then the earth is too hard to harrow and Cover the oats in. The ground is too wet to hill our tobacco grounds again, the Wheat is too miry to Roll and all this when the Season is so far advanced as makes it almost too late for the works that are still to be done. Rain all this evening till near Sunset. At midnight thunder and lightning and a very heavy rain till day.

3. *Sunday*.

Rain, thunder and lightning from 6 in the morning and a very heavy Atmosphere till 12. The afternoon bids as fair for fine weather as any day since January and I shall rejoice if it Continues.

My boys Samson and Ralph, who were taken sick the 10th of February, are not yet well, the former but Just recovering a little and never from the first clear of a fever, this latter still as poor as death and always in a quiet fever. They have different disorders: the former had at first an inflamatory fever; the latter I always concluded was attended with worms but never voided one till about a fortnight past there came two from him. 'Tis doubtfull as to him. I have again put him under a Coarse of Othiops Mineral[23] and Rhubarb.[24]

4. *Monday*.

All overcast. Clouds enough for another month's rain. I much question whether any corn will be planted in the Country in the Common time.

I began to sow oats sooner by a fortnight than I ever did and I allotted only 40 acres in my Farm for them of which I plowed up 30 the first fortnight and sowed, and I have not been able now for two months to break up the remaining 10 acres so wet has the Ground been and so Constant the rains. The rest of my oats I intended to sow in a Corn field I had turned out, but these I could only work in Patches and never one day could I sow the ground the next day that I had levelled the day before, and as to harrowing it has always been so wet that I fear the project of sowing old Corn Ground will turn to very little, although in any Common year it must needs be a good scheme both on account of levelling the ground turned out and in a Crop of Oats, for they I

---

[23] Ethiops mineralis was a dark-colored medicine prepared by grinding mercury and sulphur into a black powder. It was used for worms and recommended as "infallible against the Itch."

[24] Rhubarb or rheum was a popular tonic astringent or, in large doses, a purgative.

find by experiment yield well and always fit the ground the sooner for swading.

Sent Guy off to fetch up McGinnis from Northumberland.

5. *Tuesday*.

Still very Cold and Cloudy and a very great probability for more rain. George Garland[25] came this day to assist in making my trunk Gates but, Colo. Thornton pressing me to go to see him, I was obliged to send him back to his Master till my return.

11. *Monday*.

Go To Town. Sarah goes to work at Watts's.

JUNE 1757

5. *Sunday*.

I left W[illia]msburg where I had been ever since the 14th April and then got violent ill and continued better and was there near 3 weeks. The assembly broke up the wednesday following, that is the 9th of the month.

8. *Wednesday*.

I got home and found I had lost 5 negroes, vizt, Barbadoes Nan, Mary Lubber, Carpenter Ralph's boy Ralph, George's boy George and Nassau's son Nat, besides Ralph, [his] Wife and two of her children that dyed before I went and Betty Oliver.

As to worke, not a Corn field touched but with the Ploughs. All the time since I went spent in planting the Corn and making the tobacco hills and that in ground before plowed and spreading the dung. 'Tis said the rains were a great hindrance and that Matheny's people were very ill, sometimes 4 down at a time, but Watts had No such hindrance and yet he is in the same condition.

Very fine corn indeed but in great danger of being totally ruined with weeds.

13. *Monday*.

Went to Dr. Flood's for my health and stayed till thursday but rather worse. Violent rains fell in the time which began Monday night and held ever since.

[25] George Garland (d. 1798) was probably the son of William Garland the surveyor. A Richmond Co. resident and voter during the 1770s, he was obviously apprenticed to one of Carter's neighbors at this time.

19. Sunday.

Still cloudy after a whole week of rain. My corn fields quite Miry. No working and weeds and grass above the corn. Myself very little better. Cough returned again. Tobacco all planted tuesday last. My mill in great danger of going away and [I] see tumbling dams are dangerous things in great rains because they never vent water equal to the Increase. Therefore I prefer flood gates and will make them as soon as I can.

24. Friday.

Smart rain this day. We are over done with it and my overseer Watts as foul in his corn fields as can be. His hands and he are so dissatisfyed with each other that neither do any thing. I was obliged to help him with two more plows this day.

25. Saturday.

The oats only harrowed in in the Corn field, I find, are good in those places where they were sowed and harrowed in before the rains fell, but when the ground had been hardened by the rains before they were covered in they are not near so good.

My tobacco now begins to start and had I my worke so far before hand as to make love to it I should not fear turning out a fine Crop, but my wheat to cut and corn fields not yet out nor won't be these 4 or 5 days.

26. Sunday.

'Tis necessary to take notice of this day because it is full cold for any prudent man to keep a fire and I wish it don't introduce many of those severe Fall distempers we had last year. Nay if it continues what we now have it will be bad enough. Should the ground worm rise, as 'tis the weather he delights in, tobacco crops will also be short, for 'tis very late to replant and numbers of those that would can't, there being scarcely a plant about in this neighborhood. The flyes the last rain eat them all up.

29. Wednesday.

There fell a rain very severe in my Corn field and no where Else and I may say it could have fallen no where so improperly. The low cover that had been water sobbed this month and more was just got drye and turning green was again over done and none turned as yellow as a kite's foot. Our working of it is of little service but to remove the weeds from choaking it.

Begann this day to mow my oats. The Crop I believe will [be] but indifferent. They were first plowed almost in mudd, then sown when the ground was mere mire and the long rains after prevented our Rolling them, which I reckon is always 1/4 of a crop difference, and Cold rain since have all contributed to injure us so that we shall have none shew this year. Thus the Farmer is nothing without weather. Very Cold morning and evening. Neither corn nor tobacco grows.

30. *Thursday.*

Began this morning to reap with but very few reapers, so many Complaining of last year's reaping. I am affraid it will be a heavy Job.

JULY 1757

6. *Wednesday.*

Rain every day since the 2d of the month which retards all work. Our tobacco foul and can't weed in it above half a day together. Our corn although wed out yet so over done with rain that it can't grow but looks very yellow, even the first that was wed. The ground under it is mere mortar. A hard rain this day, no reaping hardly and every day obliged to be turning and drying what is down.

7. *Thursday.*

The poor Farmer must always feel the weather and rejoyce when it is good and be patient when it is unreasonable. Severe rains every day and in harvest time so that we can't work and tobacco grounds seem to be turning to meadows.

8. *Friday.*

The Weeds have every advantage of us possible. They out grow us and seem to flourish on our removing them. Oats a poor Crop occasioned by Constant wet that have killed the roots and made them ripen without any heads. Add to this our necessity in Sowing them when the ground was mere mortar. I see the small tobacco plants by being too much loosened in the hill in tearing the grass from them are greatly obstructed in growth and a piece of ground wed a fortnight past looks smaller than the tobacco by it which is not wed and before weeding it was the best.

14. *Thursday*.

Now drye and except one little shower it has been so a week. Matheny begun to lay by his Corn. Excessive hot. My tobacco all cleaned out. The excessive rains before and this heat after does not as yet suit tobacco. It grows but only here and there. We have only topt a little.

Finished my wheat in my Farm this day. Exactly a fortnight since we began. Only 8 reapers excepting one day or two and those 10. We have cut as much ground as last year but have not filled so much room in the barn. We had a new seeds man who could not be made to sow so thick (the life of Farming) and the winter's rain and frost killed abundance and the summer's rain washed all the coat of the roots off that they carry their proper nourishment to the grain. Their racks full in the blooming time another very bad thing and we have really stowed Closer. However we promise our selves by the room we have filled 1,000 bushels at least.

18. *Monday*.

Our tobacco ground this year is all very stiff land and I fear we shall not receive great profit from notwithstanding it was well manured. The prodigeous rains at the time it was hilled baked the ground excessively. They were turned also when so wet as to be mere mortar or else they could not have been turned in time. They were planted in a very wet season. They were also first wed in one and we have been since obliged to hoe them over but the tobacco grows very irregular. Abundance of Hornworm, Ground worm, Web worm and bud worm. I last year plowed my tobacco between the plants, with my 5 hoed plow and kept the ground light, but this they last and though I run the common fluke plow through this left the hills as hard as rocks on each side.

19. *Tuesday*.

Lucy[26] taken with a headach and fever about 10 o'clock.

20. *Wednesday*.

I ordered her a vomit. Very brisk all day.

[26] Lucy Carter, second daughter of Landon Carter and Elizabeth Beale, married in 1775 William Colston (1744–81) of Hornby Manor in Richmond Co., son of Travers Colston (1714–51) of Exeter Lodge, Northumberland Co.

21. *Thursday.*

A little before 10 cold in her hands and sleepy. This a kind of ague.

We have been on this plantation in a manner drye above a fortnight, only a small Shower or two in the time, but last night and this morning a heavenly rain but perhaps it may continue. If so it may be too much. The earth is Covered with water. We are really overdone with rain. Every place a float.

24. *Sunday.*

The ground was made so wet by the last rain that we have not been able to weed a plant of tobacco and the weeds with the first weeding being still alive the tobacco, together with the prodigious sobbing of the roots in some, drowned and a good deal turned yellow and only here and there a very drye spot has grown. Yellowness I find is occasioned by extremes either wet or drye for the tobacco turned yellow last year when there was no rain. Therefore it is a defect in vegetation and not the quality of the weather on the leaf.

Rain plentifully this day and a great probability of more, so that we low ground are like to pay for it. Many plants are lapped, a great Symptom of drowning. Am I always to be thus unlucky? I can truely [say] that from 1749 to this year I have not had one tollerable seasonable year.

25. *Monday.*

Rain again, mere april Showers. No working at any thing to Purpose.

26. *Tuesday.*

Prodigeous rain this night and one Clap of Thunder near us that had three distinct reports although the first seemed to be instan[tan]eous with the lightning. I imagined there must have been what they call a thunder bolt or ball of fire discharged in the air for by the report it appeared to contain three several explosions and each of them a Crash of a frightfull nature.

28. *Thursday.*

My method of introducing the English husbandry with the tobacco planting now seems to be exceeding good and has only this inconveniency, that it frequently happens that the divisions of 50 acres manured each year cannot be land of equal nature but every where it will be stiff and light so that in the tobacco crop it is evidently discovered that the same seasons nor manuring will not suit in the same field every where but tobacco will grow very unequal. I speak not of this year for we have been constantly mud and mire so that it must have been more care than negroes can be persuaded to to have prevented spoiling the plant either by doubling the root or pressing it too hard or planting too shallow, which are all great faults and often the occasion of a raggid Crop, but in other years it will be difficult to remedy this evil. However this we assert that either such land must not be tended at all in tobacco or, if it is, this is as likely a way to make it rich and profitable as any and although we don't always come up in Crop to the planter who culls his land yet by our grain we more than equal him and profit and 'tis evident that our lands run better into grass after such a method than theirs and of Course our creatures will improve and in time add to our profit. Had I been at home I would have prevented a great deal of the raggidness of my Crop by planting after the season was over and the land a little drye. But they followed the old way and strucke a line and sometimes the plant was plaistered in.

30. *Saturday*.

Finished laying by Corn only this day at these home quarters but not so at the Fork and David Morgan's. Wet weather has many excuses but one there is that is not pardonable, that is we never begin soon enough. I am always abroad at the time and I never can be reconciled to the trifling between March and the weeding of Corn. The fields are very good but then tobacco [in ?] a meadow Strong ground alone must support us.

AUGUST 1757

1. *Monday*.

We have been every hand endeavouring to get the weeds out of my tobacco but 'tis to no purpose for no weather kills them and 'tis now all of it to do again. The crop to tobacco would be good but it cannot for the weeds and rain which produced Cold nights. This evening a great rain indeed for more than half an hour.

4. *Thursday*.

Reflecting this day on the most effectual method to raise a tyde bank so as to have it in a little time solid and usefull to its intended purpose. I considered the impossibility of carrying earth from the land in many places and to supplye this, which is certainly very proper but very costly, I proposed to let the plain sedge be the base of the bank and in proportion to the weight of water to be kept out to raise 2 banks with the turf cut out of the marsh and by carrying these banks in strait all lines according to the necessary distance before mentioned to be governed by the weight of Water. When these turf banks are raised to the highest their own weight will bear with the turf outwards then at low water to provide large wide tubs to lye on some stage to float fill these tubs with the floaty mudd with scoups wet, [which] may be well done at low water. Then as the tyde rises conduct them to the banks and ladle them in. By this means the finer water will filtrate through the bottom or side, and the mudd consolidated which I do imagin will answer the end proposed. And when this is hard then are the bankers to go on raising the banks til evident this mud will harden because no roots in it whereas what is taken out of the ditches after the first stratrem of turf is off being nothing but mere pete it never unites and when rotten becomes mere ashes and blows or floats away. This to be tryed.

8. *Monday.*

The first easy rain that I think we have had this year and I do expect we shall receive great benefit from it.

It has been a very Aguish Season. Many of my people have been ill and are dayly falling down with. In my house my children Judith and Lucy have had their severe spells but I thank God they are well. Bobby[27] taken on thursday and has had a fever every day since. He had a natural purging which one would have imagined would have carryed it off but neither that nor a vomit which worked plentyfully upwards and downwards has done it. Neither do I believe anything will but the barke. It has been more usefull this year than common. Sukey taken ill yesterday, vizt, Sunday. Took a vomit this morning, 18 grains Ipecacuana, which brought off 4 vomits, 3 bilious, and two stools very much so and thin. Her fever appeared to day much about the same time as yesterday and I am in hopes will neither be so high nor so long for she has risen without any headach and is huskier. A breathing sweat.

Many negroe Children have been ill with the ague and fever. I gave them all vomits but the fit did not abate and from a possibility of their being attended with worms I gave them each a purge of Pulvis Bazilicus according to their ages and the fits left them without any more except in one case to whom I was after obliged to give the barke.

---

[27] The exact identity of Bobby or Robin Carter is unknown. He may have been the son of Robert Wormeley Carter and Winifred Travers Beale, daughter of William Beale of Richmond Co., who were married the previous year and were living at Sabine Hall. If so, he was probably the "fine little Boy" who died at "about 18 months old" that Robert Wormeley refers to in his daybook on July 15, 1766. (*Va. Mag. of Hist. and Biog.*, LXVIII (1960), 312).

9. Tuesday.

Sukey's fever being to all out ward appearance quite oft, I gave her of Pulvis Bazilicus grains 13 in hopes to carry down some more of the bile that the vomit might have lossened but her fever coming on at 10 prevented it working and really either the nature of the fever was such or the jarring of this purge occasioned it; so that she continued for a long time exceeding uneasy. At 4 I ordered her a common Clyster which moved the purge so that she had 6 or 7 stools. Dr. Flood came here but gave her nothing then, imagining she would wear off the fever, and left her the

10. Wednesday.

in the morning with orders to have an account sent him that night which was done. The child's fever instead of lowering at night as usual rose and she continued burning and sweating all night and

11. Thursday.

this morning a high fever which rose till 10. Then she fell into a profuse sweat, a severe head ach and great uneasyness at Stomach. I dispatched a messenger to Dr. Flood and after that was gone the messenger of yesterday returned with Medicin for her. I knew not what they were but, observing some Symptoms of Convulsions in the Child and concluding from an imperfect taste there was both Castor and Valerian root[28] in them, I gave the Child a dose as proper Nervines. However at 30 past 11 a Severe fit came on. We gave her 15 grains Ipecacuana to breake the Phlegm that usually collects in such cases in the Stomach. As much of this was lost we gave 6 grains more and by the help of a feather got a large vomit of tough Phlegm. Her fever very high and yet her sweats large. I ordered Nervine, drops of castor, Hartshorn,[29] and Lavender[30] in tea. The vomit not working any more, I ordered a Lenient Clyster to open a passage downwards but this stayed up those passages being so Contracted by the Convulsive violence. Dispatch off another messenger for the Doctor to come to her. Note: Mrs. Carter[31] in a very sharp ague all the time she tended

[28] Valerian root comes from plants of the genus *Valeriana*. It is antispasmodic and gently stimulant to the nervous system and organs of circulation. In full doses it increases heart action and produces exhilaration; toxic doses result in diarrhea, vomiting, reduced sensibility, and mental disturbance. It was used particularly effectively in hysteria, convulsions due to worms, the coma of typhoid fever, and whooping cough.

[29] Hartshorn, or aqua ammoniae, was used as a stimulant.

[30] Lavender is a volatile oil from the flowers of *Lavandula vera*. It is aromatic, stimulant, and carminative, but it was used mainly as a flavor and an adjuvant to other medicines.

[31] Winifred Travers Beale, Mrs. Robert Wormeley Carter.

the Child. Robin has been ill ever since the 4th but this day seems to be clear of his fever. A Blyster was applyed to Sukey's neck at 12 o'Clock after her vomit.

It rained the 9th, 10th and this day and this night a great gust Southwest. Northwest, and North hard wind, some hail and a great deal of rain. Dr. Flood here.

12. *Friday.*

Sukey an Ague again from 9 to 10, then a fever and high. Rain all day and mostly very hard all the morning. Fairwell tobacco. 'By Tim.

14. *Sunday.*

Poor Sukey still very ill. Severe fevers almost constant. There seemed to be a Small intermission from a little after sunset till past 12 at night. Dr. Flood got down 4 doses of bark amounting Decoction and all to 1/4 of an Ounce, the decoction boyled with Valerian root, but her fever rose high at 9 this day and continues till this past 2, which is the time that on these days she used to grow a little Cheerfull but now she has both head ach and great Sickness at Stomach, a complaint she never had before and this is her 8th day.

Judy taken ill again, a bad ague and fever yesterday and the day before it was but slight. She took a purge of Dr. Flood's giving last night which workt her 7 or 8 times but it did lessen her fever.

15. *Monday.*

Began to mow my meadow the Second time. Grass high but mostly Coarse, much damaged by hoggs. Hard to mow. Very wet occasioned by the ditches being filled up.

Began to thresh wheat. Weather Cold enough for winter. Family very ill. Mrs. Carter severe and violent ague. Judy ague and Vomiting. Sukey for a while Cold but then temperature and better. Sukey mending all this evining and from 11.

16. *Tuesday.*

Judy her ague and fever severe by the Doctor's orders in her ague, which was attended with a vomiting, weake, tasteless chicken broth was given her in great quantitys which washed her stomack clear of abundance of bile Notwithstanding all her natural vomits and the doses given her. In the evening her fever went off and at night 4 dozes of the barke given her, 30 grains in a dose, and two spoonfulls of a strong decoction of barke with each dose at the distance of 2 hours. Before this barke she took in her fever some attemperating medicine and capivi.[32] We could get nothing down her with the least appetite. I affected it with ordering a hot rasher of boiled bacon in her room. This awakened her stomach as it were and after eating of that eat other things. My meadow will yield a fine crop notwithstanding the hogs in my illness have done it much damage.

17. *Wednesday*.

I thank God Judy has escaped her ague and fever, that is to say her usual period. My daughter Carter's hers also for a while and little Sukey travels out of her room. Only some patients with out and they not bad. Now drye again. Our ground much baked. Tobacco however grows a little.

21. *Sunday*.

Smart Thunder and much rain this Night. The Season still continues very sickly; my Children I thank God are all mending but then the rest of my indoors family are falling down continually and those without in mere gangs and now the disorders more violent. Agues stronger and the fevers more irregular. Few notwithstanding much evacuation by vomits, Purges and indeed constant sweating's ever come to a regular intermittant under 5 or 6 days. The bile discharged seems now to be thicker and more rancid, I suppose owing to the obstructions being longer continued by reason of the Cold evenings. I used chiefly the emetic wine. With some it brought off great quantitys of Green and Yellow bile upwards; with others it run altogether downwards owing to the bilious matter being quite loose. These were all harder to remove and not as yet without some purges and the bark.

22. *Monday*.

There have been sick:
At the Fork: Lame George, Juba, Rose twice.
At Mangorike:[33] Martha, Billy, Willoughby, Sarah, Mimah.
At Morgan's: Peg and Mooter.
At Matheny's: Sukey.
At Home: Nat, Tom, Sawney, Sam, Nassau, Winney, Bettsey besides my whole family except Johnny Carter.

I am affraid that my Crop of Wheat for this year is all nought, the flye weavil being all in it, and what little that is threshed begins to grow warm

---

[32] Cals capivi is a product of *Balsamum americanum*, which grows mostly in Brazil. A powerful balsamic, it was used as an internal cleansing agent and in the treatment of disorders of the breast.

[33] A tract of land in Richmond Co. given to Landon by his father.

although Spread thin. My Corn is merely infested with the large bats which is a sure sign that they are there for their food is such flyes that fill the air in Clear evenings and that there do so is pritty evident. There has been a remedy proposed for this farmer's Evil said to be sent into the Country by Mr. John Tucker from Barbadoes. It seems all a Farce to me and must be a thing started by one who knows not the nature of this animal or insect. It is never discovered to be in wheat till it has done its mischief and is flying away and is found so soon after reaping that it is almost a Certainty that they take place in the Ear, as it grows like unto the pea bugg which being a layer embrio is to be seen in the green pea a Small blackish speck and appears to be perforated through the pod. These are first eggs, then maggots, then flyes and before they get to that stage eat up the grain to a hull. Now how the branches or root of Sasafrass can affect those things so as to preserve the wheat I am a Stranger unless by affluvium and if so it should be mixed with the wheat as soon as reaped and stowed away with it in the mow or else it will do but little good but to those which are not come to maturity when it is threshed. I beleive nothing but grinding can do. Or not sowing any as many have now neglected to do.

Captain Wm. Brockenbrough told me that he saw a List shewn to him by the Governour of the Servants inlisted as Soldiers by Colo. P[hilip] L[udwell] for the Royall American Regiment[34] in which List he saw a receipt of the Colo. for £10 the man in which List he read Sir M. Beckwith's[35] man, Jonathan Beckwith's[36] man, Colo. Faunteleroy 1 man and others at the same rate and that he knew, Jno. Beckwith's cost only 2 pistoles, Colo. Faunteleroy's £3.10, Franklin's[37] 7 or 10, and Parker's[38] £7.10 and so of many others. I note this for enquiry.

23. *Tuesday.*

The Wet Year continues. A very hard, gusty rain this day. Capt. Brokenbrough and I settled Accounts. Ballance due to me per Ledger 12/4 if I have

[34] The Royal American Regiment was formed in 1756 for American service with American volunteers. An account of its origins and composition is in Stanley M. Pargellis, *Lord Loudoun in North America* (New Haven, 1933), 61–66, 110–11.

[35] Sir Marmaduke Beckwith (b. 1687), planter, baronet, and son of Sir Roger Beckwith of England, lived in Richmond Co., where he was county clerk, 1708–48.

[36] Jonathan Beckwith, planter and son of Sir Marmaduke Beckwith, married Rebecca Barnes, daughter of Richard Barnes and lived in Richmond Co.

[37] Perhaps Thomas Franklin, Richmond Co. resident who died in 1794, or John Franklin, King George Co. resident who died in 1776.

[38] Almost certainly Judge Richard Parker (1729–1813), lawyer and planter of Westmoreland Co. and son of Dr. Alexander and Susanna Parker of Tappahannock. He was King's attorney in Westmoreland, member of the Westmoreland Co. Committee of Safety during the crisis of 1775–76, and judge of the general court, 1788–1813. He married Elizabeth Beale of Richmond Co. in 1751.

not overcharged him in the money paid by Wm. Degges.[39] But if I have the over plus will bring me in his debt 11/8.

24. *Wednesday.*

Now 7 people down with the fever etc. of the Season but I hope none bad. Rain most of last night. Rain today. Very unlucky in every thing. My meadow hay now above half out which will be much injured. Tobacco near ripe that will be bruised and I fear drowned. A very Cold raw rain all this morning and likely to continue drizling past 12. Rain all the evening, wind little but perpetually changing.

25. *Thursday.*

Rained all night and till near Sun this morning. Rain from 6 all day.

The disorder in my out and in family still continues only there is a change in the Circumstances or rather Symptoms that attend it. Those which were taken the middle and last July were attended with plenty full vomitings and sharp Natural purgings of bile. The bile thin, the fever irregular but gave way without any thing more than a good cleansing of weak Chicken broth. Note: the weather very rainny and very hot.

Those in the beginning of August hard, sharp agues but neither vomited Nor purged. The bile thick. I used to these Vinum benedictum[40] and they all recovered without barke or bitters. Days very hot and wet; nights cold.

These now have sharp head achs, sometimes pains in both eyes and after a fit or two Severe agues which came not in the beginning. The bile Green and Yellow; fevers long, some to 24 hours and some to 36 hours. I used after the first or second fit Vinum benedictum and the next day but one after a strong purge Jalap[41] and where I did not purge the patient was long recovering and not without a good deal of barke with which I often gave Pulvis Valerian and Rattlesnakeroot. This I found loosened and Warmed the bile and gave it motion downwards. The Byle tough and fetid as rotten egg, and much of that particolour green Yellow and a bluish cast. Weather Cool and very wet indeed frequent rains.

Began to grind up my wheat made this year. Flower looks white.

26. *Friday.*

All night raining in the morning and likely to hold so this day at least.

[39] William Degges (d. 1761) was a small planter in Richmond Co.
[40] Vinum benedictum is a mild emetic wine used particularly in apoplexy.
[41] Jalap is from *Exogonium purga* and was used as a purgative.

Clouds broke at 9 and seems to incline to be fair. Sicke people coming in dayly. Barke now of very little effect notwithstanding they are both vomited and purged plentyfully.

27. *Saturday.*

Fair but Cloudy. Ground a bushel of new wheat this day and sifted the brand out. The flower weighed 37 pounds.

28. *Sunday.*

A very clear, fine day and cool with all. The more agreeable as it is the first day for a very great while that we have not been nursing the sicke. Some few are still expecting their fits of the fever but all are clear and I am in hopes will continue so at least for a while. Note: I was obliged to give the barke at last in very large doses, a drachm in a dose. This used to be the way formerly but the modern practice has introduced much smaller doses as equally effectual but this season the great relaxation of the Stomach etc. made it very necessary after the many large evacuations of the bile to brace as soon as might be and many were even then obliged to drinke three times a day a very strong bitter infusion of horehound[42] and Sentry[43] in Small beer, half a pint or near it at a time.

By the weight of a bushel of wheat ground yesterday without any toll taken out I found only 37 pounds clear of bran. Therefore this flour can't be sold under 19/ the hundred for 'tis clear by the following account I shall not make more than 3/ the bushel for wheat and be paid for grinding, Sefting, carrying to mill and to a landing and waste.

100 bushels at 37 pounds the bushel is 3,700 pounds at 10/ per contra is:		£18.10
100 bushels at 3/ is:	£15.	
1/8 for toll:	1.17/6	
Sifting 3,700 pounds at 6 per contra. At this rate a stout boy won't earn 8d per day:	18/6	
Loss on 3,700 in moving 3 per contra is 111 pounds at 10/ per contra is:	11/1¼	
	£18.7/1¼	
Ballance for carrying etc.	2/10¾	
	£18.10/	

[42] Horehound is derived from the leaves and tops of *Marrubium vulgare* and was used as a mild stomachic tonic and in large doses as a laxative.

[43] Centaury is any one of a group of small plants of the gentian family. An excellent bitter, it was used in the treatment of worms and as a diuretic.

I find this method of manuring tobacco grounds every year requires a greater labour than I thought in my lands, especially in that of this year which is very stiff. I only plowed it up in November and then it manured and hilled in April but I see in moist years this is not enough and I must endeavour to plow my Cowpens up in August and September and as this is at least 50,000 it may very Conveniently be hilled and lye mellowing all the winter, then in November to break up the remaining 150,000 and in March give it the tother plowing. It will then be fine and fit for the hilling and Manuring in April, and in the mean time in March early the Gang may give the Cowpens a turn. This shall be the Scheme and it seems to be most feasible and after the tobacco is planted then to run through it with my machine plow of 5 hoes by which means all the sides of each hill will be stirred as well as the middle of the rows.

29. *Monday*.

Yesterday's Sun has shewn how much the last rains have Injured the forward tobacco much spotted in Stiff land how much more so then in light. But a great deal.

This day again visited with sicke people. No less than 14 taken ill and but 2 relapses so that the blessing of yesterday was of but very short Continuance.

Note: the bushel of Wheat per Contra Serch yielded 34 pounds fine flower.

The price at 10/ will then be on 100 bushels 3,400 which is £17.

Wheat at 3/ is:	£15.
Therefore if this is sold only at 10/ toll:	1.17/6
we can't get 3/ nor near it the bushell.	
Sirching and sifting:	18/6
	£17.16

SEPTEMBER 1757

1. *Thursday*.

A very foggy morning, the first we have had this year. Note: the two last days in August were hot, close and smoky weather. Both Sun and moon looked red and hazy. Many persons very sick. There is no end to their bilious state. I am now obliged to repeat vomiting to many whose agues return after being in a manner quite well, and they discharge now large quantitys of green bile. I have began to trye dogwood bark[44] merely through necessity and I hope it will come in as a bitter to brace.

2. *Friday.*

Rain a little now and then. We still continue sickly and I do apprehend some change is forming in the Disorder of the Season. I have now Frank, Jamy and Brick house Nanny very ill. They were both taken as the rest and took vomits which workt as favorably as any and Purges two days after. Yesterday I heard they were both much mended and their fevers had left them, but not an hour after my inquiry I was alarmed that Jamy was dying. He had missed his fever 2 days and had walkt about. I found his pulse full but he was in such violent Pain that I could not get out of him where his Complaint lay. I concluded it must be some windy Attack and gave him some thing to warm his bowels on which he grew easy and eructed much and, as he had been taking dogwood bark in very small quantitys, a favourite medicine with some for the fever and ague, I conjectured there might have braced too soon and therefore order a Clyster. This brought away a plentyfull stool and he grew moist and then a fever arose which seemed not over high. He Slept well all night but complained of his head and stomach. I gave him in very small doses Valerian root, Rattlesnake and Salt tartar[45] to gard his nerves and throw off by a breathing sweat the remnants of the fever. He now has a good pulse but through great weakness is low spirited and I gave him wine foods. Nanny always complained of a pain in her neck, head and small of her back, a very frequent pain I found in others, but yesterday all was easy and no fever for two days. This morning she went and sat out of doors which I suppose might checke the disorder working off in breathing sweats and she was found with every pain violent, her flesh Cold but her pulse not low. I could not form to my self any Idea of this pain in the back after it had given way to the evacuations, therefore imagined it to be some touch of the gravel for which I gave rattlesnake 15 grains and Cals Capevi in loaf sugar with wine, and lest there might be an obstruction in the upper vessels I applyed a blister adding at the same time to her backe a plaister of Comfree root[46] just scented with Oil Junaper[47] and wait the event.

---

[44] Dogwood bark was a favorite medicine in Virginia for reducing fevers and agues.

[45] Salt tartar is derived from crude tartar. It was used in treating all kinds of obstructions and to "scour the Skin of Pimples, Freckles and Morphew."

[46] Roots of comfrey, a group of European plants of the borage family with rough leaves, were used as a strengthener and to congeal wounds.

[47] Oil juniper is derived from the berrylike fruit of the common juniper tree. It was used as a stomachic tonic, diuretic, and aphrodisiac.

Jamy and Nanny better this evening. The blister has releived her neck and her back is made easyer by the Plaister and Capevi etc. Jamy complained much this evening of a stoppage below at the joyning of his stomach and bowels and vomited some Phlegm. As this Complaint Continued I imagined the bark before mentioned had braced that part too much and that it was necessary gently to open that passage. For this reason I gave Rhubarb 20 grains, Cream tartar[48] 20 grains, Pulvis Sene[49] 6 grains with 4 grains Cinnamon as a Carector divided in two doses at 2 hours distance. He Slept well two hours after the first dose and waked perfectly easy of that complaint upon which I conjecture that bowel is opened and the next dose if necessary may bring down a stool. I can't but observe that these 2 patients were made worse by the Purges taken 2 days agoe although every body before them and that a large Number were greatly releived by them and some lost their fevers and notwithstanding this some late patients have been seized with purgings after their vomits even repeated so that I shall Conclude for while to forbear purging and let nature do this last which she had done very favorably in three or four that are now ill. Jamy about midnight had two easy motions and vastly mended.

3. *Saturday.*

Rain this day. Sick people all mended and well, only weak.

5. *Monday.*

Before day wind came to Northeast and rain and at day a great probability of Gust and so it continues. A good deal of tobacco on scaffolds cut down the 2d and 3d of the month. More Sicke people come in and so it has been every monday morning for near 3 weeks, but this peculiar to negroes who refuse to complain on Sundays because they look on that as holy day and don't care to be confined by physick let their Sickness. Rain all day and gusty.

6. *Tuesday.*

Wind a while at East. Great probability of the Clouds breaking but the Northeast took place again. Rain in smart mists. There is something in this weather resembling 1750. It held so off and on for 3 days then rained and blowed for 6 days Constant. I was obliged to take my tobacco off the scaffolds

---

[48] Cream of tartar is acid tartrate. It is nearly insoluble in water and was used as a diuretic and laxative.

[49] Pulvis senae or senna is a powder derived from the leaflets of *Cassia acutifolia* and *Cassia augustifolia* and was recommended as an excellent cathartic for children and infants.

although it seemed green and house it thin. All the tobacco in the field looks Sobbed. Very high tides. My tide banks stand firm. As yet the unraised part only in danger, notwithstanding the rain and great runs from the Pocosin and the high tides that hardly let any water out. The water within the dam not near the top of the marsh. Colo. Charles Carter goes to Corotoman. The Bull run post boy returns home. Landon but getting well, Fisher[50] sick and many people. All called fever and ague. Tobacco Spotting, no oats made. The weather inclinable to break away. I put some tobacco in the Fodder house 3 days agoe out of the weather and this day it appeared some of it house burnt. I found it in a great sweat and removed it. This I think sufficiently explains the cause of house burning and what it is. 'Tis a violent sweat that the plant is thrown into by being hung too thick, or in too close a place or by the close foggy air for 'tis evidently the want of air that causes this sweat and as this Sweat introduces a kind of putrefaction the leaves grow black and fetid and, being divested of all their proper qualities and indeed moisture when the leaf dryes, it remains in a dirty black, starched and stinking state and is never more Affected by any moisture but what will carry on its rottenness. From hence we may Conclude the way to prevent this is in the two first instances is by hanging moderately thin and in proper houses open enough to let in the air and in the last state what ever we can make use of that will bring the plant into a Speedy way of curing will be a means of affecting that by freeing the plant of that watry moisture before these spells of weather come on. Such as by great Sunning, scaffolding and with care the floor sweating all which drye and bring off abundance of the wild grass or insipid water which all plants abound with besides their proper oils, Salt, etc.

8. *Thursday.*

Rainy and Cloudy yesterday and this day every thing seems as if drowned and dropping off the Stalk. Every lock of hay we get is constantly wet.

10. *Saturday.*

I cannot get a fair day to carry in my marsh hay. This is the 11th day that it has rained successively. This is a loss in every, but why complain? Has not every kind of Crop this year been thus destroyed? As to tobacco, whole fields have fired away and not an hour that a planter would use to Cut in. However I have against all the Common rules cutt every warm day and have hitherto

---

[50] Fisher, whose first name is unknown, was probably one of Carter's overseers or tenants on his Bull Run lands.

been lucky enough to get it either on fences or scaffolds and indeed some of it in the houses, but where it seemed wet or not well killed we hang it low and thin till it dryed.

The wet weather seems to be breaking away and that we shall have a clearing Northwest. God send Consideratione. No sunshine. This day except some weak patients all are well but my Grandchild who has got a cough. I am persuaded that a Skillfull observer might rank the disorder we have had under a proper head for one thing has been certain that not one patient in 20 ever lost the fever before a full weeke. The dogwood bark I find a good bracer provided 'tis accompanyed with some Correctors to prevent some ill affect it has from its too great roughness. Wind changed to Northeast at 3 and all cloudy and rain again.

11. *Sunday.*

Rain this morning, Cold, and Cloudy all day. The tobacco houses all Stink. I am affraid tobacco is touched in them although none falls. I serched one to day and find the tobacco in a sweat hanging.

12. *Monday.*

Rain now which makes the 13th day.

Agreed this day with John King to overlook my Plantations called Mangoright and Mangowrong.[51] He is to follow all my Directions in every thing. He is to have 500 Weight fresh Pork; milk of two Cows; what corn his family can reasonably use and £25 Current money the year. He is not to go abroad without my leave and to use every kind of Diligence.

14. *Wednesday.*

Yesterday a very fine and this morning bids for it.

15. *Thursday.*

Poor Sukey from being as well seemingly as a Child could be was siezed after breakfast with a head ach and fever and in less than 2 hours a very Severe Convulsion. I threw down 20 grains Ipecacuana, got away abundance of Phlegm, her breakfast and much clear water and as this did not move her downwards I ordered a Common clyster made, emolient with Cammonile flowers etc. This day last year the Child was attacked in the sam[e] m[ann]er but as she began this year and got over the disorder that then prevailed though

---

[51] Part of the Mangorike tract in Richmond Co.

with a Convulsion I was in hopes that for this year at least she would have a respite. Lucy taken since dinner; fever and head ach so that I may conclude this day's fogg has produced A return of all these disorders again. Judy has felt warm more than Common this day also. Johnny privately took a Crocus[52] vomit yesterday. Imagin his season for an attack approaching from the head ach he privately enjoyed for 2 days.

16. *Friday.*

I am sorry to find my observations on house burnt tobacco too true which see before the 6th instants. Riding this day by a tobacco house, I got off and spent some time with the people hanging the tobacco. As I went by the other end of the house I smelt a very strong and putrid smell very pungent to the nose and immediately ordered the overseer to take some sticks in the 3 tier above the ground tier, vizt, that above the joice and that below it the 2d room from the gable end, and I found the tobacco had been in a profuse sweat. The leaves were of a black brown Color and wet, the stemms were swelled, wet and had rotted near the joyning to the stalk and they smelt of the scent above. This I found had happened from their disobeying my orders which was to thin every stick as it was handed in from the scaffold for 'tis necessary in Scaffolding to hand the stick thick that the Sun may not have too great a power, but it ought to be thined when housed and this was done when I was present but overseers and negroes think the work too tedious and always from their judgments by the last year but this is a year on quite the contrary extreem and so I am likely to suffer. I have set all hands to thinning and giving air to the tobacco and have opened about 3 feet wide through the house each Way from the tier above joice to the bottom but I am affraid some I shall not save. I have found the same in another house and affraid all the first hanging every where is so. For this reason, I sent an express to my manager at Northumberland about it.

17. *Saturday.*

The 13 and 14 were fair but ever since that rain and very giving foggs. I this day in order to save the tobacco in one house made three or four Charcole fires having thinned and opened the house every where and indeed brought the tobacco to a tollerable good state and it came to its Colour and had lost that earthy putrid Scent but the evening's rain was very violent that 'tis to be feared nothing will do to make it valuable.

[52] Crocus was a name given to many preparations made after the manner of rust by corroding and opening metallic substances. It was often used in making emetic wine.

18. *Sunday.*

Rain again this day.

19. *Monday.*

Rain also last night. Cloudy and damp this day. Tobacco seems to grow worse in the houses although we have fires every morning. Nothing but relapses. All that have been sick already are growing so again, but how can we expect it otherwise? No clear air for now 20 days and more. Lucy and Sukey still ill.

26. *Monday.*

I have had the pleasure of Mr. Wormeley's Company these 4 or five days and also of some Cool Northwest winds which were much wanted to dispell disorders and drye our tobacco houses, but I can't as yet see much effect although we may presume the evil is in Cure. We began to gather our Fother last week.

27. *Tuesday.*

Very fine weather. Winds Northerly and Westerly. The tobacco house now drye and sweat but the disorders of the Season not yet abated. I have 8 in the house that were sick not a month past. Judy and Landon also ill. The latter came from Bull run so he has fevers every night and an ague every other night and a very bad pulse, sluggish attended with frequent and irregular intermissions. There is now a vile distemper amongst the horses. The first taken was a year old mare which I discovered down on the ground, and when it got up staggering before and Faultering behind I conjectured bleeding proper and by large and frequent doses of boiled Rattlesnake root that recovered, but I believe it was very soon after it was taken that I discovered, for a mare of my son's which had had it two days before it was mentioned dyed with it notwithstanding the Above application. Her young colt was siezed with it and had a large Kernel under the lower jaw. This was lanced and the Creature is still alive although the 4th day and all the while seemingly in extreme pain. My mare Bonny found yesterday dying with it and thus I fear it has been in many places all over the Country.

28. *Wednesday.*

Began to use new oats. Children still sick.

OCTOBER 1757

1. *Saturday.*

Another mare with a young Colt taken with the disorder and although instantly almost blooded and a large dose of Rattle snake root given to her she is now incapable of standing, and her neck merely drawn on one side. The Colt that lived so long after it dye[d] last night, it may be, for want of food for as it sucked and could not stand, my Coachman very sick and the owner of it a pleasure hunting I imagin no care was taken of it. This mare is the 5th taken ill and I believe will be the 4th that is dyed. This day I give her 30 grains Calomels[53] and 2 drachms of Jalap but she dyed.

6. *Thursday.*

Began this day to sow wheat but with one plow as yet and in very stumpy ground. Very fine weather ever since the 24th September and but two slight frosts the 19th and 26th of the month. Not done gathering Fother as yet. Indeed we carry it a great way and there is abundance of it.

15. *Saturday.*

Still very fine weather without any kind of interruption. We Continue sowing wheat but by reason of the dryness of the weather none comes up as yet.

Began to put our Cattle in our Cowyards yesterday both at the barn and the plantations. The Fork wheat is also sowing by means of one horse and a very pritty plow made for that purpose with one share. We plow better than 1 acre in every day the Ground is so light. I shall certainly trye to use these plows hereafter in all my light lands.

Mr. John Page went home this day. He has been here a week and much recovered he is.

My Children all mending but now the little negroe Children are again relapsed into fevers and agues.

Bottled off yesterday 29½ dozen Cyder, the old Barnaby not yet gone. The wheat mow that I kept unthreshed, expecting that the weavel would be destroyed in the embrio by means of the sweating of the mow, now Appears to

[53] Calomel is mercurious chloride and was used as a mercurial purgative. It was a favorite remedy for biliousness, glandular inflammations, and typhoid and malarial fevers.

be full of the flye and the bank or field swallow seems to be as busy as the bats were yon May, the flye crawling from under the boards and the birds keep a continual snapping with their bills as they catch at thousands and ten thousands will be destroyed this way no doubt but as every grain of wheat produces a flye there can be no hopes of their being totally destroyed. I am apt to think these flyes are come to maturity only from such parts of the mow where the air has got in and prevented the sweating such as the top and sides but this I shall discover when I thresh it out. If I find the middle is saved by it I will next year to make the cure more effectual mow all my [wheat] without a Cradle and stack it like hay, and lay a thick layer of straw on the bottom and sides and over the top, and tread it all hard down.

The first sown wheat begins to appear but the land was so baked by the summer's rains and has for want of some later rain broke up so very Cloddy that I must question whether a great deal of it will come up. However we have made our chance of being thick enough for in 12½ acres I find my man has sown some thing more than 3 bushels to the acre. I ordered him to lay it in thick but this is over doing it; however we will wait the event.

16. *Sunday.*

A Small rain and raw. Sukey I fear relapsing. She was taken with a Sickness in her Stomach on which I ordered 20 grains Ipecacuana to be given her. 'Tis Just a month since she was seized before and as it was about the same time in August I fear it is to turn out a periodical fever and ague which I once knew in my Son Robin for near a year. However I must observe it was not till the last of this month last year that these disorders left us.

20. *Thursday.*

Sukey kept cheerfull and briske after the vomit till yesterday morning when she seemed dull felt feverish till past 12 this was oft, and at bed time I gave her the first dose that Flood sent her. As she was clear of a fever she remained so all night and this morning upon which she took a second dose; but about 12 she complained of a head ach, grew Cold, laid down and fell into a fever so I fear the vomit only put off the relapse for a time.

OBSERVATIONS ON INDIGO

Having a design to take a tryal at making of Indigo and not believing it to be possible for any work in the beginning to support the great Sallerys given for the managers of it, I resolved to steal into a knowledge of it by inquiry but I found my Countryman are with this as with tobacco only slightly acquainted.

Therefore, as I could not out of the Several confused methods given of raising seed fall on one that could promise me any Certainty, I began my self as late as the 19th June to sow about 40 hills in my garden, and in this I was to depend only on what I had experienced in other things for a plant I never before saw above an inch high, and I was quite a Stranger to the kind of Land for some cryed out for the light, others for the rich, and some asserted any land would do, and although all agreed in sowing it in hills yet no two were Alike as to distance. I therefore fell on some land that was pretty rich and very stiff and endeavoured to make the hills 3 feet asunder. In these I put three or four seed. This I discovered to be wrong for but few hills had any come up in them in a fortnight after. I then put about ten in a hill and they came up, some later, some Sooner, occasioned either by the badness of the seed or the Severe rains for though water is a great softener of such seeds and certain[ly] prepares the hill to part with the germ or Sprout yet my stiff land baked much and must necessar[il]y obstruct the rising of the tender sprout. I found these young plants of a very Slow puny growth although I frequently loosened the earth with great caution about them and they were in many places much disturbed not to say injured by piss Ants. Nay although it was absolutely necessary to loosen the earth I could observe them to sicken for a time after for that operation. In about 3 weeks or more they grew so high as to admit of a small quantity of earth to be halled up to them which I found of great service in promoting their growth; at about 4 inches high I thinned the hills to three or four plants and should have taken more away had I not discovered that every little wound they received from either flye, buggs, or worms certainly killed the plant. However I must say I knew so little of the proper method of raising the moist seed and the plants looked so sorry that I conjectured my hills might have been made much neerer and therefore I was not so much for thinning the hills more as I have found since they ought. Yet I discover this should not be done till the plants are above 6 inches high for many dyed that seemed at that time to be flourishing at about 18 inches high which was just as some blossoms began to appear, I topped, that is nibbed off, the top buds of each plant and left in some hills one stalk, in some two, in some three and in some four, all which I have since found to be wrong and that hills made at rather more than 3 feet distance will not be too wide for more than 1 plant, for on the topping they begin to branch excessively and presently shad the ground and that this prodigeous luxuriancy prevents much seed growing on the main stalk when it will hang prodigeous thick when the plant has more air to its roots and not suffered to runn off its sap in branches. Therefore it must be certainly extremely necessary to observe the shooting of the branches and to top them also as soon as they get to 3 or four inches and they will also bear abundance of seed.

These things, I say, appear to me to be good in observation but whether they will be really so in practice and be most productive of seed and easy as to the labour of making of it I can't pretend as yet to determin, but God willing I shall know if the tending of seed be profitable. From what has been said by way of direction I set down the following method which I intend to pursue next year.

THE METHOD

As I intend to use about 11 acres of my last dunged tobacco ground which is naturally light and I believe pretty rich I shall within a very few days make the usual tobacco hills up and berry the rank suckers that are now ground in those hills. By this I propose to make the ground fine for the summer working and also richer by the rotting of the suckers. This ground shall be kept inclosed that the ground may not be trod down by creatures nor the hills rooted down which would prevent the rotting of the suckers. In the month of February late or March early I propose to level every hill down; this will be the most effectual way to give the ground a good working and to get out such stalks of the suckers that have not rotted. When the ground is thus cleaned and levelled I intend to lay it off in squares exactly 3 feet distance in order to its being hilled convenient for the little plow that is to be used in weeding hereafter. To effect these squares with ease and exactness by those who are to hill the ground: Set off a strait furrow with the little plow from along the longest part of the ground and with 3 or 4 sticks exactly 6 feet in length lay Another line at the 6 feet distance on any side of the line first run. 'Tis done with great expedition. Thus as soon as the boy begins to run his first line let him take his first stake stuck for his first furrow and lay it in a right angle as near as he can from the furrow he is to run, and at the end of the stake let him stick the same stake down, then let him go his first furrow till he comes to his second stake and lay that in the same manner as he did the first and stick it up, and of course he will have two stakes stuck to set his third stake by and so of all the rest as many as he shall use. Thus the ground will be laid off one way at double row distance. Then let him begin on the side of his ground and set off a strait row as he did before but cross ways to the former and so proceed as before in laying all his furrows that way. Thus will the ground be checquered all over at double row distance each way. Then set the least expert hands to making good tobacco hills, working the ground well in each chequer. Thus Will the more experienced or sensible hands have a guide between the hills in each furrow to make a very regular hill and thus will the ground be one way hilled at its proper distance of 3 feet and then by setting the hands to work cross wise to what they did before they will have the same guide of hills to direct them to make the interveening rows and the whole ground will be hilled at its proper distance of 3 feet square. See the draft:

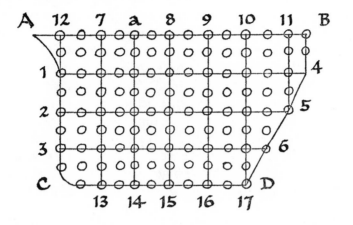

If you first plow from A to B you will have the lines (A-B), (1-4), (2-5), (3-6) and (C-D) laid off at double distance as before directed. Then by crossing and plowing in the direction of A-C you will have the lines (12-1), (7-13), (a-14), (8-15), (9-16), (10-17), (11-5) and the whole ground is then chequered at double distance. Then let hills be made in each intersection in the direction A-B. The whole ground is then hilled at double distance. Then by beginning in the same direction you have a furrow between two hills to govern you and 'tis such a rule that it must be a very dunce indeed that shall do amiss. This will hill the ground to its proper distance of 3 feet one way and those will direct you by hilling the same way as you did at first to make the hills in their proper distance the other way for there will be two hills to work between.

This is not being more nice than expeditious upon an experiment made last year in a Corn field of 130,000 hills will give a greater Certainty as to the quantity tended, much easyer to the horse that is to draw the plow and also more commodious for those who are to work it with hoes. Add to this the advantage there will to the growth of the plant by crop plowing and loosening the earth.

The ground being hilled as above about the middle or last of March if the weather is kind and moderate if not early in April or as you can with good weather, Cut off the tops of the hills pritty flat without Clapping them and follow with the seed immediately about 6, 8, or 10 just rubbed in in the middle of the hill and covered with the finest earth well Crumbled. The reason of this early sowing is evident from the weather that has happened this Year in which there is as yet scarce any ripe seed.

The ground between the hills will by the rains that frequently fall be much baked. As soon as you discover that it begins to appear so, set in the 3 trowel plow, and one furrow will do provided you open the two hinder trowels so wide as to skim a part of the hill on each side (which may be easyly done if two wings that hold these trowels are made to open and shut by 2 graduated tongues placed before and behind). To this each way of the ground, for 'tis certain the ground must first settle before the weeds begin to spring, and by keeping that light they cannot have time to spring because as this plow has no mould board the earth is only raised and Crumbled by the working, and every time a tender sprout even of a weed is exposed to the air it dyes. This work is the more necessary in that Indigo, being a plant that draws all its nourishment from the tap root, 'tis long before it can be able to Cope with weeds.

As soon as any of the plants begin to appear, if the earth should be baked about them, loosen it with such tools as you think proper, an old knife or some such, but with great care not to wound nor disturb its Situation, and from the tops of the hills take care with little sharp turnep hoes to pare all weeds.

As the plants grow draw out the weakest to thin the hills, for although I plant 6, 8, or 10 yet 'tis only to get one good one to stand with Certainty and therefore this first thinning should not leave less than 3 or 4 in a hill, for I have found although we have not yet sorted its enimies into classes it has many, both buggs, flyes, and worms.

As they grow larger thin again to about 2, and when they are about 12 inches take all out to one good one for then the tap root has got down, and the plant in any tolerable soil and with Common moisture begins to flourish. You are then with the hoes to give the plant a little of the Cool earth by way of hill but not to bury it but only lay it lightly to it. This will help to support it in blowing weather and also to keep the earth from baking round its stem which certainly retards its growth. Note: this work should be done evenings and mornings or cloudy weather for I have seen the plants sicken prodigeously if done in hot sun shine.

Watch the blossoming the plants which I find is in middling ground when it is about 18 inches or two feet at such time sure to Nibb or Clip off the top bud of the main standard. I imagin a pair of light garden sheers very proper for this purpose and then give it a little better hilling than before. Your plow should have again gone over the ground both ways by this time or near it for then innumerable branches begin to appear.

When the branches put forth they should be watched and also topped in middling land to 4, 5, or 6 inches in length otherwise they will be too luxuriant and shade the ground too much and make a great deal of the seed imperfect.

The seed is generally in Clusters all along the main stalk and the body of the branches.

23. *Sunday.*

Rain last night.

24. *Monday.*

This day near Sunset Landon Carter came home. I with great mildness asked him if he did not think that as he was to go up to Bull Hall tomorrow he ought to have staid at home to have taken my directions with regard to my affairs and if he did not think this Sauntering about from house to house only to inflame himself the more by visiting a woman that he knew I would never Consent to his marrying would not ruin him and contrary to his duty. He answered very calmly No. Then Sir be assured that although you will shortly be of age if you do not henceforward leave her you must leave me. He answer, then Sir I will leave you, on which I bid him be gone out of my house. He took up his hat and sayd so he would as soon as he could get his horse and went off immediately without shewing the least Concern, no not even to turn round. This I write down the moment it passed that I might not through want of memory omit so Singular an act of great filial disobedience in a Child that I have thought once my greatest happyness but as a just Father kept it concealed.

25. *Tuesday.*

A fine warm rain before day and this morning. Robin went with a letter to the Above Gentleman which is in my Ledger to put it in his power to reinstate himself if he chooses it.

I have frequently had in my thoughts the unhappy condition of the Country in the destruction that attends most of the wheat by what they Call the fly-Weavel, and in particular this year in which almost every grain is destroyed, and have reasoned on many methods to kill the enimy in its embrio, for no other way can their destruction be effected because they lay their eggs in the young Soft grain and no steeping of grain before sowing can do this nor no affluvian affect them in the mow. I am in hopes stacking it open as we do hay may by the heat gained in sweating, for although the wheat heats as they grow yet it is not so untill the maggot is formed, and as the heat is such a gradual one as comes on with the growth that must nourish instead of destroying it. Now although also it is by heat the egg must first hatch yet that heat communicated to as great a degree as the grain can bear without toasting it must also the same as it opens the egg destroy which we find is done in those Countrys where the Chickens in ovens where proper care is not taken. I have therefore fallen upon the following kiln to give that heat should the mow stowed as above do no service. I must own I have some where met with a hint of this Sort, but I took so little notice of it when I read or heard it, not having wheat in that Condition, that I know not the method it is to be affected by but have only found an Hypothesis to be proved by practice.

I propose then to erect the Kiln after the following manner. I shall build a house convenient to my Granary of the following dimensions: 20 or 24 feet long and 12 or 14 feet wide. This house shall consist of two Stories, the lower not above 6 feet high, and 12 feet of that part next my Granary shall stand on a Square of brick work 8 feet in the clear 14 inch walls. The rest of the house shall stand on Posts. This brick work I will carry up the full 6 feet on which the side Sills, Crop and end Sills shall lye firm and Close. This brick work I shall plaister Close every way excepting one trap door. On the end next the other part of the house of this brick work I will place an arch which I shall call a Lanthern 2 foot wide, 2 feet high and an arch equal to its Semidiameter. The sides of this arch shall be 9 inches with many holes in them to let out the heat. This arch shall extend no further 6 feet within the brick work for the sake of going round to Judge of the heat. On one side this arch at the mouth shall be a small 2 foot door to let a man in to examine the heat. The Crown of this arch shall be but 4 inches thick and no holes in the five or 6 upper Coarses to keep down any flame. This arch to be plaistered all over within the square of the brick work it stands in. The Sills of this part of the house lying on this brick work, as the house will be 12 feet wide, must not be the main sills but others put in Parallel to lye over the brick work which will admit of a passage above. All around the frame of the Kiln in these Pairrallel sills are to be placed Sleepers so strong as to admit of strong Narrow laths to lye very thick over them on these laths. I will lay a sheet Of fine Sive work made of basket stuff such as we call sand sives round the upper part of this work. I shall set a kind of Curb foot or 2 high just as Experience shall Convince me of the heat to be raised. On this is my wheat to be laid and carefully stirred so as to drye it effectually and by a kind of hoppar spout, after experience has taught me it is drye enough, it shall throw a down to my grainery floor to cool.

The upper story in this house is that part of over the kiln to be a 12 foot room close lathed and Plaister with one or two light Glass Windows to give light or open to give the workmen air. It is to be 7 feet pitch. The other part is to be a plain floor for carrying the Wheat into in order to be dryed. See the drafts.[54]

NOVEMBER 1757

5. *Saturday.*

Drye weather abundance, warm in the day, cold at night and white frosts in the morning and only one sunday's rain since 25 October, so that as planters we reaped no good from it for tobacco was like tinder next morning.

Finished sowing wheat the 1st of this month. Quantity as follows:

	bushels		*[bushels]*
At home 47 acres————————	140	from Northumberland—————	72
Morgan's 4—————————	10½	H[ickory] Thicket[55]————	38½
Fork 10—————————	23	Fork————————————	63½
	173½		174

Still remaining of the Fork Wheat, 6½ bushels and 4 hogsheads in the straw to clear which may turn out.

I shall not make a seed of Indigoe. Late sowing, constant growth of the plant and not trimming the branches of the plant timely kept the seed always green and though I was aware of a great Frost coming and gathered in order to drye it in the sun yet it all withered to nothing. My Son's was a large field. I saw but little ripe at that at the bottoms of the stemmes of the plants that were growing in May, so here again I think it must be a very good rule either to have a vat ready to steep all that does not stand before June or else to cut it up and plant the ground in tobacco. There is but one objection to this in the tryals I have made and that is they were not trimmed in time. Otherwise Perhaps the seed would have ripened. This I shall trye god willing next year when I see if, if the plants are not growing well in May, one ought to have a vat

---

[54] The drafts have not been found.
[55] Hickory Thicket was a tract of land in Richmond Co. that belonged to Carter.

ready. I mean then the ground ought to be properly prepared and sowed for cutting, for to be sure very little besides the branches and Tops of seed plants will contain any dye, the rest being merely Lignens.

Note: Countryman's dictionary says that Water and salt sprinkled over Cabbages will kill the Caterpillar worm that eats them.

6. *Sunday.*

From the Country Dictionary (word Lime) 'tis made of chalk or any kind of stone not sandy or Cold as Freestone Slate is also good to make lime of, only the harder the stone the more fire they require. Chalk is commonly burnt in 24 hours. 10 bushels of Sea Cole or 100 faggots will burn 40 bushels of Chalk which will make 30 bushels unslacked Lime. Stone takes 60 hours to burn it to Lime. If this be true the proportion of wood is easyly calculated from the time that is if 24 hours use 100 faggots what will 60 hours use?

7. *Monday.*

My Family all better. My Son missed his ague and fever yesterday. Lucy hers two days agoe. Colds better. But myself very Mawkish and under a bad digestion. Dr. Flood came last night and went away this day to Court. Very Cold indeed.

8. *Tuesday.*

Sukey taken this morning with a vomiting. Dr. Flood would not let it be encouraged with warm water, not being imagining it was anything more than a nauseating occasioned by her Cold, but I concluded it so near the Period in which she has had her intermittant for 3 months past that it must needs be return of that and would have given her a vomit. He ordered her a purge at night which she took. It workt her once very plentifully at 12 o'Clock and she slept well, but her vo-

9. *Wednesday.*

miting returned this morning the same time as she had it yesterday and with it green bile in every vomit but the first and last. She had 7 discharges this way and more stool, and finding this weakness at her Stomach encreasing I ordered her a weak Julep[56] of Rum, water and a little mint steeped in it.

The weather still very drye and my own mawkishness together with the constant illness of one Child or another has prevented my doing much business. Sukey only a slight fever.

[56] A julep is a sweetened and aromatized alcoholic or medicated drink used as a stimulant.

10. *Thursday.*

Sukey Carter a fever at 10. At one very high attended with many Convulsive Symptoms but relieved by a small Cordial of Pulvis Cantian,[57] Salt tartar, 4 grains Saffron,[58] and Mynt tea, 2 spoonfulls tincture after 8 drops made palatable with sugar And an emolient and Carminative Clyster.

Thunder and lightning this evening with but a Small Spitting of rain, then Clear at Northwest.

11. *Friday.*

Very Cold lowering day wind North. Note: this is in general a very drye spell and very bad for the grain sown which can scarcely in the Stiff ground come through the Clods and the ground very hard to break up in any manner. This makes me more determined to Sow all my Wheat land that is Stiff over with sand as Soon as the grain is well up and the wet frosts set in.

12. *Saturday.*

Go to see Colo. Thornton in Northumberland County. Lucy Carter taken ill this day with fever, Vomiting and Purging which Carryed it off.

15. *Tuesday.*

Began only this day to gather Corn.

16. *Wednesday.*

Came home. Very hot day, quite drye weather still. Wheat scarcely to be seen. Lucy her fever this day but slight.

17. *Thursday.*

Rain this night Scarcely a Season but refreshing to the wheat. Landon and Johnny set off to Bull Hall. Mangorike quarter burnt down. Nat brought the bred I bought of Jordans: 12 doublerisened loaves, 2 single ditto.

20. *Sunday.*

A very fine rain indeed and it looks as if it would continue. If so I am in hopes the wheat Crop will revive. Two very severe gusts of wind this evening

---

[57] Pulvis Cantianus, popularly known as the Countess of Kent's powder, was derived from a number of ingredients and used as a diaphoretic.

[58] Saffron is derived from the flowers of *Crocus sativus*. It was a popular remedy as a diuretic in measles and other exanthematous infections.

at West, the first with hard rain and thunder and the last Northwest drye and Cold so that work could be done in the tobacco house.

21. *Monday.*

This day quite Cold.

22. *Tuesday.*

A white and a black frost. I can perceive the late drye weather has hurted the wheat in the ground in stiff lands, which brings to mind a former observation, that of running the harrow once after plowing over all such lands, for in drye spells succeeding very wet ones such lands naturally break up Cloddy and leave deep cavities between them, and without harrowing first the seed when sown falls in those holes and is forever buryed by the harrow after and subsequent rains. I must also observe 'tis a very bad way to keep seed wheat in hogsheads or any thick heaps for 38 bushels was of my son's wheat and it is not half come up. Although mine was a little weavil eaten it may be seen, where his was sown by the ground.

23. *Wednesday.*

This finished breaking up my tobacco ground with the plows. It was exceeding and besides being swardy broke up in lumps from the drowth and the Constant feeding the ground with Creatures, and yet the two plows have in 40 working days constantly imployed broke up 80 and odd acres.

25. *Friday.*

Sukey Carter, taken with a sickness since dinner, brought up her dinner, seems Cold and her pulse very quick. Rain all this evening and all night.

26. *Saturday.*

Began to sleet in the evening; continued so till 12 at night. Then Snowed.

27. *Sunday.*

Sunday snowed this morning. Corn still not gathered not owing to any bad Conduct but too warm weather. Lucy a great sickness at Stomach and head ach.

When Sukey Carter was taken ill the 25th, she was attackt with a sickness in her Stomach and a head ach. Her pulse much disordered, she vomited once and, perceiving as she lay some hours after in a great uneasyness from her breathing in her Stomach, I threw down 20 grains Ipecacuana. This gave her 4 vomits and she grew easy and her feaverish Symptoms in the pulse left her and she continued well to the same time of day this day that she was taken ill before when she grew heavy and cold at her finger's end [and got] a head ach. She lay down and slept, and although it is now three hours since her fever is but just perceiveable but her head ach continues.

Lucy's attack to day was a violent sickness at her Stomach. I gave her 24 grains Ipecacuana which brought off only one vomit, vizt, her victuals at breakfast, and much Phlegm and although she brought off her Physick yet she had 6 stools after, two of them only purgative, which shows that her digestion is faulty and that 'tis a bilious cause.

28. *Monday.*

Rode out, it being fine overhead. The rain before the snow and the Snow since has made the earth as wet as ever I saw it. I am satisfyed there Can't be any thing of a Crop of wheat. My land is low and naturally wet but this is drowning. In Short I never saw so poor a prospect for wheat. The drye weather at first stopped it in the earth and now whilst it is quite young too wet weather seems as if it would kill it. Gave Sukey 25 grains Rhubarb which gave her only one very large stool. Her fever's left.

DECEMBER 1757

2. *Friday.*

John King my overseer entered on his business this day at £25 the year.

3. *Saturday.*

Lucy a fever last night, pretty near off this morning. Gave her 25 grains Rhubarb and 10 grains Cream tartar. Workt 6 times and seemed to be of great service.

4. *Sunday.*

A cow brought up well last night but found swelled today and appeared to be wounded in the Anus, of which she dyed this day. Note: before it was discovered she was wounded my Coachman gave her an ounce of Jalap which might perhaps be an Injury to her. It was thought she could not dung. Upon Opening her the Wen which she had on her side by a former Gore and into which the great gut had fallen was quite Corrupted and very fetid so that had she escaped this 2d misfortune she must have dyed. This brings to my mind the fate of many that seemed for a time to carry off the Wenors well enough but sooner or later they dye and I suppose by the rubs they get amongst one another after may occasion bruises and putrefaction there for it shall be a rule to fatten such up with the first opportunity.

This day came John King and Complained of a violent Running he had at the Penis and an accute pain in his back which took him the day he came, that he got it by lifting his hogsheads of tobacco where he came from. He is so bad as to be obliged to lye up for it. I'm certain this, that if he should be a Cripple I will not be obliged to pay his wages.

7. *Wednesday.*

Sukey lookt badly all this evening with a quick Pulse.

8. *Thursday.*

Better this morning. Gave her 20 grains Rhubarb and 10 grains Cream tartar. 'Tis her usual Period of attack which is now got to every Fortnight. She took the purge at day break and vomited it up at 30 of 9. Then she grew Cold and very pale with a head ach and little pulse and threw up a very green vomit. I gave her 15 grains Ipecacuana. She had after it 5 vomits of very yellow Bile and some of them very thick. At 1 her head ach abated and to strengthen her stomach I made a small mint Julep with a little rumm in it. Seems brisk and talkt cheerfully. Her fever not higher. Better at night.

9. *Friday.*

Continues better though very pale. Dr. Flood came not on Account of the rain. This is the 3d day Constant rain.

10. *Saturday.*

Sukey a fever early and very sick at her stomach and head ach. This fever went off in the night. Dr. Flood came here at 4.

11. *Sunday.*

Dr. Flood went away at 11. The Child no fever to day but I thought her pulse a little quick at night. Snow and then a little rain.

12. *Monday.*

Sukey's fever rose at 1 in the night. Sent to Dr. Flood for the medecins at 30 past 6. This Child dangerous ill at 12, dead pale and blue, a partial moisture.

I gave her a small Cordial to strengthen her, vizt, Salt tartar, Pulvis Cantian each 5 grains in balm tea. I hope for the best. Lucy taken ill. I saw it yesterday but she would not own it nor that anything ailed her not an hour agoe. Note: Flood yesterday was Commending her looks. 'Tis now Just 15 days since her last attack so that her disorder also is got to every fortnight, that is from the day of her Attack, for she was taken the 27th last month and her fever kept no regularity nor left her till the 3d of this month when she took a purge Rhubarb.

13. *Tuesday.*

Sukey's fever kept wearing away Yesterday till one in the night when she was quite clear. She took in the time 2 of the powders sent by Dr. Flood for that purpose. I went up at 6 this morning in order to begin her bark doses also sent by the Doctor. Found her flesh calm but her pulse stopping every 2, 3, and 4 stroke and with seeming difficulty recovering its stroke. I was greatly alarmed not know whether 'twould be proper to give her the bark in such a state having I think known persons thrown this year into nearly the same Condition by the bark. However as there were mixed with her doses and bitters many medicins I conjectured the Doctor had provided against such accidents and therefore gave the first dose. She lay till past 7. I felt her again and found the intermission removed to between 30 and 40 strokes and as her spirits were cheerfull and no oppression at the stomach I concluded that Symptom might have been occasioned by her rising a little before I first went up to the pot. The weather being Cold it might give a sudden Obstruction but this is perhaps only conjecture for both my Son Landon and I were both so this year and I am certain I took no bark and my fevers then had almost left me; therefore there may be something in Constitution or in the particular bilious state of us all.

Lucy's fever yesterday wore off in the night and this morning (as it was her period of Attack and she was taken with a Chilly fit and sickness at her stomach) I gave her at 6.25 grains of Ipecacuana Concluding the bile lay ready for a discharge and in 15 minutes a very bilious vomit came up and some short time after a Second.

Yesterday a fine yearling of the last summer's growth was discovered to be swelled ready to burst and could not walk. I ordered some tobacco Smoke Clysters to be given it which brought away some wind and a hard pellet or two but no abatement of the swelling. I then ordered it half a point of a Strong decoction of Rattlesnake root, soot, and 2 spoonfulls rum and in an hour some more clysters that the body might be the easier opened. Then I ordered a 2d drench of the Snake root, sut and rum which purged off a great deal of Slime. At night I ordered another drench of the same and they tell me this morning the swelling is much lowered and it eats both bran and hay. I shall repeat the dose this morning. My reasoning on this was an intire obstruction in the guts and a Viscid blood by the rains and Cold winds and therefore the drench aforesaid to remove both which I hope it has done.

It is necessary that man should be acquainted with affliction and 'tis certainly nothing short of it to be confined a whole year in tending one's sick Children. Mine are now never well. Indeed I may believe there are many reasons for it besides the Constitution of the air which has been very bad. I have none but negroes to tend my children nor can I get anyone and they use their own children to such loads of Gross food that they are not Judges when a child not so used to be exposed to different weathers and not so inured to exercise Comes to eat. They let them press their appetites as their own children did and thus they are constantly sick. Judy Carter, who has been as well for many weeks as ever child was, by being suffered after her dinner to some of her sister's barley broth yesterday took in such a load as could not be contained in her stomach and this day she was seized with a natural vomiting. I found nothing but food coming up and therefore ordered a small dose of Ipecacuana to help to clear the over burthened Stomach. The medi[ci]n I gave produced a while good effects by bringing off a good deal of filth and Bile but it had too powerfull an effect on her weak stomach for she vomited 6 times yellow bile, and whether an ague intevened I don't know but she lost her pulse for two hours and quite dead coldness and hardly alive with nervous Catchings in her hands and Jaws so that I fancyed her death near. However I gave her Pulvis Cantian 5 grains, Salt tartar 5 grains, Pulvis Castor 2 grains in a weak Julep of Rum, water and mint and in about 2½ hours her pulse beat and after a good sleep Nature seemed to recover and a Small fever ensued which wore away by night gradually and the Child mended, grew cheerfull and had an appetite to eat which I sparingly indulged but she lost all her bloom off her face this morning.

Sukey has been taking her bark powders this day and clear of a fever.

Lucy's Vomit workt but twice upwards but 6 times down wards. Her bowels always give way and 'tis some times of Service but Judy must take few vomits at least from me. Her natural weakness of her stomach make them dangerous I have now experienced with great concern though the practice was not bad. They much better.

The Swelling returned on the Calf this night and it dyed so that I begin to apprehend it had eaten something that poisoned it. I had it opened and found in the abdomen a prodigeous quantity of water and the guts and gall quite Clear and proper so it was certainly a dropsy. Perhaps if I had used Antimony[59] I might have saved it.

14. *Wednesday.*

I am much pleased with my new Cow stalls. They keep the cattle drye and warm enough and their Food drye and by the Conveniency of the roof over it a boy can fill the Cribs for 30 cattle in ten minutes because the flooring above joice is open just above the cribs and 'tis but turning over what is left of the former feed which I find is a good way and they eat it well having no taint of their breath and the fresh stuff is easyly pulled down and I am farther persuaded that I shall not make one bit the less dung for by littering the spare parts of the yard as we used and cleaning out the stalls twice a week and scattering that over the yard it seems to be a good mixture of the animal dung. These stalls are of this farther service (for by having convenient houses on the sides of the yard we not only take care of the last year's Calvs which are all fed with Wheat chaff and hay, the sorry ones if any seperated from the other) we have also an opportunity of providing for the young Calves that fall for this purpose. I bring them all up from my other pens and send down some hearty cow not forward with Calf in their room so that my thirty stalls are always full and the Calves are only suckled three times a day which I find to be a better way than letting them run with the Cow for they this way not only escape the Over exercise of running after the Cow and perhaps in bad wet grounds but by being kept from a Constant draw at the teat the Cow's milk has an opportunity of stretching the bagg which is of prime service to prepare the vessels for the reception of milk and which I have observed very beneficial to the Calf who then gets a belly fully instead of a Sup now and then. I have borrowed this reasoning from Overseer's Calves which are always the largest not because they take less milk from them but because the cow by knowing where the Calf is does not restrain her Self from hunting food as much as she seems to do with the Calf at her heels.

15. *Thursday.*

Judy her fever 15 minutes after 10 much the same time as it attackt her yesterday though her Cold fit not so violent maintaining a pretty strong pulse. She had 3 natural and very bilious vomits and her fever higher than it was yesterday so that the Ipecacuana she took yesterday might have added to the

---

[59] Antimony is an element of metallic appearance and crystalline structure, tin-white in color, hard, and brittle. It is prepared chiefly from sulphide stibnite by roasting and reducing with charcoal.

weakness of her Stomach and her loss of Spirits but her attack was a return of her fever that left her in October.

Harry from my Plantation on the other side of the meadow came here and told me his tobacco house was robbed, a full hogshead tobacco was opened and above 100 pounds taken out of it. The people stemmed tobacco till the moon went down and it was taken out by somebody that went in and out at the prize hole. I sent out advertisements offering £5 reward if the offender was convicted. And to delet such practices I wrote a little ticket of paper my name and tyed them up in the heads of many bundles.

Snow all this evening. The wheat makes but a poor appearance having never recovered the drowth after sowing and the violent rains that succeeded that drowth.

Judy fever abated at the same time it did the day before yesterday and she grew cheerfull.

17. *Saturday*.

Rain all this day and snow At night.

20. *Tuesday*.

Rain this day. 21st and 22d fair day like the afternoon and then rain. The wheat in any of the stiff land near killed. The grown quite Cold and no Sun to warm it.

23. *Friday*.

10 Young Calves a good off set before Christmass. I do hope Sukey will escape any period of her Ague and fever although the 20th she look[ed] wan and blue about her eyes and lips and so the 21st and 22nd with a rigid Cast towards her nose and an intermission in her pulse but it came to no fit, yet these Symptoms appeared at 30 past 10 and did not quite wear away till 2.

Lucy's period is not till the 27th. She looks mended as yet. Judy much mended. I hope she will have no return but that her Attack was accidental.

28. *Wednesday*.

Sukey and Lucy and Judy all well and this is a day beyond Lucy's Period, and Sukey had only a Slight Symptom at her period and the very day of Judy's period. I am in hopes they may be in a way of getting over this long holding fever and Ague which began with them in June last.

Began this day to plow Mangorike Corn field, that is I go two bouts on each side the last year's ridge. The ridge I shall hoe up when I hill it and the lacing on each side between the plowing directly, then when I weed go cross the ridge.

29. *Thursday.*

Sowed the Mangorike plant patch this day with the sweet Scented seed made on the plantation and the Fork also.

30. *Friday.*

Sowed the Patches at Harry's and at the Riverside with the plantation seed excepting 5 beds at the river side which were sowed with some seed John King brought here as a fine, broad, long, green tobacco, this for a tryal. Ordered the Fork quarter also to be sowed.

31. *Saturday.*

Sowed in the plant patch by the Old Kitchin the following tobacco seed: vizt, in The first bed as you go to the Kitchins, Orleans;
The 2d and 3d, Parker's broad Green;
The 4, 5, 6 beds, Colo. Wm. Randolph's seed.

WHEAT PAGE

Date		Bushels	Total Bushels
August	16	9½	
	18	10	
	20	11½	
	24	12	
	26	11	
	27	5	
	29	10	
		69	69
September	1	11	
	3	11	
	6	12	
	8	12	
	10	13	
	13	13	
		17 from Morgan's	
	15	13	
	22	30	
	29	42 from Bloughpoint[60]	
		174	174
		Total	243

[60] Bloughpoint was a tract of land in Lancaster Co. belonging to Carter.

WHEAT SOLD

September:	Colo. Faunteleroy	$2\frac{1}{2}$ bushels
	John Eidson[61]	$1\frac{1}{2}$
	Mr. [Charles] Carter	18
	Colo. Faunteleroy	$2\frac{1}{2}$
	Ditto	$7\frac{1}{2}$
	J. Beckwith	10

[61] John Eidson (d. 1774) was a small planter in Richmond Co.

OATS

September 29	43 bushels
October 11	54
25	$58\frac{1}{2}$
November 12	56
30	$54\frac{1}{2}$
December 20	51
January 5, 1758	40
17	49 of these sent Dr. Flood.

THE DIARY

1758

JANUARY 1758

7. *Saturday*.

It has been prodigeous fine and warm weather from the 28th of December to this day, the weather now cloudy and squally but not yet Cold. Wheat looks pretty well again but this night prodigeous Cold Wind Northwest.

We have had 3 pluerasys this winter amongst us but I thank god they were Genuin and Yielded to bleeding over and the rattle snake root in small dose 10 grains with 6 grains Valerian root 3 times a day.

9. *Monday*.

Went home with Colo. Thornton. Wet weather almost all the time I was there.

15. *Sunday*.

A very rainy night. This a Constant heavy rain.

11 Calves and but one lamb. A cow dyed whilst I was down. They

16. *Monday*.

say she was put up in her Stall at night seemingly quite well and found dead in the morning. She was old but not poor and raised a fine Calf last Fall. They opened her and found abundance of water in her belly. Surely there must be some poisonous herb eaten by her to dye so instantaneously.

17. *Tuesday*.

Began to plow for oats this day. The Corn field not quite finished owing to late rains in a great measure but more to Lazyness in my plowmen as I could not examine into their behaviour on account of my being abroad. I find the wheel plow can't work well in old Corn ground. The last year's hills incommode the wheels and drive the plow out. However this is well supplyed by the single fluke hoe which turns it up very properly.

A Cow calved and the Calf dyed by reason of neglect in putting her into a Stall at such a time when she ought to have been in a house and at full liberty; but negroes will do these things and white people are more deceitfull.

18. *Wednesday.*

A most remarkable fine day after a prodigeous white Frost but no ice. 13 Calves.

Sowed the 4 last tobacco beds up at the house with some seed that came from Colo. Spencer Ball's to see what it is that has made so much noise.

21. *Saturday.*

This is the first day that John King talks of going out to work from his coming here. He is very low with his disorder that he has had, all which time as I pay him by the year I will never allow of.

MARCH 1758

1. *Wednesday.*

I went down the 23d January and was absent to the 20th February. In that time many spells of Severe weather at every house where I was. Ever since the 20th have been sick with a very severe kind of Cholic and now not well. February has been a bad month indeed. No oats sowed as yet. I see, go abroad at what time of the year I will, the work that is then to go forward will stand. Now oat ground is not plowed and the reason is the horses are overdone in plowing the Corn field. They did the same last year and did not eat the same food and were done before this.

2. *Thursday.*

Yesterday was a fine, warm, Sunshine day; this a cold, Snowing, Sniveling one. I had brought from on board the *Union* a Servant pretending to be a gardiner named, Joseph Brown, a Yarmouth man. Says he was an apprentis to Kitchen Gardiner.

3. *Friday.*

Very Cold, hard Frost. No working yesterday nor today.

6. *Monday*.

Began this day to sow Oats. The weather till now has been so bad I could not put a seed in Sooner. I saw my wheat yesterday and every where in the Stiff land 'tis near all Killed being spewed up by the very wet weather. This whole Season hitherto has been bad for wheat, for near 2 months after 'twas Sown the weather was too drye to bring it up and ever since that too wet and we could not roll it.

Began this day every where to turn my dung. The yards every where but at the Fork seem to be well stocked and there 'tis but thin. The litter mostly marsh hay and that the creatures eat continually and but few Corn stalks, so a bad Crop of corn makes a bad cow yard. Such is the connection all through the year and in Spight of all contradiction I do maintain there is not a better litter than corn stalks. I now say it from the truest experience.

Judy Carter taken with an Ague and Vomiting yellow bile 6 times and very thick. Her Stomach very weak. I gave her a mint water Julap with a little rum after 6 grains Salt tartar and 12 grains Crabb's eyes.[1]

8. *Wednesday*.

Judy's fever came on at 5 in the night with a Sharp headach. No ague but at 11 after a long nap she vomited more yellow bile. Lucy also taken ill this day with a fever and a Vomiting of green bile.

I cannot omit taking notice of the fevers and pain in head and side amongst my Fork people. The pain excepting one in the right side, sharp fever and at the end of the disorder a Cough and expectoration. I found, after bleeding, a vomit of Ipecacuana necessary the next day and a decoction of the rattlesnake pretty strong. In the begining 2 spoonfulls every two hours and as the pain abated 1 spoonfull. They brought off abundance bile with their vomits. Those that had the pain in their left sides were made worse by the vomits given against my orders but recovered by bleeding and the use of the rattlesnake. There are now too dangerous ill at Hickory Thicket although taken but yesterday. Both were blooded and had rattlesnake given them all night but seemingly worse to day by the oversear's account. I have sent the wench a vomit. Her fever not high but I ordered the fellow a second bleeding and if no better a blister, being unwilling to give a vomit as his fever is so high.

[1] Crab's-eyes, a calceous matter found beside the stomach of European crayfishes, was used as an absorbent and for drying.

Sent home the fellow sent here for a gardiner. He knows nothing of the matter. Plowman [blank], alias Wm. Gates, I keep. He seems a workman and willing fellow.

9. *Thursday.*

A Warm rain. Gave Judy a Gentle purge at 4 in the night, vizt, Rhubarb 15 grains, Cream tarter 9, Salt tartar 3 grains in a little Syrup Solutive roses[2] as her bile seems to be loose and her passages downward obstructed and her natural weakness of her Stomach makes it dangerous to draw this off by the stomach. Her fever was attended with a Constant pain in the head which did not abate till near 5 and though the fever lowered yet 'twas with no sweating and her flesh felt much parched and drye, but in the night Nassau told me this parchedness went off and She seemed as if she had been in a Sweat. Note: by means of the fever's lying in her head she Slept almost the whole day.

Lucy's fever lay also in her head. She had only one vomit and before she was attackt had been three times to stool, twice very loose. Yet her prodigeous paleness and the sweat she went through indicated to me a load on the Stomach and the Severe pain in the head confirmed it so that I gave her 16 grains Ipecacuana this morning in hopes the quantity will be Sufficient to throw up what is loose and continue to keep the passages downwards open.

Though the dose to Judy was very small yet it vomited her 6 or 7 times and purged her 5 times and left such a dead sickness on her that I was obliged to have recourse to more cordials. This sickness of her stomach continued till 4 at which time I gave her prepared Cordial Pulvis Cantian, Salt tartar aa 4 grains in a Julep of rum burnt on Cinnamon tinctured with 6 grains Saffron a small quantity with her powder every 2 hours and it seems to give her great ease and she is grown a little lively. Lucy had an ague 30 past 1 with a head ach Succeeded by a sharp fever. Notwithstanding her vomit workt 2 and downwards five times she had also a pain in her stomach in the ague. I find they are not better. Therefore I sent my Chariot for the Doctor. Judy's stomach still complaining near 5.

Finished this day turning dung at John King's two quarters and at the Fork. At each place the quantity much larger than ever I had and as much better having made the pen larger than usual full 40 yards square for 60 cattle and indeed more care has been taken to litter thin and frequently so that 'tis all very short. Harry's dung two days agoe was finished very good and larger than common but not in proportion to his number of Cattle. He had no stock of

---

[2] Syrup solutive of roses was a combination of damask rose leaves boiled in water with liquor and sugar. It was used as a purgative.

litter. My home yards not yet finished the quantity very large and very good.

Sowed 16 hills with Indigo seed for a tryal in my garden.

10. *Friday.*

Begin this day to cowpen a broad for next year's Crop at every place but the barn and at home. Those yards not yet cleaned and as the Cattle must have lain warmer in them than common I think it as yet too soon. I have now found the method I fell upon of making Stalls to be the very best I ever knew or saw both for the food, the Cattle, the goodness of the dung and the quantity, but I want still to contrive it so as to make them moveable, for my out yards which must always be in the ground I intend to Manure for the Conveniency of carrying out the dung.

Judy's sickness at the Stomach continued till 9 at when being more composed to reason on her case I concluded that which at first was perhaps the affect of the rubarb on a stomach already vomited by the bile must now be owing to a great relaxation and emptying, and in order to give some degree of warmth to the Nervous coat of her stomach I threw down in some of her Julep 4 drops tincture Castor. She grew easy, slept till near ten, then wake with her sickness and heaved to vomit once but nothing but wind came up, on which I ordered Water gruel to be given in so small a quantity as a tea spoon full at a time that the quantity might not press on her stomach, and getting four or five of these at some distance she grew easy, fell asleep and did not wake till past 1, then eat as many large spoon fulls and grew easy and slept till day when she waked quite easy, eat a small bowl full and continued easy and clear of a fever at 9. Lucy's fever not yet off though the head and Stomach are both easy. It seems she slept all night and felt moist in her palms but it only abated the fever.

11. *Saturday.*

Judy's fever left her this day. Lucy her ague and fever at 5 this eve.

12. *Sunday.*

Lucy missed her ague this day, but

13. *Monday.*

she had it between 2 and 3. It now keeps no regular day nor hour. Mingo dyed this morning. He was taken the 7th with a pain in his right side and head and blooded before I knew of it. He should have been vomited. That perhaps would have saved him though he mended all thursday, Fryday, and Saturday, lost all pain, spit free and eat and slept well, but saturday at midnight he was attacked with a violent pain in his Stomach. Yesterday an importunation broke and he dyed this morning.

15. *Wednesday*.

This day a hard, drye, Cold Northwest; very freesing day and last night the same. Colo. Chs. Carter and Mr. Carter of Corotoman[3] here and rode with me to my Several Cow yards. Great sight of dung. Lucy her ague and fever this day. 'Tis now every 3d day and but very moderate.

16. *Thursday*.

A prodigeous warm day. Many of my people have been ill this week and although the disorders have had some Symptoms similar with those a fortnight past yet they differed greatly in others. Some the belly most violently pained even to madness. Some the head, Stomach, and side. And I found worms to be the occasion of all the Coughs only such as the titillation of those animals in the stomach would occasion, and although there was a Sort of expectorated Pus yet the pains were not relieved till the removal of those animals. I bled to releive the Symptoms and gave Mercurius dulcis[4] in Purges by which means and a Course of worm powders after many were brought away, and some patients reduced very low recovered, nay some were imagined near their end. Note: till the operation of the purges the pains did not abate and then they began to spit and the pains dyed away. I had 4 in this Condition.

I observe my oats first sown begin to put forth a root. They have been in the ground now ten days and not a rain on them. Indeed I can't help observing the great drowth of the weather in my river side Cornfield. We have near 10 days' work occasioned by the drowth, the baking winds on the former wet Spell and the natural Stiffness of the land. Mangorike Cornfield will be near done this week. The ground is lighter than the other and their hands less afflicted with sickness. Besides there is one big bellyed woman that has seemed to be near her time about 2 months. As to wheat 'tis as bad as ever I saw, drowned in the wet land and spewed out in the dry land.

We are now cowpenning for the crop in 1759 and that it may not be

---

[3] Charles Carter of Corotoman (1732–1806), planter and son of John Carter (d. 1742) and Elizabeth Hill, was burgess for Lancaster Co., 1758–76, and later lived at Shirley in Charles City Co. He was Landon's nephew.

[4] Mercurius dulcis praecipitatus or sweet precipitate of mercury was a powder derived by passing mercury through a brine. It was used as a purgative, being particularly valuable in treating worms.

forgotten what division follows the other in order of farming I here set it down.

The stone house in tobacco	1758
The Barn field	1759
The Sasafrass	1760
Hay's Marsh Field	1761
Right hand great gate	1762

Each part is sown the Fall after in Wheat and each old Wheat field the Spring twelve month in Oats.

17. Friday.

Windsor, Sukey, Margaret's son Tom all pretty well. Windsor was Seized so suddenly and so violently as to run mad and held from killing himself. His pain just below his Navel across the belly. As he never complained before I suspected wind to be the Cause and gave Agua Mirabilis[5] 2 drachms with a large draft of Strong ginseng[6] tea. This procured ease. I then found little fever and that he had had no passage for two days and Gave Pilulae Cochea Minores[7] 25 grains. His pain returned as violent as ever by fits. The Cordial continued which always eased him and after a reasonable time threw up a bitter blyster of Common decoction, with Worm wood,[8] tansey,[9] Southern wood,[10] Cammomile and Salt 1 spoonfull. This brought down much hard indurated feces and the purge workt at intervals. He was very bad with his pain till after 5 motions he grew easy, slept moderately, but the return of his pain every now and then made me Suspect worms and I gave Othiops Mineral 12 grains with Coraline[11] and Semen Sakto [?][12] aa 15 grains 3 times a day. His fits of pain lessened and were not so violent and yesterday I threw down

[5] Agua mirabilis was a combination of spices useful as a stimulant.

[6] Ginseng is a root from both the Orient and America that was used as a mild purgative.

[7] Pilulae cochiae minores was derived from a combination of ingredients including the pulp of colocynth, syrup of buckthorn, and oil of cloves. It was used in colic pains, viscidities, and flatulencies.

[8] Wormwood is derived from any of a number of related strong-smelling plants with white or bitter flowers. An excellent bitter and detergent, it was used as a stomachic and in the treatment of worms, jaundice, and dropsy.

[9] Tansy is derived from the flowers of any plant of the genus *Tanacetum* and was used against worms and in treating certain female disorders.

[10] Southernwood is derived from the leaves of a shrubby wormwood, *Artemisia abrotanum*, native to southern Europe. It was used against worms, as an antidote to poison, and as a purgative.

[11] Coraline, a hard substance made up of the skeletons of certain marine animals and found in tropical seas, was a good astringent used to treat diarrhea, acidities, and convulsions.

[12] Probably semina sago, a combination of seeds of semina and the pith of certain palm trees. It was used as a strengthener.

Mercurius dulcis 6 grains with 20 grains Pil Cochia. This brought off large quantitys of Slimy goard seeds such as all experience pronounce to be parts of the Joint worm and after them all pain Ceased, the purge moved pritty Hydragogue and he grew quite well.

Sukey asked for a vomit as being now and then sickish at her Stomach. 30 grains Ipecacuana were administered. She workt two days, then a Smart fever attacked her with a severe pain in her Stomach by description near the lower orifice and with it a Short Cough. Of her own accord she got blooded but not above a Cup full. The Operator was fear full as she had a fever (which is an error the common people are fond of not bleeding in a fever). This gave no relief. On visiting her I found the pain now and then affected her left side below the Paps but the violence of the pain and the place and Cough which did not yield to the rattlesnake made me conclude worms in the Stomach or neck of the duodennon and one other Symptom confirmed it arising into her throat of some thing that pricked her. I gave her a spoonfull sweet oil and sugar and then found the pain more distinct in her stomach whereupon I gave Mercurius dulcis 6 grains, Pilulae Cochia 20 grains. In about 2 hours her side pain increased Violently. I applyed a blister to the part and hastened the operation of the purge. It brought off 3 or 4 worms and eased the Stomach. Then the rattle snake, vizt, 8 grains Valerian root, 6 grains every 3 hours, brought on a breathing sweat and free expectoration and by degrees every pain ceased excepting now and then in her Stomach, on which I gave for 3 days Othiops mineral 12 grains three times a day, and she has been well all to a weakness now 3 days without pain.

Tom's case a fever, an ague to appearance. He took a vomit which workt well. The ague came on at dark for 3 fits running then a Constant fever and violent pain in head and lower part of the stomach. 'Twas easy to suspect worms in his case, being a lean, Scrawney creature and great eater. I gave him Pulvis Bazilicus 20 grains. Before it workt he was in extreme pain and a Constant. It brought off 2 worms and 3 came away after wards insensibly. He grew very low. I constantly applyed him with oily limbs, marshmallow tea,[13] drops of Castor, Lavender, and Harkhorne and every night rattlesnake decoction but no abatement of the pain nor fever and his flesh merely parched. I then gave sweet oil and sugar and in two hours some drops Rattlesnake 8 grains, Valerian 4, ginseng tea and Salt tartar 4. This brought on a breathing moisture and by frequent drafts of Mallow tea with Salt prunella[14] the heat

[13] Marshmallow tea was derived from mallows, any plant of the genus *Malva*. It was used in nephritic ailments and for gripes in children.

[14] Salt prunella is a crystal mineral obtained by combining salt-peter and flowers of sulphur. A diuretic, it was used to treat fevers, gonorrhea, and throat infections.

abated, he sweated gently, his flesh softened and his pulse became distinct and the dying patient as it was thought shewed signs of recovery and has been mending 4 days, walks about and now by the help of small doses of Othiops mineral throws off worms every now and then. He is well but low as yet.

Those cases have confirmed me in the change I imagined I found in the disorders of this season which were at first Pleuroben then Peripneumonick and now they are chiefly occasioned by worms—every day they grow more distinct and the pains are all in the belly below the navel and yet awhile the fever's sharp but abate on the opperation of slight mercurial purges.

Finished sowing oats opposite the barn. The piece measures only 31 or 2 acres and they have put in the ground 158 bushels which at 4 bushels to the acre should have been but 124. The negroe seeds men have no gage and therefore must have it proportioned at so many bushel to each land. There were 60 bushels sown on this side the barn and I suppose with the same profuse hand.

Still very blowing, drye weather so that I can't sow clover which I am ready for.

18. *Saturday.*

Thunder a little and a pritty sprinkling of rain. Not cold as yet. I sowed my Corn house trash dunghill this day before the rain. Fine mellow stuff and full quantity for the little grass paddock by the Corn house.

19. *Sunday.*

It proved fine and warm last night and rained sufficiently so as to refresh every thing, but March is an invidious month. It now blows hard and very Cold at Northwest. Beware of a Frost.

20. *Monday.*

A hard Frost. Yesterday's and this day's cold wind has destroyed all the good effect of Saturday's rain. The Stiff land is as hard baked as ever. As I am now Cockling my wheat I have been over great part of it. I find full 1/3 of it killed, that where the ground lyes low drowned and on the tops of the ridges and sides where the ground was dryer quite spewed out and withered. I never remembered this land so spewy before. I once thought the plowing in Number four bout lands had been a preservative against and I thought to have carted Sand over it to make it less apt to Spew but this winter seems to baffle all that kind of reasoning for where the land is apparently drye the wheat is most spewed out. This can only be owing to the Summer's rain and the wet and sharp weather in the winter, and indeed the land at the Fork which is quite Sandy is in the same condition which is certainly no common observation. However if we could come into the true virginian notion of sowing then we should have great expectations for they generally sow each grain at a foot asunder and I think mine is something thicker than that.

Began this morning to sow Clover seed on my oats and endeavoured to put in 12 pounds to the acre. I wish I could promise any thing from the seed but veryly I don't like the looks of it. However it can't be worstead by being put in the ground. The wind quickly stopped me. Finished plowing for oats this day. My horses quite wore down but as much owing to the want of care in my people that feed them. However they shall have a week's rest and then only roll in the wheat and oats.

22. Wednesday.

Yesterday moderate and summer like. Rain but at night. Cold Northwest and so all this day.

It proved as fine a night as eye could wish to look at and only a visit from Northwest at 8 or a little past I went to bed and just as the Clock was striking I waked (it proved 10). I was waked with the rocking and trembling of my bed. Being confused from my sleep I thought the noise attending it was like the passing of many coaches by under my window but a second rocking and trembling came that instant with a roaring in the heavens, not a rumbling. I went out to know if others had not felt and heard it and the whole plantation were up and out of doors seeing for the Cause, but every part of the heavens was quite rekiin[?] and clear. They say about ten minutes before these two there was a small shaking of the earth and about the same time after the two another. The first I did not feel and the last I only fancyed I did, it being so small. Their accounts and mine agree as to the two that the earth and air shook and trembled. My boys in the house all were alarmed with it and my daughter in Law up stairs waked her husband. If it was not an earthquake it must be the explosion of some vast quantity of Gunpowder and Combustibles but this we can scarce conclud it to be having no such thing but a Small magazine in Wmsburgh at least 60 miles in strait line if kept in direction from the westward and Northward to the Eastward and southward. It was very terrible to one not used to earthquakes and I never had any idea of such a thing before only from description to which this answered. I send to see if the water in the well was muddy

23. *Thursday.*

this morning but it was not. I wish I had sent last night. Snow by 30 past 8 which in half an hour covered the ground. It is remarkable this snow came on with two different winds, Southeast and Northwest, and held so till the Northwest prevailed but not hard. This snow accounts for a certain coolness in the night air that has been felt these two nights so as to oblige us to use more bed cloths than we did this whole year and, as it is made Certain by experiments that snow is partly affected by a nitre in the air and as there frequently happens small *Concussions* (tremors) in the air so as to make the windows of houses rattle Every now and then before great snows with out any apparent cause of wind, it may not be impossible that the shocks and trembling of last night may be the affect of prodigeous quantitys of nitre in the air. If so we may conclude this will be a long snow. This is but a hypothetical conjecture but I wish the end may not veryfye it, for although it may be usual for farmers to impute good crops of grain to the snows that fall in the winter yet I beg leave to say my experience tells me they do great injury when they fall after the middle of February. Beware oats which are just peeping above ground. The observations made on the preceeding tremors before sooner lead me to observe the old sign so frequently talked of by people, the fires treading snow, which seems to have some foundation in reason, for the all woods abound with a nitre, yet we find in the producing this Salt by vegetable beds as I have read of 'tis often seen that they receive great impregnations by adventitious air. Wood, therefore, cut down even a Small time may have its porousducts [?] which it abounds with emptied of its natural juices so as to admit of the introduction of air, and the nearer a snow as this air is Nitrous the wood will of course be more impregnated which as soon as it becomes raryfyed by the fire falls naturally into those little explosions resembling the treading of snow. Now according to Stephens's doctrin[15] for making Potash old woods are best which must be owing to the impregnations of nitrous air as before, and the saying woods do frequently spit when no snow follows proves nothing against it, for the intervention of Powerfull winds or melting heats of the Sun may with good reason be allowed as dispersing cause and does not prove that the air in the

---

[15] Almost certainly Thomas Stephens, an Englishman, who was granted £3,000 in England to discover a new method of manufacturing potash. He published a pamphlet on the method, selling it during his visit to Virginia in 1757. In the same year the Virginia House of Burgesses voted him £100 to help him build a potash furnace in Williamsburg (see Brooke Hindle, *The Pursuit of Science in Revolutionary America* [Chapel Hill, 1956], 208, and *Burgesses' Journal, 1753–1758*, 423, 492 [Apr. 19, June 8, 1757]).

wood was not of a nitrous quality, and as that quality is asserted to the generating of Snow it is no bad sign of signs when the wood on the fire spits or bubles as is before observed. If those shocks we felt are universal or felt as any great distance to before they must be caused by something more than Nitrous air exploding. If it be asked what should occasion such explosions it may be well answered Chimistry has discovered many bodys inflamable or explosive with the intervention of other when neither of them singly discover any such effects and the saying the air is nitrous does not exclude any body of another opposing quality rising into it perhaps from the earth. 'Tis certain it snowed constantly till past 6 in the evening and is pritty deep. Now the clouds break from the Northwest.

24. *Friday.*

Clear but very cold. The snows melt fast in the Sun.

This day Dr. Flood informed me of the Shock of the Earthquakes being felt at his. It agrees with mine exactly at ten but he says there was but one and it continued not longer than 6 or 8 seconds, but I am certain of at the distance of some minutes the first waked me and the 2d I felt distinctly.

25. *Saturday.*

In spight of all our care which I can answer for the time I was at home I have lost the following cattle this Fall.

Of a dropsy:	2, 1 cow and 1 Yearling
Found dead:	1 fine cow though put well at night she had formed a wen and that was corrupted within.
Of a load of chaft:	1 yearling having weevel eaten wheat in it.
Of a Scouring:	1 ditto
Broke its neck:	1 a young steer just taken up.
Pushed into the Creek:	1 heifer.
	7 in all

The cockling wheat this year an immense trouble occasioned by the Rascal who was overseer last year at the Fork who never saw the work well done there and from thence came most of my seed wheat.

A person (Mrs. B. of I.)[16] siezed yesterday with a violent Tenesmus for a while attended with hard indurated fever and a griping which had made her fainty. I ordered a purge Rhoobarb, Jalap, Cream tartar, Senna aa 11 grains

[16] Probably Elizabeth, daughter of Moore Fauntleroy and wife of Captain William Brockenbrough of The Island in Richmond Co.

finely powdered. In two hours after the following Clyster: 2 handfull Marsh-mallow root boiled in Milk and Water sweetened with brown sugar together with a hand full of bruised flax seed, 2 spoon full hogs' lard, and to be repeated till the purge worked. The following Cordial to be given a Spoonfull at a time: Agua Mirabilis 3 Spoonfulls dicoction of Genseng 9 Spoonfulls. This purge eased the Lady but although it was only preparatory to her cure because she did not get quite releived and had a relapse of her gryping for which she should have been blooded the good women got to dosing her with Clove Oil[17] burnt with Cinamon, decoctions of red oake bark,[18] hot firy cakes of Peper and Ginger and locked up the guts. This threw on a violent fever which Nature relieved by a violent evacuation through the other Channels and 'tis said she is recovering when there was 20 to 1 against her from the Vile practice.

27. *Monday.*

I saw my daughter Sukey yesterday. She has been exactly a fortnight under a Constant fever but said every day to intermit because when the period of the ague and the hot fit is off she becomes cheerfull. Dr. Flood could not be got to her and my fears will not let me practice on her as her case is of so Chronick a kind.

28. *Tuesday.*

This month proves the great inconstancy of the weather in this Country but more so this year than Common. We have had within this week a very deep snow, then yesterday weather almost too warm, great rain and very sharp Claps of thunder and lightning, last night a prodigeous blustering Northwest and to day spitting with Snow blowing hard and in squalls and with all very Cold. We should have finished sowing our Oats had it not been for this wind. Frequent scudds of Snow.

29. *Wednesday.*

This day hard frost, no working and very cold and windy with many snowy Clouds. No sowing a seed.

30. *Thursday.*

Hard frost, blowing day, very cold wind at Northwest and a great Sup-plye of cold Clouds.

[17] Oil of cloves or Ol caryophyllorum is derived from the bark of the tree that produces cloves and was used as a carminative.

[18] Red oak bark was a powerful astringent and was sometimes used against intermittents.

31. *Friday.*

My weaving boy pretended he never wove 7 yards the day when his Master was here and having not wove 4 since of 3/4 cloth but one day I set by him this day half an hour. He mended 15 threads in the time and moved his roller 6 times and yet he wove 11 inches and had many hindrances with his shuttle which is 22 the hour and as there are 13 hours clear of eating time it comes to 8 yards, but I ask no more than 7 which is better than an hour and a half leizure time. 95 bushels oats brought up. 10 left to finish sowing. 16 bushels wheat brought up. Finished sowing oats this day which we could have finished 3 weeks agoe but the weather so hard as not to admit of it.

APRIL 1758

1. *Saturday.*

A White and black frost this day. The ground has been so frozen now 12 days that my intentions of rolling my wheat has been greatly obstructed. The way to guard against this is to do things when they may be done and not at certain times, for this work, necessary as it is, will now be late done through these means. Yesterday the first apricot blossom appeared a full month later than usual.

The weaving boy has been as long weaving 31 yards 1/4 [by] 3/4 cloth as he was weaving 33½ yards 5/4 cloth and has used 2 pounds more of yarn in the 3/4 Cloth than in the former. He had 38 pounds 1/4 and in this 42 pounds of which 1¼ he has returned so that his villany extends far not only to weave little but to prevent his weaving at all by destroying the yarn. The whole month of March has been singularly very bad weather and he is no Planter nor Farmer that leaves many works to be done then. April has begun in the same course. Very Cold, blowing and a great prospect of Falling weather.

Oats sowed in the ground beyond the Corn 111 bushels to 30 acres.

The weaver had out 19 pounds yarn which warped 31 yards 1/4, the same Number of pins as in the former piece of Cloth.

The whole quantity oats sown is 329 bushels, about 80 acres, so that in the whole we have sown 9 bushels more than 4 to the acre although one Piece fell short that quantity and another exceeded it. 16½ bushels wheat brought up.

2. *Sunday.*

A white and black frost this day. Exceeding Cold. Frequently snowing from Northwest and the Clouds flying in squally drifts.

That which used to be called April Showers in order to produce the flowers in May are now nothing but cold scudds of Snow and I doubt not but many a poor cow goes to pot for it.

4. *Tuesday.*

17 bushels wheat.

5. *Wednesday.*

This day a Frost and so has it been this 12 or 14 days. A prospect of good weather. As a Farmer or Planter I must call it a bad Season. The cold winds attending the Frosts have had their visible bad effects on every thing. Cattle which not a fortnight agoe were in fine order are now much reduced. Oats lye just peeping the clod, poor and perish. Wheat again almost dead to the roots and nearly blown out of the ground. The earth merely dust and flying as at midsummer and from what I can see no prospect of any plants at all.

7. *Friday.*

Still Cold, hard, blowing weather and 'tis observeable ever Since the earthquake there has been a bank at West every night. The next day hard blasts. So it is to night.

Dr. Nicholas Flood has not been here as a visit to the sick since the beginning of March when he came to Judy. Neither has he prescribed since the 24th of March when he sent Sukey medicin.

8. *Saturday.*

This seems to bid fair for a fine day, the first for a full fortnight. In Short I have never been so much puzzled to do the proper works in my farm since I first began. Rolling of the wheat has been so often obstructed by hard frost that it is but just done. Rolling of the oats is but now began and indeed too soon for it as it has happened, the Frosts having kept the seed so long in the ground; but if it was not to be done I could not have time to do it for the carting out the dung must be begun in a week more and 'tis as necessary a work. Thus we see what hindrances may happen. How necessary is it, therefore, to use the present time and not comfort our selves A thing may be done next month when 'tis not impossible but nothing can be done then as it has really happened all March; how many have depended on getting their cornfields ready this very month and yet how few in low stiff lands could ever work for the hardness of the earth occasioned by the hard frost and Violent winds upon the back of the last month's rains. 'Tis now prodigeous drye. Every thing wants rain. The sun sets again in a Cloud. This day has been windy but more moderate than it has been this fortnight and only in flares.

My daughter Sukey went to Mr. Hamilton's[19] the 9th or 10th of March and was taken with an ague and fever the 11th or 12th which never left her till the 24th or 25th; then it kept off till the 3d of this month and came only a fever every night and but slight. As she had taken the bark before to remove her fits I did not think proper to repeat it, the fevers now about requiring long and gentle evacuations. I therefore the 6th gave her Rhubarb 15 grains, Cream tartar [a]n[d] Salt tartar 4 grains, Soap 12 grains which gave 3 moderate stools and her fever skipped that night. Last night she had a small return. Her maid Winney was taken ill there and not hearing of it she fell into a Continual fever which held her 6 days. I fetched her home last night and gave her some weak decoction Rattle snake. This occasioned her to vomit and seeing much green bile although she was big with child I ordered her 25 grains Ipecacuana this morning which workt easy and brought away 5 vomits, all green bile, and after 6 at night she fell into a fine breathing sweat which I would not obstruct, therefore only ordered her plenty of milk warm tea.

10. *Monday*.

Winney continued all yesterday in her fever. Her pain in the head abated a little at night but not the fever. I gave her Rhubarb 5 grains, Conutuptheus [?][20] 5 grains, Rad Valerian 5 grains, Salt tartar 4 grains in a Cup of Marsh Mallow tead with Salt Prunella in it and 40 drop Spiritus-Minderius. Four of these doses this day but no amendments. Therefore I sent to Dr. Flood as she was usefull (though careless) among my Children. At 2 I gave a spoonfull of Rattle snake decoction finding her cough hard and her pulse prodigeous quick, and as she had one stool the rattle snake I repeated hourly for 3 doses, and at 5 she fell into a plentifull sweat and as she herself owns and Continues in it till [blank].

Joe who was taken last wednesday with an ague and fever and went out on fryday after being emptied by a Vomit was on saturday siezed with a pain a cross his breast, and on Sunday by the rattle snake root his Cold broke, but on munday his pain fell into his right side for which I blistered him. That grew easy and last night and this day quite easy till 5 when he was siezed with a Chillyness, pain in head and back violent. I was alarmed at it but it abated soon and I am clearly of opinion he had chilled himself by lying in bed without his

[19] Gilbert Hamilton (d. 1768) was a planter in Richmond Co. and at one time was sheriff. He was a close friend of Carter's.

[20] Perhaps some form of aconite, any plant of the genus *Aconitum*, which grows on the mountains in Switzerland and Savoy. It was used as a cardiac and respiratory sedative.

cloths and getting up and setting without his breeches which it seems he and his Lady too are fond of. But one week had I my family clear of disorders and now there is but 5 of them ill.

My wheat now discovers the prodigeous service there is in rolling, nowithstanding it was done so late and the earth blown quite drye and hard and no rain since to settle the earth and moisten it for the roots. It shews with this one warm day prodigeous green.

12. *Wednesday.*

Dr. Flood came last night past 5 to Winney. He ordered her to be blooded this morning which was done quantity 6 ounces very morbid and almost in a state of Corruption. He then ordered great Plenty of Mallow and ground Ivy tea with Spiritus Salis Oleo[21] and Lavender aa 20 drops every two hours and one spoonfull rattlesnake decoction every two hours to break the viscid state of her blood and help on Expectoration with plenty of gruel for food. Her Pulse still very quick but the uneasyness in her head abated.

Lucy Carter taken ill with an ague this day which is one day over her monthly period and 'tis remarkable. She never look better since her first attack in August. She was siezed in a moment past 10 and though her fever was moderate yet 30 past 5, when it appeared her fever was almost off, she vomited green bile. Joe mending. His child Sarah ill. Toney's boy ill. And poor Sukey Carter who was brought to the Dr. very weak and low and in danger of a hectic. He gave her nothing imagining she might mend.

13. *Thursday.*

Winney blooded last night according to order though not such a quantity taken away as was ordered through her fears and difficulty in bleeding. It seems much mended the upper coat a little Florid not so Viscid and a tollerable proportion of Serum. Her cough breaking and she spits a tough matter by means of the rattle snake though no sweating and the pulse not much lower and near as quick as usual. She thinks herself better. This is her 11th day. Her pulse growing so much fuller than it has hitherto been and very quick withall and as yet very little expectoration although a plentiful use of the rattlesnake decoction. At 6 this evening I ordered 6 ounces of blood more to be taken away as being the only means to save her. She thinks her self she is better because her cough is not so troublesome and frequent but I observe she is under a great

---

[21] Spiritus salis cum oleo vitrioli was obtained by combining common salt, water, and oil of vitriol. It was used as a diuretic in the treatment of fevers, obstructions in the liver and spleen, dropsies, and jaundice.

difficulty in breathing and as yet no proper sweat though her flesh is grown much softer.

14. *Friday.*

Winney I think much better by her pulse since her yesterday's bleeding. Lucy's fever came on before day so I can't tell whether she had any ague. Mr. Hamilton writes Sukey is not better nor worse.

Began this day to Cart out my dung, only one horse cart and an Ox Cart by reason of Joe's illness.

Began every where to plant Corn the 11th of this month. Not the least moisture to the earth since the snow the 23d March. It is therefore extravagantly drye, hard winds, cold Frosts and now hot and smokey. Few or no Plants that I can hear of. This is some of my old luck though now I suppose it is pritty general.

15. *Saturday.*

Excessive hot day and no rain as yet. Such are the Seasons I have had to crop in ever since 1751, always on violent extremes. I can't but take notice of the death of my little Canary bird, an old housekeeper having had it here 11 year this month and constantly fed it with bread and milk, and I wish the heat of this weather did not by Souring its food occasion its death, for it sung prodigeously all the forepart of the day. At night it was taken with a barking noise and dyed the night following, vizt, last night. I know this is a thing to be a laught at but a bruit or a bird so long under my care and protection deserves a Small remembrance.

16. *Sunday.*

Lucy took her vomit last night, 14 grains Ipecacuana and 25 drops of Vinum benedictum. It produced only two vomits and 3 stools. I do imagin it was too small a dose but the reason that governed me was that the bile was loose and well accumulated by her fevers, that the Physick had been new and on the tryal made on one of the same age or near a year older who happened to be sick 17 grains and 40 drops work very much. But be it as it will she missed her fit this day which is the first instance since her Attack in July.

A fine breathing Shower this for near half an hour. The wind with it hurryed down a good deal of water. 'Tis just 3 weeks since we had one drop before. Every thing smiles already. Oh for a day of fine dripping refreshment.

A purge Prescribed by Dr. Amson for me in a Compound fever, part bilious and inflamatory. The latter Symptoms had been removed by bleeding: Rx Rhubarb 2 drachms, Glauber Salts[22] 3 drachms, Salt tartar 10 grains.

Boil them a few minutes in about 3 ounces Water, strain and add Solutive Sugar Roses 1 ounce, Agua Mirabilis 2 drachms. Mix them well together.

Received advice from Mr. Hamilton's that my daughter Sukey was now grown very weak with her fevers. Dr. Flood had sent her a purge the day before which had vomited her once and worked her 4 times. Nothing but thin Slime and she could not move with out help. Her case has in my opinion been very dangerous these 12 or 14 days. The Dr. could not be got to her till about a week agoe. He saw her and concluded she was going into a hectic, this on a very long Coarse of intermittants sometimes with sharp agues and at best a very delicate child must Needs be very bad so that I almost dispair of her. We have had a plentyfull watering this night.

17. *Monday.*

A Cold hard Northwest this day after the rain. Last night little Sarah, Winney's child, dyed. She was taken a fortnight past with a fever and ague, then very common in the family, and without seeing her I ordered her a vomit of Ipecacuana which worked well and easy but her fevers returned a night or two after on which I ordered a gentle purge of Rhubarb. This removed the fevers for some days. When they returned again Dr. Flood was then visiting her mother and, feeling the child, advised me to give it 4 grains Mercurius dulcis and 8 grains Othiops to be purged off if any Symptoms indicated the next day. This was done and brought off 7 worms. Her fever still continued intermitting every night on which I gave her Othiops and Rhubarb in Small doses and brought away 6 worms more which releived the Complaint in her belley and as her fever then left her I never saw her afterwards till the 15th at night when I only heard her complaining of something pricking her stomach and throat as it came up. Yesterday this occasioned her to vomit and she threw up some green bile. I ordered her a small quantity of Ipecacuana to cleanse the stomach and get up the worms, these which appeared by the pricking Complaint. She had two vomits and in a Stool two worms more and they told me was very brisk and eat well but in the night she complained again of this pricking in her Stomach and whatever it was it stuck in her throat and choaked her. I am of opinion she was at first so full of worms that to get rid of

[22] Glauber's Salt or Sal mirabile glauberi was obtained by separating the spirit of salt from the salt and was used as a diuretic and a cathartic.

the nausious taste of the medecin given her they eat through her stomach and into her throat. I was so engaged with others of greater Consequence sick and deceived by the constant news of her being better that I never examined thoroughly into her case and was quite easy as to her so that I forgot to administer a little sweet oil so much recommended for killing worms in her stomach or else 'tis probable they would have been destroyed before they did the injury. But she has ever been a lean, meagre, sickly child now near 7 year old.

Winney has been all along so costive in her disorder that I have been obliged to order a clyster but on Saturday, I suppose her juices becoming thinner by the attenuating quality of the rattlesnake and her foods and teas, she had two stools which prevented the exhibitive some laxative medicin which Flood recommended when he saw her Yesterday. She had 4 stools and last night I ordered her some warm wine and water a little endialed with Cinnamon Water to be check this discharge lest it should weaken her in her low state, but the person who tended her was too cautious and gave her very little of it so I suppose her bowels kept discharging in the night. I have now changed her food to rice gruel. This had been the constant going off of her disorder in others this last month when they have not had emetics very late in the disorder and they by being properly governed have all done well and I hope this may be her case for they tell me she is certainly a great deal better but I shall presently visit her.

Winney a great deal better although affected with the death of her child.

Old George and Dinah taken ill. Their complaints are agues and in the fever pains in the right side. Both took vomits and are now discovering coughs but no fever. George was for ten years a noted runaway, always in the woods and mostly naked, and now he has left that trade he is grown a sickly fellow. This is the second attack of a pleuratic kind that he has had after his intermittants. He had near dyed with the first.

The third day carting out dung and only 62 load out. The case is everything is poor through the prodigeous bad February, March and thus far in April. I will for a fancy send for an Irish cur of which I have heard so much talk work with one horse.

18. *Tuesday*.

A very Cold keen Northwest wind this day. Also very bad for the Creatures who now stand in need of green herbage even for a Natural Physical use to correct the gross and viscid bile made so by the long feeding on drye food and the very cold weather.

The wet season in plowing, the cold drye season in sowing, and the same in Sprouting has destroyed many oats in the stiff lands and some in the light.

19. *Wednesday.*   20. *Thursday.*

Cold Easterly winds and very drye warm the 20th just at night. 117 load dung carried out yesterday, to day 25 more of which 4 compleated the dung in the barn yard. The rest without the yard made mostly by the out Gang of horses. Carryed 121 load in all. Out of the yard as yet 21 load.

Sowed this day a small plant patch which I had well dunged between time and well watered immediately and intend they shall be watered morn and eve.

22. *Saturday.*

Joe's recovery has been very slow till now. His case was first of the most bilious kind of intermittant then inflamatory attended with a Severe cough and pain in his right side. He was for his ague and fever vomited and discharged much bile. He was too low as I thought to admit of bleeding for his pain. I therefore blistered him and kept him under a long use of the rattle-snake root. His cough abated by frequent expectoration and a natural purging came on which I have found if watched to be a favourable crisis of the disorder, but he was so much reduced and so relaxed at last I was obliged to have recourse to bitters, chiefly Centaury.

Winney his wife whose case is fully described before makes very little shew of recovery. She gained a little strength but I believe through aversion to medicin she concealed her want of appetite and eat frequently without any inclination. She had also a purging but it stopped too soon of its own accord. Dr. Flood who was called into her had directed upon any Symptom of sickness at Stomach or want of appetite to exhibit a dose of Ipecacuana but these She concealed and grew very nervously affected. Being with child there was danger in using warm nervines. The Dr. Therefore ordered her warm bitters 3 times a day and Spirit Lavender with 1/5 Sal Volfrigty [?].[23] She complained this day of sickness at her stomach and being affected in her sences and deaf I gave her 25 grains Ipecacuana which brought off Abundance of filthy Phlegm

[23] Probably Salt volatile olesum, a combination of salt ammoniac, salt tartar, leaves of *Marum Syriacum,* wine, oils of cloves, cinnamon, nutmeg, marjoram, lemons, and oranges. It was used in nervous disorders.

and bile. She seems a little feverish which She has not been these 5 days, but I think she both hears and speaks better. I shall begin her bitters tomorrow if not obstructed by Circumstances.

Lame George whose disorder was the same as Joe's had (if he does not as it is) like to have lost his life by a hiccup because he was known to be subject to it without any other disorder. I found him under a prodigeous difficulty in breathing attended with a return of his pain (that had left him) in his right side. I gave him 25 grains then 10 grains Ipecacuana then a Spoon full Crocus wine before I could make him vomit. He had several Gulps of thick yellow Phlegm and one vomit of the same. He certainly must have catched cold again though his pulse is not much disordered. If I don't find this pain abate I shall blister the part. He took in the morning a Laxative purge for a constant pain in his back which I imagined to be a bilious induration in the adjacent Guts.

My Dear Sukey is now most dangerous ill at Mr. Hamilton's. Dr. Flood who has in her hand has given within 8 days two purges which have brought off abundance of Green Slime but they produce no abatement of her hectic heat and she is now attended with a tickling Cough attended with a Small pain in her breast. She is so weak with the many attacks of the fever and ague she had since August twice a month and now with this present disorder that I dispair of her life. God only knows and I calmly submit. If she recovers I shall be greatly thank full for the blessing for she is the most Patient, most Sensible and most engaging infant that ever parent had. If she dyes I shall remember the rod that chastizes and learn to amend by it.

Sowed many Indigo hills this day. It took 3 men and a boy a fortnight to make them and two days to Chop off the hills and now two days to sow them. This I mention to estimate the profit.

I find few or no plants any where. Have therefore set about a large plant patch in a Nuke of my meadow, rich light and drye enough and convenient to water, and by a cooler with its bottom full of Gimblet holes and a false bottom lined with woolen they may fill it with water and when ever the beds lift up the false bottom by a String and hook it to the pole of the Cooler and I imagin the water will fall equally on the beds. This will be of great Service also in my Garden to water things there.

Finished carting out the barn dung. Quantity as follows: in the yard 121 load; without the yard 71 load. I had yesterday a peck of my new wheat cleaned for mill. It weighed 14½ pounds and has made as fine bread as I would wish to eat. I mention this because all the wheat this year is weavel eaten, but to preserve mine I stacked it as close as I could in my mow and I find excepting at top and at the sides the weavil killed in the egg excepting here and there a grain which may as well come into it from the sheeves at the side for they thresh it all promiscuously. Very drye weather again, hot, windy and smouky. Finished planting at Mangorike all my Corn.

23. *Sunday.*

Poor Sukey near her last. Her disorder encreases and her strength decreases. Mr. Hamilton thinks she must mend speedily or dye in a very little time. Maid Winney's sickness continued which obliged me to give her Warm medicin, vizt, Powder Saffron and Rattlesnake root 23/20 grains, Powder Valerian, Salt tartar, Crabbs Eyes and Coraline each 30 grains, divided into 6 doses to be taken every two hours. Three of the doses strengthened her stomach so much that she could bear her victuals. They also brought on a breathing sweat which removed her frequent fluttering in her Pulse and the intermissions.

24. *Monday.*

Gave Winney her bitters as before ordered. These made her sick again but by adding some of the powders she kept them and I am in hopes as they have encreased her appetite they will strengthen her.

Dung carryed out from J. King's: 58 load.

25. *Tuesday.*

This morning Mr. Gilbert Hamilton (at whose house my dear little daughter Susannah has been ever since her last illness) sent me an account of her death Certainly approaching, and he says in his letter, although her face, feet and hands are all cold and her pulse quite gone and reduced to the bones and skin that cover them and dying very hard under the Severe agonys of her disorder, Yet does she preserve her Usual Patience to such a degree that he never saw such an Example before.

Severe stroke indeed to A Man bereft of a Wife and in the decline of life because at such periods 'tis natural to look out for such Connections that may be reasonably expected to be the support of Greyhairs and such an one I had promised myself in this child in Particular,

> For although she did not live beyond the very Dawn
>   Of humane life
> Such were the early discoverys of her growing Excellencys
> It might be justly concluded That had the same Soul
>   Animated to a Mature Age A more healthy Frame
> She would have been a Conspicuous Pattern if not inimitable

Even amongst the most Prudent, Good, and Virtuous
Of her Sex
God Omnipotent.

Could it have consisted with thy divine Purposes to have Suffered this blessing to have continued to me my happyness would have been uncommon but as thou hast otherwise determined it It is enough to lay the Obligation of a constant gratefull return to thy divine Goodness that thou was't pleased to Suffer me to be the instrument of so Promising a humane Creature, for in this Shall I comfort my self that I was not myself altogether Corrupt or thou wouldest not have so Signally dignifyed such a Stock by a Scion so universally applauded by All who knew her and this before she could have received any of the Advantages of Education. In her therefore Pure Nature must have been pure Goodness. She dyed between 11 and 12, The constant period of intermission of her fever from the day of her attack, and it never changed this from day but once when it was beleived Dr. Flood's medicin prolonged the time of intermission for more than 12 hours, but 'tis now certain her disorder lay in her breast and I suppose the breaking of that importunation finished her.

56 load Carryed out this day.

26. *Wednesday.*

56 load this day.

27. *Thursday.*

A very cold day and drye Wind at Northwest ever since the day before yesterday ten o'clock. We have been 2 days turning our dung in at King's. The ground is well covered but the dung dryed much by the winds. Quantity of Dung from King's is exactly 200 load.

I visited my Plant Patches and those which were pritty well off on Saturday last have now scarcely a plant to be seen. Such have the ravages of the Flye been this drye, Cold weather. Order some seed to be soked in Milk and sown to morrow morning in the meadow at the Fork.

28. *Friday.*

A fine rain before day and continues to rain a fine drop but 'tis cold occasioned by the return of those clouds that were drove to the eastward by the Cold winds. I uncovered my plants to let the rains was[h] away if possible the Flye. This insect certain comes out of the ground for as well as I can discover from their smallness they have no wing though called a flye and take that appellation from their skipping when the hand is laid on the bed. I was so apprehensive there would not be plants saved for seed that I got the Frames of boxes and put round some plants every here and there in my beds and covered some with Glasses to raise the plants, and although I swept them well before I covered them and the Sun shone hot through the Glasses I discovered flyes on the leaves of the plants, from whence I conclude they must come out of the ground. It has been a drizzling day all through but this has not drove away the flye. They may be seen on the plants as thick as ever. The weather being cold is the Occasion of it but I have heard it said Constantly that 'tis only cold, drye weather that they eat in.

29. *Saturday.*

This a moist day till 2 when it cleared off with a thunder shower and a hard blowing wind at West but not Cold. Began this day to examin into the cause of the wetness of my meadow and I find near 20 strong dams made by the beavers in the Canals which rais a great pond and against the ponds the[y] bore holes through the banks into the meadow. I discover they always require sticks to Strengthen these dams which I see they get from the bushes that grow on both sides of the bank. This has obliged me to have all those cut down and in order to carry off the water that is within the meadow I must again open the middle Canal which will in very dry seasons obstruct my watering as I have before observed.

Carted dung yesterday from the Mangorike yard 36 load, this day 40 load.

30. *Sunday.*

Very Cold last night, excessively so this day. Prodigeous piercing hard wind at Northwest. This will in all probability bring on fresh inflamations, ruin those few plants remaining, prevent the sprouting of those lately sown. Note: every rain for this year at least has cleared away in this manner. I once heard an old Almanack maker say if the world lasted long enough mid-summer day would change Seasons with Christmas day. It bids fair for it this year, for 'tis very probable the 1st May will be much colder than the 1st of January was.

MAY 1758

1. *Monday.*

A fine winter's morning with Clouds all along the Southern and Western horizon like Snow and not a Frost last night only because the air was so violent that the dews could not lye but cold enough for a black one. I have not but 3 or 4 Nights this year been able to endure my quilt on my [me], but last night it felt light enough. Thus have I seen every year since 1749 labouring under such variety of bad seasons in some principle part of it as to make it impossible to make a Crop of anything to perfection but once of oats and once of wheat. It differed many times with other people but now I fancy 'tis pritty universal. The West and Northwest wind rising with the Sun.

Plants destroyed generally by the Flye at Court and the last sown seed not come up. Every body planting corn in their tobacco grounds. Very windy.

3. *Wednesday.*

A Prospect of a Shower but broke away with a most violent West wind. A dismal prospect in every thing: Wheat turning yellow through drowth and Cold winds; Oats perishing for the same cause; Mole destroying Corn most prodigeously; Milions of Flyes still swarming in the tobacco beds. There was great talk of a fine rain in Pharnham Parish[24] last saturday. We had the pleasure to see it pass by us which we have enjoyed for many years but I envy not till well some body is blessed. 6/ per bushel offered for peas to plant. Yesterday 43 load of dung. The plants sown the 20th April at night appeared some yesterday and more today which we may Call 12 days. The flye has not found them as yet. 47 load today.

Dung from the Mangorike Cow yard 208 load. Began to cart the house dung.

4. *Thursday.*

A very squally day. Clouds full of snow to appearance, and there fell several large flakes of it in a smart scudd that went down the River where it seemed to rain below us. The Plants sown in my meadow began to appear here and there so that although the place is something moist they kept the same time in the ground as they did sown in my Cow yard. Perhaps the salt of the barn there was a good ballance for the warmth in my meadow.

5. *Friday.*

This morning early a white frost in all moist lands. I thought there was one yesterday but of this we are certain.

7. *Sunday.*

We were favoured the 5th and sixth with every pleasing prospect of a warm rain, but rain and it All vanished by a gentle North gale last night. A prodigeous fogg this morning Succeeded by a Cold North wind. To last night:

[24] North Farnham Parish was in Richmond Co.

66 load of dung carryed from house, 57 of which the first dung hill on the right.

8. *Monday.*

Last night very cold indeed and this morning a Smart white frost so that if we do get plants enough 'twill be in spite of the weather. 'Tis exceeding drye with all. 22 load of dung carted out this day. 88 in all.

9. *Tuesday.*

A white frost this morning visible at 6.

10. *Wednesday.*

This is third morning running I have to observe there was a white frost which added to the parching heat in the day and excessive drye weather must certainly destroy the Crops and fruit of every kind. Plants in my meadow came up here and there in 12 days but none has started since.

The flye which destroyed and destroys almost every bed as fast as the seed sprouts I now think to proceed from the ground by their being so universal in every peace of ground you break up. The plenty of plants for many years prevented any observations for the better producing them. Therefore this year I have been more to seek in them than in any thing. However I think I have discovered that constant moisture or Urinous salts keep them off the beds in the first case and I suppose in the latter case the eggs they must certainly come from must be destroy[ed]. Therefore Cow yards have penned all the winter must needs make good plant patches provided they be near water to lower the salts that they may not also destroy the plants. Or moist black meadow grounds that will pulverize fine and can be kept constantly moist but not wet are exceeding good as to preserving the plants from the flye. I sowed one of these at my fork quarter and contrived the drains that were made to carry off the water should float round it so that I could in 10 minutes raise a gentle moisture over the whole beds and discharge the water immediately with any Current or force at all. These plants came up in ten days and this day being but the 12th the ground is covered all over with plants that seem not to be disturbed with the flye. They were covered down with light leafy brush. Those plants in my own meadow though the ground is as riche were covered as well but only watered twice a week, but finding they make no progress I have covered thicker and now water every other night. The Patch in my cow yard is but small but pritty full of plants. Here I watered night and morning but as the ground was of a Stiff kind it would [dry] a little about midday. Therefore I have ordered another Covering on.

I find Corn requires in light land some care in planting also to provide for these drye spells or else the birds pull all up as they have done at the fork for 100 hills together. Therefore for the future I shall plant early and deep and tread the earth that covers the grain well down. I did so in one piece and there it stands. The reason is the earth being settled round the roots the birds can't pull the Stalk up and only break off a little of the blade, but in the other case for want of rain the earth binds not at all and gives no kind of resistance to the [blank].

I began also to weed Corn at the Fork yesterday but at Mangorike the labour of making the tobacco hills is great and prevents me, for which purpose as my land is now in a great degree improved I will for the future make my hills in the winter and put my dung in the Step. This will be easy and the turning may be done at the usual time. The dung will not Suffer because it will be covered with earth in the Step and yet its ground rott. Now although this don't expedite the plantation work in general yet it gives room for beginning to weed Corn sooner which it Certainly must want in some places especially hard spots before the rains fall. 96 sheep sheared here. 135 load of dung this night from hence.

11. *Thursday.*

Cold wind this morning at North and so leaving easterly Clouds heavy and hazy rain seemingly at hand. God send it may. 25 load dung this day.

12. *Friday.*

A hazy morning and to appearance likely for rain but we have had these so often I cannot look on it as a sign of any, especially as the wind continues Northerly and Cold which to be sure was very sensible last night.

Finished carting out all my dung made in the Several cow yards in trumbrels measured to contain 40 bushels full.

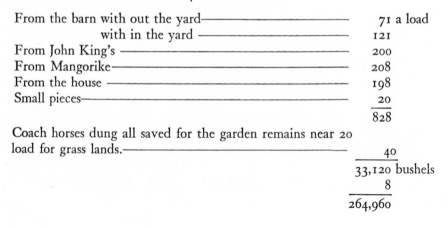

From the barn with out the yard———————————	71 a load
with in the yard ———————————	121
From John King's —————————————————	200
From Mangorike————————————————————	208
From the house —————————————————	198
Small pieces—————————————————————	20
	828

Coach horses dung all saved for the garden remains near 20 load for grass lands.————————————————— 40

33,120 bushels
8
264,960

15. Monday.

This morning it remained some time doubtfull as to Fogg or rain but at last a very small thin shower cleared up the debate which would have been an injury, the quantity of water was so little, had it not been Cloudy. We have had just two showers since the Snow immediately [before] the earthquake. One would have been enough to have refreshed the earth had it not been followed by a Constant long run of Cold, hard winds, white frosts and sharp nights. The other too little to be called a shower.

I have endeavoured all I can for plants but although I water night and day the weather is and has been such I fear all won't do. We can't long determin on any method. Sometimes the watering seems to be bad, sometimes Covering is good, sometimes it seems very pernicious. The moles have burrowed all my Corn up almost that I did not plant in hills. This I always preferred as the best way but did otherwise in some new hill sides because I could hardly dread the mole there, but this drye weather has encouraged him to run every where and the cutting him out in the weeding is nothing. He only runs lower and eats corn as well as a hog.

It rained from 8 o'clock at night by smart showers till near day, very refreshing.

16. Tuesday.

A Cool day and windy.

18. Thursday.

It began to rain at 9 at night and the earth has been most agreeably entertained with it all night and raining this morning. The prospect is once more green. I hope the plants will now be pushed on to some good purpose. Rain in the evening. A cooled night.

19. Friday.

Not very warm but very pleasant and fair.

20. Saturday.

The same weather.

Finished burying my dung and turning. All my tobacco hills ready for cutting off when plants, a work notwithstanding the difficulty attending on account of the drye weather sooner done by 18 days than last year.

Began this day to weed Corn sooner than last year by 19 days. The Corn much missing by means of the birds and mole who root every where like hogs.

I have ordered it a fourth time replanting and then I shall set it the next Shower. Rain this day with Thunder, a moderate shower.

Not one hill in 40,000 of the indigo I planted is Come up so that either every seed was bad or the planting or sowing so soon in April (which they who did last year were the only successfull people in seed making) will not do every year. If this be the case, I doubt the making of seed will be always hazardous for in a cold spring it must be sown later and this won't do in a dripping year as was 1757 with a Cold fall unless some art be used more than topping to check the overluxuriance of the plant in such years. I sow or plant all the ground in Indian peas. Began this day.

21. *Sunday.*

A prodigeous dew this morning little short of a Frost in it thickness, Complexion and great coldness. Yesterday many severe showers of hail fell all around us at Charles Beale's.[25] Very great length of time it continued there. But few ears of wheat yet shot out, only here and there one.

23. *Tuesday.*

Rain this night and warm.

25. *Thursday.*

A fine rain indeed. The plants in the meadow have grown but little. I do suppose though it is low and rich it is a little too drye and not having had any cultivation for any time before the land was not so well opened as it should be. Plants at the Fork grow fast. Here none of those causes obstruct, the ground being both moist and short from frequent tending.

27. *Saturday.*

Wheat ears this year very slowly and very Sorryly. It is above a weak since it began to ear and in the same lands where it is of equal hight 'tis not half out. This can only be owing to the Coolness of the weather which is remarkably so almost every night. The ears are very short which I think must be owing to the drowth in March, April, and the forepart of this month with the coolness of the weather, for 'tis observable that it is the same in wheat that may be said to be rank and in some grounds where by the blad and stalk it appears to be very rich. I see no worm nor rust as yet although the leaves of many shrubs are much rusted and by the Colour and the dust 'tis the same and it is the same

---

[25] Charles Beale (d. 1764), Richmond Co. planter and son of Thomas Beale (1675–1729) and Elizabeth Tavener. He married Mary, daughter of Samuel and Ann Barber.

time in the month that it came in 1753 and 1754. However the wheat is not near so forward now as then, which is a seeming corroboration of my conjecture that it is an insect and that its parent is directed by nature to choose the proper period of the vegitation of the plant it fixes to. If so I am in hopes we shall not have it in the wheat.

I have now finished threshing. My mow stacked for experiment to kill the weevil and I find by every circumstance I am right. The Wheat was prodigeously eaten at top and along the loose parts of the sides and so it appears at the bottom layer of the mow which I had laid with the sheeves erect (which I find was no good way) and by that means the air found an easy entrance. Note: there was also in this layer several worms with white soft bodys, a sharp brownish red and very hard head with a mouth hard enough to eat wood and a hard horny fork at the tail like the earwigg. It had 3 feet on each side near the head and one on each side under the tail and it would in walking extend its body near an inch. When ever it was obstructed it would raise the forked tail for its defence. I could not see any in the grain and have reason to conclude it sprung immediately out of the earth encouraged by the moist straw at bottom which was in many sheeves merely rotten. The Sun killed them in a few hours. I put one in a Phyal with some sound grains to see whether it lived on wheat. The event I shall discover.

28. Sunday.

Cool day. Mr. Wormeley and Mr. Reid[26] here.

29. Monday.

Very cold indeed this day as if it had rained much some where.

30. Tuesday.

Very cool and very drye. It must needs be very bad Cropping. Corn though clear looks yellow and grows not. Plants still labouring under the Flye.

31. Wednesday.

A rain before day this morning refreshing but not plenty full. This month has been remarkable for its dryeness and Coolness. Some rain has fallen but the cool winds after them presently dryed up all moisture and we have only two days in which a man could set with comfort without a fire. All our stiff

[26] Perhaps John Reade of King and Queen Co., planter and son of Robert Reade of York Co. (d. 1712). He lived relatively near Ralph Wormeley.

lands that were broke up since the middle of March are quite light and drye so that our corn looks yet poorly.

January was fine weather. February all winter. Windy, very wet and Cold. March the first half or near like February. The latter drye and Cold. April quite Cold, Frosty and drye. May Cold and drye. June I hope will be kind and Seasonable.

6 o'clock in the morning well watered. At last a very fine rain and still raining God almighty be thanked.

JUNE 1758

2. *Friday*.

A great rain from 5 o'clock in the evening and so all night.

3. *Saturday*.

Raining till 8 this morning. This will hurt the blooming wheat.

Cleaned the wheat I sold Cornelius Deforest[27] of the lower sort and in order to make it as good as possible we took out better than 20 bushels so that his bargain of 22d the bushel is a very good one to him as I grind it for nothing. A grey mare that left a Colt 3 weeks old at Blough point was this day Covered by Roundhead. I have ordered up again about 10 or 12 days.

5. *Monday*.

Began to mow my meadow this day. A fine crop and fewer rushes than ever.

6. *Tuesday*.

Looked over my oats this day. I dread the Crop. Every here and there they are very low, mildewed and are head not above 6 or 8 oats on a head and what can this be owing to? The ground is rich for it brought a fine Crop of Wheat. It was plowed up early and sown thick and one part which was strong cow pens of only one year was tended and fed with turneps. Had it been only in stiff land I Should have thought the rains in the beginning and then the drye weather had baked the ground too much, but the light lands are the worst. It must then be owing to the very cold weather which withered the roots and the rains being so late they had not time to put forth new roots before the heading season.

[27] Cornelius Deforest (d. 1782) was a baker in Williamsburg.

Planted in my Cow yard as you go in Colo. Randolph's tobacco for seed and the shortened howes and one row of the other side. I intend to plant the rest with Mr. Parker's and Spencer Ball's seed. Wheat now just parting with its bloom.

7. *Wednesday.*

A very fine rain preceeded by a prodigeous wind at Northwest that drove the rain through my house. There was also much lightning and thunder.

8. *Thursday.*

Very Cool morning. A fire is very Comfortable.

Planted this day at the Fork 2,000 plants from the patch sown there in April. It is Just 6 weeks from the sowing and would the virmin let them alone we should plant abundance from them. There is a young ground worm that has killed thousands of very small ones.

11. *Sunday.*

Got in half my house of hay yesterday in good order although the rain and gust within the week took off a little of its green colour. It now rains again so that 'tis probable the rest that is to come in may Suffer more. The wheat shews no rust as yet and I am now in hopes it will [not]. My observations in 1753, June 1, shew that it always comes after the wheat is eared and it appeared then the 25th May. Therefore the wheat must have been all eared now, though it did not ear so soon this year by a week and better. Yet such a length of time has elapsed since it has eared I say I am in hopes it will escape.

A Sharp flurry at Northwest this evening which brought down some of the largest hail I ever saw, long, thick pointed, very irregular, but I flatter my self it has passed by many places where it could have hurt me. It rained all the fore part of the day very plentyfully. I sent off my Waggon and Six horses to Blough point for Plants.

12. *Monday.*

We have planted at the Fork about 10,000 out the late sown plant patch. They look lively, that is those planted before.

14. *Wednesday.*

Yesterday and this truely Summer, Sultry hot and but little air. Still getting in my hay. A very large crop indeed. A pritty shower this evening.

15. *Thursday*.

Russling this morning bad for hay but fine for what we can't follow, I mean planting. However I have removed about 150 of Mr. Parker's tobacco in to hills made in the plant Patch and just 15 plants of Colo. Carter's famed Orleans which are all that came up. Visited the Fork plant patch this day. They promised as fair on monday last of affording a large draft this Season as ever plants did, but the ground worm has again rose in them, cut off and mangled and Poisoned many thousands. Upon which, as it is clouded, dripping day, I have ordered many (though no bigger than half Crowns the whole circumference of the plant) to be drawn and planted in the hills. I tryed two plants of the size on monday last in two hills and if those in the beds had grown as much we should have pitched our Crop this Season. This is the only chance left. If they stay in the beds they will be destroyed by the worm and I beleive the planters' reason for not using plants so small is for fear of the worm in the hill. Now if they are as lyable in the bed the Chance is equal if not better in the hill. I observe though 'tis a fine soil for plants, yet those beds should be laid a little higher, for now the roots grow numerous the earth is too proud and don't keep them down so as to take a long root.

16. *Friday*.

As this has been an extraordinary year for the flye in our plants every body seems to have fallen on many experiments for their preservation. I have tryed many different places. One was the bottom of a large hay stack that had lain many years and seemed to be exceedingly rich and well pulverized. The other the floor and yard of a quarter of long standing and burnt down a year agoe, very rich as it must needs be with the ashes etc. that are always found about such, but although these were sown early in March they afforded only here and there a plant. Another was in a drye part of a rich meadow constantly watered and in which a great quantity of seed was sown, and they appeared as well covered with plants as a thing could be, but although it lay open to almost every warm sun and the ground seemed prodigeous light and fine yet the flye destroyed them and they did not grow equal to any expectation, and out of a large number of beds very few plants indeed were taken. Another was in a very rich and moist black soil convenient to over flowing at any moment. These became plantable in 6 weeks from sowing but an enimy of as dangerous a sort appeared, I mean a sort of ground worm that eat the roots, and thousands dyed and the rest seemed to stand, but the favourable Seasons enabled us to plant many very small things not with more expectation but the chance they might stand in the hill, as they seemed to stand none in the beds. Another was in my Cow yard after the dung of the year was heaped. The land was very stiff and very Subject to bake in amongst some very fine rotten garden dung such as seemed fit for tender flowers. Now though I was obliged to water every night and morning even during the Cool weather in May Yet I found few or no flye and the patch had no other fault but that of being too small, a fault I was led into by the quantitys sown every where else. These plants always kept green, were plantable in seven weeks and very strong plants and have been drawn Season after season ever since So that had necessity led the way in any former year I should not have wanted a plant this year, for till the plants were really plantable the beginning of this month the weather was never once seasonable for such a growth, and had I mixed Sand with the Soil before, for the Cattle had been wintered on it, in all probability it would have been in full time had we sown it the first of April. Instead of that we only sowed the 22d. I can't but conclude as I have before done the flye is generated by eggs in the earth and that the strong salts of the Urin (of which there must needs have been many both of Cows and horses, for it was in that Corner where my cart horse dung was always thrown) destroy those eggs, for we scarcely had a flye amongst them. The richness no doubt was great but I can't suppose that is confined to a particular salt there. I do believe the soil in the other places had their share in a proper salt for vegetation, but his abounded with those only that could destroy these vermin. How easy then is it for persons cropping in my way to be always provided with such and large patches too as a Standby in such years. We heap our dung in March the first week and instead of heaping it in the yard it may be turned on one side, and let the yard be immediately broke up for such a purpose, but then we should remember to have them near Water.

It is to be noted I frequently sprinkled or sifted fine old hen dung over these plants in order to prevent the eating of the flye. Whether it produced this effect I can't tell, but 'tis a good way in that it must carry a good deal of rich salts to encourage the growth of the plants.

18. *Sunday.*

Yesterday and this morning really very cold. I had fires. Ground worms rose in my cow yard plants. Oats head here a bush and there a thing; I doubt the crop from this late doings. At least one part will be ripe and shaken before the other is fit to cut.

20. *Tuesday.*

I have just finished stacking all my meadow hay and, finding the quantity so much greater than ever I yet experienced that not only the whole Hayhouse full (which I never got by two rooms before always keeping the old hay left in it, but seeing the present hay so much better I removed it) but 15 cart loads in the rough of my home cow crib, I can't but say I am surprized at it. 'Tis true all June has been fine growing weather, but then I began to mow the 5th and it would have been all done by the 13th had not the rains prevented. It was all a miry bog rooted in many holes late in April by the hogs and stopt up in all the Canals by the bevers. I cleansed these canals up and turned off all the water and kept out the hoggs and in the beginning of May I expected a very poor Crop. To what shall I impute this prodigeous crop? Not to the Spring, for it was certainly very cold. Not to the water lying on it, for that could not be richer confined in the Mill pond than it used to be and 'tis certain no grass grew like we had drawn it all off. May not then the great rooting of the hogs by breaking through the matted roots of the sward been the cause of the grass shooting out so much more luxuriantly from the bottom? For 'twas observable the quantity was gained by the bottom and not in the hight, it having been much higher in former years, and 'tis certain that the burthens it has bore is a strong proof that the soil can't have grown richer, and 'tis as certain it has lain as long under water before. These are hints to reason on and I don't doubt but on tryal hereafter I shall find that some such kind of Cultivation as deep harrowing those grounds every 4th or 5th year will be the best way of keeping up a Crop. Note: I am not deceived in the stowage, having been often a witness to that work's being well done. There is another observation to be made. Rushes every body agrees are nourished mostly by water, and yet although the meadow has been underwater till the middle of May I had not 1/10 of the rushes I had last year. I can't but think the rooting of the hogs destroyed some of these also.

22. *Thursday.*

A prodigeous hot indeed. The rays of the Sun reflected on all the eastern parts of the Country by a long and deep western cloud that must needs threaten a very heavy discharge of wind or rain or hail. It all went off.

JULY 1758

3. *Monday.*

It has been now a full fortnight and no rain but mighty hot and very drye, and yet never did the flye eat no more nor the ground worm so much, so that all our expectations from plants are gone, and although 60,000 plants at my fork quarter would have been enough and I had a patch of near 200 thousand I shall not get 40. These occasioned by the ground worm and my overseer's letting the hogs root up the patch though under his nose.

Began this day to mow and reap wheat. The weather parched it up too soon. This night a prodigeous rain indeed and violent lightning and thunder. 5 cattle killed in the neighbourhood.

4. *Tuesday.*

Prodigeous indeed More sever rains, lightning, thunder and wind. Got in what wheat was down. Here let me observe that all the objections (against my proposal for sowing wheat from weavil) that are founded on the pretended close stacking of others are without truth for although the proprietors have ordered and fancyed things were so done I can venture to assert they were not, for I catched my own people who have the experience of it doing it in such a manner as to answer no purpose. The layer of straw all round were so Slightly trod that when I went to examin them a man might sink down to the Shoulders and yet they had leizure, straw and every thing else. The reason is the old ones in my absence lay and Slept and the boys neglected to do it.

5. *Wednesday.*

Rain again this afternoon, many Clouds thundering out, their fiery constant Winds perpetually returning back the rain that passed. Very unlucky indeed for the farmer. In England they don't mind these rains but in our hot climate they are not only very large but also very hot and set the wheat to sprouting presently.

12. *Wednesday.*

3 fair days last past. My wheat at home down to day though not all in. I have not in all the works in my farm been so disturbed as with my people in Stacking my wheat as I ordered. Go where I will I find them at it the old way so that I can't promise my self so much Success from the method as I proposed. Began to mow Oats.

28. *Friday.*

From the 9th till Yesterday nothing but hot drye weather and but a small Sprinkling last night. This has made bad farming indeed and would have been bad Cropping had there been any tobacco. My oats only finished getting in this day. Manuel's broken leg and the Election has made it late. The people not minded and Idle.

Judy Carter had her sickness at Stomach and fever the 23d. I gave 17 grains Ipecacuana with 30 drops Vinum benedictum which brought off much curdled sower Phlegm and some bile and by two motions downwards she was quite cleansed and remained well and brisk ever since.

AUGUST 1758

9. *Wednesday*.

There is no other observation to be made but that it has been excessive drye ever Since the 3d July and so it seems likely to Continue. I had but a mere trifle of tobacco planted and that now quite good for nothing.

The beginning of this month I was at my lower plantations. Very drye there and there I discovered the weevil flye in the wheat at my quarter and at Mr. Carter's and so at my fork Quarter. I therefore see there is no stacking close enough without stratum of hay or old broken Straw all around.

Last night as fine a rain for about 2 hours as I could wish preceeded by great wind. In this season of great Scarcity of plants 'tis odd I should be so unlucky. I had about a head basket full of prodigeous fine plants last monday, intending to have stuck them in the very first season, and said to my Gardiner when these plants are drawn leave here [and] there a good one to be hilled up and he immediately went and cut them all up.

15. *Tuesday*.

A very Severe flash of Lightning broke just in my face but the Wind being against me it did me no damage. Very drye and no rain though rain all around us. Corn much burnt. No turneps came up. Our Stock of Calves have been 61 in all. 2 killed. 3 dyed and the English Cow. Leave of the Common 55 alive.

17. *Thursday*.

Very Cold morning. No rain here as yet. Dew thick, almost a frost.

18. *Friday*.

Our Grass all burnt and every other vegetable. 'Tis well we have no tobacco to aggrevate this misfortune by seeing it all dye.

22. *Tuesday*.

A very fine rain this night. Began this day my second mowing of my meadow. It appears a very fine Crop.

29. *Tuesday.*

Not yet quite finished stacking my hay. 'Tis a fine Crop. Very drye now again though a very great prospect as Usual for rain, but the Northwest drives it all down the Country.

30. *Wednesday.*

Very Cold indeed. It makes us all shut close.

Rained all night and so this morning gentle and fine. Such a rain might have made a great deal of Corn last month and some turneps but now it hardly will.

SEPTEMBER 1758

4. *Monday.*

Began to sow wheat.

9. *Saturday.*

Went to the Assembly.

OCTOBER 1758

15. *Sunday.*

Came home October 15th. The weather Mostly drye the whole time. My wheat all well sowed and well up at every place.

20. *Friday.*

Sowed Timothy on all my Wheat fields not intended for oats next year after the rate of 2 quarts to the acre and in another addition to my meadow after the rate of 3 quarts to the acre. Began to plow up my Cowpens ground prodigeous hard and worked very laboriously.

24. *Tuesday.*

We have had two small showers last week and today a very fine easy rain. Began to pen my Cattle in all my Cow yards but the two at Mangorike. They have one Cowpen still to dung to compleat the Square of Cowpens. I find some weevil flye coming out of my barn. I perceived by the settling of the mows the side strata have left the wheat being lighter and the air has got in. I am in hopes 'tis only at the sides. We have been better than a week howing up a new Corn field. It being all fresh wood land two year agoe and grassed over and fed by the Cattle it makes the work excessive hard,

{Wheat 1758}

August 17   24 [bushels] Fork

{Oats 1758}

August 15   28 [bushels]

THE DIARY
November 1763—December 15, 1764

THE DIARY
1763

NOVEMBER 1763

?[Illegible] . . . 60 gallons Molasses at 2/-[illegible] cask in a Porter hogshead that I bought [illegible] gallons only and it bo[ttl]ed off only 2 [illegible] so that it hardly held above 63.[1] The cask [and] [illegible]. Mr. Ritchie's[2] measure did not fill it by 15 gallons. There is some mistery in this.

These things are at Dr. [illegible]nd's. He sells the Almonds at Just what they cost sterling but his intimate says that is a mistake. They did not cost 20/ a bushel and I know they were sold for 5/9 last year.

Coffee he sent but not the price nor quantity.

Chocolate 6 pounds but not the price.

Ginger 6 pounds but no price. I won't deal with this man any more in such an uncertainty.

15. *Tuesday.*

We have had [a very d]rye sum[mer an]d near as drye a fall. We have at the appearance of every New moon constantly observed her Phasis, and she has been mostly with the two horns tending to a Perpendicular to the Horison, which with us always denoted a drye moon and the more perpendicular as she leaned to the South a warm moon. The moon of this month alone has not yet answered her Phoenominon, for she was extremely Perpendicular and of a South inclination, but it has rained every 3 or 4 days and been very cool. The last rain began the 14th, and yesterday was almost a hard gust at Northeast and so it continued all night and it now rains from the same quarter.

Struck all my tobacco every where.

16. *Wednesday.*

My own want of [illegible] exceeding; I have never recovered this Fall from that. Every body almost had This. I thought [it] to be inflammatory and

---

[1] Printed from the original diary in the Sabine Hall Col. These portions of the diary from November 1763 to December 15, 1764, are written on the blank leaves of the *Virginia Almanack* for 1764.

[2] Archibald Ritchie (d. 1784) was a Scotch merchant in Tappahannock across the Rappahannock River from Sabine Hall. He married Molly, daughter of William Roane of Essex Co.

wanted the Dr. to bleed me, but he would not. Then the Endemial Cough seized me and has I fancy much vitiated my blood, for I have had my pain in my right Arm to a most excruciating degree indeed and the whole year it never came in any Joint. It has been for some days first in my Shoulder, then in my elbow, then in my wrist and in my fingers' ends so as to benumb the thumb and forefinger for near 2 days though now that is something better, by bathing with heat: cro made with liquid Hongary[3] and 1/6 liquid laudanum,[4] but I must bleed or it will be worse, For I am fallen away much and still fall away.

George Maynard, Hosier at the Rising Sun in Fenchwich Street,[5] Spun silk stockings 7/ a pair.

17. *Thursday.*

Rain all night.

23. *Tuesday.*

Very bad still with a Cough, and falling away quite to a Corps in my whole face and yet I walk about. In virginia a man dyes a month sooner in a fit of any disorders because he can't have one soul to talk to. If he has children some are one way and some another. And without a wife, who has a sick man to converse with?

Not done sowing wheat yet, Still a little to sow at Jammy's.[6] I see no prospect for even a tollearble crop of Corn. Things extremely short.

25. *Thursday.*

Cut out by Betty:
Boys' suits———————— 10
Men's suits ⎱
women's suits ⎰————————— 40
Davis'[7] account Mangorike Cattle
two pens——1———————— 75
              2———————— 70
Barn———————————— 24
Homeyard———————— 30
at Davis's———————— 5
204 in all besides 30 Yearlings

[3] Agua Hungary or the Queen of Hungary's water consisted of oil of rosemary and other aromatic oils in alcohol. It was used as a stimulant.
[4] Liquid laudanum was a preparation of opium.
[5] In London.
[6] Jammy was probably one of Carter's trusted slaves in charge of tending a particular piece of land.
[7] H. Davis was one of Carter's overseers or tenants.

Better something today, but a Cadaverous face.
Talbot[8] killing hogs. 11 [at] Island.
Finished sowing Wheat yesterday. Quantity as follows:

at Home, English seed——————— 16½ bushels	
Fork seed——————— 80	
at the Fork, ditto——seed——— 30	
at Jamy's, ditto——seed——— 16	
142½	

DECEMBER 1763

1. *Thursday.*

I see the Cattle eat the Burnet from England very greedily. A few plants in my plant patch were very fine and eaten up quite into the ground by a cow in a few moments. It has a large crown.

Hares eat it also prodigiously so much that I fear 200 heads in my garden won't bring me a seed next year.

Ibid., began my box of candles bought at H[obb's] Hole; quantity 13 dozon fine large candles.

2. *Friday.*

A loaf sugar, the last, not quite out.

5. *Monday.*

Began to hoe my fresh corn field at Davis's. Also to thrash out my oats.

The Burnet in the plant patch begins to sprout again since the Cattle cropt it down notwithstanding it is a constant frost though not severe. In this it has the advantage of the Lucern which does not grow now.

6. *Tuesday.*

It is surprizing to see how the Hares crop the Burnet in the garden almost every night. I fear I shall not save seed from it next year.

7. *Wednesday.*

The night before last I put a sizeable blister on my right arm Just above the place where my issue had formerly been in order to remove this long

---

[8] Talbot was a slave.

continued and violent Rheumatick pain, whose seat has constantly been just under the seam of the issue for now near 12 months, not near so bad as it has been ever since I used the Cold bath in June last. And though this blister by last night had drawn up an intire blister all over the place and discharged abundance of water, both before I dressed it with a Small hot plaister and since I have not felt the pain in the least abate except when the violent burning and smarting of the blister continued, then indeed the burning and smarting was too great to feel any other complaint, and this day as that began to abate the pain and weakness of the arm returned and is as bad as ever, nay though I had both yesterday and today several plentifull soft motions downwards. So that I think I may dispair of ever being relieved in that, and must content myself with my most deplorable condition, for certainly a more emaciating pain cannot attend a humane Creature. I am told I look better in the face, but yet I fall away in all parts of my body. This amendment in my face I must conclude to proceed from my being blooded about 3 weeks agoe, when my blood was exception[ally] viscid and in no small degree of Corruptio[n]. Yet Mortimer[9] will not be perswaded to bleed me again, but though I do give way to perhaps a better advice I must think it would be the only thing to give me relief.

The Weather is still warm and sultry so that I am almost totally relaxed and inactive.

The Phasis of this new moon is as all the rest have been this summer, the horns perpendicular to each other, which have been fancyed to bespeak a hot and drye moon.

9. *Friday.*

Yesterday rain, today the same and very giving weather. Tobaccoe planting I see is an art, to be learned not more by practice than by reasoning Justly on things. My overseer Davis this day told me Jamy's tobacco in hogsheads was all rotten. I had some of it brought to me. It was in a very great sweat, and by the scent I discovered it was in no danger. It had passed the rotting period of such and did not smell like dung fit for the ground but like dung when it is not disposed to rot.

It continues a squally wet day so that the Phacis of the new moon should denote a warm and moist moon, and so it does for the horns are not so perpendicular as they were represented to me. I saw them last night. It is now very warm, I fear too warm for the season and for a relaxed body like mine to

---

[9] Dr. Charles Mortimer was a physician in Fredericksburg and first mayor of the town (Blanton, *Medicine in Virginia in the Eighteenth Century,* 358–59).

recover much. It lightens a good deal at a distance from the South along to the West. Clouds very black indeed.

10. *Saturday.*

The thunder yesterday did not clear off the weather. It is still all Clouded and rains frequently. My Arm and head bad.

Yesterday I had the West India Coffee roasted in my Spit roaster. It was gently turned. Took near 4 hours to roast it well and wasted Just 2 ounces which is equal to 1/8 loss.

12. *Monday.*

Mr. D. Campbell Merchant of London[10] here. He was so kind as to offer to send me in anything I might want. I wrote him the following invoice:

8 pounds best Hysore Tea, 8 pounds good ditto.
8 ounces Cloves and ditto nutmeggs and ditto mace.
1 pound Cinnamon, 20 pounds black Peper, 5 pounds Paradice.
10 pounds Saltpetre, 50 pounds Ian raisins, 50 Currents.
3 livery suits middling men.
3 silver laced hats for ditto.
A Rocelo cloak for myself.
10 yards Welch flannel.
2 pair gloves lined with furr.
A warm muff for myself.

13. *Tuesday.*

Capt. Gregg[11] came here, says his freight is £7 per ton and will make his skipper call for my 6 hogsheads and carry it to the Warehouse and also agreed to take my son's tobacco as sure as his name is Gregg.

14. *Wednesday.*

A very rainy day. It has also spit with snow. Some folks fancy they have the weather at Command or that it is always Settled this season of the year, for they set out on a long visit and had precisely set this day to return on.

[10] Probably Duncan Campbell who with John Stewart formed the mercantile partnership of Campbell and Stewart of London. See Arthur P. Middleton, *Tobacco Coast* (Newport News, 1953), 151.
[11] Probably Capt. Johnston Gregg, who commanded several tobacco ships trading to Virginia.

Therefore they played at cards all the good weather and fine days such as monday and yesterday and now they must travel in bad or not come at all. I wish I had not perswaded them to carry little Landon[12] with them and I did not care what weather they had to come home in for it must be some hurt to make some people think.

Snow about 9 o'clock.

22. *Thursday.*

Sent over the River for 2 pounds Pepper. Mrs. Woods[13] says she has not had but 3½ before since February last but she mistakes.

The weights of hoggs killed 1763:

20 bought at the Island.
1 Davis had weight 141 gross
2 forward Bacon Spoilt
2 dyed
4 killed without weight some spoilt
11 the following weights————————————103

93	89	
91	81	
83	100	
87	80	
72	97	
426	550	550
		426
		976

Davis's: 12 hogs weight as follows:

111	90	383
117	80	652
103	55	1035
112	98	
109	60	1115
100	383	
652		

80 the weight of one hog missed in Talbot's account.

---

[12] Landon Carter (1757–1820), grandson of Landon Carter and son of Robert Wormeley Carter and Winifred Travers Beale, inherited Sabine Hall and married Catherine, sixth daughter of John Tayloe and Rebecca Plater of Mount Airy.

[13] Mrs. Woods was the housekeeper at Sabine Hall.

Jammy's: 10 hogs weight as follows:

101	81	309
101	61	416
91	51	725
61	64	
62	52	
416	309	

Fork: 10 hogs the weight as follows:

102	92	522
104	99	438
100	105	960
114	92	
102	50	
522	438	

The mill: 9 hogs weight as follows:

91	794
78	
98	
107	
65	
86	
90	
81	
98	
794	

Still to kill: 8 hogs at the mill.
Brought down from Park quarter: 11 hogs.

THE DIARY

1764

JANUARY 1764

1. *Sunday.*

Observed my Burnet this day. The heads at the end of my plant patch, which I had a cow turned in to see whether she would eat it the beginning of last month, by being enclosed immediately after she had cropt it close down, is now sprouted about an inch or more. But the heads in my garden are kept so low by the Hares that the crowns of them are but Just seen alive. These Hares are extravagantly fond of it for though there are near 200 heads and in two lines quite along the garden every head is kept close down.

7. *Saturday.*

Extreme cold these two days. My son Landon's Overseer Joseph Florence who came down with Fork Jammy (who's been run away ever since the last week in October) went up this day and Carryed 10 pounds Coffee from Mr. Ritchie, garden Seeds and 2 quarts of Pease from me, Some Midicines from Dr. Mortimer.

I took a vomit the 5th and some how catched a Cold that is now going to be very bad and I do suppose I shall fall away again.

I began to take the Electuary that Mortimer contrived for my Vertigo and Arm, but I hardly think it can do me any Service. I am now almost constantly giddy unless lying on my left side, and every Cold day gets into my arm, although I cloath it up very well. I can't say but I may have catched Cold at Mr. Beverley's[1] though all imaginable care was taken to the Contrary, but it is no season for me to go abroad in And yet the occasion was great the Standing for my daughter's son Wm.

[1] Robert Beverley (d. 1800) of Blandfield, Essex Co., was a planter and son of William Beverley and Elizabeth Bland. He married Maria, daughter of Landon Carter and his second wife, Maria Byrd.

Judy drew off the Jugg Molasses: 1 pound H[ickory] T[hicket] but one more left besides those 2 pounds lent to R[obert] B[everly].

Publick Ledger[2] for September 1763 Takes notice of an Ivory tooth cut up by Mr. Read, Cutler in Crane Lane,[3] in which was found an Iron ball of an inch diameter and not the least appearance where it entered.

8. *Sunday.*

Fine day, wind Southerly, but cool as yet, ground hard frozen. My Cold some what better though still bad and head Giddy.

13. *Friday.*

Mortimer sent for last night. My cold very bad; Signs of Snow and small spits but no settled snow.

14. *Saturday.*

Mr. [Robert Wormeley] C[arter] a graceless son. This day as his own wife was desirous to go to Rust,[4] and of course used my chariot, refused to let the boy Moses that I only lent to him ride postilion, And complained of his wearing out his cloths when he rode postilion to Corotoman, where even then his wife was accommodated with the Chariot, to make a visit to Mrs. Carter.[5] This is to play the fine gentleman, and on the weakest pretext imaginable, for riding a horse one way is equal to riding another so that the same distance in the ride would have rubbed out the same cloths, whether as postilion to his wife's chariot, or as servant before his Grace's Portmantua. What is this but to do every thing to thwart me who own no particular respect to Madame because she has never deserved any of me; but I say only to treat her as a Gentlewoman, as she lives in my house.

Foggy all day from 5 morn till the evening. There has been a great deal of this weather this year and I do believe it has always soar throats with it. I know it in my family. My Cold is but just mending and I feel my throat now smarting. My daughter Judy taken ill last night, head ach and soar throat.

15. *Sunday.*

A fogg early this morning, which ended in a very large white frost, but not cold. My Cough but little better, head giddy as usual though 4 of my gum pills last night with 10 grains soap have given me two large and very fetid

---

[2] The *Public Ledger* was a newspaper published in London beginning in January 1760.
[3] In London.
[4] Perhaps Samuel Rust (d. 1769), a small planter in Richmond Co.
[5] Mary Walker, first wife of Charles Carter of Corotoman and daughter of Charles Carter of Cleve.

motions. Miss Judy, better. Took 4 grains Calomels in a pill last night, and this day Rhubarb 20 grains, Jalap 5 grains, Cream tartar 10 grains to work it off.

I lookt at my Cauliflowers put into my Cellar against the wall in November with earth to their roots. They then were not flowered but now they are all flowered. 27 of them. Two we use today for dinner. I have ordered a fresh layer of earth to their roots tomorrow that they may be guarded against the frost the rem[ainder] of the winter and seed may be saved from them. I once did 10 at my father's and saved fine seed.

No lamb as yet though we had one the 14th of this Month last year. The reason perhaps that we fail this year is because that forward Ewe brought a Lamb in August also.

16. *Monday.*

Still a very cloudy day, but a small mist of rain in the night, though the appearances for it have been pritty strong these four days. I yesterday received all the opening effects from a dose of my pills (though but a small one) that I took the night before, but in the evening though I filled but moderately I found a heaviness and a constant ringing in my head, which with me has been for some time a presage of an approaching fit of the vertigo. The only thing that some authors who write upon this disorder, do agree with what I have experenced in it. And in the night I discharged an abundance of wind downwards and really slept well; Yet this morning my stomach and lower bowel have been in a perpetual tremor with the wind and one loose motion has not abated it. Perhaps my Coffee that I used for breakfast may have contributed a little to it. I shall use ginseng tea and some Aqua Mirabilis as a Cordial to strengthen again which I have before found effectual.

17. *Tuesday.*

Davis Measured the fork quarter corn, vizt: 46 hogsheads
Used in fatening and before: 10
                                                    $\overline{56}$ = 112 Bushels

Very poor crop indeed.

Laid off for the people from this 17 day 3 barrels each working hand and 1½ each child.

Jammy's corn at house but 10 hogsheads equal to 20 barrels. Nothing to feed out of it and 8 hogsheads ½ at the home house.

18. *Wednesday.*

Yesterday and this fine clear frosty morns. I rode out twice yesterday and find a benefit in it.

20. Friday.

Talbot's account of my home sheep this day is 69. Besides the fatted ones 3 of the gang have dyed and one of the old Wethers. There are also 52 of the sheep that came from Northumberland, one of them being dead.

My oats thrashed to this day, are of the 1st out of the Stack 127 bushels and of this 28 bushels Talbot is saving seed out of it as it comes up.

John Singer⁶ brought here 11 hogs from Park quarter. He scett off with 20 hogs. 4 he was obliged to return home with. 5 he was forced to sell by the way, 1 of them at 12/6, 2 ditto at 30/, the other at 25/ per [hundred weight]. It weighed 112 which comes to 28/. This cash paid me by the overseer. He also brought down a beef.

$$
\begin{array}{r}
12/6 \\
1:10/ \\
\underline{1:\ 8/} \\
3:10/6
\end{array}
$$

22. Sunday.

From the 17 to this day very fine weather, which I improved I hope both in my health and my works. Sowed tobacco seed at the following places:

At the Locust:⁷ G. P. seed of Orleans
Davis's: the seed he saved last year
Jamey's: the seed he saved last year
Fork quarter: GP new orleans.

It rains this day.

23. Monday.

Sowed the home patch GP and lettuce and cabbage and radish seeds.

Broached up of Wine drew out 2 dozens. It is remarkable I have now 18 bottles of the wine bottled up January 24, 1763, and had no other to use all the while so that a pipe will last the year out and more in great plenty. I used wine in as great plenty as ever I did. I never had so much sickness in my family as this year, and the expense in such times is very great in Wine to Gruels, Wine to drinks and Wine to Vomits and bitters.

We have this day come from the Serene temperate climate of St. Helena as

---

⁶ John Singer was Landon Carter's overseer at the Park Quarter.
⁷ The Locust was one of Carter's tracts of land in Richmond Co.

yesterday was to the intemperate bad weather of Nova Zembla, first a rain and then a cold snow. My Chariot gone for Mr. Beverley and his Lady to Clarke's[8] opposite to their house but to be sure they cannot come.

25. *Wednesday.*

Ground covered with snow and very cold wind. No Beverley this day I believe.

Tom says that I have 3 pieces of Canvass nailed up in a chest in the Store.

27. *Friday.*

The first lamb this day. My daughter Beverley came the 25th. Extreme cold ever since.

29. *Sunday.*

Most extravagantly sharp. One Cow dyed though in heart because numbed with Cold two days agoe and a yearling drowned in Hay's gut.

31. *Tuesday.*

Drew out the 2d time 2 dozens of wine from the Pipe.

FEBRUARY 1764

2. *Thursday.*

From the 28th last month to this day extremely wet. The second lamb yesterday. A most violent wind generally called a Southwest but I think more West. Mr. Beverley, his Lady and Lucy nevertheless gone up to Clarke's to get over, but it is impossible. No boat I am sure could live in such a prodigious storm. Lucy carryed with her the 4 ounzes fine thread [spun] this year. Not one day as yet from the 23 January to this day that the earth could be touched with hoe, spade or plow, that is 11 days together, so that if a planter has been negligent or is anyhow late in breaking up his stiff lands he may give over thinking of it after Christmass in a manner.

3. *Friday.*

Colo. Tayloe's Stone cutter Ralph came here to work day for day with my man Jammey who is to work at the Colo[nel's] when he goes to Walling in his Plantations.

[8] Probably the home of either James Clarke (d. 1768) or Robert Clarke (d. 1784). Both lived in Richmond Co.

Killed the 11 backwood's hogs brought down by J. Singar Overseer from my Park quarter. They are sold to my son for his Mill wrights at 30/ per [illegible] and are to be salted up for him. Their weight was 1019 neat Pork.

This is a fine day overhead, but really bad for an infirm man to walk about. I almost got my hip disjointed by walking in my garden. All hands hoing, ditching and plowing.

4. *Saturday*.

Colo. Tayloe's Fork quarter dogs made great havock amongst my sheep last night. 11 killed and 4 wounded of the home gang and 4 killed of the Northumberland sheep. It is again a rainey day and the new moon seems to be a wet moon.

6. *Monday*.

I have been very lately paid off by the cur dogs amongst my sheep. My Stock were as follows until the 2d of this month if I could believe one negroe, but I find all are so lazy that they never went to the houses to count them and are so Villanous as to confirm all with damned lies.

Talbot swears he counted:

$$
\begin{array}{lr}
\text{the Home gang February 2d} & 69 \\
\text{the Northumberland ditto} & \underline{52} \\
& 121
\end{array}
$$

But now there are only 90 in all which Nassau this day counted besides the two Ewes that have lambs so that I have lost in all here 29 and at my Fork there were 17 though this day only 16. From hence I say that though it is evident the dogs have killed them yet not so very lately as from February 2d. I have people out killing all the dogs they can see.

7. *Tuesday*.

A very rainy day mere deluges of Water, Snow and at night a most keen Northwest. My sheep are now got to 90 except the fateners so that I have had destroyed by dogs and neglect 31 here and one at the Fork. Talbot now counts them every evening and is to come constantly to me to tell me how many he counts.

8. *Wednesday.*

Very cold indeed hard frozen. Colo. F[rancis] L[ightfoot] L[ee],[9] J. Davenport,[10] P. Johnson's son,[11] three Griffins[12] and Colo. Peachey[13] all here. The Second 2 dozen of wine drawn out of my Pipe now drunk up.

13. *Monday.*

T. Harford[14] paid me 12/ his debt and 3/ towards some more corn. 6 lambs in all. Hard rain and West at Southwest. I rode out some days agoe with Corotoman C[harles] C[arter]. Got a small wrench which I did not feel for several days, but Yesterday some sharp Urine discharged, certainly provoked[?] and opened something of a Sore in the Pipe of the Glans Penis, that oozes now and then a yellow stuff, nothing fetid, but so keenly sharp so as to twinge the Part and inflame the whole Nut. I use a fomentation of Comfry, Chomonile flowers, Sumack[15] and Oak buds And to allay the inflammation in the glans Unguentum Album Camphorum[16] seemingly with effect.

14. *Tuesday.*

A fine morning after such a prodigious storm as yesterday was. My complaint easyer last night; therefore I am in hopes it mends. Use Elder flowers[17] boiled in milk and water and drink Mallow tea and honey, shake, spread the same on my bread and butter from its healing and detergent quality. The Penis still discharges a yellowish matter, but not so much of it, nor not so acrid. The first may perhaps be owing to the incumbent posture in the bed. I slept well. I feel it sharp but sore only at the point of the Glans, though I thought the whole pipe this morning seemed stiff.

[9] Francis Lightfoot Lee (1734–97) of Menokin, Richmond Co., was a planter and the sixth son of Thomas Lee and Hannah Ludwell. He married Rebecca, daughter of John Tayloe of Mount Airy. He was burgess for Loudoun Co., 1758–68, and for Richmond Co., 1769–76; member of the Virginia Conventions, 1774–75, and delegate to the Second Continental Congress, 1775–79.

[10] James Davenport (d. 1777) was a planter in Westmoreland Co. He was later clerk of the Westmoreland Co. Committee of Safety.

[11] Probably James Bray Johnson, oldest son of Philip Johnson.

[12] Probably Leroy Griffin (d. 1775), Richmond Co. planter, and two of his brothers, perhaps William and Thomas (d. 1775).

[13] Col. William Peachey (1729–98), Richmond Co. planter and son of Samuel Peachey (d. 1750).

[14] Thomas Harford (d. 1777) was a farmer in Richmond Co.

[15] Sumack could be any of several unrelated shrubs and trees of the genera *Ailanthus* and *Myrica* which were used as diaphoretics or aperients.

[16] Unguentum album camphorum was a camphorated white ointment used as a cooling agent for burns and other skin irritations.

[17] Elder flowers were derived from any shrub or tree of the genus *Sambucus* and were used as a diaphoretic or an aperient.

23. Thursday.

Better is this Complant and only the usual remainder[?] itchings of Ulcers.

I observed my Burnet both in my garden and Plant patch. The Garden has only been kept from the Hares and that is grown a little, but that in the Patch grown at least four inches and in a large field must be fine winter food for all creatures as all will eat it. But it has a second enemy the mole underground that eats the root off a little below the Crown and this in Rowes so that some care must be taken to prevent his destruction as we have numbers of them in the Country, and they always rise every warm day especially in ground any thing drye, or light.

An extract from Le Page du Pratz's history of Louisiana printed 1763. Volume 2d page 5th.[18] Wheat, Rye, Barley and oats grow extremely well in Louisiana. But in regard to Wheat one caution is necessary. Sown by itself it grows wonderfully but when it [is] in flower a number of drops of red Water may be observed at the bottom of the stalk within 6 inches of the Ground which are collected there during night and disappear at Sunrise. This water is of such an acrid Nature, as within a short time to consume the stalk and destroye the ear before the grain is formed. The Author prevents that by sowing Rye and drye mould with the wheat, the mould equal in quantity to the wheat and Rye because he says it is owing to the too great richness of the soil. In France he saw the same method practiced and the farmer told him it was because the land was New and contained an acid prejudicial to wheat, and that Rye drew that acid off without prejudice.

It is not unlikely that this evil may be the same with what many books treat of as produced from lands too sower for wheat. I know they recommend taken off or lower that with Rye or Barley, but I never heard they sowed either of them with wheat. It would be such a Mixture or Metchlin that I cannot think they ever do so for a market Crop; neither can there be any reason to run any hazard of intermixing so much grain; for the over Richness of any soil or its sowerness as it is called is lowered and cured by, cropping any thing on it and early and frequent dressing of it with the Plow. If then Mr. du Pratz is not mistaken the thing and carry[ed] the cure of one evil in France to relieve an evil of another sort in Louisiana I am mistaken. Sowerness is common to all fresh new rich lands and much experienced, but I never saw that to make the

---

[18] Le Page du Pratz, *The History of Louisiana, or of the Western Parts of Virginia and Carolina* (trans. by the author, 2 vols.; London, 1763) is the work referred to. It was first published in Paris in 1758 in three volumes as *Histoire de la Louisiane, Contenant la Découverte de ce vaste Pays.*

Ears to fall when the Wheat is in bloom. It generally mildews the stalk quite up with whitish spots and I believe frequently perishes the grain, but Every farmer knows the evil so well that none hardly ever sow wheat in New fresh lands and as they have other lands to crop on that evil is never very injurious. But as to the Particular description given by the author of the evil of Lousiana I must be of opinion it is the same with what we call Rust, because it begins at bottom just as he says it does, and as I have reasoned in my treatise on this.[19] It must come from some corrosive moisture communicated by some particular constitution of the air which is generally of a moist kind that Preceeds. Perhaps then it is only inconsiderately asserted to proceed from the land itself. There seems to be very little Philosophy in it. Acids may abound in land and we know these may be acrid and corrosive, but why it should only do this when the Ear is in bloom [is] not easily to be guessed at; But let this water be the effect of some constitution of the air. The incertainty of any constancy in the effects of that, ceases to support the difficulty, but that it may happen from some cause not yet discovered though in the nature of the several changes of the air. Now the sowing the old mould with the wheat may alter the ground, Yet after so long an exposure as from August to June so small a quantity must loose its own virtue and partake of the nature of the soil. Therefore the mould, if it is to do any good in the Louisiana evil, should be sown in June or about the time that these drops begin to appear, and though I hardly think it can do any good then what may be effected by shaking of these drops of Water and the Rope method which I mention is much better to be drawn every evening along the wheat or land by land. I have by this extract discovered some kind of certainty in this affair. The author calls these red drops and says they are acrid; We know our Rust is a kind of red Brown. Do not these seem to tally? Perhaps this very corroding water communicates its Colour whilst it corrodes. If so the Rust on every thing is explained which was my only doubt, for I had never found the water but went no farther in my enquiry then the origin of the disorder which perhaps never began to be made till the disorder had began. Again this some how accounts for the Irish practice of Rope halling their wheat, which Capt. Brereton[20] once mentioned to me, but perhaps (if they did it to prevent Rust) they only began it, when the corroded moisture had got into dust, which was certainly too late. Should it not be done often in such moist seasons at such times? Why not every noon or night? We have gangs enough to dispatch a field in a hurry.

[19] No copy of this treatise has survived. It may have been published in the *Va. Gaz.*, of which few issues of the late 1750s and early 1760s are extant.

[20] Probably Capt. Thomas Brereton. He captained at various times different ships engaged in carrying tobacco to Great Britain.

Du Pratz, Volume 2d, page 13: Louisiana has a vine at the edges of their Savannahs or meadows that resembels a Burgandy of which they make good wine, If they take care to expose the Juice to the sun in summer and cold in winter. I have done so and never could turn it to Vineager.

25. *Saturday.*

Yesterday two more of the Sheep that the dogs had bit dyed so that my loss by dogs have been 34 sheep. I have now but 88 sheep and 19 lambs only. As yet I heared only of one that Yeaned dead.

26. *Sunday.*

Just a fortnight since I complained of pinching myself in mounting my horse and a Wrench he gave me by stumbling behind, And yet not well of my disorder though I have been many days and nights free from almost every complaint in Particular fryday noon and night and all Saturday till past 12. Then things appeared as bad as they had done, yet last night quite free again, so that I hardly know what to think of myself. But Dr. M[ortimer] who says he himself has been so laughs at me and pronounces me in a good way. Indeed fine authors write circumstantial enough about such a complaint and I never met with any such thing before myself though twice I prescribed in such cases and heard no more of them; And many things may contribute to the continu[ance] of the disorder. We shall see this day.

Yesterday, Snow, hail, rain, Wind and some times in a few minits.
This day began Warm and fine but ended raw and cold.

27. *Monday.*

Extreme cold indeed, hard wind from Northwest. Preparing to plow for oats. Began also to hill my tobacco ground before the house.

28. *Tuesday.*

Very cold and hard frost. Note the quarter of beef that Dr. Mortimer had the 25th weighed 105 pounds at 4d: 35/.

MARCH 1764

3. *Saturday.*

I thought I was getting well of my wrench but two days agoe felt a pain in the part or rather a great itching. Last night the veins leading there extremely tense and hard and today sharp smarting some times. At last I discovered another knot of an ulcer, send for Mortimer immediately, much scared. This accounts for the E—— all the week after 3 in the morning.

Colo. Tayloe's stone cutter Ralph finis[hed] 16 Capitols for my Piazzas and went away home at night. He came to work February 3 and has been here 25 days, that is 4 weeks and 1 day So that Jammy is to work as many days for Colo. Tayloe.

Colo. Tayloe's stone Cutter worked 2 days more.

5. *Monday.*

Colo. Tayloe's Ralph sent back here to cut my dishing capstones for my Pigeonhouse posts to keep down the rats.

The Phasis of the New Moon the 1st of this month is with both horns up which denotes a dripping moon. March used to be famous for many weathers, but as yet it has proved the most freezing month we have had, Every day a hard frost so that it is near half a day before a tool can be drove into the Earth.

Received by the hands of Mr. R. Parker 1 hogshead W[illiam] K[irkham][21] No. 1: 1045 N. on account of Wm. Kirkham's two years' rent 1 ditto T[om] A[sbury][22] No. 1: 1182 on account of Tom Asbury's two years' rent, overplus to be paid in cash.

Drew my 4th two dozen out of my wine.

Paid Mr. Parker 15/ ballance of Asbury's tobacco Shipped this in the *Tryton* Jno. Anderson.[23]

6. *Tuesday.*

It began to snow last night at 11 o'clock and so it has continued ever since to 5 this evening. The snow is really pretty deep.

It will be late oat year, if not in other crops, and what must other people do who have but just began any hoe work?

I gave Captain Anderson of the *Tryton* in Jordan's[24] imploy an order yesterday for my 27th hogshead at Northumberland quarters. Three more he is to have here, and I sent him Asbury's and Kirkham's hogshead received yesterday so that he will have 6 hogsheads.

[21] William Kirkham was a farmer in Richmond Co. and a tenant of Landon Carter.

[22] Thomas Asbury (d. 1767) was a farmer in Richmond Co. and a tenant of Landon Carter.

[23] Capt. John Anderson commanded various ships engaged in the Virginia tobacco trade in the 1760s and 1770s.

[24] Almost certainly John Morton Jordan (d. 1771), prominent merchant first in London in partnership with Robert Maxwell and then in Annapolis, Maryland. At his death he owned extensive estates in Virginia, Maryland, Antigua, and England.

8. *Thursday.*

By the present weather it looks as if we have had no winter and all is yet to come. Snow deep, violent wind, extreme cold all day yesterday and now a wind as hard as ever.

My Yearlings dying with worms in their backs and sides. Inspected at Totusky[25] and shipped [torn] Capt. Gregg to James Russell[26] [the] following 6 hogsheads:

Crop 1763   Richmond

L[andon] C[arter] E No. 1. 1282   4. 1166
                      2. 1177   5. 1187
                      3. 1357.   6. 1126
                         3816   3816
                                    7295

9. *Friday.*

Paid Elianon Haydon[27] cash 26/3.

Yesterday promised a fair day this, but it is nothing but rain, the moon answers her Phasis. 8 lambs at the Fork quarter.

10. *Saturday.*

The extreme badness of last night's weather has made it remarkable. All yesterday a rain till between 4 and 6, then a very heavy rain, then hail and hard wind all night till two o'clock, the snow and ice in Storms of Great Guns, and notwithstanding all the whole heavens quite Cloudy much resembling more snow, the earth all Ice and snow and the trees the same and the Wind very hard at North and Northeast.

11. *Sunday.*

1st likely day for good weather. [Go]d send it to continue.

14. *Wednesday.*

Still confined and that close by the weather. There has not been one day this Month for any body to walk or ride out; Neither has there been any working the whole 14 days as my 3 acres plowing will shew for two plows and

---

[25] Totuskey was one of Carter's plantations on Tutuskey Creek in Richmond Co.
[26] James Russell was a London merchant.
[27] Elianon Haydon was probably a member of the Haydon family of Lancaster Co.

my 15,000 tobacco hills for 20 hands for I began both those W[orks] the 1st day of the Month. I tend a sort of land that won't do without early tillage and it cannot get that this year, so that unless I meet with the most favourable year of Wet and drye alternately day by day, I shall again make no crop; And how can I expect that from the long falling of all the moisture now: We are certainly to have drye weather for it and if that is to happen in any hot month it will be very bad for my lands.

An old Stear died in my pen. Two sheep died so that my number is only 86 now.

15. *Thursday.*

The earth loaded with water and still raining, but as I hear some thunder there is reason to conclude the heavy wet clouds will break and retire. No oats this year to be sure, no ground plowed for them and I fear none can be yet awhile. Richard Edwards and [Ann] Hamilton's[28] weadding day.

16. *Friday.*

Yesterday a little fair in the evening. Walked out on horseback near 2 miles but with great difficulty roads so bad. Much lightning after 8 last night and rain all night till day, so that we have now water enough as the Pool says of Snow.

17. *Saturday.*

A small frost, clear skye and promises a fine day. My stock of Sheep reduced to 85 by the death of 5 more since the dog Slaughter which were harrassed by the dogs. As yet but 21 lambs. A young Ewe Yeaned yesterday in a puddle of water. The lamb perished. I discharge some filaments I do suppose some seminal discharge to d[ay] in the Urethra and now brought off by the Marsh Mallow tea. Note: These are but small.

19. *Monday.*

Printer sent me up 50 copies of my Pamphlet against Cam.[29]
Sent 18 over to A. Ritchie to sell at 15d each.

[28] Ann Hamilton was the daughter of Gilbert Hamilton.

[29] This pamphlet was the *Rector Detected*. Published by Joseph Royle (d. 1766) in Williamsburg in March 1764, this was Carter's second contribution to the pamphlet warfare over the Two-Penny Act which he and Richard Bland carried on against Rev. John Camm. The details of this affair are traced in Glenn C. Smith, "The Parson's Cause, 1755–1765," *Tyler's Qtly. Hist. and Gen. Mag.*, XXI (January and April 1940), 140–71, 291–306.

Thomas Beale[30] and R. Tomlin[31] a pamphlet each at 1/3.

21. *Wednesday.*

The 18, 19 and 20th tollerable pleasant days but not for working in my land, for though I did work it was rather lumps of Lobloly that a dividing clod the earth was so loaded with water. I did sow some oats though I could hardly harrow them in, the ground though finely plowed was again so baked with the rain. This day a deluge of water, for the time it lasted from daybreak till past 12.

23. *Friday.*

Much rain last night; very cloudy, foggy and misty this day; all things extremely wet and no sun, nor likely-hood for any. I myself still with my [earlier] complaint and something of the Vertigoe but better a good deal I hope.

24. *Saturday.*

Still moist and uggly weather, even dangerous to the constitution. We do sow oats but harrow them badly. All my coleflower brocoli are dead, both the full grown ones that should have blown this month and the Young plants set out in November last. A hasty man would from thence conclude the plant not so durable as is represented; but that some winters will destroy them; but of this they had no fair tryal; the young plants which I ordered to be covered with bushes on Forks were also by my fool covered down with straw which rotted them, and the grown plants were all eaten along the stalks by the hares which pealed them quite bare. I am of opinion that as they grow with long stalks they ought in November to be set down deep in the earth and kept from Hares and the young plants to be only sheltered.

25. *Sunday.*

From 12 o'clock yesterday a very fine day till dark, but it began then to blow at Northeast and has continued so ever since, so that there is as great a quantity of rain seemingly to fall as we have had from 12 to 2 a small deluge, which we could have spared.

---

[30] Thomas Beale (d. 1799), small planter in Richmond Co. and son of William Beale (d. 1778) and Ann Harwar. He was the brother of Winifred Travers Beale, wife of Robert Wormeley Carter.
[31] Robert Tomlin (d. 1794) was a leading planter in Richmond Co.

26. *Monday.*

[V]ery cold raw day, very moist heavy atmosphere Just in the tops of the trees, all ready to rain and Yet the whole low grounds a float. Shall we not want this rain? I greatly fear we shall in the summer.

Fork Jammy came home at 9 this morning from working at Colo. Tayloe's so that as he went to work their this day 7 nights he has wrought 7 and one day before 8 days in repaying Ralph the Stone cutter's work here so that I am still in debt of Jammy's work 19 days. Note: as I include the Sundays that Ralph was here I also include the sunday that James was there (but there shall be no dispute).

28. *Wednesday.*

A foggy moist morning, which turned into a very hot summer's day. Thus are the seasons changed at once upon us when we are in no kind of preparation for them, neither could we be prepared, because we have not had one drye day to work in. I wish we may not have a vast [torn] [illegible] storm of thunder and lightning this year. We have had two already. The last the 15th of this Month proved destruction to a Slave at McCalle's[32] over the River and knocked down another.

29. *Thursday.*

Paid Frary Taylor his account off by a note on Mr. Jett[33] £5.19/10½.

Bottled off this day the remainder of the pipe of Wine broached the 23 January and find 27 dozen and 9 bottles only so that allowing this Pipe to have held 40 dozen which it ought we have used up 12 dozen and 3 bottles in two months and 5 days which being 65 days is 2 bottles per day and 17 over.

Really very warm and smokey.

31. *Saturday.*

Still very hazy and Warm, a long spell. This weight of 3 hogsheads more home crop which go in Capt. Anderson to Jordan:

L[andon] C[arter] E. 7. 1352
8. 1364 Richmond
9. 1323

[32] Archibald McCall was a merchant in Tappahannock. He married Katherine, daughter of Dr. Nicholas Flood. Connected with the firm of James McCall of Glasgow, he left the colony in 1775. He returned to Virginia after the Revolution and died at Richmond in 1814.

[33] Probably Mr. Thomas Jett, factor at Leeds in Westmoreland Co.

APRIL 1764

12. *Thursday.*

[No] rain this month to signifye any thing.

Cold, flyes eat in plant patches. No corn planted though every thing near ready to begin.

Finished this day sowing my oats; a very troublesome job. Ditching not quite done but near it.

13. *Friday.*

A small white frost plain to be seen at my barn on the Straw. Began to sow oats in my fork corn field between the corn rows.

14. *Saturday.*

Davis a quarter of fatened beef weight 95 at 4d.

17. *Tuesday.*

This day a writ served on me by Thos. Lucas[34] for his crop in 1752. Constantly drye and hard.

Began this week to plant corn at the Fork quarter and Jamy's; but not at Mangorike. The earth is so hard that our corn hills can hardly be made. English cow killed herself going into the Lucern.

18. *Wednesday.*

This month hath hitherto proved neither agreeable to grow or labour. It has been too drye and generally too cool for the former, And the ground so hard white and drye for the latter that neither spade, hoe nor plow could touch it to do any thing with it.

Tobacco plants now growing very scarce by means of the flye eating every where. Persons no doubt are pleased with this, at least the Rector of York Hampton[35] who wants to be left at his liberty to do with the poor as christianity directs him which by his sampling given the world lately is 50/ per centum. Divine Humanity this.

---

[34] This matter was probably settled out of court because there is no record of its having come before the Richmond Co. court.

[35] Rev. John Camm was rector of Yorkhampton.

20. *Friday.*

Very cold Northwest this morning and all night. Yesterday's rain was Just brought on by a Northeast wind that blowed near 3 days and just as it rained only so much as to give a fresh look to the grass (for it was not enough to moisten Cabbage hills made a fortnight agoe) the wind flew round to every point of the Compass and then fixed at Northwest from whence a great hail cloud passed to the North east and Just touched S[abine] Hall, hail stones very small.

Wed my Davis and home plant patches, also I believe Jammy's and the Fork; covered all down again. I wish they had not been touched. There must be a frost this night if the wind holds. Plowed my Lucern. Finished this day. It has been a week in all doing this day. Neal talks of the largest hail stones he ever saw. I don't believe him. Mine were as small as ever were seen. Though every thing foretold a frost, J. Lubbar[36] at the fork was weeding his plants. I ordered all to be instantly covered down.

21. *Saturday.*

Never was there a greater change of weather. Yesterday till 4 in the afternoon every sign for a sharp frost. The wind chopt about, has now brought on a fine rain that I hope will continue—replenish my lucern at the fork quarter.

The Park crop to this day; there is to be 9 hogshead in all: L[andon] C[arter]:	N[umber] pounds:
	C 1. 1112.112
	2. 1167.111
	3. 1268.110
	4. 1285.111
	5. 1125.106
	6. 1228.105
	7. 1223.112
	8. 1130.100
	9. 970

22. *Sunday.*

Fine rain in the night. This day very cool Northwest hard wind. I see all our rains clear up this way.

---

[36] Jack Lubbar was an old and trusted slave.

24. *Tuesday.*

Still very cold. The third day the wind has been Northwest and two days it has blown hard. I now begin to plant corn at mangorike. I hope soon enough.

25. *Wednesday.*

A frost this morning on the wind's Cutting. I suppose now we shall have a South wind and it will be warm and drye as we have been all along. The little rain that fell 4 days agoe doubly dryed up by 3 day Northwest hard blowing so that I in my stiff lands am quite baked.

26. *Thursday.*

Still very dry and very cold. Every appearance of rain only an addition to the dryeness and coldness of the weather; and now almost May day. Virginia must be shortly fit for no creature to live in, the Climate so altered the whole year divided into drye and wet spells, Warm and cold. Nothing but Lucern grown. Burnet seeding and though the ground is rich it makes but a poor figure in comparison with Lucern. However I shall go on to pers[evere] and watch it.

27. *Friday.*

It began to rain a fine moderate rain, and it has continued from daybreak to 6 o'clock; It came on gently, but very cold; however our great drouth and hard baked lands make us wish it to continue.

28. *Saturday.*

A very fine rain all day yesterday and for near all night and still very drizzling weather.

Last night through the rain came the news of my poor brother's[37] death, who departed this life the evening before; a dropsey it is supposed, joined with some domestick affliction or rather near connected concern, helped to remove him.

29. *Sunday.*

A rain all day, prodigious plenty of water fallen and seemingly still to fall.

[37] Charles Carter of Cleve.

30. *Monday*.

Paid this day one Jacob Alenthorp for Mr. Jno. Mercer[38] his fee against Townsend[39] cash 20/, the ballance 30, the remainder on the account which is to be produced when the ballance is demanded.

MAY 1764

4. *Friday*.

Pretty good weather lately, plenty of rain; but April a bad month, drye and cold.

It is half of every day too cold. My head not above a day or two easy and then giddy for as many. Began my Piazza 4 days agoe. Sukey at the hen house gave me the following account of the charge under her that I may be a Judge of her care which she has been entrusted with:

Old geeses	33	
goslings	78	two geese still to hatch
old ducks	8	
young ducks	20	Seven hens sitting on duck eggs
Old fowls	32	
Chickens	200	one hen still sitting on her eggs
Old turkey	12	
young ditto	7	Seven turkey hens sitting

She has orders for two bushels corn or meal to feed.

[38] John Mercer (1704–68) of Marlborough, Stafford Co., was the son of John and Grace Mercer of London. He was an eminent lawyer as well as a planter and merchant.

[39] Probably the Rev. Jacob Townshend who was minister of Cumberland Parish, Lunenburg Co. in 1757–58. In the fall of 1762 "the Revd. Mr. Townshend" had sued Landon Carter "for defamation and scandal" in one of Carter's writings. Edmund Pendleton represented Townshend, as John Tayloe wrote, "out of pure compassion as the poor man could get nobody else to do it having applyd to all the Lawyers," and John Mercer appears to have defended Carter. See John Tayloe to Landon Carter, Oct. 16, 1762, Sabine Hall Col. The passage that gave Townshend offense was almost certainly the charge made on p. 10 of Carter's *Letter to B——p of L——n* that "One Mr. T—nsh—d, in concert with the memorable [Charles] *Dick*—who, by giving larges prices for Tobacco in 1759, the Crop of 1758, got so much of it shipped off his own Account, that by running away before the Time of Payment, he was able to cheat the Country out of many Thousands of Pounds.—A Fact from which the said Mr. *Townshend* has indeed endeavoured to exculpate himself by a Letter; but it does not appear from his Arguments, that he is quite clear of the Accusation." The records of the General Court in which this case was probably tried are lost, and there is apparently no record of the verdict.

11. *Friday*.

Day for taking Job Pearsall's[40] deposition from Hampshire, versus J. Townsend at King George Courthouse.

14. *Monday*.

Sent to Rippon Hall[41] 8 broad hoes, 6 reap hooks.

16. *Wednesday*.

Rain seems to be wanted again; there have been fine showers lately, but the cool winds have dryed every thing prodigiously and hardly any thing has grown.

This day I discovered the rust on the under sides of the black berry leaves, and I must be of opinion it has been on it some days before; This I fear is a prognostick of the rust in wheat. It has been so in former years. I shall next week have [to] trye the ropes to hall the wheat as before hinted at to see if that will be of service. I shall particularly have the stalks examined in the evening to see if the yellow drops are at the Joints according to Page du Pratz.

20. *Sunday*.

John Newton,[42] Waddman,[43] W. Flood,[44] Gibern[45] to be examined Richmond Courthouse.

24. *Thursday*.

Much fine rain the night before last. Planted yesterday about 50,000. Very cool all the evening, night and this morning Cloudy and a shew for more rain.

26. *Saturday*.

King George Court day my brother's Will.

---

[40] Job Pearsall was a farmer and resident of Hampshire Co.

[41] Ripon Hall was a plantation belonging to Carter in York Co.

[42] John Newton (d. 1767) was a planter in Westmoreland Co.

[43] Probably William P. Waddman, a farmer and resident of Richmond Co.

[44] William Flood (d. 1775) was the brother of Dr. Nicholas Flood and a planter in Westmoreland Co.

[45] Rev. Isaac W. Giberne of Belleville was minister of Lunenburg Parish, Richmond Co., from 1762 until about 1800.

27. *Sunday.*

A fine rain.

28. *Monday.*

Replanted at Mangorike and did the same and planted much at the Fork.

30. *Wednesday.*

A very fine rain in the night and till 11 this day. Planted and replanted a great deal.

31. *Thursday.*

It began again at 12 yesterday and rained till 12 this day and very cool.

JUNE 1764

1. *Friday.*

Very cold this morning. The Season still continues. Drew a bill of Exchange yesterday to Andrew Bailey[46] on Will Hunter[47] for £25.

4. *Monday.*

To Jas. Hunter[48] on ditto———————— £27.15
ditto to Mills and Hunter[49] on ditto——— £31.19/10
This bill to Mills and Hunter was for a Pipe of Wine, freight and duty so that the cost of it in Current money is £31. 19/10
                                    15. 19/ 7.¼
                                     3. 3/11.
                                   £51. 3/ 4.¼

So dear I will never more by a Pipe on such Compliment.
The bill to Hunter was a protested bill of £25.

[46] Andrew Baillie was a merchant in Tappahannock and the owner of land and tobacco warehouses in Colchester in Fairfax Co. He left the colony in 1766.
[47] William Hunter was a London merchant.
[48] James Hunter was a merchant in Fredericksburg and agent for William Hunter of London.
[49] At this time James Mills (1718–82), prosperous merchant at Urbanna and Tappahannock and husband of Elizabeth (1725–95), daughter of Col. William Beverley of Blandfield, was in partnership with James Hunter.

Paid Capt. Thompson[50] for his Porter £4.15 an order on Stewart [and] Campbell of London.

14. *Thursday.*

Paid Mrs. Woods by an order on J. B[ac]khouse[51] £23.10.
Paid Nelly Headly[52] by ditto £ 7.
Now very drye. No rain since the long season June 1st.
Talbot Sheered 85 sheep this month. One died afterwards. The Account is: 84 old sheep, 23 lambs, Fork ditto.
Sukey's account of fowls:
Old geese 33. Gozlins 79. 4 have been used and 4 killed by the sow.
Old ducks 8. 42 ducklins. 2 used.
Old fowls 30 hens 3 cocks. 180 chickens. 30 used.
Old turkeys 9 hens and 2 cocks. One hen dyed. Young turkeys 40. Two died. 3 hens setting upon hen eggs and 2 hens on ducks. These besides the Bantham fowls under M. Betty's care.

15. *Friday.*

Bottled off Mr. I[saac] W[illiam] G[iberne]'s cask of red Wine. 14 dozen.

18. *Monday.*

Maryland Gentleman[53] to come over.

19. *Tuesday.*

Put up in the hall Closet 10 bottles Mrs. Braxton's[54] seed peas.
Garden Peas saved 1764 Mrs. Braxton's Pea 10 quart [torn] resined down, marked Mrs. Braxton 1764 [torn]. Very forwardest pea I ever had.

21. *Thursday.*

Weights of 20 hogsheads shipped from home in Quiney.[55]

[50] Probably Capt. Alexander Thompson of the *Virginia* who transported tobacco to England during the 1760s.
[51] John Backhouse was a Liverpool merchant.
[52] Nelly Headly was probably a housekeeper for Carter.
[53] Probably William Fitzhugh (1721–98), Maryland councilor and former resident of Stafford Co.
[54] Probably Judith, daughter of Christopher Robinson and wife of Carter Braxton (1736–97), son of George Braxton and Mary Carter, Landon's sister. Carter Braxton was burgess for King William Co., 1761–71, 1775–76, member of the Virginia Conventions, 1774–76, and delegate to the Second Continental Congress.
[55] Capt. William Quinney of the *Marlborough*. He transported tobacco to England during the 1760s.

No. 10. 1256   20. 1255   24064
     11. 1186   21. 1178   7200
     12. 1148   22. 1178   3700
     13. 1116   23. 1225   34,964: the whole crop
     14. 1276   24. 1093
     15. 1198   25. 1250
     16. 1202   26. 1266
     17. 1178   27. 1257
     18. 1288   28. 1159
     19. 1167   29. 1288
          11915   12149
                          11915
                          24064

Weight of Longwith's crop from Mr. Rd. Edwards. 20 hogsheads in Robinson.[56]

 1. 1172   11. 1105
 2. 1096   12. 1116
 3. 1101   13. 1178
 4. 1076   14. 1149
 5. 1056   15. 1192
 6. 1070   16. 1182
 7. 1083   17. 1142
 8. 1135   18. 1053
 9. 1129   19. 1034
10. 1130   20. 1113: These 20 hogsheads sent to
                              W. Hunter.

A. 1209   D. 1273
B. 1104   E. 1252
C. 1127   F. 1092: These 6 hogsheads: Campbell and Stewart.
1. hogshead to Jordan No. 27. 1050
weight in the whole 30419   Blough Point crop
                     34964   Richmond crop
                     65383

22. *Friday.*

No rain but perhaps a small sprink[le] for about 5 or 6 minutes, ever since the 5th of June in the night, and extremely cold, Wind at North and Northwest for now 3 days; a fire necessary and very agreeable.

[56] Perhaps Capt. Robert Robinson, who carried tobacco to England from the 1740s through the 1760s.

Mr. Gilbert Hamilton's pea [torn] bottles resined down marked G. H. [torn] next forward and near to Mrs. Braxt[on's] [torn] to have to can the [torn] original [remainder of page torn off].

26. *Tuesday.*

We have not had any rain since the 5th which is 3 weeks agoe. That rain fell just about the blooming time of the wheat, which so clogged the impregnating dust that abundance of the upper grains in the Ear are not filled. And it has been so cool ever since that although we planted some plants that have stood and are still alive; yet nothing has grown, neither can any thing in so hard a baked ground as mine is. So that the chance for cropping is as it has been for the two past drye Years; the Corn though tollerably clean has grown as little as possible, and the oats have not Stirred one inch since the rain for the Cool winds baked immediately. Otherwise had it pleased God to have spared us more seasonable weather we should have made a good Crop of every thing; but his will shall with me be the rule of my life as it has been in all things, as far as human creature could do.

28. *Thursday.*

Very pritty Season for planting and every thing my baked Stiff soil is to produce; it began yesterday about 6 in the morning and held off and on till about 1; then it left off, but did not break off, and in the night it rained again, and this morning left off again, but I hope it is not, nor will not as yet break away; for my soil was in such a dreadful hard situation, that it must require more water to produce Well. This baking state has prevented my getting all my hills, about 12,000, turned for planting, for the people could not do 1/3 of a day's work the ground was so hard and what they did, as a planter, I don't much approve of, For it is in many places very cloddy. We had been 3 weeks exactly without any rain, and all that time under a daily cold Northwest wind so that the season then availed but little to me.

29. *Friday.*

I this day rode out to taste the season but I saw very little that could be relished, as little moisture as ever made a season; and even where my land is extremely light at my Fork quarter the earth nothing more than pearled up; therefore if the weather don't continue cloudy or some more rain does not fall all that is planted will be in a terrible Case; but God send it may do both. At present I have done planting to about 12,000; but perhaps a week hence I may want 60,000 to plant, for there are few plants left in the beds.

Bottled off the Porter. Mr. Carter lent me 21 dozen. I had a few muggs drawn before bottling.

30. *Saturday.*

A fogg today as well as yesterday; a very drye Sign it is and it is most extravagantly so the earth notwithstanding the rain can hardly be hilled up and quite dusty.

D[avis?] got home. Gone ever since tuesday. Odd pretence. All a farce, vile Hypocrite.

JULY 1764

1. *Sunday.*

A very fine rain this evening all at once from West and Northwest and then Southeast. Very sharp lightning. We had great occasion of this rain. The plants planted last rain all alive yesterday morning, and this day I find by the Violent heat yesterday morning to the time of raining at least 4/5 burnt up.

12 drew a bill of exchange to
    Dr. Mortimer on Stewart and Campbell   £60
    at 60 per cent exchange —————————   36
                               cash   96

Paid off the Dr.'s Account with this to a trifle—the remainder of Garland's note on me to W. Lee[57] for £85. And a note to Marmion Fitzhugh[58] for £27 for my chair.

4. *Wednesday.*

Just began to cut my Wheat. Much has been said about the goodness of this Crop but now I come to have a survey of it, I can't see it. I still find the rainy spell about the blooming time has perished the grain. They are but barely filled for grain.

My tobacco quite at a Stand although in the richest Cowpens. The Cold weather immediately and for a month almost after it was planted, and the drye weather during that time and the violent hot since with only one tollerable soke has not done in my stiff land.

[57] William Lee (1737–95), son of Thomas Lee and Hannah Ludwell, was a merchant in London.
[58] William Fitzhugh (1725–91) of Marmion, was a planter in King George Co. and son of John Fitzhugh (d. 1733).

My corn though green too low for the 4th July. In short the drye weather and cold spell has injured that. I have it all to lay by and weedy it is for weeds grow cold or hot wet or drye.

[5]. *Thursday.*

Mary Sandys[59] paid me £5. 9 for the rent [du]e from her husband and is to leave 11/ with Mr. Garland for me.

Rode over my plantations, found my Wheat much Trodden down, the earth extreme drye and the air cold, Corn Pipes up in Stiff land tobacco much missing and that which stands not yet moving into growth. In short no sign of a crop in anything. Oats low and now a trespass committed by the breaking in of Cattle. I can't make my people work or do any thing. Indeed the 3 past days so hot I could not desire. Every wind blows drye.

8. *Sunday.*

Mr. G[iberne?] is an evidence to this being the 3d drye year on this plantation, and if I had evidences living with me, I could prove that ever since the year 1751 we had only had 3 moist years and they were very wet indeed. The year 1750 was also the gust year. So that for want of the common tryal I as yet don't know what my management in my land would have turned out had it been season[able].

This year had I sown all my dunged ground in Pease I can't think I should have made a crop. I planted some in May early and they have been wed and plowed 6 times, and they are only alive, those that I planted in June hardly up such and so drye has the weather been. As to my tobacco there has been some mismanagement. The overseer has been careless. The people have only buryed the dung at top of the hills. Therefore the plants have all dyed as soon as they touched the dung which could not rot for want of moisture; he owns it but does not seem to be ashamed of it and says he never buryed it better.

No rain as yet. Clouds regularly divide on one side and the other and 'tis extremely hot and scorching. I therefore expect nothing. It seems to be a vain hope to do so, but I thank god that others I hear are happy in his benevolent rains.

9. *Monday.*

Yesterday a prodigious fine rain for [ne]ar two hours, and the severest thunder that I think [I ca]n ever remember; one Clap in Particular after [i]t

---

[59] Mary Sandys was probably the wife of John Sandys (d. 1770), Richmond Co. farmer and at this time probably a tenant of Carter's.

had Just past my house rushed so sudden and unexpected that every body was alarmed. It split a small Cherry tree in my garden. There were many others but I thank God none did any other harm and to his great mercy be it ascribed. We had but few plants of our own and every body seems to have been in fault. They never [torn] and I never ordered them to be repeatedly wed be[liev]ing the weeds would preserve them best, but it has proved otherwise. But there is no small degree of infatuation in my people. I heard there were plants at Hickory Thicket and sent there. The tumbrel came back only with one load and they told me there was no more. I now hear my son's Overseer expected I would send for more and kept them for me.

Not yet topped a plant at Mangorike and but a few this day at the Fork. No corn field done weeding as yet. But a bad hand at mowing my wheat. It has been so hot, indeed the hottest week I ever felt. Mary Sandys paid the 11/ due.

13. *Friday.*

Yesterday about 4 o'clock in the evening came up as fine a rain as we have had this whole Summer and really, by its coming so gently and succeeding so soon the rain of the 9th, it at last has cooled and quite moistened the earth. All my plants that I planted before [these] showers died quite scalded in both [torn] the earth when we planted though moist f[torn] brand put into warm water and the Sun [torn] quite destroyed every thing. I sent off my [torn] and tumbrils in the rain yesterday and got about one tumbril load from Hickory Thicket of Plants. I sent also a boat and 6 hands up to Mr. Beverley's for a large load of his plants. As yet they are not come at past 6 this morning, but if they do get any as I hope they will, I shall stick them all in [while] the earth is so moist, for I shall [torn]. This will be as late as I can manage [p]lanting. My corn though not suffering not yet [torn] laid by; It has grown much lately. The [storm] and small rains have done good for that [I no]w hear people complaining about th[e small]ness of their Wheat grain. It is just as I [said]: the rain that fell the last of May Just in the blooming time I foretold would so clogg [the] farina or [small] dust that the grain would be [torn] perished and so it is. Colo. Tayloe says [his is] mighty small and half filled. Note: no [more] lightning nor thunder with yesterday's [rai]n, though I can't think it spread very far. The [show]er came up near Southeast and continued for above 2 hours quite plentifull and now the wind is Southwest and all cloudy. Therefore I do expect the rain will be more favourable to the planter in cropping by the shadyness of the day. It is very Cool and pleasant.

14. *Saturday.*

Another fine rain yesterday from 7 P.M. till [torn] [o']clock. It came up with as black a Northwest cloud as [perhaps I] ever saw, really dreadfull, but it divided near the m[outh] of Rappahannock creek or Belfield's [Mill?] and one half went [torn] down the South side of Rappa[hannock R]iver and the other [torn] to Potomack [woods] and between this firmly [torn]. I sent to Mr. Beverley's for more plants, those [that are the] most long legged all about 4,000 we could [torn]. [The] people returned this morning with about [2] [tumbril] loads very good, The clouds are pretty [torn]th moist and cool. The fork also got [more plants] from the Island Quarter.[60] Therefore [torn].

25. *Wednesday.*

[T]his day tasted a pint bottle of my Virginia wine made last year. It was very clear, but not quite so very transparent, as I see it might be. It had a pure fixed colour rather darker than Burgundy. There was no lusciousness in it, nor was it seemingly so rich in its flavour as the wine the year before was. It had a smartness in it, nothing bordering on an acid, but seeming [rest of page torn off].

27. *Friday.*

[Ye]sterday finished laying by all my corn. Still very drye and no appearance of rain. Talbot returned. The corn to come next week by an Oyste[r] boat. Began this day to sow turnips in drills every one of which I water with a watering pot as soon as sown.

30. *Monday.*

[Last night we] were [blessed] with a fine [m]ild shower [rest of page torn off].

AUGUST 1764

1. *Wednesday.*

Mr. Backhouse having sent me in by Capt. Gaweth[61] from Liverpool some of the large field Colewort called Brasica Arvensis, I this day sowed some in

---

[60] The Island Quarter was one of Carter's tracts in Richmond Co.
[61] Probably Capt. John Gawith, who transported tobacco to Britain during the 1760s and 1770s.

my garden to see what they are and to find out their time of sowing, for some I shall also sow early in the spring.

I hope this day to get in all my harvest every where. I have been at [rest of page torn off].

17. *Friday.*

Still in extreme want of rain, and the acc[ount]s from all parts that I am concerned with (except Northumberland) the same. It is now a most critical time in both the crops of Corn and tobacco. The former can neither shoot nor fill without it; and the latter may be too late for the season as it is and has been violent cold. [Rest of page torn off.]

18. *Saturday.*

This day Talbot told me he counted 84 old Sheep and 20 lambs out. In this he has missed 1 old Sheep and 1 lamb, for last month there was 85 old Sheep and 21 lambs and we have killed none since though he says we have.

Shipped this day Ed. Mozingo['s][62] hogshead Number pounds: 952 remarked LC. No. 1.

Also George Mozingo's[63] hogshead   939 remarked LC No. 2.

Both in Capt. Perry[64] to be consigned to Messr. Clay and Midgely.[65]

19. *Sunday.*

I would say if I could that we had a fine rain this day, but really it fell very short of what we expected. It promised much, but very little fell, only a mere turnip shower, or at least the earth was so drye that we cannot discover much. The sides of the hills are quite drye and dusty, and all appearance gone but some clouds that look too hard to drop amongst us.

20. *Monday.* 21. *Tuesday.*

A very fine rain. Now things may grow.

25. *Saturday.*

63 bushels of oats thrashed out of the first Cut of the stack only one yard long.

[62] Edward Mozingo (d. 1783) was one of Carter's tenants.
[63] George Mozingo was one of Carter's tenants.
[64] Probably Capt. William Perry, who transported tobacco to Britain in the 1750s and 1760s.
[65] Clay and Midgely was a mercantile firm in Liverpool.

Every thing does grow. Paid John Long[66] with a 20/ bill. Let my son Robert have all the cash I had which is 30/. Davis had 8 pounds of unwashed wool at 12d.

No rain since the 21st. All things grow. 'Tis very fine and warm, but it begins to be drye again.

27. *Monday.*

Opened the new york sugar in all	37 boxes
of which single refined————————	8
	29
the double weigh 7½	7
the single————11.20 ounces	203
8	14½
89	217½
	89.
	307.½

28. *Tuesday.*

The new moon by her Phasis extremely drye, horns nearly Perpendicular to each other. The last was so and it has been a drye month; but one tollerable rain in it and that yesterday Seven night. Very hot also.

60 bushel oats from the mow one cut 1 yard up and down.

SEPTEMBER 1764

2. *Sunday.*

It had like to have rained this day; It clouded up much last night and lightened frequently to the Northwest most of the night. This morn about day it over spread and began to Sprinkle, but it only laid the dust; however we are benifited by it a little. The extravagant heat from the 28 last month is much abated by some rain that fell North of us, and the wind now blows in fresh flows thence which I hope will drive off the Vile Musketoes which have during the prodigious heat been almost as plenty as bees in a hive; in short all our care could hardly keep them out of our rooms in the night which with the heat prevented all sleeping, at least very little of it was enjoyed. Mr. Berkeley and

[66] John Long was one of Carter's tenants.

his Lady here now near 3 weeks. My daughter Beverley came here the last of last month.

4. *Tuesday.*

A fortnight this day without rain; very bad for a hot August, a Stiff soil and a long drye summer and cold in generall and lastly a very late crop.

Sent to Mount Airy a loin of fine veal. Note: she sent me a quarter of veal when Mr. Byrd[67] etc. was up in July and I returned a quarter in August and now a loin. This is the year's Account of that matter. On the last year's ballance she owes me one quarter and one loin of Veale, but this the Lady disputes; I fancy she does not keep good books.

A pound of Congo tea.

8. *Saturday.*

'Tis now a very cool Northwest and all the appearance of a rain over So that 1764 keeps with me a very drye year: But two rains properly so to be called by farmer or Planter since the last of April, and one of them rather a prejudice as it was the 24th of May just as the wheat bloomed; All the other little showers of no service at all to stiff or any lands for the Cold winds that followed dryed and baked up every thing; and perhaps at the heels a frost. If so my whole labour which has been very great is quite destroyed, for my tobacco is not yet grown to any size and not above 100 plants housed.

I am pleased to hear the young planters boast of their great fine crops, those who are so blessed with fine rains, as to make them think they are better managers than others; who I believe take twice the pains with 20 times the skill and yet can't get seasonable weather to shew such youths that they do but badly requite the gifts of heaven. I have had now 4 drye years, and yet in the main I have been but little behind them.

9. *Sunday.*

Prodigeous Cold this morning. As yet no frost discovered. If this should not be the Case it must be owing to that frigorific quality in the air, called by many learned men the Retroaerial Salt which Phenomina plainly discover to be one of the Principles in air by which frost is produced; for it has been cold enough all night to produce one. If it has, all places where it is must be ruined both in Corn and tobacco for the first for want of rain is but yet soft. It has

---

[67] Probably Councilor William Byrd III.

indeed been very drye which may have prevented a frost, but This defect it is reasonable to conclude has been amply supplyed by a very great dew that has been all night on the grass and herbs.

11. *Tuesday.*

This night a very fine and plentifull rain.

14. *Friday.*

Extremely cold ever since the rain till this day, only not a frost down here, but I hear from Colo. Tayloe Mr. Lawson[68] had wrote down about a frost that had done much damage in those parts. Not unlikely for all the crops were as late as ours, and ours will not be in this month yet. Thus are we yearly experiencing that sage Prediction of old J. Warner,[69] the Almanack Maker, that Virginia would in time cease to be a tobacco Colony. We are and have been for some years past in the General too Cold till some time in June to plant tobacco and then too drye to get it to Stand till late in July and then not time enough before a frost for it to come to Maturity. This has been generally the case these 4 years. Some people indeed have been lucky in having few rains in the spring from whence they have been warmer and able to Plant sooner. Others have been lucky in having plentiful showers in the summer to let their crops stand and grow. And others as lucky in escaping these early frosts by which means their late crops have come well in; but I speak as to generals and of the fresh back lands where there is seldom any of this good luck.

21. *Friday.*

1764 will be the same quite through; Now quite hot and drye. Corn but very sorry. Tobacco as indifferent. Abundance of fevers and Agues. Little Landon very ill with one. Dr. Mortimer sent for. Mr. Carter not well. Judy and Betty mending. Robin from at his diversions at Leeds. The old Slave doing a kind of duty in taking care of every body.

Sold Colo. Slaughter[70] yesterday 30 pounds Wool which with 6/ for the new Sack bag comes to 51/. He paid me 40/. I am to get all the rest to Cleve. He will sell it for 18d a pound ready money.

24. *Monday.*

A loaf of sugar.

[68] Probably Thomas Lawson, overseer for Carter at Ripon Hall.
[69] John Warner was the author of *The Virginia and Maryland Almanac,* published by the printer William Parks in the 1730s.
[70] Col. Thomas Slaughter, planter and leading resident of Caroline Co.

NOVEMBER 1764

4. *Sunday.*

Received of Colo. Rd. Corbin by the hands of Mr. Carter of Corotoman
Cash——————————————————— £374.15.10
Drew a note on Colo. Corbin
To Colo. Tayloe, McCalle's debtor: 111.4. 2
A note to Sykes[71] for 70 pair shoes
for the C[harles] C[arter] estate———   14.—— —
                                        ————————
                                        £500.—— —

11. *Sunday.*

Gave Sam, the Estate's coachman, 3/9 to pay his ferryages in carrying up
the above 70 pair of shoes for the Estate's negroes. Paid for this Estate to J. and
Will Carter[72] Apothecaries £1.18.2.

21. *Tuesday.*

Now in pocket of the above money in one paper £186
                             in the other   £ 53 some shillings
                                            ————
                                            £239

DECEMBER 1764

15. *Saturday.*

Cash paid for C[harles] C[arter] estate to Mrs. Davenport[73] her account.

The money taken up of Colo. Rd. Corbin for the C[harles] C[arter] estate
thus

Accounted for
Cash paid Mr. Corbin and by him
delivered to me———————————————————————£386
paid Colo. Tayloe———————————————————— 100
paid Sykes for shoes—————————————————— 14
                                        ————
                                        £500

71 Sykes was apparently a shoemaker, probably in King George Co.
72 Drs. James and William Carter were apothecaries in Williamsburg.
73 Mrs. Davenport may have been the housekeeper at Cleve.

The above cash disposed of	386.—.—
To Colo. Tayloe	11.4.2
Paid George Abyvon[74]	14.3.3
Nicholas Taylor	1.18.7
James and Will Carter	1.18.2
Zachy Taliaferro[75]	119.11.11
To pay Express Ed. Dixon[76]	94.7.2

[74] George Abyvon (d. 1781) was a prominent citizen in Norfolk. He was a small planter and probably also a merchant.

[75] Zachary Taliaferro was a resident of Port Royal in Caroline Co.

[76] Edward Dixon (d. 1779) was a resident of Port Royal and justice of the peace in Caroline Co.

THE DIARY

January 1766—October 29, 1767

THE DIARY

1766

JANUARY 1766

A very drye spell indeed quite through the month, neither rains nor snows but in the smallest quantities and that but seldom.[1]

This whole month pretty drye and hardly a snow, nor very severe frosts.

The Phasis of this moon on her first appearance after her change was a very small matter leaning on her back. I take notice of this as a common observation that the more she leans on her back the weather is generally the wetter. Astronomy perhaps may condemn this, because those appearances are only occasioned by her situation as to the earth, so that the first illumined part will place her appearance either more or less on her back; and therefore does not probably affect the weather; However observation has the right to determine in a point although Philosophy can't be reconciled to it, especially where things though extremely probable are nevertheless free from absolute certainty.

Moon in her change leaning but a little on her back. But little rain prognosticated.

FEBRUARY 1766

It continued without rain or snow but in very small proportions to the 18, When the rainy wether set in and so continued very wet the remainder of the month, but no snow, only a scudd of moment now and then.

Moon's change leaning a little on her back. Not altogether Drye. From the middle of this month the weather has been very wet; and some very keen

---

[1] Printed from the original diary in the William L. Clements Library. The portions of the diary covering January 1766 to Oct. 29, 1767, are written on the blank leaves of copies of the *Virginia Almanack* for 1766 and 1767. The 1766 *Almanack* contains the following endorsement: "This Almanack came enclosed under a cover with nothing hinting from whom. I examined it to see if it had been Stampt, but finding none I ventured to set my name in it."

frosts indeed; twice the River frozen over; and many drifts of snow though none to lie anytime.

The Phasis of this moon or her change bespoke this weather by leaning pritty much on her back.

MARCH 1766

Moon on her back at change. Much rain.

This month extremely wet; some sharp frosts, some thunder and lightning; Earth exceeding cold, Oats lay a long while without coming up; even from early in february to late this month.

The change of this moon quite on her back, bothe her horns pointing directly upright. So that wet weather was Certainly to be expected, and we had it.

8. *Saturday.*

I have but 15 lambs as yet at home having lost 8, by negligence and the long drie summer, fall and winter.

13 ditto at my Fork. None lost.

24 Calves here. 4 have died by accidents. 3 ditto at my Fork quarter.

Memorandom: March 4th being tuesday The serch Warrant I obtained from Wmson. Ball[2] a Justice being yesterday executed at the House of Robt. Smith Junr.[3] and there being found there 80½ of Wool Washed and unwashed; also a Cart Rope that had been stolen. That warrant was this 4th day of the month returned and enquired into before the Justice Who ordered a Called Court on that day week.

12. *Wednesday.*

This day all the evidences attended the called Court but no Court held. At night found that my ox carter, Simon, was run away and examined Billy[4] the foreman who said he complained of the belly ake and went away, The Overseer being an[illegible]ordance at Court.

Extremely wet all through the month, but very few drye days; but no Snow to speak of.

---

[2] Williamson Ball (d. 1794) was a planter and justice of the peace in Richmond Co.

[3] Robert Smith, Jr. (d. 1776), was a Richmond Co. planter.

[4] Billy Beale (d. 1800) was manager of Carter's Richmond Co. lands and probably the son of Capt. William Beale and Ann Harwar.

APRIL 1766

The change of this moon the most on her back that it can be. Accordingly the rains have began; And I apprehend they will continue, for a whole week was nothing also at the beginning and it rained again on the 11th. In short the very light lands are miry to hoe or even ride on.

8. *Tuesday.*

A comet appeared near setting at 7 o'clock and did set by the accounts given me sometime after 8 o'clock.

9. *Wednesday.*

It appeared between West Northwest and Northwest by West and set exactly 30 minutes past 8 o'clok.

10. *Thursday.*

It appeared in the same course and set 15 past 8, So that it is probable some mistake as to its setting the first night it was discovered it must have been as late as 3/4 past 8 o'clock.

12. *Saturday.*

Sowed this day 1½ bushels of flax seed; first hoed the land in 4 feet beds in November, then Chopped the beds over fine, then hand raked it, then Sowed it with a full cart; and at the quantity of land though irregular it being a bottom between hills guessed to about 7,000 tobacco plants. So that it is about as thick as is generally sown. I had it also well hand raked in.

13. *Sunday.*

Signed my name this day three times to a paper folded for a set of Exchange to be drawn for a £100 cash borrowed of Colo. Richard Corbin for Colo. Carter of Cleve his estate which I did as an Executor and deeded to Mr. Carter of Corotoman my Coe-xecutor.

14. *Monday.*

Sowed my hemp at Jamy's this day. The ground is guessed to be 5 acres and was intended to be sown with 5 bushuls of seed. My 6 drill plow sowed 6 beds very well but then, the bricks' grit of the garden walks where the seed was dried getting in to the boxes, we were obliged to sow in broad cast. Note: This ground shift once dunged but much cropped in tobacco but it was broke up in November and in March and now and hand raked in.

Note: though the whole quantity of ground in hemp at Jamy's was guessed at 5 acres; Yet as 2 feet in every 7 feet was left for an alley to weed it the real quantity sown is but 3½ and about half a quarter which took 3½ bushels of seed so that the intention of sowing a bushel to the acre is pritty near complyed with, The loss of 2 feet in 7 being something short of 1/3.

22. *Tuesday.*

The flax come up, and what's so remarkable it was 2 days under water in the 9 days since it was sown.

23. *Wednesday.*

Tobacco flies in abundance everywhere. Those who uncovered and wed have suffered by taking away the weeds, the chief food the flye had to live on, and of course they went to the plants and they are gone. Many have sowed again.

Finished planting corn at Jamy's. Began at the fork but yesterday; but shall not begin these two days at Mangorike.

A smart frost last night. Ice at my well.

This day coming under my bank by the River side I observed on the upright of the high bank a very forward wild Plant. It appeared first like lucern but it was not that. I then took it for Mililot but it was too forward for that and did not smell of that Physicky smell; My horses were extravagantly fond [of] it. It had roots from 4 to 7 feet long as thick as my thumb. I brought some home to see what it may be; as it is so favored and so agreeable to my horses. I have planted at 2 feet distance.

We have had 3 very cold days; wind at every point of the compas, but all this day at Northwest chiefly. Note: in my observations on the above wild plant I did not take notice of a circumstance that ought to be observed upon, That Melilot to which and Lucerne it is most like has according to what I have ever seen been a thing most disagreeable to horses; but mine eat all they could get at of this most greedily. Therefore should it be a species of that plant, it can't but be a valuable sort to propagate, both as to the fondness of the creatures of it and its prodigeous early growth, for though it has been so cold and backward a spring, and the roots of the plant almost quite bare by growing almost on the upright of every steep bank. Yet it had not only a very broad bushy crown but it was above 2 feet high and its tenderness expressive of its being of this year's growth. It had indeed a south situation assisted by the reflecting glassy surface of the River; But then its soil was of the cold marly kind much hintermixed with the uppersand of the bank that had slid down by means of the winter's frosts.

I am also to take notice of another wild herbage that grows in my garden at this time with great Luxurience. It appears like what I have always heard called the blind nettle to about 12 inches high, very thick and bears a bluish flower now blown at every leafy joint. I always thought it a useless weed but on throwing it out I found my cows devour it most Voraciously, though I think my hogs were hurt by it. My garden is indeed very and I may say rich; therefore can't say of what great service it may be to trye this for a forward food for my creatures, because it may not perhaps turn out so well in any field culture not so rich. However it is Certainly a durable plant by its not being injured by the frosts.

Hitherto April has been a rainy month according to the Phasis of the moon as before.

Began yesterday to cart out my cow yard dung which I fear will be a long and troublesome job. My horses: 6 dead, the remaining 12 very poor, and nothing to feed them with. Oxen brake but badly out of 8 taken up to break to the draft. 1 broke its neck, 2 more so sullen that nothing can do with them therefore turned out again. The fellow to the broken neck oxen also turned out as much hurted by his fellow, 2 only work tolluake. The other still very sullen.

24. *Thursday.*

Simon, one of the Outlaws, came home. He run away the 12th of March and by being out and doing mischief was outlawed in all the Churches 2 several Sundays and on the 10th of this month having a great suspicion that he was entertained at my home quarter where his Aunt and Sisterinlaw lives, Mr. Carter's favourite maid; I had him R[illegible] watched by Talbot and Tom with Guns loaded with small shot and Toney withdrew. Just at dark according to my suspicion they came along my lane; over the Lucern field talking loudly as if secure they should be concealed When Talbot commanding them to stand, upon their running, shot Simon in the right leg foot and ham. He got away and Simon has stayed out ever since then so that he has been now shot to this day 14 days.

A white frost this morning and the air sharp but not so cold nor the frost so hard as yesterday's. However my overseer says the ground was really hard with a crust. It seems that Simon the runaway was shot at only about 11 days agoe. And he did not come in himself; for Mangorike Will seeing a smoke yesterday amongst Some Cedars by the side of the corn field when he was working; at night went to see what it was, and was long hunting for it as smoke is but rarely seen in the night. At last he got to some burnt Coals and saw no one there, but creeping through the Cedars he came to a fire burning and Simon lying by it; Who instantly started up to run away, but Billy was too swift and after a small struggle made him surrender and brought him in to Tom and Nassau who concealed this from me, in order to make as if the fellow came in himself. Willy says he was not lame last night, although he has now strummed it on account of his leg being shot. I shall punish him accordingly.

Ben Thrift, overseer at Jammy's, told me that his plants which had not a flye in them yesterday are now almost eaten up weeds and all. I ordered him instantly to prepare a patch in my meadow, First paring off all grass and weeds, Then barowing with dry brush, Then hoing and breaking all fine, Then hoeing it again and then sowing it. The Seed in strep in Milk and some salt Peter from 11 this day till tomorrow the time of sowing.

25. *Friday*.

Cattle are now dying with poverty and how should it be other wise? All the winter food gone and no grass yet on the earth. 2 have lain down and expired, and two or three more very near it if my Lucern patch can't save them, where I have and must bring them. One of the dead cows has a calf which must be raised if I can. This is the general time of the year when cattle yeild to their poverty; And I cannot see how it can be avoided, as it is impossible to provide food enough for any number of Cattle after such prodigeous drye years; And equally difficult to procure a green food for this time except perhaps a wheat field should be devoted purely for the very poor creatures at such a time. I fancy if I can once get that ready to be done from tailings, Rye, oats or Barley, it may do.

Sowed a meadow plant patch this day [as be]fore. Plants fine in the fork meadow. I gave orders if the flye came in them to float them off as it can be done in a few hours.

The frosts on the 23 and 24 in the morning have scorcht a great deal of wheat from the tops of the blades pretty low down; so that it in all such places looks fowey. This is the 4th day we have been carting out dung; but a poor hand indeed.

My man Bart came in this day, he has been gone ever since New year's day. His reason is only that I had ordered him a whipping for saying he then brought in two load of wood when he was coming with his first load only.

This he still insists on was truth Although the whole plantation asserts the contrary, and the boy with him. He is the most incorrigeable villain I beleive alive, and has deserved hanging; which I will get done if his mate in roguery can be tempted to turn evidence against him.

Bart broke open the house in which he was tyed and locked up; he got out before 2 o'clock but not discovered till night. Talbot is a rogue. He was put in charge of him. I do imagine the gardiner's boy Sam, a rogue I have suspected to have maintained Bart and Simon all the while they have been out And I sent this boy with a letter to the Island ferry at breakfast, but he never returned although he was seen coming back about 12 and was seen at night by Hart George at night pretending to be looking for his Cattle. I kept this fellow up two nights about these fellows before And have given Rit the Miller a light whipping as having fed them by the hands of Gardiner Sam.

5 Cattle died yesterday and 3 or 4 more in a decaying Situation. I have had them up to my Lucern field. Perhaps that may save them. My overseer Davis was advised to give me notice of the Poverty of the creatures before they faltered; but he is a sorry fellow and I beleive does not care though he pretends he does. He pretended the Creatures were out in the woods but they never went there; the wench never carried them out there at all in this day but he says it was his orders. I shall direct otherwise and get a man to see my orders obeyed.

27. *Sunday.*

Yesterday my son brought a story from Lansdown old Tom, that Johnny my gardiner had harboured Bart and Simon all the while they were out, Sometimes in his inner room and sometimes in my Kitchen Vault. Tom had this from Adam his wife's grandson That they were placed in the Vault in particular the day my Militia were hunting for them.

This Simon owned, and the boy Adam repeated it to me; but Tom of Landsdown said that George belonging to Capn. Beale[5] saw them in my quarter when he came from setting my Weir. It seemed to me so plausible that I sent Johnny [to] Goal and locked his son in Law Postilion Tom up. Note: every body denyed they had ever seen them and in Particular Mrs. Carter's wench Betty, wife to Sawney, brother of Simon, denyed that she had ever seen them; as she did to me with great impudence some days agoe. However Capn.

[5] Capt. William Beale (d. 1778), Richmond Co. planter and father of Winifred Travers Beale, wife of Robert Wormeley Carter.

Beale's George this day came to me and before Mrs. Carter told the story and in Simon's hearing That coming from the Weir he went into Frank's room and then into Sawney's room, when Simon came in to them. So that favourites and all are liars and villains.

These rogues could not have been so entertained without some advantage to those who harboured them; from whence I may conclude the making away of my wool, wheat etc., and the death of my horses. I never rightly saw into the assertion that negroes are honest only from a religious Principle. Johny is the most constant churchgoer I have; but he is a drunkard, a thief and a rogue. They are only through Sobriety, and but few of them.

28. *Monday*.

The poverty of the cattle is now most sensibly felt in their deaths. I had 5 dyed last week, two this morning and 2 more very near it, besides many so poor it is difficult to say they can live. Some pains must be taken to prevent this another year if I sacrifice part of some crop; because it must be of more service to save the cattle which evidently manure the land than even to make a fine flax, because in a little time Cattle cannot be bought. My Present thoughts are to plow or harrow up my wheat and oat patches as soon as reaped first sprinkling them with trash wheat, Rye or barley and these preserve till March.

Now to start this Rye is to be got and the creatures are to be somehow nourished to draw these plows or harrows; Perhaps as it is grass time at reaping they may be in heart enough; especially if the cowpens are hoed up as soon as the pens are removed; but my overseer loves home and d——g too much for which reason I beleive we must part.

A great flight of Mosketoes the 25 and so they have continued. A fine Climate hardly one Month in a year without a frost at sometime though hot in the day; And yet hardly a month without those plagues. If I can get turnep seed enough I will sow the hemp fields every where with turneps, if not with wheat tailings.

The flye still eats terribly. Wether very cool both yesterday and this morning and really begins now to be drye.

29. *Tuesday*.

Plants at the Fork quarter very fine, clear of flies and in the meadow patch there very large. I must ditch the patches now to drain off the too great moisture. This seems to be a fine place for plants and will admit of a much larger Patch. We shall finish planting corn there tomorrow. A Steer died there last night which makes the 5th Some by accidents this only through age and poverty. A cow then also on the lift. Sowed plants at home in my Asparagus beds and Artichoke bed. Seed first steeped in a week solution of Salt peter. A poor Cow died in the Lucern field last night, she could not eat when brought in. In all 8 since the 21st.

It begins to be drye. We have no rain since Monday the 21st now 8 days. I fear the summer will turn out much like the last; many good shows for rain wear a way with only a drop or so. God be merciful to us, we shall all perish with such an other drye disasterous year. No one can foresee the consequences of it; but they become evident in the whole creation. Few calves, very few lambs, old creatures and young died, nothing to fatten nay not to feed with, and of Course very little labour to be carryed, so that many shortages will be produced by one drye summer. What then will not 7 do? This is my 7th drye year.

30. *Wednesday.*

A cow died last night in the pen and I fear another steer will go. It was brought to the Lucern field where it has had plenty, it then stood and has eaten heartily but now it can't stand up as I am told so that new poverty may bring on many disorders. And then Cow and young heifers taken weak etc. and brought up. I see several very low and poor at the fork quarter. I have ordered them not to be penned.

This month was wet to the night of the 21st then it rained but not since, though every day great signs of it.

This day I uncovered my fork meadow plants. It is a fine patch not overweedy; but I fear by Reaping it moist to prevent the ravages of the flies, the plants are turning yellow, and the beds covered with a green moss. However I had it trenched all round and outlets from each alley to 12 trench and from the trench to the main one.

I also have had the covering well thrasht of its loose leaves and laid on again after a day's Sun. This I shall give it another day or two and cover down till the plants are used to be quite exposed.

Finished planting corn this day and tryed to divide my plantation there so that part hilled and planted and the rest only hoed and holed.

Moon very much on her back. Very great rains.

Wet and rainy till the 21st in the night when the wet weather ended with a kind of clearing rain and rained no more the rest of the month.

MAY 1766

Moon on her change leans but a little on her back rather drye than wet.

1. *Thursday.*

May day and a large fire; a fine climate this. I have hitherto my Locust trees to bloom in April, but now their leaves just begin to shade the trees with green.

I wish I had not broke through my resolution of not uncovering a plant till settled warm weather, but the meadow patch was so mossy at the fork that I could not but think it must want a little Sun and gave it to all day yesterday; but as the wind chopt about to Northwest I fear I have rather injured it by so doing; though I covered down at night. No Deaths of cattle this morning, though some are poor and low. 11 of them and 6 calves in my Lucern. There were 13 old cattle but two wanted bad to live aday in the fields.

This 1st day continues very cool and bids fair for a Stout frost; if so fare well everything. The fruit already injured even to the gooseberries; of which we had a great plenty till the last frost on the 24th of april and they are all gone.

2. *Friday.*

No cattle dead this day although the Steer that was on the lift is still down.

Finished planting corn at Mangorike and every where here. Ridge up my barley which is as soon as the wet ground and the season would permit. It is no good way in such land to drill anything from this general impossibility to plow or ridge it before for the rains and winter's wet weather.

Sowed 5 acres of last year's cow pens in hemp at the fork. I intended 7½ bushels seed but I fear the seeds man will not get it all in the ground. I hand raked it all. No flye as yet in the fork meadow patch.

It rained all night and till the 3d in the morning, but no more than a drop or so now and then till the 14th.

3. *Saturday.*

A fine rain yesterday morning and in the night. Spitting this morning and great moisture. Uncovered my plants to weed. Much flye and few plants every where, though enough. There can't be a greater certainty that the covering obstructs the flye somehow. As I saw my meadow patch at the fork turning green which I uncovered 2 days agoe to give it sun and air; then I could not see a flye. I had the brush well shaken and covered down at night; And now the flys are plenty in the patch. I see no plants which grows as used to be this month. The birds seem to pull the corn up as fast it comes up. I had a whole row in my view yesterday. All now pulled up and the blades lying on the hills.

Measured the tobacco ground in my present field to be sown in hemp because I had not dung enough to give it for tobacco and it makes 51,430 plants equal to 13 acres which shall be sown with 18 bushels of seed as soon as the weather will permit me. No cattle dead this day though the Steer and fork cow still on the lift. Moved Mangorike cow pen this day being Saturday.

4. *Sunday.*

The Steer and the no horn yearling died this day in my Lucern field, where they have eaten abundance and both dung and Urine Plentifully, so that the Lucern would have saved them, had not they [their] Poverty, laid the foundation of some fatal disorder.

My son John came from Town this day paid me 2 £10 bills for my man Jammy to be sent to work at his house for him to do some brick work for which I shall charge him 3/6 Perday from the time he sets off.

I rode out to my fork quarter. Found the birds had pulled up the corn as fast as it came up. A row of 70 hills and upwards all pulled up to a hill. And what is worse the bed corn that I had ordered to be sown for setting early; though all up very finely and sown close by the quarter all rooted up this day; Notwithstanding I had yesterday given particular charge about it and indeed ordered the fence to be made more secure by the Cow yard rails close by; but the more particular we are in our charges and the fonder we show ourselves of anything the more careless will our slaves be. Even the most aged, whilst their lives are made most pleasant to them, are the most ungratefully neglectfull. This cannot but be a strong instance against the pretended honesty of a slave founded on Religious Principles. This old fellow J. Lubbar is a favorite of that sort, but he has his inebrieties and whenever they interfere the devil may take his trash. Note: I have 3 times ordered my overseer to have the dead Carcasses burnt up and [illegible] Yesterday, but they are not as yet so done, and the plantation stinks alive.

Abundance of rain fell last night and this day; I do suppose because it was drye from the 21st of April to the 2d of may I shall hear this moon has been a drye one against its sign of wetness by lying on her back at the Change; notwithstanding it has raised much from her change both before the 21st of april and since the 2d of this month.

Note: a pint of corn usually contains 800 grains which at 4 in each hill plants 200 hills. This will be 3,200 hills to the peck and 12,800 to the bushels. My overseer has planted 11 bushels in one field which must be 12,800 × 11 = 140,800 and 12 bushels in the other field which must contain 133,600 hills.

5. *Monday.*

Drew a bill this day on Mr. Backhouse in favour of Mr. Ben Waller for £100.13/3 to discharge my cash account with him amounting to £125.16/7 at 25 Pounds.

Lost the fork cow also in the Lucern field. The rain was too cold for these very poor creatures, or they would not have died for they eat very well till this very wet spell. It must be necessary, if I keep up the Lucern field for the purpose of raising my poor cattle, to have a room by cow house in it to keep the creatures from the weather.

Wed my flax.

6. *Tuesday.*

It lightned much due South last night; Pronounced a forerunner of hot Drye weather and this day even from last night very cold all day. Wind at Northwest.

Fork Jammy went up to Bull run to work for my son John this day. I have 5/6 a day for him. Plants examined look well. I am puzzled to get out my dung, having nothing to give my creatures.

The last 24 bushels Oats in use. My son Jn. is to contrive me down 70 barrels of Corn to Falmouth in July or beginning of August. Sent Waller's letter with my bill on Backhouse by Dr. Mortimer to be contrived by some safe Opportunity.

Levelling down my tobacco hills amounting to 51,800 that I design to sow with hemp here; the ground looks well. I find that it is not so much the obstinacy of my steers that won't break to drawing kindly as the Villany of Manuel concerned; For a steer he took up and turned out because he would not work has been on the lift ever since.

All hands abroad this day and left me at home.

7. *Wednesday.*

Began to sow the hemp and rake it in by hand. Began also to bury my dung carted out.

Fires every day. The flye still eats intollerably. I only took off my covering of my beds at home and in the fork meadow patch.

Saw a dead two year old; which I blusht for my overseer, who can only say he had been told that all were ill. This to be sure is not doing but trust not to others to do; if so, my £40 a year is thrown away.

8. *Thursday.*

Mr. Edwards gave me the weight of 10 hogsheads of tobacco made by Longwith in 1765

No. 1. 1174	6. 1177	all Stemmed shipt in Somerville.[6]
2. 1226	7. 1210	
3. 1174	8. 1203	
4. 1198	9. 1181	
5. 1269	10. 1069	

Desired Mr. Edwards to settle with Longwith at 2d per pound the crop before this; And for this at 20 per cent.

9. *Friday.*

Finished this day sowing my hemp in Mangorike. The ground containing 13 acres has taken 27½ bushels of seed.

The fellow to the ox which broke his neck at breaking died this day.

Above 2 bushels to the acre.

Put 41 hides into lime.

Began yesterday [to] bury the barn dung and make the hills over it. I have seen that it is now done well.

Planted 2,200 hills of cotton this day at the Fork, some with Anguilla seed.

Planted also my Pompions 4 seed in a hill, and at Thrift's.

> *Hei mihi! Si fueris tui Leo, Qualis eris?*
> —Martial, *Epigrams.*[7]

Hemp up plentifully at the Fork. I am convinced that the best preparation for hemp ground is by hilling the fall as soon as the tobacco suckers are fit to bury.

10. *Saturday.*

A fire every day, because it is extreme cold and realy now drye for the wind is and has been ever since the last rain of the 2d and part of 3d of this

---

[6] Probably Capt. Thomas Somerville who ferried tobacco to England in the 1760s.

[7] "Oh me! If you could be a lion what kind of a lion would you be?" This is a paraphrase of *"Dic mihi si fias tu leo qualis eris?"* (Martial's *Epigrams*, XII, 92).

month at Northwest from noon to about 10 o'clock and sometimes later. So that the Southern lightning on the 6th night, instead of prognosticating drye warm weather has been the forerunner of dry cool weather. Nothing grows at all.

11. *Sunday.*

Wind now changed Southerly, but very drye.

12. *Monday.*

Wind still Southerly and still very drye; great signs for rain as usual. God send this may not be such a year as last; I well remember every moist appearance this waisted oft as it does now, and no rain.

About 4 days agoe Davis told me his corn brought up from below was gone, and that in that week's allowance he was obliged to use out of the mangorike corn house for some of the people. Note: the quantity from below as 74 began the 11th of February which has lasted about 13 weeks in days at 7 to the week. Mangorike corn measured was 100 bushels, and 23 bushels used out of it. This account to be settled.

No rain since the 2d and part of the 3d day. Therefore no rain since the change which was on the 8th. The moon but a little on her back of course according to observation. Rather Drye than wet. If so we shall have but bad cropping.

13. *Tuesday.*

Rain this morning for a few minites, just enough to sprinkle a Tobacco bed. Some drops this evening. Much in the Skye but none falling.

Rain at good distance from my house from South to near West for some hours.

Sowed peas at the fork yesterday and today 6½ bushels in drills at 3 feet distance; and in every other space between planted corn at 6 feet in the step, the ground about 30, in tobacco hills. Drilled with the hoe first chopping thick at 6 feet distance and then running drills between and in the chops. No bad way and some what expeditious. Not began to bury the dung there yet but tomorrow. Now burying the dung in the hills at Mangorike.

14. *Wednesday.*

No rain yet though very much overcast. Something like last year, great shows but no rain.

Burying dung at the fork one Ewe and lamb gone there out of the old corn field, by dogs 'tis supposed. The tobacco ground beyond the hemp in Mangorike at most by count 45,000 hills all well dunged. Rain in the night a seeming good Shower.

15. *Thursday.*

Thrift just tells me that all his corn was given out last night for the people and that he never has given out but 2 bushels a week to 5 people and 6 children so that by some means there are 7 bushels of Corn lost or wasted for they made 12 bushels that is 60 bushels and allow they began December 1st which is as early as they did there hoe since that time to the 20th of this to which the corn will last 171 days that is 24 weeks and 3 days equal 48 bushels and ½ and allow 4 bushels Planted it makes but 53 bushels which is 7 less than there should be.

I have ordered the planting of many peas and that they shall only be allowed 1½ bushels a week from Mangorike. Now as Peas may be expected about the last July there will be but 72 day from May 20 to that time which are 2 months, 2 weeks and 2 days equal to 3 barrels and 2 pecks.

Excessive cold every body shivering; ordered More Peas to be planted at Davis's. Plants almost eaten up there. Began to cleanse my meadow ditches and make a good bank round.

Filled my Spirit case this day. The last time was since I came from Mr. Beverley's about March 7. Quantity: 4 gallons.

6 yards oznaburg to Betty, Winny, Peg each for a waistcoat and pettycoat. 2½ yards wastcoat and breeches Joe, Tomm, Nassau, 4 yards each for them.

16. *Friday.*

A moist foggy morning. Paid H. Davis Cash £10.

This day Jack at the Fork told me his Corn was all gone. He made 33 bushels. Measured in February and 40 would have kept the plantation a whole year; therefore he must be a rogue. He pretends the Cattle and sheep eat it. He has but 6 calves and 15 lambs. 5 cattle have died 92 lambs and 2 oxen which was all he had.

I filled my butterpot again with brown sugar being the second time since the barrel was opened which was the first barrel bought by Wm. Lee.

Plants flourish well at the fork. So I am told they do in my home meadow. I am Cleaning and new fitting up my meadow Canal's bank and ditches on both sides. Work slow but well.

17. Saturday.

Beverley, his Lady and Children came here yesterday to dinner and continue. James Davenport has been here 3 days; Very kind.

Ordered and planting Pease everywhere to help out if possible my want of Corn.

18. Sunday.

A most glorious rain this day about sunset, some thunder and lightning.

19. Monday.

A fine warm day the first this year. Replanting corn every where. A fine gentle rain this evening for about 30 minutes.

20. Tuesday.

Still replanting corn and shall with difficulty finish this day; so great is the injury that the birds and vermine have done, it seems to be near as much trouble as the first planting.

21. Wednesday.

Fork still replanting corn; owing to lazy people. Wheat just beginning to appear out of the blade.

22. Thursday.

Rode to N. O. Lee's[8] followed by Beverley, his wife, Giberne, and Maxwell;[9] set off by myself at 30 past 5 Morning. Arrived 30 past 7 but as Old Mr. John Lee[10] could not come there My daughter came home after dinner 30 past 5. A pleasant drive untill we reached the school house; when a cloud from North and Northeast took us and though fair it blew so excessive hard that it was difficult to get home. Such dust with the wind and such a rain after that in my life I cannot recollect one equal unless one at Southwest this year. Every part of the North side of my house streamed with water. All the rooms and passage quite damp wet. Very much lightning and thunder. A hard blowing rain at night.

---

[8] N[aval] O[fficer] Lee or Squire Richard Lee of Lee Hall (1726–95), planter and second son of Henry Lee (1691–1747) and Mary Bland Lee, was burgess for Westmoreland Co., 1758–76, and naval officer for South Potomac District.

[9] Arthur Maxwell was a merchant at Leedstown in partnership with John Morton Jordon.

[10] John Lee (d. 1767), oldest son of Henry Lee (1691–1749) and Elizabeth, daughter of Richard Randolph, was a planter in Westmoreland Co.

23. *Friday.*

Much fencing blown down with yesterday's wind. Planted all the hills turned at the fork about 7 or 8,000; and about 4,000 at Mangorike; order more to be cut off and plants fetched from the fork to plant them as it is cow penned ground ready turned.

I fear I shall be obliged to use my stable dung in my hills notwithstanding so much put in hemp; so small have my heaps of dung at my pens been. I must get an overseer at my fork quarter. Old Jack is both too easy with those people and too deceitfull and careless himself. A negroe can't be honest. My Mangorike corn house broke open and all my quarter there. I do suppose my fellow Bart who is still out. I must once more get an overseer there. Davis is too indolent; it will be better to have more eyes than one over such gangs.

24. *Saturday.*

Cool from yesterday noon, that a fire was agreeable to every body. Much moisture in the Clouds but none falling. Wheat ears but short and small even the freshest cowpen ground. I can't see the reason of it, unless the 15 days' drouths from the 3d to the 18th of the month has done it.

The moon though now wet was her first quarter very drye and now though wet not over so, from whence I think her sign at change answers extremely rather drye than wet.

25. *Sunday.*

Cool enough to be a frost, and I doubt it is one some where North of this place if not here. What can grow?

The wheat that has eared is in general the shortest that ever I remember, as which the deep green full stalk and blade as the yellow thin stalked short blade, which cannot be owing to any fault in the poverty of the soil, but must be occasioned by the prodigeous cool weather every now and then, or to the great dryeness of the weather from the 3d to the 18th of the month; for even in my garden where stalks and blades are both very high full and broad and very green the Ears are but short for such wheat. Every kind of growth has been affected by the weather and the late wind laid things not 4 inches high quite flat to the ground.

26. *Monday.*

Still very cool; the flye eats still in the plant patches, and even in the planted hills. A boar destroying my Mangorike corn field, not to be seen in the daytime, but comes in every night and does the mischief rooting up all the New planted Corn. My 18 people did not do 11,000 hills on Saturday.

I find one overseer is too few for this gang unless he was more diligent than he is; but overseers tire as cornfields do.

27. *Tuesday.*

Began weeding corn at Mangorike with 10 hands, the rest weeding plant patches, and burying dung and turning hills for the next season.

Fork not yet weeding corn but burying Dung and hoeing hills for next season. I shall set in the corn tomorrow I hope.

Rain wanted though it rained the 22d in great plenty, but the cool winds after it have merely baked my soil, of such a nature it is. Weather now warm. I see nothing very promising for a crop, it has been in general too Cool and windy in every soil, but the stiff the worst.

28. *Wednesday.*

Signed another set of blank bills of Exchange on Mr. [illegible]'s account. The former signed was filled up for £80 Sterling for 100 cash at 25 percent money paid to C[harles] C[arter's] widow.

30. *Friday.*

Delivered to Captn. Tamer Walker[11] a crop note W[illiam] K[irkham] No. 1 weight 1091 Beck: warehouse paid to me by Wm. Kirkham for rent. Delivered also to the said Walker an order upon the same warehouse for Asbury. Sent note lost by Mr. Parker. These hogsheads to be remarked L[andon] C[arter] No. 1, 2 and shipt in Peterson[12] to Jordan and Maxwell.

Setting corn this day at Mangorike and at Thrift's and the fork quarter.

Mr. Tayloe's loaf sugar 5 pounds 100 weight.

31. *Saturday.*

A very fine rain yesterday evening and in the night and this morning very plentifully.

Planted and made good about 95,000 hills. Every thing in the weeds and all work very backward. People quite lazy and indifferent every where and overseer feels as bad as the worst of them.

Sent by Captn. Somerville to Stewart and Campbell 10 hogsheads Stemmed tobacco made in Northumberland; all 119 ounces, 1 hundred

---

[11] Capt. Tamer Walker probably was commander of the *York* from Bristol and London.

[12] There were a number of Captain Petersons who carried tobacco to Britain in the 1760s and 1770s.

weight, 16 grams. Wrote to Mr. Montague[13] about J[ohn] R[andolph] to get him the Attorney General's place.

JUNE 1766

This moon rather wet than drye and perhaps it will be wet at the end.

1. *Sunday.*

Very cold after the rain. A hard wind at Northwest in the night and some rain.

2. *Monday.*

Opened my Liverpoole Sugars, 12 loaves. Began to use one of them this day.

Every part of my plantation business so prodigeous backward, I must set in my Jobbers from ditching to turn the rest of my tobacco hills. Accordingly, I have ordered them to get 5 new hoes halved.

4. *Wednesday.*

A Pretty season but so late and I do suppose my overseer stupid with liquor that I shall have very little done; although I have had some thousands of hills got ready by my Jobbers. At the Fork: No hills turned but a very few, Jack Lubbar is a most lazy as well as stupid old fellow grown. All is my own fault to think a drunkard could be reclaimed, or a negroe honest enough to carry on any business long ennough for more than one year. I must get new overseers every where and I will too that 1 more, god willing.

5. *Thursday.*

Fine rain in the night so that all that were planted will stand a good chance to live though but a few. A most Glorious season this day for many hours from between 6 and 7 till eight and past. But few hills turned at the fork but all hands turning and so at Thrift's. I beleive I have hills enough to use all the plants fit; Certainly every thing will now grow, Wheat only in danger for some not quite done blooming.

6. *Friday.*

The rain returned a little in the night. The overseer says we have now planted about 150,000. The web worm I understand has got into the 1st

[13] Edward Montague was a London barrister and agent for Virginia, 1761–72. See Lonn, *Colonial Agents*, 288–89.

planted. I must then conclude that it was not winds that brought them, as they generally do. Wind at Northwest and after so much water as has fallen Cold enough for a fire, at least for an old man.

7. *Saturday*.

Fork turning hills they have planted in all and replanted 26,240 turned about 20,000 more and may have about 40,000 more to turn. Came a very fine rain this day for about 3 hours; Colo. [Tayloe] sent to offer me plants what I wanted. I sent 30 hands, 2 overseers, and three tumbrills to draw them, but there was not a plant large enough; his Man Simon Sallard[14] is a lying Villain. Much thunder this day and some sharp lightning.

At the fork I saw the following young turkey a hen with———— 8
2 turkey hens with———— 25
1 ditto with———————— 25
1 ditto with———————— 28
————
86

besides 2 turkey hens sitting.

Everything in the weeds.

8. *Sunday*.

There fell a profuse quantity of rain yesterday evening and last night. We think we have had full enough would it so please the Almighty but there is a prodigeous prospect for more even now, thunder at a distance and the Clouds very full and black. Rain for about 2 hours, this we had but moderate; Ushered in by a long thunder but not very frightfull god be praised. It is as yet warm withall.

9. *Monday*.

Rained a good deal in the night; and now raining this morning with some rumbling thunder. Plant what we have fit to stick in.

Still thundering, lightning and raining till 11 o'clock and Past. My overseer H. Davis was made blind by a flash of lightning, I do suppose by its being reflected on him, for he was walking just under a high bank by the riverside at the time. He is not much hurt. My man Juba also by running under a black Walnut tree from the rain had like to have been killed for the tree was struck by the lightning whilst he was there but by God's great Mercy he escaped

---

[14] Simon Sallard (d. 1770) was probably the son of Simon Sallard (d. 1747), a long-time overseer for Robert "King" Carter in Richmond Co.

Building Said to Be Second Capitol of Virginia at Williamsburg
By Elizabeth Russell Denison. Valentine Museum, Richmond, owner.

Norborne Berkeley, Baron de Botetourt (1717–1770), Governor of Virginia (1768–1770) *Copy by Stanley Tardrew Headley from original, artist unknown. Virginia Historical Society, owner.*

Robert Dinwiddie (1693–1770), Lieutenant Governor of Virginia (1751–1758) *By unknown artist. National Portrait Gallery, London, owner.*

Francis Fauquier (1704?–1768), Lieutenant Governor of Virginia (1758–1768) *Miniature by John Smart. Gilbert Fauquier, Toronto, Canada, owner.*

John Murray, Fourth Earl of Dunmore (1732–1809), Governor of Virginia (1771–1776) *Copy by Charles X. Harris after Sir Joshua Reynolds. Virginia Historical Society, owner.*

unhurt. This puts a common observation in my mind that it is very dangerous in such storms to take shelter under trees, especially walnut trees which are more apt to be struck than others for they Commonly attract the lightning and conduct it to the earth. A prodigeous rain from 10 to near 12 o'clock. There is a great probability these very plentiful rains will produce but indifferent grains of wheat, though we shall in all likelyhood [have] our pastures well clothed with grass again, which will be a comfort not injoyed now near 6 years past.

It cleared up a little between 2 and 3 P.M. I rode out examined my wheat. Saw no rust as yet, but coming home I thought of the black berry bushes which always show the rust first. Found here and there a bush grown rusty; but I think it used to be somewhat earlier than this. It can't be said that rain brings it; because it has been a wet season now above a week and if it does not come in ten days more I shall be in hopes it will be too late for this year and god send it may be so.

We have been able to plant all our tobacco hills that are turned at Mangorike, Fork and at Thrift's. Quantity not yet certain though there are yet many more, about 100,000 in all. I must observe that the plants which I had sowed in the Meadow by Thrift's house in April 25th were now large enough to plant out between 4 and 5 thousand of them; And I find I shall be able, before the moisture of this season leaves us to plant out some from those sown in my garden in my Artichoke and asparagus beds April 30th So that these have only been sown 41 days because I shall plant them this day.

10. *Tuesday.*

Damp and raw. Many people ill, In particular my boy Ambrose, who on thursday last assisted at planting very brisk, On fryday absconded on pretence of getting this meal from Mill and on yesterday came home and went to work, but at night was found liing on his back struggling in a fit. We could not learn what had occasioned it for he was speechless. Gave him a vomit which as soon as it worked losed his fit restored a good Pulse, but senseless, though I gave him a Mercurial pill knowing him to be frequently subject to worms, and clapt on a blister last night and this day a purge having cleared his guts by a Clyster last night to make a revulsion from his head. At 10 the Physick has not worked and his fits very numerous. A clyster ordered to make the Physick work.

Worms are certainly the case.

Still cloudy and likely to rain. My Crop of Corn and Peas at the fork near ruined with weeds. I must give over I fear a part of the tobacco and clean out corn and pease.

Meadow still to mow later than ever.

Patience and calmness to get over these difficulties.
Weights of the Rippon hall crop made 1765

No. 1–1245	No. 5–1169
2–1240	6–1221
3–1261	This goes to Backhouse in the *Tom's* Captn. Clark.[15]
4–1061	

11. *Wednesday.*

Very cool indeed this morning. I yesterday was obliged to weed my pease at the fork they were so foul. I find ridging up to the Pease to be the most expeditious way covering the grass about them well and giving them earth at the same time. I shall be obliged I fear to leave leading some of the tobacco ground there.

The Corn is so foul and every week so backward and everything coming on. I must open the hills to turn and put my marll mud in them and so round up the hill and Cut them off to plant tobacco.

Sent off the Rippon Hall man with 12 broad hoes.

12. *Thursday.*

A fine day, no more rain as yet I thank God, for my corn fields are in a bad condition with weeds and I have at least two days to do in hilling for tobacco.

Just finished my fork pease at about 11 o'clock. My people then set into the Island Corn field. Finish my hills before my house this day. About 3 set in to those by last year's wheat which may be finished tomorrow. Then to my Cornfield as done turning hills.

Weaned this day 10 calves. Jobbers all but Gabriel who is runaway go to the fork quarter.

27 more turkies hatched, so that there would have been at the Fork 113 in all; but as the old woman is a midwife and was obliged to attend Manuel's daughter Peg 4 of the former 86 dyed in the last wet weather.

13. *Friday.*

More young turkies sickly; people weeding fork corn head of the creak very foul indeed and so is every field.

---

[15] Capt. Joseph Clarke of the *Tom* ferried tobacco from Virginia to Liverpool during the 1760s.

14. *Saturday.*

A prodigeous rain at Sundown yesterday and in the night. Planting today but not plants enough for my hills yet which are all turned at mangorike to about 6,000. Thrift will plant his ground. Jake [?] can't; not all turned by 4,000; I hear there will be plants in the meadow, but I do suppose it is there as in other places; Plants much grown though none to plant such liars are Overseers etc. grown. There cannot be a greater proof that though they pretend it, they don't dung my patches enough; My artichoke and asparagus beds which are Rich have now in 46 days many plants. I will always follow this method and sow my rich garden beds with plants every year.

This is the fourth time I have replanted over my tobacco which is not above 150,000 and I can't have put in less than 50,000 which makes my cropping later than Common, for I said we have more plants than will replant as the seasons come every 4 days or thereabouts and the patches not rich enough.

15. *Sunday.*

A fine rain also last night at sundown and in the night, ushered in with some smart wind, much lightning, and some thunder.

Yesterday removed 29 pounds of tea in seperate Canisters to the drawers in my desk from my book cases; as there is a great probability that one pound has been taken away from thence much to my surprize as the key has never been knowingly but under the care of one of my daughters and myself. The 1st of January last there were   37 pounds. In January, February, March, April, twice in May we have used   6 pounds.
Gave to Mr. McKay's Lady[16]   1
                                        ──
                                        30

Therefore one is lost unless I gave it to my son John or Mr. Edwards who asked me for such a thing.

16. *Monday.*

The boy Ambrose that was taken on the 9th with convulsion fits has not withstanding every endeavour had them ever since about 11, at 1, and at 5 o'clock. They appear to be caused by worms. I have given him two mercurial purges about 5 grains dulcis each dose which have worked him and brought

[16] Probably the wife of Rev. William McKay, rector of Northampton Parish, Richmond Co.

away abundance of worms of the black or Stomach worm; he has taken several preparations of Mercury as alteratives And back with nervines as his attacks were periodical though no visible fever. I have joined Rhubarb and have constantly kept his body open twice every day. His fits were first above 100 per day. Now they are got to about 15 or 20 and 4 or 5 worms are voided every dead but not blackiest as if long killed. He does not seem fallen away as they tell me and has a good stomach. I am in hopes he may come about as he walks about very strong; though it is a strange case. I beleive I shall give another Mercurial or a Vomit.

I was inclined to think riding in my prodige[ous] foul corn field that if I my people held up we might still compass the work so as to make as tollerable crop; but my foreman Will Just as I got home came up with a violent pain in his right elbow, so that I can't tell what to think as he is a most principal hand. It is fine corn though very weedy indeed.

19. *Thursday.*

Thunder and lightning at some very distance every evening since the 14th at night, but no rain till last night and then a plentiful and heavy shower and another and another in the night. I have got all my hills to a very few about 10,000 ready and that at the Fork where I am afraid I shall be obliged to omit tending any meadow though the dung is all ready there, but the hills not turned, and really I cannot do it my meadow now to be mowed and should have begun it this day had not the season prevented it.

Brought my plows from the Fork where they have done the Cornfield to Davis' field at home. Toney ill with a Soar throat, a disorder that has been about off and on all this spring; I have given him a mercurial purge.

Gave Ambrose also a third Mercurial Purge whose fits are now got to but once in the day and these but a few. The bark with his Vermifuge; Alkalized Mercury, Pulvis Stannum[17] and Mizelo tea,[18] have done him much good. He is grown strong and still is fleshy, Voiding quantities of worms every day and Now his Mercurial Purge has brought away a great many more, So I hope we shall get him well.

Discovered this day who robbed my Corn house by Seald. Charles bringing very moist corn to Mill; It seems he and Blough Point George go halves and they brought a peck of this to Mill at the end of the week where we

[17] Pulvis stannum was a powder of tin used against worms.

[18] Mizelo tea probably came from the missel tree, found in British Guiana and a member of the family Melastomaceae. It produces a yellow edible berry.

stopped it. This corn was got out of the gable end board at the Corn house which must be altered as soon as I get leizure. All hands planting to make a finish.

20. *Friday*.

Received of Edward Mozingo, a tenant, his rents for the years 1764 and 1765: 1 Crop hogshead Beckwith's E[dward] M[ozingo] 2.979N.

Also of Georg Mozingo for his two rents the same year: 1 Crop hogshead G[eorge] M[ozingo] 2.1013.

Note: I cleared of the overplus tobacco in these hogsheads to each claimer George Mozingo 113 at 18/ and the 4/6 for the last year's overplus by a note on Mr. Parker for £1. 4.9. And a note to Edward Mozingo for his 79 pounds tobacco over by a note of hand payable when produced for 14/3.

21. *Saturday*.

Planted yesterday by plants from my son's at Landsdown and my meadow, so far as to finish at home to within 25,000 which is not yet too late to be planted with large plants.

Mr. Jordan, his Lady, Colo. Thornton, his Lady, and Col. Tayloe and his Lady dined with me. Quinny sent for my tobacco. Obliged to leave mowing my meadow to do that; I began the meadow yesterday. Obliged also to leave plowing my Cornfield on the same account.

The girl Liddy that has been out a fortnight taken and lockt up in Oat house broke out last night.

22. *Sunday*.

Rain yesterday and last night Plentifully.

23. *Monday*.

Rain a little yesterday. Inspected my poor crop which I made last year that is in:

On board Cap. Quinney

1765 L[andon] C[arter] E:		No.					
1.	1196	5.	1257	9.	1167		4816
2.	1237	6.	1200	10.	1242		4925
3.	1137	7.	1320	11.	1212		4697
4.	1246	8.	1148	12.	1076	13.	1160
	4816		4925		4697		15,598

24. *Tuesday.*

Mangorike cornfield not yet out of the first weeds. Davis's still to weed, and all the tobacco. No tobacco wed.

Fork Quarter field not yet done but about 22,000 tobacco hills wed.

Thrift's corn field just done but no tobacco fit to weed.

Still to plant about 30,000 in all and some to replant. My Meadow just Mowed. All my wheat, Barley and Oats to cut. Work enough to destroy an old man with a Vertigo and No less than 3 people out here.

27. *Friday.*

Sent by order of Mr. Robert Ferguson[19] to his ship below the mud bank a beef weight 380 at 18/. Note: I was desired to give notice to the ship when to send to my landing for the beef; this I did yesterday, and the mate promised to send by 8 o'clock, but at 9 no boat appeared and as it was very hot I sent it on board.

We had this day a domestic gust. My daughters, Lucy and Judy, mentioned a piece of impudent behaviour of little Landon to his mother; telling her when she said she would whip him, that he did not care if she did. His father heard this unmoved. The child denied it. I bid him come and tell me what he did say for I could not bear a child should be sawsy to his Mother. He would not come and I got up and took him by the arm. He would not speak. I then shook him but his outrageous father says I struck him. At Breakfast the Young Gent. would not come in though twice called by his father and once Sent for by him and twice by me. I then got up, and gave him one cut over the left arm with the lash of my whip and the other over the banister by him. Madame then rose like a bedlamite that her child should be struck with a whip and up came her Knight Errant to his father with some heavy God damning's, but he prudently did not touch me. Otherwise my whip handle should have settled him if I could. Madam pretended to rave like a Madwoman. I shewed the child's arm was but commonly red with the stroke; but all would not do. Go she would and go she may. I see in her all the ill treatment my son gives and has given me ever since his marriage. Indeed I always saw this in her a girl a Violent, Sulkey, Proud, imperious Dutch so One fit to be the Queen of a Prince as the old——always complimented her. As this child is thus encouraged to insult me, I have been at great expence hitherto in maintaining him but I will be at no more. And so I shall give notice.

[19] Robert Ferguson was a merchant in Essex Co. with interests in Tappahannock and a store near Layton's warehouse.

28. *Saturday*.

No rain since the 22. Begins to be drye; though our crops are so weedy as not to want rain as yet; fine Corn and tobacco but very foul.

Began to reap my wheat at Olivers branch,[20] much injured by a trespass of all my creatures of my cow pen on the 23; by means of two Mischievous steers.

Killed one of them as per yesterday. Reaped my Barley two days agoe.

My Thermometer from 76 to 87 for two days past. Yesterday from 82 to 87. Three people fainted, but I beleive they had foul stomachs gave them Vomits. One got out. The other a Purge today.

30. *Monday*.

Got down 11 acres at home this day by reap hooks, and scythes 5 mowers; but my horses so poor and so imployed in my Cornfields still very foul I could not set to carting it in. Therefore resolved upon treading as much as I could cut in the field; for which purpose I prepared a large treading floor more then 60 feet diameter; but could not quite finish one floor before night took us; however we took in 5 large sacks full and two empty tobacco hogsheads full which I had covered and secured against the rain and lockt up the loose untrod straw. The rest of the wheat I ficxed in triangular Gavels in the high parts of the fields; that is 3 large sheeves in such a form laid that the heads of each sheeve lay on the butts of the other so that I hope they will not take much damage.

JULY 1766

Wet moon by its Phasis. So it proved.

1. *Tuesday*.

A rain came on this day moderate at first but in prodigeous plenty in about 2 hours. I dread the effects of it. This is a certain instance that man knows not which is best for him. My missing tobacco crop and my new wed as well as grassy cornfields want rain; but my Wheat Oats and flax want none in my opinion; however let us hope for the best, and it may be we shall be convinced rain is best. Cornfields if not thus assisted and tobacco plants if not now planted would be too late; and Wheat Oats and etc. may perhaps receive

[20] Olivers Branch was a piece of Carter's property in Richmond Co.

but little damage—but we are as fainty in our hearts as we are defective in our Judgments.

2. *Wednesday.*

It was so great a rain yesterday that we could plant all day this day; but I fear I shall not have plants enough to replant all. I expected a great many from Colo. Tayloe's, and Sent 6 hands there to draw ready for my tumbril; I also set my Fork people to drawing at the Colo's. Fork quarter. From thence we got a large load; but my overseer has bean so long in my business; and from his being given to drink is become an indolent liar. From Col. Tayloe's old house my Tumbril only came back with about 3,000 and this morning they brought but a few more. My people came away and left the plants they had drawn to the mercy of other people who drew them. My garden plants were very fine and a good many; I Sent again to the Colo's. and Toney my only honest slave I hope he will not trifle and it may be I may get my crop finished.

I don't yet hear the rain has done any damage to my wheat. I fancy the floor. I began to tread before the rain will yield me 20 bushels of clean wheat. This is the 3d year my grapes have been all destroyed by foggs or wet weather, after they had bean well set for a great vintage. I find the living Standard is bad by lodging the moisture too long, I must cut them down. In this I observe Nature is not to be indulged for the vines of the Conskey[?] all grow to living trees; and that perhaps is the reason why there is seldom a crop of grapes. I must therefore this fall cut down my peach trees which will be bad as I am raising hogs in Styes.

Weeds encrease upon us. I fear I shall never conquer my crop of corn and that will be very bad. I have still 100,000 hills to first weed and can't set to it on account of the trouble I have about my tobacco.

3. *Thursday.*

O! More rain is still! It is rather too much as our experience has taught us to reason on things; and nothing but the interposition of Omnipotence can ward off the effects which will be fatal in the destruction of the corn by the weeds which now never dye. The tobacco by the weeds and worms which are ever hatching. And The Wheat and oats by the rain which never suffers them to grow drye therfore the one will sprout and the other grow musty. I have bean struggling to get some wheat in before it came but could not effect much of it. We are poor labouring men. God knows best what is good for us. Greater constancy, nor quantity of rain is not common than what we have had this day from about 10 to near 8 o'clock. I would have pulled my flax. Quite ripe for it, but it proved so wet and etc.

Every direction forbids that work in rainy weather, but I don't see the reason given, unless it may be because should it be down it might endanger the seed; but let it be what it will I should think if it can be laid without danger of beating, as it may against the sides of a house with the boles upward, I say it should not be omitted in some rains least their continuance should beat it down and then it must be full as bad. I think I have seen that some weeds that grow long should be left in the field such as come up after the flax has got a growth; they seem to be very good supporters to the flax when it grows slimer by being thick sown. Mine was so.

4. *Friday.*

It left off raining about 8 last night and began again in half an hour and continued in as Violent floods as do at any time fall all night and all this day till past 2 o'clock. The effects are to be dreaded. Cornfields are ponds of water. Wheat field are black with rain and the tobacco ground quite miry. I can only [see them] at a distance, but I am told the standing wheat is much lain down and by the grain that I saw I fear they will sprout.

I rode out and Saw to my Surprize but greatly to my Satisfaction that nothing except a little corn in the field was so much hurt as we had expected. That indeed seemed as if it would drown. The Wheat was prodigeous moist some swelled, and abundance laid down in the field. But as to the wheat laid in the treading floor, That by being laid almost upright sheeve by sheeve and covered was with the straw of the first trodden now as on opening as drye as tinder from which I learn a good method to manage another time.

5. *Saturday.*

It left off raining yesterday about 3 o'clock in the evening, and towards night had the appearance of clearing up at Northwest; and we comforted ourselves accordingly; but this morning I found another day of settled rain; which is dreadful considering I am but one week from a finish of my corn there. It seems since the 11th of February we have used up 75 barrels brought from Northumberland and 100 barrels made at Mangorike but of the 75 barrels my hogs at home are said to have had [blank]; And out of the 100 my Fork and Jamey's people have eaten. There is no account to be taken of this, because I am told the Corn houses have been robbed. I adduce my credulity and confidence in my overseer has been too great and I must believe he has found out a way to do me many prejudicial jobs though of advantage to himself. So certain is it that a man that is a drunkard is not fit for an overseer over any thing; for he that loveth drink, must love every thing, to get at it.

That man who is under our present circumstances, must be a very foolish boaster who shall think that he either can or does make anything but by Almighty permission. I am almost Starving for corn, and only comforted by the prospect of a fine crop of wheat and now ready and began to be cut down; and behold after 3 days can stand rain a fourth, and a shower as if the elements were coming together. The Southwest and Northeast winds play well into each other's laps; they have been by turns shifting incessantly, so that the rains have been violent till 6 this evening. To be sure the wheat and corn must be gone as well as the oats for every field is a sea, and there is reason to doubt the tobacco's drowning as well as the oats and other things. No clearing up as yet; it has bean raining pretty from the 2d now four days inclusive.

6. *Sunday*.

Road out this day found all the wheat that touches the ground either in Sheeves or loose all sprouted some inches; So that I may loose the value of 10 or 11 acres of wheat spoils for a market that but as I know that grown wheat may be eaten and is only disagreeable by being Clammy and sweat My negroes shall eat it as soon as I can get it thrashed; therefore I have ordered it all to be spread out in this day's sun although it is Sunday, as being a most necessary for no corn can I buy for want of ready money; Not even of the Compassiot Mr. Ritchie.

We have had for weeks abundance of musketoes, a very small narrow fly that lies quite close to the skin and smarts black and slender; it is an inhabitant of every shrub this wet spell.

We have had another domestick storm this evening as well as a heavy storm of rain. It began with a Joke as perhaps most things of the sort do. But our tempers are such that both Mr. Carter and myself forgot the bounds of our convixions; However, though I don't record it as an excuse or Justification I must be persuaded I am not the aggressor. I well remember on my ordering the boy so to do some thing about tea time Mrs. Carter then called out for Tom to come and tend the tea making. I then in a joke [said] I thought he thought we ought not to use it but once in a weak; his replye was neither ought you to use it any more than we. What Sir, can't I spend my own money. He answered, by God You will have none to spend soon. I replyed I might owe about £1000. His answered as I understood him than two would not pay it. I then indeed grew outrageous and said it was a damned infamous lie etc. For which

I do suppose Mr. Carter leaves the house as he said he would. Indeed he said abundance more and I replyed as tauntingly, he might he had been my dayly curse. After cooling a little he allows it would be insulting to tell a stranger that he had nothing to spend; but he does not think but a son ought to take liberty with his father; because (A strange doctrine) his estate is to pay it when his father dies. How, for god's sake? If it is the son's estate, he can't be obliged to pay. Therefore, the whole argument is rather forced to disguise an error in behaviour; and by such palliatives Men will never be in the wrong and if so they cannot mend. For my part if my God will assist me whether he stays or goes I will learn to destroy the right of a parent even his son and give up for I see he is too obstinate; and perhaps we are equally unhappy in temper. I am old but I should consider that it seems myself; others I find. Nay Sons are determined against the least indulgence to the Grey hour of a Parent.

7. *Monday.*

A prodigeous rain yesterday about 2 and to near 4. We had though Sunday as a work of great necessity as our bread depended on it for we could buy no corn any where. I say we had all the sprouted wheat near quite drye in the Sheeves, and should have hurried what we could of it in; but that violent rain, seemingly only here for Colo. Tayloe had none. At dark came up another as violent and as long and between 10 and 11 came on a third quite a storm attended with much sharp lightning and from a very slow moving cloud from Northwest which continued till quite 3 o'clock. Then it grew clear and at about 5 in the morning the whole skye overcast with very rainy clouds, but god be praised it moved off without more rain for our very tobacco though but young is in many places drowned and so miry we cannot stick a first plant in those hills or worm. As to the unused corn field, that is intirely drowned as well as choked with weeds and the hills so dissolved that abundance of corn has fallen down.

I was just riding out to see the destruction but was called back by my son to his wife then taken in labour the 3d time without a midwife so punctual are women or rather obstinate to their false accounts. I found every body about her in a great fright and she almost in dispair. The child was dead and the womb was fallen down and what not. I found her pulse good and even though as all women in such cases are and I believe should be; I knew that this could be no prolapses of the womb till after a delivery but from the accounts concluded it might be the Vagina swelled and inflamed. I therefore ordered it to be gently pressed up with Marsh Mallow decoction and milk. At last this proved only the protuberance of the waters through the thickness of the membrane. Those broke and a large dead child much squeezed and indeed putrified was delivered. An intire placenta but no lochial discharge. Another prodigeous alarm. I could not but say that I did not like it, but reasoned from the dead state of the fetus the possibility of such a circumstance though I never read of it in any Author; but as I know all authors do say if the woman is well and free from fevers or violent pain the colour nor quantity of the lochia is not to be regarded, and as this is Mrs. Carter's real state I hope no danger. I ordered her in some cordial gruel (which I had all along directed her) about 20 grains Ipecacuana which brought on a breathing moisture and then a Lochial discharge came on. This is a disagreeable state for me to be in where I see the ingratitude of those for whom I give myself such concern; but they will never be provided against accident with mid wives and Doctors and are human creatures. Dr. Mortimer came here and sees as yet nothing amiss. I am glad he is, it is a releif to me; for I do believe ten thousand anticipations are every moment broached without the least foundation; it is the effect of tenderness; but great weakness.

8. *Tuesday.*

Last night about 12 another most violent rain till day with abundance of sharp thunder and lightning from Northwest. This day very fine and clear. Mrs. Carter very well still with little or no Lochial discharge. If she continues so, I shall say her case is an exception to the common observation of authors and others in practice.

My people can't be back with my wheat, so Hugely ungrateful are they.

9. *Wednesday.*

No rain since the 7th in the night, but the earth too wet for any work but holling the weeds from things. I rode out. I can't perceive the wheat much hurted by the sprouting, most of the grain has got and neither tastes clammy nor sweat[y] in the mouth. Every place marred ponds And the corn really water sobbed; A good deal drowned, and pretty much tobacco. I have planted all again. The rains seem to have hurt my pease. Mrs. Carter still very well; If she should continue so books and experience have not yet amounted to all the particular cases in Midwifery; but it is evident from her situation of hardly any Lochial discharge there are such cases not dangerous, although every author says it is. Indeed Smellee[21] says that is various in women some more some less, some of one Colour some another; And nothing to be regarded if the patient is

---

[21] William Smellee (1697–1763) was a Scotch physician and author of the *Theory and Practice of Midwifery* (3 vols.; London, 1752–64), which went through several editions. A recent biography is R. W. Johnstone, *William Smellee: The Master of British Midwifery* (Edinburgh and London, 1952).

well and without fever. I am apt [to] think with him from this Case though Causes of these Lochia are not rightly assigned. Instead being the mouths of Vessells seperated from the fetus and Placenta, They may be but the smaller vessels diverted from their Course of Circulation through the secundines and by the tendency of the blood that way, those small vessels may some times burst and ooze as they do till they are healed. Therefore in this Lady's case it is possible few or none of those vessels have burst; but the blood has returned to its usual Canals.

10. *Thursday.*

From our preceding drye years we did expect that this moist year would be a good crop year, but as yet I see reason to think otherwise.

The wheat, apart from the injury of the late rains, has but very short Ears, owing to the cold weather about that time and of those short Ears at least 2 inches the grain not filled owing to the prodigeous rains about blooming time.

The Corn first merely choked with weeds which cannot be killed any way; They only who plow can save the corn by worrying the weeds from one place to the other and really the ground too miry and rocky for the young roots to receive any nourishment.

The pease quite ruined with the rain hardly growing and quite yellow. The tobacco not growing, very weedy and miry. Add to this a glut of all sorts of worms from the first planting brought on by the rains. Flax seems quite black by being pulled in the rains, and that has stayed longer almost rotten Streke.

In short all kinds of cropping in low lands in a rainy season must be very precarious.

11. *Friday.*

Could I have known of this wet season I might as I am told by tending of about 1/3 of what I do have made a good crop of every thing; For 1/3 of the wheat would only have been about 50 acres, which I will thus trye.

1st, Might have been of the best ground. Next, I could have got it in sooner and of Course have thrashed it out sooner. But against the profit must have contended; for at Present I am apt to fancy I shall get for 50 of the present

Acres	500
for 50 at 15 bushels	750
for 50 at 20 bushels	1,000
in the whole	2,250

bushels which would be a very great quantity per acre for 50 acres only to yield. So that if the present quantity can be got safe I shall about gain 750 bushels, all the additional, straw and All the chaft which is something considerable. On what cropping then, I should not have been a gainer only in the labour and Mental Concern.

Next in Corn had I tended 1/3 of the corn that is 100,000 instead of 3 I should be fare have been able to have tended it well but at present above 50,000 is not nor cannot be tended at all. Of this I really question whether I shall get 25 barrels, however suppose I do　　25
of 100,000 at 1 barrel　　　　　　　　　　　　100
150,000 at 2 barrels　　　　　　　　　　　　　300
in all　　　　　　　　　　　　　　　　　425 barrels. Now 100 barrels well tended to bring that must have been 4 barrels, 1 bushel, 1 peck per thousand which I fancy would have been too large so how I shall in all probability be a gainer, even though the 50 not tended should yield nothing for 4 barrels is very great for any 100,000 in the lower parts of the Country to bring; And as I must get more fother off the 300,000 thats the one; If I can't tend above this 1/3 I had better go on though at least 150,000 of it should be as bad as not tended at all.

Tobacco I tend at least 280,000. About this I can't reason with exactness; because no one knows how vastly larger and thicker tobacco will be when receiving every due tendence and of Course heavyer; but should we guess that 15 plants in the present way will make 1 pound of tobacco then 280,000 will neat but 18,638 pound tobacco. Now to tend no more then 1/3 of this 280,000 will be but 93,333 plants which to make 18,633 tobacco must yield near 1 pound per every 5 plants which must hoe fine tobacco and not a plant bad nor hurt by worms and etc.; so that there does not seem much profit in this small cropping, And yet in such wet years there does not seem to be a possibility of doing every thing Justice should more be tended.

15. *Tuesday.*

Still gitting wheat in and shall be longer. Yet my people work so indifferently and so much to get in though I have 5 mowers at it and no very good Prospect of dry weather now. We had a smart rain on Sunday morning which did not hurt the wheat because it was worked up and not sheaved. My horses very indifferent and pull in but little.

21. *Monday.*

Paid this day James Fraily[22] on account of his produced against me for Tayloe's work to this day amounting to £8 2s by a note on Mr. Thomas

---

[22] James Fraily was probably one of Col. John Tayloe's plantation managers.

Hodge.[23] If he pleases to accept the same. Note: his former account of £4 11/6 is included in this account and my order on Mr. Hodge is upon the back of the said account.

23. *Wednesday.*

It has not rained since Sunday the 13th, When we had a pretty smart shower in the morning just before Mr. Beverley went away with Lucy. Yesterday in the evening we had three distinct sun dogs which is the usual sign for great rain but as those clouds which I imagined reflected the shadow of the sun like a mirrour from being of a watry nature were all dispersed by Sun set I did imagine that sign would fail but then most have been something not to be accounted for by any phylosophy of mine. Perhaps a greater permenancy of some watry medium Which reflected the shadow of the Sun for this day we had first some smart showers then violent thunder and lightning a severe rain till within the night with prodigious sharp thunder at last before this last thunder the moon by rising pretty clear to the Eastward made about one third of a rainbow very visible in the night but without any colour more than that of a bright light and the foot of that segment appeared visibly to be just below my front Garden from South to North. I suppose these are the night Rainbows said to happen but rarely and appear to be generated by the moon's reflecting the light of the Sun for there was no variegation in Colour but a broad list of light. It rained during the whole time except to the Eastward and this bow appeared something to the westward. They tell me there was also one about 11 and another about 3 in the morning after it being raining. There was none sean where it did not rain.

24. *Thursday.*

A prodigeous deal of water every where in my plantations. I could not even ride into my wheat fields without miring. I have about 40 acres of wheat to stack up. It was just cut down as the rain came; As the stack we were making is not wet above 5 or 6 inches down and that is taken off to I am in hopes we shall escape any great damage if more rain does not fall upon it before we finish.

All hands setting out the double plants in my tobacco grounds every where; but I doubt I shall not have enough to make all the missing hills good. My plant Patch at home tobacco sown in turnips contains 17,442 square feet and at 6 inches square for each turnip it will require 69,768 seed to be sown. As

---

[23] Thomas Hodge (d. 1775) was a merchant at Leedstown and justice of the peace in King George Co.

40 seed are found to weigh a grain, this number of seed will amount to 8 seed or 1/5 of a grain more than 1,769 grains, equal to 4 ounces 5 pennyweights. And as a pint of seed is found a thought above 10 ounces, half a pint wanting 13 pennyweights will sow it.

Now to do this it must be lined off in beds 4 feet wide and the length of the bed in feet by 4 will give the square feet, which by 4 the square half feet or 6 inches as under will give the said in the whole peice. 36 seed then will sow 9 square feet or 1 square yard; so that one foot in length of these beds bring 4 square feet. 16 seed will sow it and every 10 foot in length will be 40 square feet equal to 160 seed equal to 4 grains; so in each proportional length.

To do this as equal as possible let the seed for each bed be well mired in some ashes a good quantity or dust of a different colour from the colour of the ground and by sowing pritty thick the seed will fall nearly at its intended distance of 6 inches as under. Note: some small allowance should be made for bad seed that may be in the bast; 20 on half a grain for every 5 feet in length of the 4 feet be as equal to Just 100 seed in rough feet.

Mr. Giberne this day from H[obbe's] Hole tells me Mr. An. Crawford[24] desires if I chose it that I may draw on him for £9 of the money which I may owe John Hammond[25] who I have sent for my corn to Potomack and who I shall also send to Falmouth for my corn there and for some Plank if he does his business well; but this I fear will not be, for he has been gone to Potomack now above a fortnight.

Some fine tobacco plants in my garden beds. I have ordered Davis to plant them this evening; and I send the same orders to Thrift if there are any plants in the meadow patches or hay house.

My daughter Judy the 17th of this month went to the great race, when it seems it was a most improper time being her Lunar period; From whence nothing could stop her going to a dance at her uncle Beale's; and there in a very hot night she danced though sick for her period came on. The next day she came home very sick but kept all secret; of course, a vomiting came on, no vomit would be taken for particular reasons which at last I would, know her period held her till tuesday the 22, no feaver as I was informed. Yesterday she came down stairs very hungry. I understood she was now and then sick at her stomach. I then said she must take a vomit if she was so any more, but did not say what this day of her own accord she got one from Tom and took it being 3 spoonfulls Ipecacuana wine unknown to me till it had workt her 4 times and brought off much dark green bile and other. I was told she was easy. I ordered

[24] Andrew Crawford was a factor for James Ritchie and Company of Glasgow at Tappahannock. He was later an agent for Thomas Jett.

[25] John Hammond was a resident of Richmond Co. apparently engaged in hauling and shipping.

some thin broth to ease the passage of some of the bile downward, but it seems she drank some toast and beer. I do suppose cold as well as windy. This about 5 gave her a severe gryping and at last brought on her sickness at the stomach again and she vomited both yellow and green bile, and it seems took a clyster for no motion had happened downwards; her sickness returned again as the Clyster brought off nothing, and I do suppose I shall have her on my hands, by her obstinacy and Secrecy. She does bear ungovernable the whole summer through, eating extravagantly and late at night of cucumbers and all sorts of bilious trash; so lavish of her health has she been.

25. *Friday.*

M[ortimer] came to Judy. Staid all night. Went away 26th.

26. *Saturday.*

Yesterday a vast plenty of rain. This day the same. Water enough to be sure. If this is a tobacco year I have no experience, or indeed stiff low lands either for Corn, peas, or Wheat, or Oats as the harvests are so hard to be got in. I have a large stock well made of Wheat 60 foot by 18; and if this rain don't hurt it another make besides all my oats still to get up.

Accepted a note on me from Richard Neale[26] to Faunteleroy's[27] estate For £3. 19/3 which I will pay as soon as I have cash.

27. *Sunday.*

A Showry morning till past 7; and then a constant rain till 10 o'clock when it cleared up. I heard this day my wheat out in the field had sprouted a little yesterday noon, What must it not now be after so much rain since?

Dr. Mortimer made this day his second visit to my daughter Judy and staid only 2 hours. Judy's fever only lower. His first visit was on fryday. He staid till yesterday morning. Her state was such she could bear nothing inwardly. I advised a Plaister to her Stomach; the Dr. was angry and for a while rejected it; but as her pulse continued very low and a dead sickness even felt outwardly; he consented and put on the plaister which in two hours by the help of clysters eased and her pulse rose. There was an attempt with a dose or two of medicine but these she could not keep.

Yesterday he went away. Said she was better; but the child was only easier for fever rose, but abated again and she had two stools. She continued easy all

[26] Richard Neale (d. 1782) was a resident of Northumberland Co. who dealt extensively in land in the Northern Neck.
[27] Probably the estate of John Fauntleroy (d. 1766), planter of Essex Co. and son of William Fauntleroy (d. 1757) of Richmond Co.

night and is so now, but still a fever and the Dr. Can't stay. Nature directs to get some help but to what purpose, such that Can't stay? Nothing as I know of but so my 10/ thrown away. Was it any other I could do as well and I beleive by being near better.

28. *Monday*.

I now see clearly that corn not laid by with a good hill to it very early in this month stands but a very poor chance of being fine corn let the earth be ever so good. After that time it gets yellow by either disturbing its roots in drye weather, or matting them to much in wet weather; And in the moistest weather in the world it will not in 10 or more days recover its greenness and of course its shoots but sorry for that yellow state is owing to some defect in its growth. The reason I have for this observation is I had a little swamp at the Fork laid by very early in Tobacco Also some corn before Davis's house and the upper end of the field also a little Corn in Mangorike field; And these 3 pieces are the only grean corn I have except Thrift's field which was mostly so done. These are fine corn. The rest will be corn, but it will be but indifferent.

It has rained again this morning and seems very likely for more. I wish it would be hold up a few days. I should save some crop of tobacco, Pease, Corn, Oats and wheat. Oats I am Cutting. The rain helps them because they would shatter, but when down they must be lockt and stackt or they will be twisted though they won't sprout so soon as Wheat.

The Wheat has been all down above two days and this is our 6th day of rain but yet my people say there is but little as yet sprouted, less than was at the Fork the spell in the first of the harvest and that proved to be but little.

A Shower of rain has fallen about 2 that in 30 minits laid all my low grounds in ponds and my hill sides knee deep so that the Corn is there in danger. A prodigeous cloud went up and another down the River at the same time. God have mercy upon us or we perish for bread.

At 5 o'clock P.M., begins a rainy night on the 6th day's very severe rain. Farrwell every kind of crop.

29. *Tuesday*.

Drew out of my Pipe of Madeira 1 bottle and the first and only one to put in my Crocus bottle. It is a great pity for it is prodigeous fine. Much rain last night; quite Cool and Cloudy this day all over.

30. *Wednesday*.

Doctor Mortimer sent for yesterday to Judy but did not come. Gone to Beverley's. I hope her bowel complaint and coldness in her feet were more an alarm than any thing else. I gave her Rhubarb, cream tartar, venice soup[28] of each 8 grains [and] Jalap 4 grains. It carried off much wind and for a good while eased her bowel. She had one motion by day, but her complaint returned a little. However, another motion releived her. Her flesh grew presently warm last night, her pulse seemingly very well. I am in hopes another dose or two may bring on a recovery, her disorder being intirely bilious but must be moved off gently as she is low and weak.

Yesterday being the 7th rainy day it sprinkled on and off all day. Last night rain all night. This morning still rainy and great likelihood of continuing. It seems to be our happiness that there is no wind. Otherwise the corn would lie down. The last 30 Acres wheat cut down just as this spell came on is now mostly green with sprouting. It was the best wheat I made. The Oats that were cut down must also sprout.

Miss Judy after growing quite chearful by means of her last night's doze and having prevented some flatulencies from settling upon her bowels by Ginsing tea eat some bite of fryed Chicken and walked about the room pretty strong herself but at 3 without much sickness at the stomach brought up some very thin and very green bile and after that another vomit of the same. I immediately ordered two spoonfuls of the Ipecacuana wine to be thrown into a pint of warm water given in thirds at half hour distance. The first and second inclined her to a small motion downwards and after that a vomit upwards some thing green like the former and then another that appeared to be clear water. As she is free from all sickness, coldness in her extreams, and regular in her pulse except quickened by the vomit and as she has no pain in her bowels I will hope that nothing will obstruct her recovery. It is difficult for a father to practice on his child but as I cannot get the doctor I have ventured the best I can and flatter myself it has pleased God to suffer the method to be prudent and successful.

AUGUST 1766

Drye moon by its Phasis. So it proved quite through.

2. *Saturday.*

Paid this day by a note on Mr. Andrew Crawford Fifty three shillings to John Hammond for the freight of 422 barrels of Corn from Col. R. Lee's.[29]

[28] Venice soup was probably Venice treacle or theriaca Andromachi, a syrupy mixture used as a purgative and as a stimulant.

[29] Col. Richard Lee (1726–95) of Lee Hall, second son of Henry Lee (1691–1747), was a planter and burgess for Westmoreland Co., 1757–76. From 1777–93 he served the same county as representative to the House of Delegates.

Doctor Mortimer being at Beverley's from the 27 of last month did not come to Judy though frequently sent for till yesterday he called in in his way to Washington's[30] on Potomack. I suppose in sending this for his third visit to the child. But I told him I hoped he would call as he came back for both of them would not make above one visit; this day he called in his return and went over the river. Upon her growing worse, that was,

3. *Sunday.*

I wrote to him to tell him of her purging 18 or 19 times since he left her yesterday and desired him to contrive to make her a visit so that he might see her period of remission or intermission which I was perswaded if ever it did happen was only in the night. He wrote me a second very severe letter treating me extremely rude ridiculous and scandalous but came this evening for another visit and stayed the whole night as it was just dark when he came. He directed his bitters to be taken in the morning, noon and night and

4. *Monday.*

went off this day to Jett's rather before day light. I wrote him a letter in answer to his two indecent and abusive scrawls in which I put forth the Parent's right to object to harsh medicines such as were condemned by the best of men and especially such as he had experienced before in a fatal manner from that imperious and audacious practicioner the Devil in human shape and that he should either obviate those fears if he could or else behave with greater tenderness and decency.

5. *Tuesday.*

Judy's fever coming on now and then and her purging sometimes frequent sometimes moderate, but I think she seems to mend though but slowly. She is aired out every morning.

6. *Wednesday.*

Weather cool and dry now though a heavy shower the 4th in the night. Wind Northwesterly. Judy mending today though her fever came on after breakfast. Her swelling in her stomach quite gone by her yesterday's purging to day but moderate. Better towards night she ate some boiled chick. One motion in the night and one towards day

7. *Thursday.*

lowered her spirits again and after riding out one more and by dinner small one took away almost all spirits from her. I will trye a small vomit of Ipe-

[30] Mount Vernon.

cacuana if these stools continue by way of check; though it is my child it can't hurt her I hope.

I accordingly this evening put 24 Grains of Ipecacuana to insure in 4 cups of water poured these off in half an hour mixed as much warm water with them of which I gave her three droughts and about an hour after gave her the powder that had been infused. She brought up at 4 heaves perhaps better than 3 quarts of prodigious stuff in sour phlegm and this with little or no strain nor sickness at stomach. She had one watry motion afterwards and a second of a moderate consistence. After that she felt an appetite and eat some minced Chicken slept well in the night with no interuption but one moderate motion.

8. *Friday.*

This day aired her out in the Chariot. She grew seemingly hungry and with great moderation pacified it. Her fever came on a little this day. I went to Colo. Tayloe's. She had one motion in the day, walked 3 or 4 times about the Passage. Her fever not very uneasy though her flesh warm at Night. She had a trifling effort at the pan and slept well the whole night through.

9. *Saturday.*

This morning Judy not so well as yesterday, her pulse rather quick and not so full. But she says she is very easy and keeps mending. I gave her a dose of her bitters. She sets up much better than ever. Mortimer wrote to me to give her a purge as soon as I thought she could bear one but I do not think that so well now as it may be some days hence. God send her recovery. This is now advancing the fourth week.

Note: the second load of plank from Blough Point came up yesterday:

				Plank	*Paling*
1st load	4,500	feet plank Wraling	quantity	272	580
2nd load	4,730	quantity 427 Plank		427	—
3d load	4,500			383	200
4th load	4,518			304	277

15. *Friday.*

3rd load of plank came up as on the foot of the preceding page. Miss Judy mending though but slow I beleive fine.

17. *Sunday.*

Every thing burn't up. No rain since the 4th, a fortnight tomorrow. And what is worse by being confined with my Child my Gardner has watered nothing. The three hills of Anguilla Cotton extremely fine in the Garden but I believe it is a plant will not do here. There is but one blossom out although it was planted at the usual time with other Cotton. Many buds tending to blossom. Worms in third and fourth glut destroying all the Tobacco before them. The greenest corn turning yellow for want of moisture and extremely hot every day. On the 8th of this month my Wench Mary did fell down with heat and I do suppose from some cause of sickness not before discovered she died in less than 3 hours. The first instance I ever had of the kind.

19. *Tuesday*.

Passed a note in favour of Wm. Jackson,[31] late Overseer to the C[harles] C[arter] Estate for 20/ on Account of his wages to any one in Hobbs' Hole that will give him credit for it.

20. *Wednesday*.

Upon examining my sheep I have found out Mr. Owen [Griffith][32] to be a damned villain, setting down every day the number of sheep as if he actually counted them. But near a fortnight agoe Davis counted them and found 7 short of the number Owen pretended. They were afterwards brought up and since then has in every day's note given in the particular number which was sheep, lambs, and fallow sheep: 83 in number. But now we can discover but 77, that is 47 Gang sheep, 11 fat sheep, 15 lambs with those in Johnny's house and 4 Ewes that suckle them.

My Daughter Judy's illness began July 17 so that to this day there has been 32 days and the quantity of butter made in that time by Owen's Account is 113¾ pounds for 475 Gallons milk which Milk ought to have yielded 237 pounds butter. But there is a pretence of Milk for fools and which ought to impose on none but fools and evidently proves a roguery in my dairy. The quantity of butter weighed in 4 pots since my daughter's illness is

	167½ pounds—48 pounds
weight of the pots leaves	119½ pounds—21 pounds

used up in peck butter makes 140½ besides the pot made before my daughter's

[31] William Jackson (d. 1776) was later overseer for Landon Carter at Ripon Hall in York Co.

[32] Owen Griffith (b. 1746) was an indentured servant for Carter from 1765 to 1770. Sent by his father from England to Virginia, he had already served in the navy for eight years as a captain's clerk and was an excellent penman and accountant. His relations with Carter were never cordial, and in 1770 he apparently tricked Carter into releasing him so that he could return home to a large estate that he pretended to have inherited. He later went out to India. The affair can be traced in *Va. Gaz.* (Rind), Sept. 27, 1770, and Griffith to Carter, Dec. 21, 1771, Sabine Hall Col.

illness. In this whole affair there is a damned villany. And this rascal Owen by giving in Accounts over different from what he keeps in his book is consenting to it for which I will have him before a Justice.

22. *Friday.*

Wildridge Smith[33] brought his 4th load of pailing and Plank to be found and on the page August 9. The whole quantity to this day as per accounts in Mr. Edward's letter:

	Plank	*Pails*
17,648	1,386.	1,557.

23. *Saturday.*

John Singar came down from my Park quarter this day. Brought down the notes to my last year's crop (to wit):

I.
G. CN.
1. 1,147.   2. 1,111.   3. 1,122.   4. 1,155.   5. 1,056   6. 1,131 weights.

In all 6,722

Stemmed tobacco of which borrowed   440 Quarter RWC.
from A. by———   19)   6,282   330 half shares.

330

4/ 660 Stemmed   660 per Share
165 added to make leaf

825 at 18/. = £7.8/6 for which I paid Singar a note on Wm. Thompson[34] I drew an order for shipping this tobacco in Capt. Carnaby[35] to Jordan and Maxwell of London which I delivered to Mr. Arthur Maxwell.

J. Singar brought me word that John Hammond the Shippers had 51 barrels of Corn and 4 bushels with 4½ bushels of Rye coming down and set of[f] yesterday from Falmouth with it.

26. *Tuesday.*

Began to cut tobacco last night and this day a small scudd of rain Since the 21st when it rained plentifully. Pulled my Male hemp Yesterday at home.

---

[33] Wooldridge Smith (d. 1783) was a resident of Northumberland Co., and at this time he was apparently in the lumbering business.

[34] Probably William Thompson (d. 1771), merchant of Portsmouth town in Norfolk Co.

[35] Capt. Carnaby sailed in the *Russia Merchant* for Jordon and Maxwell during the late 1760s and early 1770s.

SEPTEMBER 1766

Drye moon by its Phases.

10. *Wednesday.*

Rain three nights agoe after much drye weather.

11. *Tuesday.*

Buckland's[36] two men began to work at 3/6 per day. Clear of sickness and Sundays.

30. *Tuesday.*

The rest of this month has been really dry and cool withall mornings and evenings. Very little Tobacco grew much. Fodder was either a great deal or the people too lazy to get it in. Corn makes but a bad appearance. Severe fevers and agues continue.

OCTOBER 1766

Cool and dry.

11. *Saturday.*

A frost.

13. *Monday.*

Began to sow wheat at the fork. Disorders still continue amongst us but not yet inflammatory but of a great imprudence. Tobacco not all cut yet.

18. *Saturday.*

Began to drill my barley field. Sowed also my last year's cowpens in barley broadcast in all 26½ bushels sowed. Finish yesterday sowing my fork Wheat, Rye, and clover.

22. *Wednesday.*

Drye for some time till this day it began to rain and so it continued.

---

[36] William Buckland was a builder and architect. A biography is R. R. Beirne and J. H. Scarff, *William Buckland, 1734–1774: Architect of Virginia and Maryland* (Baltimore, 1958).

23. *Thursday.* 24. *Friday.*

Struck and stripped out in these day a 90 foot house of tobacco.

25. *Saturday.*

Mr. Carter and his Lady of Corotoman this day went home. The rain detained them here 3 days.

This day I measured my Corn left in my wheat house under Owen Griffith's care. He began the 3d of this month to use out of 52.4 bushels of corn that is

		264 bushels
used to this day		98 bushels
	should be left	166 bushels
I find only		130 so that
there are stolen out		36 bushels.
Measured my wheat also.		bushels
March 10th there were		135
Used For the house etc. to this day	89½	
Sent to the falls	10	
People eat	57½	
sowed	47	
	204	
Oliver's field produced		120
Falls		94
		349
		204
		145
Measured this day		95
Stolen out of this since March		50

This day change my lock on my wheat house door. One which cost me 17/6. Talbot has lain in that house every night and latched Smith's Johnny once; but this Owen only left the key with Talbot and never locked him up as I ordered him up so he may have made away with the grain or the people may have got in when he went out at night to his wife.

27. *Monday.*

Owen this day discovered to be tardy in the above, although he says it was but pure negligence. It seems he knew of the Check I had upon him by means of the morning's notes he always gave in of what he did the day before; and working to make the corn hold out he topped a hogshead of wheat with Corn so Davis reckoned that hogshead by its contents. By which means instead of 30 bushels of corn we have lost 60 bushels and but 30 bushels of wheat instead of 60. Now laziness won't do for should that be the case as to the corn which was in use the wheat was only in use once a week and in these few weeks from October 3d to this time it is impossible that the measurement guessed could be as much as is lost. Besides it is only the new wheat gone. Now Talbot always measured out that and he had only used 47 bushels and our loss is 30 bushels and the thing speaks a deception which has the face of Villany always because if he had missed the corn as he says why did he not speak of it. On the Contrary, every week when I asked him he always said his account and expence would agree.

Sowed this day the Grass seed C[harles] Carter of the Park[37] sent me by the name of the lion grass brought down by poor Col. Chiswell from the back park. House my turnips two days agoe. 3 hogsheads full. This day housing my Irish potatoes.

Weighed 15 pots of butter made in my dairy:

August 19	5 pots	134 pounds
October 27	6 ditto	288 pounds
		422 pounds.

A Proper inscription to be written under a picture of Lord Camden[38] and The Right Honorable W. Pitt.[39]

C. Pratt *et* W. Pitt
Viri Honoratissimi
Qui Britanniam Magnam Conservabant
Fovendo LIBERTATAS
America Britannicae
Contra Perdititionem
designatam
Per
G. Grenville. *Anno* 1766.[40]

[37] Charles Carter of the Park was better known as Charles Carter of Ludlow.

[38] Charles Pratt (1714–94), 1st Earl of Camden and lord chancellor in England, was a favorite of Americans because of his opposition to the Stamp Act in the House of Lords.

[39] William Pitt (1708–78), 1st Earl of Chatham.

[40] "Charles Pratt and William Pitt / These most honored men / Who preserved Great Britain / By fostering the liberties / of British America / Against [their] destruction / Designed / By George Grenville Year 1766." George Grenville (1712–70) was M.P. for Buckingham borough, 1741–70, and First Minister, April 1763—July 1765.

THE DIARY
1767

JANUARY 1767

9. Friday.

Came home from the Assembly on saturday the 20th of last Month. Brought up with me two Cheese from Mr. Mills weight 33 at 9d. Began then to use it and finished one Cheese yesterday so that 16 pounds has been used up in 19 days. Very wasteful.

Found my whole Estate under as bad management as could possibly be. Not a Cowpenn broke up any where nor a Corn hill more made than when I wen[t] from home the 30th of October notwithstanding every day since had been very fine weather till the 3rd of this month. Upon the whole my short Crop of Corn alone has been gathered now here all husked and under davis but 50 barrels husked out. From hence I may conclude I have parted with davis properly though not in right time for he ought to have gone some years ago for the bad Crops I have made lately seem not to be all together owing to these other but to his Idleness occasioned by night drinking and his villainous lying which has constantly deceived me as I have been infirm and not often able to see into his work and by the little Specimen of hilling Corn this year now carefully looked into the whole has been villainously done.

Thrift who for some days took upon him to leave me under pretence that one of his gang run away as she did last year or as I insisted that she should be one of his Gang he yesterday agreed to serve me for one share in the Crop of his hands and 300 weight of meat. So that I hope his stomach is brought down.

Ishmael Moody[1] whom I hired in Williamsburgh as a steward for £25 a

---

[1] Ishmael Moody was probably the son of Ishmael Moody who managed the horse racing at Yorktown in the 1740s.

331

year came into my business some time in the latter end of November. He seems to be a very willing man but I am afraid too thoughtless. However, I hope from his disposition he may do pretty well.

17. *Saturday.*

A very fine day after abundance of rain indeed off and on from the 9th to this time which suits very ill with my low land Plantations in which Davis during three months of fine weather had not done one hoe of winter's work. So let his pretensions to honesty be what they will he appears to be a willful villain to me just as if he intended I should not make any thing of a Crop by dividing the Plantations under separate Overseers. I have however sowed the Fork and the locust point Plant patches and have broke up about 60,000 Corn hills, 20,000 Tobacco hills in Mangorite, and near all the Fork Tobacco ground; and I must if possible by picking the ground upon good hour of fair weather push on the rest, though I have many hindrances. Particularly all the hay still to be brought over the Island Creek.

23. *Friday.*

Now a great thaw after better than 2 days constant sleet which froze as it fell.

A bad season this for old people and creatures which must feel it in their bones and joynts. It is also very bad for any kin[d of work] for none can be done.

26. *Monday.*

Still drizling and so it has done ever since Wednesday evening the 21st. Moody sick off and on near a week.

28. *Wednesday.*

Yesterday morning the drizly weather broke away with a sharp Northwest. Set in with 8 hands to getting rails. This day tolerable good.

29. *Thursday.*

A loaf of sugar in the evening. The last pretended to have lasted 11 days.

31. *Saturday.*

Yesterday the drizling weather began again and has this day turned to a down right rain. So that my chance for recovering my winter's work thrown now upon hand by the rascally behavior of davis during the good weather whilst I was on the Assembly grows everyday less and less. For there is hardly two months to come for breaking up all my Ground and getting all my rails etc. I never was in such a situation before.

FEBRUARY 1767

5. *Thursday.*

It has been fair weather from the 3rd to this day and now very fine. All hands at work but so much to do and of such various sorts it is hardly possible to keep much at the hoe. Plant patches to get ready. Corn to move to my corn house through such bad roads. Oats to sow and rails to get in such a wet swamp. I fear I shall be over done particularly as my horses are so bad but I must try for it.

11. *Wednesday.*

3 days ago smart weather. The day before yesterday a fine day but in the night a terrible wind. Yesterday hard wind very cold spitting hail and snow. Our Vestry day. Parish Levy 88 per poll. Raise 14,000 to discharge Colonel Tayloe's debt for what he paid John Beale[2] for his land. Also 28,000 for a £200 payment next October. This day a fine day. Hoeing up Cowpens. Manuel finished Carting my Mangorike Corn to the Corn house. Quantity 298 ears [illegible] each 4 bushellBarrels 119.1 bushels [illegible] carried in by the people $\frac{04}{129}$ barrels [illegible] in all 122 barrels. It may be concluded with safety that there are 120 barrels of Corn good measure in the Mangorike Corn house which will not be begun upon before the 19th of this month. Now from the 19th of this month to Nov. 5 when to be sure New Corn may be gathered as there are but 37 weeks and, the whole expence of my people being but 22 bushels a week, 163 barrels will keep them, 120 of which being in Mangorike Corn house there will want

To Spare at the Fork $\begin{array}{c}43\\59\end{array}$ Left of Thrift's crop.

13. *Friday.*

A snow at last. It began in the night. The ground is covered and it is still snowing. We have been long threatened with it for even in the fine days banks have risen here and there in the horizon and it is probably will be deep.

[2] John Beale (d. 1766), planter and son of Thomas Beale (1675–1729) and Elizabeth, daughter of John Tavener.

Note: we took out this day 16 Bushels of eared Corn from the M[angorike] Corn house to make the peoples' allowance.

17. *Tuesday.*

A fine Evening. The snow not gone off the earth, having snowed for more than a day when it fell and really continuing excessive cold ever since till after 12 this day. My Two sons and their wives gone to Beverley's. Nothing could be done but littering cattle and moving fence rails since the 13th.

19. *Thursday.*

Tolerable good weather. All hands at the hoe from yesterday 12 o'Clock. Sowed yesterday Lucerne and burnet seed in the Garden to transplant for a tryal. Set out turnips for seed. Ordered them to be covered at night with straw. Mr. Ball here to day paid me a note on Allison[3] in part of his 2,100 odd feet of plank as he says. I say 2,200 odd. He disputed with me about £5. 10 per thousand. As he brought it up I agreed at £5 for the bastard inch but the quartered inch and ¼ I will have £6. 10 for but £6 as he brought he said he would not pay it. I [said] he should or pay nothing. He wants about 200 feet more of bastard inch. I bid him take it soon at £6. 10 or he should pay more if it lay to season.

He talked of his other accounts. I told him the remembrance I had suggested to me if there was any ballance it was in my favour. He did not know my Account. Talked of hops, some tallow, etc. my Son let him have. I agreed to let those accounts drop but not the plank for that should be paid. For the rest were things that I lint as he could not pay in kind. I got his man some years ago to make some Negroe shoes. Had done him smith's work several times and so the conversation ended.

This turns out a fine day. If the weather holds, I may possibly in some measure repair the injury that Davis did me in not doing my winter's hoe work in the good weather in November and December when I was upon the Assembly. Perhaps the ground will not be so light in not being broke up earlier but I shall finish my whole Tobacco ground by to night. I hope all to about 10 Acres which my scheme was not to have tended this year but to leave to cowpenn the next that I might make two crops of Tobacco with two dungings before I put it in wheat and then two croppings in wheat before it rests as I have fallen upon a method of raising oats in the Cornfields that I turn out

[3] William Allason (d. 1800), son of Zachariah Allason and Isabel Hall of Glasgow, Scotland, was a merchant at Falmouth. His papers are in the Virginia State Library, Richmond. A few of them have been published with a short biographical sketch as "The Letters of William Allason, Merchant, of Falmouth, Virginia." *Richmond College Historical Papers,* II (June, 1917).

every year. By this means I shall tend between 40 and 50,000 Tobacco hills less. But as it will be all better dunged I am in hopes the crops will be better and I shall have an opportunity of putting in one half of my crop of wheat into the ground without waiting till my Tobacco is off as I have done. For this reason I must this year tend the last year's wheat ground in wheat again. Then my Tobacco ground of next year comes into wheat so that this advantage of early sowing wheat will after next year get into its course of succession.

I hope to begin my Corn field again tomorrow. There is about 1/3 of it broke up and of that about 1/5 begun by Davis in a most rascally manner which must be done again because neither the step nor the ground upon which the hills were made were broke up. Such his disposition to me.

20. *Friday.*

1 pound of Congo taken out. Th[illegible] last about the 3rd of January.

27. *Friday.*

We have had very bad weather the 22, 23 and 24. Snow all day the 23 and hard frost ever since till midday; but yesterday it grew milder and this day a fine day. Began to sow oats. 7 bushels from Capt. Beale's oats raised last year in my Plant Patch sowed by the mill behind the new hay house.

Moody turned away this day. A base rascal. Now 12 lambs, we have had 15 and one the dogs killed as soon as Yeaned. Corn fields go on again.

A loaf sugar; the last the 14th just 13 d[ays]. We have but 9 loaves left of S[tewart] and Campb[ell's] 90 loaves which came in and was opened in December. Each weighs 5 pounds and 1/2 so that we [illegible] have used up 60 pounds sugar in 79 days from the 10th December.

28. *Saturday.*

15 lambs this morning.

MARCH 1767

2. *Monday.*

A very rainy night all last night.

3. *Tuesday.*

Though Yesterday very fine, it rained all last night and blew hard. Pleurisis now very brisk. 7 taken Yesterday and this day.

4. Wednesday.

16 lambs this morning.

A box of candles brought out of the vault this evening; I never heard when the last was taken out. It was in December 176[6].

6. Friday.

Rained great part of last night.

Mr. Gualdo began yesterday to teach my daughter Lucy to play on the Guitar. His terms are 2 days in every 3 weeks, that is, 34 times for the year, after the rate of 13 Pistoles. These times to be at my house. All lessons elsewhere, if she is in the way to take them, are to be gratis.

7. Saturday.

Rained all yesterday all night last night. Still raining. No work to be done. We shall be late. Every thing so wet. But 3 calves as yet on my whole Estate in this County, a plain proof of the severity of last year being particular on my Plantations. Others have Calves a great many.

18 lambs this day. 8 Lambs at the Fork, 6 of them rams. Rain but small all day except about [an] hour.

8. Sunday.

19 lambs this day, 10 of them eaws. Rained last night again.

The last halfpound of the tea opened the 7th of February was this sunday put into the small canister.

9. Monday.

20 lambs. Fork great C Field begun this Morn. Fork Harry died yesterday. But 5 days ill. Something broke in his Stomach. He walked about very much on Saturday and yesterday morning complained of no pain till in the night and then in stomach where it had removed. From tuesday when he felt it in his side was blooded and took rattlesnake and grew quite as good and up on Fryday himself. His leggs left off swelling as usual spring and fall.

A loaf of sugar taken out, the last was on the 27th of february.

11. Wednesday.

23 lambs this day. We have had two days hard Southwest winds which this day turned round to Northwest and brought back a little winter.

Bodleian Plate of Early Williamsburg Buildings
Colonial Williamsburg, Inc., owner

George Washington (1732–1799)
By Charles Willson Peale. Colonial Williamsburg, Inc., owner.

12. *Thursday.*

Snowing a great part of this day and very cold, ground this morning hard with frost. O for a little good weather.

15. *Sunday.*

A tolerable day after as severe a spell as I think ever happens in a Winter. Now 4 days since any kind of work could be done.

16. *Monday.*

A warm Smoaky day. In all 27 lambs this night. 9 lambs at the Fork. 1 heifer calved yesterday a dead Calf.

The pot of brown sugar filled this day. The last time pretended to be the 16 of January but I know they have had some since.

Books to be sent for:

The holy bible O[ld] and N[ew] testament illustrated by way of question and answer £8. 6/. Printed for Hinton, Pater Noster Row.

Stevenson's *Gentleman's Gardiner,* Newest Edition, for Hinton.

Wm. Blackstone's *Commentaries on the laws of England,* Worral.

[Frorein?], *essays on Agriculture and arts,* 8 pounds, bound and lettered.

Essays on husbandry, bound and lettered, 6 shillings.

Turnip Cabbage, 6 pounds.

Large late dutch Cabbage, 5 pounds.

Alexander Jacob, *Complete English Peerage,* best Edition, Neatly bound [illegible].

British Biography, 8 Volumes, bound and lettered.[4]

Bird grass 6 ounces the Virginia grass.

The white Osnabuggs which came from Captain Dobie[5] by Emerson's[6] negroe were 50 yards in two pieces, 26 and 24 yards.

The money due to the Northumberland Collector of the taxmoney is £8. 9 and 35 tithables, at 4/. 1,450 acres of a 2/ the hundred acres to be paid in October either by Mr. Edwards who is to sell either wheat or bag or by myself.

[4] Of this list of books, only three are definitely identifiable: William Blackstone, *Commentaries on the Laws of England* (4 vols.; Oxford, 1765–69); Alexander Jacob, *A Complete English Peerage* (2 vols.; London, 1766–67); and Joseph Towers, *British Biography* (2 vols.; London, 1766–72). "*The holy Bible,*" "Printed for Hinton" and not by Hinton, may possibly be *The Christian's Complete Family Bible, containing . . . the Old and New Testament at Large and the Apocrypha. Illustrated with Notes and Comments* (3 vols.; Manchester, 1765–67).

[5] Probably Capt. George Dobie, who transported tobacco to England during this period.

[6] Probably James Emerson (d. 1777), jailer in Essex Co.

SEPTEMBER 1767

8. *Tuesday.*

Account of Butter pots from Betty:
   6 filled with Butter.
   1 filling.
   3 Empty.
   2 with Pickle.
   5 at Lancaster.
   1 Sagoe pot.
   1 Rice.

19 All large ones but one.
   1 with Tamarins.
   1 with Sugar.

OCTOBER 1767

27. *Tuesday.*

Measured the lamb house field now breaking up for corn with a 8 foot pole.

From the Mangorike gatecorner to the Corner landing up to the house 45 pole:
360 feet
From the last corner by the lamb house
to the chop's crossing that ditch in a line
from the Cabbage ground 125 pole: 1,000
                                                   360
                                        square feet 360,000

If the whole piece was square it would be 8 acres and ¼, but on the other side against the lamb house it is longer than 125 pole so that it is near 11 acres. Now as this corn is to be planted 4 feet every way, it will by the to[illegible] contain 29,942 corn hills so we may calculate quite up to the Peach orchard 32,000 and better.

Measure out of the field from corner of the road by the main road to the Cabbage ground: 68 poles of 8 feet long.

From the lower to the upper corner of the Cabage ground: 62 pole.

This being the length and the other side being 125 po[les], I add these and half them for a mean length.

125	187
62	93 pole long by 68 wide
93	68
8	8
744	544 square [illegible]
	744
	2176
	2176
	3808

9)404736   44970 square yards
4860   4840 1
(6   40130
There with then   4840 2 be in this peace
                  35290
better than [illegible]   30450 3 acres which by the table
contain 21776   4840
                  25616 4 corn hills so that
both pieces will   20776 5 be   29942
                   15936 6   21776
hills which will be short   4840 7   51718 corn
                  11096
of quantity by almost   4840 8
9 thousand now   6256   the upper part of
the lamb field will   4840 9 make that up and more
                  1416

29. *Thursday.*

Measured the tobacco ground now hilling being all the Mangorike Cowpen th[e] year 1767

along the road	131,8	foot poles	
the opposit	133.	264.132	1056
across at the upper end		70 poles	
lower end————————	74	144.72.576	
		6,336	
		7,392	
		5,280	
square feet		608,256	

Not quite 14 acres, which at 4,000 to each acre is about 56,000 but as there 4,840 square yards in an acre equal to 43,560 square feet, equal also to 696,960 square quarters of feet, Every tobacco hill at 3 feet and ¼ each way being 169 square quarters of feet the acre will contain 4,124 tobacco hills so that the above 14 acres will contain 57,736 and 56 square quarters of a foot over equal 1/8 of a hill.

The average length of the ground being 1,056 feet. The breadth being 576 feet. These into each other gives the contents 608,256 being within a little of 14 acres of ground. Tobacco hills as tended by good planters being 3,¼ feet distant; Each acre being

	4840 square yards
divided by the	9
square quarters in one hill	43,560 square feet.
	16 square quarters in a square foot

[s]quare quarter in a hill 169)696,960/4124 tobacco hills in an acre and 4/169 over

· · · · ·(4

So that the 14 acres will contain 57,736 hills and 14 times 4/169 = to 56 square quarters. But as that ground is but 608,256 square feet it will at 3¼ feet each hill contain only 57,586 hills that is if the hills but 3¼ in the step as well as row.

THE DIARY

January 1, 1770—September 2, 1778

THE DIARY

1770

JANUARY 1770

5. *Friday.*[1]

This month began with a violent as well as constant rain all the first day of it and towards the middle of the night Ever since which we have had a most violent frost and so excessive cold that the River has been in the general impassable. Our works after our Corn has been got in co[u]ld be nothing but feeding our Cattle and getting wood to burn. The Mill dam we could not work upon. We are now carrying the [h]ay upon our herds which we stacked up on the Island. [Torn] taken up this year And as we are now sending for the things we have bought of a New England man in Totuskey these two days the house has been [with] difficulty kept in wood with the young Oxen. Our Tobacco prizing could not very well go on but with my lazy people every thing seems to be an excuse.

We killed our 16 hogs from the Park on Tuesday last. The weights are but very poor only 1,541 which makes me think that the new Overseer Browne certainly took by far the best for my [torn] them when he was up [torn] very fine ones [torn] the draught [torn] we have [torn] on Wednesday last. It is [torn] fine beef the weight of it [torn] 400 neat and perhaps [torn] to the draught kept it [torn] growth. I know it was [torn] for at 2/ the gallon and a barrel of Cyder at 15/ the barrel and half a hundred of pickled fish at 15/ the 100. It is to be paid for in Corn at 9/ if taken soon and in pease at 4/ per bushel.

[1] The diary from January 1, 1770 to September 2, 1778 is printed from the original in the Sabine Hall Col. This portion of the diary was kept in a number of odd-sized booklets, most of them unbound. Somewhat less than 5 per cent of it was previously published by Lyon G. Tyler in the *Wm. and Mary Qtly.*, 1st Ser., XIII–XXI (1904–13). In the few cases where the original has been lost or destroyed since the publication of the Tyler edition, that edition has been followed.

7. Sunday.

I believe we are still under the watery effects of the late Comet. We began to feel its influence more than a month before its appearance and I think we feel it now. If the great Newton[2] was alive perhaps the same happy genius that calculated to the world the trajecto[ry] [torn] as well as appearance of s[torn] would have been able by [torn] sensibly to have discovered [torn] are the divine Instrumen[ts] [torn] the excessive seasons of [torn] moisture in the worl[d] [torn] for I can see no nec[essary] [torn] position of the [torn] vary ac[cording] [torn] or rec[torn] not [torn] an emission of a fiery nature. It rained all day yesterday. Rained and drizzled all night and is now drizzling like a fogg.

Notwithstanding this, as Captn. Beale had invited this family yesterday to a dinner and a twelfth Cake, every body showed such an inclination of obliging the old Gentleman's Compliment that they all prepared and ventured through the rain though it was near One o'clock before the [torn] was passable. Having no Company my[self I s]et out with the rest but [torn] out of my plantation [torn] [w]ished to be back for although [torn] held up a little it still [torn] and the road was [torn] [w]ith such a sudden thaw [torn] frost that our [torn] the Chariot [torn] before observed every since the death of the old Gentlewoman neither the sons nor the daughters take the least pains to keep up the usual Command over at best a set of idle and blundering Servants and the infirmity of the old Gentleman was too great for him to do any thing but be uneasy at the late coming in of a pretty good though mere remnant of a dinner. The weather growed worse and I saw at any rate a necessity for my coming home for to be without my usual night apparatus even a warm room might endanger my aged and infirm state and as Mrs. Carter was obliged to come to h[er] infant I was satisfied that [torn] in a Chariot so difficulty [torn] to dinner would make it [torn] late as well as har[d] [torn] home in the [torn] to my h[torn] difficul[ty] [torn] on his [torn] a const[ant] [torn] than four mile till I got home. I was wet the full half of my legs but as the water had not got to me till near 2 thirds of my journey was over by pulling off every damp thing rubbing my feet well warming my inside well with some Coffee and a small dose of my domestic Elixir at night I have slept well and hope I have risen with very little bad effect from such a foolish step taken. However it shall be a warning to me never more to be pressed by any youthful folly against my long experience that in winter time if the rain holds till past midday to [thin]k it will break up, which

[2] Sir Isaac Newton (1642–1727).

was [my stu]pidity of yesterday; We left [torn] there and with him [torn] a good [torn] natured [torn] who has [torn].

[Torn] morning left it intirely to Nat whether he would go for Mrs. Parker[3] who had solicited my Chariot to bring her to my tomorrow's entertainment. Nat, though he got an ague by his yesterday's drive, thinks he can go well enough but if it would not look with weak minds like an intention to disoblige I do not think it prudent that he should go. There is a pretty general perverseness in the whole sex and perhaps it is a thing not a little conspicuous in that Lady otherwise with an infant at her breast she ought not by any means to have thought of venturing out in such a season. But when Parents give up their authority in teaching Girls to submit to cas[ual] disappointments perhaps it [would be] high treason or some d[torn] resentment should [torn] in such [torn] I had a [torn] came to [torn].

My butter so long agoe expected so certainly bought and shipt on board a Vessel of one Harry Woodford's[4] was not yet got to Hobbs Hole though it is barely a day's run from Tyler's store[5] where it lay. Therefore, had I not prudently fallen upon a method of feeding my Cows with Corn very early, my family would with all my other case have wanted butter.

The day before yesterday Wm. Ball fetched in my Cart from the new England man in Totuskey a barrel of Molasses which he calls very good at 2/ the gallon, and a barrel of Cyder at 15/ the barrel, and half a hundred of fish at 9/. So I owe [the] New England man 40/ for 20 [torn] and for Cheese at 9/ [torn] [as] well as a bushel of apples [torn] the above things which [will be paid for] in Pease at 4/ [per bushel.]

[Torn] clustered pea called from the shortness of the pods the finger pea and from their roundness as well as excellency in soup the Sugar pea but of all the pea kind they are the smallest increase and are only of use from their prodigious length in Vines and as they may be tended between the drills of wheat provided they are not too near it will not be any bad Cropping for the same trouble of the hoe that gives the wheat the last. Nothing cleans these pease and as this wheat comes off before these vines begin to run the plow by breaking up the stubble may give a good earthing to the pea. So that 50 or 60 barrels made will in this new England Trade contribute to the little [neces]saries for house keeping.

[3] Mrs. Richard Parker, the former Elizabeth Beale, daughter of William Beale.
[4] Harry Woodford was probably a small merchant and shipper operating in the Potomac and Rappahannock areas.
[5] Probably the store of Thomas G. Tyler who had an ordinary at Acquia near Landon Carter's Stafford Co. lands.

14. *Sunday.*

We have had a sufficien[t] [torn] quantity of bad weather since the [torn] taken notice of and till I can [be assured] of the contrary I shall hold [myself per]swaded we have some how [been influenced] by the late Comet in this [particular]. For my part I see no [reason why] Comets may not be co[nsidered] meteors of a watry kind as well as of a fiery nature.

My annual entertainment began on monday the 8th and held till Wednesday night when except an individual or two that retired sooner Things pleased me much and therefore I will conclude they gave the same satisfaction to others.

I can only say that my business may not [have] been carried on with life as usual perhaps from a reason its being bad weather. But suppose I allow another reason, my indifferent engagement in it, the time lost as well as the family expence may easily be repaired by a little Oeconomy.

Will Lawson[6] my Overseer tells me though my bulks of Tobacco in the barn seem to be much larger than they were in the mud house yet he does not [think] they turn out quite so much [prize]d Tobacco. If so I shall fall short [of my fi]ne late expectations which were [founde]d upon the quantity of the [bulks a]nd indeed my Tobacco hung [torn] it possibly might be more [torn] the gust than that in the [torn] lambs better than a week at the fork and one fell here [last] night.

My Oysters lasted till the third day of feast which to be sure proves that the method of keeping them is good although much disputed by others.

Fitzhugh and Lucy came down on Tuesday last and with them Col. Carter of King George which added to the life of the Company. Every body expressed the highest satisfaction and I hope every body was pleased.

18. *Wednesday.*

Ever since the last rain the frost has been very intense and the weather extremely cold Perhaps from some fund of snow either in the air or in the upper parts of the Country. Our work has been under Will Lawson: at the fork husking and putting up of Corn, At Mangorike getting the hay or litter over from the other side of the Creek of which [we can] do but little as the water is so cons[tantly] freezing, At Dolman's[7] burning the [plant] patches, a tedious work also throu[gh his] forgeting to cut down the b[ushes neces]sary

---

[6] Will Lawson, not to be confused with Thomas Lawson, overseer of Carter's York Co. plantations, was overseer of Sabine Hall in 1770 and later at other of Carter's plantations.

[7] John Dolman was one of Carter's overseers.

for it in the summer [So that] with Gardner Johnny's ga[ng helping] them they still have a day's [work to do dow]n at the river side and the Locust [p]atch besides. We shall then burn the fork. The Jobbers are all getting wood. Manuel and the little Cart bringing it up and it seems to be as much as they can or will do to keep this house in fire wood. Mulatto Peter has in one of his bleeding fits brought himself very low and many of the people are sick but I thank God we do very well and none of them are dangerous ill. Tony goes on with his scheme of old age creeping and whindling about often pretending to be sick when nothing ails him so that the paling in of my Garden is still to meet with every difficulty for this rascal has been trifling it off now four winters and as to Mr. Guy he has learnt so much diligence at Ring's Neck and [Ripp]on Hall under those sprightly [Overse]ers Boughton[8] and Lawson that [he ha]s not now in three months got [anyth]ing as yet for a new Cornhouse [torn]. Indeed his partner Mr. Jimmy [has also] got into his swelled legs which [comes] from his wearing of leathern skin boots many years agoe so tha[t] the best way will be to sell him off as a very sorry fellow. Frosty weather is bad for prizing. Therefore we have not got our 21 hogsheads out yet. Owen says one of them is about 1,000 pounds. We must do things as well as we can but they are very badly done this year. I see if cold weather keeps me in the house it makes every body idle. Mrs. Bridget I find has had a pain in her guts six days without the least fever and looks well that is she has her Mother's Cabin to loung in and Nassau so constantly drunk that I cannot with every day's inquiry hear who pretends to be sick but there will come a warm day for the punishment of these things.

23. *Tuesday.*

We had a little snow on Friday and some on Saturday last but nothing to speak of. I rode out yesterday for the first time since my entertainme[nt]. The weather has been so very hard it [was] dangerous to venture and for what? [For] of my own wheat barley and [torn]thing doubtful whether many people [torn] not want grain to continue in even the grou[nd] [torn]. I never remember to have seen it so effectually killed. The reason is plain, severe dry frosts and no snows.

We have 4 lambs at the fork of which they have been careful and but one here and as yet but only one Calf.

I am repairing the fork dam and have near finished burning all my plant patches. Manuel began this day to carry manure to them.

---

[8] Ring's Neck was one of Carter's plantations in York Co. John Boughton was overseer there.

I fancy we shall be obliged to get dry sedge out of the marshes for Dolman's Cattle. During my entertainment the Gentlemens' servants not only took the hay from the Cow yard to litter their horses but used all the blades out of the stack. My Scoundril Nat, the ringleader of this impudence, it seems was too fat to go the hay house.

Tony has been 2 days morticing Cedar posts for paling in my Garden. As to Mr. Guy it is well he has a lame partner to lay his idleness to. If Jimmy had been well he says the Corn house [w]ould have been finished but from Jimmy's sickness he has above the plank [to] saw and the stocks to get. I believe [he] will t[ell] another tale by tomorrow night. Lawson has resolved to take him [u]nder his care. As to Jimmy his lameness appears to have been occasioned by [wear]ing very small shoes. Such a splay footed rascal wants to be a small footed fellow. He could not walk nor stand but I found a way this day to make him do both and work pretty heartily. I have forbid him coming home to his wife at night and shall have him watched for they that cannot work for me cannot without great deceit walk 2 or 3 miles in the night.

We have begun in good earnest whilst the weather is hard to husk out all the mangorike Corn. I have ordered all that has been used to this day to be given in Account tomorrow and to keep an Account from this day that we may not only know how much we have made but how much we shall have by us.

We have not yet got all our Corn stalks into the Cow yards and yet I think they are pretty dry. We sent 6 sow pigs to the fork that there may be a new stock of breeders there. I have ordered them to be kept up for about a week and to be penned in the stye every night which must be done ve[ry] punctually.

24. *Wednesday.*

It has rained pretty smartly in the night and till near 11 this mor[ning so t]hat Mortimer who was sent for to Mulatto Peter taken with a bleding at the nose off and on ever since this day sevennight cannot come.

To humour other people I have sent for Fauntleroy[9] and Mortimer to this fellow although I have several times stopt the bleeding and really there is something in his case not regularly to be accounted for. It seems twice or thrice before in his life he has been subject to this bleeding but after every violent touch it has been stopt and left off. His state of health then nobody can give any account of but as to his present state till this bleeding we all can pronounce him a boy in great health and what should occasion such a bursting of the vessel of the nose without a fit of sickness or other visible cause is the difficulty.

[9] Dr. George Fauntleroy (d. 1770) was a Richmond Co. physician.

Had it been periodical I should have conjectured an intermittant and bleeding the crisis of it but it has been irregular in every bleeding of it and sometimes at 2 days' distance. I have kept him upon a low and cooling diet, given him cooling medicines, blooded him in the arm and foot a little at a time, Cupped him between the scapula [bo]th with and without scarification, have used warm baths to his feet for a delivation of the blood from his head besides many styptics of the shops and all the old women's methods of cold water to his head, to his privates, Vinegar cloths, and what not and all to no purpose. The evening before yesterday imagining it to be a divided state in the blood I administered 30 grains of the bark with 6 drops of Elixir Vitriol[10] and have continued the use of this ever since with every now and then a cup of Comfrey decoction with saltpetre[11] and gum Arabic[12] in it in order to unite and thicken the blood. He has not bled to speak of since monday 4 o'clock. Fauntleroy was here and seemed to think I gave too little bark, but sure I am small doses administered frequent have the best chance of entering the blood. I have not much expectation from such practitioners in such extraordinary cases for it must require a great length of practice to meet with such an one. However it is the duty of a Master and I have sent for them to satisfye that.

Mr. Corrie[13] for 4 or 5 messages has been letting me know he had wax candles to sell at 18d the pound. Not dreaming but they [were] myrtle wax I sent for a sample yesterday by Nat and got 2 dozen which I must look upon as a mere trick both in price and quality, and I fear that private character often given him is now coming out. I will be upon my guard.

Note: I had ordered of the hogs that came from my Park Quarter 2 to be weighed, cut up, and salted by themselves to see what they would lose in their weight. Mr. Ball[14] paid that pork to Wm. Lawson for part of his allowance as he desired I might have his meat salted. The meat was killed the beginning of this month. 249 of it laid by and this day it weighed but 240 so that Lawson's allowance must be rated by this that is as 240 was made out of 249 what quantity of freshmeat did it take to make the 80 pounds of salt he had before.

Nat, notwithstanding the rain, has sent Nassau's horse to the ferry for the Doctor. As yet the boy Peter don't want him but I suppose the Doctor might

[10] Elixir vitriol was a mixture of spices and oil that was used to strengthen the stomach.

[11] Saltpeter is composed of equal quantities of fixed and volatile salts and was used as a diuretic.

[12] Gum arabic, arabici gummi, was a substance of white color that flows from the acacia or Egyptian thorn and was used to soften or thicken "the thin Humours" in diarrhea and fluxes.

[13] John Corrie (d. 1785) was a merchant at Tappahannock and justice of the peace in Essex Co.

[14] William Ball was apprenticed to Carter to learn estate management. He was an unusually competent man even by Carter's standards and later married Ann, Daughter of William Beale.

order this horse that he might get his little girl home from Mr. Giberne's and I suppose he will endeavour to earn a 10/ the same time he fetches her over.

25. *Thursday.*

The yesterday's rain cleared up by 10 o'clock with as fine a day over head as could be wished but under foot from the excessive hard frost the earth was as miry as could possibly be. It was overshoes even to my little house in the hard gravel walks. I took notice of some clouds passing from the Southward and prognosticated from them there would be thunder and lightning. Accordingly, in the evening we had a flash or two with some thunder. At night there lay a northern bank which I also foretold would be snow in the night. The wind was sharp in the Northeast with a good deal of rain and this morning we have a pretty brisk snow.

Note: in salting up the quantity of pork that Will Lawson was to have that I might be satisfied what it would lose I found that in about a month it had lost near 2 per Cent. Ball never considered this but paid Lawson his full compliment for which I called him a foolish fellow, a word that he stomach much. But I was at last able to convince him that it is always foolish to say no worse to do injustice knowing it to be such. However Lawson took more time to be convinced which I did by representing a quantity of Corn under his Care and asking who[se] loss the shrinkage should be as he might be able to prove he had embezzled none of it. This so far satisfied him that he was ashamed of holding the dispute. But comes a blade that can't see right and justice because perhaps not wrapt up in £100 and he asks what use was the disputing about 12 pounds of pork. My answer always is truth and justice have no virtue if it does not shine in a farthing as well as in a million for then such virtue is only covered by some accidental quality that may attend it as in a case like the present the quantum to be gained by it.

28. *Sunday.*

Hard and cold weather and spitting of snow frequently since the last account.

Mr. Ball went out for 60 pounds of Coffee from Corrie on friday last. Corrie pretends that he informed me that his Candles were Myrtle wax Candles and that he could have sold them if he had not kept them from me but this is one of the fugges that deceiving men make use of when their tricks are discovered in order to disguise their intentional cheat for every letter of his speaks of wax candles only. Therefore I will set this down as an instance of that Gentleman's dispositions. He will not part with any sugar under 55/ the hundred, I suppose thinking that my necessities will compell me to submit to his extravagance. But he is mistaken. I will go without at any time rather than indulge the least villanous imposition.

We had yesterday 6 lambs at the fork and one Ewe brought two here last night so that we have now 4 at home besides those at the fork. Great care shall be taken of them if orders frequently repeated can do it.

Colo. Tayloe and John Wormeley[15] came here on friday. I gave them my opinion upon old Tayloe's,[16] Wormeley's father-in-law's, will. Mr. Wm. Digges the younger,[17] Wormeley's Son-in-law, came here also yesterday. A passable man enough.

31. *Wednesday.*

It has been thawing and showing signs of good weather both above and below so that I was in hopes not only of getting to the hoe but that we should have been able to have got some Tobacco seed in the ground. But a part of it the earth is too wet to hoe and before it got dryer the frost has set in again so that we have got to our old work of husking Corn.

It seems my hay is every where out. This has obliged me to go to mowing the marsh sedge dry as it is otherwise my Creatures but soon be without food.

Tony is preparing my garden posts but at so slow a rate that his boy and he only mortices 7 of them a day.

As to my fork Corn house I believe Gerry will never get ready to frame that. It will be a good one when done and a lasting one but I fear a dear one by the labour.

My lambs drop very slow as yet but 7 at the fork and 2 here. I had 4 but the Ewe that brought twins produced such rats that they could neither suck nor be suckled.

I must kill my last beef this day feeding it with Corn is very expensive and so is the feeding of my Cows in order for my butter.

I have given directions that no more of my husks be burnt but all of them preserved for the Creaturs. Other people find them good food and necessity has made me try them.

I have now had a very bad cold above a week.

---

[15] John Wormeley (d. 1785) was a planter in Lancaster Co. and son of John Wormeley (1689–1726).

[16] William Tayloe (d. 1770) was a planter in Lancaster Co. and son of William Tayloe (d. 1710) and Ann Corbin. John Tayloe of Mount Airy was his nephew.

[17] William Digges, Jr., was the son of Col. William Digges (1742–80) of Bellfield and Elizabeth, daughter of Col. William Digges of Denbigh. William Digges, Jr., inherited Bellfield and sold it in 1787.

FEBRUARY 1770

5. *Monday.*

February began on Thursday last and I have been confined with a cold from the monday before which in spite of all my care I catched I know not how and in my infirm state as I could not proceed with any degree of hurrying evacuations I am not yet well. However I think I mend.

Mr. Beverley and Billy his son staid here till yesterday the weather being so far from being inviting as to confine them and Mr. Giberne the whole time in the house. Cards was the only diversion and though very little was played for my Son according to his usual devilish way with me could not bear me either with him as a Partner or against him. Constantly ridiculing and insulting every thing that I said or did so that he fairly drove me from the game and then got his heart's desire by playing the dead man as it is called. I am [?] have made many resolutions but I believe I shall keep this for putting an end to Cards in my house.

6. *Tuesday.*

I laid in a large supply of them in hopes that this Gentleman who is always fond of them would stay at home and divert himself, but I have found a greater evil in it. He pretends he does not want to play. Then he must want something else only to abuse me which I beleive he does so that perhaps the resolution of no Cards will only introduce some other point to insult me upon. However this I beleive I shall gain. He will be seldom at home now and in that I may be happy for it is much better to be without any object that we have an affection from nature than to enjoy such an insulting Companion. As R composes many parts of play it is no wonder that it is more harmonious than L and of course more agreeable in every sound of it.

Mr. Carter of Corotoman lost his Lady the last day of January and a great loss it is to a young man with a house full of very young Children. The letter I received from him I have put by as a standard of the greatest good sense and the greatest affection to a departed friend in a mild, a simple, as well as an expressive language. Poor fellow. I pity him because I know and have travel[led] in that very road of affliction. He is now entering into a course loaded with every disappointment and concern which he must daily feel though he marry again ever so agreeable for as he has many girls he will see how constantly they must want the tender and instructive care of their natural Mother.

Amongst our bad weather we have had snow upon the ground now the third day which makes bad for every kind of work particularly for our yeaning sheep. One has brought 2 lambs which being but mere rats died in a day perhaps through my indisposition and a strange easyness in Ball not to be distinguished from indolence. They were not properly taken care of and now another Ewe is yeaning two but from her long continuance at it she and the lambs may all die. I have got as yet but 10 here.

My greatest puzzle is now wood for my fires and the keeping my people to get it for me who with no better authority than what I see is exercised whilst I am sick will do nothing.

The yeaning Ewe taken notice of before was delivered of two distinct bodies of lambs with all parts compleat only joined by one neck and one head. Bodies as big as usual for lambs just yeaned only one something larger than the other but both rams.

I made Nassau open the bodies of this extraordinary production through the one mouth. He pursued a distinct gullet into each body but could only find but one large heart in one body and in the other none at all. Perhaps it is not in the power of man to assign a cause for such a pervertion of nature.

9. *Friday.*

The atmosphere though rather warm by much too moist. I rode out yesterday and excepting the day before I have not been out of my house occasioned by a very bad cold and hard winter for above 12 days. My cold still obstinate and to be sure in my extreme age I must look bad though I feel neither pain nor fever. I have not dared to evacuate by bleeding excepting two small cuppings and purgings. To be sure my age cannot bear but my alterative openings have failed me by at least a week from what they used to do in every cold. The cough racks my head for some little time after it is over I colup [?] as well as usual but expectorate very little which has really been the nature of most of the colds during my life, a thin slimy matter dripping from all parts frequently spit up but not in any quantity and seldom thick enough to denote an expectoration. A vomit would be the proper method to discharge this phlegm but as I am so old I don't care to be busy with them.

I like my ride out yesterday as little as possible. The ground quite rotten and poachy. Nothing hardly alive. The fields full of water so that no kind of work except husking of Corn can be done Although the Cattle must be taken care of for which purpose as all my hay is gone I have been 10 days at least moving the sedge in Mangorike marsh and getting it over to feed my Creatures. They really eat it tollerably well though it seems to be dry. I have not got in all my Corn stalks yet and there are at least 4 days of hilling to do and not one hoe struck in a fresh Corn field such has been the winter although I was so forward with my work before it sat in. I am trenching the fork plant patch which is the last we have to do and then all will be well manured but we are not as yet able to lay off even the dryest ground in beds for sowing. Johnny is going to try again this day.

The number of lambs fallen yesterday were 17 here besides the little twins that died and the monstrous lamb, and Mr. Ball tells me he has seen a little shenkin lamb in the old field which I suppose has been the case why in years past we have thought all our sheep have not yeaned and, as this villanous shepherd Jesse manages, I suppose it will continue to be the case for he lets the sheep jump over the ditches and miry slashes which can never be proper for yeaning Ewes. Therefore if I live and can effect it I must every fall have a pretty large field well fenced in to keep the sheep in during their yeaning time and if I can put some winter grain in for a winter food but then I suppose being infirm and old myself it will be the general pasture for every bodies' creatures for I can hardly keep my wheat patches clear.

Rode out this day as damp as the air is in hopes to mend my cold. Whilst I was out I felt very well but since I came in a perpetual trembling in my bowels. Perhaps the Alterative I took last night is now ferreting out the wind from the several parts where it had gotten or possibly it is the forerunner of a vertigo for I have observed the same thing just before a sharp fit of it especially in the chamber of the heart attended with great palpitation and frequent stoppages in the pulse.

I see in this length of time though but a few days comparatively this has discovered in my work the want of my eyes to put the Overseers in mind and they will in spite of my teeth catch at any little foolish excuse rather than own a neglect though the thing seems certainly evident.

We shall not get all our Corn stalks in towards making our dung heap unless I set apart a time on purpose for it to make it a work to be done and not an odd jobb as it has been.

I must look into the expence of the Mangorike Corn that is just done husking and the Corn house not above 3 parts full. To be sure the Corn left will not quite fill it and yet we had a greater quantity than ever I used to have by near half a Tobacco house full of unshucked Corn. But Lawson says they eat prodigiously at the Great house.

11. *Sunday.*

Still damp foggyness and impossible to sow tobacco seed and indeed to do any thing else. I never saw my hill so miry and poachy before.

Mr. Ball tells me my wheat is just gone which is very quick work in expence though just perhaps in account and if I don't alter the expence of Corn I shall be soon told that is just gone and how to get my Mill done I cannot tell in such accountable wet weather so that the effects of the gust is every day coming upon me and I believe my people all out of their senses for I cannot get one of them to do a thing as I would have it and as they do it even with their own time they have it to do again immediately. Tony himself is just such a Rascal.

13. *Tuesday.*

Still very wet weather yesterday and great part of the night a constant and violent rain and now a thick fogg equal to a great shower over and through every thing that it passes.

On Sunday last Frank Lee came to dine with me. Poor fellow in a very low state but yet I think easy to be amended. It is my opinion that his whole intestines are smeared over with an acid slimy phlegm which should now and then be brought off by gentle pukes as well as carried down by Alterative appealings but some how his Physician who seems to think as I do has mistaken his medicine. Pukes he has not ordered. The appearlonts [?] directed are mistakenly called Neutral salts for they are the Vitriolated Tartar dissolved in Cream of Tartar whey a little sweetened with Manna[18] and from experience I know them to be so predominantly acid as in no sense to agree with the ideas of neutrality and this poor Lee has found them for they bung him up from dose to dose and every now and then his throat is merely tortured with gulps or belches of the sourest verjuice which is evidently contrary to his Physician's intention for he forbids Rhubarb appealants because of their generally having such an astringency behind them. Therefore he must be a stranger to the effects of those salts which he prescribes as neutrals. I am certain frequent draughts of warm water would be more so and am convinced that many Rhubarb preparations guarded as they are and may be against that astringency would cure this Gentleman. I could not but recommend to him this method with a pill of mild soap every morning 5 grains in quantity. He told me he had tried 2 pills and had received their good effects.

Yesterday my butter so long expected came to hand By Colo. Anthony Thornton's[19] letter. It was shipt on board some vessel the beginning of October but not said what vessel nor by whom so that when I got the letter I could not tell where my butter was. By accident one of Colo. Tayloe's people saw it in

[18] Manna is a sweet, white, dewey substance that forms on the bark of trees in summer and fall and has been used as a cathartic.

[19] Col. Anthony Thornton of Ormesby was a planter in Caroline Co., where he was also justice of the peace and occasionally sheriff. He married first Sarah Taliaferro and later Susannah Fitzhugh.

Ritchie's warehouse. A rascally practice begun by that Gentleman of whipping every thing in there whether sent to his care or not for the sake of Storage and as he takes no trouble to give notice of the Goods people very often as I was are put to seeking for their things and only hear of them when they are spoilt or wasted.

My Casks should be two hundred weight. I tried one of them. It was 95, Cask and all, the butter not rank but very Cheesy and tending to rankness. I have ordered it to be carefully washed, new pickled, and potted up.

By means of this butter I have taken away one half of the Corn to the Milch Cows and will upon the first spring of the grass take away the whole.

My wench Betty tells me we have just finished our last summer's stack of potted butter and have three pots though but small of what we have put up this winter. I see I could have done without this butter that is come to me but it was at a dear rate for every pound that I have made this winter has cost me 12 d in Corn alone besides a prodigious stock of peashaving greens etc. Therefore, I must have more care taken in summer butter making for it cannot be worth while for the sake of a little fresh butter to feed cows with Corn in the winter.

14. *Wednesday.*

It still rains although it has thundered this morning and I did expect that that was a sign for clearing up. It was so evident yesterday that we should have thunder and lightning from the frequent rolling and returning of the clouds. Notwithstanding, it rained most of the time I ventured to pronounce it.

There was yesterday an appearance that carried terror in its look. If it was a vapour that rose immediately from the water it descended upon it like a great storm and went with rapidity and violence the whole breadth of the river but before it got out of sight it dispersed into a long heavy fogg that settled in the horizon. I discovered no wind with it at my house but to be sure it looked dreadful and must have some thing of the kind in it.

The house were we have no fire is constantly as wet as if we were hourly swabbing the walls and floors. Yet nothing of this prevented my Son from his Corotoman journey round to Beverley's although he complains of a cold, two of his Children with violent colds and sometimes quartans and the little infant smart fevers every night which they will do nothing to because I have advised that they should. Nay, nothing of this prevents Mrs. Carter and my Girls from a visit to old Beale's because he keeps his son's birthdays on this day. I could not but laugh that they should think of carrying me out in such weather. I have been once this year a fool to accomodate their humours but having got over the effects of that it shall be my fault if I do again.

I rode out upon my hill but was obliged to return in by means of a hasty shower. My people can do but very little. Cattle they must feed and therefore turn out in all weathers. I hardly think my Creatures that bring in wood can stand the roads although I feed them so well. I don't remember ever to have seen such roads before. Up to my very door is quite miry and no Tobacco seed yet sown, but perhaps we may be the better for this for I think with so much rain it must burst and rot in the ground.

15. *Thursday.*

A sign of fair weather at last. Would to God it may hold that our works may go on for we shall be very backward. No Tobacco seed sown and not only no weather to do it but hardly the least weather to prepare the necessaries. Not a foot of ground to be worked. The last rains by washing off the dirt that the frost had thrown up over the wheat and grass occasions a little verdure which some will call a spring but perhaps the first frost removes that fancy.

For these 5 or 6 days a great singing of frogs. Perhaps by the rains being warm these animals are wakened but I much doubt of frost soon to set them to sleep and don't expect our winter going because of their melody. Irrational things which act by instinct are certainly not more secured from mistakes than rational and we see how often they are deceived. An instance where instinct seldom exceeds reason as some fools chatter. For my part, I think reason an improvement rather upon that which in every body is impressed by nature and therefore man has his instinct as well as the brute creation and his reason to govern it.

The earth is extremely full of water and if that has not time either to evaporate or sink before frosts set in our roads will be as bad as ever which in Clayey soils have really been intollerable. To morrow if the weather will favour Lawson will begin his new Corn field and must husk the Riverside Corn in the night.

Dolman who has made a long jobb of the plant patches has now the brush every where to get for covering them when sown so he will be a day or two latter before he can get to his hoes.

Jack Lubber will undoubtedly finish my prizing this week. I have but 24 hogsheads which I apprehend will fall a little short of my expectation of 30,000.

There are many reasons for this without saying one house did not yield as much as another. One reason can hardly be prevented for where there is a large Crop which people are obliged to stem in the night the Negroes in spite of our teeths will throw a good deal of their task away, which I see has been the case this year. But, if I live another, should I make a great Crop, I will endeavour to prevent it by making each person keep their stemms by themselves till the morning for inspection and a proper correction. Again as to my Crop the blowing down of the tottering part of my barn rackt by the gust, I say, that blowing down in January has evidently destroyed me a great deal of Tobacco for Lawson being a fresh overseer and not knowing where the bulks were laid at last found one of them so exposed to the weather when the barn was blown down that when it came to be opened it was spoilt to a very little.

17. *Saturday.*

We have a frost again though not very hard. It has brought the water up into the earth and of course my Garden Peas cannot be planted.

We are hoing Cornfield at Mangorike and the Fork. Began but yesterday. I have order[ed] Lawson to count each foreman's work and rectifye the gang by that. For if the foreman does not work the gang will not.

The Cotton patch is ready dug and manured there for the planting in proper time. I believe it will be all I shall plant here. It is the fittest soil and others not so fit may require more working than I can spare time for.

McGinnis[20] is boarding up the partition in the Tobacco [house] where I must put some of my Corn until that Cornhouse is finished for the old house is quite full which holds near 90 barrels and perhaps there may be near as much more to put up.

I have forbid using any Corn out of the Riverside warehouse that I may always know where my reserve is.

I have ordered Guy, as he must be done plank sawing before I come back, to get new sills for the mudhouse where they are rotten because he may make a mistake in framing that Corn house and as I intend to keep that plantation for Corn alone except a little hemp and flax and find I can dung a field of at least 60,000 every year I must provide me a house to put the Corn in.

Johnny is throwing up my beds in my quarter patch at home but I see the rascal does not intend to finish by contriving that all his lambs should get out of their yard that he may be trifling about after them. I have 29 lambs here and 12 at the fork.

18. *Sunday.*

Promises a very fine day. The right smokey look of spring weather in the morning.

[20] McGinnis was probably a slave, though he might have been Richard McGinnis, a Richmond Co. farmer, whom Landon Carter may have employed.

Last night a long distant growling broke forth, I suppose from a consciousness of never having shown the least gratitude to a person constantly indulgent in every thing and a daily maintenance of a large family besides an assistance given to look after the Children and an assistance too not used for that purpose but daily in spinning for other peoples' advantage. I concluded that this must some day militate against the behaviour of so much ingratitude daily shown and therefore where there was the least conscience it could not bear the reflection without the invention of an excuse.

Somebody mentioned housekeeping. I said I hoped that term would not be used where nobody showed the least disposition to such a care. A person then broke out that until I sent Mrs. Woods to take the keys from her every drop of Milk, Spoonful of butter, of fat, every ounce of sugar plumbs, etc., passed regularly through her hands.

I laughed at the care we then experienced in Milk, butter, fat, sugar plumbs, soap, Candles, etc. Not one of these innumerations lasted my family half the year. New soap was obliged to be made in June. Fat gone by July. Sugar continually bought in and old expended plumbs a large barrel of 300 weight bought of Grieg, Captain of the *Admiral Hawke,* and paid for by Colo. Tayloe for me. All gone. No body knows how. Butter merely vanishing. I never listened to Negroes and therefore gave no ear to the pots of butter, the aprons of plumbs carried away. And when people grew too heavy to do anything but trust to thievish servants I directed Mrs. Woods to offer her service and can be sworn when these inconveniences were removed the old Lady went by my direction to offer the keys again at the bottom of the stairs. I heard the insult she received. But Lucy remembered when Mrs. Woods went for the keys and said it was by my direction. Lucy was a Child and might retain that in her memory without the circumstances and she might not hear after people had got well that Mrs. Woods went again by my directions to offer the keys up, but these circumstances being put they could not be denied.

I have written this, let who will read it, only to show that I have long seen this little cloud ready to burst and after I am gone let such people clap their hands upon their hearts and say whether it was not their own determined pride in resolution that kept a person from doing any thing below the dignity of a princess. Let them reflect, if they can before God, whether such behaviour was not the effect of resentment for my not cordially giving in to a particular affair, An affair cooked up against my advice when I only suspected it and carried on in secret without the least knowledge of mine only to insult me about 30 minutes before it happened with an invitation. Yes! There is no Christian conscience that can deny this truth.

From hence have I dated all the ill usage and barbarous treatment that ever parent met with, where no indulgence, no tenderness, no presence, nor the most endearing expostulations could ever purchase the least quiet doing. Other people have eyes and ears but if they have not seen and heard these things as the scripture says they have not made use of them. Every day proves I am right.

A very fine day. I rode to the fork. By means of George's laying off the ground there was not much hoe work done yesterday. He says Lawson told him he was obliged to lay off the work at Mangorike, but that is a mistake. Tom Pantico lays that off and keeps it well before the people. There are but 12 lambs there. I saw the ten remaining sheep which looked very well and some as if big with lamb. The lambs are really well taken care of and look fine. One of the 3 sows I sent there has brought 8 pigs. Lawson said 9, but he was mistaken for George who put them up says the sow had no more.

Wm. Tutt, it seems now Colonel Tayloe's Overseer at the fork, came last night to order George to keep my Cattle out of Colonel Tayloe's old fields. I am always ready to do this and that fellow knows last year when he was my Overseer it was my constant orders to him, but Tom Reynolds, then Colonel Tayloe's Overseer would be always pulling my fence down to let his or the plantation horses into my pasture and take them out when he pleased so that through those gaps my Cattle got into Colonel Tayloe's grounds. It is the very same thing now. Tutt suffers his horses to be brought into my pasture and put the gaps up often as I will they are taken down night or morning for those horses and George says he put them all up but on friday and now they are down again. I ordered him to go and put them up immediately and bid him tell Tutt I was willing to keep my Cattle out as he knew and he must keep his horses out. I shall write to Griffin Garland[21] upon this head. That whole partition fence is my own and has been ever repaired by me.

I have now a pretty good opportunity of discovering the difference between spelt and Rye for winter pasturage. Neither of them grow much in the winter. At least they have not done so this year and do not show the same disposition towards it as barley does. But as to the feeding, the yearlings in particular keep constantly upon the spelt. Therefore for them I must believe it is the better food. But the fattened sheep, perhaps because the Rye has not been fed so close, keep upon the Rye. However I shall prefer spelt as it is a more pleasing food and because it yields a better grain Crop which is itself a very fine food.

[21] Griffin Garland was a small farmer in Richmond Co. At this time he apparently worked for John Tayloe.

We have 32 lambs at home.

For a Curiosity I walked into my garden and it is really a curiosity for I do not believe there is a single thing alive in it except a bunch of spinnage or two. Such has been this winter. Every strawberry vine is infallibly dead, the lettice all rotten, the broccoli near mulch, the parsley killed down into the roots, and so I suppose are the Artichokes, The Clay thrown in the walk up above the brick rubbish. I had before taken notice of the pompous Account of Cabbage turnips being all a randum lie. But I now [have] seen. Plant them when you will and let the growth be what they will our common winters would destroy them for I had them covered in November and those I planted in July are nothing but mush. In short the damage to my garden if I consider my table cannot be less than £50.

I went into my Cow yard where I saw my 4 draught oxen. They have been broke this year and have been fed like stalled beeves but I am pretty certain these Creatures can do nothing without plenty of hay or fodder of which I have scarce had any by means of the August rain and the September gust and it was my misfortune to tend no wheat last year on account of the weavil. But I see if the weavil eats it all up I must tend it that the straw may save my poor Creatures. In short I never expected half so melancholly a sight as I have now seen. One more such year must put an end I fear to all schemes of subsistence.

20. *Tuesday.*

Yesterday I had appointed to go with Mr. Giberne and my Grand son George[22] to Blandfield, Mr. Beverley's boat being to meet us at Rappahannock Creek mouths. We were all ready to set off when a Southeast wind brought up some rain blowing as it advanced and vearing round to the Westward so that by night when it got to Northwest there had fallen rain enough according to my notions to satisfye any plantation that had been even 6 months dray and a gust very little short of that which all the Country calls such. The wind has blown extravagantly at Northwest all night and now blows so hard that I fear there will be no water doings this day. However as Beverley's boat did not come yesterday and I thank God we escaped without much damage as yet heard of perhaps all will be very well. We can go when the weather is milder.

By Owen's Account my Tobacco except to about 200 is all prized up in 24 hogsheads neating [?] 24,950. This 300 which Robin is to have makes the whole Crop 27,250 and I am very certain that I had even after the Tobacco was struck 30,000. At least 1,000 [was] stolen away and so with its large bundles to

[22] George Carter was the son of Robert Wormeley Carter.

Tom Smith.[23] The neighbours saw it in his possession but the identity could not be proved. And by the heaps of stemms many bundles were thrown away by the Negroes to have it said there task was finished besides a pretty great bulk quite spoilt when the remainder of the barn was blown down.

We have now 37 lambs. Mr. Ball tells me another Sheep was missing the night before last and when he sent Lydia for it that bitch took one of Johnny's Ewes belonging to the lambs [?] and brought it up and that Sheep was missing last night for which I have ordered her correction.

My Spinners, imagining I was gone yesterday, instead of their usual day's work spun but 2 ounce a piece. And because the woman, I have directed Owen to set it do[wn], Peg my Cook wench, broke out in favour of her daughter, one of the Spinners, for which that Lady and the three spinners are all whipt this morning. It has made me order Mr. Ball to look into their spinning every day that I am gone.

26. *Monday.*

Went up on Tuesday last to Beverley's, took boat at Rappahannock Creek, the wind and tide against and the boat so small we were 33 minutes getting opposite to Col. Fantleroy's, it being very cold and my little Grandson George with me. Unwilling to frighten him his first trip by water we turned into the Colo.'s, Giberne the Child and myself. There we dined, borrowed Colo. Brockenbrough's boat, which was larger, and in the evening reached Bland-field w[h]ere all were well.

[The] next day rode to see Beverley's [new] building just raised to the surface of the earth. I believe it will be [torn]omly but in order to make it so I wish both the fronts are not spoiled for I find there is to be a building at each end which goes no higher than the first story and as I understood Mr. Beverley, in order to keep some range in the funnels of his Chimneys, he intends to carry one of them over the ceiling of the roof to the main funnel. I endeavoured to advise him against this, being satisfied of the danger if not of the certainty of its smoking but I suppose a plan laid will lead him at all hazzards into the resolution of doing it.

Thursday was a very rainy day Friday a good one but Saturday all the seasons of the year joined together. Sunshine, rain, snow, hail, and prodigious gusty. It was with great difficulty George and I got home. We left my Son and Giberne there.

[23] Thomas Smith (d. 1782) was a small planter in Richmond Co. and brother of Robert Smith (d. 1776).

At night found Nassau most excessively drunk so that I suffered as much as an old man could suffer, it being very cold without fire and without the least assistance for Tom coming round with my horse got not here till yesterday.

Moore Fauntleroy[24] my ward just returned from England came to see me. It was so extremely cold with a most violent Northwest that very little warmth was enjoyed even in my house but indeed coming home so late I could not see the provision of wood and by the logs that was very scarce.

Begun this morning to enforce my resolution of correcting the drunkenness in my family by an example on Nassau.

Such weather with but little food will lessen the number of our Creatures. Two Cows it seems have died and a young bull since I went abroad and also two lambs just yeaned and more must die for I cannot see how such rats occasioned by this miserable spell through a long winter can live.

28. *Wednesday.*

Once more a tollerable appearance of a good day and if it does not turn out as every good day this year has done. The certain sign of a bad spell. We may get to work with the hoes tomorrow morning though at present the ground is extremely hard.

I wish this year may not by its several circumstances be recorded for the severest weather in the memory of our people. The circumstances are many. The dying of the Creatures will be one very sensible one. The food all gone to a very trifle. The Creatures extreme poor though until the bad weather in January in as fine order as ever I saw them and the giving them corn which never has been customary if it saves them must introduce another circumstance of record for I doubt the Crops will not maintain the gangs the year through at least since the 3rd of January. I myself have used here 200 barrels more than I ever did which I call a certain consequence of the August hours rain, the September hurricane, and the severity of the winter. Hardly a day without falling weather, severe frosts, pinching colds, and violent winds.

Another consequence of the gust is the destruction of the timber which perhaps no future age of the world can repair for the standing trees are in a state of death mostly being so shaken by the winds the roots so broke and the violent wet weather since disposing of them to hasty rots.

It has been usual to wheel earth in the winter upon Mill dams where wanting but this year we could not wheel a barrow for mud and clinkers. Not

[24] Moore Fauntleroy (d. 1790) was probably the son of Moore Fauntleroy (d. 1758). He studied medicine in England and later resided in Essex Co.

a ditch could be repaired and fence rails, got only at the hazzard of the people's lives, in ponds of water. And although we have not above 5 weeks to the planting of Corn season not a day as yet that we could break up ground in. Therefore these necessary works with the turning of the dung in march will make the sucheeding [?] crop so late before it can be got in the ground as to leave another memorable circumstance of the severity of the weather.

I have indeed sowed all my plant patches but two but really I dread the constant wet weather will render that diligence ineffectual and perhaps the want of plants may be another circumstance of record to the severity of this weather.

My Garden I have before spoken of. It has hardly one thing alive in it and must all be new planted.

MARCH 1770

1. *Thursday.*

This month begins as the last began continued and ended. The appearance of a good day in February was the certain sign of bad weather and yesterday's tendency to a good day is almost as certain of some cold falling weather this day. However we are got to our hoes to catch an hour whenever we can.

I met Tutt just now with his Gun who had been to Spencer Watts' for thick joint Tobacco seed. He has hoed no Corn field and could not find a good day to do it in. I believe it must not be only one but many good days if he finds one to work in.

I shall sow my last plant patch and that in the fork meadow next week, God willing, having sown every where else. I ordered Lawson to break up the Quarter plant patch there for Irish potatoes which I intended to put in it.

Guy and Jimmy it seems have been 3 days getting new sills for the Mudhouse, some of which are rotten.

3. *Saturday.*

It rained all day yesterday according to its usual sign this year of a fair day the day before. It was very remarkable that all at once in yesterday's rain the water hanging on the trees turned into ice immediately and looked quite beautiful although the weather was really soft and warm and the air had a smell something like the washing a gun. Indeed every pissing puss upon the plantation gave up its stench notwithstanding it has been so well and so constantly washed with rain from the beginning of 70.

This day a very fine as well as inviting day but I am doubtful of its continuance for although it was so warm last night we have had a general white frost.

4. *Sunday.*

I was in hopes by the prodigious fineness of yesterday and the northerly cast of the air that we should have escaped the certain effects of a fine day and a white frost in the morning which are constantly denoted a succeeding bad spell. And then by a week of good weather a diligent planter might have got himself in some tollerable order for the succeeding Crop but this day appears beclouded just as we used to have it before a great rain which if it should come added to the last great quantity that fell will be by much too great for my lands and how we shall get in order is not in my power to guess for we have but little more than a month to the usual time of planting Corn and all my old ground to be broke up, Some of my new fields not done listing, and some of my ground for dunging still to be hilled up, all my dung to turn, and indeed, which I much desire to do if I can, my stiff land Tobacco hills to be made again before they are turned for planting as this severe winter must in a manner have baked and consolidated them although I got them all made before the winter sat in. As to my cattle I fear they must go. Two of Cows just calved quite upon the list and many others with hardly strength enough to walk about and not a shive of food to give them but a few shucks, the husks of my Corn when shelled, a very few hops, and what trash I can get out of the great marsh every day liable to be burnt with fire. Here then arises another circumstance to record the bad winter preceeded by the gust for the want of butter the succeeding year will be greatly dreaded because there is no prospect for making any in this wretched state of my Cattle at Calving. But to all this we have this comfort that we are under the direction of a merciful God.

We have been entertaining ourselves off and on for these two days with a game at whist for pistereens and I think I have added to Billy Beale's old debt to me upon that account 7 pistereens more so that as he says he owes me now 14 and with all the rest I am quite clear.

7. *Wednesday.*

Yesterday evening it broke up fine after much spitting for rain but I fear we shall still have it though our earth is full loaded.

Wm. Kirkum paid me at Court a hogshead of Tobacco for his rent. An honest man.

Sam Griffin,[25] though he promised, indeed offered, to pay me £50 for Dick Adams,[26] yet as I suspected my note upon Adams to Thos. Reed[27] had been accepted I desired him to pay the money to Mr. Reid which I say he not only promised but swore to do, never paid it to him but upon pretence of some quarrel carried it back as he sends me word by Tom Beale. However I understand by Reed he had not the money and offered Tobacco for it but at a price that Reed would not give so that this worthy fellow I fear is not as good as he should be and indeed I cannot help thinking Mr. Ried too artful with me for it has now come out Adams accepted my note a twelvemonth agoe to a correspondent out of Reid's but because he did not get it indorsed truly he comes upon me for the money.

At last I have got Charles Yates'[28] receipt for the £50 paid upon Younger Kelsick's[29] account but it seems I have 50/ to pay for the interest because truly there was no money in the Treasury. Mr. Yates also has not behaved genteelly for he got a note of mine on Tom Slaughter accepted but Slaughter, owing him money also, he transferred the payment to that account and applied to me as if the note was not accepted upon which I gave him an order upon the Treasury.

9. *Friday.*

I will for once perswade myself that good weather is coming at last. This day has mended much upon yesterday's fine day a great sight two of them together in the year 70 yet awhile.

The cattle that have died this year are 8 in Lawson's penn, 5 in Dolmon's, and 2 steers killed in the same place by Mr. Manuel and the Boy Kit. They were ordered to drive them to the fork to be raised where they had plenty of food and they drove them through the same marsh in the Corn field where each mired and died. When people can do this notwithstanding they have a plain level main road to be sure correction can never be called severity.

I must always take notice that my fork Creatures fare the best in the winter. The reason is evident. That land is light and dry and all the rest of my Quarters are stiff and very wet. I have several times resolved to build me a large Cow house there and carry all my food to preserve my Cattle during the

[25] Sam Griffin was a resident of Richmond Co. and probably the son of Leroy Griffin (d. 1749).

[26] Richard Adams (1726–1800) was a merchant in Richmond, a justice of the peace in New Kent Co., and burgess for New Kent Co., 1752–65, and for Henrico Co., 1769–76.

[27] Thomas Reed was a merchant with businesses in Northumberland Co. and Richmond.

[28] Charles Yates (1728–1809) was a justice of the peace in Spotsylvania Co. and merchant in Fredericksburg.

[29] Younger Kelsick was a small planter in Richmond Co.

winter but I am puzzled how to get my dung from thence for my Mangorike ground. Nevertheless, I must fall upon some kind of a stage to float it down the Creek for I cannot help thinking the savings in my Cattle will pay me for it. However the matter must be well considered.

I have 14 lambs at the fork where not a lamb has died. I have but 13 here and indeed have not lost many but from the young Ewes who drop their lambs and will not own them. Perhaps it would be a good way to pick these young Ewes out after rutting time and winter them there for I am satisfied This disowning of their lambs can only be owing to the wet weather.

12. *Monday.*

We have been this 3 days much threatened with rain. Missting, cloudy, and windy, and now much over cast and very cold.

Tony will next Wednesday have made a complete month about the weir which allowing for the timber and Carting it down with the peoples' work that helped him at setting I must value at 40/ and reckoning his own work which I used to hire at 3/6 the day which at 21 working days amounts to £3.13/6 so that the fish that I eat will cost me better than £5 besides the loss of time in fishing for them every day.

Tony it seems although he had a stout boy will not reckon this work was done but by one person. His boy has now been going on 3 year his apprentice.

We are not finished breaking up our ground to be dunged as yet and there is at least three days of the Cornfield to be broke up.

Tony begins this morning to paling in my Garden.

The Jobbers are scourering the wormditch round by Lawson's house in order to fence in the new Corn field.

This cold night has been the death of two lambs. One died yeaning, the other as soon as it was yeaned, though both in the house. So that we have but 55 lambs and we should have had 80 in a moderate winter.

14. *Wednesday.*

This weather that threatened us ever since the last good day came on in the night with hail rain and wind so that our old fields are as much afloat as ever they were and I do suppose such a violent check to the poor Cattle that were just beginning to lick themselves and grow chearful as it were upon the juices of the buds that I almost dread to hear of more deaths amongst them. And to mend the matter one of my draught Oxen well fed this whole winter with Corn, Pea vines, Rye straw, spelt straw, and wheat straw, the night before last broke his neck intirely by Manuel's carelessness. He fed the Creature and then turned him out of the Cowyard and I suppose going naturally in search of grass it stepped into the ditch or gully and so brike his neck. This is the third draught Steer put to a violent death by that cursed villain. The two former for the sake of a short cut in stead of being drove along the road to the fork where they were ordered to be taken care of. They were drove first one over the marsh where it mired and died. My orders were to whip that boy severely for it but this did not deter Manuel for above a month afterwards, the other steer being ordered to the Fork for the purpose of a plenty of food, he drove him over the same marsh where he mired and died. Certainly for these things no justice can be done without a most severe correction.

This bad weather continues fatal to my young yeaning Ewes. They drop their lambs, disown them, and the Creatures die for want of the cleaning care of their mother so that by disasters of this kind I cannot have lost less than 8 or 10 lambs.

Other people lose lambs at more than a fortnight old and they conclude it must have been by housing them with their mothers. Perhaps in Tobacco houses not cleaned but strewed over with little scraps of Tobacco that may be some cause for such an accident. Otherwise it is against any experience of mine for talk who will a lamb is certainly too tender a Creature to endure such violent dirty rains. But I never put the Ewes after three or four days yeaning to lie with the lambs. They are turned out as soon as they have done suckling and I wish I had a house to keep them in at nights at other times for a shelter against such weather. Such an one I must get, God willing.

I visited Mr. Giberne yesterday. A worthy good man but a little too unfortunately attached to some oddities that will injure him. His friendships are extremely strong but not always fixt upon proper objects and I think he is so blinded to them as often to forget evident facts and sacrifices his own reason. I have known him intimate with many who even as to their behaviour to him ought to have been despised by him as rascals and without naming them I can see that even now he is attached to some who I will venture at the forfeiture of my judgment which has been very intuitive as to men and things. I say I will give up my senses if these people don't deceive him. I caution him against them but still I think I see he will go on in that sacrifice rather than suffer reason and good sense to wean him from such attachments. It is the failing of a well disposed mind but I confess but it cannot be the prudence of any sensible man and therefore I pity him.

15. *Thursday.*

This weather I am afraid will turn into a deep snow and if it does must effect a great destruction amongst Creatures of all kinds where the food is very scanty and the herbage only the buds of bushes in which the sap is but beginning to rise.

But bad as this weather is it could not stop Nancy Beale who run mad with inclination must go home to her Mother at least 46 mile off although the weather threatened during the whole time and to mend the matter my foolish daughter Judy because she had promised to go home with her in spite of every reason that I could give her would go for which as to Judy she shall never have my leave again and as to all other silly creatures I will not fetch them here since they do not know how to accommodate their inclinations to the least obstructing circumstance.

Mr. Toney shall as certainly receive ample correction for his behaviour to me as that he and I live. The day before yesterday he began to pale in the garden and only fitted the rails to seven posts. When he began to put them up I was riding out and ordered him to leave the gateway into the garden as wide as the two piers next the gate on each side. Nay, I measured the ground off to him and showed him where the two concluding posts where to stand and the rest at 8 feet asunder from post to post to answer to the tenons of his rails and I asked him if he under stood me. He said he did and would do it so. I had been 2 hours out and when I came home nothing was done and he was gone about another jobb. I asked him why he served me so. He told me because it would not answer his design. The villain had so constantly interrupted my orders that I had given him about every jobb this year that I struck him upon the shoulders with my stick which having had ten year made out of hiccory so very dry and light had been long split and tied with packthread therefore shivered all to pieces and this morning, for that stroke which did not raise the least swelling nor prevent the idle dog from putting up the posts as I directed in which I convinced him that every thing answered, I say this morning he has laid himself up with a pain in that shoulder and will not even come out to take off a lock that he carried but 2 days agoe to Buckland's smith on purpose to get the spring mended which broke again this morning. I might as well give up every Negroe if I submit to this impudence.

16. *Friday.*

Yesterday was a bad day all day indeed. Abundance of rain and a good deal of snow which melted as it fell.

I do believe my old Carpenters intend to be my greatest rascals. Guy does not go about any jobb be it ever so trifling that he does not make three weeks or a month of it at least. The silling my Mudhouse, a jobb of not more than 3 days, he has already been above a fortnight about, and this morning when my people went to help to put the sills in, though he said he was ready for them, he had the rotten sills to cut out and because I told him he should certainly be called to account for it as I came back truly he was gone and no body knew where and had been gone for sometime but not about my house.

Mr. Tony, another rascal, pretends he is full of pain though he looks much better than any Negroe I have.

17. *Saturday.*

Tony came abroad and was well entertained for his impudence. Perhaps now he may think of working a little.

Guy actually run away. Outlawries are sent out against him for tomorrow's publication.

We have been putting in the sills under one side of the long Tobacco house, called commonly the Mud house, but cannot finish it till the dung is taken out for it must be raised a foot or two higher than it was.

Lawson heaping his Cow yard dung. He shall then go to collecting the dung of the Mudhouse and the barn. His Tobacco hills are all finished but his new Corn field too wet a little of that to do.

One lamb fallen today which would have been 56 but one died last night through Johhny's carelessness. He wants his correction.

A Calf also died under Johnny put up for a Veal. He has had it up a week and now pretends it would not suck. It was a motherless Calf.

The weather very cold though beginning to look fair.

Mr. Page at Colo. Tayloe's sent for me to dine there. I have a bad cold and could not go. This cold I catched at Mr. Giberne's by means of the familie's keeping the room door open.

18. *Sunday.*

I find the complaint of other people about losing their lambs has at last got into my stock that yeaned yesterday and one other died last night. The weather was cold but as the house is warm one would think from their number it cannot be the cold that has killed them. I am rather inclined to think the Ewes have no Milk and how should they, poor Creatures, for notwithstanding the provision I made of near 40 acres of Rye it is so killed by the frosts and constant bad weather that they cannot get a bite. They are fed with Corn but perhaps not enough. I raised more lambs in the same house last year than I believe I shall do in this which is another consequence of that Gust for I fed with meal last year but cannot do so this because my mill is not yet put up. I must have a larger house with divisions in it that the Ewes may lie with their poor lambs.

19. *Monday.*

It is an old observation that after a storm comes a calm but in this year 1770 it has been something inverted. Instead of after a bad day expecting a good one, whenever we have a good day we are certainly to expect a very bad spell after it. I thought after we had got so far into March and indeed approaching near the sun, for it is now nigh the time of his vernal equinox, I say, that by his heat more and more every day this system of weather would have changed but I see it is otherwise. Yesterday turned out tollerably good and with a Northwest air but today we are all overcast, very cold, and clouds swagging as if big with snow.

I cannot help thinking of the folly of my daughter Judy. She went on Wednesday last with her perverse Cousin Nancy who suffers no weather to obstruct her inclinations down to Lancaster more than 40 miles off and a prodigious bad day of snow and rain it was. Judy knew my Chariot would be wanted on Sunday and pretended to be resolved to come home on Saturday but although that was travelling weather and yesterday a fine day she has staid I suppose till today to complete the stupidity of coming as well as going in bad weather and it is very presumptive it will be such. Surely where there can be such a folly the resolution of never indulging it any more cannot be amiss in one. No, if girls will sacrifice their good sense to the ridiculous inclination of others, as a Parent I ought to prevent it.

I had my Ewes first on my bowling green yesterday and then on the hill sides so that the poor Creatures made a shift to get a belly full and this way I intend to conduct them if possible to save the lambs for it is certain they suffer for want of milk and that their mothers could not get without food.

22. *Thursday.*

Colonel Fauntleroy's feast day where I suppose my family must go.

We have heaped our dung at Mangorike, the Mud house and the barn. Those people are finishing the hoeing their new Corn field but up here Dolman though 3 days at it has not finished heaping the dung in the Cow yard quite and has the Tobacco house and sheep house to do.

Guy came home yesterday and had his correction for run away in sight of the people. The 2 sarahs came up yesterday pretending to be violent ill with pains in their sides. They look very well, had no fever, and I ordered them down to their work upon pain of a whipping. They went, worked very well with no grunting about pain but one of them, to wit Manuel's sarah, taking the advantage of Lawson's ride to the fork, swore she would not work any longer and run away and is still out. There is a curiosity in this Creature. She worked none last year pretending to be with Child and this she was full 11 months before she was brought to bed. She has now the same pretence and thinks to pursue the same course but as I have full warning of her deceit, if I live, I will break her of that trick. I had two before of this turn. Wilmot of the fork whenever she was with Child always pretended to be too heavy to work and it cost me 12 months before I broke her. Criss of Mangorike fell into the same scheme and really carried it to a great length for at last she could not be dragged out. However by carrying a horse with traces the Lady took to her feet run away and when catched by a severe whipping has been a good slave ever since only a cursed thief in making her Children milk my Cows in the night.

Mangorike marsh burnt yesterday and according to my lay observation it betideth rain which I believe will happen now but in this year every good day was a token of rainy weather. There is a phylosophy that with me accounts for the rain after burning this marsh. It is of 2,000 or 3,000 acres very rank in its captail sedge and of course must through up abundance of smoke which unless agitated by violent wind by inveloping the common rising moisture of earth must at last condense and descend in rain. Therefore from such a moist earth as we have had we are not only to expect rain but really a heavy one and such the clouds appear at present.

Paid Schakleford[30] this day 30/.

23. *Friday.*

Yesterday snow hail and rain but upon clearing up a little I went with my daughter Judy to the feast. There is a time when Company will divert especially that man who can relax from the true modes of thinking and reasoning properly. Otherwise perhaps there is not quite so much diversion in company for now adays go where you will there is such a sameness in action speech reasoning and expression that you would think every body only learnt from one another. Add to this that unhappiness in laughing, the evident token of the fountain that only bubbles nothing relative to the water that flows from it. The old Gentleman is with me an honest man with good principles.

I believe every body begins to laugh at English education. The general importers of it now adays bring back only a stiff priggishness with as little good manners as possible especially when the particular cut of a waiscoat, the multi oval trim of a hat, or the cast of a buckle does not attract great admira-

---

[30] Richard Shackleford (d. 1794) was a farmer in Richmond Co.

tion, but if they do, then the tongue becomes extremely multiloquous upon the learning of the foppishness of the fancy.

I came home but without Nassau or Nat, a drunken father and Son. The latter first mired my horse up to his saddle in crossing a marsh that none but a blind drunkard could ever venture upon and Mr. Nat so engaged with boon companions as never to get my chariot by which means I was to plung home 5 or 6 miles upon this mired horse without one person to assist me. I got home near sunset and about 8 o'clock came the Chariot with the drunken father and Son. This morning I ordered the son his deserts in part. The father I shall leave till another opportunity for though my old Servant I am too old a Master to be thus inhumanely treated.

This day the same as yesterday in snow and slet and yet it is the 23d of March. Perhaps we shall have very short Crops this year for I am sure we have no time of a year to work for them.

At last Mr. Molleson's[31] *Trimley* is arrived. I think she should have been called the *Trimmer* for after such pompous letters it is but a poor account to get but £9.15 a hogshead when but only now the Tobacco is found fault with. And what is the fault? The Brokers say it is not in condition, otherwise very good. A happy word this without any meaning to be comprehended and therefore capable of any explanation that the maker out of the sale shall please to give it. There is one unhappy thing that strikes me. Molleson says he can send me abundance of depositions from the brokers as to this want of condition. This Gentleman has been at depositions before. I wish he may not be too fond of them because they are always suspicious of the facts and often of the principles upon which a man acts. And in this particular case I wish he may not be too fond of them for by profession a broker is a villain in the very engagements he enters into. He must buy and must sell as cheap and as dear as he can which is the very trade of a Jockey and when a man becomes broker for both Merchant and Smoker it is the most villanous part of his roguish employment because he must be perpetually counteracting the interest of either one or the other and therefore must add to his villany by doing it as secretly as he can. And as it is no doubt who he will prefer in this trade, although the planter alone pays him, we may presume he substitutes these unfathomable words to justifye his breach of engagement to the merchant when he sells the poor planter's Tobacco for nothing to keep in with the Smoker who it seems will not buy but with his own broker and then only as he shall please him in what he has bought. Is the Merchant then so stupid as not to see this? Yes, he sees it,

---

[31] William Molleson was a London merchant.

but as he pays nothing for it he suffers it to go on and perhaps for the benifit of borrowing money of these brokers that he may oblige the poor planter to make good the proverb that whenever he goes a borrowing he goes a sorrowing. I wish this may not be my friend's case. However I have borrowed very little and will borrow less for although I intend to preserve honour I will not put myself out of the way at any time from keeping out of a Lion's mouth. I have writ to him I shall ship as usual but if I cannot upon the terms of living I must Ship no more after I have cleared this account which I hope will be this year. It is a strange thing that there should be that trade upon earth in which no man can continue honestly in or rather it is strange that a man will not continue so at all hazzards. This Gentleman in his first letters and ever since till these Sales did endeavour with me to keep up the Character of a Gentleman and it may be upon my expostulations he will continue to do it but I confess these sales with their excuses carry a different blush.

24. *Saturday.*

This may be called the day of days for it seems as if the coldness of the whole winter was annalized into one prodigious keenness. There is hardly any venturing for an old man into the air. My very bones are pierced with it.

Captain Grieg came here yesterday wanted to know how Molleson's Sales of my Tobacco pleased me. I told him how much I was disappointed. He then said he saw some of the Tobacco at home and it had not been well handled. I told him it was a joke that for Molleson complained only of the condition and that in 4 different parts of his letter but what that was I could not understand. The Tobacco he says was otherways good but I had reason to suspect from his referring me to depositions from the Smokers that he could get that he was somehow unhappily fallen into their hands. I read Grieg my letter to Molleson in which with great temper and friendlyness I admonish him not to be too fond of depositions especially from fellows by profession obliged to be rascals, for from every definition of the employment of a broker he was to buy or sell for the person that engaged him as cheap or as dear as he could which naturally obliges him to advance or depricate the goodness of the Commodity. And as in the Virginia trade one man was to serve the Merchant as a seller and the Smoker as a buyer Such a naturally seperation in interest must teach him to study arts to disguise the person he must prefer and of course as the Smoker, the person on the spot, will only employ such brokers as best serves them, him he will prefer. The Merchant, as the poor planter is the only man that pays for it, though he sees the Villany, cannot be expected in every case to be disturbed at it and especially if those brokers are rich, as it is said by their Trade, and lend their money to the Merchants they must be doubly armed with power and of course can easily invent unintelligible words to disparage the Commodity. However I told Molleson as I engaged with him upon principles of honour if I should not meet with a reciprocation it should be no plea with me for any ungenerous action and Grieg should have all the assistance I ever proposed him which really is all that I have in my power. Only I should take care not to sink myself too far in his favours for unless I could live by such a correspondence he must another year load his Ship how he could. Grieg said the letter was very genteel but he was damnably vexed about the sales which I shewed him. I told him they fell short of my expectations about £130 but nothing disturbed me but Molleson's hopes given me in every letter of agreeable prices and not one word of my Tobacco as to any fault even when Somerville came away. On the contrary, he says in that letter all the Tobacco was well sold. Therefor, I must believe this revived report of his being in partnership with Russel especially as both their Accounts now generally turn out between £9 and 10 a hogshead. This made Grieg mad but I found he could only speak of a very few Sales of Mollison's where there were more. In short, I have too much reason to think amiss. However it is Solomon's advice, a soft answer yet awhile will be best.

I can borrow no Candles at Beverley's and if Thompson's purchase from Norfolk don't come up soon we must be contented to sit in the dark which I get by lending Candles myself. Mr. Carter of Corotoman had 2 boxes containing better than 5 gross. Mr. Parker had some dozen but these are Gentlemen who only think of favours when they want them.

The severe cold last night killed me one little young lamb. I must project another lamb house if I can to suit even these winters. I have discovered that little lambs when together will lie all of a heap and I know from the nature of a sheep an over warmth or pressure upon their loins kills them dead. Therefore, I shall in the first place project length enough a low building and width enough to have 2 divisions, one latticed with seperate cross divisions to contain a few lambs together and the outer one lathed like a shed for their dams to lie in and upon the South side a large yard for the day suckling and basking.

27. *Tuesday.*

As certainly bad weather after every fair day still as it has been through this year hitherto although yesterday from its smokyness I thought it would be otherwise. I am afraid we shall not get ready to plant Corn in any time. Our ground is so naturally stiff and has been made so heavy by this constant falling of moisture that my people can't do much but as to Dolman's gang compared with Mangorike they do nothing at all. I must join the hands together as soon as possible and every fellow that does not work as much as the Mangorike fellows and every woman as the Mangorike women shall be whipt to it.

Ball yesterday found some shelled Corn as well as eared Corn in Manuel's quarter with one of my bags. Thus has that rascal made good my suspicion either of not giving all the Corn he was allowed to the Oxen he drove to the horses or else has robbed me of Corn as he brought from Mangorike. I have contrived that he shall not fail of a good whipping. He pretends the bag Bart brought to him and he found the Corn amongst the shucks in the Tobacco house but this is a presumptive lie. I thought it to be impossible that those Creatures should look so poor when they had all along been so well fed.

Bart this day goes to work with his Gang, the first stroke he has stroke in the Crop from the beginning of November. If I should want more wood cut I shall put a worse hand about it.

This day we intended to have Bob Carter's little child baptized. By the whim of our Minister all Children must be christened in Church. I wrote to him yesterday that we should be there unless it was bad weather and asked if he could not, should it prove bad weather, perform that service at home as Mr. John Wormeley who is to be a Godfather was here and impatient to get down. His answer acknowledges he had done so for others but as he had gained nothing but censure in such compliances, imagining I hinted at them, he was determined in preserving in his resolution in baptizing no Children out of the Church. I gave no cause for this and am only convinced it is a full explanation. That this Gentleman rather makes a use of all instances relative to me [to] confirm his oddities in these things imagining that as others see he does them to me to whom they must reasonably conclude he lies under some obligation for the long time he lived here at free cost they will not solicit him to break through his obligations to others. But upon the whole I must say his pleading his oath to conform to the Canons not settled with the least view to the situation of [torn] Countries where the professors [of] Christianity must probably live at [Gr]eat distance from the Churches I [say th]is conformity is rather an excuse [torn] off for him to avoid to trouble [torn] the same conformity must [torn] man not to marry people but in churches. However as he is paid a fee there both for the license and even for marrying upon being asked in church he prefers going to houses where the fee expected is greater than allowed for a license and as to the asking fee by marrying them always at home he gets the money without the trouble of going abroad. Besides if they will go to the Canon that I believe directs the Baptism to be performed during divine service which by the by is never done and much in the mode of gratifying the aversion to trouble for it is easier after divine service is over to go to the font than to be walking backwards and forwards during divine service which I fancy my friend is not fond of for he goes as seldom to the Alta[r] in the church service as any Min[is]ter as I have ever been acquain[ted] with. However I impeach his [torn] fault. He has many good qu[alities] and I wish he had not this [torn].

28. *Wednesday.*

Yesterday a bad day. Colo. Lee and his Lady came and dined here. No Parson came this day. A wet fog till past 10. The horses not to be found. If they should be in time, the Child will be baptized for the day seems to intend fine at the latter part.

Tony began yesterday to nail my pails up.

Lost two Lambs more yesterday. It must be the house. Perhaps their urine, dung, or something must be the cause of it for these were young lambs very brisk at night when put into the house. Yesterday another lamb fell so that I have now but 49 when if all had lived and fared well I should have had near 70. I have 14 at the fork there and have lost but one.

31. *Saturday.*

I hope the weather is changing. The mornings are dewy and smokey though I think by the appearance of the moon we shall have wet weather this month yet. We are doing every thing to get ready for planting Corn and I hope by Easter which is the 14th of April we shall be about it every where. In some places sooner.

I understand from below many little Children have died with tumified throats. The swellings begin in the almons of the ears and if they are not immediately discussed they gather inwardly low down below the view of the eye where they frequently burst and there the matter choaks the Child. Little Martha's child from being at one time or another full of swellings all over its body at last about three weeks agoe fell into one of these. I only heard of it two days agoe, ordered the saffron and Camomile poultice and the uneasiness of the Child seemed to abate, but last night it broke inwardly and died. There's a Child of Johnny's taken in the same manner but Nassau says his will break outwards. If it does I am in hopes it will not be difficult to cure. He runs and plays about and perhaps may not mind it. I have known this disorder many years agoe when I lost several Children. Doctor Parker[32] then alive could only save a few.

[32] Probably Dr. Alexander Parker (1690–ca. 1760) of Essex Co.

I think my man Tony is determined to struggle whether he shall not do as he pleases. He has with McGinis been 2 days only pailing in the dairy and henhouse yard with the posts ready hewed and morticed for him. I told him when I rode out this morning he would certainly get another whipping. He was ranging the pales at least one pannel above another full a foot pretending the ground was uneven. I asked him if he could not pare the ground away. He stoopt down like falling but I imagined it was the Negroe's foolish way of hearing better. I rode out. When I came home the pales were all laid slanting. I asked him why he did that. He still laid the fault on the ground and as his left shoulder was to me I gave him one small rap upon it. He went to breakfast afterwards and no complaint. This evening I walked there and then he pretended he could not drive a nail, his arm was so sore. I made Nassau strip his Cloaths off and examined the whole arm. Not the least swelling upon it and every now and then he would tremble. I asked him if I hit him upon the legs he said his stroke was in his bone which made all his body ach. At last, looking full upon him, I discovered the Gentleman compleatly drunk. This I have suspected a great while. I then locked him up for monday morning's Chastisement for I cannot bear such a rascal. I thought this a truly religious fellow but have had occasion to think otherwise and that he is a hypocrite of the vilest kind. His first religion that broke out upon him was new light and I believe it is from some inculcated doctrine of those rascals that the slaves in this Colony are grown so much worse. It behoves every man therefore to take care of his own. At least I am determined to do what I can. Mine shall be brought to their [p]iety though with as little severity as [possible].

APRIL 1770

2. Monday.

Yesterday a very good beginning was soon changed into a very bad day but nothing like the night for we had at first Snow then hail then sleet and at last a very rainey night quite through till this morning when it began again to Snow which has already whitened the earth and if it continues it must be deep. Too bad weather for the poor planter who has been all this winter kept for [from] preparing his ground for the succeeding Crop for he ought very soon now to be planting his Corn when there is hardly anything done for it. Add to this his Creatures without food very little grass and too weak to range the wet woods for the buds of trees. I have been obliged to give over feeding with Corn except to the Chariot or Coach horses and a little to the poor suckling Ewes for the expence [of] this wint[er] has been [illegible] more than I have used in other years quite through.

The winter disorders among my people are again come about. I have 5 or 6 with pleuretic pains and full pulses a kind of inflammatory disorder joined with a bilious one with pains difficult to be removed except with blistering. Two days agoe a little Child died by means of the swelling of the almonds of its ears which burst inward and choaked him. I never heard of its illness till a week or 10 days after it had been taken and then the matter was formed too much to be discussed and had such a tendency to ripen within out of the sight of the eye that no art that we knew of could draw it to the skin. Otherwise possibly it might have been saved for by the methods we did use the Child was made easy and seemed as if recovering but in the night it broke and I suppose by means of a sleepy mother the Corruption choaked it. It had taken one vomit and I am vexed I did not give it another because the action of vomitting frequently breaks such tumours and throws up the matter but this was a very small infant and indeed from its birth full of gross humours, a kind of family tendency through that particular race of Negroes, The mothers seldom bringing a Child without one inflammation or another and the Children generally born or quickly running into foul tumours. I had one of them that lived out abundance of such tumours but at last when a young woman the grossness of her constitution collected in the spile of her back below the ribs where even the Surgeon's knife could not reach it though he very skillfully cut for it that broke inwards and by the greatness of its discharge killed that girl. Things of this kind have happened to every one of great Betty's breed and that old Jade herself has been saved only by a large Excrescence in the nature of a wen on her neck. However, there is a disorder of this kind raging down the Country that has killed many Children though I believe had it not unluckily seized this little foul infant or had I been made early acquainted with it I might have been more happy in my applications.

Gardner Johnny has a stout boy taken with it but as he is bright and runs about we are under no apprehensions about him.

Mr. Carter went up to a sweep stake race that was to be this day at Boyd's hole. Curious weather indeed for a planter lavish of his own health and regardless of his Cropping to be travelling about. I might also add a Burgess having the duty of his County as a Justice of the Peace for had this been a good day it is our Court day and every body must know how few courts have been held this year—but one, and that in March when Mr. Parker the Lawyer could not attend.

Perhaps in a future day it will not be much credited that after a winter perhaps the hardest that any person living can remember that there should on the 2nd day of April happen the severest day that we have felt this winter. I imagined that if the snow continued this morning it will be a deep one although it melted nearly as fast as it fell till about eleven but it has continued so constantly all day in spite of its melting that I believe every thing will be sufficiently covered to denote its depth and now at 6 o'clock it is snowing as hard as ever and from a Northerly and Northeast bank of clouds that seem almost inexhaustible. Indeed every rational Creature must see his duty to look up for the mercies of heaven for even under seemingly natural causes without that assistance such is the helpless situation of man upon earth that he is able to do nothing. Therefore the Lord pity us all. Hardly a mouthful for our Creatures and difficulty even to get fire for ourselves but I will not dispair for where a sincere belief and confidence in divine omnipotency solicits such blessings the religion I profess teaches me to know that all things needful will be granted unto us.

I must say a great many years ago I saw a deep snow on the 23rd of April with all the Creeks frozen over. I was then going with my first wife down to Mr. Charles Grymes's[33] and had many of the Mangorike gang to break Totuskey Creek with pestles before the Scony could carry us over and I desired old Miscal[34] the inspector there to record it upon his year book which I have since seen. I also remember some time in my second wife's days a covering of snow that whitened the houses and grass plats in the month of June that fell before day and vanished almost with the sun not comparable to this but only mentioned as to the time of the year when according to natural reason the prodigious warmth of the sun in this Climate we cannot easily expect snows. However as we often meet with hails in Summer and raining large spicular Ice perhaps those two bodies may have a similar generation in their phylosophy and the same quality in the air that produces hailstones or Ice may grannulate though in a lesser degree and feather impending rains into flecks of snow.

3. *Tuesday.*

The snow held till near day this morning. The Overseers tell me it is now up ankle deep notwithstanding it has been melting ever since it began to fall and in the thin places it is frozen. One young Calf last night lost its mother and there is a Cow of Dolman's somehow gored by the cattle attended with a probable death which are all the losses that I have yet heard of. However there

---

[33] Charles Grymes (d. 1743) of Marattico was a planter in Richmond Co. who married Francis, daughter of Edmund Jenings (1659–1727) of Ripon Hall.

[34] Probably John Miskell (d. 1744), Richmond Co. farmer.

is one that must be felt and may probably be a great one. We were in a fair way of planting our Corn by the 14th or 15th of this month but I fear that the going off of this Snow and the water that it will leave behind will carry us now a fortnight back. This delay carries also through the working of our Tobacco hills, will perhaps injure that Cropping. And I cannot help suspecting some injury to our fruit. We have had as yet no spring till about 3 days agoe when the Apricot trees began to bloom and to be sure such a coating of snow hardened into ice must destroy them and every thing else in the least forwardness but as it is all the work of heaven we must patiently submit to it.

The Bankes of snow are but retiring in the heaviness of Clouds to the Southward and perhaps we may be again visited too soon with some falling weather. Indeed by the appearance of the Moon when she changed I saw there would be great reason to dread a very wet month for she still lay quite on her back and I don't well remember a moon in that situation without very wet weather in some part of the month. I have somewhere attempted to account for it by her pressure upon the atmosphere which must be very great from a full weight of her diameter at least greater than from a part of that diameter which by her appearance we have the greatest reason to suppose and as the moisture of the earth is probably from the atmosphere preserved by the continual exhalation from the earth whenever the moon in her Changes makes these appearances we must reasonably expect wet weather but I know not whether this phylosophy is a true one. However it probably accounts for our experience of wet weather in such appearances.

4. *Wednesday.*

I think yesterday was full as cold as any we have had this year and a great reason there was for it. A sheet of snow upon the earth and one continually passing over us in the clouds driven by a very keen Northwester So that the water froze in our basons within doors and yet to show the power of the sun the yard was in puddles till he was declined too low to give his warmth. We have felt the effects of this weather in the death of Two Cows, a lamb, and one yearling and perhaps shall hear of some more for we have but little food and both the night and this morning have been and are extremely cold.

I am puzzled to think what can kill my lambs. I have lost 10 or 12 pretty large and that very lately. I fancied the house might injure them. Accordingly I gave them a range all day and a large yard to lie in but still they died. They have small homony beat fine besides fodder and the Ewes have been well feed with Corn and have been pastured about upon the hills and sometimes below where there is a green food to be pickt. I begin to think as our fodder was cheafly blown into stemms by the gust that these lambs have been hurt by eating those stemms which to be sure were not very digestible in tender stomachs or it is possible that this gust besides ribbing it may have given it some noxious quality. I have ordered the lamb that died yesterday to be opened as it was pretty large to discover if we can whether any of its food was amiss in its bowels. In short I don't know what to do but we must try till something shall do.

At the fork Quarter we have only lost one lamb and 3 little pigs which were eaten up at first but there is a Cow that has been sickly in the beginning of the year and unhappily got mired a fortnight agoe. She is still ill and may die. It is hardly worth while to think of the badness of this winter but it has exceeded any that I ever remember and as our Climate is thus changed I must wonder what succeeding years will do for firewood. We now have full 3/4 of the year in which we are obliged to keep constant fires; we must fence our ground in with rails build and repair our houses with timber and every cooking room must have its fire the year through. Add to this the natural death of trees and the violence of gusts that blows them down and I must think that in a few years the lower parts of this Country will be without firewood but pines have a quick growth and we must find out a way of burning them unless we shall be happy in discovering mines of coal. There are some such in the Country and perhaps time may discover more.

As yet I hear of no plants of mine that are come up. I had seed from many people and it is hard that all should be bad. Mr. Ball talks of his plants being up but as they are the only plants I have heard of I wish it may be any thing more than talk. By the By this is another effect of the gust. I turned out seed enough but my fences were so blown down that the Cattle whilst we were saving the Tobacco got in and cropt off all those heads that had stood the gust.

Nat tells me the Coach mare, Moll placket, brought a Colt on Sunday last. I think the Creature has had fine weather for her lying in.

5. *Thursday.*

Still very cold hard froze in the mornings. Snow in patches upon the [g]round and the earth too wet to work though worked it must be if we plant any Corn this year.

Two lambs more died last night. I had that which died yesterday examined within. The fodder it had eaten lay in sticky stemms from its stomach upwards into its throat and downwards into its bowels and the small homony quite dry in its maw without digestion. Poor Creatures, they can get no grass and the loss of my mill prevents their having meal which would otherwise assist their digestion. I have therefore ordered them no more fodder nor homony and have turned them with their Ewes to brouze for what they can get about the hills. There must be some unknown cause for this death of lambs. I have lost 14 or 15 here pretty well grown since the 20th of March, Mr. Giberne 29, and so it is said with other people all about. I did think the way I was in as it had turned out well for at least five year was the proper method of raising sheep but now I see how true that saying is that the race is not always to the swift nor the battle to the strong and I might ad[d] nor success to the man of rational care. However this may be in the system of ups and downs that governs in this unstable world and we must not from the least dispair give up our care.

This morning 5 hands out of Mangorike Crop came up sick—two of them I am perswaded mere lazyness and the boy Sam, Kit's son, because put to work with the people has taken himself off. The wench Nelly must be brought up to the house. I think she is far from being well though out at work. I wish that rascal Pantico, her husband, and his new comrade may not somehow have injured her. I understand he gave her beating before she was sick. I wish that may be the worst.

Lawson whom I sent to my plant patches yesterday told me they were coming up in every one but Mr. Ball insists they are not plants. He may be mistaken and I hope he is.

6. *Friday.*

This morning has once more a good appearance but I fancy I shall never have done hearing of my losses. Yesterday 2 more yearlings died, one at Mangorike, the other at Dolman's. I never took more care of these Creatures in my day. There were but 24 of them. They had from November 30 odd acres of pretty good rye to eat whilst it lasted, were constantly housed in the Tobacco, fed with homony, Corn shucks and fodder till within these few days, but a Calf is such a creature that if he does not lie out he will get lousy and if he does he perishes which was an odd dilemma for this bad winter. However neither my Overseers nor myself thought of lice before they were too far gone. Otherwise by washing with ambur they are always killed and the Creatures live.

Robin came home yesterday. Volunteer beaten and of course all the money lost.

Colonel Harrison's weaver run away and Judy's Cotton is to come down without weaving after being there near 12 months. Thus weavers out of one's own family will never encourage the least manufactory and I do think it is intirely owing to this that more people do not make a better hand of it. Molleson was to have sent me one but I am afraid every friend of his as well as himself have talked too much of his earnest inclinations to serve his Correspondents.

7. *Saturday.*

We still have not any spring warmth in our mornings occasioned perhaps by the excessive wetness of the year hitherto, for as the moisture the earth is continually giving up condense after the sun has left us it must hang in a cold heavy atmosphere until the sun shall come again to rarifye it for an easy fluidation or dispersion.

I heard of no dead lambs of my own yesterday but my Son brought word from Totuskey bridge of the loss of whole stocks of lambs constantly fed with fodder and homony and the Sheep with Corn besides Salt as often as it could be thought to be wanted which I am apprehensive in such a prodigious moist year [as] this should have been at least once more per week than my usual custom which has been but twice for yesterday I saw my Ewes that have not yeaned greedily picking the earth where they have Salted and all the houses where Salt had been scattered. For my part I have forbid all feeding of either Ewes or lambs excepting the giving them frequently of Salt in hopes that this may prevent their deaths.

It seems Mr. Dolman has lost one of his young calves pretending the Cow came up without it but I suppose I shall find that Calf somewhere mired for it was a fortnight old. This fellow is too great a Rascal to live with me. He took care of his Creatures last year and lost none but this year he has made up for it by no care at all.

4 Goslings brought out this day for the first time this year. Hatched 4 days agoe. Notwithstanding the severe weather every egg brought its Gosling.

10. *Tuesday.*

We were deluged with rain from Sunday evening till yesterday and then excessive cold. It obliged my people to go to work in the Riverside field where the ground is not quite so stiff, but I had hardly any people to work yesterday. Sick persons, Cow keepers, bread bakers and markets took up ten hands and as fast as one gets well another is laid up with every kind of disorder—Maggots, worms, bilious intermittants, inflammatory fevers and watery purgings.

The Cattle likewise have by means of this wet weather a new complaint added to their poverty: a Rheum distilling from their eyes hardens into a horny scales called the hooks. One died yesterd[ay] one last night and 4 more ill with it, so that I wish this year may not be too fatal even to carry on the business of Cropping or even life. I have set to try to cut this horn out of the eyes. Lawson says he has done it at his father's.

Ball set off yesterday to take a full view of Rippon Hall for the genteel Mr. Thomas Lawson by a nack of lying pays no regard to his words, engagements, or bonds and, I am almost convinced, not to his actions. There is a public story now of his carrying my Cows and Calves to his wife's mother's and his own maintaining all his people out of my mill Corn.

12. *Thursday.*

I hope in God we shall now be blessed with what we call spring weather from our expereince in life for as yet really during this whole '70 we have had nothing but the severest and worst of winters and by plain observation the spring is full 6 weeks more backward than it was last year. Severe weather indeed in all its effects. Out of Dolman's stock I shall by night have lost of Cattle young and old 12 head. Out of Mr. Lawson's stock with the two now appear to be dying 15 head, Of lambs 18 and at my fork Quarter but one old Cow and 1 motherless lamb. I discover an error I have been guilty of in not carrying all my Calves and yearlings as soon as the winter set in to be taken care of at the fork. I did it 2 year agoe as that soil is dry and really a better chance for winter food and there I succeeded well but last year William Tutt behaved so scandalously that being obliged to part with him I was in doubt which of my Negroes I could put there with care and honesty enough to preserve and feed these Creatures. However if George continues as he has behaved it will be to my advantage to have a convenient house for all my yearlings and also for all my lambs and by putting a woman under his particular management to help him I may effect a great thing for although we have lost some Cows the most of this 27 head have been 2 years old and yearlings which can only be owing to the excessive wetness of this plantation and so I think with respect to the lambs, for their food has not differed from ours and yet I have lost none there, Although I am now convinced that this fellow Johnny is too damned a rogue to be trusted with any kind of care and so are all his family bred under him. A stout Girl of his put to attend the Ewes and lambs this day carried all the Ewes to the old field convenient to a bottom where she could have a fire and sleep and coming home from the fork I found a little lamb asleep upon the bank of the ditch and all the Ewes 3/4 of a mile from her. I sent Nassau to hunt for her but he could not find her whilst I staid.

I rode yesterday to see Colo. Lee at Colo. Tayloe's through my fork Quarter and so along by Colo. Tayloe's old plantation. I came by Garland and the Overseer where 3 Carts were carrying out the last year's dung which I think was hardly more rotton than mine is of this year and to be sure must have less salt in it as they have had a whole year to evaporate. The fault was this. All fermantation which produces rottenness must have one certain moisture and any thing below or above that degree will prevent it. Now when they heap their dung they raise it to 5 or 6 feet high. This setting down makes the lower stratum extremely solid. Of course there is very little rotteness below 3 foot from the top. They were carrying this dung out pretending in their usual method every load to 12 hills square but I am certain the heaps could not be nearer than 25 or 30 yards in the rows and perhaps rows of 40 feet wide. This is the reason that upon one of the best pieces of land probably in the Country for Cropping the Colonel seldom makes near so much as I upon one of the most difficult clayey soils that is. This last year he has but prized 12 hogsheads and I have made 24 hogsheads and more Carts and plows I never saw upon any plantation in my life, 5 plows checking off his Corn field and 4 Carts carrying out his dung, very few Tobacco hills made and no Corn ground hoed but large wide lists to be broke up with the plows.

I think that estate is an instance in proof of what I have ever advanced and have always practiced up to: Carts and plows only serve to make Overseers and people extremely lazy and it is a certain truth that wherever they are in great abundance there is the least plantation work done there for both Overseers and Negroes imagine this or that work will be quickly done with the plows and Carts and of course are very little solicitous to do their proper parts of the business and when the plowmen and Carters see that others don't work it must be next to an impossibility to think that they will work till in the end every thing is to do and of course every thing must be slubbered and harried over which is no proper mode to advance the vegetation of the soil. Again in order to effect these bad crops they proceed in a very indifferent way. Instead of half a peck which should be the manure of a Tobacco hill they put in a little handful in the step between the hills this being long and not rotten. When they turn the hills upon it and cut them off there is hardly a finger's depth above the long dung and every body knows a plant is or nearly ought to be put in that depth. Of course the young fibres of their roots are immediately to shoot in this dung which I believe is an absurdity in the doctrine of vegetation. I talked to Colonel Lee as well as I had done with Garland upon these points. Lee was perfectly satisfied of the disservice introduced by Carts and plows and really the impossibility of their doing any service by their being late worked for as to his own plantation where he is building and intended to make use of his hands to assist his building. He intirely laid aside all thoughts of a Crop of Tobacco and imagined to be sure he should be vastly forward in getting his Corn into the ground but he declares he knows no one so backward where they have not a Cart or plow so that the lazyness introduced by it must needs be evident And then told me a story of his brother Phill.[35] He had one Pritchard for his Overseer who without Carts or plows always made large fine Crops of Corn and Tobacco. Colo. Phill imagining that more might be made with Carts and plows with no small expence provided them in abundance but Pritchard upon one year's tryal being satisfied that his people had laid aside their diligence in working resolved that unless his Master [took] his Carts and plows away resolved not to live with him and never since has that plantation afforded a good Crop. The Colo. has now taken to his hoes again and is satisfied he is in a good way for a Crop.

I almost wish I had not thought of dunging my other fork Corn field for as it must be done well I do not think by the distance the dung lies off the people can finish it before Saturday and 7 days is too much time to be employed now in preparing for planting. However to compensate this I will soak my Corn in warm water and as the hills will be warmed by this dung I am in hopes I shall lose nothing in the main.

13. *Friday.*

Fine weather indeed and I hope in God it will continue but I think it is rather too windy for stiff land that has been made so extremely wet. It must quickly bake it very hard. However, by tomorrow night at farthest I hope we shall have got all our Cornfields compleatly hoed, Those that are stiff quite hilled and ready for holing and planting on monday. The light land as it is all hoed may be all hilled and holed in one.

I fancy the fork people will have finished dunging by this night or tomorrow very early. Therefore I have ordered Corn to be put in soak this day at 12 o'clock that we may hole and plant tomorrow. There is one Calf there and another Cow ready to calve. Dolman's two Cattle that were taken blind died last night, although yesterday the Cow eat Corn very heartily. Her case seems to have been poverty joined with her blind disorder. Out of Lawson's 4 that were sick Sukey thinks 3 are getting about and 2 of them are feeding with the Cattle but the gored steer Nassau thinks will die. We heard of that accident

---

[35] Philip Ludwell Lee (1727–75) of Stratford in Westmoreland Co. was a lawyer and planter. The eldest son of Thomas Lee (1690–1750) and Hannah Ludwell, he was a member of the Council, 1757–75.

at least 3 months after it happened and there is a cyst of matter which I suppose has corrupted his gutts. To open that must let them out and I fancy he has not strength to digest it off.

I must repeat it that I never saw such a spring in my life. Even at this day there is hardly a bud to be seen in the woods any thing swelled but the sweat Gum and not a spire of green stuff of any sort to be seen in the marshes excepting a few flaggs which is a sight I never saw before for early in this month I have for many years past been solicited by the forresters to let them put their poor horses upon Mangorike marsh.

Robin Smith the younger some weeks agoe was seen by Williamson Ball, Walker Tomlinson[36] and others feeding his hogs upon my land by my meadow and as they then told him it would teach those hogs to get into the meadow it has accordingly happened for by means of Dolman's not going there so constantly as he should they have rooted up a very large and very fine plant patch. Will Lawson says the beds that did escape are the finest growing plants that he has seen. I have rectified the beds and sowed them again this day with Goores' seed. Dolman has spent several days in repairing the V fence but hogs can always root under and so it has been with these devils. I believe Dolman will not steal and I have employed him this second year in hopes to make him a good Overseer but I fear his want of diligence will prevent me. I cannot spirit him up to make his people work and it is now evident that with the Mangorike Gang playing before them their lazy sweat is pouring out. It is vain to think of any care in the man that is not diligent and has not life to make others so.

14. *Saturday.*

Yesterday a very sharp wind from Southwest, West and to Northwest. The whole air filled with a cloud of dust after that some thunder and lightning for a few hours with little sprinklings of rain first from one quarter then another. This morning a very damp thick fogg.

For Wednesday and Thursday we were quite clear in our hospital not one sick person in it, a circumstance that has not happened for near 6 months before and yet I thank God not a loss but an infant of a few months old mentioned before. The disorders have been every one of them inflammatory at first then bilious and frequently attended with worms. The pulses always denoted where bleeding has been necessary. Rattle snake root has proved a sovereign attenuent and great expectorant and there hardly has been a case wherein sooner or later an emetic has not been necessary and in some of them

---

[36] Walker Tomlinson was a resident of Richmond Co. and probably a farmer.

the bile has been so acrid that without attemperation it has not been easily removed but has been attended with sharp located pains. But blisters on the parts Rhubarb soup and alkalized mercury have even relieved these. Yesterday 2 patients came up after a long spell before attended with this acrid bile. Vomits relieved one but the other from whom many maggots have been drawn by mercury has got into an intermittant which the same doses of Rhubarb must be administered for and then probably a little bark.

We have at last catched this infamous jade, Manuel's Sarah, who has been out now a full week yesterday. She at first pretended to be sick but having no discoverable complaint was sent out to her work, run away and not heard of till a robbery for meal. Yesterday in the evening Lawson observed her going to her Lodging and by a fair run catched her. She pretends to be big with Child and perhaps may be so. I had her corrected and intended to lock her up till I could sell her. She begs hard and is turned out to work.

Notwithstanding the moist fogg and indeed a bad cold by cloaking wrapping and muffling myself up I went to the fork Quarter where my people having finished dunging their corn field yesterday were making holes to plant corn and had according to my directions put near a bushel to soak into warm water at 12 yesterday.

18. *Wednesday.*

Yesterday a very fine day indeed till near sunset a North Easterly wind springing up beclouded us much and blew very hollow all night. It continues cloudy as if preparing for rain.

Made a very good beginning in planting Corn at Mangorike yesterday. The fork I expect near half done by breakfast time this day.

By a letter from Dick Edwards of the 16th they have not begun there. There crops of Corn for 1767, '68 and '69 most scandalously mean indeed for near 40 hands but 288 barrels last year and never 300 in one of the years and yet by Mr. Carter's account of Corotoman and my son's chattering I am always told of great management there. To be sure Dick Edwards must give them the information. There are but 13 hogsheads of Tobacco there and were but 20 last year when mine was 30,000 in 1769 and now 24 hogsheads notwithstanding the gust. I will venture my life there is not either a Crop of Corn or Tobacco tended there. Longwith like Davis here has had those plantations too long for the common honesty of the world to do any thing upon them. I have actually used in my family at home already more Corn from Mangorike alone than those 40 hands made me in any of the 3 years.

Mr. Ball came from Rippon Hall on monday last. His accounts from there are as wretched as can be. Almost every plantation work still to do and so far from planting Corn that there was near a mile of fencing to be got in place. The whole Crop of Corn used up but about 8 barrels and all the Mill earnings. No tollerable account either of the expences or of the sales of one thing last year or this above 40 head of Cattle though only 8 have died different from what were there when Lawson went there notwithstanding the increase of 20 Calves last year. A pretended Account made up by Lawson of his sales last year with a very trifle of butter but a little pork sold and only a few beeves and a most extravagant Smith's account charged to me without any bill or receipt as a voucher and even my own transfer Tobacco in payment of my levies charged to me. In short a greater rascal cannot be produced upon earth than this Mr. Thos. Lawson. I know not what to do about my this [year's] levies. Ball shall go there and turn him off the plantation and Davy Goldsby is hired for £8 till Christmas next constantly to attend the people.

Mr. Carter's mare, the Queen of the May, was walked up yesterday expected to be with foal ready to foal but I am certain she will bring none this year. To be sure these Chickins were reckoned before they were hatched, a usual hunt of that worthy Gentleman's whenever I promise myself with any pleasing expectation.

Last night a Cow constantly fed for the sake of Milk this whole winter and really extremely fat taken with the blind staggers. She was blooded and dosed with a large draught, to wit, my little red slop bowl of rattle snake root decoction, and looks lively this morning and eats Corn heartily.

19. *Thursday.*

A fine day again. God be praised! Yesterday really very cool. The flye eats in my home plant patch but no where else. Some how they never burn that patch right.

Planting Corn away apace. George at the fork pretty far advanced in the 3rd Quarter of his Crop. His first planted Corn near upon coming up the roots but little short of an inch long. This Corn put into the ground last Saturday, the 14th, soaked first in warm water from 12 on friday to Saturday morning.

Dolman destroyed a Crow's nest this morning with 4 young ones whose heads are saved for Northumberland where we are to be taxed for Crows and squirrels heads every titheable. I have promised my people half a pound of meat for every 6 Crows heads which they will catch on sunday next as they are now so easily to be taken in the nest. I wish I had an opportunity of writing to my Northumberland plantations to get this done. I am sure the hands there would amongst those pines catch a great many now they are so young.

The Nohorn Cow taken 2 days agoe with the blind staggers they tell me has now got pretty well and feeds about as usual. I had her at first blooded then gave her of rattle snake root decoction in warm small beer a good dose, although [she] is with Calf, and yesterday gave her 2 more doses of the same, to wit, my red slop bason full, so that rattle snake root after a proper evacuation by bleeding that has not that bad effect upon brute creatures big with young as I have been apprehensive it would have upon women with Child. I gave it upon a full perswasion that this disorder in the Cattle was somehow occasioned by a thick visid blood perhaps made acrid by an ill temperated bile.

Ordered Cucumbers to be sown this day. The home Carrots sowned in my wattle plant patch come up.

21. *Saturday*.

I find we work by our eyes faster than we do by our hoes for Lawson was to have finished planting the Corn on the left side of the road to the fork yesterday early but he has not finished it today.

I lost a yearling yesterday, a Cow last night, and it seems the Nohorn Cow is again very bad. I am puzzled for the cause of this. They get their bellies now pretty full of green food and are not much purged with it. It must certainly be some noxious vapour rising out of this wet soil for I lose none at the fork where the land is sandy and dry.

From Friday last to last night Guy, Toney, McGinis, Jimmy, and two boys have been getting pales of Chessnut. Two of them only have been sawing. The rest getting stocks and they have only got 317 five foot poles 4 inches wide.

McGinis went yesterday to fixing a tongue and Ax tree for a pair of Cart wheels that are to go to Rippon Hall. He is then to fix up a horse tumbril which I am to send there.

We have been much alarmed in this house about a Jail disorder brought into the Neighbourhood by Colo. Frank Lee's servant bought of Somervill. The man has never been ill himself but only weak with imprisonment and a hard faring sea voyage. However every death that has happened in the neighbourhood has been imputed to that cause and many more that have not had it have been raised to strengthen the report from the frights and apprehensions of the women greatly cultivated by Bob Carter who brought one foolish story or another every time he went out and would not let me reason either to show the inconsistency or falsehood. I sent to Colo. Frank Lee and it is all turned out a lie. There have been a few deaths but those owing to causes of another nature.

22. *Sunday*.

A very fine day God be praised.

I repeated yesterday the rattle snake root to this No horn Cow. We have again got her about to walk, feed, dung, and stale and I am endeavouring by bran and sulphur to deturge and Cleanse her bowels, giving a dose of rattle snake root every night for it must certainly be some vicid or coagulating state in her blood.

I got Mr. Ball to measure the pease left behind and instead of five bushels which he measured after the New England man had his quantity There is now but 3 half bushels besides the peck sent to Mrs. Wormeley and as there has been none used five pecks must have been carried off. Owen, from being an ingrained villain as well as a noted lyar by his rascally lies, rendered himself suspected for he swore the door had never been opened whilst Ball was away. However the door must necessarily be open every day to get the taylings out to feed the pidgions. Thus does the liar and the thief constantly unite in one man and often to the prejudice of the thief for had not an accident discovered the possibility of others taking these pease Mr. Owen must have been had before a Magistrate for flogging and all upon account of this devilish lie. It seems the key of that door has been frequently left in the wheat house and whilst some of the people were shelling the corn for use they have probably taken them out from time to time for Tom Mooter, a shell[er], was once catched with a wallet full of them and was made to carry them back. There was a fault in leaving that key there. It used to be locked up in my desk. Ball neglected it when he went away and Owen continued that neglect but it shall be so no more for although Mr. Owen by the circumstance of Mooter may be innocent I know him so disposed to lying that I cannot help imagining he that pays no regard to his word will never regard his actions. It is a prodigious pity. This fellow is capable of getting a plentiful and comfortable livelihood as any man upon earth and could he be honest he would be worth old gold to the Gentleman that should employ him. Half the honesty of Will Ball would make him valuable to me but this he cannot be.

24. *Tuesday.*

No rain since the 18th and then only sprinklings. However It has lightened pretty much from the Southward to the westward and thundered in the night. They tell me it also sprinkled.

Mr. Owen begins again some of his roguish care. I had every thing Counted yesterday by Will Lawson in Owen's presence both in the wheat house and in the store that is moveable which that fellow shall answer for now without the least excuse and to no other place will I trust him. Nay, I will make his going to any other place a crime.

Upon my riding out this day I found that the Corn which I had planted in

Mangorike upon the light ground had also began to appear above the earth and this without soaking So that I am apt to believe the earth is warmer than we imagine it to be.

Ordered Kit this day to begin getting bark for his leather. It seems there are 49 hides of one sort or another. Of these a few above 30 are the deaths I have sustained, a mere stock of Cattle indeed but unless I could give up the advantage of making winter's dung I cannot see how it can be avoided in any severe winter upon low st[iff] land so loaded with water as mine has been this year, although if I could be happy in an honest man to [illegible] my Oxen I might accomodate even this point. For I am well satisfied by the success I have met with at the fork where I have lost but one Creature that I might by winter cowpenns there upon such a dry soil as it is avoid all the inconveniency of this wet soil, but then I shall have the trouble of getting my fodder there from Mangorike besides the inconveniency of removing the dung in the spring. Perhaps between this and next year, please God I live, I may fall upon some method of remedying this evil for it is a prodigious great one to lose more cattle in one year than there is a chance for raising.

25. *Wednesday.*

Cloudy but dry and with too cool a wind. Plant patches must certainly be paid off with the fly especially those who have uncovered and wed. But this is none of my practice. Before the plants have g[one] cleverly [out] of the way of the fly, that is, have [gr]own too large for them to eat and have taken a good hold of the ground with their roots to grow out a little bite and not mind it, which is seldom the case in any year by this time in April but more particularly this year when our spring has been at least a month backwarder than usual for I hold to these rational principle[s]:

1st. Insects though they may be delighted with one species of plant must nevertheless be intended in their formation to feed upon what they can get and the wisdom of Creation never could have fixt them in that land at all where this particular favorite food had not been in vegetation.

2ndly. I have discovered that these flies eat of every wild vegetable more or less except lettice and poppies which I suppose instinct may have instructed them to be too noxious and I have also discovered in a plant patch green with all sorts of vegetables as well as plants they have eaten the finest plants. For these reasons [I] have thought plants have only been devoured by the flies when no other kind of food has been left for them. Therefore I never force them through the necessity of removing all other weeds to eat my plants.

Again where plants have not got a good hold of the ground to uncover and weed them is certainly to expose them to the weather that may happen which if a hot sun must destroy them and if a dry windy day must wither them and all this if even you should cover again immediately for then you take away the shade of the weeds which are a preservative in every instance of experience to the tender state of every plant.

Yesterday we finished in the afternoon the planting the Mangorike Corn-field with Corn and Wm. Lawson tell me it took by the fairest measurement in the world 21 bushels and that Dolman and he particularly watched that none should be made away with.

Allowing this to be the case 21 bushels at 800 grains to the pint carefully counted must contain 1,075,200 which at 3 grains in each hill are 3,58.400 hills. Now as 7 foot and 2 will plant in every acre 3,111 hills, it must follow from this quantity of Corn planted that this ground contained within 10 hills by the planting 115¼ acres.

To prove the people were pretty honest in not making away with this Corn I counted their first day's work when they had planted 10 pecks of Corn to about a pottle and that day's work was better than 40,000 hills planted and according to the above account 42,666 hills must be planted by 10 pecks at 3 grains to a hill.

I imagined always that this field had been mistaken in its first survey for that it evidently looked larger than the other divisions and they were made 87 acres so that in all probability this field may be about 30 acres more but this I can try.

From this imagination I resolved to give Dolman his Crop of Corn in the Mangorike and river side fields and therefore have tended none other for him but I shall see the quantity of the hills in the Riverside field which I began to plant yesterday evening.

We finished yesterday planting the fork Corn. It has taken 11½ bushels to compleat those 4 fields equal to 46 pecks which contain 588,800 grains which at 3 grains to a hill is 196,266 hills. But each of these fields being by measurement 18 acres and each Acre at 7 foot and 2 containing 3,111 hills these 4 fields would contain 223,992 hills. Therefore the people must have failed to drop 3 grains every where. Otherwise the Corn used would have been more for only the Cotton patch, the Tobacco house negroe Quarters, and late Overseer's house are not planted with Corn. Upon the whole we may well reckon these 4 fields at 200,000 hills good.

We are planting the river side field and was I to be with my people I should finish it tomorrow for we have really made the ground light by our working though it has been late.

Mr. Archibald Ritchie came here [to pay] his long pretended visit of respect though his attachment to gain could not help informing me that he came to settle that disputed balance about the difference in Exchange between receiving my bill on the 25 of April 1766 which paid off his account then and his selling that bill for £4.15.4¼ less. I told him I should settle nothing about it. It was unjust and I would not pay it. He offered to settle it by arbitration. I refused that because few Gentlemen now adays care to engage as they may be privately interested either by their dealings with him or affection to me. He told me I would not like my Character called in question by a petition for a trifle. I replied it would give me no concern for as a trifle it could not affect my disposition to justice. A suit would only prove how much I was convinced that his demand was unjust. He offered to refer it to me whether I did not agree when that bill was drawn I would allow the difference. I then solemnly declared that I did not. I might, as it was before the Court settled the Exchange, say that if they settled it at less than 30 per Cent I would allow the difference as I do in many instances where people are in a hurry for their money before that time, but it would neither have been prudent nor indeed consistent with the mode of doing such business which the law had fixt the trade in. I asked him why he did not let me know of this difference of exchange before such a prodigious length of time as 2 years and 2 days had elapsed and that he ought to have returned the bill as he did one sometime before drawn at 40 per Cent which he wanted to get at 37½. He said he would if I had been in Town. To which I replied if he had done that I should have got 30 for my bill for it is easy to be proved that some bills sold at 30 in April 1766 though when kept by artfull managers who wanted to get more till the month of July they fell to 25 per Cent which was his case. I asked him to dine with me but he was going to Mount Airy and imagining his proposal of an arbitration was with a view to discolouring my dispositions only to be satisfied with a suit I wrote to him if he could satisfye by any other proof than his own say so that even within that 2 year and two days he had given me notice of this difference in Exchange I would pay him the money and, as justice and the course of Trade must determine, that he ought to have returned my bill rather than sell it for less. To be sure my allowing him such a length of time was giving him all the opportunity possible to complexionate his claim if he could.

26. *Thursday.*

A frost this morning with an exceeding cool drying wind which cannot fail of being curious weather for the laborio[us] planter especially on a stiff soil that has been almost mud from early in January to the middle of this month. I have made a shift by more labour than ever I used in my life and by being sixteen days later to get my work in order for my Corn that is planted in it which will be all done this day and the spelt wheat drilled up at the river side. Tomorrow, please God, every bit of my Corn field fences shall be compleatly righted. On Saturday the people shall have a holiday to draw the Seine, if the Overseer can get one, to plant their potatoes, or what they please.

At the fork they will plant me a bushel of beans in every other Corn hill before the quarter that they may be protected against thieves of which I must have abundance or I could not have so many pease and beans stolen from me every year. Tomorrow they will get their flax ground rehoed in order for sowing which Talbot must do. I have rakes made on purpose and have ordered George to send for them. This night we will have the [gr]ound first fine raked then sowed and [ra]ked again.

Mr. Manuel has at last compleated every scheme that he might have in hand to ruin me. Before this winter came in I was possessed of 8 oxen, 4 of them well used to the draft and 4 newly broke. In a little time he contrived that 3 of them should mire and die only because he would not see 4 of them when spelled drove to the fork to be rested along the road over the dam but suffered a rascally boy to drive them over the marsh where they mired. The other he contrived to lame. I constantly allowed 2 bushels of ears besides fodder to feed those 4 that were worked every day they did work and I am certain from the honesty of Ball they had this food. But now, as they were but 4 to work, two horses were allowed to go before them that I might spell them two and two. For my horses I constantly gave half a bushel of shelled Corn every day they worked. In a little time Manuel consigned two of those horses to death and so he has continued behaving till last week when I wanted to Cart out my dung I had neither horses nor Oxen to carry a loa[d]. He proposed breaking 2 more. I gave him leave on Friday. Now although his wife was the Cowkeeper he never troubled himself to direct her to keep them up in the penn and on Saturday morning came so late from his night revellings they were turned out. He took me two hands half the day but could not get them up. On monday with the same two hands and another he yoked a pair and was tuesday, and wednesday all day walking them about as he pretended and this day he turned one of them out. It did nothing but lie down and when I saw the other in a yoke with one of the old Oxen, that creature he pretended was so sullen, it would not draw. This is too much to bear. However I kept my temper and resolved to sell Mr. Manuel. He was once a valuable fellow, the best plowman and mower I ever saw. But like the breed of him he took to drinking and whoring till at last he was obliged to steal and robbed my store of near half the shirts and shifts for my people besides other things. For this I prosecuted him and got him pardoned with a halter round his neck at the gallows. For a while it had some good effect but returning to his night walking he turned thief as before killed beef which was found upon him but no proof of the property to be had. He again escaped. Since then by means of the same practices he has killed me 20 or 30 horses and as many draught oxen. He sleeps now at night and must do it in the day and to make up his work by one barbarity or another he has as certainly killed these Creatures as ever he has been concerned with them and now I will part with him.

Gardner Johnny was so pleased in being turned to the hoe that he came this morning at day break to tell me he was going and the rascal took his row next to hindmost man in my field. But to show him I did not intend the hoe to be his field of diversion I gave him the place of my fourth man and have ordered my overseers to keep him to that. I observed it made him quicken the motion of his arm which up here used to be one, two, in the time of a soldier's parade. I am necessarily obliged to put postilion Tom into the garden but I have him to learn. However I cannot be worse off than with Johnny for with him I have not for some years got anything in my garden and hardly ever a piece of work done like a workman who has been at least 20 year a gardner. His perpetual pleasure is to be always stupidly drunk and right hand man to young Robin Smith who has sold him every thing even to my plows for the sake of his throat and in this stupid state has he for many years neglected to do me the least pennyworth of service. I have therefore thought it time to remove him to where he may be made to work or else I will sell him also for a greater villain cannot live. Notwithstanding this, out of opposition to my real experience and Robin's knowledge of them, he would willingly buy them but he has already if he would look into them people who by idleness and villany turn out as trifling a penny as ever such a number of slaves did in the world and if he had a house to keep they must be sold to provide for it in two year at the most. It is the same at all my out plantations. Although I have many to work and fine land to be tended, I hardly make more than what cloaths them, finds them tools, and pays their Levies. Perhaps a few scrawney hogs may be got in the year to be fattened up here. If these things do not require the greatest caution and frugality in living I am certain nothing can do.

Sir Marmaduke Beckwith came here, a Gentleman of great age but with a declining look though in chearful spirits. It seems Moore Bragg[37] had purchased a Piece of land of Jesse Thornton,[38] part of which Sir Marmaduke

---

[37] Moore Bragg (d. 1792) was a resident of Richmond Co. and probably a farmer.
[38] Jesse Thornton (d. 1779) lived in Richmond Co. and was probably a small planter.

fancied to be his and, although Bragg had got it in tending and sown with
Oats, the Knight without any legall proofs ordered some of his slaves first to
chop a line along that part which he fancied his, then to ditch it. Bragg in
support of his possession ordered the people away without any kind of violence
and filled up the ditch which they had dug. I suppose they inflamed their
master with many idle stories for they came again and insulted Bragg very
frequently up to his house. Upon which he got a warrant from me rather than
carve his own preservation of the peace, and the Knight came here to justifye
his slav[es and] Brought papers to prove his right to the land. I could not
help telling him that as a Magistrate it was neither my business nor power to
determine the disputed bound but as a Magistrate I was to preserve the King's
peace and as it was evidently infringed I was sorry to see those ignorant
creatures pushed on to such behaviour by a Gentleman who must know that
the law in preservation of the peace of the Community had directed other
methods for his recovering his right. But he would not distinguish between a
man's coming to dispossess him of his own possession and his going to dispossess the man by violence. In the first case he would have had a right to resist
force by force, but in the second case the law would allow no force but would
imploye every attempt not legally pursued a violence in him to dispossess
another. Therefore out of compassion to these Slaves I only ordered them 15
lashes apiece. I am sorry to say that from my first acquaintance with this old
Gentleman to this moment there is the same tendency in his disposition. He
smiles even in the bitterness of his resentment and whilst he seems most
pleased he is most earnest in calculating revenge for he wanted me to give an
escape warrant against Jesse Thornton, one of the evidence in the half of
Bragg, who 2 year agoe had broke jail upon an Execution obtained by his Son
Duke Beckwith.[39] I begged of him not to be so warm. He laughed and smiled
but was still resolute. I told him upon the oath of the Officer I was ready to
grant that warrant but the Sherif said he was sure the Jailer had taken out one
if he had not he himself would apply in a few days for one. The Knight in
order to discover himself wanted a warrant against Bragg for stealing his two
spades which these ditchers had left there and informed him Bragg had taken
with great friendship. I advised him against such a measure, but he was
resolved to pursue it and told me he would get some other Magistrate and
make this Thornton and Will Bragg, the other evidence, evidences who must
forswear themselves if they would not own they saw moore Bragg take the
spades. I told him, if they should, Moore was the Criminal and, if they should

[39] Marmaduke Beckwith (d. 1790) was a Richmond Co. planter and justice of the peace.

not, Moore would be relieved in great damages by a civil prosecution for false imprisonment and a vexatious [lawsuit].

27. *Friday.*

I fear I shall be again as unlucky as I was in the year 1757. A Cold April then brought in such swarms of flies to our plant patches that they eat me up as they did almost every body else without the least chance of a crop. There were some lucky ones then that escaped them and no doubt there will be some now but luck is very bad for a man only to crop upon. There should be some reason to govern what he does and I am mistaken if they have made use of any. But no doubt we shall hear of prodigious management should this happen to be the case. However Will Lawson tells me there are still a great plenty left and it is possible if the weather turns warm as it seems to be growing and a little moist that these flies will leave us. Notwithstanding I have soaked a good quantity of seed for sowing another large patch tomorrow morning. I do remember that both last year and the year before I sowed patches so late as the 11th day of May and by constantly watering them night and morning with water impregnated with hen dung I made large plantings out of them in June and it may be so again. I think my fork Corn is coming up very prettily and as yet few birds have disturbed it. I am getting ready my flax ground for sowing there and should put the seed in the earth tomorrow but I have agreed to let my people have it for a holiday. I shall then put in my hemp and after that run over the fencing into hoing the lists of my Corn field immediately.

I intended this day to right up all my fencing at Mangorike, having yesterday finished planting there but I thought my winter grain, to wit, spelt, barley, and wheat, wanted a good hoe dressing and have accordingly set all my hands about that. Between my river side spelt I have sowed a drill of Carrots. Between my barley, as the rows are 6 foot wide and the barley will come off in June, I put a row of Tobacco plants. Between the wheat rows at the same distance I put a row of pea hills. The barley would have been a good Crop but for some places where the winter has killed it and many ugly tresspasses about which the Overseers have been negligent and I fancy the same of the wheat. The spelt now florishes and after this dressing I will hope all will grow.

30. *Monday.*

On Saturday last my daughter Beverley came here. It was a fine morning till about an hour before she got here when it began to blow very fresh and very cool at the Northern and so it has continued ever since. Yesterday so cold at Church that it was really doubtful whether it would not snow and last night extremely so and must have been a frost.

It's needless to repeat what a dangerous situation of our plants must be in as to the fly. Billy Lawson but on friday had gone round all my plant patches and though the plants were but thin in most places yet he was satisfied I should have a great plenty for my Crop and in particular in this meadow patch he saw those which had been sown since the rooting of the hogs thick and well come up and in the other beds though thin and really much eaten there were many as big as pistereens.

My Son with young Billy Beale[40] went to that patch on Saturday evening. The walk there and back again took them up better than hour and therefore they must be presumed to have looked with some care and excepting the young plants just come up and that very thin he could not see a plant of any sort. This made me put in a quantity of seed to steep in a solution of Saltpetre water which I took out yesterday and put to drain in a Cullender and laid thin for sowing this morning. And I have set Billy Lawson with a few hands to take off that covering, pull out those weeds, and, as I am told the beds were all in clods and most rascally prepared when first sown through the villany of Gardner Johnny and the base carelessness of John Dolman who has discovered his want of trust in these instances of the plant patches, I ordered Lawson to make his people with little small sticks break every clod to pieces and when the beds are fine which the sun will dry them to to s[illegible] and cover it down [with] naked brush. About a pint of the seed was Goore's and better than a quart New Orleans raised 176[9].

I am told that earth is rather moist although we have had no rain. Therefore I hope the sun will get between the naked brush.

Billy Beale, the younger Son of the late John Beale, a lad of about 18 came up to me on Saturday upon a letter I wrote to his mother. He brought with him Mr. Eustace's[41] and Mr. Edwards' consent, his guardians, that he should be bound to me in the place of William Ball, which the young Gentleman very willingly agreed to and signed the same indenture as to the tenor of it as Ball had signed. He is to come here the 6th of may and to serve me three years for £10 the year in order to be instructed in the Stewardship or management of a Virginia estate. [I] ordered him as he went down to his Mother to see my lower plantations and bring me an account from under the hands of the overseers what quantity of ground they are tending, how far they are advanced in it, what Cattle they have lost and what stocks are remaining; and I wrote to

---

[40] Billy Beale was the younger son of John Beale (d. 1766), a planter in Richmond Co.
[41] Probably John Eustace (d. 1786), planter and justice of the peace in Northumberland Co.

Mr. Edwards who at present overlooks that estate to go with him and let him see every thing for I now began to be so uneasy about making nothing there, the best land almost that I have and near 40 acres, that I was determined to prosecute my Overseers if they did not comply with their express articles of agreement.

Captain Kelsick dined here yesterday with Giberne and Wadman. Giberne began to express his sorrow for Tom Lawson's behaviour at Rippon Hall. I asked him how he had heard it. He told me it was the general town talk [and referred] me to Kelsick who had been there. Kelsick said that numbers talked with him about it and in particular the Inspectors who declared that he had almost ruined the plantation, had sold off all the draught oxen, broke others, employed them at his own plantation, made away with my Cattle and Sheep, and sold all the Corn, and was satisfied that although he had received the money he had not one penny of it. As to the fortune pretended to be got with his wife it was only 3 negroes which he had also spent and they did believe such another man could not be found upon the earth for extravagance, idleness, rattling diversions, and infamous lying. Wadman said that he was convinced long agoe that such a liar as he knew Lawson to be could not [an]swer because in his life he never knew a man who paid [torn] said that [illegible] he did. The very position [illegible] I have been preaching and laying down to every such unhappy fool being convinced that the vain of lying could only have a foundation in the [in]tention to de[ceive] and such man must be a villain in his very heart and I am satisfied through the faithfulness of time it must be discovered in every such thing.

The last of April exceeding cold and dry. Flies contrary to observations eat the large plants and let the small ones alone. I ha[ve] seen every patch but the meadow and locust point in 50 or 60 places sitting upon my horse had them [illegible] plants were and where were not and at that distance as they were pointed to me did see what I am perswaded as yet awhile will be plenty enough. But nothing grows and creatures are yet poor. The lambs not filled, the Ewes very spindly, and the Cows with young calves [are pitifully] thin. Birds pull up the Corn as [soon] as it appears above ground. Shall [have] sowed my flax [illegible].

MAY 1770

1. *Tuesday.*

No rain from the 18 of April till this time so that the earth has not been moistened for the least kind of vegetation and joined with the cold Northerly winds. The planter must needs stand a very wretched chance, and May begins in the same cold dry manner that April ended.

I was yesterday entertained with abundance of information as well as reflections that seem to have been swallowed more through the unfortunate tendency to popular interest than from the wisdom or affectionate prudence of the person who brought the information.

It seems Edmund Northern, who more than 4 years agoe had been employed as a Sawyer for Mr. Neale at my Bluff point quarter, This fellow out of a resentment founded he knows not why has at last carried his violence into reports against Longwith because he could not gratifye his avowed aversion to [torn]. It seems when they left off work there Longwith returned to me the quantity of the provisions he had had for the year's service. This was referred to two Arbitrators and they allowed me to charge in Account for the ballance of that year in which he moved. Northern, of course, had this trifling sum of about 7/6 deducted out of his wages. This made him in the County here full of indecent resentment against me as it was about the Election time. It also almost led him to death's door in a fit of sickness before he would apply to me for assistance. But com[pelled] by necessity to it I had the pleasure of relieving such a monster, and now the fellow, sensible no doubt of the shame of ingratitude after such a particular instance of service, yesterday took an opportunity of locating his resentment gainst Longwith. He told my Son out of 15 Cattle that died at Bluff point when he was there 14 of th[em] were actually mired. Longwith measured all his Corn in by [the] hogshead but delivered it out by a half bushel by which he got a great deal of Corn to his own use and Northern said that John Carter, a tenant on Kendal Lee's[42] land, could prove that Longwith sent half a barrel of my wheat every week to mill. Northern further urged against my imprudence in employing Tom Lawson without inquiring into his character in the neighbourhood where every man could have informed me of his known worthlessness. I could not but reply then every such man must be a villain in his heart because they all knew Long before Lawson went to Rippon Hall that he was going to live under me and if they had either gratitude or religion none of them had wanted a motive to let me know that character. Although they do advance it in justification their not caring to speak amiss of a Neighbour, they really valued old Daniel, the [fa]ther of the man, the same reason [co]uld hold good for their silence now.

---

[42] Kendal Lee (d. 1780) of Ditchley in Northumberland Co. was a planter and justice of the peace. The son of Richard Lee (1691–1740), he married Betty Heale of Lancaster Co.

5. *Saturday.*

Rained Thursday in the night but from a cold northern quarter and so it has continued ever since. I ventured to open those plant patches where I could not see the fly in abundance and wed them but I must say The prospect for plants is too discouraging for any thoughts of a Crop this year. There are small ones which the flies have left but what expectation can there be from them till very late in the year unless we should be blessed with both moisture and warmth which really we have no right to promise ourselves for according to my foremer[?] nothings this world, though not supinely given up, has some-how been established upon the principles of number, weight, and measure, and I think I have experienced long and large spells of one sort of weather have been succeeded by the contrary extreme. By way of ballance therefore the lesson should be that the divine being might be averted from making the land barren through the iniqui[ties] of his people.

I examined the Corn planted in stiff land and even the Thursday night's rain has but just begun to make it swell so that we shall be late in the coming up of that from this last 28 days drought for I am certain no rain has fallen to wet the earth since the 6 of April. There was a sprinkling for a few minutes the 18th.

Yesterday I rode to Colo. Tayloe's to see Mr. Dulany[43] of Maryland and young Wormeley.[44] Dulany perhaps has passed for middle age. A serious easy man in his behaviour and when he does speak very agreeable, but I think under that prodigious silence his own opinion of himself or rather self suffi-ciency is easy to be traced. I could not help observing a little of that leaven relative to the dispute with America, which, although he at first [had] written in favour of, he seemed to have recanted by a paper of his own writing and signing shown by the memorable Colonel Scott who passed through this Colony. I had heard Dulany's friends, Wormeley in particular, pretty ex-travagant in vindicating him from that aspersion, but I think yesterday I could observe he was not quite clear from it. No opportunity was given me to debate upon the point, yet this Gentleman was supercilious enough in reading the extracts of Lord Chatham's and Lord Camden's speach. The first was condemned as a parcel of nonsense, which to be sure could not have been

---

[43] Daniel Dulany (1722–97), was a Maryland lawyer, politician, and pamphleteer. A good biographi-cal study is Aubrey C. Land, *The Dulanys of Maryland* (Baltimore, 1955).

[44] Probably Ralph Wormeley III of Rosegill (1744–1806), Middlesex Co. planter and son of Ralph Wormeley (1715–90). He was appointed to the Council in 1771 and after 1776 served in the House of Delegates.

spoken in the house of Lords, and the last was Sophistry and Chicanery for let Camden say what he would the Lord Chancellor was always in the Law the keeper of the King's conscience, and Camden's [e]steaming it that the Law indeed was the keeper of the King's conscience but the Chancellor no ways bound to intrude in any point in which he was not consulted was mere Chicanery and he was justly chargeable with a duplicity in his conduct for having been silent whilst these measures were pursued and now openly opposing them. Here I ventured to throw in Lord Chatham's nonsense conveyed to me not only a firmness and integrity in the Nobleman but indeed a sting upon the villany of the Ministry, and, as to Lord Camden, it is certain that villany was carried to such a heighth that he neither was permitted to offer his advice to the Sovereign nor the Sovereign to consult him but in all cases borne down by the violence with which they resolved to pursue their measures and if the King's Conscience could have been directed by the sentiments of the Chancellor it was evident he did not want them if the public papers are ever read for every weekly paper certainly conveyed his sentiments to the public in very strong expressions and the very solicitation to engage him to accept the Seals after they had been taken from him from his avowing those sentiments was a full conviction that he was wanted to continue in office only upon the terms of accomodating his opinions to the extravagance of the measures and this was further deducible from his being made Chancellor after he had so gloriously supported the Liberties of the people by his judgment on Wilkes' case as Lord Chief Justice. There was an endeavour by means of that promotion to make him alter his sentiments but he has shown that he chose rather to sacrifice his interest than his conscience. The Gentleman made no reply to this. Therefore I dropt the argument and I will venture to pronounce his soundness is less conspicuous than his knowledge.

I cannot yet get to breaking up the lists in my Mangorike Corn field. That Gust has kept me a full week repairing my fences and it will be Monday first before I can get to the hoes or all my chance of next winter's food will be destroyed by the Cattle of the Neighbourhood who lie down bellowing by the very fences that I have put up.

My hands, 4 of them, worked yesterday ditching the road from hill to the main County road and there they are at work today so that I cannot have their assistance which otherways would have enabled me to go again to the Mill dam next week, a work that must be done, for without this Mill I evidently see it will require 2 large crops of Corn here to keep this family a year for I am certain there is an iniquity practiced at most of the Mills about. No bushel of Corn of mine now ground ever yielding more than a bushel of meal and it

never yielded less than a bushel an a half at my own Mill. Such is our present
Trade.

9. *Wednesday.*

Monday and Tuesday they have been Court days and this is to be another.
I had thought that by a kind of diligence in this spot of public business we
should have been able by this time to have brought our Docket into a very
small size but I see each person concerned with the Court will reserve their
lazyness and I am certain, let what ever will be advanced in the public Gazettes
to spirit Gentlemen up to a diligent discharge of their duty to the public, I
believe every man of them shows the least inclination even to incomode the
least private concern for the sake of the public and I wish I may not find a kind
of surly obstinacy in some of them against doing this duty as they should.

Our Clerk[45] truly omitted entering an order for the Grand Jury although
it had been the practice of the Court to make that order at least two Courts
before the grand Jury Court for fear of a bad preceding Court day. He justified
himself that he was not clear that it was his duty to do it upon which I moved
that the Court should enter as a standing order that in all instances wherever
the Justices by law where required to do any particular public service that the
Clerk should as of duty enter all those orders in the same manner as he would
do upon any particular order of the bench. This motion was growled at by
every member on the bench and indeed Mr. Parker who seemed to be willing
to show that he thought he had an influence rose up in his King's Attorney's
seat and opposed it pretending such an order would look as if the Justices were
designing to lay the blame for every such omission from off their shoulders.

I could not help replying first to the growling bench that my intentions
were only to serve the public and that I had been perswaded from under the
shelter of my own vine to take the chair which I had lived into that I could
easily retire and would do it if Gentlemen instead of supporting me in the duty
of the chair should show themselves so disposed as they had done in every
instance to overrule my endeavours.

I further observed that the law as to Grand Juries which directed the
Courts to cause them to be summons was silent as to the particular mode and
of course in every construction it would be implied the Court had a right to
direction the most discretion anyway. Therefore as the only possible omission
of duty in such points must arise from forgetfulness I could not help asking

[45] Leroy Peachey served as clerk of Richmond Co. from the death of his predecessor, Traverse
Tarpley, in 1768 until 1793.

who in point of just reasoning would be condemnable for such a neglect. Of course, as the Clerk who was only paid for doing such as duty must certainly be looked upon in the highest light of delinquency he must be the proper person chargeable with such a neglect for I would presume that a bench crowded with the determination of a vast variety of businesses must needs be more excuseable for such a neglect than the Clerk could who might by a public Table of his duty upon the establishment of such an order have it ready upon his minutes without the least chance of forgetfulness.

Mr. Ball who for sometime has taken a pleasure in exposing his weakness by opposition to many of these things and said he did not see the use of such an order that the Court ought to remember those things themselves. I could not help replying it was some wonder then that the same Gentleman had not done his duty in such a remembrance with this particular case of the Grand Jury and indeed with respect to abundance of other matters for he had certainly shown himself greatly deficient this way in many points. Coll. Smith[46] also opposed it. My Son consented to it, though he thought there was no occasion for it. Coll. Brockenbrough was Clear it was the Clerk's duty, that [he ought to have] done it, and, therefore, since he was doubtful of the duty, the order was a good way to keep him in mind of it.

I next showed their worships what a prodigious mistake in judgement as well as injury they had made many persons liable to by neglecting a former motion with respect to swearing the Constables relative to the laws against tending seconds. But by the perswasions of Mr. Parker they became satisfied that there was no law in being against seconds and by a confidence peculiar to that bar had asserted that both the Legislature and the revisers of the laws were of the same opinion. Therefore I should [imagine] those Revisers had discovered their opinion by printing those very Laws as the Legislature certainly had done by attempting the very last Session a bill to repeal them all which the Council would not consent to. Parker, Lawyer-like, denied that to be his argument when he opposed any former motion. But I told him I would produce the minutes of that day. The Court at last entered the order. We had many tedious businesses for these two days in which I must say every Lawyer at the bar seemed quite ignorant how far he was engaged in the causes, as they were called, what had been done in them, or upon what point they turned. This was one of the evils of delay that I had pointed out to them and they have shown not the least tendency to amend it. Mr. Boyd[47] wanted to introduce a

[46] Col. John Smith (d. 1794) was a Richmond Co. planter and justice of the peace.
[47] Probably David Boyd (d. 1781), lawyer and planter of Northumberland Co.

new mode of interrupting the process of Common Law by a species of bill in Chancery that should not have the decree to rules of injunctions and yet should stop all further proceedings upon any action at common Law though it had not even been brought to tryal. For this extraordinary motion he met with 2 upon the Bench of his opinion and of course the Court was divided. As I was obliged to be of the side of the Minority, I gave this for my reason, That give his bill what name he pleased it must have the nature of an injunction which were always only allowed upon an oath made to the moving equity and theirfore if he would not proceed in that form I could not indulge his motion because I was satisfied some specious allegation of equity might be advanced against every common law acts and of course the subject must be deprived of his modes of freedom and every thing would in time be thrown into a Court of Conscience, which I beg leave to say would be a Court of the greatest latitude in the world whenever the Judges shall be allowed then to throw aside the evident rules and doctrines of the Common law. Of course, this cause was contrived for its trial in the form it was brought.

Mr. Carter of Corotoman and then Mr. Beverley came here. My son John, it seems, gone home without writing a letter. He had visited Rippon Hall, told Beverley something he could not recollect but that every thing was very bad there and it would be impossible for Ball to make a Crop of either Tobacco or corn, the quantity by much too small and but little dung to improve any more and not one good fence then upon the plantation.

Beverley further told me Jack had paid Hodge, Stewart and Campbell's demand against me without any orders of mine and indeed against my inclination. Of which I shall give Mr. Hodge a pretty stinging memorandum.

Plucked cotton yesterday at the fork.

12. *Saturday*.

We have had no rain as yet though every day very cloudy. On Thursday in the night we had a little smart sprinkling which only held long enough to make the plant patches moist in order for our weeding them but we were obliged before we have done to make use of our watering pots that the pulling the weeds might not injure the plants.

It is now that my aged eyes cannot see the stock of the plants that we have and I believe from the number of patches sown we shall have a great plenty, that is, if it pleases God to bless us with rain.

My Corn in the stiff land is but as yet coming up so great has the difference been between the stiff and the light ground.

We shall finish this day hoing the lists in the new Mangorike Cornfield but by one means or another the fork has not got so forward. Indeed they had the flax ground both to prepare, rake very fine, and sow. Also the hemp ground to pulverize and drill. Also pease hills to be made and planted of the Nottoway pea, which has been discovered, though a wild pea, to make prodigious fine soup. It cures quite green and in size very like the Chichilin vetch called thus, who imported it from England, the everlasting pea though it is not such for the vine dies after every bearing. But the everlasting pea I believe never left any man's ground in which it was on[c]e planted. Besides the everlasting pea is from every trial I have made very difficult to be set to growing for to be sure I have saved quarts of seed and have planted them without one of them sprouting though at the same time I must confess G. Johnny was the seedsman who I have now discovered was never sober and therefore has been turned to the hoe above a fortnight. I was fond of raising these everlasting pease because from the prodigious harvest that they bear and always green they might be made a very great winter food as well as a perpetual one. I will venture once more to try them. The pease sown at the fork differs from them only in the vine for that runs up but the everlasting pea will cover the earth.

Lawson somehow made George at the fork fancy he was to have a plow there and I do suppose it has made the fellow some thing easy about his Corn field but I told him he shall have no plow and shall look well into the dispatching of his business.

On monday next, God willing, I shall begin to turn my Tobacco hills. The ridged ground where I burned the suckers first and then to dunging the other stiff land and when that is over I shall part the gangs.

13. *Sunday.*

Every prospect for rain now seems intirely removed by a Northerly, though gentle, air that has swagged the clouds from us. This spell of dry weather though very severely felt by us will be easily forgotten by those who have been more happy. Yet it is necessary to be remembered that ever since the 6th of April we have only had a small sprinkling or two which hardly moistened the earth so much as to bring up any seed and without the assistance of watering pots could not have afforded a real opportunity toward a plant patch of any size.

I cannot in the course of my conversation help taking notice of the strange as well as quick impressions which some people take so strong as not to be removed even when relative to common justice and the constant practice of the world.

Yesterday I heard as an opinion formed: however directory a man might be in his will and express in his devises, yet if one devise should in any instance or circumstance that might attend it could effect the least inequality a Gentleman with as little knowledge of the law and indeed of equity as ever fell to man's share said it was his opinion that in every case a court in Chancery should rectifye every such devise according to the common rules of equality.

The case was this: a devisor leaves to 5 or 6 daughter a certain portion to be paid according to his directions and in his directions expressly says that if any of those Legatees should die before a Son younger than the eldest of them should come of age it was his intention that such Legacy should be divided between his two youngest sons. This mighty opinionst said this eldest daughter ought to be paid her portion upon her marriage because some of the daughters by being younger than the younger sons would otherways stand a better chance for their portions than the eldest would and from thence called it injustice. I ventured to ask where the justice would be in preventing a man from giving his own away in any manner that he pleased and certainly the man would in this case be prevented if in the instance there should be as an opinion that could deduce such a species of justice from the possible accident that might attend a younger child in the course of nature. Should this doctrine prevail it hardly could be known how far it might extend. In the first place, the rule without respecting justice is generally to prefer the male inheritance but by this doctrine it would in many instances happen that because the younger male children might in the course of nature stand a better [chance] of living to any future period then the elder females, the elder female ought to be preferred in justice before him.

Another instance of the absurdity of such hasty impressions was this. It has been the constant practice of all the world that bills of Exchange when taken by the person to whom paid should be deemed an immediate payment, but lately a Creditor, although he took the bills, has ventured to charge interest upon his debt to the time when according to the practice in trade the bills became due.

I say this impression supported the justice of such a claim against the practice of the whole world as well as against every reason of equality in the very nature of bills of exchange although the same opinionist had just before so positively affirmed that equality ought to be preserved.

The person receiving the bill according to the nature of Exchange had certainly a right to negotiate it away in ready payment to anyone that would receive it in discharge of his dealings. And where could the equality be if the same ready payment was not to take place in the dealings of every man with the same bill should anyone receive it. Certainly then the first payment should be as good a discharge if taken of the debtor as it ought to be of the Creditor who had the right of negotiating it away or not for himself.

Mr. Berkeley, my daughter, and all their family came here on friday evening.

It is impossible in such a large family of Children and grand Children but some one of them may be indisposed and as I have bent my studies and indeed my constant attention to consider and relieve the case of the sick I have ventured to advise my daughter Beverley to give her Child Molly a few opening powders which she did and though they were very few and really but small in quantity [the] Child became lively after they had had their effect. But her disorder being of a slimy as well as weak state in her stomach returned again. I then, as I saw the humours by the medicines I had given were made very thin and fluid, advised a gentle puke of Ipecacuanha, but poor Mother, weak in her knowledge of such things as well as her tenderness, refused to give it because as she says the child had been always taking things. I smiled and must smile when ever a parent shall suffer herself to conclude that because she knows not how to direct in such tender cases others do not know. But I can presumptively conclude that if that Child was now and then to take one of these pukes she would be more speedily relieved than she can be by any other intention to carry off this slime.

15. *Tuesday.*

We have no rain as yet although by a North Easterly wind yesterday we have been supplied with moist and cold clouds over the whole heavens and even now a thin fleeting moisture which only serves to make the human body chilly.

John Dolman is such a fellow of determined laziness that I ordered him away yesterday, being fully satisfied of what I every day discover in him, that that laziness has even contributed to so many deaths among his Cattle. The last year the fellow lost none by means of a six months that he made up of after he got into my business. But as soon as the Summer came in that all died away into allmost a walking indolence which is to me surprizing for he is a fellow of spirit enough but it only serves to make him impudent and I am certain he must have such an example of Will Lawson's daily diligence that could he himself bring into such a way he must have done it before this. Therefore, I bid him go off. The pitiful puppy has been this morning crying about the unhappy situation that he is in so that I have been obliged to try him a little further. He has promised to amend, but I really much doubt it.

Mr. Ball from Rippon hall gives me a more pleasing account than I had
before of a possibility of his making something. I am glad to see his spirits and
shall encourage them. But he tells me Dick Edwards informs him that he can
only send him 20 barrels of my Corn at which I am much astonished because
in his letter on the 9th instant he tells me that he shall send off the next day for
Rippon 50 barrels.

Mr. Ball informs me he understands Mr. Carter, the Councillor, has a
large quantity of Corn at his plantation adjoining Rippon. I have written to
him as he is now in Westmoreland to desire he would spare me what he can
conveniently do and although I have not told him so yet it seems Mr. Ball
writes me word that my plantations there have frequently assisted him this
way.

Sam tells me they have done at Rippon making all their Tobacco hills,
and Ball says he shall go to dunging them immediately that he may turn for
planting about the 22nd of this month. He says nothing about his Corn field
lists. As soon as I get Mr. Carter's answer I must write to him upon that subject
because they ought to be now hoed that the ground may be of service to the
growth of the Corn.

We began yesterday turning our Tobacco hills here and making the earth
extremely fine. It is a tedious jobb as it must be well done and the ground
really very stiff. We have hoed all the lists in our new Corn field but I do not
see the Corn well come up in the stiff land.

George at the fork will well nigh finish the lists this day in one of [the]
fields, full a quarter of the whole quantity. The flax seems prodigiously well up
and the Corn in the light land.

Yesterday I left off feeding the Chariot horses that I may carry my year
about well with the Corn that I have.

16. *Wednesday.*

I believe the trying of Carrots, Cabbage, Turnips, and all these experiments for winter food will be quite useless in this Climate for we have not now
a spring commonly moist for any such things to grow in and we can hardly
water what little we raise in our Gardens. Every prospect for rain abates and
none we have had since the 6th of April.

Nassau is become intollerable. I saw he had been drinking on Saturday
when he could not bleed his Master. I told him of it every day and now he has
got to stinking so much with it that he is not to be endured. Last night I could
not be waited upon. His pretence was his wife was taken dangerous bad. But
now I have found out that it is his state of drinkinness. Four of my people of

the Mangorike Gang are lying up through his negligence and two more of the house servants have been quite useless for some time.

17. *Thursday.*

A pretty thick mist all over us and with it a descending moisture. Really no rain. From our great want of it we were very willing to expect it and as these things seem generally to be governed by some particular direction or possibly some concurring cause that we know nothing of it may turn out a rainy day. But I confess this conjecture is not supported by my observation nor indeed by the appearance of the clouds which as the sun advances seem to grow thinner and drier. Therefore, having been told that the plants in the River side plant patch begin to scorch much, I have ordered my watering pots down there to give it a substantial wetting if Mr. Dolman will follow my orders, but that I greatly suspect from his prodigious proneness to lazyness.

I cannot help remarking that although in November I had hoed my Tobacco ground, made my hills very large and full, and indeed buried my suckers in them, yet such has been the winter's prodigious moisture and so dry the weather lately that that part of this ground which is naturally stiff has been full as hard to work as if it had been a mere highway. So that my best hands could not reach 700 hills and beat them fine in these long days. This makes the quantity I tend a very heavy jobb and some of it I am doubtful will be late in its tending. I mean not the Tobacco ground so much because the growth of our plants will give us time enough for that but perhaps the Corn field may be a little weedy. However I cannot touch those lists till moister weather from the stiffness of its soil.

19. *Saturday.*

Cold and dry as before nor can there be a symptom of rain whilst the Northerly winds prevail as they do.

Captn. Quiney came here yesterday and brought me accounts of sales for 20 hogsheads of Tobacco and 2 of Robin Carter's which went home by mistake by my mark from Falmouth. It seems as my Tobacco was last put in the Ship it had the misfortune of being sold first a few days before the news of the hurricane arrived. Otherwise it would have fetch[ed] near 9 [torn] pounds more. However what it has sold at has exceeded the London Market by above 25/ the hogshead In which there is a great mistery only to be solved by examining the Accounts. The Liverpoole sales although they deduct 6 per Cent from off all Tobacco Yet by a very few other knavish charges there is at least 30/ difference in each hogshead for the London were most of them from a farthing to a half penny per ld more. Of course, it must be madness that can continue attached to such a trade and the favour or whatever it is that inclines a man to trade to London is very dearly purchased. I shall write this to those Gentlemen with whom I am concerned and must give over if they will not remedy such an evil.

20. *Sunday.*

It is written and indeed a greater truth cannot be written that unless the Lord watereth the labour of man that soweth is but in vain. We may dung, pulverize, weed, and indeed water ourselves, but what can it avail without the assista[nce] of that benign hand. It has now been near 8 years with me that in my Garden in this month of may of particularly I have been obliged to water night and day and what has it produced, some little perished matter that instead of better we have been obliged to make use of. I ride and walk for the sake of exercise but with how little pleasure can I do either when not one part of my labour has the least promising aspect. We have had no sign of a moisture for 44 days to this moment even our dews are so trifling that in the earliest part of the morning they will hardly make the shoe leather damp.

Our present labour is burying our dung. Such weather is not really good for that for the earth although well broke up for pulverizing by the frosts is now so hard that it is great labour to make even the holes into which we put our dung and yet this is the only work we can do in stiff land.

Corn fields not yet properly up is a miserable sight at the last of this month and should the frosts set in as early as we have been accustomed the chance for making bread except in very light lands must be very precarious. In short, our Climate is so changed that should it go on it must be difficult for the inhabitants in a course of years to make even food from any grain that I am acquainted with. Our winter grains after perishing by winter severity almost every year even in stiff soils produce very little by means of our spring drought. And coolness Every evening and morning requires a fire but as God is merciful we must not be impatient and hope for the best.

22. *Tuesday.*

Still no rain and but little dew which makes the 46th day that we have been so unhappily attended.

I have heard no complaints about the scorching of any plant patches but the River side patch. I have watered that once all over very well, if my directions were follow[ed], and partly so a second time. This night they shall do it all over a third time. It has been very unusual in my experience for plants to scorch so very young. Therefore, [I] cannot be certain of its consequence but reason tells me it must be very bad.

We have dunged all this field on this side the Cow house to about 1,000 or 2 and I think very well dunged. Yesterday they began to bury the dung in the Cow field from the Creek up to our last fresh Cow penns and will finish, if they do not overrate their work, that jobb this night. We shall then bury our home dung both in the wattle gound and behind the Stables which to be sure will make us a Crop of rich ground if we can be so lucky to have it planted.

I shall then go to hoing my riverside Corn lists and at the same time weeding the Corn there. When that is done I must turn all my hills, but I wish for moisture that I may work the heavy ground very fine.

George I understand finish[ed] the full half of his Corn field last night.

At last I began my Mill dam again though but with 4 hands. This day I shall have five there and in a day or two more make it up [to] 6 or 7 hands.

My barley by the Mudhouse where the land is rather stiff began yesterday to fax at the roots as the farmers calls it. I set in 4 hands to give it another earthing up to see what that will do but I fear neither broadcast nor drilling will save a crop of grain in such excessively dry weather.

My Carpenters are now about my paling again. I wish that jobb done because I really want to right up my barn and new cover my Mangorike Tobacco house for if I should have a Crop I may have housing to put it in and I must new thatch my fork house to serve at least for putting in my Corn this next year as well as build that Corn house. Besides all this My Mill race that is to be must be lined with boards and Chestnut posts.

25. *Friday.*

The cloudy weather yesterday and last night turned to a pretty rain about 5 this morning and promised much but went off in about half an hour so that all the moisture we had did not amount to more than a mere plant patch sprinkling which did not last us the day to weed our plants through but as there was a necessity for the work I ordered the deficiency of moisture to be made up by my watering pots.

Several people I hear were busy in planting but I wish abundance of them don't repent it. In the first place, I discovered no season above half inch deep and as they generally put plants in a finger hole it must be very bad to have those little roots squeezed together with dry earth especially if they don't cover the whole plant over to near the tips of their leaves for the hot sun which we have since had must burn a great many of them. In the next place, after such a long dry cold spell I never knew but these slight showers brought the ground worm up in a great plenty so that they have reason to expect every plant will be cut off. I know this day my cabbage plants in my garden that have merely spread the hills have many of them been already cut off by them. And for my part I know no plant patches this year so thick sown as to endanger the plants by their being longlegged in their growth and those that are thin I am very certain will not be injured in their beds should they be suffered to stay there yet a while till the moisture and warm weather has burst the worms and I am certain from all my experiments that such large plants had better be planted in dry weather provided the ground is made fine than in such scanty seasons as this was after such a long spell of cool drought as 49 days. For these reasons although my overseers wanted like other people to be sticking their plants in to the tune of about 30,000 I would not let them plant one but made them weed the several patches out watering them to close the earth in after they had done and I am perswaded I shall see my advantage in it.

I have not yet buried my house dung. It will take me tomorrow and I fear some part of Monday and then I shall have the ground in my barley field that was sowed with Carrots but did not come up to be dunged for which purpose Manuel is and has been casting dung from this year's cowyard below and when he has done that he is to Cast the rest into the last year's dunged ground between the two years' Cow penns which I am in hopes will make all the ground that I tend exceeding rich.

Whilst this Carting is going forward I shall first set my Corn in all my fields where it is wanting, [have] the missing hills well hoed and holed, and the plants with their clods put in pretty deep near to their blades which are to be cut off that they may not pipe up and stop the shooting. I shall then hoe and weed my River side field and after that, if it is done, bury this cooled dung and then to turning hills and making the earth fine whereever the hoe can be got into the ground.

Note: Mr. Guy has again run away. I found fault this morning with his idleness and his bad work and as I went down the hill ordered the Overseer to give him a trimming. Somebody it seems has told him of it and he run away. He shall be again outlawed and I believe not excused as he was before from a whipping for it.

I went this day to Captain Beale's who gave his Son Thomas a public dinner upon the bringing home of his late married wife Miss [illegible Ball]. It is no business of mine but for a Lady so much talked of and for whom so many young fellows has pretended to run mad I think there is as little to be seen as ever I saw in any one. There is a silence but not graced with quite so much good humour as to bespeak the wisdom of it. One thing struck me. This Gentleman by his first wife had a couple of pretty Children neatly dressed playing about who seemed as if they wanted to be fondled by their new Mama but indeed She did not seem to take the least notice of them. Which to me would argue a want of prudence had she really a proper affection for certainly no woman willing to oblige her husband would according to the tenor of the Scripture have missed so fine an opportunity as the taking notice of one of these little ones must have been to engage her husband['s] affections. He passes for a phylosopher but I believe he is only happy in wanting the power of judging with propriety of such things for he seemed as if unobserving of this behaviour though it was really so contrary to natural prudence and conjugal love. There was a large Company there and I met the famous Hudson Muse[48] going there of whom I took no notice always bearing in mind his opening and exposing private letters that did not in the least affect him.

26. *Saturday*.

There has fallen by appearance a pretty refreshing shower in the night which may have been of service to those who were eager to plant yesterday As to the setting their plants for growth but I believe as evidently as can be to their prejudice with respect to the ground worm which I thought would be the case for I saw my Gardner planting cabbage plants this morning where I knew they had been in full growth and he assured me he had carried in an armfull to the Rabbits which the ground worm had cut off in the night.

I expect to see the Corn much refreshed. My Riverside Tobacco beds not quite wed out this morning. When that is done all hands are to set their Corn.

I rode out this day and don't discover much of this fine shower that was talked of last night. Either the earth was excessive dry before it or the effects of it are so suddenly gone off that we cannot see it at all upon the stiff land hills which are really only not dust and very little in the light ground for I observe in the River side and fork plant patches which were not finished weeding when I went down that the pulling up of the weeds left the ground very crumbly and would without watering to close it in to the roots of the plants certainly destroy them.

I have seen a further reason why I believe I shall not repent planting this season. In the first place, I have not many plants really fit and the taking them up without a good deal of rain more of which we don't seem to stand any very

---

[48] Hudson Muse (d. 1799) was the brother of Daniel Muse, a merchant in Richmond Co. In 1771 he ran unsuccessfully for burgess in Richmond Co. and in 1777 he became collector for the port of Tappahannock, a post he held in 1790 when he married Agnes Neilson.

great chance would evidently kill the rest besides the havock now made by the ground worm. It cuts off Corn pease in abundance and I believe every thing tender enough to [be] bitten.

George with his fork gang makes very little progress in plant weeding. I have therefore sent my Mill dam gang this piece of a day to help to finish that patch that I may save those plants for I do suppose the same damned idleness that could not engage Dolman to see the patches well covered prevented him and the people from their having them well dunged for the plants have certainly grown by very little So that I wish I may have enough out of so many that I have sowed.

29. Tuesday.

Yesterday I rode by my fork plantation to Coll. Tayloe's and if anybody could have seen the least sign of those scuds of rain that happened on Friday morning, friday night, and the Sprinkling Saturday in the night we must have discovered it. But excepting in the plant patch there did not appear the least moisture so that little profess that George who was setting Corn there had left off upon account of the dryness of the earth and had got to weeding his field.

As we rode round we had the opportunity of discovering the Tobacco ground which Coll. Tayloe had planted on friday. On horseback we could not see above 3 plants in the whole 30,000. I sent Nassau in. He walked deep in the rows but could not see one alive and it was it seems the general complaint on Sunday with every body that had planted that the ground worm had cut off most of that which stood.

We have this morning just such another little sprinkling which promised so much that really I had inclined to have some hills cut off as my plants at the fork are fine and large but I had scarce given my orders when I found occasion by the ceasing of the rain to send to the overseer to keep on dunging till it should rain to some purpose. Indeed it is a difficult matter to act because, though planting without rain might be done very well and the plants in a manner so covered with earth that the worms could hardly cut them under ground, yet with wet earth the Cover would bake and injure the plant.

I find this business of dunging is a heavyer jobb than I would chuse it to be as the people yesterday were lazyer than common for what, the dung [was] not very far off. They seemed when I came home not to have done much.

Sam arrived from Mr. Edwards' with a particular account of Longwith's and Freshwater's Crop. Longwith does not tend but a little more than 10,000 Cornhills and not 20,000 Tobacco hills for 26 sharers and has not left for Freshwater 7,500 Tobacco hills per head at Blough point. But Freshwater himself has taken in 15,000 Corn hills a head so that from this we may discover the reason why we have made nothing for seven years there. Longwith had 3 shares which were profitable enough to him at the same time very indifferent for me considered in the real proportion and so I have written to that fellow very largely. It seems I have made Mr. Edwards my overlooker there very angry but I cannot help it for I will not starve and such management any longer there must bring me to it.

By accounts from all parts above and below very dry. The Assembly is sitting but only finishing the business left undone last session. Nothing said about the repeals of the Revenue Acts. The Association met and formed a Committee of 20 to amend that scheme but it seems they are so divided that at present there will be very little chance of agreeing to the amendments. Some of them are full as hearty as I thought they would be. Persons parading from no principle but only to make a show of Patriotism and Mr. T——[49] is at last found out to be the man I always took him, a noisy declaimer on nothing or next a kin to it he and Pendleton at the head of a party who were for meeting the Parliament half as they call this partial repeal of the acts so whilst we were inslaved by those that were not repealed we must go our half and give up that point.

Fine Language this, just as if there could be any half way between Slavery and freedom. Certainly one like of the former preserved must be the hold to which the [rest] of the chain might at any time be joined when the forging Smith's thought proper to add to it.

The rain, as I imagined it would do, left us almost as soon as a man could say John Smith Pease. I went down to see the hills cutting off and so little water had fallen that they were quite dry and dusty to a mere shell at top. However I have ordered there 18,000 to be planted this night in that dry dusty earth and covered over as I have done for 2 years past. The night moisture possibly will keep the plants alive as they are large and laid in full growth as to their roots till we can get a rain and I have observed that ground worm very seldom eats within the earth so that the covering them over will probable be a preservative against his ravages till the warmer weather shall put a period to his rising.

I have now the 2 Cow keepers, the sheep woman, 4 stout hands, sick, one lain in and Mary Ann in the Kitchin o[illegible] of my Crop gang at this very busy time.

[49] Robert Carter Nicholas (1728–80), son of Dr. George Nicholas and Elizabeth Carter, was Landon Carter's nephew. He was often referred to as Mr. Treasurer, a reference to his position as public treasurer of the colony from 1766–77. He was burgess for York Co., 1756–61, and for James City Co., 1766–76.

30. *Wednesday.*

Went to Mr. Ball's yesterday with Mr. Berkeley. A great prospect of rain but none as yet fallen which from the 6th of April 55 days including since the earth here has been blessed with any real moisture. It has mizzled, scudded, and sprinkled four times in the time once half an hour, once 15 minutes, once three minutes, and once perhaps 10 minutes, all of which did not even make moisture enough to hold out picking any thing of a plant patch. Nevertheless, having some very fine plants at the fork, I ordered Lawson yesterday to get about 15,000 of them ready drawn to plant between 5 and dark in the way I pursued last year, that is, open the hills with my hand put the plant with its roots at full liberty, press the earth close round upon those roots up to the level of the hill, then bend the plant to the sunrise and lay a handful of dry dust over it to the tips of the leaves.

But Lawson stranger like to the time such a work might be done in did not get above 8,000 plants drawn and planted in the place designed.

This day finish covering in my dung upon the hill. The whole ground replenished to beyond the valley going to the Mill and about 9 rows in the wattled ground for which we must contrive and scrape our stubbs another day.

Set the people this day to turning the rest of the hills in the last year's Cowpen ground by the gate below to compleat that piece in order to be planted every night in the same manner if no rain falls. I believe the natural moisture of the earth perpetually rising will keep the plant alive till we may have rain and the covering prevent the attacks of the ground worm who never eat below the earth. If so, the hastiness of others has not put them in any forwardness before me. Mr. Ball told me his people wormed over the day before the 30,000 he had planted and got 8 measured quarts of worms and yesterday he himself took 8 worms out of the same ground and five off from many hills.

Captain Quiney's boat brought my Goods, to wit, Billy Ball's box, A small cask of earthern ware for ditto No. 1. No. A cases for myself and 25 bags of salt, a Cheese, a speaking Trumpet, Some Seed, and a fan, and one last No. 1 R[obert] W[ormeley] C[arter].

It seems it took the fork gang all day yesterday setting the right hand corn field which is but one fourth of the ground they tend. The hemp wed out by Gardener Tom though very indifferently come up by means of the dry weather and I will fancy the badness of the seed for tutt was a Rascal in saving it. Lame Johnny has been 3 days weeding the flax and as he goes on will be three weeks but he says the young crab grass is coming much in it. We must take a day all hands to do this jobb at once.

We set in the Riverside Corn field tomorrow to hoe and set the corn if the ground [is] moistened.

31. *Thursday.*

At last a mighty blizz of rain is come. It come on drop by drop from about dark last night so that we may reckon a full 30 days' dry weather in May and 24 in April.

I pursued my method of dry planting yesterday to the number of what my Overseer calls 15,000 but as he overreckoned the day before dry planting above 1,500 plants I have sent to have these counted.

My situation is such that, although I have more plants big enough, the ground I have cut off being of the stiffest land and quite mucky by the rain all night as I have no over abundance of plants I must run no chance of throwing them away in such a wet season.

Again as the hills I have turned is in the same stiff land it will evidently be making mortar of them to cut them of. Therefore the season must dry away more before I can venture upon that. Of course my hands can only go to setting Corn in my light fields till this season and its very moist effects shall abate. Then I must prepare a good stock of hills for dry planting or what moisture may happen and in particular turn all my hardest ground by which time I do suppose I shall have a great plenty of plants fit. But during this my river side corn field has all its lists to break up owing to the quantity I tend as well as the hardness of the Tobacco hills that I have turned and the vast heaps of dung I have buried. However I am in hopes the great breadth of the ridges which I hoed to plant Corn in will keep that from suffering or being in the least injured till those lists can be hoed and as the Fork are better than 3 parts done weeding I do imagine I shall have 6 of those hands at least to throw in and help out with this work very soon.

I receive this rain with prodigious pleasure. The earth dearly wanted it in all my cultivations as well as the old fields and every thing I hope will be benefited by it for my plant patches were all cleaned wed out.

JUNE 1770

19. *Tuesday.*[50]

. . . whole one unplanted from his joining yesterday's planting with the

---

[50] Most of the June entries have been lost or destroyed. What remains begins in the middle of the entry for Tuesday, June 19.

rest. [H]e [i]s much ashamed of it and I believe will not give occasion for a re[buke] of that kind.

I find that although there is a certainty in this planting and covering of plants even living in dry weather, yet either by its being a new way, the willful neglect of the people, and really the carelessness of their Overseers, it is attended with some inconvenience. They either cover all the plant over and then for want of air it is late in shooting or they do not plant it all, and a careless Overseer, knowing he cannot see the plants at a distance, concludes that they are planted when they are not. Again as soon as they do shoot out the ground worm eat in the hill cuts them off which has been the case to a very great degree in those hills dunged [illegible] [suc]kers so that it will take me the [be]st part of this day to repair their damage. [Torn] way. Upon the whole if I could have [it] done and with large plants in a careful way I should be inclined to follow it but carelessness though equal in both ways is easiest discovered in the old way.

I believe by friday or sometime in that day my hills will be all turned if it does not rain and on Saturday if my own plants are not large enough I will send to Coll. Tayloe's patches which Garland has promised to preserve for me.

I have visited all my plant patches. Together they will afford me a great many plants perhaps sufficient. But replanting I believe must be done by plants from abroad. I confess I have contrary to my practice suffered myself to be alarmed that I have the business of planting still to do the 19th of this month but if I look back I shall find I never have with a full crop got done before July and indeed last year it was the 9th of [torn]. It at all but as it was if no gust had happened I should have made a great go having even with the gust made near double of what other people did with a greater number of hands who were all so long done before me.

I am also much alarmed about the looks of my Corn fields, full of grass still though most of them wed out before the rain and all of them about half done. But still I recollect the same thing has happened in wet years before and yet I thank God even I have made plentiful Crop of Corn who crop it upon stiff moist lands and so I hope I shall again for it is not too late to conquer those weeds in the growth of Corn.

At the fork it is enough to scare me to see such a matt of grass in one week's time and one of my best hands there taken sick. Otherwise I intended that gang to assist my Tobacco Crop here. But we will do as well as we can since it has been in our power to do as well as we would. [Illegible] has made [illegible] slow days [torn], but have done it very well and says he shall go on much faster now having got his Oxen into a better way of turning.

The corn there is but low yet strong and green except in a few patches where the grass has matted it.

Tony, McGinis, Guy, Jimmy, and Lame Robin have been replanting at least 20,000 in my stiff Tobacco ground this day, and I cannot but express my astonishment at what I saw. Plants appearing as if in real growth and yet as soon as you touched them they came up and without the least root to every one of them there was the hole of the ground worm big enough to take a man's little finger in. The season is gone or I would go over the whole plant by plant least I should be so served in the rest. I must observe that this very piece of ground has been always remarkable for ground worm and I do not remember that I ev[er] [torn] there before the middle of June and, as we have added to their growth by endeavouring this last fall to lighten it with Suckers, to be sure the destruction must have been greater than common. My blough point plantation in old Wist's days always had the same evil attending it and that old man never planted a plant there before the 15th of June old stile. Now we think we have no Crop if we don't pitch it in May truly.

I visited my gangs three times this day staying with them about a couple of hours each time. I had taken notice when they worked up the hill of the same strong heavy stroke which they had got into turning the stiff land before the rain. I put them out of it one day and they turned me then 40,000 and this day by going from hand to hand every now and then I have got better than 30,000 turned. The earth was prodigious weedy though otherwise light and clever. I have dunged it all again though it was made extremely rich last year and I am certain, all holding well, that I shall by Thursday midday at farthest have turned all my hills. I have some plants of my own that are pretty large and these I shall put in if I have no season. If a season should come by that time I will break off plowing and fetch plants from Coll. Tayloe's Marsk quarter to complete the whole, although I had much rather my own Tobacco should be planted there and as it is if seasons are not very late I will stick in my own plants by the others that I may prefer as I like it.

Yesterday I sent Talbot for a barrel of Sugar at Mortimer's from James Gilchrist[51] of Norfolk by the order of Mr. Jno. Thompson[52] at 45/ the hundred weight. The neat weight in his Account was 290 pounds but by weighing it off into my butter pots we have got only 277 pounds. Thirteen pound is not much loss but I shall write to Thompson to have an abatement made for as I pay for what I buy I ought to have what I pay for.

[51] James Gilchrist was a merchant or factor in Norfolk.
[52] John Thompson was a merchant in Norfolk.

It has been very unlucky that my best wench at the fork should be taken ill yesterday and today because really the situation of the Crop is too bad for such an accident. However we are all subject to them and must submit without murmuring.

I see the horn fly very busy about but I have no Tobacco for the Creature to lay its eggs upon and therefore need not be very apprehensive about this first glut.

If no season happens tonight Tony and the Carpenters go about their Mill waste and the Mill dam Jobbers set into the pease. Perhaps we may save a crop of them and they will purchase many necessaries for housekeeping. We were all day threatened with rain so that what Tobacco we have planted does not seem to have scorched much.

21. *Thursday.*

Yesterday Mr. Saml. Hipkins[53] came here. I settled and paid off his Account to the amount of £23 odd. Also engaged him to pay Tom Reid of Northumberland in ballance of James McCall's[54] Account £27 odd and a draft on me to the said Thos. Reid by John Longwith of £25 which three sums were discharged by a bill of Exchange I drew payable to Mr. Hipkins upon Mr. Willm. Molleson of London of this date amounting to £66 odd at 15 per Cent discount.

Yesterday I made my Carpenters replant all my Tobacco ground upon this hill going over it hill by hill and sticking a plant in where ever they did not see a growing bud and as a convincing proof plants plan[ted] in dry weather and properly covered over are more certain of their growth than if planted in any oth[er] manner this whole piece containing full 100,000 was replanted by those 5 fellows out of not more than a third of the full grown plants in the small patch under my garden wall which to be sure could not exceed 3,000. I mentioned to them the place where they would be missing if any where and there they met with more than they did in the whole field cut off by the ground worm after the plants had uncovered themselves by their growth. The time they spent in this Jobb was mostly owing to their searching carefully in every hill. Note: it was cloudy and likely for rain the whole day but it did not rain.

I perceive I shall not finish turning my hills near as soon as I expected. The earth, though light, is prodigiously full of weeds, which must be carefully turned in as much as possible. However finished it shall be and to be sure

---

[53] Samuel Hipkins was a merchant at Totuskey Bridge in Richmond Co.
[54] James McCall was a merchant in Great Britain.

Saturday will compleat it. It is a large piece of ground. More than I thought it was. We shall then go into our Corn field and if it does not rain take every evening to plant this ground and not work in the night about it that I may have it done well. If it does rain all hands shall go to it.

Cloudy and warm but no rain.

I am apt to think there was more haste than good speed when my this year's Cowpenn hills were made for they work very hard upon turning and by being weedy we shall be longer in that Jobb than I expected.

At the fork the people have got over seemingly the most difficult part of their weeding. The Corn low. The ground but stiff and not dunged. It is a little yellow, perhaps owing as much to a wetness in that part as to the grass. With life and continuance we may save the Corn there.

Coming home I had occasion to take particular notice of the wheat. I see some of it is rusty and perhaps the whole may be so soon but that is more my pity than my observation. It is very remarkable that one part of this wheat was last year tended in Pease and the wheat by being sown this year where the Pease grew is if possible 20 times better than that sown in the Tobacco ground which was all dunged last year and only brought a crop of Tobacco. Perhaps this observation may convince me that the drilling first in Pease is a noble manuring for wheat but I must take notice that although the wheat is better the ground between the rows where I am now tending pease is much fouler than the Tobacco ground part so that although the tending of pease is of great advantage in point of manuring yet the tending of Tobacco is by far the better dressing.

Sam came home this day with letters from Mr. Ball. I never had a great opinion of his extraordinary sagacity and I think now his letter has confirmed me in it. He affects to show himself nettled at what I wrote to him although it was only to prevent his being dispirited. I am glad to see he has a spirit of some sort but must endeavour to perswade him to apply it properly and not against the advice that is given to him.

22. *Friday.*

Very hot a part of this day. Three of my wenches turning hills grew fainty. I had them up and ordered them a vomit a piece being satisfied from long experience that this sudden faintyness with heat is occasioned by a stomach loaded with bile too thick to be vomitted without an Emetic. I[t] sometimes happens that a large draught of cold water occasions this but, as that is generally fetched a great way, the coldness must be pretty well off and therefore I formerly suspected another cause and happily found it a bilious one of course. I give a vomit as soon as possible and am lucky in their recovery provided I can hear it in any time.

There is this day a prospect for rain but it seems to wear away. I want a shower and do not want one that is a shower would assist the finishing my planting and it would not be quite agreeable to my grassey Cornfields.

This morning I set my Carpenters to lighten up the missing hills in the stiff ground by mangorike gate in order to replant them this evening but I find they are more missing than upon the hill. The ground worm has eat more there than any where. Those fellows have spent near the whole day and have not lightened up in rows even 5,000 hills supposing they were all missing under pretence of the earth being very hard when in fact the hills were made before the frost and turned not quite 14 days agoe. I will order all the hills lightened to be counted that the Rascals may be severely punished. Tony I see is the conductor of this idleness. He leads the gang and just as if every man had an equal number missing not one goes a hill before him which is a certain proof of villanous lazyness and all shall pay for it tomorrow.

23. *Saturday.*

Great prospect for rain but none falling. A cool Easterly wind.

I am certain no man but myself would tend the piece of ground by my great gate in Tobacco or indeed in any thing else and yet I have been labouring to bring the parts of it which are runy into tilth for 12 years and better and when I can follow it with the hoe every now and then especially 4 or 5 days after a rain it will produce as well as any other land but with common work. It is so in spots with the rest of the field. That it is quite disheartening. I observed it to be very grassy this day and set my pea gang into it to weed it deep between the rows and nurse up the growing Tobacco with a good broad hill, a method that all planters have agreed [with] me in it seems through an apprehension of the webb worm. But I know nothing of the matter. If the man who keeps his ground clear of weeds ever has a web worm but in universal gluts indeed, and certainly by a cool earth put broad and round the plant the tender roots will certainly be protected from the scorching sun and upon this principle have I made even this spot of earth produce good Crops for this broad hill at the same time keeps the land from backing and of course the plant must grow. Even now had not this soil been a favorite spot for every kind of insect there would have been pretty Tobacco in it for that which has stood looks very well but there is abundance missing. Replanted last night and replanting this day for I still hold to it where the earth is light and fine anything of a large plant is better planted and covered in dry weather with its roots unconfined that it can be in wet weather where they must be confined by being stuck in the holes with [the end] of a small stick. It would have been happy if this field had not baked. So I am certain more Tobacco would have stood for I saw where the buds took the advantage of the lightness of their leaves as they were covered down and have shot out through them.

I observed ground worm, piss ants, grasshoppers, and even Crickets centreing themselves under the leaves.

My pease will stay well enough now till the next week and that gang shall brush out what Tobacco they can between this and Wednesday next and one day will finish the pease.

There are but 13,000 Tobacco hills to be turned this day and they may be done plentifully by the gang. The women who fainted yesterday have two of them got to work very well. The other two, I suppose near the period of the return of their fever and ague, have still sick stomachs and headach. I have ordered them another vomit and have given direction if the weather should be hot to let the women sit down for about an hour at midday.

Talbot is a great rascal. Whilst he should be drawing plants, for as it is cloudy I will plant all day, he is gone to look out for the boar and I suppose is to idle a day away. Indeed, I have always observed it when any work is in a hurry you will have abundance of lazy fellows unwilling to go about it.

George at the fork is going on but I think but slowly. He pretends there is so much grass he is obliged to hoe the whole as he weeds.

I cannot but observe that every thing, growing or not, foul or clean, has a yellowish cast which to be sure with those things that are really clean can only be owing to too great a moisture below that the plants have not as yet recovered and too much binding above about their stemms even in light land. The only cure for this must be stirring with the hoe, but then the planter with a full crop cannot give it that assistance and if he contracts his Cropping another year, when probably the seasons for tending will be more favourable, then he cannot make a crop from the smallness of the quantity.

It seems they will not finish turning the Tobacco hills this day though the whole gang with but two sick, the two Cow keepers out and one shelling of Corn, had this morning not above 14,000 hills to turn. The pretence is the ground has grown hard near the Cowyard. It may be so but I believe it is rather too hot for the people to work.

I had the curiosity to look over my last year's June book.[55] I find that I begun planting Tobacco then in May but was to the 22nd before I finished

---

[55] This June book has been lost or destroyed.

turning all my hills owing to the excessive drough[t] of the weather for it seems it did not rain all June through last year. But then I had wed out Mangorike Corn field and was in the River side field near done by the 27th of June. Now I have touched neither with my hoes so that though I may possibly get done planting this year before I did last, for I find even at the last I had 80, or 90,000 replanted and that I did not finish till the beginning of July when I dry planted all, yet I shall not be near so forward with my Corn field for to be sure it will take me late on Monday if it should not rain before I can get into it. However by my last year's observation my Corn though weedy is vastly better this year and I will not dispair should I lose a little. It can't be much. I also found that by the 21st of June I had wed over a piece of Cowpenns though it was prodigiously missing so that in Tobacco the two years are nearly alike. I have about 90,000 still to plant and by this day's replanting I am afraid a great deal to replant for 4 hands have not done this whole day much above half this 56,000 piece under the hill. But it must be lazyness in them for they have not kept Talbot and one boy full employed in drawing this day. They send me word it is the stiff land next the wood side and I do suppose by lightening those hills with a kind of spudd which I made each of them provide himself with they have been the longer about it. I see the ground is hard though the hills were turned not above 12 days agoe for in weeding with 5 hands this day from about 7 o'clock they will not have gone through above [blank] thousands. These things are taken notice of that I may not be too much depressed by my late management and I could not have been earlier for the cold dry spring through April and May has thrown me backward by making the ground too hard for the hoe to work with because upon a fair time of a day's work a gang of 26 hands did not turn me 10,000 hills although it was then cool before the rain. To be from hence I may say I tend too much and perhaps I must lessen the Crop by little and little every year. But the proper remedy must be to get the Corn field broke up sooner which I could not do as early as I did last year owing to the very wet winter.

25. *Monday.*

The blessed lovely rain yesterday which gave me an opportunity this day of finishing planting all the Crop of Tobacco I intend to tend and replanting full 200,000 of it. This day's planting alone not being replanted but as the hills were so lately turned and the plants with such good roots besides every now and then a sprinkle in the day I am in hopes there will be little occasion to replant that. However as Lawson was doubtful that we should not have plants enough of my own and had fetched a small Cart load from Coll. Tayloe's I have ordered them to be stuck in double in my Cowpenn ground that when I come to weed it I may prefer which of the two sorts of Tobacco I chuse.

I had indeed with a view if I found I could compleat it laid dung all along the road by the barley ground and had hilled up the same in order to plant it with Tobacco. But ever since these rains set in which brought us such a world of weeds and indeed the cold dry spring which made our hills so hard to turn I have given that thought out and intended to spread the dung in order for drilling upon it with barley this fall which I believe will be the case for I fancy I have full crop enough to employ me.

I think I trespassed a little upon the old man today by a most hearty day's work of gangs, Jobbers, Carpenters, and even spinners. For every toe has been as active as it could possibly be. I wish I may not have a little overdone myself but I was willing to make one push as so favorable an opportunity had offered and therefore by 4 o'clock I had planted and replanted full 200,000 plants and by God's blessings I do not fear at laughing at those forward people for certain I am whilst these weeds are floating the Corn fields their Tobacco grounds must suffer by them.

27. *Wednesday*.

Cloudy all day with a great probability of rain at night.

I got into my Corn field with my Mangorike people yesterday after breakfastime. Much work was not done, their weeding hoes not being helved, and really 4 of them sick besides the two Cow keepers, Phillis shelling Corn, and Mary Ann worming Tobacco, and Peter at the plow, and old Dinah quite given out in all 10 out of 32. So that I had but 22 at work.

This day the same people out. Not much work done and cloddy withall though very fine till this day when they began to complain of the weeds by turning yellow.

I had occasion to look into the expence of my flour which came from Bull run. 939 neat pounds. Used up 629¼ pounds. Left in the house only 185¾ pounds. Notwithstanding my directions about weighing out every grain there is a loss of 104 pounds of flour besides what is set down and what is expended which I beg leave to charge to the article of house keeping.

This little inquiry has made me attempt to settle the question whether it is cheaper to use flour bought at 12/6 the 100 which I am told my Son sells this at or to grind up our own wheat as we used to do when wheat sells at 4/ the bushel.

I allow this 939 pounds of flour to last just 91 days Upon an average one with another equal to one fourth part of the year. This flour at 12/6 the 100 comes to £5.14/7½. Four times as much for the year is £22.18/6, which buys at 4/ but 114 bushels and 3 pecks.

My usual allowance in wheat was half a barrel the week, equal to 130 bushels wheat the year which at 4/ [is] £31. Of course then flour at such a time at 12/6 would be cheaper than wheat by £8.1/6 the year and allow for the want of bran. 65 bushels of bran to be gained out of 130 bushels of wheat that at 12d the bushel would be £3.5. So that flour is still cheaper could you buy your bran at 12d by £4.6/6 and if we should reckon the cheating of Miller's the nibbling of wheat cleaning it and scanking the flour all of which have their ry and waste it must be much cheaper to buy flour at 12/6 even in such times when wheat sells at 4/.

How then does the Merchant Mill make so much profit? The answer is quite clear. The grudgeon or seconds which are wasted in families he may get 8/ the 100 for and 12d the bushel for bran. Or else by feeding stock he doubles that advantage by the ease in which he raises besides out of every good bushel of wheat he can get 30 pounds of 12/6 flour and about 15 pounds of 8/ flour besides his bran. Now allow the want of honesty to be equal in the Conductors of Merchant mills and the grinders etc. of wheat for the house. It must then be evident that though the merchant mill gains by the wheat he grinds yet the house keeper will lose by the wheat he grinds.

28. *Thursday.*

Fine growing weather acknowledged by every body. But at present I cannot see it in even rich Tobacco ground quite clear of weeds and that in the lightest as well as stiffest land. I suppose the latter may want stirring and I am endeavouring to have it done where ever I think the Tobacco has taken hold of the earth. As to the Corn, I do suppose that would grow had it always been kept clear of weeds but the clearing of it now must for a while sicken the plant and of Course make it turn yellow. However I am in great hopes as we are going over it now it may so clear it in its young state as to recover it again.

I think I have the clearest evidence in the world that kindness to a Negroe by way of reward for having done well is the surest way to spoil him although according to the general observation of the world most men are spurred on to diligence by rewards. However this species of gratitude is seldom experienced in a slave.

My man George at the fork whose care and diligence had carried on the plantation to a very fine prospect in Corn, the only thing they tend there, has been rewarded by me very frequently with meat from my Smoak house to encourage his continuance in doing well. And now his weeds are come upon him he takes double the time to do any one thing. Yesterday I was pretty early there. They had but 17 rows in the morning to weed out to get to the other Corn field which was little better than 2 rows a hand and George himself had but 1 row to do, these rows shorter than all the rest by the depth of the Cotton patch. And in the others they used to do 4 rows apiece per day and this morning when I went there the women had better than a row apiece to finish that field and Mr. George was but in his second row in the other field. I looked particularly and carefully to see the work yesterday that was to be done. It was perfectly light and far from being as foul as what had been done when he did 5 rows the day and the rest 4. Therefore, I ordered them all a sound whipping and George should have been well paid only he had an excuse of removing the Cowpenn. The wench Judy sent to my house for broad hoes full an hour by sun did not get here till I was going to bed. I gave her a sound basting and Mr. George, instead of being rewarded with meat for doing well as before shall receive a sound correction, if by tomorrow I find he has not mended his pace.

Mary Ann worming my Tobacco had but a few rows this morning to finish the ground she was in and has not at 12 o'clock got into the other piece. Indeed she laid a foundation for this lazyness for after I came away she sent me word there were abundance of worms and she wanted Sukey, I suppose to keep her company in her lazyness. But she shall have but one reproof more and the next shall be a sound whipping.

I am puzzled to account for a very plain observation at my fork Quarter. My rows of Corn at 7 feet distance and [in] the Cowpenned part of it I have sown a little flax. The Corn there is laying by and it is remarkable that it is all very fine except here and there a row which looks very yellow though not near so foul before it was laid by as the rest of it. The ground is equally light and if the Flax had occasioned this the wonder would be why more of it was not so. The Corn was equally high with the rest and has not changed till yesterday though it has been some time laid by whilst the other carries a deep green. George tells me those rows were set Corn but how they came to grow so much and turn yellow all [a]t once is still the mistery.

Grieg took his leave today. I showed him Hopkins' and Bayley's[56] letter to Mortimer wherein on the 10 of March last they bid Mortimer tell me Molleson refused to pay the £5.16/1 for the medicine which he had bought on my account the July before. I also showed Grieg where Molleson had charged it to me as paid to them but in March he tells them he had no effects of mine. Grieg

[56] Hopkins and Bayley was probably a firm of druggists in London.

was very wrath and swore it must be a damned lie or some impudence of one of Molleson's Clerks for it must be impossible that he could be without £5 or that he should scruple to pay it even for my honour when he had paid my Son's bill for £50 upon my indorsement and to be sure if he had not effects to pay this £5 he had not as yet any remittance to pay the £50. I allowed his reasoning and wrote to Molleson in that stile expressing my astonishment at the thing and desired to have it explained immediately and if it was a behaviour in his Clerk such a rascal ought to be showed his door instantly.

I have written to Hopkins and Bayley for [a] clear explanation of this affair also but would not send the letter by Grieg and shall send it to Mortimer to go by Carnaby.

29. *Friday.* 30. *Saturday.*

Heavily engaged in my corn field; it is so very stiff, most part of it, so very cloddy by being broke up really wet or we must not have broke it up at all such was the winter and the spring after it, and by means of the late rains so full of weeds and grass that I cannot tell what to think of it, for really we cannot, the best hands, do a tollerable day's work and yet as to higth and indeed strength in the general the corn looks well except as to its yellow state which to be sure will come about again from the visible strength of the ground as soon as the weeds and grass are taken away.

Note: we do this weeding with a good hill least we should be late in laying it by.

JULY 1770

1. *Sunday.*

I am almost afraid I shall lose some Crop this year. My ground through the wet winter down to March exceeding wet was obliged to be broke up when too moist and it is now too hard for the best hand to do a common day's work and a great sickness amongst all my people that I much question whether this week will clear my Mangorike Corn field and the River side is still to lay by.

At the fork George, the principal hand, the half of every day sick with a fever and Ague. Vomits cannot cure him as usual and there is still a great deal more than half of his Corn to lay by.

The Corn every where but in a few spots looks well but as it is wed the under leaves every here and there fire at their ends.

My Tobacco still a good deal missing, and very little in any growing state. I shall tomorrow, god willing, have stirred and wed out about 56,000 and I have a great deal more that wants the hoe. I must not dispair but I hardly know what to do. I have attempted to assist with 2 plows but oxen can do nothing in hot weather and horses are too poor as I have no Corn to give them and one of my plowmen very sick yesterday. However tomorrow we try again. It may be things will turn out better.

The Barley not yet ripe and I believe very sorry at last. I had a head gathered though large and burley yet the grain excessively shrivelled and this was tended in drills and twice wed.

In short for such a wet winter and so sickly a gang now I must conclude I have over cropt myself. Yet as no endeavour has been wanting I will go on with prudence and contentment.

I am certain that I tended above 80,000 more Corn hills last year and had early in July laid by every plant of it but then June was a dry month and the winter before it not a wet one.

5. *Thursday.*

Our court set from the 2nd till yesterday noon at which time I understood they had finished every thing laid before them. But I imagine it can only be with respect to two indulgences, one to Coll. Smith who was engaged in repairing his Mill dam and begged the Court to put off his causes, [and] The other to Mr. Plummer[57] who was taken ill the night of the 1st day of the Court. I was attacked with a pretty wrapping lax on Tuesday night and could not attend yesterday.

Neither could I see my plantations but I understood from my Overseers that the Corn field was so hard as well as foul that all my people did but little day's work. The foreman in particular did not quite finish one row up the left hand side of the gate in all yesterday. Indeed it is a long row but I am astonished at it for one part of it every body must acknowledge is light ground but as he was before the gang he is either doing nothing to keep them back or because he saw they could not keep up with him. They tell me what with the stiffness of the soil and the weeds the Corn pipes up in its blades in the middle of the day. I might add the dryness of the weather also for such land cannot want rain a week and it has been a week last monday since we have had any rain though by the prodigious coolness of the weather now it must have rained very much to the Northwards for besides my getting intirely into thick cloaths

---

[57] John Plummer (d. 1771) was sheriff and justice of the peace in Richmond Co.

I could bear a fire this morning. But perhaps I myself may be something bilious in my constitution at this time and therefore subject to be cold for by the purging which I had I discovered a vast discharge of bile and, although I did nothing to check it but lay quite still all day and let it stop of its own according as it had no gripping effects, I still imagine the load of it is not quite removed for by some eruputions I discover the taste of rotten eggs which is always a symptom to me in every constitution as well as my own of abundance of bile growing a little putrid and indeed I fancy there may be a similarity between that and the contents of an egg.

This cool weather produces some advantage to us for the day before it I think I never knew more Musketoes at this place in my life and this weather has made them a little quiet.

My ground every where is exceeding hard to work even in my upland Tobacco hills which have been but very lately turned. The rains that fell have baked it much and they are obliged to hoe the whole of it.

I understand I have still in some places much Tobacco missing in the hills though it has been so intirely planted and replanted. If we get a rain I shall go over it again, late as it is, for last year I planted later than this and made fine Tobacco of it by topping it low.

I cannot help observing as I have before done that this climate is so changing unless it returns to his former state Virginia will be no Tobacco Colony soon and if the winters continue so wet and the springs so long, cold even into the summer, no stiff land can grow any Tobacco very shortly. What then can we tend? Our wheat what with rust and weavil flye seems now to produce no Crop even though drilled and our Corn by one disaster or another produces very little. There is a great scarcity of it in the Colony now by means of the gust last year and I have heard it is so low and foul in abundance of places that none or very little can be expected to be made this year. Plows are much talked of but who without food for their Creatures can find strength enough to work them properly and what can this scratching of the ground do with one horse as it [is] now practiced. I am told that even in the low grounds of Northumberland where they all plow in the scratching manner the corn is extremely low which I know unless deep worked will not produce any thing though if it can be worked deep I am perswaded it may for I once had a field in which I discovered the Overseer had not broke up his ground but only covered it over with a slight weeding. I made him July hoe the whole field over and although the Corn was low I had an ear of Corn for every stalk near as long as the stalk after the tops were cut off.

We have had an appearance in the sky something like a Comet though without any tail. It is a week last Tuesday since I discovered it and by its possition it must have been then in view about a week before. But it takes such changes first from East to West then from West to the Northward of the East then from Northeast obliquely to the South that I believe it will be difficult for anyone to say what it is. Last night it could not be seen any where and indeed I did imagine so, for the night before within about an hour of day it rose above the horizon in the North East and hauled away to the Southward for that hour in which I could see it. But the daylight advancing, it necessarily disappeared which it seems is one of the circumstances attending Comets at their first appearance in their greatest distance from the sun they emit only a burr around their nuclei as this did and as they approach near the sun acquire their tail from the sun's influence upon that burry atmosphere which is always opposition to the point of influence.

Tom Reed of Northumberland who acts for James McCall would not receive my ballance which Sam Hipkins had offered to pay him according to my Account drawn off and wanted to submit it to arbitration. I refused that because from Long experience I had discovered Arbitrators not generally sworn acted partially upon one side or the other and therefore I chose to settle the matter if he pleased by a Court.

It seems Mr. Edwards who last March was 12 months wrote me a letter about a hogshead of Tobacco of mine that he had paid into Mr. McCall's hands for 25/ the Centum to be carried to my account. Now wrote me by Reid that he paid it to Reid for 20/ the centum and Reid returned it to him. Therefore he let him credit me for what he would give and this he says according to my directions though in his letter of March twelvemonth he expressly says he paid it to James McCall for 25/ if he kept it according to my express directions. And indeed the last letter is so contradictory of the first that I cannot help thinking that some influencing circumstances has made my friend Richard write this last letter to favor Tom Reid's method of drawing up this account for he by keeping that hogshead from my Credit till the next year deducts 6 per Cent off from it as old Tobacco and then allows me but 20/. The difference is but small. However this Mr. Reid shall not easily worm me out of his 5/ the Cent and 6 per Cent for I find I can easily know from the inspectors where this Tobacco passed when it was taken out from their Warehouse and could I be allowed to swear in my own case I could swear that James McCall sometime before he left the Country told me at Coll. Tayloe's that Edwards had paid him that Tobacco and insisted upon 25/ but believed he could not allow so much. However upon my telling him he allowed it to others on Account he said he would have no dispute about it and agreed to allow me 25/.

6. Friday.

We have had no rain since Sunday the 24th of June which in my stiff land is enough to make me dispair of making any thing either in Corn or Tobacco for the ground is really so hard that the people cannot work it to do a tollerable day's work neither in the Corn nor in the Tobacco ground and what is worse than this the ground worm which to all experience used to leave us before this time of the year has risen in my Tobacco ground and cut off since it has been wed. The paddoc in Particular which I saw all well standing and spreading the hill long since I last replanted it now as they are weeding it hardly seems to have a plant in a row so that instead of dispair things are almost got to a certainty that we shall make very little if any Tobacco this year. Add to this my hands are every day taken sick with both bilious and inflammatory fevers. God knows the end of this. These 3 cold days have produced me abundance of misfortune.

I send this day to Mr. Adderton's store in Northumberland to lay out 1,550 pounds Crop Tobacco. He is to allow me 25/ the Centum and sells good Oznabrugs as the store keeper told me last Tuesday at 9d the yard. I well remember that formerly grass hoppers used to eat only a hole here and there in the leaf of a Tobacco plant which would grow larger as the plant grew but I cannot say except once within these 10 years that I ever knew grass hoppers eat up whole plants and whole fields before this year which they really have done very completely for as to horn worm I have been able to keep them under but whilst the wenches having been going over a field to destroy the worms the grass hoppers have followed and eaten that very Tobacco. Perhaps they are more numerous now than they used to be or it may be plants by being young[er] than they used to be in those days for every body pitch[ed] then in April or May they are sweeter to the grass hoppers than they used to be formerly. But as Mr. Berkeley wrote me of this complaint the beginning of June this hardly can be a reason and we must look upon their present destruction to be owing to the vast increase of numbers. But it is to be wondered why the plenty of grass has not furnished food enough for them for it is very remarkable they are only in the cleanest ground. If this does not in a few years destroy the possibility of making Tobacco they must meet with some destruction themselves. It is not the green grass hopper but one of a sooty dusty colour and except in size resembles much the Asiatic locust. We must submit to all such destruction and do as well as we can, but I believe it will be difficult under such a staple to make a tollerable subsistence. It might be wrong to call them judgments and as these things are by the permission of the great Creator we ought to hope for his mercy.

I am told that even in the richest low grounds in Northumberland the prospects are so bad that at our last court many people did not expect there would be Corn made this Crop to keep the Inhabitants. Yet we know there is between this and probable frosts some months and things may turn out better. Therefore I still hope for the best.

I had a purging of a watery nature which seized me on Tuesday night [and] held me all day on Wednesday for as it was without pain I would not check it. But yesterday although the disorder had stopped itself my bowels felt very trembling and I had a great lassitude upon my spirits. Note: for an old man I took the best method and kept still during the disorder and did not use any food but broth and a teaspoonful or two of a cordial.

This has been called a seasonable year but I think from my experience in the growth of every thing except in very light land it has been far otherwise and I never desire to see such another. We have had rains it is true oftener than for some years we used to have. But they have been remarkably so hard that where the land any thing stiff has been but just turned nothing could grow away by the baking of the earth to get out of the way of the insects that abound at this time of the year. Perhaps the prodigious wetness of the winter may have put the stiff land into this situation of baking after every sharp shower.

This morning just as I expected having said I should make very little in either Corn or tobacco I was told by the most insolent as well as most impudent person amongst men (my son) That was because I would follow my own way. Pray Sir, what are my ways? Planting your tobacco drye. That Sir is evidently all the tobacco I have that looks tollerable and in the same field though on the other side of the run it was planted in a season where it is not near so well standing and does not look half so well. Then, Your ground was lighter by G—. By the same oath it is if possible a million of times harder and stiffer.

I was then asked as I planted the same time as they did at Marsk[58] why was not my tobacco as forward. Sir you don't know what you say. In the first place, that tobacco is forwarder than Marsk. In the next Marsk tobacco is sweet scented and of a quicker growth; and that earth I'll be sworn not half so stiff as mine. To which the dutifull child replyed I would swear anything. An impudent rascal. But so it is, a scoundrel determined to abuse his father will be contradictory and as Confident about what he does not know.

He then told me I always broke my ground up wet. I answered this year it really was so; and I was obliged to do it or not break it up at all, for it had

[58] Marsk was one of Col. Tayloe's tracts in Richmond Co.

not been drye since the September gust, and indeed before, from the 23rd of August. I was answered that was Strange when his wheat at Hickory Thicket had wanted rain All the Spring. To be sure Sir, that might be, and mine be too wet; besides the dryness and the Coldness of the Spring, though it baked, it had not dryed it; for it was evident on the turning those hills they turned up in moist Clods which the hoes were obliged to pound fine.

In short, this man is a brute to his father and if he is so contradictory in the H[ouse of] B[urgesses] it must be impossible anyone should answer him or indeed mind a man who regards not what he says. He has not seen my estate this whole year but in Passing by, and yet he will find fault because sworn to do it with his father. If I ask him why richer lands in my neighbourhood don't exceed me in cropping, Then I am answered they make better tobacco. Ask why they don't Sell better, then I am boldly told they do which is too gross a falsehood for a man to utter.

This great manager has a lightland plantation and mine is stiff. He plants early, breaks up drye, and what not and yet how much does he make? A question to be asked to a man in debt and one that keeps no house and except in wearing cloths and a little corn to two hands no kind of Expence whatever.

7. *Saturday.*

Yesterday agreeable to our ardent prayers about 12 o'clock there came on a rain which from its mildness and quantity we will pronounce a great blessing. It now rains and looks as if it would continue which will be no disadvantage to a Crop so missing as mine was. I replanted last night all upon the top of the hill and to the mudhouse which makes twice replanting with some and three times with others. I am also replanting the great piece by the Chessnut tree. It contains 47 acres in the whole which at 4,000 to the acre is 188,000 plants. They have got full half way this morning but I am a little doubtful my plant patches will not afford me fine plants enough. However though the tops are small the roots I see are very large. I will stick them in and have sent to Tutt's and to Hiccory thicket to see if none can be had there. I know the present Cow penn ground was stuck with a plant of my own and a plant of Coll. Tayloe's. I understand many of them are missing but in abundance of hills there are 2 plants alive. I shall therefore order should we fail to draw each spare plant and replant the rest as the season is so good.

I find I am not to act without fault to be found with me. My method of nurcing up my plants when I weed is condemned because some careless fellows throw now and then a clod over them just as if the bad execution of any thing was a proper rule for condemning the practice. A careless fellow in the old way of weeding might cut up a plant, perhaps a more dangerous accident than the covering of the plant. It also was objected to me that I had here and there a plant top which had not been wed. I own it and am really glad of it though I don't commend it as a planter. However it is a proof the ground is good for it has not been so long planted. Neither is it weedy. But I may venture to pronounce the same accident has happened to many a man with a full Crop.

I have ordered all my Corn not weed to be suckered now it is so wet and had my fork Cotton suckered last night. It is very fine and has received no small benifit from a hoeing I gave it after the weeding between the rows last week.

I confess my full Crop this year has been an inconvenience because it has proved a hasty dripping year at the time of weeding the Corn so that all that has been to do again and the corn has been injured by it. But I am of opinion from the experience of many years the man that has calculated by a little Crop for a wet year has lost greatly by it. I found that last year and made almost double of what better lands have produce[d] by tending a large Crop.

9. *Monday*.

Sent up by my Son the Transfer note for 528 pounds my light hogshead in Falmouth warehouse to be paid as far as it will go in discharge of my Levies there, If James Broone, my Overseer, has not got them paid. If he has the transfer to be sold and paid to the person who has been kind enough to discharge my levies.

Rode out this day with Billy Ball who came on Saturday from Rippon Hall. I went on purpose with him to judge of the Character which he had given of my Crop under his care there. Indeed the friday and Saterday's rain had altered the Crop vastly here especially that part of it which had been wed out. But he was so pleased with it that I began to imagine the Rippon Crop was but indifferent but he assured me the Mangorike Corn in the general was better than any he had seen even all the way he came up and as to the Tobacco it had really spread the hill much better than any he had seen and comparing the fields in their size to what he had seen he concluded without accident I must make a large Crop. He had seen none cleaner of weeds than mine. Some people indeed had topped a little more than I had and he believed he had at Rippon but he did not like any body's Tobacco half so well as mine. As to the fork Corn that on the left hand side he looked upon to [be] very fine. Some little of it looked fady which he would imagine was owing to the near distance in which it was planted in the step but I told him it was rather the weeds which had been so lately taken away and hilled up and that it had not as yet felt the effects of the rain. To convince him of this I showed him a pretty large spot full as near in the steep and yet of a deep black green only from those weeds being cut down and the Corn hilled up 10 days before which I had done least it should suffer.

It will take me till Tuesday night at least to finish the Mangorike Corn-field. George will finish the field he is in as to his own rows this night but the women will be some time tomorrow in it. He then lays by the last field of the four which has been now three times worked and he must again lay by the first field by the quarter for that is very green yet. The weeds are shot apace again and ought to be cut up before that corn is done with.

Manuel by means of the rain on friday and saterday will not have done the River side field before some part of tomorrow. He has made a long jobb of it. Near 4 weeks.

Tomorrow I sow my last year English broccoli seed but I must soak them in saltpetre water for those which I sowed in June are hardly any of them come up. Gardners are now rogues. Their seeds only sprout a few when sown in the spring and broccoli gets its growth so much if sown then that the winter frosts kill it but Coll. Frank Thorn[ton][59] told [me] if I sow it in June or July he has found it will stand the winter very well.

My plows having been 3 weeks about the same work which they did last year in 12 days, that is 19 days, sundays deducted, which is an excess of 7 days, I have been considering (supposing the people equally diligent) to what this difference can be owing; and as I planted in 4 feet rows at 4 feet distance last year, and have this year planted at 7 feet rows and 2 foot distance, I have calculated the real work in both ways.

In either way the work of the row must be equal, whether planted at 2 or 4 feet distance, therefore to prove what difference there is in the work from the number of square feet in an acre (to wit), 43,560, deduct the distance in the step out of those square feet and it must give the quantity.

In the 7 feet rows the distance to be deducted is 6,220 feet because the contents in rows are 3,111 which leaves 39,338 square feet to be worked; And as 4 feet distance gives 2,722 Corn hills, their distance at 4 feet will be 10,888 to be deducted out of the square feet in the acre, which leaves but 32,672 square feet to be worked. Of course, 7 feet rows work in every acre 6,666 square feet more than 4 feet rows work. Now as the River side corn field is 82½ acres

[59] Col. Frank Thornton (d. 1784) of Society Hill was a planter and justice of the peace in Stafford Co.

multiply this excess into that, and it will show perhaps a good reason for this length of time in working.

6,666 square feet more in one acre give in 82½ Acres 137,486 square feet. Therefore if the 4 feet way they workt last year was done in 12 days this 7 foot way ought to have been done in [blank] days so that my plowmen have not been diligent.

11. *Wednesday*.

Though I was made to believe by every message from Manuel that he should be done the River side field yesterday, yet I see nothing of him in the Cornfield at the fork. Neither will he be there before 10 o'clock today. Therefore my long taken resolution shall shortly be put in Execution.

Yesterday I cut my barley down. But a very trifling Crop. Talbot is bringing it in today for I must tread it out under my own eye.

This day we are cutting down my wheat. I fear a crope will be more trifling than the barley for this wet winter in my low stiff soil has been very bad for all kinds of winter grain.

Lawson will not finish the Cornfield before some time early tormorrow which will make 12 days and the people have been in that very heavy tending Corn. Indeed at this rate my whole Crop would cost me 25 days' work at each weeding and therefore I think whilst I tend in 7 feet rows I must contrive to work the spaces between with plows if I possibly can.

Could it be done with Oxen I might do it but then to go a serviceable depth those Creatures even with shifting every day that is a fresh yoke at midday will not hold out without corn feeding as my people manage and to feed them will be an expence that no crop can bear. Upon the whole then the working without plows must be a greater profit unless I should content myself by a little thin scratching the earth out of all heart.

George at the fork thinks he shall finish going over the third time his whole Crop of Corn early tomorrow. He must then go the 4th time over 3/4 of it for it is not high enough to lay by as they call it and indeed though dunged many nolds look very yellow but I suppose they rather dunged these worse than the other and perhaps the weeds which never died upon this nolds may have contributed to this yellowness. But I believe the principal error has been upon all my plantations here the not thinning this Corn soon enough and that even those spare stalks have injured the other. I remedied it in one of the fork fields which is very fine.

Last night my people tell me they saw 2 distinct comets with long tails about an hour and a half after the moon rise tending to the Northward with their tails before them as they advanced. Their accounts are so wild and uncertain that if we have clear weather tonight I will contrive to look at them.

To find out what difference (if there is any) there is in working an Acre laid off in 7 feet rows or in 4 feet rows: Every 28 feet makes 4 rows 7 feet wide. Of course it makes 7 rows 4 feet wide. Multiply this 28 by 10. It gives 280. Then A piece of ground 280 feet wide gives 40 rows at 7 feet distance or 70 rows at 4 feet distance. Now a piece of ground 152 long by 280 wide gives 43,560 square feet which is the full contents of an acre. Of course then that 280 feet laid off in 7 feet rows will be 40 rows and laid off in 4 feet rows will be 70 rows.

As then these rows in both ways must be equal as to their working where the Corn is planted, it will be necessary first to deduct the number of 4 feet rows out of the square feet in the acre, to find the quantity of work in tending Corn that way: Then deduct the number of 7 feet rows to find the work in tending Corn that way; and on which soever side the excess shall be, on that will be the overplus labour:

4 feet rows	7 feet rows
43,560	43,560
70	40
43,490	43,520
	43,490
	…30 more work

in the 7 feet way, then in the 4 feet in 1 acre. By this every Acre then in the 7 feet way works 30 square feet, more than it does in the 4 feet way.

In my whole Complement then of 82 Acres, I had only an excess in labour of 2,460 square feet, which employed my plows this year full 7 days in the 7 feet way, more than it did last year in the 4 feet way; which to be sure must be a proof of the extraordinary idleness of my people.

This work then may be shortened by calculating the difference between the rows for where there are fewest rows there must be more work. And in 82 acres it appears there could not be but 2 rows and a little better than a third more at 152 feet in length, in the whole 82 acres.

12. *Thursday.*

Mangorike Corn field will not be finished weeding before near 12 o'clock this day.

It was begun tuesday, the 26th, in the evening for all monday 25th of June we were planting tobacco and till the evening of tuesday. So that allowing 3½ days in June then the 2, 3, 4, 5, and half the 6th which was fryday when it rained and so it did on Saturday when we again replanted our tobacco there must have been 8 days working in Corn. Then the 8, 9, 10, 11 and half the 12. It makes in all 12 and a half days' work in that field. There is no telling the quantity per day each hand for they were never all there by 8 and 10 hands. Add to this 1/3 of the ground prodigious stiff as well as weedy and the other 2/3 vastly full of grass and weeds.

The corn everywhere very yellow; the last rain has only recovered what was wed before it, and not all of that. I almost think it has been injured by not being thinned sooner. It must be a good way to thin immediately after Setting it, provided that is done as early as it was this year.

I thought I should catch manuel; he pretends the river field was as much work again this year as it was last year, but I told him it was bare 2 rows and 1/3 more.

Oxen are not the thing to plow with, they are slow at best, and tire every hot day. And the plowmen unmercifull to them by constant beating them; a villanous fault always in Manuel; and if I get horses, then they are rode out in the nights by the negroes. So that on all accounts hoes are the surest and best way of tending, except where a man manages and plows himself and then he must take care of his horses also.

In short to do this work well there can anyway only but small crops be tended in wet years; and as no man can tell how the year will be he must be contented to lose a little in a wet year and keep a large crop going in Case it Should be a drye year when he can tend it with his hoes full half as much again as is generally done.

My overseer seems certain of a fine Crop of Corn this year. I believe the rains will continue, but unless the ground is very strong I doubt of it, for it is too late in the year to have yellow corn. But then every body's is so, plows as well as hoes.

Musketoes excessively numerous.

My wheat all near housed. I never expected any crop, and I believe I shall not be disappointed in hardly getting my seed, now it is got together it is but a handfull. I tended it in drills; but I see in wet winters without laying the ridges very high, the broadcast must be the best way. However, I s[h]all trye it once more before I give it out and if I can I will contrive to lay the earth up in very high ridges, and as it will be at 6 foot distance by making two drills in each ridge I am in hopes it may do especially if it is not another wet winter again. And as I intend peas between, perhaps with both crops something may be made.

I find I am always to be unlucky in my tending for winter food for my Oxen that cart in my wood; for I had last month at least 6,000 hanover turneps planted out which grew away well, but being old and not going to see them often; the two Ewes that suckled my lambs, by the carelessness of my new gardener have been in and eaten them all down. That rascal told me it was my hogs; but I at last found him out. I see by his carelessness I am not better off than I was with Johnny. [H]e was a rogue that sold every thing and this is a villain that lets every thing be [r]uined even by weeds, for nobody walks the garden and he does nothing.

I am thinking that if another year when I tend corn in 7 foot rows I should the first weeding instead of working all abroad as I now do I should ridge up the middle between the rows as we used to do, and cover down the grass in that ridge, and at the same time give the corn its proportion of earth, it would not [be] quicker done than we now do it. This ridge then is to be halled to the corn when we lay it by; So that although the first weeding only one hand goes in a row up and down to ridge it well from the corn in both corn rows: Yet in laying by each hand takes only half that ridge and goes up one side a corn row and returns on the other side the corn row halling the earth still to the corn from the ridges of both rows. By this means each row of corn being dressed by one and the same hand it must be best done.

Lawson proposes to clean the tobacco below the hill, then what is left above, and give the pease a hilling, and then to the river side. Note: as the great piece of tobacco is but just planted, as it were, I shall allow them to weed it into the middle as they used to do without making a hill round the small tobacco as it seems to likely to continue moist.

Lucy went to lay out about 1,500 pounds tobacco in Blare's store[60] for linnen and cotton for my people. He allows 25/ per Cent goods at 75 per Cent.

13. *Friday.*

Last night we had a very fine rain which will give us an opportunity of replanting our Crop of Tobacco now for the 4th time if any should be missing. And as it is but the second day of old July planters know that something may be made of it. Therefore it is much better to work the ground with a plant in every hill than without one.

This rain I also receive as a prodigious blessing for my Corn. It [is] still in a jaundiced state and with moisture. The ground stands the best chance to recover it.

[60] Tom Blair was a small merchant in Westmoreland Co. who kept a store at Nomini.

My daughter Lucy yesterday went to Tom Blair's store on Nomony and laid out for me in brown linnen and Cotton for my people Mozingo's hogshead of 974 pounds and 30 for the Cask and also the transfer notes paid me for Mr. Parker by Ben Bramham[61] which reduced to Crop make in all 1,550 at 25/ the Centum, the goods at 75 per Cent upon his first Cost. Reasonable in the linnen although without the boundty taken off in British Oznabrugs exported from England. The whole amount to £19.7.6.

I was raised this morning by a complaint in my left arm which I have had more or less every since february last. It is no swelling nor wasting hardness or too great a relaxation but a real pain in the muscles from the shoulder down to the bent of the elbow. I have tried every species of fomentation, Embrocation, and strengthening plaisters of various sorts as well as constant friction of the part and have been offen perswaded of great relief from many of them as for many day[s] together I have been quite free from pain but lately I have not been able either to put my Arm behind my back upon my head or to push any thing out wards from me without great pain.

I remember just such a complaint in my right arm 6 years agoe in the very same part which yielded to no application that I could be advised of or could think of myself but by keeping a perpetual friction upon the part it wore away and I fancied the friction had by degrees rubbed it out. I can also remember that by being then addicted to lie upon the right side and of course upon the right arm frequently with head I was by means of my Vertigo obliged to change that position in lying so that by accident I fancied I got into the true cause of that complaint and removed it by this change in lying which though it did not bruise it certainly obstructed the circulation in those juices whatever they are that pass in and about the muscles and nerves and I now think my left arm is affected by the weight of my body and head frequently getting upon the arm in my sleep. But how I am to relieve that is to me a great puzzle for if I lie on my right side I am almost sure of a vertigenous whirl from a constant discovery that all the wind in my body rushes up to my stomach and by affecting the nervous coat occasions that swimming in my brain. However I will put on a soup plaister a little impregnated with the oil of Turpentine to give a warmth to those parts at the same time that it keeps the muscles tight.

There was but a very small sprinkling at the fork. George will be in a few hours out of that cornfield begun 3 days agoe. He then goes into the third field to hill that up which is the 4th time that his hoes has been engaged with that Corn.

---

[61] Ben Bramham was a farmer in Richmond Co.

I think if ever man had a fair trial between plows and hoes, that is, the plows drawn by oxen, I no[w have] one to convince me that those who argue for plows only argue for an extraordinary indulgence to the people regardless how much such contend against them both for profit and dispatch. They pretend they can tend much more with plows but unless they feed I assert and can prove that they cannot tend as much as the same number of hands for every Ox, horse, plowmen and plowboys can do.

In the first place the fork land is extremely light and as it has been wed over twice before though it is still grassy the labour in cutting or plowing that grass is certainly as easy as any such work can be in the Colony.

My fields there are each of them exactly laid off into 18 acres. I tend the Corn in rows at 7 feet distance. The ridges in which the Corn grows are exactly 4 feet. 5 women and 1 man began and finished cleaning and hilling up this Corn in less than 4 days. The number of rows were 36 each day.

Two days agoe two plowmen, 2 plowboys, 8 steers, and 4 horses set in to plow up the middle space which is barely 3 feet wide because 2 foot on each side the Corn reduces the 7 feet distance to 3 feet. These two plows in cool days do but 30 rows and in warm days not above 24. However set the average at 30, the 5 women and man does more work in 4 days than the plows do in 5 days. Of what use then are such plows to go a serviceable depth to make the Corn grow they cannot work with the hands and only to scratch the weeds is to do no service at all to the Corn. To feed the Creatures with Corn no Crop can support it and with it upon bare grass no Oxen can hold out in a warm day one half of the day. All the advantage then I get is to kill 4 or 5 of these oxen by beating them to make them draw and that is the sum and substance of this mighty business of plowing.

17. *Tuesday.*

Tollerable growing weather though the mornings and evenings are something cool. Indeed they have hardly been otherwise for our Corn and Tobacco growth above a week if that in the whole year.

My Son came home from his visit to Park and Acquia yesterday. The wheat all rusty. The people eating purchased Corn and that at a very great rate. No method of allowancing them to a peck a week. Very little Corn tended. Not field enough to make a proper allowance to keep them. Coll. Slaughter as yet got them no Carpenters to build their Tobacco houses. Tollerable good Tobacco though but a short crop of that and yet the Overseer wants his [p]ay increased. Proposes to manage both the plantations for 1/10 of every thing which he makes which is 2 shares and a half and as the Gentleman keeps eating his wheat his maintenance will be probably 2 shares more so that I suppose in hopes of making something he is to contrive to get the whole profits.

Wed out my uphill Tobacco and hilling up my pease. I shall from thence finish laying by my Corn at the fork and at the Riverside but I must first weed my large piece Tobacco.

No news of Ambrose as yet.

18. *Wednesday.*

My pease completely done with till the gathering time and really in the general a very fine patch. If last year I saved 60 bushels when they were not near so good out of one fourth of this ground I may promise myself without accidents near 300 bushels. But 200 will be an agreeable profit to me for I sold them for necessaries for my house at a reasonable price, and the pease fetched me 4/ the bushel.

I was very tauntingly criticised upon last night though these pease cost me but one day's work of making pease at a dear rate. What was the matter? A large piece of Tobacco not wed out. It is very true. A large piece of Tobacco planted only the 26th of June of which perhaps not one tenth lived by means of the ground warmth the 2, 3, and 4th of July in that very cold spell and only replanted last friday by the Thursday night's rain. Therefore in its nature the ground dangerous to be touched for fear of disturbing those late planted roots but because a very few plants looked clever the management of the planter most execrably arraigned. However I have got into the ground and by tomorrow night perhaps there will hardly be a weed seen. There is a growing bud in every hill and I doubt not with common chances I shall make every such Critic grit his teeth with envy at my success.

I could wish the right hand of the fork Corn fields began to show a little greenness more than they did. They have been clean above a week but it is the knoles that look yellow and I am afraid they were not so well dunged as they should be. I shall get out laying by my third Corn field by thursday night or very early on friday. That is fine Corn all but a very little low sunken ground behind the Quarter. I will then give another brushing to the first field laid by and allready 4 times worked for the grass will not die.

I am determined never more to tend a seed of flax between Corn for if my pease which only took one day's work are looked upon as such a dear jobb to me that flax in about 3,000 Corn hills will be certainly much dearer for although the Corn is as high as you please it has made it look fading at the bottom.

No news of Ambrose as yet.

19. *Thursday.*

Without more rain very little can be made in my stiff land. That which fell last Thursday in the night only made a season for replanting where the hill had been fresh turned and the Corn received no benefit from it for I dug this day to the moisture and it was above the depth of my own wrist from the fingers' ends and at the fork there has been none since last monday 3 weeks, the 25 day of June. The people at work don't turn up the least moisture. I have been very unfortunate in working my stiffest land this year. It was too wet during the winter and really too moist when broke up which I was obliged to do or not tend it at all and now it is nothing but clods notwithstanding 2 weedings besides the breaking up. The Corn is yellow and will remain so without more moisture.

My left arm continues still very uneasy to me. It is seldom I can lift it to my head, pick my nose with it, and never turn it behind me, and hardly ever dare reach any thing with it ever so little out of a direct line before my body, there is such a certainty of pain in the muscles between my shoulder and the bent of my elbow. I have tried every thing I know of for it: Vinegar and herb fomentation, embrocations with oil of Turpentine, and spirits strengthening plaisters and even malaxing plaisters impregnated with Chymical oils. I have bathed it with Oppodeldock[62] and camphorated spirits. It neither swells, grows hard nor softer than the other arm, neither does it lessen, and there is not the least pain either in the joint above or in the joint below, only sometimes an uneasiness by a seeming consent of parts. I have now taken to a very frequent friction of it which seems to give it the most ease and have almost an inclination to cup it. I shall with Dr. Arbuthnot[63] make an embrocation of Liquid Laudanum and spirits.

I cannot help taking notice that the long time I have lived, the care I have taken of my family, the paying off Children's fortunes, and putting out 3 sons with an Estate very well to pass in the world, still maintaining a large family at home, and all this without being in debt but a very trifle, I say, I cannot help taking notice that these circumstances well considered as they ought to be in a country almost universally enthralled do not preserve to my with my Son the character even of a tollerable manager. Every thing that I do must be excessively wrong although vastly superior in the produce to any proportion of his profit and much greater than better lands have produced for any number

---

[62] Opodeldoc is a name for a number of soap liniments sometimes compounded. Carter could also be referring to a kind of plaster.

[63] Dr. John Arbuthnot (1667–1735), English physician and literary figure. A recent study is Lester M. Beattie, *John Arbuthnot: Mathematician and Satirist* (Cambridge, 1935).

of years in my Neighbourhood. If this don't denote a perverse disposition either to quarrel with me or provoke me nothing can.

It is really grievous to hear any accidental bad prospect which will happen almost in any year imputed solely to my bad management. One while I am told I shall not have half plants enough for my Crop. Another while when my Crop is not quite so full standing as every body must really wish then no body ever had so many plants. If I, to preserve a reality in my conduct, happen to have not quite so sightly a field as others have upon a road then how much better do they manage and for God sake what is it I do? I tend double the Crop of other people because I know I am able to tend it in tollerable years and in a wet year I am certain to have at least as much come to perfection as they have. Again in order to make us[e] of my plants when full grown I plant them in dry seasons and cover them down which evidently appears to be an unexceptionable way even this year for where I did it there the Tobacco is largest which the ground worm did not cut up and as ground worm are common to all kinds of planting why is this method to be condemned when they have only destroyed it there in the same proportion as the[y] have done in planting with seasons. Again when I weed tobacco in order to save the tender roots from the sun I give it a light earthing instead of leaving it quite bare according to the common practice and this does save it evidently for where the Overseer did not earth it up but wed in the common way many young plants died which did not do where it was earthed up, If there is any truth in a constant daily observation.

I never omitted planting and replanting in every season and this I have done 5 times in some pieces where the ground worm have continually destroyed me and because those plants not put in the ground yet a week are some of them missing by the hot suns when they were very small this is called my method of planting just as if I could be supposed to do wrong out of obstinacy. Certainly there is not only a damnable deal of ill nature but a hellish stupidity in such an abandoned conversation that I am every day of my life tormented with whilst the Gentleman himself knows that out of the small crop which he tends he hardly has a plant equal to numbers of mine and none superior and as to his produce poor fellow that would make me pity him if his behaviour had not shut up every such bowel.

20. *Friday.*

I have rid out this day for exercise purely for really there seems to be no other temptation. The forward planter perhaps upon his light soil may please himself with a singular happiness in dry weather for let who will say to the contrary our Mills could not be so dry if the weather was otherwise and I am certain my Soil is too dry for any Cropping stiff as it is.

I reckon I shall pull my flax by breakfast time. It is but a so so Crop for the chance I have run in losing the Corn amongst which it was sown. However such strong stalks by giving it a speedy broad high ridge may possibly save it. It is both tasseled and silked and really very fine all to a fading just begun at bottom.

Manuel will be early in the other field. Really a very good one and he shall go over the 4th and last field. He says he shall be done all next week. George and his gang come to help Mangorike as soon as this flax Corn is ridged up which may be to day. But tomorrow early without accidents it will be done.

Ambrose it seems by the Children's Account is every day in fork Jammy's house. I have set a watch for him and shall send another in hopes to catch him. It seems he brings his meal in there and bakes his bread.

21. *Saturday.*

No dew this morning and so it has been ever since the great fogg this day sevennights. Indeed I dreaded that fogg as preceding a very dry spell and as it came on with a Southwardly wind I am the more confirmed in it for I think that a Southerly wind in July has not for many years promised any moisture nor produced any where it was constant.

This weather of course must make all my Cropping precarious and I am doubtful that most of my last piece of Tobacco which is a very large one will not stand it out for I saw no moisture in the ground yesterday as they were weeding it. The chief of the plants but live buds, many of which seem to be dying and the ground worm was cutting off what had begun to grow in the hills. This is a melancholly circumstance and would be a mortifying one was it not for our hopes in the merciful protector of all things. However I have done my best. My Crop large as it is was all planted and most of it replanted and abundance of it three and four times replanted by the 26th day of June and that in hills fresh turned which to a planter of any common experience is not of the latest for planting and to be sure those hills in little danger according to expectations of being quickly foul against. But that rain was heavy and the second that fell on the 13 of this month whilst it served to replant the ground again raised abundance of the grass and weeds so that whilst I was obliged to weed those hills I am very fearful it was only putting the plants into a way of dying from the hot dry weather.

I had all along dreaded the effects of that gust last year not only in what I immediately felt but in what I had reason to conclude for in earth so dissolved as mine was and remained so for a full month after I did conclude the whole would be reduced to as solid a state as ever it was and accordingly in November I broke every hill of it up in hopes the winter would divide it again. But the winter was so constantly wet that it rather contributed to consolidate it and the spring so cool and dry till late in May that the whole became as lumpy and cloddy as ever. The breaking and turning up of this could not be attempted before the rain set in and then the weeds made it light and hollow so that I apprehend that to be one cause why the Tobacco planted last friday did not stand as I could have wished and really endeavoured it should. Therefore let our state be what it will we must be contented and it is in vain to spend a disquieting thought about it could it be possibly avoided but my constant misfortune is that if my labour and pains at home produces nothing I have experienced that no labour used abroad at my plantations had a right to expect any for they never make any thing.

22. *Sunday.*

I went yesterday to Coll. Tayloe's where it was extremely hot but as the moon had changed in the morning we promised ourselves rain that evening and really if any thing but actual raining can be a proper sign of approaching rain I thought there appeared a very great one for a very heavy deep cloud arose quite from the North near to the Southwest but according to my constant experience that whole weight of clouds emptied itself below our horizon so that we get not of it. I say experienced because I don't remember since I have taken notice in my life that ever a Southerly wind of any continuance in the month of July ever afforded us any moisture either in rains or dews.

Dry weather is too universal a topic in this climate and we only live according to the particular seasons in which it happens.

I had great experience last year of a very dry May and a very dry June quite through. But July proving wet had it not been for the gust in September perhaps this part of the world had never experienced a greater Crop notwithstanding that dry May and June. But I never knew a dry July in my whole life turn out a tollerable cropping year.

I see no instance of it now and I remember the same oftentimes before. However we have our usual resource, our hopes in the mercy of God, and let who will boast of extraordina[ry] art in management without his assistance man is but a weak and babbling fool.

It is necessary however to do all we can to help ourselves but I am very certain that even my people under my Overseers have got quite out of that rule. They are satisfied they can weed 50,000 a day at least of Tobacco when altogether There were 4 only of them for these 4 days past sick and yet these 4 days have been spent in weeding a piece of Tobacco neither by measurement nor count above 180,000 and I am sure by the plants in it no ground that could require any very extraordinary care for it is much missing at last and yet the piece is not done by near 30,000. It was indeed hot and if the overseers indulged themselves and the people a little it was not much amiss, but they pretend to say they were hard at it all the while which is an assertion against a fact. As to Mr. George and his gang at the fork, They have just as many rows to a fraction as they had to do yesterday in hilling up their Corn. Their pretence to me they were all day till fair dark tying up a little flax that had been pulled out of the ground. But Billy Beale tells me they had just begun that work when he went there yesterday about 2 hours by Sun so that from 7 o'clock in the morning when I left them to 5 in the afternoon full 10 hours they took their pleasure. If I do not punish them for this my resolution must quite have failed me. I see clearly their view. They do not want to give the least assistance to this prodigious Mangorike Crop, a thing which they did last year even under old Charles, their forman, and lazy Tutt, their Overseer, bedrid the whole time. They came here by my book the 12th of July, all their Corn laid by, and worked the rest of the year till gathering time. But now the 22nd we have just had 2 days work of them in hilling up the pease and full one half of their Corn must be again laid by provided we get any rain to give it a green cast. It begins to look well but as yet too starky for another hilling because such work as it is not weedy unless it is done in some growing season generally does injury to it by adding a hot earth too perishing growth.

I have ordered all these creatures here tomorrow under my own eaye where I will try to make them work.

Mr. Ambrose brought home this morning. Catched getting in at his sister Frankie's window. I knew that bitch entertained him and there laid the scheme for Simon to watch for him and he was accordingly taken. The punishment I will refer tomorrow and the whole week.

23. *Monday.*

Yesterday it rained and filled us with a joy of a great blessing. But upon riding out this day except in the Tobacco upon the hill and that bit by the gate below the hill we had none in either Tobacco ground or Corn ground not even in the pea ground but at a corner of it. At the fork they did not know it had rained at all and even with the little dew that fell in the night not a blade of

Corn was moist but piped up clean to the tassels. However at the Island just over the Creek the people told me it rained a smart shower. It came here very suddenly and as surprizingly went away.

Mr. Giberne wrote me yesterday lamenting the death of my Grandson Landon at Bull run and praying for my Son's and other children's recovery from the flux. My daughter Lucy came from her uncle's and told the same story that Reuben[64] said he had read it in a letter of Johnny Hamilton's to his brother Bob.[65] There might be something in it but I could not help thinking it strange that John Hamilton who lived at my Son John's should meet with an opportunity and my Son not to let me know how his brother did. Therefore I wrote to Mr. Hamilton to see that letter. It came this morning, mentions the death of my grandson Landon, a young wench, and 2 Children by the flux but does not say one word about my Son Landon or the rest of the Children having it. It is usual for people to aggravate all bad news but one would think Gentlemen who read letters might avoid that especially when they must know such news would give parents great uneasiness as it really did me and robbed me of the best part of my night's sleep for I came out after 11 and did not find myself sleepy till near 2.

It began to rain this evening and really with every one but myself it was concluded there would be a great plenty of water. But I have too long taken notice that these southerly winds in July must blow a great while to produce a cloud of weight and generally before that happens the Northwest sky as if impatient of so long a sun against it clears up gradually and bears the watery clouds back again. It happened so this evening as I had foretold when every body seemed to be sure of a rainy night and we had only a very slight sprinkling which I hardly think in 48 hours could have given sufficient moisture to the present dry state that the earth seems to be in.

It seems by Mrs. Hamilton's account the letter from her Son John that mentions my Son Landon and 2 of his little Children being ill with the flux was written to Reuben Beale which Lucy recollected though she did not at first speak of it. So that the poor fellow may still be in a dangerous way in his family by that disorder. Should it be so I shall hardly know what to say to John Carter, his brother, for to be sure when that youth was once violent ill of this disorder in my absence at home his brother Landon acted the brotherly part and attended him through the who[le] of the disorder and that when he was by the Doctor's Accounts in a most dangerous state. But Mrs. Hamilton truly

---

[64] Reuben Beale, son of William Beale (d. 1778), married Landon's daughter, Judith, in 1774.
[65] Johnny and Bob Hamilton were probably sons of Gilbert Hamilton.

out of a partiality to her daughter says Johnny has got a family now and must not venture as he used to do. I could not help telling her that gratitude and humanity knew no such boundary as that of a partial family concern and it was often thought out of tenderness to that virtue that mankind were providentially saved from infection.

24. *Tuesday.*

The Southern clouds contrary to a general observation last night at dark rallied back again and when the whole heavens appeared without the least symptom of rain it began at bedtime and continued moderately as it is said all night.

I rode out in hopes to relish the good effects but excepting in the Tobacco ground where little buds that had in a manner seemed to be dead but were now spread the hill I did not enjoy the satisfaction I wanted. Perhaps the Corn has not as yet received the advantage and I am really doubtful whether it will to much purpose for this month's dry weather though the stalks were thick had faded them every where and spotted most of the top blades with a kind of burning starkiness so that the sight was rather melancholy. Yet through hopes we certainly live and may possibly continue so.

There is an oddity in the situation of my plantations this year. It has rained plentifully below me and quite near to me and at the Island plantation not a stone's cast across the Creek they have had frequent showers but none at my fork till last night from the 26th of June. No doubt as their Corn from their very rich land, the small quantity tended, and this happiness in seasons must needs be better than mine. We shall hear much of fine management but this I am certain of that I have been 3 times over my Corn with my hoe and that the dry weather might not bake the earth too much the plow has gone again between the rows a considerable depth and will by Saterday night, God willing, have finished the whole. If the Corn should get green I will then give the rows another coating of fresh earth.

I am quite out of conceit with tending flax between Corn rows or any thing else that is not to be cut off before the weeding time of Corn for I see that whatever grows there draws the nourishment from the Corn.

Yesterday about 11 it seems my Mangorike people got into my Riverside Cornfield to lay it by and, although I gave orders to clear between the rows each person half way and lay the earth up to the Corn, had I not rode out this morning I perceive clearly it would not have been done for a middle pace of more than 2 feet was left between the rows. I asked the foreman particularly how he dared to work so and before Dolman he told me he was order[ed] to do it. I set them to rights once more and could not help telling them the contradicting of orders was a treatment I would not bear.

I have 6 hands going all over my Tobacco ground to search for the double plants and set them in the good ground where missing. It is indeed a troublesome jobb but better done than not for otherwise those plants would injure the plant in the hill and must be cut up by the hoe.

I sometimes divert myself with talking to my old people to worm and top my Crop and as they had told me it was all in the main very well standing I could not help seeing through their treachery. But Sukey told me there were now buds spreading the hill where it was said to be missing and she would answer by September I would see a good Crop of Tobacco for she knew the ground and without water with warmth it would not be as quick as others.

My arm continues still bad and I do not know what to do with it but I am trying Dr. Arbuthnot's oetherial oil of Turpentine, honey, and camphorated spirits made into an embrocation. I think, as I have done with every other trial, I made every now and then a little easy by it but I fancy it is from the friction more than any thing else.

My Son wants me mightily to sow the River side Corn field in wheat this August. I have not the grain. Otherwise, could I get it, the work might be done for I am of opinion Manuel by the end of July old stile will have run all over my Corn fields with his plows and then to be sure they will have little to do to keep them from covering in the wheat Should I sow it. However it will all depend upon the last year's crop made in Northumberland as mine here was rusty. If that is good and can be got out for Talbot to bring it up the first week in August I think it may be done well enough. Therefore I shall send Sam down to Mr. Edwards about this.

25. *Wednesday.*

It is just as I expected. Yesterday the rain that we thought a fine one at the fork was no rain at all. I observe the dust rise as I rode along but had not the time then to go into my Cornfields. But this morning I see manuel plowing up dust and indeed the Corn shows there was no rain for although high and strong it is fadey and scorching which in rows at 7 feet distance can never be thought too near and unless my people were villains in the first breaking up of this Corn ground and only covered over their work I can impute it to nothing but the dry weather we have had this month for with respect to the field except in that part where the flax grew it is as comparatively as a field can be as clean as the house floor. I am plowing it that the Corn may draw nourishment from a loose earth. But it [is to be] remembered, this year I gave in to that damned stupid way of planting all my Corn in holes without hills. Last year I hilled all and made a fine Crop out of Corn not near so high but it was not dry in July. This year I hilled none and shall pay for it by making very little. Therefore for the future as to my ground as long as I live it shall be hilled for to my reason there is no better way of keeping moist[ure] in a root than by a roomey covering over it.

I think my field where I imagined I should have very little Tobacco begins to look pretty lively from one end to the other of the rows and I have again demanded of my wenches to know why they chose to deceive me by saying the ground stood well when it did not. Sukey told me some plants had died she believed since she went over it last week but she would be hanged if any planter seeing that ground would not say the tobacco stood tollerably well. I told her it was too small. She replied she knew the ground, knew how it was dunged, and would be hanged if it did not turn out good Tobacco. However one thing I do intend to get out of that stiff soil as soon as I conveniently can for to be always doubtful of Success is but a bad situation for a planter and that is really the case with this ground. With no rain nothing can grow. With smart showers every thing will make and it is prodigious labour to be hoeing the ground deep when other people are only paring it.

This day we went to divide the land called Juggs formerly a purchase made out of my mouth by the roguish fellow old Ben Rust but in such a manner made as to vest the fee simple of it in his Son Richd. Rust to defraud his then wife out of any dower in it should she outlive him. Richard Rust, dying an infant, the Estate fell to his 3 Sisters, Mrs. Vass, Mrs. Lowry, and the present Mrs. Corrie. Samuel Rust, her first husband, wanting to secure the whole piece bought Lowry's part, the fellow being a drunkard, after he had sold it to me though had not confirmed it. I then bought of De graftenreidt[66] who intermarried with the Heiress of Mrs. Vass that part of the coparcenary by which means as Sam Rust gave his purchase of Lowry to his Son Ben the whole 100 acres was to be divided into 3 parts. The Commissioners appointed by the Court with the Surveyor made every part equal to 39 acres and a third, and as it was determined by lot the Riverside became my property with but very little marsh however by far the best land and [an] old house upon it that may easily be repaired and moved and a tollerable orchard when the Trees are cleared of the Cedar bushels. So that I imagine two or three hands may be conveniently seated there to some advantage and as I have the only spring and

---

[66] Probably Baker Degraffenreed, a small planter in Richmond Co.

indeed command every road from Corrie's over to the other two parts by inclosing my own property I may perhaps in a little time obtain the whole for I am perswaded the causeways from the other side for their coming and going to their land will be worth full as much as the land is. This has been called an uncharitable thing but if it is considered the first disappointment was occasioned by the right they hold and that in a fraudulent manner I think it cannot be any injustice to endeavour to recover that. Willmson. Ball one of the Commissioners and really as partial as a man could be against me took abundance of liberty to asperse such an intention in me. However, a gentleman putting him in mind of his filling his wive's third in a house of Connaway's in Northumberland with his own Negroes to compell the woman to lay off his third in the land in a rich and convenient spot for him, the simple fellow could not but see himself condemned. Just as that Survey finished It began to rain and really we were blessed with a most heavenly watering till late in the night, by far the finest I have experienced since the rains in May. And if the Corn was not too far gone by the dry weather of a full month I must think this rain will happily bring it about. It is now the 27 Friday and as yet too moist to hill up tobacco in. But Lawson tells me he shall compleat the Riverside field this day and with his whole gang tomorrow with the fork joined brush out his tobacco. Therefore I have agreed that the fork hands shall finish that field and on Monday next, God willing, they return to their plantation and again hill up their Corn.

Rode out this morning. Fancied I saw the Corn something greener though I don't know how. The small Tobacco in the hills has not to my thoughts started any thing. However the toppers say it does and as they go over it twice a week if they are honest they ought to know best. I think the ground is rich enough unless the gust washed its goodness away. It produced very fine Tobacco last year.

I had again an opportunity that seeing that oxen will not do in the summer in plows. A creature not really poor in its looks but a little weak, it may be allowed, lay down in his yoke at 7 this morning. The sun was warm but not very fainty as one would think and as soon as his yoke was taken off he got up turned about and went out of the field. Now if such a piece of sullenness can be depended upon in any Crop I must be mistaken. The Creature had not worked but 2 rows. This tells me that should my lowland wheat be thrashed out I shall really be puzzled to get it in the ground in August unless I can do it with my hoes which to be sure will depend upon the growth of my latter Tobacco that I would not willing wish should give us this opportunity.

Manuel declares he shall finish at the fork tomorrow night. If he does he shall set in the mangorike Corn this side my bridge, and Lawson's gang shall begin at the pease ground to lay by and indeed meet the plow. The fork gang must go over their right hand Cornfield and if they do it quick I will give another stirring to the left hand field but all with patience and resignation. I think a crop must be in a bad situation when at this time of the year the planter knows not [what] to promise himself which I declare I do not, every thing seeming to be so uneven.

30. *Monday.*

Very growing weather. No rain nor want of it since last Wednesday and Thursday. Endeavouring to give my Tobacco a hill and then compleat laying by Corn which is now brave and green and allow some of it but low the stalk strong and burley. But as to the flax Corn as I call it at the fork I shall never again put my middle Crop in Corn ground till after it is set for its ear for the flax that I raised there has made me pay dear for it. There were but 3,000 Corn hills and it has evidently spoilt one half of it I believe beyond any chance of recovery. Noble high Corn large stalks but pinched in the ears and firing at the bottom by means of that middle growth. It did not serve me so last year because it was dry weather and no crab grass grew there. But this year by means of the Wet weather just as the flax was riping a growth of crab grass started up and I am satisfied injured both the Corn and the flax. I pulled the latter immediately and set a plow to break up the crab grass and the fellow assures me he never had harder work in his life. 4 oxen, although the soil is light, could not in two plows break that ground up in two days. I am giving it a stout hill but believe nothing will save some of it.

I rode out on Saturday as far as the Rappahannock bridge to view it and receive it for the County from John Redman,[67] the undertaker, but, although I told that fellow at Dickenson's Mill[68] the Gentlemen Commissioned would all be there and notwithstanding he promised to follow directly, at past one o'clock we saw nothing of him. Therefore I surveyed the work, found it very substantially done, and believe had the [man] pursued the agreement strictly in making the Caps of the sleepers of Chestnut and nailing down every plank with a spike instead of every other which he has done it will be a work of duration. The plan was my own taken from Vitruviusis[69] bridge over the Rhine in Julius Caesar's days. Two stout freshes have gone over the bridge

---

[67] John Redman (d. 1773) was a small planter in Richmond Co.

[68] Dickenson's Mill was on Landon's Richmond Co. property. It formerly belonged to his father.

[69] Vitruvius was a Roman architect and engineer who probably lived during the ascendancy of Augustus.

since finished above 3 feet but as it is part of a sphere the water rising not possessing the whole length had had very little effect upon it for when it gets to the crown of the arch the springs on each side are so deep in the water that they add nothing to its buoyancy. I was told there travellers going by expressed a satisfaction at the Architecture and Naval Officer Lee told me yesterday he believes it will be a model far and near for he never heard any thing more spoken of. But we will not receive it because it is built 20 foot above the old place and on Sir Marmaduke Beckwith's land, who although I heard he had directed the workman to build it there from an ill natured principle intends now to dispute it with the County. I said nothing to it and if he does not cut it down before next Court am determined to move to have the road turned over it.

I am obliged it seems now my barrel of flour is finished to thrash out my this year's crop of wheat for house keeping. I never thought it was worth any thing being so shrivelled with the rust but now I think much worse of it and have put in 130 grains to the ground to see whether it will come up for really I doubt it. This has made Baldy Ritchie try to screw me out of a penny. My Son John sent me down 900 and odd weight of flour from his mill as good as ever I eat at 12 the hundred besides the waggonage to the landing and this fellow this day though I sent privately about it sells his flour at 14/. I may buy a little but it shall be a very little and sent off yesterday to John Carter for enough to serve the year. I wish he would send down a cargoe of it that I might cut Mr. Ritchie's comb a little.

31. *Tuesday*.

Contradict it who will it is as certainly proved to me to be as great a truth as human reason can suggest that these violent rains such as our last September gust do so intirely dissolve to a great depth all the upper stratum of any stiff soil that upon their settling off the Glebe is restored to its primitive state of cohesion. I have now from the first breaking up, turning, weeding, and all to this moment at least 6 times gone as deep as the eyes of the hoes would let me and a piece of Tobacco ground wed quite deep and light no longer agoe than this day week is by the succeeding day's rains baked as firm and as hard as the yard before my door seems to be. If this is the case with how much reason do we conclude that the richness of the soil whatever it was that was put into it must be greatly evaporated and this certainly accounts for the prodigious unevenness of every Tobacco crop. I have seen this year Some parts of the land by being rainey and light the plants are easyly kept in growth but whereever it is the least stiff without a constant rain nothing can grow unless we are perpetually lightening the earth up with our hoes. I hardly have a field that this is not prodigiously verified in and scarcely a plant answers its manuring and cultivation as it used to do last year.

Fork George is once more going over the Corn field by his meadow in hopes if possible to make something of it but at present though not foul it promises very little.

Manuel is now with his plows in the Mangorike Corn field. The Corn very green and strong but yet low.

Mr. Edwards from below by my man Sam yesterday is to send me up this week a full account of my wheat.

AUGUST 1770

2. *Thursday.*

Excessive hot weather. No rain now for a week. However, it is called growing weather by everybody. Indeed it is of that sort which we used to experience as growing weather but I can see nothing of its effects either at home or abroad with any thing in a young state and that that does grow in a fuller state grows but slender and narrow and really in what I would call a sickly manner for it all grows standing up as if it had no substance. Some people may make good crops but I really doubt it. As to my own I have too much of it in a near immovable state to think it will do any thing, and yet to be sure the ground may be called rich if such cowpen and [dung]ing can make it so. But there is such a cohesion in all the earth I tend, even immediately [a]fter every rain, that nothing [re]ally moves. I have gone over abundance of my tobacco to see what stirring will do which is the second time with all, the third time with abundance, and the fourth with a great deal. I have still a large field of Corn to lay by and what is worst of all it is too hot for creatures to work and the people are tumbling down sick in shoals. I think yesterday I had near 14 of them ill with fevers and agues and one with a real plurisy. There are about 5 of them well enough to g[o] out. I have all along dreaded the fall of this year to be a very sick[ly] fall and I am much mista[ken] if it does not turn out so.

I seldom promise myself good Matters. I had a view of doing something this year by the provis[ion] I have made. But I have long learnt tha[t], although our common philosophy sh[ould] lead us to think this or that the [best] method and indeed something li[ke] experience may have taught us [that] it is so, yet I am apt to b[elieve] that some circumstances frequently attend which over set all our reasoning. What else can be the case this year? Rain except once in great plenty. People healthy enough to work and really did work and yet as mean an appearance as I ever saw any where where I go in years much less encouraging. Has not then that prodigious solution which the rain of the gust and that of the whole winter made destroyed in a great measure the very vitals of vegetation? We look upon the cause or spring of vegetation to be salts of some sort or another and do not we know that the way for all salt loses it is to put it in a way of evaporation by an intire solution? Therefore as this has been the case we ought to conclude it to be the real cause of our present want of growth.

4. *Saturday*.

For two days it has really been blowing, a little showed of rain would seem, and yesterday a most threatening sky from the Southwest to the North point almost made it certain, but it blew off in a very hard wind and in this part we had a very trifle of rain. So that it will. The violent hot weather, the hard drying wind, and eleven days' want of rain—we are really in a bad state again as to moisture.

Lawson tells me the Tobacco in the large piece of 180,000 has been kept down and still is so by the grass hoppers, an evil I know not how to prevent, although I have before had near a whole Crop destroyed by them.

Mr. Carter of Corotoman, Coll. F[rancis Lightfoot] Lee and Mr. Giberne came here yesterday from Mount Airy in the evening of the day. Coll. Tayloe wrote a complaint about four of his horses being shot and the Guns that did it were heard at Buckland's. It seems the boy that brought the letter in the way came by my Charity school. Rigmaiden,[70] the Master, told him that Mr. Neale had been at his schoolhouse and had written to Tayloe's Gardner that if the horses came to his field again where they had been the day before he would shoot them and I do suppose directed John Northern, his overseer, to do so who is a fellow of such a surly disposition that I am persuaded would shoot his own father. The Colonel wrote to me for a warrant to have a view upon Neale's fence that he might sue him upon the Act of Assembly.[71] I told him the express words of the Act did not give the injured trespasser such a warrant but, as the equity of the Act certainly directed that in all suits for trespasses the sufficiency of the fence should be proved by viewing, it was a reasonable

---

[70] William Rigmaiden was at this time master of Landon Carter's Charity School.

[71] The act relating to trespass was passed in October 1748 and may be found in Hening, ed., *Statutes*, VI, 38–40.

warrant to be granted to the injured trespasser as well as to the person injured by the Trespass which the law had directed. Therefore I sent him a warrant to Mr. R[ober]t Tomlin's, Wm. Thrift,[72] the elder, and Dan[ie]l Lawson[73] to go and view the fence, directing that Neale should have notice of their view.

The fever and ague still continues through my own family excepting a very few about the house. Nancy[74] has had hers 6 days successively, Billy Beale his 4 days, and all the rest everyday for a week. No vomits as yet h[av]e stopt them and the intermission is so constantly in the night that the bark is with difficulty to be administered. My Quarter is every day full of them.

5. *Sunday*.

The weather continues too dry for the excessive hotness of the days. We have had no moistning rain now for these 12 days. My Tobacco is all again gone over but I suppose what little was wed in the wattled ground upon the hill on Thursday was sevenight last may want it again. But I know not when I can get into it for I have all Mangorike Corn field still to lay by with the hoes, and I am certain George at the forks will yet be a week finishing his. Besides this, I see my pea ground is again grown weedy for, although we have had nothing grow with us that fetches its nourishment any depth in the ground from perhaps an insufficiency of moisture, yet the grass by rooting superficially has never failed to grow from the slight moistures which we now and then get.

Fevers and Agues still continue with us day by day. Little Nancy has had her 6th fit, Beale his fourth and looks like a lark[?], nothing but skin and bones. He has taken a vomit, then a purge, and at last we venture upon the bark with rhubarb in it because of his excessive quantity of bile discovered to be in him. The first intermission we got down a dram and a quarter. His ague and fever after were but moderate and we have got down to this morning two drams more of the bark. The Rhubarb keeps his body open and we are in hopes that we have stopt his fit. As to little Nancy she has never been under my care. Her wise parent let her disorder run for 2 fits, gave a slack vomit himself, and then sent for Dr. Mortimer, who gave her a very sharp one, I am certain of the Crocus kind, under pretence of Ipecacuan wine. But still her fits go on day by day. The Physician has forbid the bark, thrown in much saline mixture, and I wish the Child well.

[72] William Thrift (d. 1776) was a farmer in Richmond Co.
[73] Daniel Lawson (d. 1789) was a farmer in Richmond Co. and father of Thomas Lawson, overseer of Landon Carter's York Co. plantations.
[74] Nancy Carter was Robert Wormeley Carter's daughter.

8. *Wednesday.*

Still very dry. Yesterday promised much rain, yet like former weather it went off in a little missling and this morning it was really very cool, perhaps the effects of the rain somewhere.

My ride confirm[ed] me in my long opinion there can be nothing of a crop made this year in any part where the gust of last year and the excessive wetness of the winter has been felt, for nothing deeper rooted than grass grows any where that I see. Stir it as often as you will the stiff land runs into cohesion with every little moisture and the light land has lost its vegetation certainly from the evaporation of its salts by means of that prodigious dissolved state it was thrown into from the moisture as before.

I have not seen a good plant nor really a good Cornfield but perhaps on some dunghills, and this weather does not suit with any growth that I know of, let the superficial judge say what he pleases.

Mr. Edwards, after having given me reason to expect an account of my wheat on the 28th of July by the week following at farthest, first sent me word it was not thrashed out and then by a letter there is not above 40 bushels of it, though no complaint about the rest. I am astonished at these things but I need not, having been certain of much bad management there for now upwards of six years. I cannot easily guess the reason of it. Indolence in the Overlooker perhaps from some inward disturbing cause and a rascally abuse in the under Overseer who has been too long in office and no doubt has fallin upon some method of enriching himself that I can't learn and nobody will discover to me. For to be sure a just proportion of what I get cannot have raised him the estate in land and Negroes which he has got, and this year I am not to expect any thing.

Mr. Edwards' mother is dead and he intends to remove up the Country. I have written to him he is right, for with the present management it was [to] be as impossible for him to live as it is for me with no greater profit under his conduct. Another overlooker I will have who shall live upon the spot and grow rich with his Industry or else not at all under me.

Young John Beale[75] offered his service and offered it in a decent way, leaving it to my honour to reward him in proportion to his services. I told him I should depend upon him and that I would reward him with honour if he deserved it. He replied he should look out no where else.

Our Court sat 2 days. Parker not there. Gone upon some wild Goose chase

---

[75] John Eustace Beale (d. 1790) was probably the son of John Beale (d. 1766) and became manager of Landon Carter's Northumberland Co. plantations.

after Barley into Maryland. I wish that man well but doubt his modes.

Fevers and Agues continue by dozens in a day and where they are most obstinate I have discovered worms.

I fancy the project in sowing my Cornfield with wheat will be abortive for want of grain unless I can have it from the upland Gentleman, Coll. Carter of Nantzatico,[76] I expect down on friday. Perhaps he may let me know whether he can supply me.

9. *Thursday.*

It is dry and has been so ever since the moderate rain last Wednesday was sevenight. Nothing grows, but it is no news to say so, as I am perswaded from this cool Northwest wind that has been blowing for now two days we have a long spell of dry weather. Every body I find dreads it and perhaps it will continue till the change of the moon upon the 19th. Ten days more then according to human expectation. Farewell all chance of a crop. For to be sure, if these wet clouds which went and discharged themselves to the Northward can have produced such a cold air that even fires would have been welcome for two days, we may expect an early frost. If so, good night to you Nicholas, both with Corn and Tobacco.

10. *Friday.*

I need say nothing about the weather because that seems to be an established dry spell and very cool withall. Of course, it must be very prejudicial to all growth.

Last night was our Corn night and I ordered Owen to look well into the quantity that was left at the fork. He tells me that it was Lawson's opinion as well as his that it is not as yet quite half used out of that Corn house. We began it by Owen's account June 21, which is exactly 8 weeks giving out to last night. Now suppose it to be half used. If in the next 8 weeks we don't use more than we have in the last 8 weeks it must hold us to October 4. Then we shall have to Account 13 just 10 weeks, for which purpose we have all the Corn at Dolman's still to make use of. Our present expence is from 28 to 28: 2 bushels a week besides the house use, which is about a barrel a week; so that we use one week with another near 7 barrels. Therefore for these 10 weeks we shall want 70 barrels out of Dolman's Corn, and unless I have been robbed there I have ought to be better than or near 200 barrels there.

[76] Charles Carter (1733–96) of Nanzatico, King George Co., and later of Ludlow, Stafford Co., was a son of Charles Carter (1707–64) of Cleve. He represented King George Co. and subsequently Stafford Co. in the House of Burgesses.

11. *Saturday.*

Very dry and very cold. No Cropping weather to be sure, for, if I myself cannot be pleasant in the circulation of my own juices without qualifying the air of my room with a fire, how can I suppose any succulent plant not accomodated to winter air to be so. Certainly the salts of Vegetation inveloped as they are with the juices of the earth must be clogged by them and lose their activity. It would be a frost was the earth moist enough. Nay I don't doubt but it is one somewhere.

Mr. Carter of Nantzatico came here yesterday.

12. *Sunday.*

Neither rain nor dew. Dry weather still going on and really nothing growing. We have had no rain from the 24th of July to this day in all 19 days. Yesterday it began to be cloudy quite from the South clear to the last but the clouds advanced so slow that I believe as I conjectured they were shedding their moist contents below in the Country, and at night the Northwest air which has been for sometime moving went gently off. It now looks graesy, as it is called, quite from the North almost to the eastern horizon. But whether this is not the lightning evaporation of the earth settling below the horizon as usual I cannot tell.

13. *Monday.*

No dew this morning. A small gathering last night towards rain, but by means of the Northwestern air which arose as usual about bed time all those clouds were presently dispelled.

This day we begin to get marsh hay with but 2 mowers and 6 or 7 in Gang, but I will contrive to set more at it as soon as I can, for it is upon a good shock of that stuff that I have experienced the Cattle are to be supported.

I cannot help taking notice that the same Number of hands have been three weeks mowing and securing the meadow hay which they did last year in one week. The pretence is a prodigious burden of grass but it seems they have now only 8 stacks instead of 18 which they had last year. I am then told these stacks are abundantly larger than those last year. Indeed, I have made them get the hay out of the meadow upon the hill sides, well remembering the rain in August last year floated all my stacks in to the River, so they may have had more work to do. But I believe the principle cause of this delay has been my being an old man and prevented from visiting them by means of my left arm, which has now in spite of all that I can do been 5 months at times very painful between the bend of the Elbow and the Shoulder that has almost got to a fixt pain. And though John Dolman pretends to want more wages I cannot see that he is one whit either more diligent or more careful than he was last year, and I am pretty certain I shall not make so much as I did last year, especially if this dry weather continues, by a vast odds.

14. *Tuesday.*

The first judgment denounced against man was that he should sure die. The second that he should get his bread by the sweat of his brows. Every day's experience demonstrates the truth of the first and every year's labour proves the latter, especially in a Climate divided as this now is between rain and drough[t], generally one half of the year wet the other very dry. Extremes in any thing are bad but in this Country more than commonly so because they happin too frequently when it could have been wished to have been otherwise. Rain during a whole winter season cannot be so advantageous to poor man as it would be if intermixt in the summer season. But instead of that, whilst the sun like the human invention called the solamander is burning and browning every thing, it passes over. For want of moisture no labour can succeed. The Corn seems now quite past prevention not only parched but burnt up quite through. Shoots in perfect withering away. And as to Tobacco, it is really bad excepting in the very small stuff. What service rain can now do it, for that which was green two days ago though with very little growth is now brown and mottled, and must in a few days fire. However, rain may do for the sowing of wheat, a cultivation absolutely necessary to be within the chance of bread corn for this part of the earth, for I much apprehend the produce of our Corn fields will be too short for any such purpose. And what is melancholly to behold: a large field of pease well set and covered over now burning up with hardly a pod to be seen. It took me near 4 bushels to sow it and I fear it will be a happy produce to get as man[y] off. Yet this amongst the trifling spunlatists is every day called a fine seasonable year. I have looked at them with much concern that they should deduce from one possible happy spot the happiness of a whole Colony.

I find a day's or two's indulgence at home is in spite of every reward and every care a compleat destruction to my business. The hogs I had at the fork not 4 days ago intirely at the command of a little Girl, by being neglected for want of my every day's inquiry, are now ranging over the Cornfields. That Slut has turned sleepy and Mr. Foreman George, having no body but women to press him in his work, quite indolent with respect to any kind of care. His very sheep penned close by his door ranging over the Cornfield. And why?

The Girl did not put up the gap well. This is the scoundrel whom I have rewarded week after week preferable to the rest of his fellow slaves with many a good meal of Meat so that I may say my kindness has contributed to spoil him, for instead of taking care of every thing as he used to do he has been even too lazy to see the gap of the penn put up at his own door and I am certain his cattle not penned. I have ordered Lawson to correct them all with sharpness and him with severity at the head of them. Mr. Beale was ordered to examine into the hogs every day. He went there but I suppose he forgot it. If he did not, he never mentioned this affair to me. I wonder at such young fellows. He is the second person that has somehow been too indolent to speak to me about anything.

16. *Thursday.*

On Tuesday night it pleased God of its infinite mercy to shower down on this part of his unworthy creatures that prodigious blessing of rain for which we had been so long panting aggravated with every circumstance that could attend a drough[t], even the prospect of the want of bread. And may we all be gratefully thankful for the same, for every thing that could be relieved by moisture had in that rain one glorious drought to revive it into growth from whence we will hope that our fears and apprehensions may not be so great as they have been. Yesterday there was a prospect of another fine blessing. It began at darke but immediately cleared up. Perhaps the same mercy may think proper in due time to give us a second refreshment, for as the first rain coming upon such a d[r]ough[t] must in well worked ground be immediately soaked up into the assistance of vegetation, a second in our way of reasoning will not be improper to push that growth forward which has been so long delayed by the dry weather that the tenderness of our Crops may be sufficiently protected against the approaching frosts that we have for some years past experienced both in September and October.

Talbot set off on Tuesday morning with the Pettiauger to Nantzatico to fetch down my wheat that I bought of Coll. Carter for the sowing my riverside cornfields.

I was done laying by all my Cornfields both at the fork and here before the rain came and had begun to whip out my wheat, the little that I had made, and my Rye which I intend to sow at the fork in a Cornfield there because I think I will winter my young Creatures at that dry plantation and I would willingly have a bite of green food for them. But the 3 people who went to thrash out the Rye, one of them taken with only [illegible] and fever, the other two, too lazy to work, only thrashed out one bushel. By such management I am pretty certain I shall be a long while getting in this Rye. Lawson tells me one day more will finish the wheat and as I have not had above 7 bushels from the Crop I fancy it will be extremely small owing to the rusty situation which it was in. Note: this was drilled wheat. Therefore rust is not so presumptively the effect of moist weather, for rows at 6 Linear foot distance must have stood every chance of being well dried by the air from the moisture that fell in the spring. It was never my opinion that it was occasioned by wet weather but by some particular corrosive constitution in the air to be seen. I well remember in a dark red drop at the lower joint of the wheat from whence it ascends and burns the stalk, as it were, clean to the inward vine of the straw; and the ascending juices instead of going to nourish the grain ouze out into a dark reddish powder like rust for which I neither know nor have read of any remedy. Some people by accident this year have escaped this malady by sowing their wheat early last year from whence early sowing is greedily adopted as a preventive cause, but me thinks such a remedy is even presumptive against reason, for in the first place, if either wet weather or this corrosive constitution of the air should be the cause of the evil, these very causes must be presumed always to come late in the year. Otherwise, the early sowing can be no remedy to it, for certainly the grain not sufficiently filled cannot but be affected with it whenever it does come. However, as the latter sowed wheat has this year been all affected by the rust and the early sown escaped it, the hasty farmer thinks now he has got a perfect remedy against it by sowing his wheat in August. But I have experienced a year in particular noted and observed upon before that the early sown wheat was only affected with it when the latter sown by being late in earing escaped it, and this seems to be most natural and did indeed fix my conjecture as to the probable cause of the rust, that it was some corrosive quality in the air. And come when it would it must affect all grain in a filling state and may as well attack us early as late in the year. But of this experience only is to convince the farmer and I wish it may never happen that he may be fatally convinced.

My Chariot carriage must now be thoroughly repaired and as it is not worth employing a perfect artist about it my Negroes, Tony and MGinis, are set to do it which will be a delay upon the fixing my waste dam and pier heads to my mill as well as lining my Canal. However, I hope to get it done in time by the finishing of my Crops, for really the want of a mill cannot have been less loss to me than even £100 this year. My people have suffered by getting meal. No creatures could be fed through the prodigious expence of Corn more than Meal and, what is a shame to think of, no mill that I have ground at has really allowed me above one half of the meal that my grain ever made at my own mill.

18. *Saturday*.

Yesterday and in the night we had another very pretty rain so that if anything can bring my perishing Crops about it is to be hoped this weather will.

I finished thrashing out my Rye. There are but 13 barrels[?] of it. There was no prospect for a Crop. Neither does the sort of grain ever afford one.

We have thrashed out all our wheat below perhaps about 13 barrels[?] more, the winter's wet weather and the rust together having in a manner totally destroyed that.

We have also thrashed out our spelt wheat that grew at Mangorike, another very short crop, and I am now whipping out my barley perhaps as short as any of them for the quantity of the ground tended in it.

The spelt wheat shall after this be thrashed that I may with the Rye finish sowing the fork field to be begun on Monday next, God willing.

Talbot came down last night from Coll. Carter's of Nantzatico with but 30 bushels of wheat. It is there was no more ready there, which is curious after what I heard.

I shall, God willing, on monday next sow this wheat in the Riverside Cornfield. Talbot must go for more that I may make a good trial of that jobb, which I confess I have no notion of. Neither do I believe one of those boasting creatures who talk of such prodigious crops made in their corn fields. I rather think they are all in debt and fancy this puffing way to keep their Creditors in temper.

This day it seems I am 60 years of age. I thank God that he has suffered me to see the day another, although according to the common run of man's age, I may say my days are full. I cannot say they have been attended with more than uncommon misfortunes and, as I plead no preferrence above the rest of the world, I do with an unfeigned heart return thanks for this and all other the mercies of heaven. Perhaps a few friends may come to see how I look upon this birthday. Excepting my left arm, I have a tollerable share of health, and I doubt the pain that I feel in that will never leave me. I am too old to grow it out. It has been too long upon it to think of removing it by any kind of application since all that I can yet think of has been done with but very little effect although every thing that I have done relieves it for some small space. I cupped yesterday and drew two spoonfuls of blood behind the joining of my shoulder to my Collar bone and was easy for near the whole day, but at night, after my first nap, the arm as usual seeming to be breaking off. However the pain it got to the joining of my elbow where I have never felt it before, but this possibly was only owing to some agreement from the great muscles where it has constantly been and returned to this morning. Rubbing is the only speedy relief that I do find but from a cupping. I am sensible that would my age admit of it bleeding would be a prodigious service to it. I have now only that and blistering to try, but I try to rub out this bilious season of the year before I apply to either of the[m].

20. *Monday.*

It has been raining off and on here in plentiful showers ever since Friday the 17th, and yesterday in particular very smart showers though not very long so that I hope my Crops have suffered no damage by drowning; and if any thing can bring them about this prodigious growing weather must needs do it. But all will depend upon the holding off of the frosts this fall. If they do not come early, we shall have the blessing of making tollerable good crops of Tobacco and Corn.

The rains prevented my sowing wheat this morning in my Cornfield, it being much too wet. How ever I am sowing the Rye at the fork which if they chop in well deep and level as I have ordered it will probably made a good winter pasturage for my young calves this year.

Note: I have had 4 lambs dropt at the fork this August and am apprehensive the same Ewes have yeaned again that yeaned last year in the spring for by my overseer's account I have but 18 Ewes there and I had 14 lambs, one of which died in the spring, so that these 4 which have yeaned lately make up the whole complete and yet Nat tells me when he went to draw the old Ewes for fatning he found three of them very big with lamb. If he is right, I must have two to lamb. Of course, then some of the forward Ewes in the spring are yeaning now, but it is possible that my overseer may be mistaken in his number of Ewes. Therefore, that shall be looked into.

My people are worming and suckering today and some of them beating out my barley. I have ordered the rest to go round the river side Cornfield fence where it seems Mr. Parker's boar and sow get in just as they please.

My Son set off this evening for Hobbs Hole from thence to Rings Neck.

I had thought that my last Cupping upon the joining of my arm upon my shoulder have contributed much to relieving that complaint which I have now had better than 5 months, for it was easy near 3 days, but all at once in my sleep last night, though I did not lie upon my left side, I was waked by a pain as if my arm was breaking in the bone. I cannot but Imagine that was I not afraid of bleeding on account of my age that would relieve me. I shall therefore venture to draw a little every now and then by the Cupping gourd till this bilious season is over when if I am not easy I shall either bleed or blister the corn.

21. *Tuesday*.

It seems it rained great part of last night and now it is all clouded over, spitting every moment, which makes me think we shall have too much of it, for upon riding out I observe my Tobacco shows as if it was much sodden at the roots and now the toppers and the overseers think that it grows. It is to me strange. There is hardly a plant with a leaf ten inches wide and indeed in my thoughts it is morally impossible that it should be wider, for the stalk has not thickness enough to produce a wide leaf, it has been so stunted by the dry weather. As to the Corn, to be sure abundance of shoots are come out since the rain where there were none before, but these shoots as yet not thicker than one's finger, and how should they be large, the stalks that bear them are but like small walking sticks and I think hardly with substance enough to bring a good ear. But some people, who perhaps have made observations by memory alone, which seldom comprehends all circumstance, These say, that they have know[n] such stalks produce good ears in favourable seasons. I have known very short stalks bring long ears, but then I think I can remember that although they were short they were thick and from that instance have ever since comforted myself that where the stalks were thick it would be a good crop however low they were. I remember many years agoe cutting the tops of such a field that the very ears reached the ground. I wish I could say that there is any prospect of its being so this year.

I saw Manuel sowing the Rye at the fork. He is very sure that the 13 bushels of feed will sow full 13 acres of the 18 acre field so that I shall have 5 barrels[?] of spelt to sow in the rest. He prudently left off sowing till what is upon the ground shall be chopped in, which I think was right as it is still raining. Note: that ground with all this rain is dry enough to work with the hoes, and the Rye covered in but yesterday morning has a sprout of 2 or 3 inches long.

My Cotton patch which is very fine from a redness in some of the leaves alarmed me for fear the rust was coming on it and I made Nassau pull a handfull of them. The stemms are quite clear and Lawson tells me that all the rust he had ever seen first came upon the stemms. The leaf is bold and flourishing but yet with deep red spots and the Negroes say Cotton always turns so whilst it is blossoming. The pease now look very white with blossoms but are also run up thick with crab grass so I know not what they will produce.

Mr. Edwards from below the 14 of this month having written to me that from that day he did not intend any more to be concerned with my affairs there because he found it was impossible f[or] him to give me satisfaction by his m[a]nagement expressing how ready he shall be at all times to befriend me and how thankfull he is in acknowledging past favours.

I could not but propose a letter for this Gentleman to show how inconsistent his gratitude for past favours came in with such a declaration of his resolution to be no farther concerned for me. If he discovered by his management that it was impossible to give satisfaction, his produce for many years ough[t] to have shown him that before now instead of inclining him to throw up a business before he had finished his year. And as he could not complain of any restraint of mine upon him except in not allowing him to buy plow horses when he could not pay for them out of any produce and it is very evident with the few that were bred there he never had care or resolution enough to prevent their being destroyed and ride[n to d]eath. However, with very little objurgation I returned his Civility in expressions and desired that my spinning wench lent to him, if he had not been as punctual in returning her to the quarter from where he took her upon the day that he discharged my business, that he would be pleased to send her up by a note to my house, for according to former reasoning of his there was one while too many hands for the land and another while too much ground tended for the hands which made the turning out of some thousands very necessary. I thought I could do better with that wench up here. And as to any Act of friendship that might contribute to his future well being I would be bold to say that in spite of his lowland experience no one was better disposed towards him than myself. I informed him it long had been my intention if he could not do it to oblige the person that overlooked my overseers there to live amongst them that my own directions should be punctually obeyed as well as ordered, which I was satisfied had been no part of his concern. Otherwise, he would have complained of the disobedience of the Overseers and I should have turned them away, but that he never did.

22. *Wednesday.*

Yesterday's cloudy weather notwithstanding by and before sunset we had designed our approaching Northwester by a clear horizon all at once settled into a Northeast gale which has brought us down perhaps water enough in the night alone to have recompenced all the past dry weather as much as rain could do and, if we add to it what we before had already taken notice of and what by the situation of this morning it is very likely we shall have, we may possibly be convinced that it is too much for our Crops. At least the lowland man will pay dear for the natural richness of his ground and the stiff land planter probably as dear whatever goodness in tilth his artificial labour may have produced for to me it seems evident that abundance of Tobacco if not of Corn must be drowned. But perhaps it was not intended that man should do more than secure a livelihood by all his bustle in the Year 1770 for if we consider the weather according to the several periods of it the chance of doing more can have been but very little. Indeed, every blush of a growth has been enough to raise the labourers' spirits but something has constantly attend[ed] in every moment of such a favourable circumstance that must have depressed any phylosophy but that which is fixt on the revealed mercies of God.

I know some affectations of piety that are always arraigning every man that discovers how much he feels and apprehends when these several dispensations attend. But if we reason upon man as man it must be natural to feel such an apprehension and if we reason upon him as a Religionist it cannot but be just that he too, [that] is to feel the rod, should be sensible of it even before it comes; and I do think such a disposition may be justified by the example of our Lord and Master in the Gospel upon which our Religion is established, for there in his human nature he prayed that the cup might pass from him when assisted by his divine nature he knew it certainly would not and then reposed the whole of his sufferings in the will of his Father besides. The inspired pen of many a writer seems to recommend that we should kiss the rod of affliction which I believe we could not so heartily do as a rod were not the horrors of it greatly impressive before the punishment had fallen upon us. Therefore in the sincarrity and force[?] of religion I say unto my heavenly Father not my will but thine be done and may thy mercy extend this blessing of rain in such a measure unto us that we may feel it as a blessing. Things must be so much in the way that they were yesterday that there seems to be no occasion to take further notice of them than that of their being in a way of suffering. I thank God that although we are now labouring under a Northeaster there has not been as yet no violent wind. Otherwise I see not what can prevent it from being what was usually called here an August gust, for the earth now fortified with water ponds it every where.

23. *Thursday.*

It now begins to be fine warm weather again and if it continues we may and ought to say the Lord has been on our side, for notwithstanding our apprehensions by riding out this day I think I hardly see that we have had a drop of rain too much. It came into my head to ride over my large piece of Tobacco ground, and there I am prodigiously concerned to see what I must call very bad management and partly owing to myself. I suffered all that ground almost from the chesnut tree to be too foul before I turned the hills and by the people's turning them upon the grass so rank as it was the hills became quite poachy so that the Tobacco planted in them by means of the dry weather that followed had not the least chance of living. For although those weeds are dead they are nevertheless like so much long grass or straw. From hence became the cause of the webb worm every now and then and in the month of July of the plants dying, for although a stout rain fell when we planted the ground and just after it was done that only settled the top earth down to give the plants a little growth and as soon as their roots got down to this grass they withered and died away even as large as plates by which means perhaps there is more than one half of the Tobacco quite missing and a great deal as yet but beginning to grow.

If ever the accident my ground again should be too weedy to turn I will first weed all the grass off between the rows and then turn the hills resolving never more to let a hill be turned upon long grass, for I see there cannot be a greater evil.

The rest of my Tobacco begins to look very fine, and I believe will make a Crop. But I must keep this Cowyard part from possible trespasses for even the Neal cows have got over the ditch and broke me several plants.

I have ordered the hands from whipping out the spelt wheat directly to hill up what Tobacco there is in that large piece, for that is growing and, as the earth seems to be dry enough, a good hill may help it forward.

I am resolved to stay till Monday next before I chop in the riverside wheat. By that time perhaps it will be dry weather. The weeds upon the Corn ridges will be killed by cutting down and working deep with the hoes. I may be able to let that wheat have a tollerable chance in growth.

The fork people will sometime tomorrow be done chopping in their Rye and spelt wheat so that I may have them to help in with the riverside wheat and to brush over the sluggish stiff part of my Tobacco ground.

Mr. Carter of Williamsburgh[77] having written to me that David Goldsby informed him of Mr. Ball's illness at Rippon Hall from the 9th of the month to

[77] Robert Carter (1728–1804) of Nomini Hall lived in Williamsburg from 1761 to 1772. He was the son of Landon Carter's brother Robert (d. 1732) and Priscilla, daughter of William Churchill, and the grandson of Robert "King" Carter. A member of the Council from 1758 until 1776, he has been treated at length in Morton, *Robert Carter of Nomini Hall.*

16th, which letter I got but last night, I sent Sam off upon a horse this morning to know how he does.

The Councellor also informed me that the crops there were generally said to be indifferent, but how to credit that I cannot tell, for on the 5th of this month Ball wrote me a letter by Sam in which he tells me because he would not be sanguine himself some of the Neighbours who came to see him he got to look over his Crop and they told him it was a very good one. Now he could have no view to deceive me because from his going there really so late as the 13th of May and not having a hoe struck either in Tobacco ground or Corn ground excepting the holes that were dug in the old field for planting the Corn, he could not be answerable if the Crop was indifferent, especially as the neighbours who I desired met upon Ball's coming there and certified under hand that through the same preparation made at that time of the year there could be no chance for any crop either of Tobacco or Corn.

But I know in this neighbourhood people are very fond of speaking meanly of their neighbour's Crops and I am certain mine has been so characterised. However, when I ride out, I declare I do not see any so good and although I have so much missing yet by the quantity I tend without any accident things going on just as they do I will venture a wager with the best of them both as to quantity and quality. It would have been much cleverer could I have got my whole Crop to have stood.

I rode also in my Corn fields. There are abundance of shoots come out since this rain and I think the stalks are grown quite green again and something thickened in their size. Perhaps that may prove a better Crop than others expect and by their talking I believe wish not that they worry me but because of their vanity in condemning my management and praising their own.

25. *Saturday.*

It is still raining. Rained all night, very much yesterday, and so it has continued from the 13th of the month off and on to this time day by day almost with very little interruption except now and then a few hours in the day. I have thought the Tobacco had rather too much and so I thought when I came from Coll. Tayloe's last night, but I hope in God I shall find myself mistaken.

Owen Griffith, having heard of a packet or two in the post office that had been there for some time, got me to find an order for the taking them out. When these letters came home, there was one principal one from his brother Edward, which I keep in my Custody because that letter, having given an account of a pretty considerable estate in money and reputable rents falling to

Owen by the death of his Uncle his father and Mother.[78] The money said to be lying in the Duke of Montague's[79] hands for which he is to pay 4 per Cent interest. And, as Owen's time is near expiring, the letter directing him to make haste home by the first ship, provide himself necessaries to appear in, when at home to call at Brecolough house if he went by Scotland to endeavour to get the money for purchasing these necessaries by a bill of Exchange drawn either upon the Duke of Montague or upon Messrs. Hyndman and Lancaster[80] for £100, where his brother tells him the money shall be lodged for taking up the bill. And under an oath this letter dated at Montague house May 26. An attestation of the truth of every part of the above Letter under the signature Montague in a large indolent character after the usual manner of Noblemen. I cannot but conclude this to be a genuine letter and therefore engaged with Mr. Sam Hipkins for Owen's taking up those necessaries and some Cash he might want to fit himself out for sea to indorse a bill of Exchange of Owen's drawing upon Hyndman and Lancaster for £30 sterling. The circumstances in his brother's letter being so strong, however, if I should be deceived I shall only make it an instance to refrain for the future from the least good nature or humanity to such a creature. The reason of my being suspicious really arises from many circumstances in Owen['s] Character that I wish he could repent of. Otherwise they must bring him to the Gallows. For in the first place, a man totally disregarding truth will as certainly disregard what he does as he is alive and what can keep the gallows from such a man when he is in the least pinched? I make Owen write this and he also shall write a letter to himself, seriously written from my wishes for his welfare. But still I doubt it, for however the matter has been denied he certainly must have assisted Tom in getting the spare key of my bookcase and keeping it so long that my liquors might be at their command. Now such a circumstance carries the deepest die of iniquity with it though but a trifling profit unless the pleasure of getting drunk whenever they pleased can be satisfaction enough for the fraudulent method in which it was gained, and

[78] Many of Landon Carter's friends thought this letter had been forged by Owen Griffith, but Carter proved to his satisfaction in a long letter to Rind's *Va. Gaz.* (Sept. 27, 1770) that there was no logical reason why Griffith should have forged it, and he therefore pledged himself to cover Griffith's expenses up to £100. However, subsequent passages in the diary and a letter from Griffith to Carter, Dec. 21, 1771, revealed that the letter was a forgery and that Griffith had "contrived" the entire hoax "many months" before it was put into execution simply to outwit and embarrass Carter, to whom he referred as a "Boisterous Tyrant" and an "outwitted Cunning Man." In this letter Griffith indicated that he had no intention of repaying the £100 and expressed his intention of "going to India to remain forever."

[79] George Brudenell (1713–90), 4th Earl of Cardigan, was Duke of Montagu at this time.

[80] Messrs. Hyndman and Lancaster was a mercantile firm in London.

Owen, take my advice, repent heartily of this, for your denial has not in any manner exculpated you from that base action. God only knoweth the heart of man, and if you will not fly to him for a perfect forgiveness, although by act and contrivance you may have secured yourself from the punishment of man, he will suffer the gallows to overtake you for this iniquity unrepented of. For this you know that you were acquainted where those spare keys lay, were promitted to go there as my clerk, and, when one of them was missed, accounted for it by a villanous lie of which not one word upon inquiry had the least blush of truth in it till at last the key was found concealed in the lining of Tom's waistcoat so far from being injured by opening any other lock as you had asserted that it appeared as if it was just come out of the Locksmith's Shop. It is not aggreeable to me to repeat such a story to you and I only do it out of that principle of humanity for my fellow creatures which leads me to wish that you may be intitled to the forgiveness of God by a hearty repentance of such an abandoned, such a stupid piece of villany.

Our fevers and agues which have been almost universal seem to be returning again and with this oddity in circumstance, the gangs employed to do particular works are all taken with it at once. I have not now a Cowkeeper to go after my Cattle, every one of them being laid up with the fever and Ague. I thank God I have been successful in the care of them all and hopes I shall continue so in the removing of this relapse, but this wet weather is too bad for that as well as for other things.

It will be impossible for me to get any wheat in to the ground, the earth is so wet. But to be sure the business of sowing so very forward has proved last year rather accidentally good than certainly so for every Crop. For as to the rust I am so convinced that it comes sometimes on the latter sown grain and sometimes on the forward grain that I am satisfied whether it is produced by excessive moisture or some other corrosive quality in the air that unless we certainly know such causes will only attend a Crop of late grain or a Crop of forward grain it is ridiculous to think we shall prevent it by the time of our sowing.

Again it cannot be moisture that produces it for two reasons. It evidently begins near the bottom of the stalk and so runs up the vine by which means the juices instead of nourishing the grain ouze out and dry into a rust. Therefore, moisture cannot affect it because according to our idea of wetness that would rather cool such a corrosive quality and wash it off. Besides, wheat drilled this year so wide asunder and scanty in growth must have been dried by the air from all moisture and till this year it has been advanced that the drilled wheat has generally escaped the rust. Besides, the light land has been destroyed with it as well as the stiff.

29. *Wednesday.*

Monday and Tuesday have been fair and I took the opportunity of sowing and chopping in wheat in the Riverside Cornfield. They had sowed yesterday morning above half the quantity we had from Nantzatico and Manuel was sowing so that I fancy he has pretty near sowed the 30 bushels. If Lawson has kept near him in chopping in, it will be well for the rainy weather is now come back again.

Note: the Nantzatico wheat has got the fly weavil in it and so I wrote Charles Carter yesterday by Talbot who went to fetch down the rest of my wheat from thence and the son wrote me word from Evans's ordinary[81] in his way down the Country in Company with Beverley and Hunter that Hunter showed him a sample of Coll. Carter's wheat that was the fullest of weavil he ever saw any.

Freshwater[82] was here on Monday last. He has a good Crop of Tobacco according to the quantity he tended, for Longwith did not leave him Tobacco ground enough for what I call a full Crop. He lives with me again upon the same terms as he did last year, but Mr. Longwith truly will not leave[live]. Under John Beale I did imagine he would not, because he would then live under some eye that would take care that he did not convert my property to his own use, which I begin to think he has done and Mr. Edwards quite too indolent to inquire into any such thing. Longwith, therefore, may go by my Choice, and so I sent him word.

My Son came home yesterday. Mills whom they all went down to part with does not leave the Country. I knew that he must be a fool if he did, for where can he make a shift to live as well as he does here? Every body fancies he has a good deal of money, but I know it is impossible, for if any man can live as extravagantly as he has done and save money by only carrying on the Trade of a storekeeper and I have always heard not selling at the dearest of rates and yet lay up money he must have an art that I know nothing of. My Son went to Rings neck in his way back. That fine Crop at last is to turn out nothing. These rains have fend the Tobacco just as it was ripe and fit for cutting. If things were so, Boughtons is no planter. I know it to be the general rule Tobacco must not be cut in a rain and I would not do it to chuse. But having had Crops

---

[81] Evans's Ordinary was in Essex Co. and was owned by John Evans, Jr.
[82] Tom Freshwater was manager of some of Landon Carter's Northumberland lands.

much injured by the rainy spells which generally happen in August, I once broke through that rule and found it answered so well that I have never let a Crop suffer since, provided it was ripe by means of any rain. For in the first place, warm rains will at first coming kill Tobacco as well as the sun and if it is carried out upon the grass the rain nor the sand can't hurt it. In the next place, should the rain be too hard and the Tobacco begin to flap, we see it is so much like the effects of the sun that it cannot hurt in that falling state if it is cut and laid upon the grass. I saved in a gust year when every body lost their Crops 12 hogsheads of fine Tobacco by cutting the plants, sticking them in upon the tops of the hills because the water was between the hills until the people could gather them up and carry them out.

Planters have a wild notion that rain brings the juices of the Tobacco out of the pores of the leaf, but, whenever it does so, it is only out of Tobacco not ripe, for I have lowered by a weight a ripe plant to the bottom of my creek and four days after taken it up, sunned it well, and it cured as thick and as fine as I desire Tobacco. I did for experience and I gained it.

31. *Friday.*

On Wednesday morning we had a rain till near 12 o'clock that unless we had really been blessed with two fair drying days before seemed as if it would have drowned every thing. However, I thank God everything this morning seems to have escaped. Nevertheless, there was a coldness last night that really threatened a frost and the dew this morning almost grandulated. But nothing that I hear of has submitted to it. It continued cool all this day till a little before Sun set but in the night it turned extremely cool.

Mrs. Hamilton came here to day and in her usual strain wanted every thing particularly that I should part with the wench that I had only lent Mr. Edwards to spin for him. Then she wanted to purchase her. But I withstood all her silly importunities and foolish method of endeavouring to bring me over.

Talbot not come down and I do suppose even notwithstanding every promise that was made and all that heard there was no wheat ready for me.

I rode to the fork, saw the Rye that was come up and indeed the spelt wheat, but I am afraid it is the second time that I have sown Rye in my Corn too soon to do any service, for I see the grass that was cut up and seeming dead till the Rye was sown is now taking root again and if that grows it must outdo the Rye in its young state. Just so I dread it will be with the 30 bushels of wheat that I have sown. Therefore in all these lowland Cornfields, loaded as they will be with crab grass at this time of the year, it can be no good way of sowing wheat so early and if we do not I am perswaded the ground has not strength enough to produce it. Of course, this new kind of husbandry can only be fit for upland Cornfields where the earth is yet awhile too fresh to be thus loaded with this late fall grass.

I wished yesterday that I had had my hands to spar[e], for I am certain that in one week only pulling the crab grass from the Corn ridges I could make a stack of hay as great in quantity as two people could mow in a marsh and as much better as can be immagined.

John Dolman it is seems will be next Monday three weeks that I have employed him with 3 mowers and six hands to get me the marsh hay and certain I am that he has not got half the quantity that I used to get with 2 mowers in a fortnight's time. Indeed, Dolman is too lazy to push any gaing of nigo and I am too old.

A boy from John Longwith brought me another pot of butter this morning weight about 11 pound, which is the 4th pot of the kind that Longwith has sent me this year. This boy brought me a letter from John Beale, who I am going to employ below, telling me that Longwith had a good prospect for Tobacco and but an indifferent one of Corn. The boy assured me that both Corn and Tobacco were very fine. The letter dated the 30th of this month, I asked the boy when he got it. He told me he came off on Thursday morning and walked it up with that pot of butter in one day, which to be sure is upwards of 40 mile. I asked him particularly if any Tobacco was drowned. He said not a plant. Neither did John Beale speak of such a thing in his letter, and yet Mr. Hamilton who came up two days before said he heard Mr. Edwards say that only he and I had suffered by the rain. He lost his whole Crop and I, 90,000. However it is so impossible to believe that I imagine Dick Edwards only guess[ed] the one case by feeling his own for I hardly think a man resolving to have no further concern with my business could go to see it after he had left the business when perhaps he recorded[?] the same thing before. John Beale seems a little disturbed that I had ordered all my 35 bushels of wheat to be sown down there, imagining it would injure the pasturing. But I sent him for answer 35 acres only taken from my land out here and would be but small detriment to Cattle who had such a prodigious range that Cornfields from the gathering of Corn to the making of wheat seldom produced much feeding for cattle excepting in their browsing upon the Cornstalks which might be carried out to them in their winter Cowpens as I should direct and as I did up here. Besides, those hands below might any time produce me 500 bushels of wheat which they could not do when sown in Tobacco ground unless they took too much from Tobacco to make a crop of that. Therefore, I hoped he would let my orders go on and to shift of Cornfields he might begin and cut down about 15 or 20,000 joining to where I began and, by a ditch or two into the natural drains, that swamp would every foot of it produce good Corn and some of it fine Tobacco.

It seems my Son Robert is now once more determined to tend only Orleans Tobacco and never to prime it, laying aside his own reason and possibly adopted the following of others. For as to not priming Tobacco, although they would carry more leaves to the house, I will venture a wager that a plant primed and topped to 10 leaves should be thicker and weigh more than one of these unprimed plants. I have tried it before, have won a wager upon it, and this is the reason why my Tobacco every year is thicker in the leaf and carries a better grain to the felling of every one of these unpriming Gentlemen than any they make.

SEPTEMBER 1770

6. *Thursday.*

It has been moist and rainy from the beginning of this month till now and we have cut some Tobacco so thick to the admiration of some Gentlemen here on Tuesday last, the 2nd day of the Court, that one of them ignorantly was going to seperate the leaf, immagining it had been double.

Every body complain of firing. But as I have nothing of it in my land I must conclude that my method of hoeing the ground after I have wed and hilled it and indeed working it always as deep as I can although it is condemned by many people is the only way to keep the Tobacco in a full growth; and when that is obtained there can be no such thing as spotting or firing but from some bruise or wound. Again I am always condemned for topping too low, that is, not priming high enough; and the pretence is the Tobacco touches the ground. It should be observed that way of hilling Whilst I [torn] weed my Tobacco, also much condemned, has this low priming in view as well as sheltering the roots of the young plant from the sun, which would scorch even in the ground as the top of the hill is pared away if such earth were not put to it to make up the hill again, and by thus making it broad as well as high as the plant can bear without something it, when I came to prime low this very hill takes the whole leaf very near to the stalk of the plant; and by that means cannot be battered by the winds that blow so much as higher primed plants generally are, for they frequently get their points quite fazzled out; and I am certain, by having the 10 leaves up on a stalk shorter at least by an inch than the high primed Tobacco is generally topt to the thickness of that inch of stalk, must go in to my leaves when it does not into higher primed Tobacco.

This day I rode to the fork. Two of the people which I left there to take care of the stock are sick at home and Ross only is to do that business which she cannot with Cattle, sheep, and hogs; and the hogs are kept up in the Stye then, for I sent away Judy to help her till the other two hands get well.

I have before endeavoured to observe the difference in growth, etc., between spelt wheat and Rye, and I remember I took notice that the spelt wheat sowed in the same field was much more resorted to by the Creatures in feeding than the Rye was as long as it remained a good bite; and this I observe was generally as good as the Rye. But this day I have seen it is Really much better for it was sowed the last in the field and yet I think it is as high again and this in a worn out Cornfield. But I must observe one thing. It does require more seed to sow an Acre of spelt wheat than it does of Rye, for as near as we could guess we sowed the same quantity of seed of Spelt as we did of Rye but the Rye is thicker. Therefore upon another year, as I shall be fond of changing Rye for Spelt, I will allow a bushel and a half to the Acre instead of a bushel which I have sown this year.

I begun yesterday for the first time to gather dry pease. 24 hands only gathered me 10 sacks of pease in the hull and a half from a little before 12, Lawson the Overseer being sure that the hands can get a bushel a day apiece. I offered his salary to prove they did not, and now he is to try. Like other people inexperienced he thinks su[ch] a bet would be sure to him, and I immediately offered to lay it that he did not from Monday morning to saterday night produce 6 bushels of his own gathering. He tells me the pease are very thick, but I see by his gathering he knows very little of the matter. I am certain the wet weather [h]as made the vines too rank for a [lar]ge crop, for pods will not grow as fast [as] vines. However, I don't fear but [w]e shall have a reasonable crop of [t]hem to b[u]y necessaries from the new England men, and I am now satisfied [tha]t the pease are not changed in growth but were so done by some black eyes which Beale accidentally suffered to be thrown among them—a circumstance well worth taking care of for this little pea at 4/the bushel destroyed the market of the neighbourhood last year who offered their common pease and black eyes at 2/6 a bushel.

It is three year ago since I observed a large flowering weedy shrubb by the edge of my marshes and called it from its shape the Carnucopia Sylvestris coloris flavi commodore melliflorse. I gathered many seeds of it and sowed it ever where but none came up and this day in the place where I first discovered it, I have seen it in full bloom. It is a flower [torn] pretty lively in colour and of a [torn] fragrancy so much [torn]ally full of bus[?].

8. *Saturday.*

This day 12 months w[e] had that terrible gust, the effects of which I am certain, we have not yet recovered. For in the first place many have been and are still starving for bread. Ag[ai]n it seems to be certain that the rich[ness] of every soil so deluged with water has been vastly exhausted, by an evaporat[ion] of the Vegetating so greatly fluid [faded]. And I fancy the timber lost is quite irreparable.

Yesterday we had a very great rain for the shortime it lasted. I had a pretty deal of Tobacco, but upon looking at it after the rain was over I don't think it hurt in the least.

I was pleased to hear Mr Carter, forgetfull of his constant endeavours to expose any management of my crop, now obliged to own the real goodness of it. But still, as if unwilling to app[rove] the management, it is all impute[d to] the accident of the rains; but to ask why the same accident has not be[en so to] others as much is to make a [two lines torn and faded].

I say whoever attempts to make crop[s] or anything without the assistance of heaven? Why then should it be called an accident when my crop turns out well, because the rains have helped me, anymore than the same may be said as to the management of others? However this I assert: if our July had not been so drye and hot also, My management would have appeared more conspicuous than that of others; for I dare bet anything that none of the Tobacco tended as they have done can be thick as mine. And this is one cause of it firing. It was never so workt as to keep the plant in growth, and rain upon such plants must make them fire.

Buckland came here yesterday to get some plank and did against my wish get above 900 feet.

Buckland went yesterday into my Tobacco ground, and said it was by far the thickest and finest he had ever seen.

He laughed and told me peoples' tones were vastly changed. One while he heard I should make no crop and now people were fancying I should not find house soon for my crop. But here I said they were as much mistaken as they were before; for I did not tend Crops without calculating where to put them; although what we had as yet cut would not do more than fill three good rooms.

We began again to sow wheat in the Riverside corn field, Talbot having only come down last night, after a full week's trip to Nanzatico for 50 bushels. It seems there was no wheat ready after all their mighty talk. And I fear the whole is talk.

Note: the first sown is said to look very fine; but no more is to be sown till monday that we may hoe in yesterday's sowing and get in my Tobaccoe cut down.

This day riding in my Cornfield I observed an upright sucker from the roots as strait and as small as a switch whip with a tassel at top but no shoot for an ear and about one third of that tassel with perfect grains of Corn in it, which bring to mind a long dispute I once had that the dust of the tassel was the true essential to the production of grain, for although nature intended the husk for a matrix to raise it, yet, if that dust can fall any where so as to be protected from drough[t] or rain or other bad weather, it will produce grain; and I once remembered a little cluster of grain growing upon the blade as it joined to the Stalk, and this sucker which I have gathered proves the whole.

I see if we intend to produce wheat in our Cornfields it must be done with a good plow, for although mine that was hoed in is pretty well come up, yet it no where looks so well as where it has been hoed very deep, and this the Negroes cannot be got to do always. Again, as we must sow it at this time of the year, our lowland fields are too subject to be grassy, and although the grain comes up very well amongst the grass which the hoe cuts down, yet I see if the weather is any thing moist that grass will not die soon enough for the wheat to grow much among it and a great deal of the wheat will be choaked. Therefore the field intended to be sown with wheat should have one plowing more than common in order to destroy this grass as well as to make the ground light.

Observing Mangorike Will carrying in a turn of tobacco and raising it with some strain I asked him if it was heavy. He told me that it was by far the heavyest he ever carryed in his life. I had it counted and it was only 18 plants.

In order to have my tobacco as much under my own eye as possible I set my Carpenters this day to make my prize house fit for hanging tobaccoe; because by hanging that first I am in hopes to get it cured by the time I shall want the house for prizing.

Sam, god willing, goes off to morrow for Rippon Hall. I have written to Ball blaming him for not answering my letter by Coll. Tayloe's Harry, when he had not written first by Sam the post before this on account of his being Just recovered from his illness.

I cannot avoid miniting down part of a Conversation with Mr. Boyd the day after our last Court. That Gentleman had frequently talkt to me about the bad management of my affairs at my plantations below in Northumberland

County; and I always answered him that I had trusted to Richard Edwards who I suppose on account of his mother's long illness had been for some years very remiss in looking into my business.

But that day Mr. Boyd informed me he had heard three reasons offered by way of accounting for that bad management.

1st. My negroes were never cloathed well enough; and therefore they could not do their winter's work.

2. I would not allow any plows.

3. I had ordered my corn to be tended in a different manner from what was usual and therefore the people could not tend their Crops.

As to the first charge, I could not help saying that my people were as well Cloathed as they always used to be and I clothe none other any better at home where I always made double of what they ever made down there with fewer hands. And I asked why they had not made the same crops for these last 6 years that they always made before. I allowed them but one shirt and I allowed no more up here. My people always made and raised things to sell and I obliged them to buy linnen to make their other shirt instead of buying liquor with their fowls. He said he did not hear Mr. Edwards give this excuse but it possibly came from him.

As to the second reason, I use no plows any where nor ever did use any, and I asked why they did not now do as well with out as they did formerly. But this excuse was a lie for they had my leave to break oxen, and they did break them and had killed them into the bargain.

As to the 3d excuse, I said all till this year they had tended their corn and planted it as they pleased; therefore the alteration now made in planting corn could be no reason for the last 6 years' bad crops. But as to the alteration, I had experienced the advantage of it, and others up here, seeing the crops I made by it, had of their own accord got into it. Besides, allowing all the ground in a field to be worked which way you would, An Acre was but an acre. And I would maintain that a field laid off at 7 feet and 2 would bear soon wed at any other distance [for which I refer to the whole method stated in my June or July book where I have shown that 7 and 2 is much easyer managed than even 4 and 4].[83] Boyd said he knew no thing of these things but only told me what was said. I then observed the management has been so bad that they wanted some excuse; and Unfortunately they had fallen upon what any man of sence or honesty would be ashamed of.

But I believe the true excuse is behind, which perhaps time might discover. Longwith once would have told me some thing, but I would not hear

[83] The brackets are Carter's.

him; and I do suppose, he finding I would not hear him, made an Advantage to himself by doing himself the same thing by which means neither could tell of the other.

10. *Monday.*

I everyday discover more and more that whatever may be the cause of fevers an[d] agues they have certain periods each fit which it will keep. We imagine them to be owing to a redundant bile greatly Obstructed; but evacuate them in what quantity you will, it will not or does not for a considerable time, that is, during the period the fit has formed, alter in the least. Therefore any thing more than lessening the quantity of the bile and assisting that evacuation which nature may be submitting must be doing wrong. However the bark, both a bitter and an Astringenct in the first instance, mixing with and thinning the bile, may be very proper in the intermission provided its last quality, that of its Astringency, is not too strong at first; but after the quantity is abated and the Obstructions are removed, then that Astringent quality must be most serviceable.

Little Nancy now in her relapse has her 5th quotidian; every day attacking later than the day before; and this day she took her second vomit which mo[ved] her moderately. And between while the bile was assisted downwards, but I see no change. Perhaps A little bark to morrow with Rhubarb if her fit goes off well may serve to Alleviate as well as carry off what remains of the bile, and when that is gone which I doubt will not yet awhile be affected I am in hopes this relapse will be Removed.

My Son Robert went up to the Acquia Quarters.[84] Robert proposed our joining under one management. I agreed but as to the proposition of Slaves that each of us had; And to my astonish[ment] his wife then said, then all the bargain should be off; to which I replyed, with all my heart. She asked if he was to have nothing for his trouble. I could not help thinking he daily received a full reward for more trouble than he ever took for me. In short, this woman every day discovers who is at the bottom [of] all the ill usage that I receive. The devil cannot be more busy; A mean spirited creature and sordid without remission; That cannot see her All, alredy rising out of me: but unless I part with my all, she will not be satisfied. And I am certain then I should be turned a grazing, and by her means. And yet she finds a way after she have secretly raised a hubbub, to wonder at it, and shew as if she was concerned at it. I am certain she is always concerned in it.

A fine day and we have made a great Cutting. Besides worming and

---

[84] The Acquia Quarter was a plantation of Landon Carter's in Stafford Co.

suck[er]ing a week, we must be at tomorrow also. Thus by means of Talbot's stay for the Nanzatico wheat, I shall not be able to get that in the ground yet a while; for I must Save my Tobacco by housing, and by worming and suckering; and then my pease and my fodder is to get; besides a constant working in tobacco, for some is as yet very Young.

Sent home Mr. Parker's English boar left here for him by Somervelle. He was too mischievous to live on any plantation; for although with a boy to attend him constantly, he would get into the cornfield in spight of every body, and tare down abundance of Corn. Therefore I told Parker of him, and at our last Court he desired he might be sent home, which I did in a cart this day by Manuel; but although the day was really cool, according to the Custom of hoggs' impatient of being tied by the legs, it seems he died before he got there.

Mr. Parker wrote me back by Manuel. He found him the Gentlest creature in the world; and was satisfyed he should not be obliged to pen him.

Irony not intended, either to rebuke, to deride, or Upbraid, must be quite out of Countenance; and one intended as such, must be unpardonable in this Case; for to be sure I had every thing done that could have been done, to get this boar safe to his Master. And if this letter was intended as a joke, I must say an Irony is too edged a tool to play with.

11. *Tuesday.*

Last night and the night before very cold. I was (the last cool weather) told there was a frost up the country; but not to do much harm I am certain. This weather is also cool enough for a frost; and by their frequency in coming, harm must be done. We are cutting every day; but we have so much to get in. I fear a great loss; besides my corn is much too green and soft in the late shot Ears. But we have a most mercyfull god, and I will place my confidence in him.

As to my soil, I am certain these early frosts must prevent my making tobacco; for none of it will grow before the warmth of July, when it is hotter than any month we have in the year; And if ever that shall prove drie as it did this year, we must be late with both tobacco and corn; and then the early frosts ruin us. And what to tend for bread or profit I cannot tell; for Wheat rusts or is eaten Up by the weavel flie every year; so that our expectation from that must be very precarious; for we cannot prevent either of these evils. One year the rust affects the forward sown wheat, and another the latter crop: And the weavel every crop that is not rusty. And this I see is advancing up the Country where they certainly have the earliest of frosts.

Holy David said the days of man were threescore years and ten, and if he chanced to live to fourscore years it was but labor and sorrow; but either the period is now shortened or besides his inspiration he was blessed with prodigious Strength for I can find that even after 3 score years it is labour and sorrow; for I think I may say no temperence and care has been wanting on my part and yet I feel pain and that I was a Stranger to before 60; but perhaps my father being 50 before I was born contributed something to this.

Latter crops, though sometimes they sometimes turn out better than the forward crops, are attended with many inconveniences besides the constant dread of an early destructive frost, and the bad chance of getting the fodder in well is not one of the smallest.

I could not but take notice of the want of Experience or rather hasty way of speaking in my Overseer Will Lawson. He imagined this day's cutting would fill the 60 foot double shedded house.

He has but 2 rooms in it filled and a scaffold of near 2 more; and there are 8 rooms more in the house. Now it is a prodigious cutting indeed that can fill 2/3 of a 60 foot house. Note: my old Stagers in the Gang lookt with some contempt at his saying so and when I askt them if they thought so they were certain the cutting would not fill the house by 4 rooms at least.

John Purcell,[85] master of the Patrol in this neck, told me that, going after a fellow of Colo. Tayloe into a tobacco house of Spencer Watt's in the Island full of tobacco, the fellow getting, threw down some sticks of tobacco quite dung rotten and the house stunk most abominably. This tobacco I know was very high topped, and I suppose by its firing for want of deep working it was cut down not half ripe and of course it was too thin to stand the sweat of the house. Thus is 9/10 of the tobacco spoilt every year; and, although I have constantly pointed this out every year, these conjurors will go on. It is more than probable one cause why I always outcrop this very rich plantation upon a clay seemingly good only to make bricks with. I ordered after this tobacco is got in Manuel, Guy and their boys to go to filling up the tobacco house called the mudd house up the sills to be out of the way of the winter's water.

12. *Wednesday.*

The barrel of flour I had from Mr. Webb's mill[86] having been all expen[ded] the 8th of this month inclusive, Billy Beale this day gave me in from his book the dayly consumption.

---

[85] John Purcell (d. 1778) was a landowner and farmer in Richmond Co. as well as master of the patrol in the Northern Neck.

[86] Webb's Mill was probably the mill in Essex Co. owned by James Webb (d. 1771).

32 days used up 213 pounds flower. But by the book it wanted 1/4 of a pound which is really is very exact for I must think the horn of the scale generally went with the flour.

My expence then for this number of days being 6 pound 10 ounces and 1/2 per day. It will be a good rule to Judge for the whole year. Thus 365 days will at this rate require 2,430 pounds 12 ounces 3/4. Allow then 12 barrels at 2/3 each and it will produce 255 barrels of flour so that I shall have over and above this rate of Expending 126 pounds of flour for very extraordinary uses for we have not been without company these 32 days and my birthday happened in the time.

Finished housing my prize house all to two rooms before the door and a little in the roof of the tobacco room at one end. I think there was full tobacco enough to do more than fill it but as it was well kiled in the sun I suffered them to hang it thick and I wish it may not be too thick; however if the weather keeps fair I hope no damage will attend it. If not, I cannot think there will [be] less than 3,000 pounds of good tobacco in it for I never saw finer put up.

Mr. Carter of Corotoman came here [and] is surprised to see how much my tobacco is come on. I asked him why? He told me it was his thought when last up that it would be nothing. I observed to him he had joked himself into those thoughts for it always promised to me that it would be unless the weather should prevent it. Now he fancys I must make 100 hogsheads. I laughed at his going from One Extreme to another. I only promised myself 30 good hogsheads and not that if the frosts did not hold off.

Lawson cannot till about mid day go to Chopping in my wheat, because he has not yet done worming and suckering, a work that must be done.

Killed a fine house lamb this day and I will endeavour to ride out with Mr. Carter to his quarters.

I must forever be astonished that my cows now don't bring above 20 Calves a year and a Veal or two or so besides; but I have observed that very drye years throw the brute beast back in their breeding and there is a good reason for it; for to be sure plenty of food must [make] the blood disposed to generation.

I made Rose at the Fork, as she stays at home to keep the Creatures from trespassing, to begin an[d] Cut the tops of the flax corn and I think I shall really have fine corn there.

Dolman's but just done getting the hay on the fork side of the Creek. The island overseer made the people leave off getting hay on their side. And now he begins to think he shall not be able to get what he had reserved. Therefore I have ordered Dolman to go over and get what the overseer is sure he shall not want. Indeed, I do not beleive he can get any more of it; for, poor fellow, he is plagued about taking his tobacco out of his houses again.

13. *Thursday.*

Road out this day in my Chariot with Mr. Corotoman Carter to see his totuskey quarter under John King the Younger.[87] I remem[ber] to have heard this Gentleman the last time he was up praise his crop as much as he condemned mine. But I must confess myself astonished. Thinner tobacco I never felt. Neither did I ever see tobacco so indifferent. Most of it hardly a hill about it and none of the Ground workt well enough to bring Peas. The Corn in most places pritty Good but not enough to make a good crop for the hands. And Yet by calculating 2½ and 3 barrels to the thousand he deceives himself with a large crop; but I know nothing if the 70 thousand which he tends for 9 sharers turns him out 140 barrells.

I felt in his tobacco houses then hung with tobacco and that not half full. The tobacco just hung the day before was really stinking and dung wet, all I am persuaded to its not having the least substance.

14. *Friday.*

Lawson hoeing wheat yesterday; by tomorrow night he thinks he shall finish the long rows in the field.

Very cool last night. A Northerly air and a great dew began to fall before Sunset which continued Cool all night; but thank God no frost to be seen this morning.

Mr. Gibern, his Lady, the widow Faunteleroy, Colo. Lee, his Lady, Moore Faunteleroy, Mr. Carter, and Mr. Hipkins dined with me. A pleasant Company.

I ordered Talbot to sow the wheat something thicker. I see that 1 bushel an acre will not do in Cornfields. But indeed this hoeing it in with a large Crop of tobacco and the fetching the grain a great way is no good Scheme.

Mr. Beverley wrote me a letter to tell me Talbot informed him I had but a mean crop.

15. *Saturday.*

My people came up from hoing in the wheat at the Riverside to working and suckering the tobacco by the cowyard here which is the second time that is gone over this week.

[87] John King the younger was probably the son of the John King (d. 1771) who had earlier been an overseer for Landon Carter.

We have sown all the long rows in the corn field which is up to the light piny land. The Overseer would sow a few rows more as far as a peach tree there. I find by measurement I have sown [blank] bushels of which at 1 bushel each acre makes near [blank] acres.

Yesterday I was surprized that, after having every day directed Billy Lawson to examine my tobacco house below hung all to 6 rooms with tobacco to see that it did not spoil, and constantly hearing it was in fine order, Yet to find it beginning at Northwest gable door. So it was at Colo. Tayloe's houses. His overseer did not care to go to taking it out to the scaffolds, pretending it would go through the Sweat. But I could not think it a sweat but rather the weight of the great dews every night and, though I might be certain if their tobacco cut down before it was ripe and really very thin would rub through such a prodigious moisture, Mine, much thicker and not obliged to be cut on any account before quite ripe, would certainly do so. Yet I could not run so dangerous a risque and had it directly taken out and Scaffolded.

This morning I found this upper house so, although it was only hanged this week. I took that also out and am this evening putting it in again.

I am so certain it is the effect of these dews that I send to order the gable and doors to be shut at night.

We finished thrashing, cleaning, and measuring the pease I had gathered; and to shew how little these or anybody who tend pease know either of the quantity of their encrease; and what they can gather a day I have been very particular this gathering. Lawson said to be sure he could gather 2 bushels per day. I offered him a bett of his sallery that he did not from Monday morning to Saturday at night himself produce 6 bushels. However I would not let him bett; And as he had 24 hands gathering I bid him to keep them diligently at it. They gathered two days till night. And upon cleaning and measuring they turned out just 12 bushels and half a peck.

Note: we may for the future know the quantity gathered, for a Liverpoole sack, filled up so as to be well tyed, 22 of them just made the quantity. Now 24 baggs just made at half a bushel each 12 bushels. Therefore the baggs may be said to hold one with another half a bushel of these little peas. And of the black eye Peas 1½ bags only made 3 pecks.

I endeavoured to keep the sort clear of mixture. Therefore pickt them as well as we could before thrashing; however some will get in them so that we must be careful in picking 5 or 6 bushel out for seed.

Nassau got devilish drunk yesterday and run off at night. He has been in that trim the whole week and we have 8 or 9 down with the fever and Ague.

Mr. Corotoman thought I should make a very great crop. Colo. F. Lee, who saw it all down the hill, was of the same opinion; but I said every large crop must have some missing plants, and some hedgebudds so that I would not be sanguine in my expectations.

18. *Tuesday*.

It rained last night, though very moderate yet plentifully enough. I had a pritty good cutting of tobacco, but I got it timely enough upon the grass.

Lawson finished hoeing in all the wheat I intend to sow in the riverside field and that is as far as the piny points.

We then cleared Dolman's spelt wheat ground of the crab grass and weeds in order for plowing to sow barley in; but I must first finish filling up the floor of the mud house.

Lawson worming, Suckering, cutting tobacco, and tending what was cut yesterday.

Sam returned Sunday night from Rippon Hall. Wm. Ball very well, in high spirits about his crop. But no hay as yet got and but a poor produce of pease, though a very fine Cotton patch. And the plaguy distemper broke out amongst my cattle again. Ball perhaps the occasion of this by turning them out of the pasture to wean the Calves; for I heard the infection was in the neighbourhood.

I have written a long letter about everything to go by John Goldsby[88] who is going in quest of Owen Griffith's things that came in Captain Barron[89] to Norfolk, a ship from Hyndman and Lancaster.

Last night talking of tobacco my son told me he would give me 30 hogsheads for my crop. I understood he had been challenging Marmion Fitzhugh above to weigh plants with him. It is a strange thing that a man should have sacrifized his reason so long; this crop has never been worth anything but a curse from him till now, although every part of its growth except in the drowth of July has been extremely Promising.

On Fryday last I went with Corotoman Carter etc, to Mt. Airy, and left Nassau at home to attend Mr. Carter just taken with a lax. But I was surprized he would not let the boy Ben that waited upon me ride the bald face horse, Pretending the horse ran away with him. Lee thought this a good thing in Nassau; but I suspected what has happened. He kept this horse to ride out for a drunk; And so he did all day just till I got home when no Piper was ever drunker, and so confounded improvident there was no bearing him. At my

---

[88] John Goldsby (d. 1786) was a small farmer in Richmond Co. and probably the son of Edward Goldsby (d. 1758) of Richmond Co.

[89] Probably Capt. James Barron of the *Molly* who arrived in Virginia in August 1770.

going to bed he could not wait upon me And went off, and has stayed away till this morning. He will not tell where he has been; but I beleive it must have been Robin Smith's, because I went there to enquire and though they denied him I do suppose they concealed him.

I clapped a pair of handcuffs upon him and locked him up for a serious day of Correction. I have been learning to do without him, and though it has been but very badly yet I can bear it and will. And then perhaps by a course of punishment I may do the rascal some good.

My Arm last night as bad as possible. It suffered me to sleep till 12; and after that I never got another wink. It seems as if there was some fault in the circulation of some of the Juices that flowed better in an upright posture of the body than in any inclined situation.

Miss Lucy went to John Beale's child's Christening, and kept my Chariot all night, went then to Captain Beale's. And yet this girl pretends she never goes abroad. I almost think she is seldom at Home.

It cleared up in the night last night and I did imagine the weather would have been settled; but about 10 this morning the wind came at Northwest and lookt much towards a frost; however I hope in God we shall escape for it has grown warm this evening. However the wind is at Northwest.

My prize house has been hing too many plants on a stick; for in spight of every thing but scaffolding it will everyday grow wet and funkey, though I have large air holes cut every where. I gave orders for only 10 large plants on a stick.

19. *Wednesday.*

Longwith's boy came up yesterday with the 5th. pot of butter, weight 11 pounds.

The boy says they have 12 calves that they milk the cows. Therefore I wrote to Longwith to know as their pastures are so good what is the reason they don't send me up above 10 of butter in a month, when with but 18 cows besides the milk that I use and the butter consumed in a very expensive family I pot at least 60 pounds in the same time.

The boy says the overseer has filled all his Tobacco houses except one end of one; and that he has a large cutting still to house for which his Overseer intended to strike a house and that the day before he came up the people had examined the houses and there was not a plant spoiled; and that everybody reckoned they would make a great deal more than ever they did. I know this has been the crye every year immediately after housing; And yet neither Mr. Edwards nor Longwith ever could account for above one half of what they guessed. Therefore, I always used to direct Edwards to watch and enquire about; for certainly if they were not ignorant planters they must have been better able to guess their crop after housing. But Dick either never did or never would complain. Now as Longwith has put about a report of having had abundance drowned I began to suspect some trick as before intended this year. Therefore, I asked the boy whether he had any tobacco drowned; and he told me he heard the people say there were about 1,000 plants hurt by the wet in the swamp; but as to any being spoilt in the house he was certain not a plant was hurt.

To prevent then any trick to be played undiscovered I wrote to John Beale who lives at Mr. Eustace's and is to succeed Longwith and Edwards; to go and take good notice of the number of feet in the tobacco houses that are filled, also what quantity he strikes; and privately to watch that fellow; for I was clear from former years he had made away with my tobacco; which he might easily do as the Warehouse was so near, for it was without a difficulty to get any rogue to carry a hogshead to the warehouse in any other name.

The boy also told me of a very fine and large Cotton patch. This I ordered Beale to have lookt to good Shared only when he was by. But I dare say the villain robbs me there also.

I sent again for my Spinning wench which I lent Mr. Edwards. Mrs. Hamilton said she was sent away when she was down before but that was not so; and I perceived it not true because the old woman wanted to buy her of me, pretending the girl had a fellow of Edwards for a husband; but I absolutely refused selling. And Yet the boy Joe told me she was still there. Upon which I ordered her up with her child this next week without fail.

Yesterday's cutting upon the hill must have been a large one indeed; for all my people were hanging on the scaffolds till near 2 o'clock in the night. And 6 of them have been at [it] till past 1 this day.

And we came cutting down below the hill.

I examined the Mangorike tobacco housed. All seemed to be sweat. They have still 6 rooms to hang there.

My son thinks this tobacco had better have been fenced this year, 'tis so large and stout. But my enclosure is all wathing. However if it was fencing I don't think that a good way. I allow it cures sooner on the fences and cannot be hurt in the house; but then I fancy it is very much hurt by the weather on the fencing.

Fodder and Pease will certainly be injured for want of gathering. The former begins to drye and the Patch is quite covered with the latter; and Unless I take the hay gotten from the Marsh I can't yet go about either of them; And I am certain that will be as bad. However, what I can't help I must endure. Particularly my arm which has been full 8 months painfull to me without any releif; and yet nothing visible as to be felt upon it. I begin to fancy old men have many pains not to be accounted for.

We had yesterday very great reason to be very thankfull that the sudden change to Northwest died away in the warmth of the sun. And I fancy we shall want the same mercifull protection; for about 2 in the night it blew very fresh from Northeast without one cloud; and by day it got round again to Northwest and so it has continued all day but rather a cool air than a wind; And as the day declines I think it continues cold. I wish we may not have a frost. That would put an end to all my labours for the year except the Corn for I have abundance out. But I have a mercifull being to trust to. Nay, possibly it may be only my Apprehension from the risque I run.

Killed a beef this day for my negroes, honestly worth £5 as meat now sell, but I would not part with such another for that money.

Sowed spinage seed this day. I remember I did not use to sow it before November; but a few years last past All our November sowing has been killed.

20. *Thursday*.

No frost I thank God but yet a very great fog this morning which I have endeavoured to keep out of my houses; for every adventitious moisture can be of no advantage [to] tobacco, which certainly has moisture enough of its own to throw off. Yet a moisture may sometimes be necessary to well Colouring of tobacco in the curing. But then it should never be admitted in drops.

Cutting tobacco this day. And tomorrow, to gathering the Pease for which purpose Dolman is to spend tomorrow and the next that there may be a compleat gathering of the Patch over.

Manuel gone to plowing for Barley at Doleman's.

Lawson sends a hand or two to fill up the remainder of the tobacco house floor.

We shall not be able to begin about any fodder till next week, when George and the Fork Gang must work at their own the for a part of every day at least, and in the evening to help with the tobacco.

Fevers and agues still very constant among us and that in Number of the Principal part of my Gangs, so that my work heavy upon hand is still to be heavyer because I have nobody to do it with.

My painfull arm let me sleep last night till 4 o'clock which I have not done this week before; but after that it grew most painfull; and yet nothing is to be seen or felt but the pain.

The tobacco cut below the hill, though not so large and thick as my upland tobacco, is nevertheless very good. I felt of it just now as stout as little boards and Some that I saw just cured is charming.

I don't think Lawson has made the people work as they should have done. Indeed they are sickly every now and then.

Manuel a Villain, and must be whipped. He broke the Oxtree of the cart going with tobacco, by driving into the ditch. He has not halfe raised the tobacco house floor although he had been a week about it, and then truely he laid up sick; And was not plowing although then ready: pretending the grass roots were in his way. Whipped he shall be; and I saw Carpenter Jamy well laid with the Cowskin.

I see it will not do to sow any stiff land cornfield with wheat without a plow; mine was hard deep and came up well, but heavy rains bake such unplowed earth so hard that it is all grown spindling so that this £20 for seed I fear is thrown Away.

If I don't mistake my riverside account of Corn will be a flemmish one; the door open for the bitch that shells, do what she pleases with it; and every grain now is a penny to any body that will steal it.

Ordered the overplus wheat up here directly.

Doleman's very dear bargain to live with any man; Parking himself and his wife truely upon the last; so that he cannot or does not assist in any thing not even in locking the Corn house door.

Abraham Clark who weaves my cloth course and fine for 4d truely says he must [have] 12d for my bed ticks.

21. *Fryday*.

This morning we had a complaint about a butter pot's being taken from the dairy door where it was put to sweeten last night and that it was seen there after candle light. Unfortunately for the theif that night was a very particular one, everybody that was well or could move was sent down to hang a prodigeous cutting of tobacco on Scaffolds at the Mangorike tobacco house. So that it must be done near home. Owen had gone over the River at 12 o'clock with John Goldsby and did not come back till 2 in the night. So he could not say whether the Servants that lay in house had done it or not. How[ever] I sent Billy Beale to search all their holes and boxes; And in their loft it was found, but both of them solemnly deniing they knew anything of it. I have desired

Colo. Brokenbrough to come here within these few days that I might pay those gentlemen for it. It seems such a theft was committed on two butter pots last year but nothing was said about them that I might not be angry; And I do suppose it was expected this would be past over in the same manner.

I got this day a dreadful fall from my horse. I was walking down the hill from the Gate by my watled tobacco ground and just as I got in to the level road at the bottom; a little creeping bird came out a bush and put my horse into a mere tremble; He fell upon his nose and not being able to recover himself, as I had but 1 arm to help him by pulling the bridle, although I sat well upon him, at last he fell upon his leftside: Of course, I came to the ground, but being blessed with a presence of mind, I quitted my Stirrops and kept my arm close to my breast; so that by taking the ground first with the hinder part of my hip and then my elbow I got but little hurt except in my knee occasioned by some part of the horse's Neck beating that to the ground as he fell upon it.

I rode afterwards to see the Pea gatherers and found, notwithstanding my 11 hay gatherers were put to assist them, there were only 27 people. 6 were sick. 3 were finishing scaffolding the tobacco. 3 with Manuel clearing the grass before his plow. 2 filling up the tobacco house floor; and 3 nay 4 Suckering and topping. Thus it is and has been, at no work can the hands be kept together but at the hoe; for then all other works in the crop are merely done with.

I discovered this day what I never knew before, nay what I had positively forbid years ago, but negroes have the impudence of the devil. Last year the suckling wenches told the overseers that I allowed them to go in five times about that business; for which I had some of them whipt and reduced it to half an hour before they went to work, half an hour before their breakfast; and half an hour before they go in at night. And Now they have made the simpletons believe I allow them to eat their morning's bit. So that a wench goes out to bake for that, then they must have time to eat it, then another bakes for their breakfast. But these things I have forbid upon their Peril.

I see clearly that the giving this beef this year will be of full as bad consequence as it has been years before; for I did not observe one hand imployed in the pea Patch with any shew of diligence.

I cannot avoid taking notice of the agreeable change in the weather; from real apprehensions of a frost we are got again to summer weather. God send it to continue that the two necessary fruits of the earth, our bread and our clothing, may be preserved to us If he can own tobacco which is our only real profit when the wheat crops are destroyed. I remember last year after the Gust we had till very late in October a very drye spell and no frosts.

Little Nancy's Ague and fever returned again Yesterday and this day again; She took a vomit this morning but under father's directions.

The wheat left after sowing was 8 bushels which was brought up. So that out of the 80 bushels we have sown but 72 bushels; and that I beleive is all thrown away; for I can't say that I like sowing any thing, more specially wheat, without deep plowing in my land which I am certain I have proved from experience, in particular in my tobacco and corn crops and when I did tend wheat and oats in those crops also.

22. *Saturday.*

Pease, if they could be so cultivated, as to afford a reasonable encrease, must needs be a fine succedanium for corn; but by all my tryals hither to I am doubtfull of it, and to be sure nothing is so tedious as the gathering of them; have not at two tryals this year with an overseer at each end of the rows reached more tha[n] 1 peck per hand with a large gang. Now as these sold at 15d is a very great price, the bare gathering alone is worth more than the pea when made besides the breaking up the ground, planting, replanting and the twice weeding them besides the fencing them in. There are inconveniencies that want remediing.

The encrease possibly and the replanting them may possibly be helped by drilling them, if we can. Barley drilled, and the weeding them will at the same time be a good dressing for the drilled grain especially Barley which comes off the ground before the pea begins to run; and it will then have two good dressings one at preparing the spaces between for drilling the pease and the other at the first weeding the pease; but then the second weeding the pease is an expence only to the pease. However, the drilling saves the replanting. And if it does not add to the encrease I am persuaded nothing can; for otherwise they will seldom yield more than 10 bushels the acre and hardly so many. Indeed their haulm makes fine winter's food. But I must make one more tryal.

No rain, I thank God, though very likely for it. So that I have had all my up land scaffolds of tobacco house[d] and ordered in the outsides of the Mangorike scaffolds in.

My people have not quite gathered over my pease so that I shall not begin my fodder as soon as I expected for I must finish my pease and on Monday, besides taking the lower scaffolds, I must cut more tobacco both above and below. However, I have experienced that in tending Pease as well as flax that in this climate it is no good way to grow either of those crops two years running in the same ground. For after either of them are properly said to be done with as to growth, Crab grass either in the months of July or August with the least moisture, and by seeding will evidently destroy the succeeding crop do what you can. Flax will be prodigiously injured by the early springing of that grass. And Peas, after they are blossomed and even Podded, will be smothered and perished by the grass, An instance we had very full this year in both.

23. *Sunday.*

I am much mistaken if I have not [done] this year, as well as I should have done last year had no gust intervened, that we all in general Cultivate our Staple Commodity from no Principle at all; and therefore whenever we are successfull in our low land worn out soil that it is more owing to accident than to any rational expectation.

1st. As to the earth we crop; how often do we delay working it, till just before we are to plant, on pretence truly of having it fresh for the roots of the plants, when in reality that freshness which we fancy is generally in a cloddy unpulverized soil. And I have more than once been insulted by being asked whether I intended to plant tobacco by Christmas, because I had all my hills made before November was out. Nay, a conjurer or two once declared they would not thank any man to break a hill for them before the last of March. Certainly these creatures form no Idea how earth is and ought to be pulvarized by the frosts and snows of the winter which cannot get into the glebe if not broke up before they happen. But they say the winter's rains will bake those hills hard again. Very true. But which is easyest to break up again, a Soil broke up before the frosts or one that has never had a hoe in it from the last weeding of the plant till the last of March? Or I may more familiarly ask which ground will be hardest, that broke up before the winter sets in, or that which has never been broke up before for above half a year and has had not only all the winter's rains but All the fall rains and winds to make it hard? This I say without the least regard to the nitrous impregnations of frosts and snows because some late assertors tell us there is not such a salt as nitre to be found in frost or Snow; a thing to be contradicted even by a fireside in the highth of summer for a real Ice may be made by nitre and salt; which I have often seen; and the Natural History of many nitrons can [illegible] tell us of frosts and Snow almost every morning during the summer season because the earth abounds so much with a kind of Native nitre. Besides in our own climate we frequently see Winter plants vastly impregnated with nitre shall throw up ice many inches high About their roots. And clay lands, in Particular mire, throw up icicles when other soils are hardly frozen; and this purely owing to the quantity of nitre with which clay is always found to be impregnated. Again our tobacco house floors when cast out having been long impregnated with the juice and dust of tobacco, the most impregnated plant probably in the world, are soonest observed to be covered with hoar frosts; for which very reason many planters cover their floors over with straw, and more would do so wer[e] it not from the great danger of fire.

As to manuring land for tobacco, As we know not the particular salts that support vegetation we cannot [say] so certainly which is the best manner, nor indeed the proper time to put it in the earth; but this we may be certain of that nitre seems to be the rustative principle in vegitation; and allowing that the time certainly for putting in this manure Must be before those salts are evaporated by rotting the dung as it is called. We see the best manure is the dung of animals that feed on grass and vegitables. Therefore, we ought to conclude that nitre that plants mostly abound with is the enlivening salt carried to the earth by the manure. Therefore, that is best which abounds most with it, which makes our tobacco past etc. so admirable a manure. And to me it seems most rational to lay this manure on before the fermentation of the manure has produced that rottenness, as every rottenness must be the effect of some fermentation. Therefore, I use it before I turn my hills; and this I do for the same reasons by burying it deep in the steps between my hills; for as I do not think it prudent to let the manure be quite rotten, if I did not cover it deep there to rott and quicken the soil the roots of the plant stuck in the hill must be injured either by the unrotten trash or by the strength of their fermentation. Therefore, I chuse to receive it by evaporation than by immediate contact.

Again we have without reason fancied that all plants must die if not planted in a Season; but my reason tells me that there is a perpetual natural moisture ascending from the earth too much rarifyed by the Sun to be much seen in the day, and only to be experienced in the night dews returning to the earth. Therefore if a well grown plant, at any time in the day put with all its roots in its easy free state of growth, could be protected from the scorching sun, every night's moisture must dispose those roots to shoot out their young fibres for the nourishment of the earth. And experience has taught me that the lightest dust taken from the hill is the best to cover the plant with all but the tips of the leaves left as rixpipes; for by laying that on a plant bent to the rising sun as being the least exposed to the perpendicular rays of the sun; it must and will be secured from the scorching heat of the sun, especially if a handfull is laid on, for, being pointed or round at top, the rays are broken from their immediate effects on the earth where the roots of the plant lie. I did this in 1769 in the driest and hottest months; and also in 1770; and I was so far from discovering any failure in those plants that I really observed they faired better than those planted in a season. But as I tended a vast crop and had some missing plants, the Eye of folly and malice was always sure to impute it to this cause of planting; although I only planted so when my plants were full large and no seasons offered.

Again, I often with concern wondered at the practice in the first weeding of Tobacco to see the hill pared quite bare and the young roots of the plant robbed of that security they had against the burning sun and really not a few I always found died by that means and unless favoured by a good rain those which did not die always seemed sickly. The constant reason given for this was to prevent the webb worm. This led me to e[n]quire in the natural history of this worm; and at last I found in a full weedy tobacco ground a little duskish fly very busy among the weeds after sun set; and, by particularly observing that ground when wed, I had reason to conclude that flye had laid the webb worm egg on those weeds; which by not carrying the weeds out when cut up hatched on the dead weeds and for want of food all travelled by instinct to the plants in the hills. By this mistake of its being a worm that came out of the earth, the practice of paring away the earth took its rise from those young plants; and by doing quite otherwise after taking away the weeds and burying them deep and giving the plants a good broad hill my tobacco all continued to flourish and preserve a constant state of growth; which I assert to the life of a tobacco plant as I shall have occasion to show presently.

Therefore, in order to keep away these webb worms it may be necessary to observe this Caution: never to let your tobacco ground be weedy, for it will tempt these flyes to come then to lay their eggs. Again, if at any time after the warmth of May is set in the hills you are to turn should be weedy, rather weed that ground first and bury those weeds deep between those rows and then turn your hills but not upon the weeds by any means; for should a drye spell come those weeds die under your earth but never rot and when the roots of your plants get to them, as in the case of long unrotten dung as before, the plants without great moisture must then die. This I say from experience having lost many thousands this year this way; though A hasty eye by also seeing webb worm or two would have it that they had destroyed it, notwithstanding both reason and truth did really evidence to the Contrary.

It is also a common way to pare very thin every time tobacco is hilled; but, having with care observed every plant in a manner checked in its growth, I ventured to digg between my rows eye deep at the same time that I hilled, and found that I kept the plants in such a constant full growth that not a rain ever spotted a plant of mine.

Again 'tis the practice of priming high that you may get your ten leaves to hang clear of the earth. I could not but examine into the injury that would ensue from their touching the earth and I found the ends of the leaves would be fazzled off by the winds against the ground and frequently they would be muddied by the rains. Now as I knew an inch of stalk must require more juice than four or five leaves, I resolved to trye to remedy those evils and prime very low that I might also get my ten leaves by topping low. The evil of whipping the ends of the leaves I remedyed by the making my hill broad as well as high up to the lower leaf of the plant, which by taking the hill all the way upon every puff of wind did not hurt it nor wher it out at the ends. And behold what prodigious plants I have produced by thus topping very low, abused as the method has been by every body; and the evil being a little dirtyed is fully compensated by a vast weight, besides the thickness will bear a great shaking to clear off that dirt.

After managing according to the foregoing principles, by being carefull and early in topping, worming and suckering, which I always do by hands that have no other thing to go about, I have produced I beleive as to goodness as fine tobacco as ever was seen And as to quantity very large, though not ever so much as it would have been had it not been for that error of turning my hills upon my weeds and the weather being drye a full month afterwards.

Many things are also said about my tending such a Vast quantity of Corn, tobacco, and indeed Pease. As to these latter, the tending them would be really nothing, for with a gang of hands where any wheat is tended, for instance enough only to serve a reasonable family; for more should not nor cannot be grown, where it is not altogether gone into; then I say some of the stiffest tobacco ground being spared, vizt, about 95 acres, that put into wheat in double drills every other row, that is, every 6 feet and 1/2 in the fall; and as plows are rather a plague and an expence too great for a crop of corn where the best hands and of the most honest disposition are not imployed are to conduct them, and no crop can allow of that, I say in the fall, let every other row of tobacco hills be hoed in a wide bed and two drills at one foot asunder, the wheat sowed and covered in by the hoe, and just before winter sets in the space between hoed and the earth thrown up to the wheat drills; for Mr. Tull's[90] method of plowing from them will not do in such a rainy as well as frosty clime.

24. *Monday.*

And in April if the spaces are drilled with one row of pease, the grain being earthed up at the same time. Again, at the first weeding the Pease, the

---

[90] Jethro Tull (1674–1741), English agricultural writer.

grain is easily earthed again; and generally speaking the grain is fit for reaping before the last weeding of Pease which is easily done by halling the stubble on one side and earthing up the Pease. But as to the encreasing and the gathering, if they cannot be made to yeild better, it is not worthwhile tending them, for as is before observed the very gathering is worth more than a pea Sells for.

But as to all work I lay down this rule: My overseers tend their foreman close for one day in every Job; and deducting 1/5 of that day's work, he ought every other day to keep up to that. Therefore, by dividing every gang into good, Middling, and indifferent hands, one person out of each is to watched for 1 day's work, and all of the same division must be kept to his proportion. And I can truely say that I never found 20,000 per hand of corn and tobacco too much to be tended except in very wet years. In such years, therefore, I would rather chuse to turn out ground than never to have a full crop. And the only difficulty I find is in getting plant patches large and forward enough; and some years, when my crop is latter, my fodder will suffer. But then by gaining greatly in my crops I certainly make up for a little loss in fodder. And the hawns of my pease, besides the hulls, wheatchaff, and straw is often a full equivalent for a little fodder that may be lost. And in a full crop of corn some of it may be spared to keep up a Stock.

As to manuring Ground, everything will turn to good manure, which ought to be a winter's case.

Rode out this day. I observed at least a good cartload of tobacco not brought in on thursday last; by accident it was not hurt by lying on the ground.

My 60 foot scalded house well filled this day and 3/4 of it may be struck in ten days. I am obliged to take Manuel from plowing to bring the overplus tobacco from that scaffold to the 90 foot house which is to be hung with the next cutting below.

A very cloudy day, often Spitting, but at 12 the sun broke out; I ordered up my tobacco Cutters to Stay up here: And to humor my Son they slit the stalk thre[e] parts down first. I know it cures sooner, and as it is late and the tobacco large, if my people can do it right, it is a very good way.

The 60 foot house very fine tobacco. Near 2 rooms hung in the 90 foot house called the mud house.

25. *Tuesday.*

It rained yesterday till 12 o'clock and then clear away a little when I set in 6 hands to cutting, first slitting the tobacco stalks down the two lowest leaves; but contrary to all observation it thickened and rained again. However we had time to get a pretty smart cutting on the grass—It rained frequently in the evening, so it did in the night and this morning pretty smartly.

I must observe both the August and September new moon kept their points of their horns pretty perpendicular over each other, which is a general sign of a drye moon, but the one was a wet month and the other now bids for the same weather. So that perhaps this sign took place by some accident in the weather when the moon did so appear. But I have really fancied a reason for it.

Note: my tobacco in the houses as yet appears very good. We have got the 60 foot double shedded below full and a great deal in it near cured; this 50 foot house above near full; And the prize house in a manner quite full, which I reckon equal to 30 if not 40 feet of housing; And I am certain more tobacco up the hill than will fill the 90 foot riverside house. And I may be positive the two mud house [lots] will do plentifully to fill the [90] foot house of fine tobacco. And to be sure the great Piece of Ground by the chesnut tree which has hardly a plant cut out of it will plentyfull fill the Fork 90 foot house; And we shall be able to strike the Mangorike 60 foot sheded house. Now as every plant almost is really thick, large, and fine, why are not we to expect 40 hogsheads? I shall lay out for that Number and more, if it pleases God to indulge us with no early frost.

			foot
3.	90	are———————————	270
1.	80	———————————	80
1.	50	———————————	50
1.	30	———————————	30
			430

All very full hung and perhaps we don't mistake to think the overplus by rehanging will make up the other 70 foot in all 500 foot of house. Now 70 foot in tollerable tobacco yields 1,000 pounds tobacco. If th[e] prize yields more we shall have 50 hogsheads; but to be sure 40 hogsheads.

26. *Wednesday.*

Mr. Hipkins came here yesterday and settled Owin Griffith's ac[count] for which he drew a bill of Exchange [on] Hyndman and Lancaster for £30 payed out of the money lodged in their hands on his account by Edward Griffith of Montague house, Privy garden, Which Bill I endorsed out of humanity; and if I was deceived to present the Bill to Mr. Wm. Molleson who I hoped would pay it for my honour.

Note: I printed a little L.C. in the tail of my L as a private mark to pay it by. Of which I am to advise Molleson.

Our yesterday's cutting was so large that although All hands began at 12 we could not get it out of the grass in the ground before the rain came up; and it endured a pritty heavy Shower; However all our Scaffolds were hanged, abundance floored in the tobacco house, and abundance still to bring out.

Wind now at Northwest. Nothing injured. The prize house, a few stacks with a few plants touched, but nothing bad. These we hung out.

We have Sun this day and it has turned out warm. I wish I may get all my tobacco well cured. Every day some of it gets reeking wet, owing to its thickness and being hung a[l]t[oget]her too thick.

27. *Thursday.*

Went to Dr. Faunteleroy's Sale of medicines, but none sold, not Doctors enough.

Whether cleared up finely last night. This day a tollerable good one, but cold and windy. It seems a little like a frost, but I see it warms away. Cutting this day below the hill. Hung up all our yesterday cuttings on Scaffolds.

Guy promises the riverside house this night ready for handing. Note: all the sticks gone.

Talbot drilling barley at Doleman's, the very first.

Manuel gone to H[ickory] T[hicket] for my hogsheads staves. He bought enough for 10 hogsheads. Goes tomorrow for more. This is a most lazy impudent dog. I ordered him to lay off Dolman's ground first two drills for Barley at a foot asunder, then to lay off 4 feet, then two drills, and so quite through the ground. He went to the Carpenter's and got a 4 foot stick to do it and told Dolman he was to do so, and yet he laid the drills only 2 feet from each other by which means the piece not two acres took 5¼ bushels of Barley so that we cannot tend pease between that.

28. *Fryday.*

Yesterday a very sharp northerly wind, which almost scared me about a frost; but God be praised it grew warm again towards Sun Set and this morning no sign of a frost, but still it keeps cold and Northerly.

We shall have this day at least scaffolds out for near two 90 feet houses, and I begin to think we shall do more than fill the other two 90 feet houses, for we have abundance out yet and are cutting away. I hope we shall get all in safe. I can't say the last cutting of any one piece is as large as the rest was, but it seems to be of a good size and really feels uncommonly thick so that perhaps I am not much too sanguine for ordering 50 hogsheads to be got.

Miss Lucy gone to Mr. Beverley's. All my people every where almost ill with Agues and fevers; and the Stoutest fellows generally the worst.

Owen left me on Wednesday. Ball sent me a hasty letter. I sent an answer to it to tell him he is very indecent to me, I suppose owing to his odd temper, but I bid him be cautious for although I knew how and always was generous and kind to those under me I could not tell how long I should bear such warmth of temper from him. He is angry when I find fault with anything. How then am I to instruct this man who can't bear to be blamed?

My son and his family to come home to day, that is, if they chuse it. I read yesterday; that none but madmen know the pleasure there is in being mad, Gamesters only taste the pleasure of gaming which mostly proceed from the desire of being wealthy and powerfull; which like a dropsical thirst encrease the more they are indulged. Perhaps Mr. G[iberne] and this Mr. C[arter] and his connections are strong instances of such evils; but how does this gaming square with their several professions in life? Perfect friends as they stile themselves are always endeavouring to ruin one another. Loving husbands and affectionate Parents are daily bent upon ruining their whole families.

I have been obliged to Send Nassau, although he is very ill himself again, to Mr. Buckl[an]d's son. I never heard of that child untill the parent thought him very dangerous ill; I sent him some gentle powders to open his bowels; He took [it] which had its effect; Then I understand Brokenbrough[91] was written to. What he gave him I know [not]; the child had got better; but all at once grew bad again and I was sent to. I was sorry to meddle where another was imployed because I did not know what had been given and so I wrote; but importunity made me Send Nassau. He brought word the child had worms. I recommend 2 or 3 grains calomels and Sent it to be administered. Nassau brought word last night the child was better; but now the Father writes word it must die this day. I don't care to be concerned with such people for he says it has a regular pulse, and yet he fancy's he is dying. The child may die. All men must die, but I hardly believe any one with a regular Pulse.

This evening even this alarmed parent sent me word the child is much mended, and begs pardon for the weakness of his apprehensions.

Again the fever makes an advance and then the boy is bad again and the father Frightened.

[91] Dr. John Brockenbrough (1744–1804) was a doctor at Hobb's Hole and son of Col. William Brockenbrough of Richmond Co.

29. Saturday.

I sent Nassau with orders to give the child a gentle Puke or two with Ipecacuan tea, a little stimulated with the essence of antimony, and wrote to his father, that he knew it had been all along my opinion the disorder was of the growth of the Season, a load of slimy Phlegm in the Stomach constantly disponating there from a fund of Acrid bile seated in the passage below the orifice of the Stomach; And, if we did not attempt to remove that by pumping some of it out, the child would not stand a rational chance of a perfect recovery; for I had observed that all the present complaints of Spleen, in those who have been attackt with this bilious fever, were absolutely owing to the not evacuating this bile properly. That as to the child's weakness, such a Stomach would at any time bring on such a languor, but as soon as that was discharged even children grew stronger.

The rain that has been lowering and ever spitting for these many days is now settling, and I fear it has catched my upper scaffold at least; however, I hope it is in no danger for what few plants had begun to cure on the outside of the scaffold I had taken in. I fancy the pease not gathered will suffer; by the quantity of the ground there may be about 20 or 30 bushels. This will be a loss; but I hope all my scaffolds will escape, for they are as yet green, all but a leaf or two. And I hope this rain will not continue; for it began at Northwest and then continued at North and afterwards I did observe it got to Eastnorth. It does not get to Northeast. I hope it will not continue.

OCTOBER 1770

3. Wednesday.

The weather on the 29th, Ultimo, broke up as was expected and really warm and Clivet[?].

The 1st was our court day and very good. Much tobacco was taken in from my Scaffolds and hung in my houses; but not all of it.

In the night or just before day of the Second of the month A western cloud came up thundered and lightned, and, instead of discharging all its contents, rained pretty much and spread over the whole heavens and Continued a Cold rain at Northeast and at North all day and grew excessive cold so that not only fires were necessary but even very good ones. Mr. Parker, his Lady, children, and many Gentlemen here from Court staid all Tuesday and this morning.

Although there had been much expectation of a frost, there is nothing like it, but it is most prodigious Cold, the rain over, and the wind as yet but at North. The Clouds seem all broken and scattered. But if the Sun does not soften the Appearance, a frost seems to forbode this night. I have abundance of tobacco not cut; have ordered if the Sun comes out that every thick plant shall be Cut, and as soon as it can be moved to the grass there carried and stacked in little sugar love stack of about 4 feet deep diameter at bottom with the buts out to ready for brush[?] carrys.

Mr. Parker's English sow yesterday morning farrowed 10 piggs. She was ordered and had a great litter of straw in a close house with liberty to come out if she would, but the weather was too bad and she never Came out and was daily fed and watered. However 4 of her pigs [died] either by being over laid or by the effects of the weather.

Colonel Peachey sends to town within these 10 days if Raleigh Colston[92] does not; if he does or does not I hope he will send to let me know it, because I have a letter to write to Mr. Ball at Rippon Hall. Colo. Peachy to be informed when Mr. Carter gets down to Corotoman.

The wind at Northwest blowing very fresh and very cold indeed. All hands cutting tobacco.

Buckland's child died last night. He had been 11 days before I was applyed to, and had been under Dr. Brockenbrough's directions for Worms; it seems every dose he took had made him worse. Dr. Flood also had been with him. Griffin Garland sent this day about his daughter who had been ill ever since Fry[day] last was seven night, 13 days, also a boy of his 3 year old ill about 7 days ago.

4. *Thursday.*

A very fine day this, but yesterday's fresh Northerly wind produced a frost; and it is remarkable that it is about the full of the moon so that now the weather wise are always certain the October full moons bring in the frosts; but it seems it must be rainy about that time: and at last the September gust left us near 2 months almost too wet to move on our plantations, and yet we had no frost till the middle of November; and now considering the 11 days this is but a September full moon.

It was lucky for us the frost has hurt nothing of any consequence in the crop. I had cut all down to about 80,000 of my large crop. I can't say all very fine tobacco, but I am in hopes in the general tollerably thick. But I am of

[92] Raleigh Colston was a farmer in Richmond Co. and probably either the son or brother of William Colston (d. 1781).

Opinion that we shall hardly get it all taken care of this week. In the first there is so much of it, near 3 ninety foot houses to hang and two of those very far off, one at the River side and the other at the Fork and but one cart to get it in, and at least 10 people out of my gang ill with fevers and agues, cuts, and biles; for at these times I commonly see, if people can't be sick to lay up with the rest, they find out a way of disabling themselves. Thes[e] can pull backs and of course a great argument against tending a full crop, at any time. I confess it has been unlucky this year so that I shall loose, I suppose a little tobacco, a great deal of fodder, and some pease; and I wish from the lateness of growth I don't also loose some corn too young to be drye.

My Grandson taken ill two days. He took a vomit yesterday that worked him well; and also one today which has brought up a great load of bile. I wish the Child don't conceal his sickness long before he speaks of it, for it is impossi[ble] such a load could be to come off without a complaint sooner: he scarcely owned a sickness at his stomach and pretends he has been at stool yesterday, but I fancy it is a mistake and have ordered a Clyster in about an hour or two after his vomit is over, and must tomorrow give him opening powders before I can venture with the bark.

Mr. Ford[93] and Billy Beale here yesterday. My son remarkable for having shot at two large bucks standing close together within 20 steps of him and missing them.

I shall be very late with my barley. One of the pieces of ground intended for it is quite full of Young tobacco, and the other excessive wet and low; and my oxen that should plow them all busy about getting in the crop.

5. *Fryday.*

A very fine morning and no frost, so that my tobacco left out was not injured; and it is well for, what with sickness Jobling about and I believe idleness in both people and Overseers, the gang does nothing.

This morning when alone with Mr. Parker I enquired of him whether he had discharged that Bond to Mr. Moore Fauntleroy of the Clifts, which Colo. Tayloe and I had long agoe by letter engaged to be his security in; And he told me it had been long agoe paid off and cancelled.

I am afraid we have been a little too large in reckoning the houses that we shall fill. We thought this uphill tobacco would fill the river side 90 foot house; and by this last cutting which has been pritty close it is now thought we shall want some to fill it; but I am persuaded it cannot be much. Again we were certain the two pieces by the mud house would fill that, besides the 60 foot

---

[93] Probably William Ford (d. 1783), a small planter in Richmond Co.

double shedded house; but just now the people hanging the Mud house thought they should want a little; however I do not think it will be much if any, for the tobacco is all at the house and except the middle room the rest are all brought down to the joice and some of the other gable end here below the joice hung, and there seems to be a good deal of tobacco still to hang. The Fork 90 foot house was hanging and abundance of tobacco there to fill it and at least two good days' carting to carry there; And really a prodigeous cutting still in the ground, and really for the last cutting, tobacco pritty large and thick so that possibly we may fall short very little if any of our expectations, provided we get a week more clear of frost.

It is a pity Overseers have not more contrivance. At the Fork I saw the cleaning out of the house going as a tedious jobb; but by a little alteration I am in hopes they are in a way of doing business faster.

9. *Tuesday.*

Good weather ever since fryday. Employed all that day and saturday in cutting, killing, and hanging my tobacco.

The Mud house wants about 2 rooms.

The Fork wants near 30 foot filling.

Carryed down my upland Scaffolds this day. It took near all day with the Cart and 4 hands.

Began to cut tops at the Fork and Mangorike: The marsh gang went to finish the pease and are to continue at it till all are pickt and the vines pulled up.

Struck some tobacco at the 60 foot house. All that was in case; very fine and but little of it under tobacco.

I would this day have struck tobacco up here, but neither the prize house nor the tobacco house cured.

My corn seems pretty good now the tops are cut.

Toney getting hoops for setting up hogsheads. Guy and the Carpenters gone to build Jamy and Jugg a 12 foot house, then to new fit their house and remove it for Doleman to live in.

Manuel begins plowing for Barley sowing.

Ordered all my tobacco to be cut down this day.

We examined the Prize and other tobacco houses but [did not] see any cured enough to strike.

I can't but take notice that only 60 feet and a little more are filled of the Fork 90 foot house so that out of the 3 90 feet houses we may have 40 feet to fill, but then this day's cutting will certainly over do it.

I begin to think Old age will have many sensations that cannot be well accounted for. I am as well as common and yet all yesterday long and this day, every motion that I make with my head so as to move my left Ear, my right begins to tout, tout like a horn calling up hogs and this whether sitting, walking, lying, or standing. It is certainly wind Sounding through the meeker aurium; and it is not uncommon to have a ringing in the Ear, but that this particular motion should cause it, is the difficulty.

Sent Manuel and Billy Beale for my brandy, the here of my Still to Wm. Northerns.[94] They brought the cask home, but it seems they know not its contents; only Beale knows that Northern put in 75 gallons of his own brandy to fill it. I directed him to do so and am to pay him 3/ per gallon for it.

12. *Fryday.*

Still fine weather. Yesterday we stripped out the first bulk of tobacco in Mangorike 60 foot house. Very fine and very little under tobacco, and really no trash at all.

My people getting in their tops. The Jobbers pulling up the Pea vines.

John Beale from Northumberland came here last night; he went to bed with an Ague. This morning we come to an agreement about his looking after my Northumberland quarters; He is to live where Longwith lived; and he asked 2 shares for the middle and that quarter. I told him, that would be going on in my old error, for then he would take no care about my other interest there; at last, I offered him a twelfth of all the growing crop after all wages or shares to other Overseers were deducted. This he agreed to take. I then asked him what he thought he should get, he said about 25 pounds. I said I would give him 30 pounds if he did his duty, and if he did not get more I should make but very little.

This evening Daniel Lawson and one Saunders,[95] Thos. Lawson's wife's father-in-law, came here; about his son's Mortgage to me of two slaves. Daniel wanted to get me to stay longer for the money. I told him Ball had heard he was to go out of the parts the last of this month. Mr. Saunders began to denye this. I said I placed a confidence in Ball, he had told me so, and I would believe it. At last I told old Daniel if he would secure me the debt I would stop the sale. But this he did not care to do; and for my Part I would not press him to it for I did beleive Thomas was a base man and perhaps not a little helped to deceive him.

Sam, returned from Rippon Hall last night, brought a penitent letter

---

[94] William Northern was a small planter in Richmond Co.
[95] Probably George Sanders (d. 1794), a farmer in Richmond Co.

from Mr. Ball. By his account, except the getting of Hay, things in good order; he had stripped out about 3 hogsheads, some very fine and some but indifferent.

Toney says he shall be ready to set off to Rippon Hall tuesday next and shall leave 32 hogsheads behind for my son and me besides some old hogsheads new trimmed up. Note: I will have those from the Fork sent for.

13. *Saturday.*

Every appearance of rain very comfortably cleared off with a moderate cool Northerly air. I say comfortably because all our fodder is as yet upon hand; and indeed some tobacco to get in, the Ax tree of the cart very unluckily breaking to prevent the doing it yesterday; by which means I shall be very late getting my barley into the ground.

I really think it should be a just observation that any one thing put backward in working, is the real cause of late doings in every part of the crop.

Dolman will not by this day, if so soon, finish pulling up the Pea vines for fodder, and they must be done for there is not a better provender to be got even in the marshes.

John Beale, who is here took a tartre Vomit this day; surely never was a Stomach so foul. 7 Vomits. Every one of them green and Yellow. He must have been very ill without it.

14. *Sunday.*

My son who would not go to Mr. Beverley's, because after his saying I pretended to be serving him, but yet never did it, I put him in mind that he was even then going in my Petty auger. I say he ordered his horses to meet him this morning at Randal's;[96] but [who] was to carry them? My boy Ben and upon one of my horses. So that this Passionate fool is every day obliged to be beholden for the very thing he denyes.

Mrs. Carter taken ill yesterday and was to be seen so before, though she would not own it. And the poor little baby Fanny is every time to share her Mama's disorder by sucking her, and this because she should not breed too fast. Poor children! Are you to be sacrificed for a parent's pleasure?

I have been a Parent and I thought it murder and therefore hired nurses or put them out.

---

[96] Francis Randall (d. 1777) was a small planter in Richmond Co.

15. *Monday.*

Yesterday came a letter endorsed from Colo. Tayloe with the death of Ld. Bottetourt,[97] our Governour, who left us the 13th in the morning. A melancholly piece of News. A fine Gentleman is dead and truely Noble in his Public character. He, as anecdote says, was pitcht upon to be the Agent of a dirty tyrannic Ministry; but his virtues resisted such an employment and he became the instrument of a dawning happiness; and had he lived we should have been so: for through his active and exemplary virtue, order everywhere revived out of that confusion that our own dissipative indolence had thrown us into.

I may say of him as Dr. Huxham said of his Master, Boerhaave, when writing about his character. *Mortuus est! Proh Dolor! Quem nulla secula hujus [C]oloniae tace lubet.*[98] Our loss is too great to be expressed. The chicanery of profession [faded] which was paving the way to mercenariness and corruption will again begin the great work of enslaving this Country and in it all America.

The General Court will run into the necessity of a longer time, and of Course greater Salleries to do their business, which this man shewed to be affected only by a little diligence in the ordinary assigned portions of time very well. The county Courts will contrive to be paid for doing their duty from that pretence of a closer attention [t]o the duty; when I have proved that by only a [d]iligent care the whole of Justice might [b]e done in the ordinary months; And when we get into the way of corruption, he will [be] the cleverest man that gets the most by it. Clients will turn bribers; and the transition from the sale of private justice to that of Public liberty will [be] but easy and short.

Mrs. Carter and little Fanny very ill and [y]et this child is to continue to suck the poizon; she can't live, it is said, without the baby and it is certain she can't live with it. Of Course, the death of the child is inevitable from such an absurd way of reasoning: I hope my Lord and my God [faded] clear of this death. I would [faded] under.

Once more we go about our fodder. Our bulks of tobacco all to this day's striking are stripped out into large bundles.

[97] Norborne Berkeley, Baron de Botetourt (1717–70) was governor of Virginia from 1768 until his death in 1770.

[98] Dr. John Huxham (1692–1768), English physician of Plymouth, studied for a time in 1715 with Dr. Hermann Boerhaave (1668–1738), professor of physic in the University of Leyden. The Latin may be translated roughly as: "He is dead! How terrible! No generation of this colony is disposed to pass him over in silence."

Again we are getting much hay; and the weather quite suitable for such purposes, but also productive of Aguish and feverish returns. In short, we run too much summer into our winter climate.

16. *Tuesday*.

The clouds that have hung as it were in the Horizon from the West to the North for 3 days, now discover their sharpness by a steady and gale. Which, if it releives us by clearing off the Epidemic disorder[s] of a most bilious nature, may be a great service to us to compensate for the loss of most of the fodder tha[t] is dryed and now blowing away. This was an evil I dreaded from a large and a late crop; Although had my people been but healthy, everything would have been in before this. But such has been the Putred biliousness of the season that we seldom can have half my people out to work and those that are out hardly in a working state. I wish the rushing in of the winter season may not add inflammatory disorders to this bilious situation that cannot as yet have compleatly discharged itself.

Toney went off this morning for Rippon Hall.

19. *Friday*.

I was pleased to see that in a field at the Fork in which I was almost certain there would be but little corn by means of its suffering as it did with the weeds, I say, now the tops are cut off, to see very fine corn in it. Indeed it yields but few tops and what blades there are seem quite good for nothing. This was ground which I dunged the year before after Tutt's careless manner; but by an oddity in our Seasons it was injured by the weeds, although twice wed and early enough.

The first time I wed it before a weed had sprung from the driness of the spring and before I could get into it the second time the June rains brought on such a thick mat of grass that the corn after it had got a growth fired quite up. And when I did weed it the second time a 6 weeks' drowth prevented its recovering any green look at all; therefore, I expected nothing from it, but I dare say it will produce a reasonable crop.

Got my prize house struck. Fine tobacco and the crye of it not being cured enough turns out about as many plants with swelled stems as will make 5 or 6 sticks, which I have had pickt out and rehanged and carried to the tobacco house, where they will stand a Better chance of being taken notice of as they cure. I find striking tobaccoe except in rainy seasons my overseers have not been acquainted with, and seem to be very willing to leave that till it does rain. But experience has taught me that tobacco in every 24 hours after it is cured comes in case at some time or another unless prevented by outward cold air or winds; therefore, to prevent being catched with my crop hanging at times when these cold winds and rains do happen I have it watched as fast as it cures and taken down. Tomorrow I shall order the Mangorike 60 foot house to be struck quite down, that I may get that out of the way for my corn.

Little Fanny Carter ever since fryday last has had from 4 to near 8 a daily ague, the most violent by account that a grown person generally has, and then a fever.

They would follow no advice of mine. Dr. Mortimer was sent for; saw her in one of these agues, ordered her a vomit, which I had done before; he did not stay to see it work, but expressly forbid the bark to be used pretending the fits would return, and yet directed nothing to keep them off, though he was as certain they would keep on whether she took bark or not; and these weak or rather Obstinate Parents were against using the bark to this poor babe when every fit was a mere death. However I was at last [indulged] in the use of 3 doses of 6 grains each with a little Rhubarb yesterday. The fit kept its period, but my wench told me not so violent nor so long; and as the fever went off in a plentifull sweat I continued the doses encreased to 10 grains; but now the child will only suck its mother's milk poisoned with her very bilious habit; and madam pretends she will spit spoon victuals out and will not give her any even as a medicine. In short, I never knew such a vile, obstinate woman, even beyond a human creature, whilst her husband tallys in with her stupidity. And I suppose by and by if the child dies the creature will be then whindling for what she herself has done.

Very fine weather but still I can't get in my barley to the ground; my oxen are too poor to work, and my people so sickly.

Molly Beverley[99] very puny. At last her worms begin to come away, by my medicine which Lucy now allows her to take.

Nancy a great Cold and a return of her ague and fever with it. But I thank God my gang this day are all apt except those at the Fork whose laziness has made sick. My old midwife alarmed me two days agoe about Chriss in labour saying the child was dead, so that Mortimer in his way home got a fee of me which he should not have had; for the wench was not then in labour, and after he was gone, by my ordering a clyster to be administered her labour pains came on and she was delivered of a fine child.

[99] Molly Beverly was Landon Carter's granddaughter and the daughter of Robert Beverley of Blandfield and Maria Carter, Landon Carter's daughter.

I was obliged this day to send two of my spinning girls to get my cotton at the Fork, Mr. Rose being laid up.

The Fork people still about the fodder very bad, but yet it may help.

Mangorike people gone to cut tops in the Riverside field.

20. *Saturday.*

I fancy our good weather will leave us soon. It grew cloudy in the evening yesterday, mizled a little at night with the wind at South by East and quickly changed to Northeast and North and continued cloudy all night, and is now cloudy.

Yesterday the two wenches that went to pick the Fork cotton brought home about 40 pounds in the seeds.

Last night, I thank god, little Fanny missed her terrible Ague; it was thought she had a fever; but it is common for the flesh to feel warm on the period of the ague when it leaves them, especially if that is obtained by the bark, which I fancy this was. Note: the day before the child only took 3 doses of 6 grains each with Rhubarb in them and yesterday 3 doses of 10 grains each without Rhubarb; and if my advice is followed she shall take 2 doses this day with a small quantity of Rhubarb, this for 2 days and then some drops of Elixir Proprietatis[100] to prevent any ill effects of the bark and carry off what remains of the bile: But unless they wean her, still sucking from a morbid breast will in spight of fate bring on a return. Poor baby.

I cannot help taking notice of many writers ridiculing the general complaints of mankind as to the weather, and charging it as an uneasy disposition; but I think the contrary, and that is rather a greater sensibility of the rod that may be used, and, of course, it must argue a Submission to it with a due concern, whilst he who discovers no emotion at it shews either a want of due concern, or a stupid inconsiderateness of what he may suffer. But let it not be argued from hence, that I am for indulging others desponding in an Outrageous anxiety.

At last poor Fanny attended with a violent Phlegmy cough and a fever with it; how she got it is not known; she took another vomit this morning first, and brought off abundance of tough Phlegm.

Mangorike tobacco house all struck but what was rehanged in it. I don't imagine there will be quite 10 hogsheads foot packt of leaf of what was struck in 8 rooms and about 2 of stemmed; and out of the remaining 6 rooms

---

[100] Elixir proprietatis, a mixture of myrrh, saffron, and succotrine, was used as a warm stimulant and aperient.

we must get at least 8 hogsheads more to make up our guess of 8,000 in the whole house which I fancy we shall not do, although I see Simon, a heavy fello, treads it down well and it is thick tobacco.

This day clears off Surprizingly, and promises to be warm again. I wish the people may also mend; the air is growing clear and who knows but it may remove these terrible agues and fevers which have now attended the Colony pretty generally for almost 3 months.

Yesterday I again heard the Governor was not dead so late in the day as 4 o'clock on Saturday the 13. It seems he had been attended with periodical convulsions from the day before and was imagined to be diing in one of them when Colonel Tayloe came away, which occasioned the report of his death. God's will be done, but I hope he has in this instance been mercifull to this poor Colony; for it seems it has been this good man alone that has prevented those devils from attempting to distress this Colony.

22. *Monday.*

This morning rain from a good time before day; but at last it cleared up with a Northerly coolness.

I kept out the bulk struck in the prize house on fryday last.

Put two hogsheads under the prize. Note: these foot packt hogsheads don't answer their expe[c]ted weight. One I saw received but 428 pounds which was expected to be 500 at least.

Struck the first hanging in the 48 foot house on the hill.

I somehow fancy this tobacco of James Englishe's[101] sort is a wasting sort in the house and does not turn out so fine as the Orleans kind. Therefore I shall preferr that sort.

Little Fanny mended yesterday, had two stools by the Clyster, no fever, her cold quite mended and the baby lively yesterday and this day so that through God's favour we hope she will get well, as she continues so this day.

Nancy a great cold which gave her a fever last night that did not leave her at 4 this night.

Molly Beverley a cold. She took a vomit that worked her moderately 15 grains Ipecacuana and 3 teaspoons of Crocus wine.

24. *Wednesday.*

My sons Robert and John set off for Town by way of Rings Neck Plantation.

[101] James English (d. 1773) lived in Richmond Co. and was probably a farmer.

A very fine day. Little Fanny growing better. Nancy brisk, clear of a fever, and running about.

Note: I signed a blank bill of Exchange to pay Esqr. Lee, the Naval Officer, his account of £41.10. My son Carrys the bill to town to be filled up at the settled exchange for the money.

People taken ill yesterday could not fill up the 2 hogsheads under prize; and was obliged to fetch George from the Fork.

Not yet done getting fodder either at the Fork or Riverside, and this day a great frost indeed. Our prize house bulk stripped out.

Wrote to Ball at Rippon Hall about Candles, Plums, and many things relative to my plantations, particularly to send Toney off to Northumberland as soon as he has done his hogsheads.

I am now satisfyed John Dolman is too lazy and liing a fellow to be hated. My sons, going to the landing, saw abundance of hogs in the corn field, and the people in the field and yet Mr. Dolman told me that nothing had been in. I find abundance of the corn from the little gate destroyed by creatures of every kind. Dolman, it seems, has kept two cows all this year, to wit, the cow he had last fall and that which I let him have this year. I have therefore ordered those cows up here and his calf to be carryed to the Fork.

I have given Wm. Lawson his first scold this whole year about the fence. I am promised that all the fence shall be gone quite round pennel by Pannel and well mended.

Manuel is to be done plowing for barley next the gate tomorrow by 12 o'clock. Note: his boy Harry has runaway. I shall order the drills to be immediately made and sown and indeed the fence carefully made up. Then he shall go to the field by the chesnut tree where I will either sow Spelt or Barley.

I was cautioned yesterday against the stories I heard of J——B——d.[102] The person who told them is vastly prejudiced against him.

27. *Saturday.*

Fine weather now and ever since Saturday last; but by reason of agues and fevers but little business done. Every body that are well too lazy.

My prizing stopped for a day by means of the rottenness of the wheels, and Master Beale could not speak to me about it for near two days. I imagine it will be difficult to give this boy spirit.

The last bulk in Mangorike tobacco house finely heated and stripped out two days ago. The Overseer frightened about it.

[102] Perhaps John Boyd (d. 1781) of Lancaster Co.

My home bulk not warm yet owing to the difference in Bulking.

Buckland had 7 or 8 of my hands to help about Mr. Carter's tomb stone and he kept Jimmy the whole day though it is not yet done.

Dolman, a rascal. He has kept 2 of my cows to his pole all this year. I ordered both away and directed 1 pint of milk from home to his Child.

Nancy and little Fanny a return of their fevers and indeed poor George.

Fanny poisoned with her mother's milk, Nancy's a Cold catched, and George took a Vomit 20 grains Ipecacuana with one cup of tartar water made from 2 grains in a quart of warm water, the rest thrown away. This worked 4 times very bilious and it is imagined it will work more.

Three, nay 4, patients from Griffin Garland, all relapses by means of leaving off and not taking my former medicines sent.

Wrote this day to Tom Reed of Northumberland to tell him if [he] will not give me timely notice that my evidences might be present I would agree to no arbitration; and he must know Richmond Court days very improper, for I for more than a year have constantly devoted those days solely to the service of the bench. This letter I gave Mr. Hipkins to read and convey to Mr. Reid at the race.

28. Sunday.

An ague this day. I ordered a Clyster after the fever abated as he has not it seems had a motion for more than two days; but this it seems he would not admit of. I was abroad and resolved to have it administered. Mama talked of his going into fits: However, after half was spelt, it was given, and of Course did not Operate.

29. Monday.

I ordered him an opening dose. This boy is made a fool by his mother and she full as bad, Sick and yet full of obstinate fright. I wish the child somewhere else. I am certain there is a chance for a whole winter's disease by such doing. Powders can't open and dissolve hard baked excrement under such a contracted Sphincter. Besides, order what I will, drunken servants and a thoughtless mother forget to give them, so that I expect Nancy soon to be laid up and Fanny is still sucking her poison. I have at last opened the Mama's bowels and hope that will reletve the child.

The stiff ground turnout of my tobacco crop is sown every other row in barley. The method I took was to make a bed of 4 furrows and then one drill in the middle, this sown with a full hand because it is later. Intend to sow the spaces between with Peas next Spring in a drill Barley, 15½ bushels, 70,000 hills.

Manuel preparing the ground turned out up to the Pear tree, which is also sown with barley.

I fancy this day will finish getting my fodder every where. Then towards next year's Crop.

31. *Wednesday.*

Weighed yesterday one large bundle of tobacco which we first sort our tobacco into. It contained 3 plants and it weigh[ed] 20 ounces so that each leaf weigh[ed] above half an ounce. Now my people tye up every night 30 of these bundl[es] into small hands. 4 leaves and a tyer therefore at one hand weighed 20 ounces. 30 must be 37 pounds each hand. Then, allowing all my gang to be at both places, house and garden people to be 40, it would be 1,500 pounds tobacco a night which I am certain they do not do: therefore, Overseers are either deceitfull or mistaken.

Weighed also 21 Small hands in my prize house 3¼ and 21 ounces of Mongorike but 2¾ so that the home tobacco was half a pound heavyer than the Mangorike in that quantity so that this way each leaf weighed above half an Ounce up here and below not near so much.

Note: my daughter Lucy had the curiosity to weigh the Cotton I pick every [night] and it was just 1 pound so that as I began the 5th of the month and perhaps did not imploy myself that way some nights I certainly may be said to compleat my pound each month.

Put under 4 more hogsheads of tobacco to be prized, two of them from the prize house and the other from Mangorike for I want to see what crop I made upon this hill.

Only finished my fodder yesterday very late and but indifferent fodder. But our late and large tobacco crop besides our large Cornfields were the occasion of this.

Gathering up my pea vines which the creatures have consumed a great many of; but, as it was the Colts and draught oxen, that damage is not great. I stuck them in the field and have it fenced in till I have leizure to bring them up.

I propose to put up 4 beeves but I am afraid I shall destroy too much corn.

Manuel not done plowing for barley yet.

I wish I had thought more of my pea vines than I have done. Had I stacked them sooner, besides the advantage in quantity, they must have been an excellent provender. My horse set greedily to eating as I stood by the stack. There is a quantity of them now; but they seem to be above half used up by the creatures.

Tutt's horse again in my Fork corn field. I sent him home with a message that I would shoot him if he came again.

I am amazed at the fevers of Betsey and George Carter.

George has 3 fits of an ague and fever every other day. He took first one Vomit. Ipecacuana and tartar emetic, which Nassau told me brought off much bile. The next fit he had I brought off stools by clysters and between 2 and 3 I gave another vomit on this day which was no fit day. It workt well as I was informed and this day an ague and fever seized him so that it must be dangerous to give him bark because his fits are grown more irregular.

Betsey took a vomit with tartar which workt her well, and gave many stools, then the night her ague and fever, and the next morning her ague and fever, after that another vomit said to work well, and this day two agues and two fevers. To be sure she must have another vomit; but I can't tell how such irregularity gets ground of us after so many evacuations.

Perhaps it may be in the air of the day for 5 of the Gang people came up this day and poor little Fanny again taken with a relapse, or it may possibly be the children's eating too much this day or what is most likely Nassau's drunkenness preventing him giving a just account of the working of the vomits.

Wm. Lawson taken with a violent cold some days ago and very bad yesterday although out with the people. I advised him to take a vomit at night.

NOVEMBER 1770

2. *Fryday.*

Mr. Parker sent a barrel of his beer here yesterday; his tumbrel carryed back 16 bushels of barley.

Sowed this day 6 bushells of barley in the great Piece of tobacco ground and we shall finish that piece to the Pear tree tomorrow.

Weighed a common large bundle of the tobacco out of the mud house, 1¾; so that if Lawson's people tye up 30 bundles they must tye up every night at least 52 and ½ each, but this they do not; so that either overseer or people must deceive.

I hope George's Ague and fever is stopped but I don't know what to say to Betty's. She had her ague last night, though she took her third vomit yesterday morning, and had her ague this morning, although she had taken two doses with bark and Rhubarb. However, tomorrow I hope we shall get more time to use the bark. This child like all the rest keeps her fit just a week.

3. *Saturday.*

We shall finish putting in all my barley this day. The first sown last fryday is sprouting, but I fear these cool nights will keep it long from coming up. However I once remember a good crop of Wheat sown in December.

I am obliged to go to righting up all my cornfield fences. Most of that work is done at Mangorike and we are all hands going to the same work at the Fork. Colo. Brokenbrough's hogs attack me on the swamp side, and my own and Col. Tayloe's on the other sides.

Tayloe's overseer is a vile fellow, always abroad and his hogs constantly in his own field, from whence they get into mine. And my hog wench is a very bitch, never to be seen and the hogs strolling about. I ordered her a whipping.

Will Lawson very ill. It seems a week agoe he opened a warm bulk of tobacco and the scent of that gave him cough, which continuing for 3 days I was satis[fied] it must be a foul stomach and I recommended a vomit of tartar wa[te]r [?] which brought off vast loads of green and Yellow bile; but his cough continuing I ordered him to be blooded and by rattlesnake brought on an Expectoration; but yesterday being pretty well he went out and stopped his spitting which brought on a fever, but by the rattlesnake root that going off this morning and his Expectoration free and plentifull as Nassau tells me.

Old Mrs. Garland came to pay for her plank. I said her son Griffen had settled with me. I beleive she had something else in view for she interceded for Rigmaiden['s] continuance at the free school. I said he was a pert Prigg, but he might stay if he wanted to do so. She said she was sure he did. Buckland wanted him, but she advised him not to go. He is a tight little fellow, and the W—— loves a glass, and it may be a pipe with it but this under my own rose.

9. *Fryday.*

It began to rain in the night which we have not had from the 23d last month just 18 days.

From the 5th to the 8 court days. Levy Laying, Grand jury and abundance of other business done. Levy, 16 per poll.

Very little work done in the time Lawson sick.

We struck on Monday in the night a good deal of tobacco every where, all, it is said, that was cured. It did not rain but at 12 I sent for a plant and found it in Case. The weather being calm, we have burnt the Hay house, [the?] Riverside, and the Locust point Plant patches. The meadow to burn. The Fork, Lawson says, getting brush to burn that.

Not a Stroke struck with our hoes as yet. Indeed our ground too hard for want of rain.

The barley coming up yesterday by the gate.

Mr. Parker had 16 bushels of Barley sent to him. There is more to send. My Son came home Court day. Jack not returned. I fear that fellow's gaming.

I say I am affraid of my son John's gaming. He did not come home with his brother as he said he would. And was gone to Norfolk on pretence about his flower; but he had no business there. Tucker's bond to him he never went after. Before I heard of their being at dice, but Robin will not say a word. [Sure]ly he hopes he will not game [a]ny more. A Sure sign he has lost, and that a great deal, for let their resolutions be what they will to tell nothing, I always hear of winning; and this I don't [faded] of. I must alter my will.

10. *Saturday.*

Yesterday's rain broke up with a Southeasterly wind in the night, very [wa]rm and only blowing a little too much and I did prudent to begin to strip [torn] bulks I struck down on Mon[day] night last. Some of them were [torn] warm yesterday but by [torn]. [Torn]ay Nove[torn] have been too hot and spewing by next Monday. We shall finish them all this day every where And all that I have seen are fine tobaccoe.

I observed the barley sown below the hill by Mangorike gate is coming up. And that sown by the chesnut tree is sprouting.

Note: The 4 beaves put up here and at the Fork were put up on thursday was Sevennight last. The 1st of them. They have just one peck of shelled co[rn] apiece, that is, 2 bushels of ears for the 4. And it is all boiled with a little salt in it.

Our 15 hogs eat just 1 bushel of [torn] corn a day, 2 bushels in the Ear.

I have ordered the 16 piggs that get into my riverside cornfield and root my [torn] to be put up in a pen by Doleman and fed with the trash corn in the Warehouse.

My Carpenters will get the House I had of deGraftenreidt ready to roll away to the Spring there by monday for Doleman where he is to live.

My people getting hay At the bottom of my meadow; there being very little in meadow; the after growth's being too [torn]. I shall order my cattle to gaze in t[he] meadow. Rain again after 1 o'[clock] produced by Southwest wind. I have often [torn]. [Torn] all day and cryes towards night.

12. *Monday*.

Rain yesterday and yet very cloudy. This day we were to begin hoing my tobacco hills.

I fancy these rains will injure some of my cotton not gethered; and I doubt some harm to my flax put out to winter roll. Although I am quite a stranger to the practice of that, I know its nature and that water is to dissolve the gum in the bark that cements the fibres of it together; and perhaps the rain that falls may be of Service to do that.

My Son John returned from Town last night. He seems so much of the gamester as to appear composed, but perhaps to ask him about his loss if any may discompose him.

He promises to have my flower down at Falmouth the last of this month and with it some cloth to make me some cloathes according to our associ[a]tion. I gave him a memorandum that it might not be forgot. I am to send Talbot up to Falmouth for these things certainly the last of the month.

My son John paid me 2 double bloons at 4/6 each and two £5 notes in all £18.12.

15. *Thursday*.

The rain monday and Tuesday made my ground too wet to begin to hill my ground as I intended; so I only could begin last night. I took the advantage of the wether and made my Cowyard below; and have ordered the corn stalks of the corn pulled off to feed the hogs and beeves to be cut down and brought to the cow yard.

Doleman says he made 40 barrels of corn in the River side corn house when he measured it two days ago. I ordered 20 barrels to be brought up yesterday [to] feed my Coach horses and have directed them a quart at a feed, that is, each 2 quarts a day, which is 1½ peck of shelled corn.

The carpenters removed Jugg's house as far as Doleman chose to have it from the spring. They are to fit it up and then to setting up my Fork Corn field house; however I can't as yet find the plan I drew although I ordered Owen before he went to lay it out somewhere in the way. I must take another hunt for it amongst my Papers.

Dolman shall leave off getting hay as soon as he has got that [?] in at the bottom of the meadow.

George has only made 14 head baskets as yet. I must have 14 more before I begin to gather corn.

Send this day my tumbrel to Blain's store by Nomony ferry for the Cotton I bought, and Lucy goes there to buy me 6 pieces more, 2 peices of Oznabrigg, and some Coarse thread.

Counted in the road 53 old geese this day.

A home cow calved this day and put up to fatten. In hopes it may be fitt by the time of our feast most annually pursued. It will be a fortnight old in this month and a month in December and about 10 days in January.

Lucy only brought home 2 peices British Oznabrigg, 6 pair Coarse stokkins, and coarse thread.

17. *Saturday.*

Rode out this day, and went to see the business that Doleman has been upon, and found him irreclaimably the same lazy rascal that he ever has been, although I have often exhorted him and indeed persuaded him to be otherwise; but I am satisfyed my people have all been lazyer under him than they ever were without him. Add to this I have found him out to be a most deceitfull liar. I had 16 piggs that got into my cornfield that I never heard of untill my son John Returned from Town although Doleman had at the landing and was obliged to come every day through that very corn field. I particularly ordered him to have them put up and fed out of the trash corn in the ware house there. But in a full week after, this was not done, and at last I heard Mr. Beale he expected would send them down. Then I ordered him to have them carried down, and not longer than yesterday asked him if they were up in the Pen to which he said yes. I then ordered him to count them every morning and to tell me if he ever missed any of them. This morning I rode to see them, and found only 7 there when there ought to be 14. He told me that 7 had got out, one was dead, and one was put up to fatten at the house. I asked then where the other 7 were. He replyed the English sow had broke the pen down. I saw this to be a lie and I ask every body. All vowed never more than 7 had ever been put up, that Robin had let the other 7 go, and said nothing about it, and Old Lubber told me Doleman put them up in the Stye this morning. The Lowsy puppy could not denye the lie, and acknowledged I had always charged him never to deceive me with a lie. For this reason I turned him away as his year will not be up before the 24th of this month when I will pay him off.

Lawson gone to Mr. Gordon's[103] with leave. Almost all my people pretend to be sick. I have but 22 at work [ou]t of 30 and better.

Billy Beale returned from John Fowler's Store[104] in Essex with the Cotton and his own things which I sent for, but he did not get quite 200 yards of Cotton although I think the goods are a little more reasonable than what others sell at.

[103] Probably John Gordon, a small planter in Richmond Co.
[104] John Fowler was in partnership with George Fowler in Essex Co.

Mr. McCalle wants to buy corn to be taken away in March and paid for in April; also he wants wheat but then it must be by weight. I beg his Pardon for this. I never sell grain by weight.

Received of Colo. Landon Carter the sum of forty Six shillings cash to be carried to his credit this 17th of November 1770.

Rd. Shackelford

21. *Wednesday.*

It has been very fine weather for some time and rather moist in the morning frosts. I got all my tobacco down two days agoe.

Took in my flax yesterday well rotted as my [son?] says who is a Connoisseur.

Put out the rest to rot this day.

Colo. John Randolph, his Lady, and daughters with Colo. P. Lee and his Lady dined here on Monday. All appeared agreeable. I had no wine, and made only this apology, That I had neither estate nor constitution to Justifie the use of it. As to the latter, experience had proved that, for I had injoyed more health, although growing older these 3 years, since I used none than I ever did before. As to the former, I could not do as others, be continually saving every drop and spoil a fine fresh bottle by pouring it on the flat dreggs of an old decanter.

Rigmaiden came this day and desired to continue in his place. I told he might do it on the very terms of last year, as the people seemed to like him. He wanted to be excused coming to George. I told him that he must do, if I found it necessary, and he agreed to continue just as he was last year. So he continues.

Rain I beleive this day.

22. *Thursday.*

It began to rain in the night and continued all this day till near 5 in the morning the next day.

23. *Fryday.*

My daughter Beverley got here before dinner, detained from Wednesday by the rain till this day.

I was lucky in getting my flax off the grass as I did. For although not quite rotted enough, it must have been spoiled, had it continued on the Ground till this time. This seems to be the only inconveniency in this way of winter rotting, provided a man has a field of enclosed grass to do it. And though he may not have place large enough, Yet, if happened to cure and drye it well enough after he pulled it, it is but laying out another and another field to rot after the 1st and 2d is done, which is my case. I laid out another field after I had taken up the first. It is but turning every other day, especially after every rain, and I think it rots even of a good bright Colour. The time is according to the weather. In that which is moist it may require a fortnight or more time; and in drye spells to be sure longer time. It is easily known when rotted enough by bringing in a little drying it by the fire and, if it breaks well and easy in the pith without snapping the bark, it is rotten enough and not too much so.

24. *Saturday.*

Rain again from 5 in th[e mo]rning till near evening.

Yesterday a 2 year old girl of Winny tumbled in a ditch of water and is got very ill with a Violent cough and great pain somewhere. We know not what to do with it. Nassau took a way a little blood and I beleive must gave it a little vomit; how ever I have order a little weak rattlesnake root to be stewed and given to it.

Paid John Doleman cash £5 and turned him away for an idle lying fellow. Due to him about £3.

Nat very ill by getting wet or gitting drunk when he went to fetch Mr. Beverley from Frank Randall's.

Stripping out our bulks last struck. They are growing warm. I wish they may not Some of them [be] too hot by Monday which will be as soon as we can get them all out.

Guy, M'Gennis, Sammy and their two boys began to frame the fork cornhouse yesterday.

This evening very blustering indeed first at South then Southwest and in the night Northwest very violent with some snow.

25. *Sunday.*

Very hard Northwest wind and for the 1st time very cold.

As I had my bowling green and other grass in the garden covered with flax and that very short I did imagine that would all have been blown away by these violent winds; but I see this morning little of it removed out of the rows it was laid in. I do imagine the rain that first fell might have settled among the Grass and after that the snow kept it down.

My Son set off yesterday as soon as the weather held up. I fancy he must wish himself at home again this bad weather; indeed any prudent man might have seen it coming; for at this time of the year I seldom discover rain holding up as this did without some great blast after it.

Nassau in spight of my hourly caution got yesterday most inhumanly drunk and what is worse blooded a two year old child and his father in that fit. It is a great wonder he did not [do] each of them a mischief. He came in and formerly of his own accord told Me he had given the Child a vomit in its choaking cold and that it brought off much Phlegm but no bile: All of which was a most audacious lie and the rascal swore he never told me so. I clapped him in Irons to lye all night and feel his drunkenness.

Very blustering till near night and then very keen, though Calm.

I never knew the like of my family for finding fault, at the same time they will not mend things when they might if they could. Every person speak well of my table but they who constantly live at it.

If the meat is very fine. It is not done says one, although Perhaps nobody eat hartier of it.

If the bread is white and li[ght] [torn] musty; but yet many [faded and torn].

If the Sallad is fine, the melted butter it is mixed up with is rank although every mouthfull of sallad is devoured.

The pickles are quite brassy though Crisp and green, and so the good folks go on disparaging and devouring.

The beer too bitter although my brewings are the same. My Coffee too weak although no body spends so much in their houses.

By accident this day a certain Gentleman's going home and not going came into Conversation. I saw I gave offence by saying, Perhaps he could not go. I was understood, though I said no more. And was told if he had not got money they did not see how any body could have it. I replyed if he had money, nobody need dispare of getting it; for nobody took more pains to spend it in v[ai]n shew than he had done; and I [torn] notion of trade. Money was to be saved, or it could not be got in trade; for few would advan[ce] but where remittances were punctual, and where there was so much expended there could not be much punctually. Besides I am mistaken if a late Partner taken in has not been spoken of as the only man that has made money for him.

29. *Tuesday.*

A very rainy morning and has rained ever since last night.

No weather to gather corn nor do any thing but strip and stemm tobacco.

This morning, wet as it was, came old William Northern thundering at my door whilst I was at breakfast; As soon I heard it was him I got up and went and saw him at my pails. I asked him to come in; he sent me an account of £54.4/½ against me, and an order of John Doleman's for £3.2/2. I continued asking him in out of the rain. He vowed or swore he would never come into my house again. I asked him w[hat] was the matter; he told m[e] I wanted to whip him; I asked him [what] he meant by that; Sure he did [torn] [a]nd to arraign my opinion given in Court against his negro for killing Shackleford's hog. He said I then said it was a pity the court could not order him a whipping. I told him I saw it was a pity the law would not countenance the whipping Masters for giving such orders to slaves to kill their neighbour's trespassing creatures bef[ore] they had complyed with the law relative to tresspassers. I offered him a doubleoon to pay his account and [de]sired he would come in and see it weighed; he said he could not change it and would not come in. I offered to let him take it home and the ballance should go in discharge of Doleman['s] note, which I would pay in a few days. But he would not take it nor see it weighed. I told him he had insult[ed] me for my opinion I gave in Court and I would bring his Spirit down. I had Billy Beale to see me offer the doubleoon which he again refus[ed] [torn] I offered to let him take it hom[e torn] me send my Stewa[rd] with [him]. [Torn] is insolent and I [torn] to see if they will [one and one half lines torn and faded].

DECEMBER 1770

3. Monday.

This month began with very bad weather and a snow at night which is now on the ground Pritty full. Excessive Cold.

Yesterday my cart came up with 15 bushels of Oysters from John Beale at my Northumberland quarters below. The oysters very fine but quite frozen so that we shall not be able to eat them good.

By a letter from my son Landon at Bull run I find my intention to seat Leesburough land[105] is to be defeated from the Unwillingness of those gratefull gentlemen to send my own negroes out to do.

My son Jack sent me down according to his promise 5 and near 1/4 yards of 6/4 cloth with 3 dozen Coat, 4 dozen breast buttons, 6 yards Shaloon and mohair to make me my cloaths.

Shackleford carried them ho[me] to make for me and has promised to make them the next weak and bring them home.

I must send to Ball to know the reason why he does not send my cart with the bottles, etc., up to me for the people's cloths.

[105] Landon Carter owned a plantation called Georgia near Leesborough in Loudoun Co.

The Northumberland Cart carrie[d] down 42 people's Cloths, three of them boy and Girls'. I fear they make but a bad crop of corn there.

6. *Thursday.*

Yesterday came three casks of butter from Mr. Alleson at Falmont at 8d per Cask and 3 shillings freight £7.9/8 weight 220 Pounds Number.

Gave my son a five pound Note and a doubleoon to pay for the same as he is going up the Country this day.

9. *Sunday.*

Good weather till this, and now cold. We had as large a white frost as ever I saw. Almost equal to a Snow.

Mr. Beverley offered when here [to] let me some bottles, but when I sent for them, he sent 10 dozen but wrote he could but badly spare them upon which with a decent letter I sent them back again.

Rippon Hall people came here the last week only. Brought the lugg of plums. I sent their people's Cloths and ordered Ball to send Candles from Town as the Norfolk man had sent none as yet.

And also ordered up my cart with the wool and everything.

Many Gentlemen having discovered the meeting of the Associators call the 14 only done by the Merchants who want to dissolve the Association. I wrote a sharp paper against to go to Rind[106] tomorrow.

We put about many addresses to be signed against the meeting in order to Countenance a Previous question whether any Alteration shall be considered till a more favourable time for meeting.

10. *Monday.*

Sent postboy Sam off to Rippon with an order to Ball to deliver my letter to Rind and to get Mr. Nelson's 3 feet 8 millstones if he can.

This day has turned out tollerable fine. I rode out to see my corn gathering and although my people pretend to be possitive, and so is the overseer, that we shall make as much as we did last year, I fear we shall fall very much Short. I see, although there were many places that lookt very fine, there are too many but very indifferent now we are gathering. Lawson's book of last year's corn accounts for more than 700 barrels and I know that

---

[106] William Rind (d. 1773) came to Williamsburg from Annapolis in 1766 to set up a rival to the old *Va. Gaz.* that would be less under the influence of the governor's party. He called his paper the *Va. Gaz.* and published it for nearly eight years until his death in 1773. The paper here referred to is almost certainly the one printed in Rind's *Gaz.* of Dec. 13, 1770, under the pseudonym "An Associating Planter."

Doleman's field at home turned off better than 60 barrels. It should have been 80, but as it grew near the house it was Easily Pillaged; but I think this year if we reach 600 barrels in all, it will be great.

20. *Thursday.*

I have had a cold ever since the 10th and know nothing about what they have been engaged. However all the corn is [in] but two days at the Fork. I fear not so much as we made last year. We are Prizing 26th hogsheads.

Drew on Mr. Waller.
To Mr. Rind————————————————£3. 0/3.
To Purdie and Dixon[107]———————— 2.16/9.
To Richard Charleton[108]for my Wig——— 4.—.—.

21. *Fryday.*

Killed one of my beaves put up to fatten here November and fed only with 1 peck of Corn which being in ears has been constantly boiled and the beef weighs better than 600 pounds.

My cold still continues bad though some little better.

Sam Walks again to Rippon Hall to bid Ball send me the Candles from Town, the Norfolk tallow chandler having not yet sent me those so long ago engaged.

My ditchers have been a full week scowring my ditch round the London orchard which has a double ditch and fence upon it; and I believe will be sometime longer, there being a large piece of ground and the fence to be put upon it.

I wish the corn made may not be much less than last year, for the house room it is put in is much less.

Note: I finished getting it in everywhere Yesterd[ay].

23. *Sunday.*

Rippon Hall tumbrel came up. She set off with 15 dozen and a half of bottles, and broke 4 and 1/2 dozen. Ball it seems Packed them up first in Wool, but finding he could not put them all in, he took them out and packt them loose and put only a little wool between a layer or two and said on his

---

[107] Alexander Purdie (d. 1779), a Scot and assistant to Joseph Royle (d. 1766) on the *Va. Gaz.*, and John Dixon, who married Joseph Royle's widow Rosanna, published the *Va. Gaz.* together after Royle's death in 1766 until 1774, when Purdie founded a *Va. Gaz.* of his own.

[108] Richard Charlton (d. 1779) was a wigmaker in Williamsburg.

letter he was sensible they would all be broke. I wrote to him he had neither Sence, contrivance, nor obedience to my orders in so doing, for I had ordered the cart and the bottles to be packt in wool in two hogsheads, and he had empty hogsheads enough, for, although now he says he never expected to make 20 hogsheads tobacco, he made Toney set up 20 hogsheads.

This man has shewn his folly in the candles he was to send. I ordered him to get them from Norfolk. He sent me word they were to be at Hobbs hole within a fortnight. That [then] he wrote me word the man had disappointed him and if I would he could get them in Town better and Cheaper. I ordered him to do so and he went to do it, but the Norfolk man again assured him they should be up here at Christmas, and he beleived the rascal, so that I have got no candles and now Ball writes he will buy them in Town, if he can, if I want them. I also ranked this to him amongst his folly.

He shewed it in another instance. I sent him a tea kettle to get mended; that man was to do it from time to time but did it not. I then ordered Ball to buy me one and fetch the old one home. He went to do this, but the man promised to mend the other immediately and did not and now Ball will buy me one if I have not got one. I have stated this as an article of want of sence and disobedience. In short, I fear this man is either turned or grown quite forgetfull of me, himself, and everything.

24. *Monday.*

Toney came up from below. He pretends he set up 20 hogsheads at Rippon Hall, a rundlet for plums, two rundlets for Oysters, and one for small beer; that Ball would not have any more hogsheads set up, having still 20 for next year and certainly 8 left out of those set up this year.

Toney also set up 36 hogsheads in Northumberland, which is about 10 hogsheads more than Beale talks of making and has got 24 hogsheads for next year.

I sent Ball two spades, a grind stone, and two girls' and 2 boys' suits, and a woman's Petty coat wanting there.

31. *Monday.*

The last day of the old year. We have had very fine weather now for above a weak, but upon riding out this day for the first time these 3 weeks I can't see but very little. The days indeed are of their shortest till now, and very short they have been; the mornings have been many day hard till about 10 o'clock so that with the feeding the cattle morning and night I own there has not been much time to work, but there has been very little done for that time. They have been 4 days hilling only 26,000 tobacco hills and not done that as yet.

And but a few rails as yet brought into place, and, excepting one or two days, but little house wood brought in.

I also lookt into the corn brought into the houses to be sure we do not fill above 2/3 of the housing we filled last year. I shall really be affraid we shall not have enough for every thing, although by care I hope we may do, because last year I used 50 barrels to my cows to make butter and I don't now use but 1/4 as much and I don't feed my oxen with it as I did then, but I fear I shall repent this, for 3 of the 4 which I sent to the Fork to winter are extremely poor. But then we are fattning 4 beeves, one however is killed, and I shall slay another tomorrow sevennight.

Lawson boasts of his cattle looking well, but I understand one died last night; he says really taken very ill; but I daresay its disorder was poverty. I talkt with him and did suppose of these fine looking cattle he would at least loose 20 this year, but he wished to lay a good sum that he did not loose 10. I see he is a burley fellow and I do suppose we shall fall short of even his late reconing about tobacco, for we have not done 26 hogsheads as yet and where the other 10 are to come from as he talkt of I can't see. Indeed he is a prating man. It is good not to dispair; but he talks too much.

I have partly agreed with Colo. Brokenbrough for the corn that is to spar[e] on Kelsick's estate; he is to let me know our next court, which is this day Sevennight.

THE DIARY

1771

JANUARY 1771

16. *Wednesday.*

From the 1st day of this month till this day we have had prodigious fine weather indeed so that I have enjoyed my three days' festival, to wit, the 10, 11, and 12 with great cheerfulness to every body in all about 60 people, of whom were Mr. Carter of Corotoman, his Lady, My nephew Charles Carter, late of Nanzaticoe, his lady, My Nephew Fitzhugh,[1] his Lady, Colo. P. Lee, his Lady, and all my neighbourhood except Colo. Brockenbrough who did not come although invited and really promised to come.

During this entertainment John Boughton, overseer at Rings neck, came over, but did not care to be seen by me; for it seems his mighty all of tobacco and corn which was this year to be more by my 16 tons account when going to the assembly or town than what I should make any where else is at last turned out not more than 5 hogsheads tobacco and not above [blank] barrels of corn to tell, although he has no stock to raise, no children but one or two, and but the working 10 hands on the plantation to feed.

I may call this my son's Management, for I have not here interfered in one thing. Can it be any other then than either a devilish disposition always and at all hazard to quarrel with my management or an ease in him to be deceived by any fellow that shall applaud and flatter him?

Just so is his management at the Park quarter; they don't make bread to eat there, and the excuse is so much wheat tended; but ask where is the wheat? Then it is all eaten to maintain the people. Sure it is time for me to give over

---

[1] William Fitzhugh (1741–1809) of Chatham, King George Co., was a planter and son of Henry Fitzhugh (1704–42) and Landon Carter's sister Lucy. He married Ann, daughter of Peter Randolph of Chatsworth, Henrico Co., and was a member of the House of Burgesses for King George Co., 1772–76, a delegate to the Second Continental Congress, 1779–80, and holder of several posts in the new state government.

such A partnership. I cannot but observe how constant I am blamed about my method of Croping, when certain I am that not one of them do half so well. I am persuaded I shall make 35,000 pounds tobacco at home with not more than 30 hands that ever do work, although I have 6 constantly tending the Cattle, Sheep, and hogs. And as to Corn, although I am sensible I fall much short of last year's Crop, yet I am convinced I have made a saving crop. I can't sell any to be sure, for I fatten 4 beaves for my family, 30 muttons, and feed milch cows to boot, besides 18 hogs, shoots out of Number to keep my family feed, 12 or 14 horses constantly, and besides all these many comers and goers fed, and even hogs from below which were obliged to be kept a while before they could be killed. Perhaps I may at last be obliged to buy some corn.

Mr. Parker sent his farmer this day for his Sow and four pigs. The day is very rainy and too bad the man cannot carry them away. I keep 2 of the pigs, to wit, a boar and a Sow.

The Possimon beer that I brewed turn out very fine only not quite hopped enough. I send 1 dozen of it to my daughter Beverley.

Began two days agoe to put some more pones in steep for another brewing.

17. *Thursday.*

Yesterday was as bad almost as a day could be with a constant blowing rain till in the night. And this day as warm and inviting as could be.

I rode out, but found very little done since my last ride last saturday was a week. But what disgusted me was to see the only cow yard out of my view as miry as possible. Lawson I see is deceitfull and the negroes lie to serve him for one told me the yard was littered last night with stalks and there was not one to be seen on it. Another told me it was covered with Marsh hay, but both was a lie. That fellow boasts of his cattle looking well, but how long can they do so with such management?

A Lamb fell this morning at the Fork.

I saw the three Jobbers setting round a fire. This is the 3d day they have been making away over a small Gully by Juggs. I have ordered all to be whipped.

Guy was to have finished the Fork corn house this day, but as Mcginnis was imployed at home tomorrow will not finish. The old trade, take one hour from any Job and it makes two day loss in work. Whipped they shall be.

18. *Fryday.*

Two lambs more at the [torn] Fork quarter. Note: the cattle there look very fine. George is a carefull fellow, [has] used no hay as yet. This shews that cornstalks cut up and carried to the yard are a better food than any we use. These creatures have not before last night eat[en] one lock of hay; And these yards is war[m] and drye.

My ditchers this day, 3 of them, began a new cornfield ditch which I hope will be done time enough for my peach orchard ditch.

My Fork wenches hilling Olivers branch.

George cutting down his new ground and then to cutting off for rails at all places round his Plantation.

The 3 ditchers in hard weather to get chessnut stakes on the creek side; because I intend to watle the new field along the road and stake and [illegible]er it.

Sent this day my bag of New Orleans to[bacco] seed to Billy Lawson to sow my hay house plant Patch. Note: it is a large one, has [faded] first well burnt with drye brush before it w[as] dug, then every root of dock Poke and [faded] carefully dug out, then trenched across the beds, those trenches filled with very rotten m[a]nure, then the tops of the trenches hilled over the dung, then laid off into beds, then [illegible] over with drye brush and then sowed, [illegible] in because the earth is very light, and is to be well covered over with small Pine branches and [faded]eighted across.

The former part of this day very fine as yesterday was; but this evening threatning with cold clouds either of Snow or bleak Northwest winds.

To save turning back I writ it down here. 3 lambs at the Fork since Yesterday morning; the first I have heard of this year. I must observe sheep my [faded] their Ewes be made to yean almost at any time, provided the rams are made wanton by feeding. I put these rams into my cornfield in August where they got so fat that for a trial I turned in some ewes; and ob[served] that after some day teizing they took ram and three of them brought lambs in November which I killed as soon as good meat and then I turned out the rams to the Gang who seem to be near yeaning at this time.

19. *Saturday.*

Very cold the first part of the day, but from 10 to 12 it turned [o]ut fine again. I rode out from 9 to 12, and ride I must if I intend to live, for even with that but little is [torn]. I found at least 8 getting Pine brush to cover the 16 beds last night at the Hay house; and all quite idle, the overseer gone they could not guess. I went then to the hay point where we are bringing over hay, they had never seen him and were Idle. Simon brought over only 7 floatload yesterday Although the day before when the float was to fix up they brought over 8. This not to be borne and Simon shall pay for it.

I went to the Fork. No overseer had been there. George had only cut down

7 trees, pretended to have been making a Sowpen for the young sows big with pig. There are 4 lambs there.

At last I went to the wood cutters. They all idle and no wood cut, and Manuel brought in only 2 load by 12. I was resolved to find the overseer and went again to the plant patch where I found him sowing the remaining 6 beds; and Some Covering those sown yesterday. I jobed him a little; he is determined to get that part done and Covered and the Locust point patch burnt sown and covered. I offered to bet him his Sallery, of it, which he was willing to lay: I told him I would not rob him with such a bett, but he had not diligence enough to make the people flye, as he saw they did when I spoke to them.

21. *Monday.*

Yesterday as variable in its changes as possible. I went to Church but the parson instead of 12 o'clock going as he advertized was better then half done by 30 minutes after 11.

This day a perfect spring day indeed, but I could not ride out because waiting for the Colonels Richard and Frank Lee and Colonel Tayloe meeting by appointment.

26. *Saturday.*

These bilious fevers now turning to Perepnumanices. I have so many people sick, and others pretending to be so that I can not get any work done. Indeed my overseer is not quite so brisk as he pretends to be.

Our weather has been not amiss for working had anybody to work.

Yesterday sent Sam on foot to Rippon Hall and so to Town to get subscription Papers printed for the establishing a Store to accomodate the planter with goods above 50 percent than he has yet bought them at.

7 lambs at the Fork and not one here.

I fancy I must put a Watle fence round my new corn fields for I see what with idleness and sickness I can't get rails ready nor all in place.

30. *Wednesday.*

Fine days till the 28, when I think I saw the present weather; however it held fair and fine till last night when I beleive it had every bad composition in it; And I am affraid we [see] the winter setting it at last.

There has been 8 lambs at the Fork ever since Sunday.

Done Prizing all to the 30th hogshead which will not I am affraid reach 1,000 Number. So have we been deceived or rather have deceived ourselves.

I ordered my corn yesterday to be all husked out, either my thoughts or some of my dreams suggest to me that I shall find some spoiled. The overseer all at once tells me it is warn at the bottom; but I fancy this is a mere excuse for but a small crop of it. However it is good to save it. I am to have 20 barrels at Kelsick and all we made at Rings Neck if my son can't get 12/6.

John Beale from Northumberland writes me word Mr. Edwards can't get the money he promised to let him have to pay for the Corn he has been obliged to buy there.

31. *Thursday.*

A fine clear day after a bad night and day; but we are merely drowned with rain.

My Northumberland boy went down this day with 12 hilling hoes. The rest Mr. Beale is to have made.

FEBRUARY 1771

8. *Friday.*

The weather still continues very fine excepting now and then a sudden and indeed according to the looks of the heavens Smart rain plentiful in quantity though I cannot say it can be unexpected, for to be sure such a winter I never knew. But I doubt where the earth has wanted its Proper purgations by frost and snow and indeed its certain impregnations by nitre I cannot but fancy when it comes to throw out its vapours we shall have cause to complain of Violent disorders. At present we have scarcely had one inflammatory cause in the air but all prodigiously bilious.

But little work is yet done through all this fine winter; and as our corn is not yet near huskt out, it must puzzle everybody to say what we have been about; nothing that I know of.

I could the 6th out of my memory.

We begun on tuesday the 5th to hoe my fresh corn field. I hoe in 7 foot rows and to break the ground up well after it is laid off I make a hand go up and hoe on one side of the Chop 3 hoes wide and then he backs it on the other side with 3 hoes more and throws the earth into the middle like a ridging bed. So that the space between to break up is hardly 3 feet wide.

9. *Saturday.*

Yesterday a fine day till night and then as bad almost as I have seen not to be a gust. All night this morning till 7 fine again, but then it began to blow almost insufferably hard.

Yesterday we had at the Fork but 14 lambs; but not one as yet at home.

We had also 26 piggs at the Fork. I have ordered the Sows between the two Corn house a tight warm snug place, and have ordered in case any of them should be overlaid to have them lookt at every now and then and the dead ones removed and burnt, for it appears to be that which makes sows eat their pigs having those putrid dead ones to learn upon.

It seems two of my Guinea breed here have strayed to the Fork as they are boars. I have ordered them home and all of them shall be markt and, if above two boars, the rest to be cut.

Mr. Giberne, Mr. Lomax,[2] Wm. Beale, Walker Tomlin,[3] and Moor Brokenbrough[4] here yesterday, and I hope, as it is now bad weather, as Brokenbrough went home, the rest will stay.

12. *Tuesday.*

No Wormeley here yesterday though it was their own appointment.
Beverley sent me some fish by Sam. Sent up to Randal's for them.
Ground wet yesterday and hard freeze.
Great rain last night.

John Beale came here last night. I find he is going to be married. I talkt to him about it. And would have removed him out of my business could I have a got a careful person to succeed him. He promises not to put me to any expence but the allowance to himself and never to be absent from his business. I agreed to trust him for this Year and if he proves a tom of ten thousands I may continue him in the business.

At last one lamb fallen last night and 15 at the Fork.

I fear the winter is setting in at too inconvenient a time for the planter. Had the bad weather come in the beginning of the Cold months we might then have employed our time in husking and putting up our corn, but it was too fine to work in the house then and now it is too cold to be out so that I fear we shall be late getting our corn ground ready for early planting, at least with my stiff land it will be so.

I go to Beverley's on thursday next if my cold mends any. And shall leave behind me a letter to Mr. Ball at Rippon to go by Solomon Redman[5] if he

---

[2] Probably Lunsford Lomax, Jr. (d. 1771), planter in Essex Co. and son of Lunsford Lomax, Sr., of Caroline Co.

[3] Walker Tomlin was a small planter in Richmond Co. and probably the son of Robert Tomlin (d. 1794).

[4] Moore Brockenbrough (d. 1793) was a small planter in Richmond Co. and son of William Brockenbrough (1715–78) and Elizabeth, daughter of Moore Fauntleroy.

[5] Solomon Redman (d. 1783) was later a planter in Westmoreland Co. and was probably the son or brother of John Redman (d. 1773), planter in Richmond Co.

complies with his engagement to rebuild my Mill there. I wrote Sol. Redman a letter if he calls when I am abroad.

13. *Wednesday.*

Very cold indeed. I fear the winter is really coming in, and perhaps it will be too bad for my Visit to Beverley's tomorrow.

I have set the ditchers into the great Marsh to cutting Sedge for littlering the cowyards which now begin to be very wet.

14. *Thursday.*

Two lambs here and 16 at the Fork by Lawson's and Beale's information. I set off for Beverley's, but with a Cold.

20. *Wednesday.*

Came by the way of Hobbs hole from Mr. Beverley's. Dined with Mr. Wormeley, Beverley, and Jno. Fitzhugh[6] at Whitlock's Ordinary,[7] a very shocking place indeed. Mortimer, McCall, Wadrope,[8] Rankin,[9] and Pitman Clemons[10] dined with us. We had a bad coming over the River; and I think my time was very disagreeably spent among some laughing Gentlemen who ever make and often swear to wha[t] they make to raise a laughter on somebody.

I cannot help miniting that my trip to Beverley's on thursday last was not guite so engaging as I really wish it, and perhaps shall make it another time, God willing. For no boat came to me at F. Randal's for near 3 hours; not very Comfortable on a Cold shore with my Cough. Indeed, although promised, the boat was not even launched, although promised, by at least an hour after we had smoked a great deal for it.

I dreaded Bad winter, and it came up in the Fryday night after we got to Beverley and snowed all Saturday and most of Sunday and the River was frozen over immediately after. Therefore to get home was to come by Hobbs hole.

I arrived here at night. Found I had lost 3 lambs out of my home gang which froze in Yeaning and one of them in the lamb house by her mother though the house was as warm as could be made.

[6] John Fitzhugh (1727–1809) of Bellair, Stafford Co., was a planter and son of Henry Fitzhugh (1687–1758) of Bedford, Stafford Co., and Susanna, daughter of Mordecai Cooke. He married Alice, daughter of Rowland Thornton of Crowes, King George Co.

[7] Whitlock's Ordinary had been opened by John Whitlock in Tappahannock in 1766.

[8] William Woddrup was a small merchant at Tappahannock. At one point he was connected with the firm of Andrew Crawford and James Ritchie.

[9] George Rankin was a resident of Tappahannock.

[10] Pitman Clements (d. 1778) was a merchant in Tappahannock.

22. *Fryday*.

Lost two more lambs that yeaned yesterday and the boy says two that are alive can't suck so that I expect my Number lost will soon be 7 out of 11 yeaned; And as the Snow still continues on the ground and a constant hard frost I fear as the Ewes are now Yeaning I shall loose many more if not all; for I cannot divise how I shall save them. So that this year the forward Yeaning has proved the best time, for it is really a very dangerous time when such spells set in.

I must say I grow more astonished Every day at what I hear.

24. *Sunday*.

I can remember that I used long ago to dread the Snows that lay on the ground in February, from the injury produced by them to all young Creatures, and indeed to the winter grain if they continued after the 20th of the month. But I thought that creatures might by care be preserved from their affects. Accordingly as to lambs I provided a very warm house and boarded it at bottom that by the straw laid on the floor they might be drie and sweet. By doing this and feeding the dams twice a day with fodder and 3 times with small homony I was able for 4 or 5 years to save all that yeaned; but I see by last year and this that it was all but chance. The last year the lambs died pritty old and large, which upon opening I imagined was the fodder stemms that choked them, but This year I have lost 11 out of 16 that have yeaned at home.

Last night I was informed I had 9 alive and all very brisk, and that they were Sunned out in the day with their mothers; but this morning news came up that 4 of them had died. So that I am at a loss to know what can be the cause. To Say that it is positively the snow may be wrong, because I have 17 at the Fork where there is and has been snow as well as here, and I have not lost one. However they were hearty above a week before the Snow came; but then some of these lambs were a weak old before they died. It is the business of man to find out causes where he can in order to prevent any evil that may attend but here is a case which nothing seems to indicate the cause of.

I have ordered another house upon the hill to be used as a lamb house, perhaps that which has been so many years in use may be infectious.

Again I will have the old house turned on fresh ground and the floor taken out, and will continue to make a baracade all along the Cold sides of it besides the Clap boards with a double row of watling and hay trod in between, to see if possible to prevent this fatality. Some pretend to say they do best left out without any care. I have not found that in any sort of Experience and whenever people have experienced it it must be mere accident for certainly it could only be loss in anything that first introduced can. And it seems against reason that if a cold shall be so intense as to freeze to death any that are yeaning the taking care to preserve them from that cold, should not be a means to save the creatures.

One thing more I will have done. The ground shall be all covered with sand a foot thick in order to make it resist any damps that may arise from the earth; and this I do because my fork land is a light soil and there I have not lost any.

25. *Monday.*

We have now 9 lambs at home, none died last night.

I wrote to Naval Officer Lee to get me some Coffee and molasses if he can spare any.

Weather now fine again, but my ground is so wet that it is not in my power to stick a hoe into it; and I have abundance of such work to do, to get in order for my next crop and from this time we have but 34 day to the first of April when corn ough[t] to be planted. I suppose then I must please myself with the 11 days new stile to be within the planter's time which will bring the 11th of April to be the 1st day and then 7 days more is but the 2d week in April. However this is not cropping.

I fancy if my crop of corn turns out this year half as much as it did last year it will be the out most with all Billy Lawson's talk.

He says he has lost but 2 creatures since he put them in the Cowyards, but I am certain of three that have died. It seems another of Manuel's oxen has died at the Fork which makes three that have died. And I do suppose all for want of care, this is so great a rascal. He first kills them and then turns them there to be fed [found?].

I have heard B. Bramhann has but 16 Ewes and he has got 14 fine lambs. I asked how he kept them and was told he put them all into a fodder stack.

Fodder stacks are not larger than my houses, and would not think they are warmer than my houses. It must be some chance then, but I heard they have been along while yeaned. If so, then I am as lucky at the Fork, for I have 17 alive and have lost none.

26. *Tuesday.*

It was rather warm yesterday and [had] not the earth been wet we might have done some work; but I could [not] help apprehending a bad day from our hardly seeing the Sun a[t] day by means of a hazy skye; An[d] last night it began to rain and rains t[his] morning. It seems as if it would carry off all the Snow but the junction of both waters will be too much for a working planter.

Solomon Redman came here yesterday and appointed Next monday for his going to repair my Rippon Hall Mill.

I write this day to my sons Landon and John by Tom Beale, bread at Tayloe'[s] mines, who goes off tomorrow if the weather Permits.

27. *Wednesday.*

Yesterday we had one entire day of rain and as much wind almost as a good h[faded] could stand under first at East and the[n] at Southwest and it has continued blowing all night.

I had yesterd[ay] 14 lambs alive whic[h] with the 11 dead made 25 that ha[ve] yeaned; but this morning I ha[ve] three more dead so that I have b[ut] 11 alive now and 14 dead, the better half, and they must all die. H[ad] this not happened in very bad [wea]ther I should have thought my ewes had [torn and faded] home too poor; but [faded] some of them do die, yet none bu[t 1] that has yeaned is dead; and Beale tells me the Ewes have good bags and a good deal of milk in them.

A Sheep is a strange and tender creature. I can remember whenever I had got a stock to any number, that I have always lost them by one way or another—Now it is said those who go with the sheep keep them from feeding; but this then would make poor Sheep, and mine have been always thought otherwise, Except the last year's latter lambs and 'tis they only that have died of the Gang.

With the latter lambs for the future I must take another course. Pick them out, and put them into my cornfields. And as to the Ewes I must all January feed them, a thing I did [be]fore; and what made them die [the]n? I thought it age and have every August drawn them out and [f]atened them. In short, I must [torn].

Yesterday the remainder of my barn blew down and my bull in it but he escaped unhurt.

My Riverside tobacco house blown quite down the whole 90 feet, just as I had got my corn, all but the rubbing, out. I have many husks in it and must feed with them to save it.

My Poor crop of corn made up here is as follows:

Riverside   72 barrels
Fork   91
Mangorike   184

347. barrels. 7 we have used as follows, so that I have not made near half of what I did last year. I don't blame anything but the badness of the Year except the mighty boast of the overseer.

My door of my Riverside Warehous[e] burst in which was neither East nor Southwest wind and must have been an Eddy wind.

The Lord Gave and taketh away and blessed be his name for all things. I have to be sure in the Course of a long life as 60 years are now called seen and experienced much adversity and met with difficulties; but I do suppose [as] they happened to me when I had Youth I made light of them by my Struggles to retrieve the losses. But unless it be the incapacity of my years I can't well account for my being so much affected with losses that now happen, though they do not exceed what I have experienced—I have before made scanty crops—before had houses blown down about my plantations; and I am certain whole gangs of sheep and lambs destroyed, and this without much complaint; but now it seems to be heavy, if I did not return to my creator and Preserver and say that what he seems to permit is best to befall me; he is able to restore all things in his good time. Therefore my God let thy holy spirit prepare me with fortitude to bear all things, that I may without murmuring become worthy of thy future blessings, and be thankfull for th[y] [torn]ast.

28. *Thursday.*

Lawson's Account of new corn used to this day:
People at Mangorike and home: 50.3/2¼ barrels
House: 19.2/3
                                 70.1/–¼.

Note: the corn used of the Riverside house when first gathered was 10 barrels, which is not to be deducted out of the Audit made becaus[e] it was not reckoned in the measurement. Billy Lawson gave me this account himself.

As soon as I told my overseer Lawson that as the earth was so wet we must give over all thoughts of breaking up the new cornfield this year and would content our selves with what tobacco ground we had and not break up more than the fresh cowpens and put all the dung made into the ground taken in, he skipped with Joy; but I bid him not be too sanguine which he saw he had been this last year.

I see it is a good thing to have some business to keep our thoughts employed for the man who cannot divert the present moment falls naturally into a disponding way and makes even the common cares of life a very heavy weight upon himself. It was so last night for a while with me, untill I shook myself and roused into a religeous mood of doing all I could, and depending on the mercies of my Preserver, who has often surprized me with pleasing events not in my power to foresee.

This a very cold blustering day wind at Northwest.

It seems two more lambs have been yeaned and died which makes 16 dead ones and but 11 alive out of 27 yeaned. It must be something that I can't find out either in the want of care or that the Ewes have been hurt by some means or other. I fancy drunken Gardiner Johnny was a much better shepherd. I never lost so many with his care. Perhaps the Girl drives them about or it may be the ewes hurt themselves Corning or Jumping over some Stacks.

MARCH 1771

1. *Fryday.*

I rode out this day and endeavoured if I could to find out the care of my sheep. At the Fork I found 19 lambs which are all they have had and as Rose, the old wench who us[ed] to take care of them, was sick, I wen[t] to see the Ewes and found them very poor. I asked the wench in her room how she fed them? She told me only in the morning about 1 pint to the whole 19. I asked the overseer whether he did not charge me 1/2 a bushel a week. He told me that was their allowance; and it seems they have only a little dirty corn in the morning. Mr. George it seems says they had half a bushel each week, and as Rose was to clean it, he supposed she did not care to give it to the sheep. So it is, I dare say, every where. Overseers trust to the people, And they quarrel and the creatures suffer.

I see Rye is of no use; for although these Ewes have had it to pick all the time they look no better than those who have none to pick.

It also is a further proof that a snow to be on the ground in February is as bad as can be; for even this food is covered from the creatures and they suffer more at such a time than any in the whole year. These Sheep on the 13th when I saw them looked as well as sheep could do. The snow fell the 15, and they have been perishing ever since till the rain two days ago that melted it off.

So my home gang has been quite perished. They may pretend they fed them, but I cannot beleive them.

Began to hoe my Fork corn fields this day. I have but 3 hands at it, 2 sick, a third taking care of the creatures, and a fourth malling rails.

Hilling my mangorike Cowpens this day and burning my home plant patch.

2. *Saturday.*

Looks rainy again. Sowed last night 20 beds of my house plant patch. 16 to sow, but not yet ready.

By enquiry I find the method of feeding the Ewes of the lambs has been done contrary to what I have ordered and used to follow. It used to be to turn all the lambs into the yard and take in a lamb and her dam at a time, put the homony allowed in the trough, which the Ewe [ate] whilst the lamb suckled and was rubbed; but now all are turned in at once, of course, no one can tell whether every lamb has sucked, the apparent cause of its death, and of the mother's poverty, for weak Ewes will get none of the food. Therefore, I have ordered it to be altered.

Borrowed of Mr. Tayloe 20 pounds of coffee three days ago, but none of it used yet.

Billy Beale went yesterday to Squire Lee's for 20 Gallons of Molasses with Manuel.

In all 12 lambs and a last year's lamb yeaned a dead one so that we have had 30 lambs yeaned here, although but 12 alive. 18 dead.

Robin, an odd fellow, thinks it hard there should be a wheelwright here and yet that he should buy wheels. It is odd that a father should have anything to live on; or that other children should be maintained when an elder son is alive.

I have persuaded him at last to have his hand full of oats sown in my garden under the pailing leading to the Bee house. It is rich ground and was it not for the ground mice very fine for forward Peas.

4. *Monday.*

There were 14 lambs last night alive by Billy Beale's account, which makes 32 Yeaned.

Memorandom: Oil of Lilly's[11] the most cooling to an inflamed Posterior and white ointment Camphorated the best lip salve as well as infallible cure for a gall in riding or any extraordinary sitting.

News from the Lamb house. The lamb yeaned yesterday dead; the mother young and foolish did not own it, and no care could raise it. This makes 19 dead and 13 alive out of 32 yeaned. A very flemmish account.

8. *Fryday*.

Rain these two days, no working. 15 lambs at home no more dead, but one died at the fork, nobody knows how.

2 calves yesterday, the first fallen at Mangorike. Ordered one of them, a bull calf, up to make a veale of this day.

The 4th began to use the 20 pounds Coffee borrowed of Mt. Airy which I do suppose will not last us long according to the modes of our family, who are perpetually calling out things are too weak, notwithstanding much weaker at other places are very good.

John Boughton on the 4th carried away to Rings neck two Sows and a boar of Colo. Tayloe's guinea breed, my own raising. I find he is a great favorite of my son's, for he treated him here as a brother, but I told the rascal to do better or I should think we were too unlucky to be connected together any longer.

Toney, Guy, Mcginnis, Jamy and their three boys all went yesterday about a Weir. I was obliged to take them from my Mill. The mills going away has been almost an irreparable loss to me. First the Gust after it blew down and wounded so many houses that I was obliged to repare those. Then I began the job the winter before but ear[l]y in the winter and then the winter began so wet that when it ended I was obliged to leave off though it was good wether and this winter I waited and did not begin till towards the end and then the first of the winter proved fine and it is now only turned bad.

For instance, this the 2d day of hard rain.

10. *Sunday*.

This weather has pursued the course of the late memorable gust too years ago last September. It began the 6th in the night, and held all the 7 and 8, 9 with a constant rain except now and then. People seemed to promise themselves it would clear away, but remembring that gust so perfectly which continued with swagging clouds, I could not help dreading that it would fix at Northeast. If so we should still have much more of it and Perhaps as bad as we

[11] Oil of lilies was a mixture of lily flowers and olive oil.

then had. Yesterday in the evening it did fix to that point and has blown and rained prodigeously ever since, So much that all below my hill seems an ocean of water, the land only to be discovered by the ridges in the fields and the trees on the ditches. And still it continues blowing and raining. Should it clear up at Northwest and dreadfully hard as it sometimes does, God only knows our fate. But a God of Mercy can and will still the raging of the winds as he has heretofore done.

I have now but 77 old sheep and had 100 and better the 14 of February when I went to Beverley's. The Snow on the next day and the weather ever since has destroyed 27 of them besides 20 lambs. I perceive the poor creatures were put up in their shedds, and, as they were open to the Northeast and East, they died.

11. *Monday*.

It held up raining at 12 yesterday; and very cold this day. The overseer says the earth is excessive wet.

Ordered my beef to be killed this day. The last of 4 fattning this year.

Ordered the poor ewes half a peck of corn per day.

It is now a very cold rainny day.

There came some trees of many kinds from Mr. Parker for Mr. Carter and they were this day planted out in Jack Lubber's Garden under Mr. Comtroller's direction.

12. *Tuesday*.

On the 8th I had 15 lambs and now I have but 13. Two are dead, And Mr. Tom says anybody that tells him he has not taken care of them lies, for which I keep him in irons all night, then whip him and turn him out to the hoe. He may have been the cause of the death of all or most of the lambs, for at first he did not care to come to work in the garden; I thought he might only be unwilling that his wive's father should be turned out, and obliged him to take to the garden and I fear I have now paid for it; having lost 21 or 2 lambs that we know of and perhaps many that we never heard of for there has not been any complaint for the want of food and though they may not have had it given to them I am charged with it as given out.

I have put Johnny into his old place who promises to lay aside all his old tricks and mind his business that he may grow old in peace.

We scorn as yet not to enjoy the blessing of the Sun, All over cloudy still and the face of my ground covered over with water. Nay the fork fields I am told were yester[day] all covered with water.

Yesterday and to day turning our dung.

I find it has not for some years been less than £400 the year that has maintained my family in everything, tools etc.

Rode out to the Fork, perhaps as bad a rode as could be travelled in many places up to the horse's knees in water and any where out of the path up to the foot locks in mire.

19 lambs again there and a few more Ewes to yean.

Gave William Rigmaden a note this day of Mr. Samuel Hipkins for £20, being his Salary at my free school for 1770.

17. *Sunday.*

Very cold and hard frozen ever since 15 in the night. We have now 14 lambs at home. Johnny's care has saved all since he became restored to his place.

I have I hope also stopped the dying of my old sheep, having lost since the 14 of February 35; so that I have now 73 besides the fatning sheep.

The method is one spoonfull of the Juice of Rue and one spoonfull common salt mixed twice a day. I heard it would save even in the rot if not dying, and certain cure if taken early. I think it has been a sovereign remedy as to 6 which were near death.

I remember some years ago to have seen after much rain in the winter and then drye freezing winds, that my ground though naturally very stiff yet by my early as well as frequent working has become so light in the hills as to blow almost away in a very great dust; I saw this last year and now yesterday it continued so all day. The effect of this before was that although I had made it extremely rich it had become really but indifferent. From hence I may deduce the only evil that attends the early making of my tobacco hills, which is a misfortune in my land, for if I do not pulverize it well to break the cohesion of the particles and give vegetation a greater surface to draw its nourishment from it produces nothing; and I know of no method to do that so effectual as to raise the land for the penetration of the snows and frosts; and if I do, it may be quite impoverished; for If I only hoe it up flat, then the rains that fall every winter, make it as clingy as it [torn]. So that I am still to seek in this poin[t]. From hence I must observe that however just the present practice with regard to good farming may be as to its principles, there is a deficiency in what husbandmen should call their theory.

This year has also furnished me with another observation. I have for many years found that our corn stalks laid in our winter cowyards for the cattle to bed up do make a most excellent manure. Just heap about 3 feet high and level early in march in order to ferment and rot so as to occasion their fibres to break asunder easily when they are put into the earth. And this I have always done to dung my tobacco grounds. I have had many frigid connoiseiurs laughing at this long dung as they call it; but by making a deep hole between the step of the tobacco hills as soon as the dung has got through that fermentation as before and putting near half a peck of it into that hole and covering it over with the earth taken out of the hole with a handclap; and after by turning the hill over it, I say I have found that by the time the plant put into the hill has in its growth sent its roots near the dung, the dung then has got such a ground rot as to be ready to receive them, and give the plant the assistence of all the urinary salts, the most adopted to vegitation of all the whole tribe of salts, howsoever distinguished. This assistance the plants could not receive if those salts had all ev[ap]orated in the dunghill which they must do to reduce the dung to the state of garden mould which some people argue for; And by this means a greater Number of hills according to this Philo[sophy] are assisted out of the same heap of manure before it is quite pulverized than there can be when it is reduced to garden mould. But whilst we are thus providing to enrich our lands, I say I saw that this year we in some measure have injured our cattle; for in long lying snows I discovered that those cattle about, which had corn Stalks to brouze upon whilst the snow lay, though it was but a very poor subsistance untill night when they were fed, yet the[y] fared better and lookt better than those who had no stalks to go to.

This may be remedied and make use of the stalks too for dung making; but not as some propose by racks of provender laid in open fields about; for in a large stock that cannot so easily be done; but I think it may in some sort by standing racks made in sheltered places in the Plantation about, into which the gang, who in such times can do but little else, may put the provender.

I see it is too good a way ever to be omitted again, to have wheat tailings or other sorry winter grain, Spelt in particular, sown in corn fields, ready to be turned out at the last weeding the corn; for the young cattle as well as sheep to graze upon during winter; for although I raise my yearlings well enough by giving every day a small matter of meal or homony; Yet when they get to be two year olds without the same care, they cannot fare so well as the grown Cattle do; and it is owing to this out of 11 lost everywhere 8 at least have been 2 year olds this year.

My overseer told me yesterday that had not the frost been so hard he should have finished hoing the corn rows of one field, which will be one half of what I shall tend this cropping, And that he has got all the lists between the fork corn rows hoed already for Oats which I shall immediately drill in them.

But he alarms me about the chintz bug, which frequently comes among grain sown between corn. However I shall try it; for what I do remember of thos[e] buggs which I have more than once taken notice of; they come only where the winter grain has been sown, the reason of which I take to be this, that by that grain's being in the land the winter, these bugs resort to it for a Shelter; and this is the reason that they do not always infest corn fields where no grain is, the common severity of the winter either kills them or their eggs; which I hope may be already done before the oats are put into the ground. For I cannot bear the Vulgar error that any thing can breed a living animal from its particular nature, the thousands of things are to be sure both nidus and pabula for these insects.

I shall trye this experiment, because I have heard that one Brookman in King and Queen, has sown and raised fine Oats in his corn fields these many years, As my son once saw at his plantation; and that without any injury at all complained of to the corn from the Oats. Should it turn out so to be sure my Philosophy as to the buggs must then be right.

18. *Monday.*

I rode out this day, a very fine one excepting a little too much wind, but it was very pleasant which made me ride out for the sake of looking into my plantations as well as for exercise.

I saw the wheat sown in the river side corn field; had it been put in with the plow it seems as if it would have been very good, but what with the bad covering it in the late snows, violent rains, and cold weather after it, I can't think it will even be tollerable. I must trye it once more and that with plows. Otherwise it seems as if I could not crop in wheat here without injuring my tobacco crops, and the plaguy wood flye has convinced me that will not do, and make anything to live upon.

I went also into the corn field now hoing up. Perhaps they might finish at this day provided I let the overseer leave out all the stiff land; but as I rode in it I thought it was now drye enough to be hilled up as they hoe it. Therefore I shall order that is not wet to be hilled up as they hoe it as it is stiff.

I lookt at my drilled barley as I went along. I fear that in the low stiff land is mostly killed for notwithstanding I drilled it in high ridges the prodigeous rains lately have nearly drowned it all. However, there is not much of that low stiff kind and the rest may do if I can but get it drye enough to give it a dressing in a week or two which I must attempt because I intend to sow the Spaces between with oats.

I rode also to my fork. The spaces between the corn rows there that I intend to drill with oats are all hoed up, and should have been drilled ready for sowing to morrow, but it seems that meadow plant patch which has been hitherto too wet will imploy this day to get burnt and sown. I think it rather too wet now, but as the beds are rounding it will, I am in hopes, do. I told the overseer I was affraid those people would be late for they have near 5/6 of their corn ground still to hoe and hill and all to dung besides heaping all their dung and hilling their new ground tobacco ground as yet only hoed up, but not loged up.

I went also to see my ditches. Sam and Will have not above a day to get to the corner of the corn field ditch next mangorike woods, and as they are to come all round to the great gate and so up by the Mud house to the chesnut tree I have made them keep on, whilst Tom and Fork Jammy are new banking the ditch at the Fork.

There are 19 lambs there and two calves, an Ewe or two more to yean and the wench say a pritty many cows to Calve.

She has 17 chickens, and 2 dozen duck eggs to set, but no turkeys nor geese lay as yet.

Toney began this day to set my Weir[s.]

My son went to Essex court in my Petty Auger. I never saw a thing so abused in my life. I ordered some enquiry to be made abot turpentine at Hobbs hole; and as soon as the Wear is done Toney shall fit her up; and Mr. Talbot's hyde tanned, for his rudder Irons are broke, and the steering lines gone and the cover of the lockes broke and lost. Suppose this to be true, he has never spoke one word about it to me or any body but he is as damned a Villain as ever was for lazyness and lying.

If Rhue and salt saves a Ewe I saw, I am certain it must be a valuable thing in raising sheep. But what is Mister Billy Beale, who did not see one drooping Ewe this morning? The Sheep girl said she beleived Gardiner Johnny had given that a dose this day.

20. *Wednesday.*

The sick ewe died yesterday, 'twas too bad before discovered, and then they have not given the medicine fair play; they made a decoction of it, instead of pressing out the juice.

A fine day yesterday but too windy to set my Weirs. This day very fine and about 12 moderate.

I sent Nat for 30 bushels Oats Colo. Tayloe lent me. Good measure and clean grain. Talbot is drilling the corn with Mulatto Peter at the Fork.

Fork Plant patch sowed yesterday. Trench this meadow patch to sow also.

My Cough splits my sckull. I have passed some Crem Tartar whey through me to remove the cough.

Mr. Corotoman Carter complains that my people don't come to his mill, but go to Eustace's. I don't know the reason of it.

22. *Fryday.*

Yesterday and the day before were really fine days and I made use of them to drill in 12 bushels of Oats in the Fork corn field, and up to the chessnut tree in my barley ground. But this day begins with a very heavy shower, indeed, not unlike the last great rain which will again put us back in planting our corn, for we cannot get ready in any good time. However in all cases let us do as well as we can.

Yester[day] Mr. Wmson. Ball told me Mr. Mills at Essex court read a letter from his nephew, John Mills, who went home either in the ship with Owen Griffith or about the same time; which told him that he had seen that rascal's father alive, that he showed my advertizement in the Virginia Paper to the Old man, who said the plaguy rogue must come to the gallows, for the whole of his great estate was a forgery.

And it is such a forgery that can only have been practiced for the imagined witness of it, for I had agreed to set him out and pay his passage before the pretended letters came to hand; and when they did come he only asked me to endorse a bill for £30, which could not be much more than what his outfit and Passage would come to. That money I have not altogether lost, for he had a box of goods come in from his father which did not come to hand till he had sailed and this I took care of, and opened yesterday after I heard of the deception; And I find in it a great many good things which perhaps cost £10 or £12, all of them of use to my grandson Landon. Besides his father had written to me to let him have now and then some pocket money and as though this bill was a mere act of humanity, Yet, if that old man has anything, he must out of gratitude repay me what I lost.

But what if the arch rascal should get hanged by it; for I had set Molleson to enquire about the estate, etc., some months before the villain could get a way and to [have] him apprehended for a rogue if he found it a forgery; but I believe the dog will get on board a Man of war.

I received a letter from Montague the late agent very kind, and I will trye to set him to endeavour to get my money if he can.

28. *Thursday.*

None to be called rain since [faded] 22d, but that was so much that some of my lands is scarce drye enough to be worked.

Fogs every morning, they lye along the horizon so as to conceal the sun at Setting, and come on about midnight. It may be a sign of drye weather or only the excessive moisture rising out of the earth.

I have ordered all my stiff corn field to be first hilled, least it should rain, and my light may be then hoed.

Sent Sam off to stop Ball's coming, and to order the 10 hogsheads to be inspected.

The bilious intermittants which attackt us in the Fall, kept here more or less all the winter, some attended with great colds and sometimes tinctured with inflammations; but now they have regenerated into downright Agues and fevers. Little Nancy had them and has continued puking ever since, looks Pale and has her belly Pretty open. She has taken 2 Vomits for it. Having observed it don't yet care to seem the type of a tertian I have order[ed] some soap, Rhubarb, Alkalized Mercury, and Crabs eyes to assimilate and bear it away Gently.

Little George is now in his second fit not quite a tertian but as near as the second fit commonly shews.

And Many wenches, even those ready to lye in, have it sometimes everyday. I cannot help observing this disorder seems to have been the ruling Site as it were of all the diseases since the fall, for catch a Cold or what you will it brings on an Intermittent.

George takes a Vomit this evening.

Yesterday an accidental visit to the hen house introduced a strange Conversation. My geese don't lay half their eggs because they have no corn. A fine excuse for the laziness of an Old Bitch that has left off taking care as she used to do, because no body goes to examine into her conduct as had been before done. This devil has had half a peck every day of the shattered corn just as she used to have, which always did before, but now truely it won't do. I enquired how many geese had laid; She told me the 4th was now begun; that she had 23 eggs setting under two of them and 2 hens; the produce of 3 geese and not all they had laid, so that this was only a lie to conceal her neglect. She wants truely more girls to look after turkeys, ducks and chickens when she has none of either. In short, I shall have no house keeping this year except from my Stalls, only because Ladies are now grown too delicate to look into family affairs. Lucy could not be got to walk out. Judy has been near a year at Hanover, and Mrs. Carter has her children to take care of. In short Owen, as great a rogue as he was, proved of more Service to me than all this management.

We shall be forward enough in Planting corn at Mangorike; but at the Fork unless Lawson leads great help they will be backward, People sick and one complaint or another. It is, I suppose, owing to such idleness that we have such sorry corn about. The fields are never half hoed before Planting.

I hardly think my big bellyed are to be matched in Virginia. As soon as a wench is with child I have been used to indulge her in not carrying weights on her head or shoulders; but they have now got to such a pitch that they cannot work truely and not only fall behind, but come in, stay as long as they please, and care not ever to go out though close by their homes.

I hope winter is now fairly gone; the weather is very fine; but according to the general observation it will be summer immediately without any Spring. If it was not to be so, last year we should not have had any winter; for untill the 15th of February our chief winter was our rain; but from that day till about the same time this month I hardly knew worse weather.

Grieg is arrived, has got my orders for my thirty hogsheads, but I don't know when I shall have my goods.

29. *Fryday*.

I could not avoid dreading the weather of yesterday for some days before it came. Every morning foggy, and the Sun could not set clear any evening but there was always a bank from Southwest to North which wore into a fog all night and next morning. Untill at last about 5 it began to thunder at a distance and about sunSet came up. I think for so early and the first thunder in the year we had it most severely here. Crack after crack for a full hour, and abundance of I expected of rain. However I had prudently enough hill and hoed what stiff land I could before it came. I suppose I may still have 3 days work of that sort to do, but I understand it is now too wet.

31. *Sunday*.

Esther. Yesterday terrible from in the night. We had a most powerful rain, and all this day which has laid us all under water so very much again, that although I had got things in tollerable order for corn planting I fear now it will be a full week before it will be dry enough to hoe the rest of the ground we intended to tend, some of it being very Stiff land and lying rather low.

About 11 in the night of last night the people in the house were raised by Kit to go to Daniel who he said was taken with a vomiting, Purging and such a pain in his bowels he thought he would die. I sent Nassau down to the Mill to him and ordered him to give him in some weak mint water 20 or 30 drops of liquid Laudanum And after an hour a Vomit of Ipecacuana. He went down, found no Vomiting nor Purging only a motion of very hard lumps indeed and a violent pain below his Navel; he guessed it be wind and gave him the Vomit which brought off a mere constant roll of wind which made the fellow easyer. Then he gave him a clyster a little strengthned with one spoonfull of crocus wine which brought away a pot full of those lumps and his pain eased a little. The fellow then walked up to the house. When here, I ordered a mild softning dose of Ellexir Salutis,[12] 2 spoonfulls, 15 grains of Jalap, and 10 of Rhybarb, adding 2 Spoons of Peper mint water, and gave another Clyster to meet it. This brought down two motions of the same hard stuff and the fellow seemed easy, lay down to sleep, and in that Sleep died. It seems he was very well all the day before and has not been sick this whole year but once with a pain in his Shoulder for which he was blooded and got well many months ago. But two of the people said just at night on Saturday he said he was griped and he thought his belly had swelled hard. However he went to his lodging, eat his bread, and went to sleep and in his sleep waked bad as before.

He is the Son of Mary Adam at Rings neck, who had 5 children by one Adam at George Ball's, 4 of whom, being like him and I suppose partaking of his nature, all died Suddenly about the age of 35. The other not like him but her mother is still alive though not quite at that age, but she seems now well.

I take this case to have been an abounding bile not carried off by stool, nor at first acrid enough to make him complain but meeting with an acid in his guts must have concreated with his excrement and in the region below the Naval lying first destroyed the Motion of his guts to throw it off, and possibly as the fellow had not be[en] often sick he might have endured it expecting it would go off, by which it brought on a Mortification that killed when with the least complaint beforehand he might have been saved.

I was convinced that nothing harsh given as a purge to such complaining bowels could be but an injury to him. Therefore I gave him none Such; but I wish I had added soap in that dose. And indeed that I had repeated the Opiad till Nature had been releived from Pain and then Perhaps she might have done her office and brought off all the hard lumps lodged in his guts, but I apprehended the Mortification and doubted Opium might have aded to

---

[12] Elixir salutis was a mixture of sena, jalap, coriander, and powdered sugar candy that was used as a carminative and cathartic. It was especially recommended for those who had become habituated to strong drink and those who had flatulent and colicky complaints.

it. But I need not have entertained that fear for I fancy Mortifications in the bowels are more instantanious, and ever rapid in their effects. However no one had time to use any method but what circumstances suggested, and all these I considered and God's will be done.

APRIL 1771

1. *Monday.*

Morning. It cleared up last night and was quite clear all night but this morning quite overcast. A great fog and likely for more rain. God be mercyfull unto us.

7. *Sunday.*

Indeed we have [been] many days since very Stormy and abundance of rain. So that I am still two days short of finishing hoeing my Stiff ground field of corn at Mangorike and one day more putting up my fence there.

The Fork dung not yet quite heaped. They do that tomorrow, dung out that other field; and put up their fence and then to planting their corn which will be at least 3 days there.

I find I am still loosing sheep with the rot, at last I am told there is no Rue. This fool Beale will not speak. I think I can see in everyone I get his bane. A certain R[ichard] E[dwards] had always a lazy disposition and no proper notion of Gratitude which will carry him to the dogs sooner or later. Then a W[illiam] B[eale] before this Excessive proud and morose, so that by his own great love for his person he cannot long continue as he should be and I may be satisfyed not only Gratitude but everything else will be lost in him. And as to this W[illiam] B[eale] want of spirit and acursed indifference as to all that can be said to him he will turn out Nothing.

I rode out and found I am still to loose cattle and at the Fork where I thought I had both food and care, but yet is near dead. My loss in sheep and lambs has been a mere gang, here near 40 [sheep] and 35 lambs and at the fork 3 lambs.

I can account for it all. I am old and even my old servant Jack L[ub]bar quite passed all labour. [And] to this I had for his ill beha[viour] turned Gardiner Johnny out to the ground, and his successor Tom too impudent and sawcy to follow orders; And the solemn fool no command to make those do anything who will without good thrashing. How to mend myself I cannot tell, as I am so old.

9. *Tuesday.*

Hard Northwest all [faded] yesterday and this day. This [was to] be foreseen three days ago, but I was laught at by a man older [in] observation than his fath[er].

Flys eat prodigiously in the [ha]y house patch.

I fear we shall hardly plant [faded] week. People lay up [faded].

17. *Wednesday.*

[Yes]terday I returned from Corotoman. [Found] my daughters Lucy and Judy at home [an]d everybody well.

Could not go over to Mr. Wormeley's whi[ch he] had appointed to be last monday; the [w]ind really blowed so hard, and so it did [f]rom the 10th when we went down to this very day; and indeed every day exceeding [c]old, frosts every morning below and understand we had Ice here.

It seems we began to plant corn on Fryday last being the 12 of the mon[th]. We have about half done everywhere so that it takes us just 8 days for that Job, owing the prodigeous Stiffness [an]d dryness of the soil although all but [faded]st tilled.

I saw my Northumberland Quarters. I [can] not see much reason to expect any [croppin]g there. They cannot get to planting [cor]n before the 20th and then Blough Point will not have much above [faded and torn] and a head in c[or]n. But as [faded and torn] will have more probably [faded and torn] usually have tended. [Two lines faded and torn. . . .] remove from Blough point what hands are more than equal to 10,000 a head to the Ware house quarter.

I could not but look upon Mr. Edwards' management. All the old fields on the middle plantation quite grown up with Pines. And all the ditches at Blough point quite filled up; so that these have been the reason why we sometime hear there are too many hands; and again the land lies mighty low. No water that falls can now run off, and not one pin[e] is ever cut down.

As to John Beale he promises much and seems to be diligent; but I am afraid must be something hare brained, Otherwise he could not so easily forget my orders; but perhaps he thinks it too trifling to obey me. I beleive I shall be indifferent about imploying such a person any longer.

Edwards ashamed to come to Corotoman where I was.

I can't but say I have found out Mr. J[ohn to] be a lyer. I am certain of two he told [torn]. I do suppose I shall hear of [more].

I should have road out this day, but my horse Bearskin was sick. He neither eat last night nor this morning. When I carried him down, he performed the journey very well to Corotoman, and the next day carried Nat to my Plantations in my company and two days after that carried me about Corotoman estate with great Satisfaction; but in the evening he discovered as much agony as a creature could endure, and this without any releif although Saltpetree and many other things besides raking him were applyed. At last Mr. Carter recommended 2 penny weight of bluestone[13] both as a safe and certain remedy. Seeing the creature in danger as well as pain I consented, though the medicine to my thought extremely dangerous itself. In about 3 hours the horse grew easier and by tuesday got well enough to come home; but he is not yet quite well.

It seems no English Potatoes have been planted in the Fork cornfield, Beale an ass pretending the fellow had nothing. Thus are my orders obeyed by these impudent jackanapes. This day by account from W. Beale's servant we have from the 5th of March till this day inclusive used up 10 pounds of Coffee which are 44 days in all inclusive. So that 1 pound coffee at this rate must have lasted above 4 days and a half. Vastly longer this than before.

18. *Thursday.*

The weather it is to be hoped is now mending from what it has been with but a Small exception ever since the 14th of February. As to the Phasis of the new moon last night it is moist and warm according to former observations. But we had the same bank from the North to the South round by the West that we have had almost for two months; a very certain sign of wind and cold.

Yesterday we could judge between Stiff and light lands in almost any work, Particularly planting corn. 6 people will plant 160,000 in 5 days which is more than 26,000 a hand and [in] the Mangorike Stiff land they [did] not plant 25,000 a hand in [torn] 8 days.

19. *Fryday.*

Yesterday was a fine day. I went to see Mr. Loyd[14] at Mount airy. A young man paying for his youthful and indeed imprudent habits of that kind of

---

[13] Bluestone is hydrated copper sulphate.

[13] Edward Lloyd (1744–96) of Wye House was a Maryland planter. The eldest son of Edward Lloyd III and Ann Rousby, he married Elizabeth, daughter of John Tayloe, in November 1767. A member of the Maryland House before the Revolution, he later was a delegate to the Continental Congress from Maryland in 1783–84.

intemperance generally called good living; which corrupts the whole machine with one kind of Morbidity or another; that is thought happy to be centered in the gout. But how short and indeed how painful is such a life.

I saw his Brother Richard Loyd who seems to me to be a pretty youth, Modest and agreeable in behaviour, and one Sensible of his own want of improvement, which is really a blessing to him, for I observe he never is impertinent in Company, a rare circumstance in Youth.

I could not avoid as I rode by taking notice of my neighbour's [pro]digeous backwardness in his crops. At this time not a fence up, dung only carting out to level old fields not tilled or hoe[d], Corn fields not yet even listed to plant, And if I mistake not I saw the cause of all this. His manager really top full of liquor and that early in the morning. Now to conceal this is unneighbourly, and to speak of it I know will at any time be reackoned impertinent, and at this particular time much suspected because I have lately been obliged to take that fellow to task, who possibly may have been ingratiating himself by too officious an attempt to do his duty as he calls it. In short, had I experienced less of a certain Person I should have known better how to have acted; but with such late management now, we have [r]eason to expect what will be hereafter [an]d I shall be mistaken if he does anything.

Yesterday I put in some bushels of Irish potatoes in the rows of the Fork cornfield where I have drilled my oats. By not cutting them, though many bushels, the seed, as it is called, only planted 6½ rows. I took this method from the jersey men who now live above. They put their potatoe in the corn hill, but, having heard that some times hurts the corn as I had reasonably suspected, I planted mine between the hill, that is at 2 feet distance one way, supposing the corn hills to be 2 feet asunder.

It is said that it rained last night. If it did, it was but a small sprinkling for I could not see any of it this morning.

The Fork done corn planting this day and have fenced in their dung hill at last and are moving their Cowpen this evening. Then to turning and tilling their new ground. Tobacco hills very hard and all the clods to be brok[en].

Mangorike will be done planting corn early tomorrow: all but the stiff barley ground which I intend on monday to dress and hill to plant corn between those drills having enough in the light ground to drill peas in every row of oat and barley being 3¼ feet asunder. So that pease drilled between every other row will be at least 6½ feet asunder.

20. Saturday.

It may not be amiss to remark that the clouds before taken notice of; although with a rainy tendency, cleared off according to the mode of '71 with a Northwest again so that we are really drye now. However, Clouds are now Showing themselves in the Morning along the Eastern to the Southern horison, and perhaps [there] may be rain.

Rode out to the Fork this day. A violent hard Northwest wind, cool and excessive drye with all. Almost every thing not of animal creation merely white with prodigeous cold drye winds.

I have always known such spells to be destructive of Plants; and as these Spells are generally to be expected I have every year been upon some experiment to destroy these flies in their eggs. I have known them in every piece of earth broke up or not, and as they cannot even hop far at a time I have concluded that the extent of their territories cannot be very large not greater than the square upon which their eggs are laid and hatched, and abou[t] the environs of that square for their foo[d]. This conjecture led me first to keep the covering of my plants on that, by keeping the earth moist, the eggs should not hatch; and, if they should hatch, that the weeds might be their food which I supposed full as agreeable as tobacco plant. In this I have been [satisfied] that the conjecture was right as to t[he] eggs being laid on the earth. It became necessary then to find out the time when; that these eggs might be more readily destroyed. And this I conjectured might from the early appearance of the flye in the Spring be sometime before winter sets in. Accordingly I resolved to burn my earth intended for a plant patch before I ever hoed or dry it; having these two things in View: 1st. Killing the eggs of the flye if laid on the weeds or grass about on the surface of the earth. And 2dly to destroy all the seeds of grass and weeds. And this I think I have succeeded in, now ever since I have tryed; especially this year for I can hardly see a flye in any patch and really considering the drye weather the plants are very fine according to the time of sowing. If others have no flye any more than I; we must then impute it to some cause not with the Common experience of a Planter.

I do expect Mangorike will have done planting corn before dark Yet; but then I intend to plant all between my stiff ground barley; which I shall begin to weed, hill, and hoe, ready and plant all as we go.

My Fork people making their new ground tobacco hills; I have them knockt fine, and indeed this drye spell is favourable to that work everywhere so that though the land is cold and stiff I shall break the cohesion of the earth and then as the roots being broke up before winter are all disengaged from the Clods I am in hopes by good dunging to make a crop from it. There are very little above 20,000 hills in the ground; and if this should do I have more to add to it another year. I do not expect to get more than 25,000 plants at the fork and that I intend shall be well dunged. Manuel may be spared to get the dung convenient. Two days will be full enough.

I am fencing in my meadow again but I cannot say new doing it, for really I have not time to new ditch it, a work that must be done this year, god willing.

Robin must go to take care of my hogs at the Fork. There are 30 old hogs there and 65 piggs. I see my guinea boar will be there also although the boar from Parker's Sow is a very fine one. Have ordered Lawson to cut the Plantation young boar on Monday. Jesse is a most vile dog indeed; he is never to be found with his hogs and they are finding out ways to get into the Corn field.

By my Son's letter to me whilst I was at Corotoman: We began to plant corn at Mangorike Yesterday seven nights and curiosity led me to examine the first planted. I found that swelled and sprouting which is prodigeous considering it has not rained since and all this a cold violent drying wind. It can only be the depth and the lower moisture of the earth constantly ascending. For as to shallow sowing I have an instance in Some timothy seed sown between my Riverside barley that has not as yet began to sprout which can only be owing to the constant Cold drying winds which must have a very parching effect on shallow sowing and that seed cannot be buryed deep. The barley there is the finest I have seen. Robin thinks the wheat sown in the cornfield by it last fall will be good; but I cannot promise myself much about it. However I this day reflected that I might make a shelter for that crop out of the roof of my 90 foot tobacco house blown down; if I can raise it on Pins of fence rails which I hope may be done Provided Guy and Jamy can come in any time from my Rippon Hall mill.

Toney had a great flogging for his yesterday's lazyness and impudence.

Sow this day in the garden some of Stewart and Campbell's Turnep Cabbage.

Billy Beale to be charged with 3 new shirts of Owen's at 7/6, being 1/6 linen, and Fowler's goods.

About 15 past 5 my people finished corn planting at Mangorike, and came to hoing and hilling between the barley by the old gate. By the glass it seems excessive hard after such a winter of rain, etc., and a mere Spring to this time of hard baking winds. If anything could convince a certain ——, this work must, how much more difficult it is to break up ground in the Spring which has not been broke up in the fall. I know the ground good, therefore Am in hopes the play will be worth the pains and Time.

21. *Sunday.*

It is a truth, whether melancholly or not in its effects we cannot say as yet, but we have had last night both a white and a black frost and so great that I saw even large dock leaves quite black and prostrate with it. Perhaps in the whole 21 days of this month we have scarce had two in which it has not been cold enough for a frost, though it is possible the air may have been too much agitated to produce it; but then, if as some late moderns say, frost is only produced by Coldness, may not this disturbed Coldness be equally as bad as a frost? For my part I think the principal ingredient is Nitre, and as that is by the operation of the cool air drawn out from the earth and plant, I do think it must thereby receive that injury which kills the plant or disjoyns its several parts; for I imagine nitre to be not only its animal salt, but also that active fluid that perpetually connects the several parts of a plant together and when that is forced off by evaporation or cold the injury is derived in proportion to the loss sustained. Therefore I do not think a cold night without a frost to be equally injurious.

22. *Monday.*

A Cool morning. I heard yesterday that some had not yet planted their corn, imagining as it is pretended the ground is too Cold; but I wish it may not be that they have been too lazy; for to be sure corn that is intended to make a crop ought to be in the ground. I fear my Stiff ground barley will be a long jobb to break up; it appears so very hard this very drye windy Spell.

I also heard a great crye about the want of plants; some people have scarce one on their plantations. It gives one great concern, notwithstanding I have often heard my management laught at in particular as to the time and trouble I take about my beds, by first burning them before I break them up, and then scorching the beds over after they are made fine. I have already taken notice for what I do this; and as the killing the eggs of the flyes is one reason I will fancy that I have found out a way to prevent in a great measure this enimy; for as yet from every eye that I set to look at the beds I have a great abundance and hardly a flye to be seen in them; some few there are indeed, but with an enimy in such swarms, it must be an extravagant expectation to think of destroying all of them.

23. *Tuesday.*

Yesterday a cow at the Fork that had calved a very fine calf on Saturday last, run mad and wanted to lye down in the Water. I had her lais and tail cut and by cutting her skin I got to her vein and blood.

24. *Wednesday.*

I then found out the creature could not stall, gave her Oil Terebinth[15] a spoonfull with sugar and a draft of Marshmallow decoction with an ounce of Saltpetre in it. This made her dung and brought away her urine and in the night her swelling abated and she owned her calf.

I really think it is prodigeous drye. We have not as yet 30 in Number quite hoed and hilled up 56,000 last year's tobacco hills in corn at 6½ feet distance and 2 feet step. Indeed there is no earth that can be workt.

My Son John came down this day about 2 o'clock.

25. *Thursday.*

If I mistake not this fog after such a long drye spell is as discouraging a sign as we can have. I never knew one that preceeded any rain after March in my life by months.

I beleive we shall this day finish the Stiff ground barley and plant it in corn. It has been the hardest jobb that I ever undertook in my life. And had it not been good tobacco ground I declare I would have given it quite over.

We have some tobacco hills a few to make and then to breaking up stiff ground Cornfields.

We have had a pretty sprinkling upon the top of the hill here; but a little towards the Fork, although at Touskey and up the creek to Hickory Thicket it proved a plentifull shower.

I did expect to finish the stiff ground barley but I begin to fear that I shall not.

26. *Fryday.*

There is an agreeable freshness in the look of everything and in the air this morning, which I think if it grows warm is more than we had a right to expect from last night's Northwest which the rain broke up with.

My overseer says the rain was in a great Plenty at the Riverside, so that the Wheat and barley there received it and of course all the plant patches

[15] Oil terebinth was distilled turpentine and was used as a diuretic. It was especially recommended for "cold rheumatisms" and stomach disorders.

which all lay that way except one at the Fork, but as to the barley the corn and oats at the Fork and Mangorike they got hardly more than laid the dust.

I am surprized indeed and cannot solve my difficulty unless it is resolved into the great complaint, Old age. For if I bite my tongue ever so triflingly it hardly can get healed and so of any part or complaint.

My tongue got sore this way about 3 months ago; and it has been worse and better off and on ever since and not well now, although every mouth water and gargarizm that could be thought of has been used. Indeed my old teeth are grown sharp and I cannot file them down and they renew the cut. Nothing seems to avail, but touching the sore now and then with Camphorated Spirits; and taking some doses as often of Gentle openners.

Rode out. Cold enough, God knows. The Northwest returned this morning and all is quite drye again. Indeed there was scarce any rain at Mangorike, nor above a drop at the Fork. And what is odd the corn planted in the light land at the same time the stiff land was planted is not yet swelled though it has been in a fortnight this day; when the Stiffland corn is sprouted.

My corn everywhere up here compleatly planted. Finished the barley ground this day about 9 o'clock. Note: W. Lawson tells me the whole planting has taken 7 barrels and 3 pecks; which I fear is a proof that some must be stolen; but this I will trye for I ordered only 3 grains in a hill so count one pint and that will give the Number of the hills which I fancy cannot be really so many tended.

A fine evening this, though some little remains of the cool air is passing.

I don't think but the people have been so accustomed to work slow in the stiff ground that now they were got into the last year's Pea patch they have not worked but very indifferently.

29. *Monday.*

I beleive I was right about the last fog's being a drye weather sign. We have as yet no rain and all the clouds promising moisture seem to roll off drye. In the last cloud that went by we had only a small Sprinkling, and in the night the clouds at going to bed produced nothing more.

I hope to finish the remainder of my tobacco hills that I may get to work in my corn field stiff land.

After that, God willing, I will turn and plant before I engage my light land corn.

This day I rode out. Corn up in many places to be seen along the Rows both at the Fork and at Mongorike.

I find there are evils that mankind cannot guard against. Life is but one continued anxiety to live, make the most of it you can; call it pleasure or what you will, the sum of all care is but how to live: And yet there are many things which that care to live cannot guard against. Death is not only certain in ourselves but also in Every living creature. But although care may for a while prevent that it cannot do it in numberless instances. Therefore in those as well as in all other things do we stand in need of help. Let me instance in the case of this and the last month. Former drye years brought our time of encrease in our stock to this month. And now this prodigeous cool drye weather makes it death to a Cow to calve; Excessive poor by means of the long winter and now no food to give strength to encounter the difficulty of Calving I have lost one cow calving already and now two more dying. The[y] say the grass purges them so; but I say they are not so happy to have any grass to purge them: that would be a kindness even to Nature. Gave W. Lawson some Water Melons to plant. The same to George at the Fork.

Sowed in my garden the sugar loaf Cabbage seed brought by R[obert] W[ormeley] C[arter] from Marmion. As also the Early Cabage.

We are to wait with patience for God's blessings; but are we not to pray for them; when all nature, look where you will, seems to lament its severe drowth? Everything dwindling even in the garden.

Now but a very few of Naval Officer Lee's Cauliflower seed sown in March are come up. Perhaps they should have been sown in warm places or hot beds.

Gardiner Johnny is growing a Villain again; he pretends to have been watering, but the earth is crackt where he waters.

This evening the most like a Summer's eve of any this year. But how unhappy has it been that our Spring has been totally overcome by an overlong continuance of the winter.

Wm. Beale had Owin's three new shirts and this day he is to have his two pair thread stockings. The shirts at 10/ and the stockings at 2/6.

30. *Tuesday.*

A Small cloud yesterday with a little thunder demonstrated the goodness as well as power of the Almighty, because it blessed us with a most agreeably refreshing Shower and this morning the heavens are clouded over as if we should have some more rain.

I removed my flannel waistcoat from beneath my shirt to wearing it above.

My overseer wanted to go to uncovering my plant Patches, pretending that the plants were not so large last year. I could not but laugh and tell him the growth of the plants must show they did not want uncovering, and he might be sure as they grew the weeds could not; therefore I would willingly see how the rain cleared up. If warm I should uncover and weed; but if cold I should not. The Pea patch ground cannot be less than 65,000 plants. The people go to the stiff corn ground taken in at Mangorike.

I have often heard people pleased to have their work before them. I sup[pose] that must be when it is done; for [to] be sure to see one's work before one when it is all to do almost must be [a] most discouraging Sight. Just such a [sight] struck me this day. My plants near ready and not one hill turned. All the Spaces between my corn rows to be thorough hoed; and my corn coming up so that by the first of old May it will require weeding. My plants all to thin. The Covering then to uncover and to weed. And my peas to plant, etc., together with a cotton Patch and all my tobacco ground to be dunged and only 3 oxen to help to bring the dung in or near the place besides some fencing to right up and my mill race to be new dug so that I cannot get the least help from one Jobber. However to see how easy and how cheerfull my hands go about everything affords the promising comfort that we shall, God willing, do everything in time.

I began the hardest corn field first and I must say it surprizes me to see how the Stiff clods give way to our resolution. [It is] a just saying that a constant diligence will effect great matters.

I must not forget rolling my tobacco landing soon.

I ventured half a penny weight of blues[tone] to a worm eaten shoot or two this day. If it does I shall persuade myself of its great value.

Manuel getting the dung to the Fork new ground. I fancy I shall have great plenty there.

Note: the tobacco ground from Pea Patch last year contains by my account 54,188; but by Lawson's better than 70,000. There is a me[faded] in some part at this upper end he says they are 275 hills deep which I don't make them but 195.

I am at last informed.

JUNE 1771

1. *Saturday.*

Yesterday morning we finished the Mangorike old corn field which we began with our hoes on the 24 of last month at 4 o'clock in the evening, and worked during all the rain as the work was so light and drye. The quantity Per acre I will remember to be 82⅓ so that at any time it may be seen the Number of corn hills or holes tended in it, supposing it all level and tendible, but there is a long branch running through it however in the general but narrow 256,657, and we had with the bread baker 24 hands sick and well that is sometimes 3, then 2, then 1 sick and laid up.

We then set in turning the Pea patch ground of last year, and did near that half in quantity, so that we have this day's work to finish that. We planted to a very little all that we turned from [faded] fork and the hay house plants.

[Faded] last thursday (to wit) the 30th [da]y of May we began to give out co[rn at] the Fork. There ought to be [there] 76 barrels of corn after all the use that had been partly made of it, to be found in May book, May 27, 1771.[16]

I am come to a resolution to go on turning and only plant the remainder of this Peice out, untill the whole crop is turned. As to my corn I know according to all the observed rules of working, it was always reckoned that a man was in time of growth if he got his first weeds out by the 10th of old June and I am sure I have full 21 days to that day: so I will not be uneasy, being certain but very little can keep us to that time and if weeds do grow so unmercifully a man can only be sorry. He should not condemn himself. And as to tobacco I know the best planters alway counted their chance good who got all his hills set by the 20th of June so that with the 11 days new stile we can't have less than 31 days yet to be good planters and do that work.

I cannot but take notice that in that cornfield we averaged round the whole gang 1,858 hills, supposing the whole 82½ acres had been all planted at 7 feet and 2, and this we clean weed and hoed the spaces between. Now in this number 23 allowing every body was well we had of boys and girls 8 so that in fact the work was done by 19 whole shares so that in fact we wed a 2,000 round each day. But turn out that branch and the overplus will well nigh bring it to 2,000.

It will be imagined ever[y] corn hill stood and was in good land, but it did not, nor could not be so, but nevertheless all was workt.

Sowed Yesterday in Lubber's garden Peachey's dwarf homony beans, half a bushel.

Sow this day; the Lettuce, Radish and Brocoli seed that came in in Captain Quinney.

2. *Sunday.*

Sent off the Park boy that came to bring the news of the fresh and with [h]im 6,000 10d nails for the tobacco house.

[16] This May book no longer survives.

I observe my Mangorike people yesterday because I had Company did not finish their turning hills in the Pea field tobacco ground by many of the short rows.

Neither did the Jobbers plant all they had turned by 24 long rowes. This is always the case. Overseers are too lazy themselves to make a push at any thing. It is not of gr[eat] consequence, but 'tis nevertheless very extraordinary.

Just so at the Fork, although they did their day's work in the cornfield, Yet by the quarter where probably the ground was hard the weeds are hardly cut up.

Just so with the ditchers. They only pared weeds from the corn but hardly earthed up the corn; so that it is paying dear for the few vereations which a Master takes. And yet to give overseers shares it will be no better, they are quite easy [and] let things go at the [ir] wil[l]. The plows alone seem to have done their work true and well.

I find there is no making my Carpenters understand me. I only ordered those two roofs of the River side cornfield to be put on pens made of logs to lap in across one another; And they have got plates, posts and sills as if for a new tobacco house. I also ordered to mend the rafters here and there just to make the house serviceable to stack the wheat in that is growing in that cornfield, and they have got an intire new set of rafters. I understood by Toney, Guy first made the mistake and though I forbid it he has spent a week more in doing it his way. Thus it is each rascal will be a directer. I must now add to it that we may also hang tobacco in; therefore it will be still of a greater service than I intended it should be.

Maryan also and her gang setting corn told me this morning she had got to the short rows down the hill in the cornfield and I sent Nassau to see and she had only got opposite Fork Jammy's house.

The Number of the short rows to turn are 7,360 hills and the long rows to plant are 5,492 so that we have to plant in that Piece 12,852 hills. These taken out of 60,000, the whole piece leave only 47,148 only, equal to 2,357 each evening. Very little indeed for a number of hands where there were no want of Plants. So that it is in this as Planters said it was in an army. Where the General is absent, Idleness is Preferred to all business. We cannot then plant any more untill a season.

3. *Monday.*

A summer's morning.
Sent down this day one Cedar pail and a butter pot to Mr. J. Beale.

Sent also Mr. Ronand's[17] account against me for my daughter's silk amounting to £17.8.0. for which I sent Mr. Beale the money to pay him in paper which over paid him 9d, which Beale is to receive and to be accountable to me for.

Give also to my son to Pay Mr. Tho. Blair his account off at our Court to witt

Paper	£	15.7.6
Gold		12.–.10
	£	27.8.4
account		27.7.1
My son to	£	1.3 receive balance.

Left now in hand Gold £8.–.3.

Note: Colo. Corbin to have the bill to Ricd. Lee for £34.11.8 to be renewed by £36.10.1, being the damage of the Protest occasioned by the Villany of Owen Griffith.

Began to turn and cut off my Paddock hills.

6. *Thursday*.

Ever since monday we have had very great Shews for rain; but as I had before observed they have as yet turned out but drye weather signs. However as the last rainy Spell came on with such preceeding signs many people would Promise themselves rain from these signs; And Perhaps as they do continue it may turn out so at last. I must own if I was a planter with but a few hills to plant I should wish for it; but as I have still abundance to turn, and am turning I am inclined to hope for a few more days yet before it does rain. Perhaps though the plants may be very large by that time, I may be planting them very deep be able to get a good crop in yet a while. I can't yet pronounce it Any thing too late for a crop of tobacco. Indeed, as the corn is not yet out of the weeds, if the tobacco was all growing the hoe would be wanting in it before either the corn or the harvest could admit of it: especially if other people's tobacco should grow as my few forward planted hills have done. I have even 60,000 now that would take the hoe now, but my corn will not let me attempt it before Wednesday next, God willing.

I have been now three days attending the Court, and anybody may see by the people's work that my evening's eye has been absent. In the main below the hill the people have done tollerably well. But two hands put on Monday to

---

[17] Probably Thomas Ronand of Lancaster Co.

turn a day's work for planting it for the seed did not all the day turn 800 hills although the same people below did and would have done 1,500 each.

Memorandum: I paid off Mr. Blair's account 27 odd money and told him I can't deal any more. His first cost is excessively buttered.

Simon begun to weed the last corn field at the Fork (to wit) 56,000 hills. The wenches one row apeice to get into it. I expect it will take near 5 day[s] to get it out which will be about Wednesday night. Then I shall set and thin the corn, after that weed out the tobacco, And then perhaps I shall be able to help Mangorike in their 30,000 tobacco plants. For I intend to turn out all My hills and perhaps by about thursday or fryday next that work will be done. And I shall dread some part of my corn by even that time. Some people fancy from its being so young it will come about; but this I only wish for, because I otherwise dread it will not.

7. *Fryday*.

The same shows for rain still continue, but I am apt to think we shall have none as yet a while. Robin it seems had a season at Hiccory Thicket. Indeed I do not want rain because I am not yet quite ready for it. So many hills to turn. This work must be some how contrived otherwise another year, but I hardly know how it can, if I tend so much tobacco ground and Corn ground. However by putting my dung in the hills in the fall I shall save that trouble of dunging in the Spring and possibly by getting some plows I may fall break up my cornfields So that that by turning up a bed for a row one way and checkering it in the Spring for planting I may have by such use of Plows the Liberty with my hands to make and turn my tobacco hills much earlier than I am now able to do. But then I doubt if I don't make my hills before winter I shall again introduce groundworm as I used to have it. The way then must be to make the hills first then to dung and cover between the step and in the spring to lighten that up and turn the hills upon it.

The plows by this means as soon as the corn is planted may go to breaking all the corn ground up again. This method I must attempt if Possible.

I never knew the Mole before to be rooting up my corn as it has been this week, even corn full a foot high and green. I do suppose some want of other food has pushed them to do this.

Lawson is resolved to set in with his hands this evening. As soon as he turned out the Sasafras ground he set into the corn field and tomorrow he thinks will finish that. So that Monday next he goes on with turning. The Fork will finish I think if all keep well on monday. It is very fine corn except on a ridge on the right hand which I cannot think was well dunged.

They shall then thin and set. Then weed out their tobacco. And so to weeding the Mangorike cow pens.

The plows begin the Pea ground Corn field this evening, and as soon as that is done they go into the stiff ground corn.

Robin, the hog boy, gone somewhere, and Postilion Tom sick.

Note: I have this year drawn on Mr. Molleson to May: To Mr. Waller £43. June 7, To Colo. Carter to renew a Protest before to R. Lee's account £ 36.10/1.

Also I drew our Court day on Mr. William Lee to Colo. F. L. Lee for the claret which I had £5.13.4.

Thunder near 12 o'clock. Rain to be expected.

It rained a little about half past one, and by 3 I was planting, but in a very sorry season. No overseer there at 4. He truely went to breakfast about 12 and not seen since. I must enquire about this: it is not very like Billy Lawson; but I have seen something like this before. Which makes me think Billy Ford had heard something when he asked me if Lawson was to stay another year.

I planted with Jas. English's tobacco from under the garden Wall in the small day's work done by Panticoe and Ambrose on monday last. These are intended for tobacco seed as the place is enclosed.

My people are finishing planting and replanting the Pea ground; but I see no overseer as yet: to be sure this is great fidelity. I fear it is clearing away, if so it is but a sorry reason. We could hardly fasten a plant up here.

8. *Saturday.*

It did rain yesterday, and though not a very long season or rather a very short one. Last night we whole planted the 60,000 Pea ground and replanted the same as well as the fresh cow pens of 30,000. And this morning, the earth being full moist, the plants full large and fine, and really a very favourable cloudy, We Set in the 113,000 peice by the Sasafras bottom, and planted all that we had turned of it, that is near all to about 1/4 of a day's work, not more than 5,000 to turn.

Note: the Plants were from the Ketching Patch, the garden Wall, hen house, Hayhouse, Riverside, and Fork patches.

I kept my wenches still setting the corn, because a rain for that work is as necessary as for tobacco planting.

I had my Carpenter Jobbers and all my Fork Gang assisting at Planting.

The clouds look full and heavy and should it rain this evening it will be clever, as we have done such a Job.

It may not be amiss to observe that our Strawberries have held out plants fully untill yesterday So that perhaps we shall not eat Any more in the year 1771.

Billy Lawson, it seems, got to the people just as they had set in to planting; so that it was something better than I thought it was with him.

Mr. Richard Parker hired me when he was here his Stump footed negro Taylor at 30/ the month, whom I sent for yesterday by my man Nat. So that the Count begins this day.

We have finished planting all the hills which we had turned. No rain any more here, but a small scudd below the hill.

Settled accounts with Mr. Sam Hipkins, of all matters between us or relative to the Store he kept for Archa. Ritchie; and paid All off.

9. *Sunday.*

A foggy morning. I sent Nassau to bring me some of the crop grass from the tops of the cowpen ground tobacco hills. It is too long, and I have ordered the hoes in there tomorrow to be wed abroad least Webb worm come there.

10. *Monday.*

Very warm indeed this day. Last night, Although no Musquetoes before, we had a mere swarm all at once.

Began this day to weed my cowpen tobacco, 30,000 at least, almost too grassy. I rode all over my Plantation with John Beale from below. He says it is a much finer crop than his below, and his nevertheless very good.

The Fork will finish their cornfield tomorrow some time, and then to thinning, and setting their corn and to weed their tobacco (to wit) 30,000 good plants.

As soon as I finish my cowpen tobacco I have one day's work in Corn; and then, god willing, I will finish turning my tobacco hills at least 170,000 hills.

11. *Tuesday.*

Thunder and lightning in the morning in the West betokeneth rain says an older man than I am: And cloud advanced with a good prospect, but as no wind accompanys it, perhaps there will not be much.

Mangorike Cornfield would have been wed out if nothing prevented it this day except the stiff land, which does not yet require it because when well hoed it was generally well chipped of its weeds. The plows however are in that ground and after that we expect time enough to give that corn a flourish.

I hardly expect the Fork to finish. It was very close and hot yesterday and really the ground much stiffer.

Talbot sheared the home sheep yesterday, to wit, but 72 and 3 sheep that had parted with their wool and but 13 lambs in the gang. So that this year's produce has been a great decrease. He went also to share the Fork sheep, 30 old sheep and 19 lambs. A good encrease. I have ordered the Pea patch cornfield to be wed out, it is really very fine. Then two of the wenches with the Setting gang finish that work and thin the corn. The Jobbers are as soon as the cornfield is finished to mend the upland tobacco watled fence and then into the stiff land corn after the plows.

The plows are after the stiffland is done to go again all over The cornfield to make this prodigeous crop tended easyer to the hands. And whilst I can use such strength, plowing, as I go deep, may be of service.

I see it was but a part of the Cowpen ground tobacco that lookt so well And I am satisfyed that the crop grass made me go too soon into that tobacco. The plants were not as much spread the hill as they ought to be. Note: I had the grass wed abroad and did not make up the hills as I wanted to do; but I feared Webworm in that weedy ground. The barley seems as if it would want the Sickle soon. I wish it may because the corn between it very fine and will want its carefull dressing.

The barley amongst the oats is not quite so ripe. I shall want that off also for I have fine pease between and they should be shortly dressed.

12. *Wednesday.*

The first day of June old Stile. The 2d day it has thundered and lightned to the West and so round to the Northeast and but very little rain as yet and I do not beleive there will be much. So that the Signs are little to be regarded.

The Fork not yet done their cornfield. Indeed this end of the field is something stiffer than the rest and they have made that a plea.

Mangorike done their corn and now in their hill turning which shall be done before it is left off. The beginning is hard in the rows and stiff, but in the [end] it is really very fine and crumbly and if I could find out a way to prevent the coats of weeds and grass I would always chuse to work such land just as it now is. I fancy a plow run a couple of furrows in the rows of such soil once if not twice in the spring and just before turning would do the whole that I want.

We have just done setting corn at Mangorike and have go[ne] to thinning.

At last a letter has come from Mr. Ball to tell me the mill is going, but he rather chose to spend 10/ to set her to going than send up. This man is fond of spending money though he knows not where nor indeed [how] to raise a Shilling. He has also hired a Miller expressly against my orders for I have over and over repeated that I would have a hand of my own taught to grind While Millers are no honester and we are to pay them for thieving from us. I have written to Mr. Ball about these things, but I beleive I may write, for he does not seem to mind me only to be affronted with me. Now he has parted with Glass, the young fellow that lived with him, And now he wants John Goldsby, as worthless a dog as any living and he has said as much, but now, at the same time he complains of his own hard living, he wants to introduce a family to maintain; but I will clap a negative on it; besides he does not tell me what Glass has left him for.

It seems my overseer Lawson will have it that the ground now hilling is 40,000 at least. I have ordered him to count it this evening, that I may know what it is tomorrow morning. He says they will be done there tomorrow and not before. If it is 40 they cannot be done.

My Cook wench cannot now dress a dish of beans or Peas but they come in quite raw.

I think every chance of rain is so gone off that it looks as if the thundering sign for rain was a sign that it would not rain whenever that had happened.

I walkt out this evening to see how my very old and honest Slave Jack Lubber did to support life in his Extreme age; and I found him prudently working amongst his melon vines, both to divert the hours and indeed to keep nature stirring that indigestions might not hurry him off with great pain. I took notice of his Pea vines a good store and askt him why he had not got them hilled; his answer was the Prudence of Experience, Master, they have not got age enough and it will hurt too young things to Coat them too closely with earth.

I then lookt at my beans said to be of the dwarf sort of homony beans which I got from Colo. Peachey. I had them planted in drills and they look much finer than the common sort planted a month before them in the Cornfield and have not been wed till yesterday. Nevertheless, I cannot but think that a vine so luxurient must be formed by nature for climbing some standard. Therefore I shall trye some rows with stakes to see which yield the best.

I sent also to have some of the timothy grass seed brought to me which I had sown in drill, between my Riverside barley; as yet it is but small and was it not for its being in drills I should fancy the seed had never come up. That barley is turned but is not yet hard. Neither is the Cornfield barley nor the pea ground barley.

Old Lubber's observation about his pease being too young to be hill[ed] comforts me about mine between the barley which I cannot yet a while hoe and earth up.

I understand my 40 barrels more of Corn is come up. I thank God for it because I dreaded much that the late fresh had met the vessel which went for it in Matapony.

Tomorrow I order it to be taken out and all the corn to be thrown quite back on the Warehouse floor.

13. *Thursday.*

The second [d]ay of old June. Yesterday a surprizing change happened in the wether and that almost in a moment. A small shift of the wind to Northeast occasioned a shiff into our thick cloaths and really fires in our Harths, and so it continues this morning. The cause is but conjecture. It must either be from much rain having fallen or a great deal to fall; the former we have not experienced. But it may be so in other places.

I find I have done wrong in point of working to keep in any of the stiff ground tobacco ground. The Piece my people went to turn yesterday although 25 hands was so hard in the rows and stiff that they turned only 12,000 in the longest day in the year. I must observe that whole piece is not all so, but it contains 38,270 hills, and I have only recconed it at 30,000.

Such things should be better managed or we should not depen[d] on our working. I wish that I could have plowed up each row two furrows, but I could not unless my corn had been left to suffer, and some of it will do so I fear as it is. For instead of 6 days we shall be much more turning the 170,000 hills.

I have known many a frost in days not so cold and I am persuaded without a change there will be one this night.

Everything looks as if it complained of the Cold weather.

The Fork not yet done their cornfields though but 4 rows to do. I ordered them to go to setting and thinning the Corn [and] After that to weeding out the [tobacco] to lighten up the missing hills and to set them with double plants if any near, if not to plant with the hand and cover as formerly.

The River seems not yet to have lost its red Colour which it got by the vast fresh in May last; or else there has been another fresh.

In the *Annual Register* Vol. 4, p. 126 from the beginning, Dr. Hill[18] tells the Public of his having tryed the Napir and Norway turneps sown in hills in bogs without draining, according to the Bishop of Pentoppedon's recommendation; and he had them then growing very large and fine in a bog in his garden at Baysen. But he does not say when that was, or when he sowed them. I sent for seeds of these sorts to Wm. Lee, Merchant, and got them in. Therefore to find out this Critical time when to sow these serviceable things. I this day ordered a dozon hills to be made in my Marshs at 3 feet distance for each sort, to be sown with a few of these seeds, to see what they will do. And so I shall doe every month, till it becomes too Cold weather. I wish it may not be another deception, such as Wm. Wyn Baker of Ireland[19] palmed upon the Society of Dublin, as to the true Cabbage turnep, which though exuberant in growth, is one of the tenderest plants in the whole world, even a slight frost kills it dead in its most flourishing growth.

Drew upon Mr. Samuel Hipkins payable to Richard Blade[20] the sum of £3, the first order on him since my settlement with him June 8. Note: this Blade has brought me from Rings Neck 90 barrels of Corn. But I have paid him 12d the barrel for 100, it being his agreement to fetch me so many from that quarter at 12d the barrel. By my account of the barley field Corn it is 20 acres. For the piece tobacco ground Contained 65,000 hills; and it is now but 40,000. So that 25,000 in barley with the other piece 56 makes just 81,000 which at 4,000 to an acre is just 20 acres, rather more. Now 20 acres planted in Corn at 6 foot rows and 2 feet step makes the quantity of corn 72,600 Corn hills.

14. *Fryday*.

Number 3 of Old June. A great dew, but rather drye weather.

I find, now we come to look in the matter, our corn has been prodigeously missing; and as yet we have not done setting it, and of Course not done thinning it. I find I must fall upon another method for this work, and make it another year the business of the whole gang under the overseer; for as it has been this year we shall be nigh three weeks about it with 4 and 6 hands and of course we do it at last too late and perhaps don't half do it; for negroes cannot be either carefull or diligent without an overseer.

[18] Probably Dr. John Hill (1716–75), prolific writer in natural history and philosophy. The article referred to is actually on page 127 of the *Annual Register*, IV.

[19] Almost certainly John Wynn Baker (d. 1775), agriculturalist and rural economist, who was connected with the Dublin Society from 1764 to 1770. His influential *Experiments in Agriculture* was published at intervals from 1766 to 1773.

[20] Richard Blade was apparently a teamster or a small shipper.

That devilish tobacco ground below, not quite 40,000, has taken me Up this the third day with 25 hands. No more stiff land will I tend if I cannot do it quicker in tobacco.

My Jobbers now go to the cornfield again to cut down from the corn those cursed white weeds, which the plow is to follow them in.

Toney, Guy, Mcginnis, and Jammy with their boys have now been a full month about preparing to lift the roof of the tobacco house fallen down. Cursed Villains indeed.

Simon falls off Vastly at the fork. He has been two longer about the last corn field than he was in either of the other, the same quantity of ground, under a pretence of the work's being hard; And yesterday he had done but little at setting and thinning the corn. As soon as the tobacco is wed he shall have a good whipping and George take his place again. I see those people will not do without an overseer.

My people came up after breakfast time to turn the Paddock hills and in my life I never saw harder work. Certain I am that such work must ruin my corn for instead of 8 days in turning such hills I must be twice 8 in doing that. This what I really dreaded when I refused to tend tobacco upon this hill. The soil, though made rich, is subject to bake after every rain, and the winter and spring have been nothing but rain. I must either contrive to break up again in March although I make my hills before winter, and then Perhaps I may be able to turn the hills with more dispatch in May. Or else I must give it many plowings. This whole Paddock is but 73 rows of 70 hills each which is but 5,110 hills. It took 2 hands a whole day before to turn but 1,400; and I beleive at least 21 hands will not turn the remainder from 12 to night.

15. *Saturday.*

Number 4. Old Style. The Fork weeding their New ground tobacco. The Jobbers in the Mangorike Old Cornfield, the rough ground, fine corn. The 6 wenches thinning the Corn. The plows finishing the rough ground up to the long tobacco house. And the Gang, what there are, well turning the home hills, the Earth very hard.

Nassau cut and marked 16 piggs, marked and turned out 2 black Cows, mark one sow pigg at the Fork. 20 or 30 still to cut and mark.

16. *Sunday.*

I was sorry to see what I did yesterday, and therefore sorry from the sinc[e]rity of my heart to say that if wanted or could be gratifyed in knowing that my son would have a full measure meted to him of all the insults which he has frequently though imprudently offered me, and often confessedly for his diversion; for his son not void of sence but void of all filial decency will from a temper too visible in the appearance of it to be denied from whence he inherits it, in a very little time become the most outrageous of all children that ever lived. In short, his indulgence of that temper is so constant and extravagant that I doubt not but in a little time he will turn everybody out of doors if he can. It is now above ten days since he began to unrein it, and except when he wants to be obliged in anything that he cannot get, he never behaves now with common decency to anyone Soul, either to me, his Father, his mother, his Aunts, his sister, his brother, nay even to the smallest babies when out of temper, and that is now almost always.

No rain but heavy in clouds is the morning as for some time past.

I made it my business out of duty to talk to this Grandson and namesake, and set before him the unhappiness he must throw everybody into as well as himself, for he must be dispised by all his relations. At first he endeavoured to avoid me, and went away. I bid him come back; he pretended to be affraid that I wanted to scold at him. I told him no, it was my concern that made me earnest to advise him to imploy his good sence which god had blessed him with, and not to sacrifice that to a temper which must in the end make him miserable. At last he seemed to listen, and indeed shed tears at what I said. I hope in God then he will learn to behave better.

The clouds that had all drawn up Rappahannock Creek according to custom and indeed Philosophy, when not attended with a wind to overcome the sucsion of that creek, Came back with a brisk gale, and rained about half an hour, a very plentifull shower; and had it been a work day I should have planted and replanted all my ground ready; but perhaps the season may hold to plant tomorrow and possibly my ground may be easier to be worked after by this blessing.

17. *Monday.*

Number 6. Old Style. It is very likely that this rain produces what we used to call the long season in June, and I am not yet quite ready for finishing the crop I intend and have prepared to tend. Young hasty forward Planters would grieve at this; but I cannot be much concerned at it. All my large crop of Corn is quite secured from the weeds; and it can be no difficult matter to turn about 120,000 hills to be ready to be planted between this and the end of Old June; for though we have changed our stile I have not been able to observe as yet that in our climate and time for Planting is therefore changed; I certainly can well remember that he was always a timous [?] planter (as the Scotchmen call it) that got his crop well in the ground by the last of June Old Stile; and this is but the 6th in June according to that old stile. I must say this change of stile seems to have been the cause why many people tend too little to make a good crop of tobacco. I do suppose I shall hear, a little ground very rich and early tended, will make a better crop, than a good deal of ground late tended. I am ready to answer that this way. He that tends a large crop, may to be sure contrive to have as good ground as others for at least the same Number of workers; and to be sure may tend that as well as others: Therefore, what he can manage though late of ground not quite so good, must be clear gains. ·Again I have ever found it better to have some ground to weed one after the other, and not altogether, because in such a case as richness of soil must give a growth to weeds as well as to plants, when it is all in the weeds at once some will suffer, and I have often seen though but a small crop for the hands, that not a little has been lost by being all at once upon hand.

I cannot pass over some behaviour in my people. I sent on Purpose last night to George at the Fork to take his whole gang to drawing plants for Mangorike, for I should have two carts at the plant patch by daybreak. Lawson very officiously sent one of the carts to my home plant patch, and because George heard that he only drew for one cart and took all the people to weeding tobacco, so that when the 2d cart went there, not a plant was drawn. I asked him the meaning of it, and he said he thought I did not intend to have any more than one cart drawn. I have ordered him to be whipped for thinking to disobey orders.

Again although everybody knew that I was for dispatch Mr. Pater was nodding in his cart going for Plants, and the little driver was obliged to be running from one horse to the other. That rascal shall pay for his ride. I must suppose that he was out all night upon one of my cart horses.

The women thinning corn must be very diligent to save their backs, for they did but little on Saturday and Mr. Talbot must pay for his want of trust. He spent with two more a full fortnight in pulling the corkle and rye out of my barley, and I see almost as much in it as I saw at first. He is a cursed lazy deceitfull fellow.

I have sent Johnny to thin my Cotton and indeed to set it where it wants.

I wish my Barley ripe that I may earth up my pease and my Corn amongst it; they are very fine and want earth though not weedy.

Notwithstanding such showers here yesterday and today, the plants could but barely draw and we hardly had moisture to replant that tobacco there.

Nassau finish[ed] Cutting and marking the fork piggs, to wit, 17 Sowes, 24 boars cut, 2 turned out, 3 not yet up, 3 fatning, 4 eaten. In all 53. So that there must have been 12 died and I never heard of more than 8. I fancy the Swineherd may have made use of some of them.

Captain Walker came here. I gave him a note on the Indian Creek Inspector's at Indian Creek Warehouse for that hogshead weight 950 which the assistant Inspector passed when Sydnor[21] through resentment against J. Beale would not. Which will make 3 hogsheads shipped (to wit) 2 paid me by Mr. Blain for Uriah Sandy[22] besides the half of the 4 from Rings neck Shipped by my son.

We made a shift to plant all the hills we had ready, and then replanted all our former ground over, but the Season except in the part of the Plantation near the hills was very scanty and it is said in Sasafras ground we had abundance missing, most of it planted last season having fairly died in the hills.

Note: Mr. Ball had plants from the Locust patch.

Mr. Giberne and Wadman dined with us upon Veales. We after played at whist. My old ill luck attended me and I lost to Wadman 11 pistereens, 3 of which he turned over to my son. The other 8 he balance[d] a debt of 7/6 upon account and there remains 2/6 due to him.

18. *Tuesday.*

Number 7 Old Style June. A small drizzling this morning; finished planting the 25,000 piece from the Smoak house to the ditch beyond the old Smith's Shop. Began turning at 6 o'clock the Uphill cowpens by the Oat-house. We have now got to turn:

The Cowpens near	15,000
The Watled field	26,000
The Cutdown to the Mill	35,000
Olivers branch	40,000
	116,000

which at 20 a day will be more than 6 days. And yet Lawson thinks of being done by Fryday. But by Monday night will be as soon as he can unless the work is lighter than I imagin it will be. However I don't intend Olivers

[21] Fortunatus Sydnor (d. 1781), tobacco inspector at Indian Creek Warehouse in Northumberland Co.

[22] Uriah Sandy, later a planter of moderate means in Westmoreland Co., was probably the son of John Sandy (d. 1770), a Richmond Co. farmer.

branch shall be done before I give two days work in my corn that it will want to clear the hills after the plow.

Very cool again, every wind blows so. Certainly there must be great rains about. This summer is properly a very cold one as yet. Hornworm eggs in abundance.

19. *Wednesday*.

Number 8. Old Style. Very cold still, a fire quite comfortable to me.

Robin, his Sons Landon and George set off in my Petiauger to Mr. Beverley's.

People began to turn the Watled ground tobacco hills, 26,000 in the whole.

The Napir and Norway Turneps sown in hills in the boggy part of my meadow according to Dr. Hill in the *Annual Register,* Vol 4, p: 126, which were put into the ground in order to find out the proper time for sowing them, as Dr. Hill has omitted that material Circumstance, 13th of the month so that they have been in near a week.

20. *Thursday*.

Number 9 Old Style. It began to rain about 5 in the morning.

The *Marlbro'* came below the Mud bank yesterday; and immediately a boat came to have my tobacco ready. I was going about it, but if it should rain anything I shall leave it off. For Merchants wish for any excuse for a bad Sale, and should B[ackhouse] hear my tobacco had been in a rain, it would be made use of by him. Otherwise, why should my last sales complain of the Gust when nobody else makes that complaint in their sales.

I am not yet ready even for this rain should it be a season; but I have above 30,000 to plant ready and it will be a good time to replant what has been planted, much of which I see are missing.

We had a little rain this morning and it has spit every now and then since, but nothing to make a season; however I ventured to stick in to the fresh turned ground as long as the large plants lasted, at least as long as my people would own they were large, for no body went to see the patches. I believe I have got in in all about 24,000, expecting more rain, and I beleive we shall have more, the wind has got to Northeast and the clouds seem to be heavy. If it does rain, it will be a point gained and if it does not we shall only loose the plants and the time.

We are getting down our tobacco for Captain Quinny, but I have been obliged to be cautious.

I thank God the rain begins to fall something like a season, and I beleive at 3 o'clock in the evening. But my overseer could not think of beginning again to plant because I was out in my cornfield.

I fancy my tobacco will get wet in the carts as they are carrying down the hogsheads. I observe this Quinny like a man seems in his interest is much inclined to be, and do as he pleases. It is thus I fell the little money I owe Backhouse, but it shall not be so long.

22. *Saturday.*

Yesterday we finished planting and replanting all the hills I had turned; and in the evening finished turning all the Watled ground: Note: the people were very lazy; and so was the overseer but he was sick.

Got all my crop down this morn, which are 30 hogsheads to go on board Quinny. This has been a great hindrance to me.

Lawson took a vomit last night and went to the Warehouse with my 4 Carpenters to Inspect the tobacco. This tobacco law is a very troublesome one to every honest and diligent Planter; And I must get a house built at the landing that my tobacco may be got down in times less troublesome than when my crop is on hand. A house 16 foot wide, 30 foot long, and 10 feet pitch will hold 90 hogsheads.

I must also use brakes to get the tobacco down, for I had one and two Oxen carried 1 hogshead with much more ease than 4 in the Cart did two.

Manuel got to Plowing by 9'. I rode in my corn. Most of it very fine, especially where I planted it in hills. That planted in holes low, though green.

We are dunging the mill cut and shall do that I hope and hill a good deal of it this day though Lawson is at the Warehouse.

It rained I understand a fine shower in the night. I hope that saves my yesterday's replanting.

Quinney Carry off the remaining 15 hogsheads of my 30 to the Warehouse.

I have often heard it imagined that our crab or crop grass was of the quickest growth of any plant; but I fancy that I have a water grass in my present Corn field full as quick, for not 6 days agoe I saw it but just coming up on a part of corn rows, and now it bids fair for a Scythe, and yet the Corn is large, high, and strong.

I am resolved as soon as these upper hills are turned which God willing will be early on Monday to set in with my gang and releive the noble corn that is threatned by it. It cannot require more than a day's work if that, for there are but very few thousands so. Perhaps 20 at the Utmost. I know that I have still 40,000 tobacco hills to dung and turn. But I am satisfyed the corn cannot wait and a day later in tobacco cannot stand so great a chance of being injured.

I must on tuesday cut my barley.

We have got all hands to turning the hills on the buryed dung at least 2 hours by Sun; so that I will hope, god willing, to have a good piece of monday to go to the releif of that corn as above.

My first 15 hogsheads inspected. They weighed but 15,796. One hogshead had been so damaged as to be cut off to 780 pounds weight. I got this in the house. I do suppose that by the skidds being too low it damaged from the moisture of the earth. It was said to be very fine tobacco and of a fine scent. Now what the merchant will give me for it will be the question. These hogsheads Numbered to Number 15 inclusive.

23. *Sunday.*

A Sumer's morning with a great dew. I walkt about in these home fields planted, and sent Nassau all over them. I thought it stood as the planter means very well indeed, and Dr. Nassau says he has seen much tobacco, and never saw any stand better.

24. *Monday.*

Number 13 Old Style. A fine Prospect for rain but it went off, and really we want it in my Cornfields for Corn wed 6 days ago, though green ever since, turns yellow now.

This day I have the experience of the expence of Plow horses. On Saturday night the boy pretends he turned out his plow bay mare after feeding her. He says he could not find her last night and now she is not to be found anywhere. I am certain some of them has carryed her off and left her by some Mill, and I do suspect Old Charles.

We shall be late before we get these hills turned. The ground is so hard.

25. *Tuesday.*

14 Old Style. My daughter Judy in Company with Rd. Parker, jur.,[23] set off to go up to Bull run. A little rain and but a little.

Begun this day to cut my barley about 3 acres at the riverside which was done but not got in.

[23] Richard Parker, Jr. (ca. 1752–80), was the son of Richard Parker and Elizabeth Beale. He was an officer during the Revolution, rising to the rank of colonel of the First Virginia Regiment in February 1778. He died of wounds received at the siege of Charleston.

My Gang about the last piece to be turned, after having cleaned some very foul and very fine corn.

26. *Wednesday*

Number 15 Old Style. The inspectors let my tobacco go on board Quinny. They had pretended to keep 2 hogsheads because under 950, not considering the law only sets that weight as to what they prize and not as to what a man freights.

The Fork began to lay by their corn just at night.

29. *Saturday*.

Number 19 Old Style. No rain for many days, though very likely for it every day. And it did rain about.

Just finished turning hills. Cut down all my barley and almost got it all in.

Our Pease will be our next concern if it does not rain. The Jobbers begin this day.

The Carpenters thatching the new raised Old tobacco house near the Riverside. I made them reap and thrash out the wheat to get the straw and to thatch on each side regularly so that I hope by monday that house will be in order to receive the wheat.

I shall then begin my wheat harvest.

The Fork finishes their first cornfield began to be laid by this day and the Cotton patch near it.

On Monday go in the next field which if well they will finish in 4 days more and so the next so that by tuesday sevennight next they will be ready to reap their oats or Rye.

Manuel Ploughing down in the Old cornfield takes in this year down to the Fork dam. Then to the Fork by Wednesday next.

JULY 1771

1 *Monday*.

June 20 old Stile. It rained on Saturday night very powerfully, and has proved a great refreshment to everything; but yet such a rain on any working day would have answered the purpose also of my finishing Planting and replanting for this year; however I will trye to make use of it by every means in my power.

There is every small to turn yet.

The Pease just began to be hoed and they look very fine.

The Fork within half a row finished the laying by their first Corn field. The cotton still to weed.

I observed a possimon tree almost 3 times as thick as my body quite split through the middle from top to bottom, its limbs crashed down and its bark peeled quite off from within. The top branches to the bottom Very dreadf[ul] indeed to behold.

The blessings of heaven seem to await us. It rained plentifully on Saturday night, and now just as our hearts could wish a Soft silent rain is coming on, that we may make use of this comfortable moisture in our crops to morrow.

Yesterday one Marshall who lives in Turner's business[24] came to down to me at night to take my Park Quarter. I could only tell him, that if my son the last of this month or beginning of August saw that Brown[25] did not do his duty I should imploy him, but then I would not give more than 1/12 of what he grew neat proceeds as it were (that is) after Levies etc. were deducted. The man went away seemingly agreeable to it.

I promise myself that we shall plant and replant every hill that we tend this year. It was a most blessed rain yesterday in the evening. I cannot but remark the difference between, the owner and the Overseer of the Crop. Upon Saturday's rain I sent to W. Lawson my Overseer, to be ready before day this morning that we might make a finish; his answer was he would be at it long before day as it was moonshine. I got up before two o'clock, had all the people sent for, but no overseer at home. Neither did he come till full day when I had planted at least 1,200. He had an excuse that my honesty could not have admitted off were I in his place: he went to see his father, and the rain stopped him from returning.

4. *Thursday.*

June 23 Old Style. All the 3 days before this spent at Court, chiefly in obliging the Lawyers to say anything out of the causes that they are engaged in, and making the most absurd motions imaginable, one of which I must take notice of. Mr. Boyd wanted the Jury to find a S[worn] Verdict in the cause before them; They found such of his notes that appeared to them to be proved facts, but because he wanted all his notes found he moved they should be sent out again. The Court indulged him. The Jury then found more of his notes but

[24] Perhaps Col. Thomas Turner (d. 1787) of Walsingham and Smith's Mount in King George Co. He married Jane, daughter of William Fauntleroy of Naylor's Hole, Richmond Co.

[25] James Brown was the overseer of the Park Quarter at this time.

in the manner that they really appeared to them as to the facts proved. He then moved to send them out again. The Court would not but received the Verdict. Then he moved for a new tryal; the Court would not grant it, because that motion must implye an evident contradiction to their opinion Just given on the Verdict.

My friend I think leaving his old sincere road and following him.

Began mowing my Wheat yesterday, this day I rode out, and found but a little done for 3 scythes which it seems was all that would own they could mow. However I set in one more. I see there some few heads mildewed, Some people call it rust. It may be so. And if it is rust it confirms my Philosophy of that evil, to wit, a corroding moisture in the Constitution of air, which beginning early shrivels up the stalk; but when it begins late it only Shrivels some heads of the wheat. And this being only accidental here and there on single stalks Shews it is, if confined at all, only confined to [so]me peculiar state in the Particular stalk at that time predisposed to be affected as that moisture passes over it.

I cannot avoid taking notice of an uncommon accident. I before mentioned a Possimon tree in my Fork Pasture dreadfully struck with Lightning on Saturday last; but it had then its top and top boughs standing and only the lower branches and all the bark crushed and Peeled down. A second flash attackt in on tuesday night and shivered that top and all the boughs off to one small branch.

Anybody may now see, how well my Fork Cornfield was dunged when I ordered it, here and there in some places and in intire rows rather low and firing when those on each side are large, green and very fine indeed, and all certainly wed at one and the same time.

Counted my barley cornfield and found it to be about 50,000 stalks. Thus the Gate Cut 32,075. The upper cut 14,480; which makes 46,655. And the short rows in both 3,345. In all 50,000.

5. *Fryday*.

June 24 Old Style. My Sorrel Mare Polly de Bell brought a colt last night.

Finished laying by my barley Corn field, vizt., 50,000. Note: the land was stiff and it took the work of 17 and 19 hands for two days so that the whole was 36 hands in all. One day equal to 14,000 and better each hand; good work as the rows were 6½ feet wide.

We are now in the 60,000 Pea field tobacco.